The Victorian Studies Reader

What does the Age of Steam have to say to the Age of the Internet?

New ideas about gender, race, language, space and material culture have transformed the way the Victorians are being discussed today. *The Victorian Studies Reader* brings together for the first time the best of these international writings about the period. Not only do Kelly Boyd and Rohan McWilliam consider familiar themes such as parliamentary reform and poverty, but they also look at the mesmerist, the barmaid and the cosmopolitan man about town. New light is shed on the Chartists, the British Empire and Darwinian evolution, while other Readings challenge conventional views about Victorian religion, morality and hypocrisy. Each Reading is prefaced by a helpful commentary placing the work in context.

In their wide-ranging introduction, Kelly Boyd and Rohan McWilliam not only illuminate how the Victorians have been imagined since the death of Victoria, but they also make a powerful argument for the importance of the Victorian inheritance today. They reveal how the field has been reshaped over the last generation by the rise of cultural history and cross-disciplinary conversation, and establish a challenging agenda for Victorian Studies in the twenty-first century.

The Victorian Studies Reader will appeal to all those who want to know more about the world of the Victorians.

Kelly Boyd teaches at the University of London. She edited the *Encyclopedia of Historians and Historical Writing* (1999) and is the author of *Manliness and the Boys' Story Paper in Britain: A Cultural History, 1855–1940* (2003).

Rohan McWilliam is Senior Lecturer in History at Anglia Ruskin University and author of *Popular Politics in Nineteenth-Century England* (1998) and *The Tichborne Claimant: A Victorian Sensation* (2007).

Routledge Readers in History

The Decolonization Reader
Edited by James Le Sueur

The Enlightenment: A Sourcebook
and Reader
Edited by Olga Gomez, Francesca
Greensides and Paul Hyland

The European Women's History
Reader
Edited by Christine Collette and
Fiona Montgomery

The Fascism Reader
Edited by Aristotle A. Kallis

The Feminist History Reader
Edited by Sue Morgan

The Global History Reader
Edited by Bruce Mazlish and
Akira Iriye

The History and Narrative Reader
Edited by Geoffrey Roberts

The Irish Women's History
Reader
Edited by Alan Hayes and
Diane Urquhart

The Nature of History Reader
Edited by Keith Jenkins and
Alun Munslow

The Oral History Reader
Edited by Robert Perks and
Alistair Thomson

The Postmodern History Reader
Edited by Keith Jenkins

The Postmodernism Reader:
Foundational Texts
Edited by Michael Drolet

Renaissance Thought: A Reader
Edited by Robert Black

The Slavery Reader
Edited by Gad Heuman and
James Walvin

The Terrorism Reader
Edited by David J. Whittaker

The Witchcraft Reader
Edited by Darren Oldridge

The World War Two Reader
Edited by Gordon Martel

The
Victorian Studies
Reader

Edited by

**Kelly Boyd and
Rohan McWilliam**

Routledge
Taylor & Francis Group

LONDON AND NEW YORK

First published 2007 by Routledge
2 Park Square, Milton Park, Abingdon, Oxon OX14 4RN

Simultaneously published in the USA and Canada
by Routledge
270 Madison Ave, New York NY 10016

Routledge is an imprint of the Taylor & Francis Group, an informa business

Selection and editorial matter © 2007 Kelly Boyd and Rohan McWilliam
Individual chapters © the original copyright holders

Typeset in Perpetua and Bell Gothic by
Florence Production Ltd, Stoodleigh, Devon
Printed and bound in Great Britain by
Cromwell Press, Trowbridge, Wiltshire

British Library Cataloguing in Publication Data
A catalogue record for this book is available from the British Library

Library of Congress Cataloging in Publication Data
The Victorian studies reader / edited by Kelly Boyd and
Rohan McWilliam.
        p. cm.
    Includes bibliographical references.
    1. Great Britain — History — Victoria, 1837–1901.   2. Great
Britain — Social conditions — 19th century.   3. Great Britain —
Civilization — 19th century.   4. Readers — History.
    I. Boyd, Kelly.   II. McWilliam, Rohan.
    DA550.V543 2007
    941.081—dc22
    2006036108

ISBN10: 0–415–35578–8 (hbk)
ISBN10: 0–415–35579–6 (pbk)

ISBN13: 978–0–415–35578–0 (hbk)
ISBN13: 978–0–415–35579–7 (pbk)

To Our Supervisors
John Gillis and John F.C. Harrison

Contents

Preface   xi
Acknowledgements   xiii

Kelly Boyd and Rohan McWilliam
INTRODUCTION: RETHINKING THE VICTORIANS   1

PART 1
Periodisation   49

1   Richard Price
    SHOULD WE ABANDON THE IDEA OF THE VICTORIAN
    PERIOD?   51

PART 2   67
Economy

2   Martin Wiener
    CAN CULTURE EXPLAIN ECONOMIC DECLINE?   69

3   P.J. Cain and A.G. Hopkins
    GENTLEMANLY CAPITALISM   83

PART 3
Consumerism and material culture   97

4   Erika Rappaport
WOMEN AND THE DEPARTMENT STORE   99

5   Christopher Breward
CLOTHING THE MIDDLE-CLASS MALE   110

PART 4
Society and class   127

6   Patrick Joyce
THE FALL OF CLASS   129

7   Mary Poovey
REPRESENTING THE MANCHESTER IRISH   136

PART 5
Space   149

8   Simon Gunn
PUBLIC SPACES IN THE VICTORIAN CITY   151

PART 6
Politics high and low   165

9   Jonathan Parry
LIBERALISM AND GOVERNMENT   167

10 Gareth Stedman Jones
RADICALISM, LANGUAGE AND CLASS   177

11 Anna Clark
GENDER AND RADICALISM   191

PART 7
Morality   207

12 Gertrude Himmelfarb
IN DEFENCE OF THE VICTORIANS   209

PART 8
Intellectual history   221

13 Stefan Collini
CHARACTER AND THE VICTORIAN MIND   223

PART 9
Religion   **233**

14   Boyd Hilton
RELIGION, DOCTRINE AND PUBLIC POLICY   235

15   Callum Brown
HOW RELIGIOUS WAS VICTORIAN BRITAIN?   244

PART 10
Science   **253**

16   Adrian Desmond
EVOLUTION BEFORE DARWIN   255

17   James A. Secord
DOMESTICATING EVOLUTION   268

18   Gillian Beer
DARWIN'S IMAGINATION   282

19   Alison Winter
SCIENCE AND POPULAR CULTURE   288

PART 11
Gender and the family   **305**

20   Leonore Davidoff and Catherine Hall
SEPARATE SPHERES   307

21   John Tosh
MEN AND DOMESTICITY   318

22   Ellen Ross
WORKING-CLASS FAMILY STRATEGIES   324

PART 12
Sexuality   **339**

23   Michael Mason
WORKING-CLASS SEXUALITY   341

24   Lynda Nead
THE MEANING OF THE PROSTITUTE   347

25   Judith Walkowitz
JACK THE RIPPER AND THE DOCTORS   360

26   Elaine Showalter
HOMOSEXUALITY AND LATE VICTORIAN ANXIETY   370

27   Peter Bailey
     SEXUALITY AND THE PUB   380

PART 13
Monarchy   **395**

28   John Plunkett
     RESTORING THE POPULARITY OF THE MONARCHY   397

PART 14
Race, Empire and national identity   **411**

29   Catherine Hall
     BRINGING THE EMPIRE BACK IN   413

     Index   431

Preface

WHY ARE THE VICTORIANS STILL IMPORTANT? What does the Age of Steam have to say to the Age of the Internet? *The Victorian Studies Reader* is an introduction to current debates about the nineteenth century. The purpose of the collection is to provide a sense of how the Victorians are being discussed today. The bulk of the Readings that follow are by historians and the book can be read as a guide to 'the new Victorian history'. However, we have also included a number of works by non-historians because one of the themes of this book is the way in which Victorian history has acquired renewed vitality through inter-disciplinarity and the dissolution of formal academic boundaries (we reflect on this in our introductory article, 'Rethinking the Victorians'). The other major theme of the book is the rise of cultural history, which is currently providing new interpretations of the Victorian era as well as many other periods. Our argument in this volume is that all those who are interested in the Victorians need to participate in the interdisciplinary dialogue. It is the richness of this academic conversation that *The Victorian Studies Reader* attempts to reproduce.

Inevitably, this is a heavily personal selection. We have included works derived from academic articles and books that have been published since 1980. Our introductory article reflects on the post-1980 generation of Victorian histories by placing them within the larger trajectory of Victorian Studies since the beginning of the twentieth century. There have been two criteria for inclusion. The first is that a work has proved to be particularly influential, agenda setting or much discussed by other scholars. The other is that the work is a good example of a particular tendency in the literature. Many of our selections fulfil both criteria. Although the inclusion of a work does not necessarily imply that its contents are endorsed by the editors, a reading of this selection will, we believe, provide an understanding of the kinds of questions that are now being asked about Victorian Britain. We have deliberately included the work of some younger scholars as they are the people who are likely to shape our views of the Victorians in the near future. We explain our reasons for the inclusion of each piece in the short commentary that precedes each extract.

To write about the Victorians today is not the same as to write about them in 1918 when Lytton Strachey published his exuberant hatchet job, *Eminent Victorians*, or in 1934 when G.M. Young's elegant essay, 'Portrait of an Age', first appeared. We also find ourselves in a different historical moment from the 1950s when the modern academic discipline of Victorian Studies first emerged. In 1973, Peter Stansky undertook a similar project to ours by editing a useful collection entitled *The Victorian Revolution*. His Reader featured some of the leading political and social historians since the mid-1950s, such as Oliver MacDonagh (concerning the Victorian revolution in government) and James Cornford (on the transformation of the Victorian Conservative Party). Ours is a collection that reflects the priorities of a different age. The categories that shape our volume include race, gender, science, sexuality, the uses of public and private space, consumerism, and material culture, as well as a number of enduring categories that the earlier generation would have recognised such as class and religion. We have included unconventional topics (such as Peter Bailey's study of the barmaid) but also shown how conventional topics have been rethought. *The Victorian Studies Reader* is therefore a 'Portrait of our Age' as much as it is an analysis of the Victorian era. It is not exhaustive and there are many important themes or topics that we have not had space to include, such as the countryside, Ireland (although see Mary Poovey's Reading), transport, technology, crime, education, childhood, the military, and relations with Europe and countries outside the British Empire.

We would like to thank Victoria Peters and Eve Setch at Routledge for their work on this volume, for their enthusiasm and for their patience. Similarly, we are very grateful to the anonymous referees for their useful comments (two of them — Hugh Cunningham and James Epstein — have subsequently 'outed' themselves). Thanks also go to the following who have provided us with guidance, references and good advice during the creation of this book: Simon Avery, Joe Bord, Arthur Burns, Pamela Gilbert, Michelle Hawley, Martin Hewitt, Clive Hill, Kali Israel, Mark Knight, Christine Krueger, Mary Clare Martin, Steven Maughan, Andrew Maunder, Farah Mendlesohn, Clare Midgely, Elizabeth Prettejohn, Amber Regis, and Krisztina Robert, Norris Saakwa-Mante. John Gardiner, Keith McClelland and Susie Steinbach provided us with helpful readings of the introduction (but are in no way responsible for any weaknesses). Susan Thorne, however, is indirectly responsible for the whole book as she introduced the editors to each other in 1987 (and is presumably also indirectly responsible for their marriage). The editors were privileged to be supervised by two remarkable and gifted historians of the nineteenth century — John Gillis and John F.C. Harrison — two men with a passion for the Victorians and a commitment to the present. The book is dedicated to them.

All of the Readings in this book have been previously published. The spelling, punctuation and citation structure of the originals have been retained, but where we have made cuts in a text, the deletion is marked with [. . .]. Readers are warmly recommended to consult the original for the complete version.

Acknowledgements

Richard Price, 'Historiography, Narrative and the Nineteenth Century', *Journal of British Studies* 35:2 (April 1996), The University of Chicago Press. Copyright © 1996 by The North American Conference on British Studies. Reproduced with permission.

Martin Wiener, *English Culture and the Decline of the Industrial Spirit, 1850–1980*, 1981 © Cambridge University Press, reprinted with permission of the author and publisher.

P.J. Cain and A.G. Hopkins, 'Gentlemanly Capitalism and British Overseas Expansion', *Economic History Review* Vol. 39/4 (1986), Blackwell Publishing. Reprinted with permission of the authors and publisher.

Erika Diane Rappaport; *Shopping for Pleasure: Women in the Making of London's West End*. © 2000 Princeton University Press. Reprinted by permission of Princeton University Press.

Christopher Breward, '"Each Man to his Station": Clothing, Stereotypes and the Patterns of Class' in Breward, *The Hidden Consumer: Masculinities, Fashion and City Life, 1860–1914*, 1999. Reprinted with kind permission of the author.

Patrick Joyce, *Democratic Subjects: The Self and the Social in Nineteenth-Century England*, © Patrick Joyce 1994, published by Cambridge University Press, reprinted with permission of the author and publisher.

Mary Poovey, *Making a Social Body: British Cultural Formation, 1830–1864*, University of Chicago Press. Copyright © 1995 by The University of Chicago. Reproduced with permission.

Simon Gunn, *The Public Culture of the Victorian Middle Class: Ritual and Authority and the English Industrial City, 1840–1914*, 2000. Reprinted with kind permission of the author.

Jonathan Parry, 'Introduction' in Parry, *The Rise and Fall of Liberal Government in Victorian Britain* (New Haven and London: Yale University Press, 1993). Copyright © 1993 Yale University Press. Reprinted with permission.

Gareth Stedman Jones, 'The Language of Chartism' in James Epstein and Dorothy Thompson (eds), *The Chartist Experience: Studies in Working-class Radicalism and Culture* (London: Macmillan, 1982) pp. 3–16. Reproduced by permission of Palgrave Macmillan Publishers Ltd.

Anna Clark, *The Struggle for the Breeches: Gender and the Making of the British Working Class,* California University Press, 1997 © by The Regents of The University of California. Reprinted with permission of the author and publisher.

Gertrude Himmelfarb, *The De-Moralization of Society: From Victorian Virtues to Modern Values,* copyright © 1995 by Gertrude Himmelfarb. Used by permission of Alfred A. Knopf, a division of Random House.

Stefan Collini, 'The Idea of Character: Private Habits and Public Virtues' in Collini, *Public Moralists* pp. 104–113. Reproduced by permission of Oxford Univeristy Press.

Boyd Hilton, 'From Retribution to Reform' in Lesley M. Smith (ed.), *The Making of Britain: The Age of Revolution* (Basingstoke: Macmillan Education, 1987) pp. 37–49. Reproduced by permission of Palgrave Macmillan Publishers Ltd.

Callum Brown, 'Did Urbanization Secularize Britain?', *Urban History Yearbook* (1988) reprinted by kind permission of the author.

Adrian Desmond, *The Politics of Evolution: Morphology, Medicine, and Reform in Radical London*, ch.1 'Evolution and Society: Setting the Scene', University of Chicago Press. Copyright © 1989 by The University of Chicago. Reproduced with permission.

James A. Secord, 'Behind the Veil: Robert Chambers and *Vestiges*' in James R. Moore (ed.), *History, Humanity and Evolution Essays for John C. Greene,* 1989 © Cambridge University Press, reprinted with permission of the author and publisher.

Gillian Beer, *Darwin's Plots: Evolutionary Narrative in Darwin, George Eliot and Nineteenth Century Fiction*, © Gillian Beer, 1983, 2000, published by Cambridge University Press, reprinted with permission of the author and publisher.

Alison Winter, *Mesmerized: Powers of Mind in Victorian Britain*, University of Chicago Press. Copyright © 1998 by The University of Chicago. Reproduced with permission.

Leonore Davidoff and Catherine Hall, *Family Fortunes: Men and Women of the English Middle Class, 1780–1850*, copyright © 2002 Routledge. Reproduced by permission of the author and Taylor & Francis Books, UK.

John Tosh, *A Man's Place; Masculinity and the Middle-Class Home in Victorian England* (London: Yale University Press, 1999). Copyright © 1999 by John Tosh. Reprinted with permission.

Ellen Ross, '"Fierce Questions and Taunts": Married Life in Working-Class London, 1870–1914', was originally published in *Feminist Studies* Volume 8, Number 3 (Fall 1982): 575–602, by permission of the publisher, *Feminist Studies*, Inc.

Michael Mason, *The Making of Victorian Sexuality* (Oxford: Oxford University Press, 1995) pp. 139–43. Reproduced by permission of Oxford University Press.

Lynda Nead, 'Forms of Deviancy: The Prostitute' in *Myths of Sexuality*, Blackwell Publishing. Reprinted with permission of the author and publisher.

Judith Walkowitz, 'Jack the Ripper' in Walkowitz, *City of Dreadful Delight: Narratives of Sexual Danger in Late-Victorian London*, The University of Chicago Press and Virago. Copyright © Judith R. Walkowitz, 1992. Reproduced with permission.

Elaine Showalter, 'Dr Jekyll's Closet' in Showalter, *Sexual Anarchy* pp. 105–16. Reproduced by permission of Abner Stein and the Elaine Markson Literary Agency.

Peter Bailey, 'The Victorian Barmaid as Cultural Prototype' in Peter Bailey *Popular Culture and Performance in the Victorian City*, © Peter Bailey 1998 published by Cambridge University Press, reprinted with permission of the author and publisher.

John Plunkett, *Queen Victoria: First Media Monarch* (Oxford: Oxford University Press, 2003) pp. 13–67. Reproduced by permission of Oxford Univeristy Press.

Catherine Hall, *Civilising Subjects: Metropole and Colony In the English Imagination, 1830–1867*, The University of Chicago Press and Polity. Copyright © 2002 by Catherine Hall. Reproduced with permission.

While every effort has been made to trace and acknowledge ownership of copyright material used in this volume, the Publishers will be glad to make suitable arrangements with any copyright holders whom it has not been possible to contact.

Introduction

Rethinking the Victorians

KELLY BOYD AND

ROHAN MCWILLIAM

T HE VICTORIAN ERA came to an end at half past six on 22 January 1901 at Osborne House, when, surrounded by her family, Queen Victoria finally passed away. Eighty-one years old, she had reigned for sixty-four years. Not long after she came to the throne in 1837 her contemporaries began to describe themselves as 'Victorians', usually with a celebratory or bombastic flourish. In one of the earliest usages of the term the Congregationalist minister Edwin Paxton Hood proclaimed that the 'Victorian Commonwealth is the most wonderful picture on the face of the earth'.[1]

Most eras take on some kind of mythological quality and that is certainly true of the last two-thirds of the nineteenth century. Even though the political power of the crown waned during Victoria's reign, the ceremonial value of the monarchy (what the great political commentator Walter Bagehot called the 'dignified part' of the constitution) still retained an imaginative hold over all except extreme republicans and few contemporaries had any problem with their Victorian label.[2] The term 'Victorian' gathered strength after 1901, as it was called upon to evoke an historical period, a series of styles in fashion and architecture, a moment when the novel flourished and a lavish empire continued to grow, but, perhaps most of all, a state of mind. It meant earnestness, prudery, hypocrisy, overly ornate and elaborate design, bold entrepreneurialism, double standards, snobbery, sentimentality, utilitarianism, imperialism, narrow mindedness, cosy but stifling family life, rote-learning, extreme religiosity, racism, respectability, corporal punishment, hard work and drudgery. It meant town halls built in the gothic style and Isambard Kingdom Brunel's bridges. It meant St Pancras Station, the Great Exhibition and the paintings of the Pre-Raphaelites. It meant the age of Gladstone and Disraeli but also the exploitation of workers, particularly children. It meant the London of Charles Dickens but also the city of Jack the Ripper and Sherlock Holmes. It came to describe a sepia-tinted age that trumpeted high ideals and Christian virtues but presided over an underworld of poverty and prostitution. And its usage did not stop at Britain's borders, but evoked recognition across both the English-speaking and non-English-speaking worlds.

The deep certainties on which nineteenth-century life depended were eroded in the twentieth century with its climate of moral relativism; the term 'Victorian' quickly became one of abuse. To be modern was to disdain the overpowering world of the Victorians with its fussy furniture, stiff upper lips, lengthy sermons and inward-looking, repressed lives. Victorianism cut Britain off from exciting ideas on the Continent (such as sex and socialism). Perhaps the disgust it evoked was best expressed in 1918, when the poet Ezra Pound commented: 'For most of us, the odour of defunct Victoriania [sic] is so unpleasant and the personal benefits to be derived from a study of the period so small that we are content to leave the past where we find it.'[3]

Yet, to live in the world since 1901 is to be haunted by the ghosts of the Victorians. We live in the houses they built, or, if we do not, regularly stroll past buildings they erected. We work in the global market place that they did so much to construct. We recognise that their world of mass consumerism and mass marketing prefigured our own. We continue to read their novels; indeed some novelists have been so enthralled by their literary legacy that they have written their own 'pastiche' nineteenth-century fiction.[4] The Victorians have also haunted subsequent politicians and policy makers. The 'other' of modern social security is the workhouse. The 'other' of modern feminism is separate spheres. Even if we want to distance ourselves from the Victorian past, we remain fascinated by it. The Victorians are our contemporaries.

This essay considers the culture of twentieth-century Victorianism and the rise of Victorian Studies as an academic discipline, with particular emphasis on the role of historians. By 'Victorianism', we mean the ways in which the Victorians have been imagined not just by scholars but by the culture at large. The essay places in context the Readings in this volume, which reveal how the Victorians are being discussed today. It explores the reasons why the Victorian world continues to provoke controversy and tracks some of the political and psychological forces that have continued to draw people back to Victorian Britain as a point of reference.[5] Such a broad canvas means that we have to be selective; nevertheless, we do highlight some of the most important trends in modern Victorianism.

Chronologies and terminologies

Of course, there is no such thing as 'the Victorian'; there are only ways of seeing things as 'Victorian'. The term is more a convenient than an accurate description. The use of the term 'Victorian' is usually a simplification as it stands for what was a diverse and complex society. There is, for example, no consensus about when the Victorian period actually was (apart from the dates of Victoria's reign). Some historians link its origins to the political movements and reforms of the late 1820s and 1830s, particularly the expansion of the franchise.[6] Indeed it is common to refer to the early part of the period as the 'Age of Reform' although even the dates of this era vary.[7] This moment was also seen as one when industrialism had taken hold and the railways were about to transform both commerce and travel. It was assumed that society was altered by these events, but, more recently, historians of social attitudes have found many of the distinctive 'Victorian' traits existed in the eighteenth century (and indeed even earlier). Proponents of 'the long eighteenth century' suggest that the Victorian rupture with the past is illusory and that continuity is as evident as change. **Richard Price** has provided the most dramatic recent critique of nineteenth-century periodisation by arguing that the notion of a Victorian period does not make sense and that nineteenth-century economy, society and politics were merely a continuation of earlier social and political currents (authors of a Reading in this book are rendered in **bold**).[8] His is the ultimate 'long eighteenth century' argument. There has been no agreement on when the Victorian period ended either. Did it finish in 1901 or should we run it up to 1914 (or even the 1960s)? Like most questions of this sort, dates and chronology depend on what questions are being asked of the past. As a subject that encompasses more than just the political or economic or cultural changes taking place during Victoria's reign, Victorian Studies must be open to constant recalibration as new questions are posed.[9] Scholars of Literature and the History of Art may well find themselves using different chronologies from historians or employing ways of naming an age (such as the Romantic period) that historians find less appealing. There is clearly nothing definitive about periodisation; it remains a moving target.

If the start and end points of the Victorian period remain contested, the subdivisions of the era have also exercised scholars. While some have assumed there was such a thing as a unified Victorian age, there has also been an influential scholarly convention that divides the period into three distinct phases. The early Victorian period is usually held to have lasted from about 1830 to 1848. These were the years of Thomas Carlyle's 'Condition of England' question, of Chartism and the Anti-Corn Law League and of Engels' portrait of the Manchester working class. It was what the Hammonds later called 'the Bleak Age', a time of economic depression.[10] The social conflict of this moment was echoed in the industrial novels of Mrs Gaskell, Charles Dickens and Benjamin Disraeli among others. However, the improvement of the economy in the 1850s is usually held to have launched a new era, mid-Victorian Britain, which was characterised by rising standards of living. Commencing after the defeat of Chartism in the year of European revolutions (1848), it was epitomised by the Great Exhibition of 1851, which served as a symbol of increasing prosperity, middle-class confidence and the belief in progress through science and technology. This period also saw crucial intellectual and cultural developments with the publication of Charles Darwin's *Origin of Species*, John Stuart Mill's essay 'On Liberty' and Samuel Smiles' *Self-Help* all in 1859. Quite when the mid-Victorian period ended varies according to who one reads. Asa Briggs runs it up to 1867, Geoffrey Best's survey of the mid-Victorians lasts up to 1875, while K. Theodore Hoppen's Oxford history of *The Mid-Victorian Generation* takes in the years 1846 to 1886.[11] The period was perhaps most elegantly described by W.L. Burn (who ends the period in 1867) as 'the Age of Equipoise'.[12] The final years of the century (late or later Victorian Britain) were ones of powerful contradictions. The British Empire was at its height and British money drove the development of a new world economy. British culture was exported around the world through the operettas of Gilbert and Sullivan, the fiction of Sir Arthur Conan Doyle and the plays of Oscar Wilde. Yet the confidence we associate with the Victorians began to decline in the years after the Second Reform Act (1867). This was a period of doubt as the economy began to face real competition from abroad, conflict in South Africa led to the Boer War and the possibility of Irish Home Rule threatened the nature of the United Kingdom. Poverty became a major political issue in the 1880s and with it came a more organised labour movement that was increasingly sympathetic to a new ideology — socialism. The rise of the eugenics movement, the hysteria over the influx of immigrants, the development of new consumer patterns with the spread of department stores, the increased visibility of women in public life, and anxieties about manliness were just a few of the issues that dominated this era. This is why the late Victorian years are often viewed as a moment of crisis and a time of relative economic decline (when measured against the rise of Germany and the United States), although Britain remained one of the world's most successful economies.

Another problem is the relationship between the category of 'the Victorian' and its successor 'the Edwardian'. Did society change dramatically between Victoria's death and the First World War? The term 'Edwardian' has achieved a resonance in the popular mind, partly because of the transforming political and technological changes of the era (the Liberal welfare reforms, the campaign for female suffrage, the advent of the motor car and the aeroplane) and, in a contradictory way, because it was seen as a moment of relative stability before the outbreak of war. The Edwardians were often viewed as essentially people of the twentieth century (although others hold that twentieth-century society was ushered in by the impact of 'total war' in 1914). On the other hand, many of the changes of the period were rooted in developments that had been building during the last third of the nineteenth century, making any notion of a decisive break with the past in 1901 questionable.[13]

This leads us to the question: who were the Victorians? The obvious answer would be: anyone who lived in the British Isles in the second two-thirds of the nineteenth century. The term 'Victorian', however, has always seemed to connect far more with the world of the middle classes (and perhaps the aristocracy) than with that of the working classes. The word conjures up in the first instance the comfortable, upper middle-class home ruled by a paterfamilias, waited on by his loving wife and several servants, while his children are seen and not heard. But the term must also presumably apply to the labouring population, especially as the nineteenth century witnessed the diffusion of the iconic Victorian identities of respectability and hard work within society at large.[14] Should we also apply it to the diverse peoples of the British Empire? Such a move inevitably replicates the imperialism of the era and yet we lose some of the distinctive characteristics of life in nineteenth-century India and elsewhere if we do not employ it. The word 'Victorian' has also been employed to describe the middle-class environments of other countries. Peter Gay applies it to European culture and it has also become usual to talk about 'Victorian America'.[15] The term 'Victorian' is therefore not straightforward. It can be frequently misleading and (occasionally) politically loaded. It implicitly underwrites a view of history that gives undue prominence to (and perhaps therefore inadvertently supports) the British monarchy, though the reader can decide whether that is a good thing or not. The authors included or discussed in this book have also varied in their identification with the label 'Victorian Studies'. Some have thought about the nineteenth century more broadly and others have been concerned with social patterns taking place over an even longer period than the years between 1830 and 1900. Should we abandon the use of the term 'Victorian'? There is clearly a case for doing this and yet it remains so colourful, evocative and widespread in the culture that it is difficult to dismiss. We should regard the word as an invitation to think more deeply about the nineteenth century rather than as a definitive statement about it.

What the present volume demonstrates is that the Victorians continue to be the source of debate and disagreement, provoking an enormously distinguished body of scholarship on their public and private lives. Victorian Studies in recent years has been more interdisciplinary than the study of many other historical periods. The province of historians, literary scholars, art historians, geographers, philosophers, political scientists and many others, it draws together scholars and writers from across a number of disciplines to explore the culture of Britain at one of its most dynamic moments. The field has always been characterised by a dialogue between these groups, each enriching their own studies by a familiarity with adjoining debates and methodologies. The effectiveness of this interdisciplinary urge, however, varies over topic and time. Examples of interdisciplinarity might be located in the way historians and literary critics used each other's work to enrich their study of the period. Dickens scholars, for example, benefit from research into urban history and the impact of the Industrial Revolution. Interdisciplinarity lies at the base of Victorian Studies and animates this collection of essays.

But what is 'interdisciplinarity'?[16] Most would acknowledge that it means more than a historian sticking in the odd reference to Thackeray or a literary critic citing Asa Briggs' *The Age of Improvement*. Historians have long drawn on ideas derived from political and social science, which they have considered cognate disciplines. Martin Hewitt trenchantly observes that much of what passes for interdisciplinary work is really a form of 'multi-disciplinarity', juxtaposing historical and literary approaches.[17] There is little attempt to make disciplines speak to one another. But, as Joe Moran argues, interdisciplinarity has to be transformative in some way.[18] It needs to produce conclusions that cannot be obtained through the normal academic channels; otherwise it would have little to recommend it. An interdisciplinary approach has to do more than just demonstrate an awareness of what other disciplines are doing. The distinctive quality of interdisciplinary work is its readiness to ask questions of the different kinds of academic explanations available. This generates a self-consciousness of technique but also an awareness of the varieties of explanation that can generate new insights. Historians thus need to learn from English departments not just to consult contemporary fiction but to also read all sources as texts, deconstructing their assumptions and use of language. Literary critics need to learn from historians that a statement in a novel is not necessarily indicative of a general trend. The historian of art needs to uncover the social context of artworks (as opposed to acting simply as a connoisseur) and also to teach others not only about the problems of interpreting visual sources but also about the act of seeing itself. Similar points could be made about the historian of ideas or of science.

Interdisciplinarity need not mean an analytical porridge in which disciplinary approaches fight it out with no clear shape to the material, although it is true that cross-disciplinary encounters can often be uncomfortable. Rather, it is founded on respect for the forms of knowledge and techniques taught by specific disciplines, but it also requires an open-mindedness, a feeling that the map of learning knows no boundaries. The task of the interdisciplinary scholar is to uncover the complex ways in which people see the world in all periods including the present, exploring the influences of culture, language, economy, geography and much else. Many (but not all) of the scholars in this collection evince an interdisciplinary sensibility. In an age where there are sometimes pressures on scholars to focus on one discipline alone, Victorian Studies stands as a beacon.

The Victorians 1901–1945: the 'Age of Recrimination'

Disdain and contempt

From the 1890s onwards, it became fashionable among the intelligentsia to despise their fellow Victorians. Oscar Wilde's reputation was built on mocking the high seriousness of his contemporaries. After 1901, many of the truths that anchored Victorian civilisation were challenged. Samuel Butler's novel, *The Way of All Flesh,* when it was finally published in 1903 (it was written between 1873 and 1885), was soon celebrated by the younger generation as a rejection of Victorian hypocrisy and repression (even though it is arguable whether Butler was attempting to dismiss the whole era). One of Butler's targets was the stultifying nature of family life, a theme taken up not long after in Edmund Gosse's memoir, *Father and Son* (1907), a remarkable portrait of the author's childhood in the earnestly religious home of his father, the zoologist Philip Henry Gosse, and his desire to break with the rules of his father's generation. The image of the Victorian family with a stern, tyrannical paterfamilias whose priggishness and prudery damaged the imagination and the exhilaration of human existence became one of the great themes of twentieth-century anti-Victorianism.[19] The solution was to personally or politically rebel rather than be swallowed up by bigotry and small-mindedness.

As far as the Victorians were concerned, the first half of the twentieth century was an 'Age of Recrimination' (our term). The Bloomsbury Group helped shape the negative image that the nineteenth century enjoyed until at least 1945. Modernism also disliked the literalism of Victorian culture, its obsession with the allegedly real. Hence some artists frequently favoured the abstract and the subjective rather than the pretence of realism and objectivity, which, they believed, had been the stock-in-trade of their forebears.

By about 1910, the standard subdivisions of the period (early, mid- and late Victorian Britain) had begun to emerge. Expressions came into use such as 'the hungry forties', a powerful image of the Chartist years that was actually rooted in the contemporary debates over Joseph Chamberlain's tariff reform campaign and the cheap loaf that free trade was believed to offer when the Liberals won the election of 1906. The last decade of the nineteenth century acquired a mythology even before it ended; it became the *fin-de-siècle,* a decade of delicious decadence that cherished novelty, and where the word 'new' acquired a rich vitality. The idea surfaced that life itself could be turned into a work of art.[20] The nineteenth century had apparently been seen off by a combination of Wilde, Wells, Beardsley and (most of all) Ibsen.

The first major historian of the nineteenth century was not British but French. Elie Halévy commenced his career by initiating the systematic study of the Utilitarians and Philosophic Radicals who had helped transform the British state and made Victorian Britain into a liberal age.[21] Halévy was not the first person to put Jeremy Bentham on the map, but he demonstrated the role of Benthamite ideas in shaping liberalism and the modern state, setting the agenda for political and intellectual historians thereafter. He went on to produce his monumental *A History of the English People in the Nineteenth Century* beginning in 1912.[22] Frustratingly, Halévy's history was never completed. After a major reappraisal of the period between 1815 and 1841, he leapt ahead to the years between 1895 and the First World War (when liberalism began to decline), leaving out the larger part of the Victorian age.[23] Nevertheless, his contribution to Victorian Studies was considerable and his work was reprinted throughout the twentieth century. Along with the Hammonds, Halévy pioneered an early form of social history even though he was himself mainly orientated towards the study of politics and ideas. He was particularly interested in the stability of Victorian society. Why had Britain managed to avoid the wave of revolutions that had continually convulsed Europe and despite the pandemonium of industrial change? In the first volume of his history (*England in 1815*), Halévy attributed Britain's avoidance of revolution to Methodism, which taught working-class people to accept their lot in life (the social role of religion and the avoidance of revolution became two of the great themes of nineteenth-century historiography).

The Halévy thesis was part of an historical moment that witnessed the development of a liberal-left analysis of the nineteenth century. J.L. and Barbara Hammond researched a series of passionate but scholarly works about the experience of the labourer during industrialisation. They took their concerns as Edwardian Liberal Progressives into the archives where they rediscovered moments of resistance (such as the Captain Swing riots of 1830) and unpicked the lives of dearth and makeshift that were common for so many in the Industrial Age. The socialist husband and wife teams Sidney and Beatrice Webb (friends of Halévy) and G.D.H. and Margaret Cole researched the history of the labour movement and its institutions (such as trade unions and the co-operative movement).[24] Although this version of the nineteenth century was sometimes ignored, they established a wider form of nineteenth-century history that resisted the celebratory tone of many Victorian commemorations. In this they were unwittingly assisted by Charles Dickens, who has probably done more than any one else to shape the modern view of the Victorians. The continuing appeal of the author who produced so many heart-wrenching accounts of Victorian poverty (not least in arguably his most popular work, *A Christmas*

Carol) meant that, in the popular mind, the lives of the Victorian poor would never be lost, although they would often continue to be viewed through a soft-focus, sentimental, Dickensian lens.

Another of the dominant figures shaping the initial interpretation of the Victorians was Sigmund Freud. In the light of his work on the subconscious, it became common to believe that the Victorians lived double lives and were tormented by the demands of the libido. Many of the recriminatory early accounts of the Victorians were Freudian. Freud influenced the book that really put anti-Victorianism on the map: Lytton Strachey's *Eminent Victorians* (1918). This was a scorching attack on four heroes of the nineteenth century (Florence Nightingale, Thomas Arnold, General Gordon and Cardinal Manning) whom he revealed to have been weighed down by feet of clay. Believing that the Victorian world had come crashing down in the First World War (and a good thing too), Strachey established debunking as a form of biographical method. Ever one for the *bon mot*, he kicked off by claiming that 'The history of the Victorian age will never be written: we know too much about it.'[25] The brevity of his book and the waspish acidity of his comments broke with the worthy biographies that had previously been written about the Victorians with their respectful tone, elaborate reproductions of letters, and lack of concern for the inner life of the subject. Strachey was associated with artistic modernism and with the Bloomsbury Group. Their liberal views and bohemian life style were deliberately intended to undercut what they perceived as stifling Victorian prudery which suppressed the kind of creativity and honest conversation (particularly about sex) that they valued.

What was most noticeable about this period was the alteration in tone of criticism from one of earnestness to mocking irony. Virginia Woolf famously claimed that 'in or about December 1910 human character changed'.[26] Perhaps it was simply Virginia Woolf who had changed, but her observations of the way her friends acted is also suggestive. She recalled a telling moment when Lytton Strachey asked Vanessa Bell about a stain on her dress:

> 'Semen?' he said.
> Can one really say it? I thought and we burst out laughing. With that one word all barriers of reticence and reserve went down. A flood of the sacred fluid seemed to overwhelm us. Sex permeated our conversation . . . We discussed copulation with the same excitement and openness that we had discussed the nature of good. It is strange to think how reticent, how reserved we had been and for how long . . . When all intellectual questions had been debated so freely, sex was ignored. Now a flood of light poured in upon that department too. We had known everything but had never talked. Now we talked nothing else.[27]

This episode defined Bloomsbury as a very non-Victorian group. As intellectuals and artists they were atypical, but it is fair to say that the later twentieth century eventually adopted this new attitude towards openness about sexual matters as a rejection of the hypocrisy and cant of an earlier generation. Anti-Victorianism was the order of the day.

The greater dissemination of Sigmund Freud's ideas about sexuality meant that, by the 1920s, no self-respecting bohemian could use the word 'Victorian' without a snarl. In 1924, the young actress Elsa Lanchester enjoyed a huge success in the musical revue *Riverside Nights* at the Lyric, Hammersmith, with a sketch called 'In Queen Victoria's Ampler Days'. She sang a range of old music hall songs such as 'The Ragcatcher's Daughter' and 'Please Sell no more Drink to my Father' and brought the house down, because the sentiments described appeared to the cosmopolitan audience to be so absurd and out of date.[28] Margaret Barton and Osbert Sitwell employed a similar technique in their 1931 collection, *Victoriana*, in which the words of eminent Victorians were set down without comment for the most part because their views were clearly ridiculous. One page is made up of a single sentence in which John Ruskin praised Turner as 'the greatest painter of *all* time' (italics in original). Gladstone was traduced for his platitudes and pomposity; he was 'a much more ludicrous figure in his own way than ever were Tennyson ... or Swinburne'. For Sitwell, Gladstone was merely 'a kindly master of intolerable platitude, with a genius for finding the inevitable phrases in which to clothe the most banal thoughts'. The Grand Old Man was dismissed for his 'underlying and perhaps unconscious hypocrisy'. By contrast, Disraeli was excluded from the book as

> almost everything he said or wrote contained ... an enormous residue of wit and wisdom (an uncommon attribute for then as now for a statesman). Moreover, his words convey meaning to other generations besides his own, and thereby betray their lack of our requisite quality: *Victorian* wisdom.[29] (italics in original)

Bloomsbury's critical disdain also applied to Victorian art and architecture, which was routinely dismissed as ugly in the inter-war years. The literary historian Richard Altick recalls that:

> The Victorians' fine arts ... were so little valued that in 1935 John Martin's last apocalyptic canvasses, a trilogy so sensationally popular in the 1850s that they had been toured in Britain and America as a profit-making exhibition, had brought at auction a total of seven pounds. The nadir, however, was reached about the same time when a London dealer offered to give a customer one of John William Waterhouse's paintings, which was taking up space in his showroom. The customer ... would have removed it, except that he found he could not get it inside a taxi.[30]

One of the most important anti-Victorian representations in the inter-war years was Rudolf Besier's play *The Barretts of Wimpole Street* (1930), a dramatisation of the romance between the poets Elizabeth Barrett and Robert Browning and the obstacles posed by Barrett's tyrannical father, a stern and hypocritical Victorian paterfamilias. The play confirmed the worst anti-Victorian prejudices. In the repressive Barrett household, the children have lost their ability to feel passion or any emotion. At one point, Elizabeth Barrett tells her brother that he has become an automaton as he has cut everything out of life that makes it worth living. The play embodied what was essentially a Freudian view of repressed sexuality and celebrated the lovers for breaking free of convention when they escaped the stern world of the Barrett home where Elizabeth had been infantilised. The play enabled audiences of the 1930s to recognise they too had escaped the strict world of the Victorians, a message to which they responded. The play ran for two years in the West End of London. It was filmed in 1934 with Charles Laughton and remade in 1957. During the 1950s there were four separate versions aired on American television. It was even turned into a musical in 1967 (*Robert and Elizabeth*). The play epitomised the allegedly loveless world of the Victorians. Another popular play of the 1930s, Patrick Hamilton's *Gaslight* (subsequently filmed twice), also featured a view of the Victorian domestic space as a place of terror where a woman is convinced by her tyrannical husband that she is mad so that she will not detect his search for the jewels that have been hidden in the house. Not long afterwards, Roland Pertwee's play *Pink String and Sealing Wax* (1945) contrasted Victorian family life (including the ever-present stern paterfamilias) with a terrible murder.

But anti-Victorianism never commanded total allegiance before 1939. As early as 1908, a soldier employing the soubriquet, 'One of the Old Brigade', penned a volume titled *London in the Sixties* in which he celebrated the licentiousness of the mid-Victorian world and claimed it was the tail end of the Regency. Recreating the atmosphere of the Cremorne pleasure gardens and of Holywell Street (noted for its shops selling pornography), he insisted on the *un*-Victorian character of the period, which he preferred to the do-gooding atmosphere of Asquith's Britain.[31] Later, Ralph Nevill (son of society hostess Lady Dorothy Nevill), in his book *The Gay Victorians*, proclaimed that Victorian London was 'much more free in its life and amusements than that of today when "Dora" and an excess of regulations have stamped out all so-called Bohemian night resorts, together with music-hall lounges and supper places of a free and easy kind ... Puritan fanatics and cranks have triumphed all along the line'.[32] In 1924 the humourist Arthur Machen hit back at the contemporary idea that 'The Victorians couldn't write, couldn't paint, couldn't think, couldn't properly be said to be alive at all. They lived and moved in a world of prim, feeble, old-maidish, curatical schoolgirlish preferences, their chief object being to avoid telling or hearing the truth about any subject whatsoever.'[33] Instead, Machen focused on their pleasure-loving sociability. Nor did the cinema avoid the nineteenth century; it presented versions of Victorian novels from its earliest days. In 1937 the film *Victoria the Great* starring Anna Neagle (a stirring chronicle of the Queen's reign) was so successful that it was remade in colour the following year as *Sixty Glorious Years*, suggesting that, outside Bloomsbury, the world of the Victorians was not inherently ridiculous for a large number of people. In a very different way, American horror films in the 1930s (especially the popular cycle produced by Universal) featured gothic terrors against an essentially Victorian background, acknowledging the nineteenth-century roots of the horror genre. *The Strange Case of Dr Jekyll and Mr Hyde* was filmed three times in the United States between 1920 and 1941. While some intellectuals viewed the Victorians with contempt, within the broader world of popular culture, the Victorians were objects of fascination and even perverse pleasure.

The greatest intellectual defence of the Victorians between the wars came in G.M. Young's 1934 essay, 'Portrait of an Age', a panegyric to the previous century. The age he portrayed was one of energy, creativity and possibilities. Young was a former civil servant who developed a passionate interest in the Victorian era. He set himself a course of readings on the Victorians, employing what became his famous methodology when he advised historians to 'go on reading until you can hear people talking'.[34] An ardent Tory, he was depressed by reading Strachey's *Eminent Victorians*, commenting dryly, 'we are in for a bad time'.[35] Young was not alone in developing an historical interest in the Victorians. His essay first appeared in a multi-authored collection that he edited entitled *Early Victorian England*. He took this to be the period from 1830 to 1865, demonstrating that the modern convention of confining the early Victorians to the period 1830 to *c*.1850 had not been set in stone.[36] Young was in effect adopting the chronology of the nineteenth century that Albert Venn Dicey had employed in his famous lectures on *Law and Public Opinion in England* (1905), which assumed that an age of liberal individualism had come to an end in 1865 to be replaced by an era of collectivism. Young also suggested that the later nineteenth century remained fairly contemporary in the 1930s; only the period before the 1860s was beyond memory. (Young himself was born in 1882 and could remember the Victorian period vividly.[37]) The sense of the Victorians as living in a historical period that was distinct from the world of twentieth-century moderns took time to develop.

Young's collection, *Early Victorian England*, brought together a wide range of authors, including the leading economic historian Sir John Clapham. His *Economic History of Modern Britain* (1926–38) had opened up a broader and more rigorous history of Victorian society as a whole and had begun to question the extent of economic growth during the industrial revolution thereby anticipating much of the revisionist literature of the 1980s. Although the essays in *Early Victorian England* have been superseded, they were not amateurish, and represented one of the first attempts to understand the Victorians in a serious and rigorous way.

Young's volumes also demonstrate that interdisciplinarity (or, at least, multi-disciplinarity) has always been integral to the agenda for Victorian scholars. They contained a strong assumption that history must include art and literature; indeed the original title of the book was *Dickens' England*, and there were ninety-three references to the author in the book. Beginning with a note on costumes, the essays ranged over theatre, architecture, town life, travel, and the army as well as other subjects; in other words, they aimed to present a rounded social history and not simply situate the Victorians within the world of political and constitutional history which was then in the ascendant. A few years later, Humphrey House's important study, *The Dickens World*, leant heavily on Young's books for providing the social and historical context.[38] Indeed, literature was an important stimulus for studying Victorian history. It was important to write the history of the Victorians in order to understand the mentality of Dickens and other writers at a time when the novel was establishing its literary ascendancy or, in the case of Sir John Clapham, to correct mistaken impressions provided by the literary record.

Victorian Britain was a contested space in the early twentieth century. It was the object of disdain in the world of Bloomsbury — but disdain can also involve fascination. The Victorians became a measuring stick for modernity. They represented the creation of the modern and yet theirs was a world that had to be left behind if modernity was to continue.

The Victorians 1945–80: the 'Age of Evaluation'

Class and economy

In 1948, BBC radio's 'Third Programme' broadcast a series of fifty-seven talks on all aspects of nineteenth-century life and culture. In his introduction to the series in the *Radio Times*, Basil Willey noted that, in the 1920s, 'The Victorian Age might . . . have been considered more appropriate to a Light programme, for to that decade it meant little but antimacassars, side-whiskers and all that those symbols denoted: stuffiness, prudery, hypocrisy, complacency, philistinism. Today, however, the scene is changed, and the anti-Victorian myth seems more "dated" than the Eminent Victorians themselves.'[39] Contributors found much to admire in the Victorian inheritance. These included the rising Labour politician Richard Crossman who, in the final programme, talked about the ongoing relevance of the Benthamite reform tradition: 'I find the Victorians of the 1830s to the 1850s as close to me as Plato, who is also, of course, as close as anybody could be today.'[40] The Victorians were seen as people living through a time of social, political and economic crisis, who yet had been able to cope with the challenges of their time. The producers of the radio programmes noted that 'Genuine specialists in the period are surprisingly few'.[41] That was about to change.

As the post-1945 era began, Bloomsbury disdain gave way to a reappraisal of the Victorian world that took place both in society and in academia. Each post-war generation felt the need to rescue the Victorians from Strachey's contempt. The period from 1945 to about 1980 saw the foundation of Victorian Studies as an academic discipline. It was characterised by being less concerned with recrimination than with attempting to develop a serious understanding of the Victorian world in all its complexity. Social and economic history became increasingly important, edging aside political and military history, which had previously dominated academic study. The ambitions of social history in this period were vast. Nothing seemed beyond its scope. The lives of ordinary Victorians and, especially, the working classes (who had played only a small part in previous histories) became central. Social class and the emergence of a class-based society became the guiding themes. Post-war economic recovery in the 1950s and 1960s was reflected in a concern with the consequences of growth in the nineteenth century. The Industrial Revolution was seen to have created modern society; to understand modern society, it became necessary to understand the Victorians. We call this period the 'Age of Evaluation', as a way of capturing the spirit of this pioneering moment when journals such as *Victorian Studies* came into being and a remarkable wave of books and articles thundered off publishers' presses offering new views of the Victorians. Some of these were influenced by that eminent Victorian, Karl Marx, but even non-Marxists shared a concern to comprehend how this society actually worked and functioned. Studies of specific aspects of Victorian Britain were often written with one eye on how they fitted into a larger story of the development of capitalism, industry and class. There was a concern with social conflict (especially class conflict) and with the tensions that underlay the certainties of Victorian Britain but modernisation (in the form of urbanisation and new forms of transport) was another theme. Scholars often thought they were looking at the whole of society when in fact they were really looking at the lives of Victorian men alone but (as we will see) this evaluation of Victorian society came to include the lives of women as well.

One explanation for the Victorian vogue after the Second World War is that Britain was still being run by Victorians. Prime Ministers such as Winston Churchill (Conservative) and Clement Attlee (Labour) were very much products of the late Victorian period into which they were born (as were many key intellectual figures, for example Bertrand Russell). Their Victorian youth explained their subsequent careers. Churchill had been steeped in Empire, and fought in a range of imperial conflicts culminating in the Boer War. He saw the maintenance of Britain's role in the world as his most important task. Attlee's engagement with the Victorian legacy stressed a completely different set of problems. Educated at the public school Haileybury, his eyes were opened when he commenced social work with the poor in the East End of London in 1905: these were people completely different from any he had previously encountered and yet worthy of respect. For Attlee, the British state needed to engage with the needs of the masses. If they were not lifted from the Victorian misery embodied in the investigations of Booth and Rowntree, Britain had failed. Each agenda was shaped by the Victorians.

Another reason for the fascination with things Victorian is that Britain in the post-war period was very much a class society. From the 1950s onwards, however, rising standards of living, assisted by economic growth and the welfare state, began to transform the lives of many of the old working classes. There was much talk of 'embourgeoisement', and the class system seemed to be changing. This fed into a concern not only with modern class structure but also with its roots, a terrain that nineteenth-century social historians explored and which gave their research a wider importance. Moreover, Victorian Britain was the first industrial nation, which meant that it could be viewed as a case study of modernisation. It had also spread its influence all over the world through its Empire. In the age of decolonisation that followed the Second World War, there was a need to establish how this small island off the coast of Europe had managed to exert such influence in the first place.

In cultural terms a dialogue was established between the post-war present and the Victorian past. The Festival of Britain in 1951 was intended to echo the 1851 Great Exhibition in its optimism about Britain's role in the industrial world. Although it included a miniature version of Joseph Paxton's Crystal Palace, complete with models of Victoria and Albert opening the Exhibition, the 1951 event was intended to emphasise the modernity of Britain, to show how times had changed since Paxton's building had entranced contemporaries.[42] This tug-of-war between the modern present and the Victorian past was also clear in the Ealing film comedies, most notably *Kind Hearts and Coronets* (1949). Set in Edwardian Britain, its protagonist (one cannot say hero), Louis Mazzini, is denied recognition by his mother's noble family, the D'Ascoynes, as she had married beneath her. He proceeds to murder those who lay between him and the dukedom (all played by Alec Guinness). The tone is both Stracheyan and also cognisant that this world is doomed. Its popularity confirmed the extent to which the Victorian period remained a relevant setting for satirising the class system. Yet the world before 1914 was oddly comforting. Edwardian clothing became fashionable in the late 1940s partly as a reaction to the drabness of 'Austerity Britain'. Initially promoted by designers such as Hardy Amies, the dandyish New Edwardian look was eventually reinvented as the costume of the Teddy boys.[43]

By the 1960s, there was a reappraisal of the Victorians by the culture at large. Although the notion of the 'swinging sixties' has been overplayed, sexual liberalism, moral relativism and the pleasures of consumerism defined themselves against the Victorian inheritance which many felt still held sway. Women's liberation, for example, was premised on getting women out of the home (the antithesis of the Victorian celebration of the domestic). Paradoxically, this gave the Victorians even greater importance; they served as a vehicle against which fashionable people could define their identity as peculiarly modern. Yet it also became possible to find the Victorians sexy. John Schlesinger's 1967 film of Thomas Hardy's *Far from the Madding Crowd* with Julie Christie, Terence Stamp and Alan Bates offered a view of the Victorians that was almost *chic*.[44] Victorian clothing became fashionable once more, as the rise of Laura Ashley can attest. The Beatles were presented (ironically) as Victorians on Peter Blake's iconic cover for the album *Sergeant Pepper's Lonely Hearts Club Band*. The new wave of gothic horror associated with Hammer films was based on a Freudian interpretation of repressed Victorian sexuality. Christopher Lee's Dracula unleashed the sexual content in Bram Stoker's original, making the Transylvanian Count into one of Steven Marcus's 'other Victorians' (see below, p. 21). The nineteenth century could also offer a way to critique contemporary international events. Tony Richardson's 1968 film *The Charge of the Light Brigade* was viewed as a commentary on the Vietnam War, the futility of the Crimean War being taken as an analogy with American involvement in South East Asia.[45] Richardson's film contains traces of a Stracheyan view of the Victorians as, from 1969, did the Flashman novels of George MacDonald Fraser with their mockery of nineteenth-century ideals of heroism.

One characteristic of the 1960s' encounters with the nineteenth century was the frisson of being able to express things that the Victorians could not express. In Jonathan Miller's television version of *Alice in Wonderland* (1966), the alleged innocence of Lewis Carroll's children's story was replaced by a very Freudian nightmare in which a young girl teeters on the verge of acquiring an adult sexuality. John Fowles' extremely influential *The French Lieutenant's Woman* (1969) toyed with the form of the Victorian novel, using it to explore non-Victorian themes of sex and eroticism. He also subverted the Victorian belief in providing narrative closure: his novel had alternative endings.

At the same time, a changing world made the Victorians into objects of nostalgia, symbols of an innocent and stable time before the World Wars and revolutions of the modern age. *The Good Old Days* ran on British television from 1953 to 1983, featuring recreations of music hall songs and routines. The BBC partly defined its commitment to quality through adaptations of Victorian novels. These were also among their most popular exports and made Victorian Britain more familiar overseas than any other period except the Second World War. It was no longer fashionable to write off Victorian art, furniture and objects as ugly. Indeed 'Victoriana' became a byword for stylish items of material culture that were increasingly collected and therefore became more expensive.[46] Victorian fittings in houses were no longer covered up but proudly displayed. The Victorian Society was founded in 1958 to preserve period buildings, especially when they were under threat of demolition. Figures such as the poet John Betjeman managed to save St Pancras Station when it was under threat, but failed to rescue the magnificent arch outside Euston Station. For some critics, this kind of nostalgia buttressed a conservative heritage industry, reinforcing the notion of Britain as an old country: a theme park of aristocratic or old world values where people were taught to know their place. For others, particularly Raphael Samuel, the 1960s witnessed a wave of popular history that was democratic and allowed people to access the past in new and exciting ways.[47] It is significant that the late 1960s and 1970s (a period of economic crisis) witnessed a wave of popular portraits of the Victorian and Edwardian world. The 1970s BBC series, *The Onedin Line*, a recreation of mid-Victorian shipping and trade, was filled with the romance of capitalism. Other series such as *The Forsyte Saga* (1967) and *Upstairs, Downstairs* (1971–5) as well as the phenomenal best-selling book, *The Country Diary of an Edwardian Lady* (1977), represented nostalgia for a time before the uncertainties of stagflation, power cuts and the three-day week that occurred in the 1970s. For all the focus on servant life, the squalid nature of much working-class life was ignored and the class system rendered as quaint (a version of British life that played well abroad).

Children were not neglected in this ongoing resurrection of the Victorians. From its earliest days, the BBC's Children's Television Unit had commissioned versions of the Victorian classics it considered to be child-friendly. Adaptations of Victorian novels were shown at teatime on Sundays specifically for children, promoting the notion that the Victorians were a crucial part of the cultural inheritance. Most enduringly, Doctor Who commenced life as an elderly Victorian gentleman (indeed the first four Doctor Whos were distinctly Victorian figures). The Victorian costumes provided a deliberate contrast with both modern-day and futuristic stories. *Doctor Who* also represented an ongoing engagement in fantasy fiction, which (like the horror genre) has frequently returned to nineteenth-century settings, largely because this was a foundational moment in the growth of science fiction (the age of H.G. Wells and Jules Verne) and, more fundamentally, in the development of the technology and ideas of scientific progress that made the genre possible.

The growth of academic studies was propelled by the expansion of higher education in the post-war world. The removal of fees and the provision of a grant for living costs for students in the 1960s, accompanied by the creation of new universities, meant that the numbers of literary critics and historians grew and that their social origins varied more widely. This expansion of the university sector also assisted the growth of the social sciences. Sociology, in particular, offered new ways of studying societies past and present. Concomitantly, historians' interests began to range over a greater number of subjects. In Britain, adult education (in the form of institutions such as the Workers Education Association) provided a space where new approaches could be developed. Tutors such as the young E.P. Thompson were able to offer courses about labour history that offered a corrective to the history of high politics.

Different types of history sparked different kinds of analysis. Political and administrative history became less fashionable, although it flourished nevertheless in the 1950s and 1960s. The major themes included the development of the party system and the state and the coming of democracy.[48] From considerations of the 'Victorian revolution in government' and its implications for the treatment of the poor to analyses of the influence of Victorian educational reforms in the maintenance of class structures, important works emerged. One of the paradoxes that sustained research was the argument that the modern welfare state involved a rejection of the Victorian laissez-faire approach even though the roots of the welfare state could be discovered in the nineteenth century.[49] Historians debated whether the Victorian period was defined by individualism when it was clear the state could be extremely interventionist.[50] Serious treatments of Victorian statesmen were produced, even though biographies in the 1960s and 1970s had become extremely unfashionable because they seemed to be a form that did not engage with larger social and economic forces.[51]

The world of monarchs, soldiers and statesmen (which had been the great theme of a lot of history up to that time) were joined by studies that delved into the rest of society. Even a political historian such as George Kitson Clark (who played a key role in encouraging the study of the Victorians at Cambridge in the 1950s and 1960s) broadened his scope to look at the social forces that made Victorian Britain.[52]

Social history, although not an entirely new development, increased in importance, and eventually transformed itself into the most vibrant element of historical study by the 1960s and 1970s. Employing the methods of social science led historians to discount earlier impressionistic accounts and to aspire to a new precision in documenting the past; they were not interested in producing a 'portrait' as G.M. Young had done. They demanded something far more rigorous that interrogated how society operated as a system.[53] As a discipline social history emerged out of economic history but it was also shaped by both Marx and the sociologist Max Weber, although British historians notoriously tended to prefer empirical approaches (working from the evidence) rather than engaging in theoretical work. It seemed to be extremely democratic, promising 'history from below'. Social historians believed their research could make a difference in politics. The best example of this would be the members of the Communist Party Historians Group, but this ambition was shared more widely by labour historians, who disproved suggestions that the working class had no history because there were no historical records. In this pioneering age, the lives of workers and the poor were not only rediscovered but it was insisted that they had agency (they were not just acted upon from above by economic forces but created institutions and a culture that sustained them). Historians were concerned with both the structures that governed people's lives but also the way they engaged with and made sense of those structures. This approach was adopted for many historical periods and countries but the body of work on nineteenth-century British society was widely admired. Victorian social history soon gave birth to a new sub-discipline: urban history. Historians such as Asa Briggs (who did more than anyone else to establish the field of Victorian Studies) developed the field by comparing patterns of urban development and showed that Victorian cities were dynamic forces for change, a view that reflected the repeated calls for modernisation in the post-war period.[54] The Victorians had much to teach. Even political history was influenced by the new social history. Historians and political scientists created what has been described as the 'electoral sociology' school, which evaluated political behaviour at all levels by employing social science methodologies.[55]

The nineteenth century drew scholars to it because it seemed to offer clues to the origins of modern British society. The Victorians, as Michael Wolff has put it, were 'the first moderns'.[56] Historians drew inspiration from the work of the late nineteenth-century social reformer Arnold Toynbee (not to be confused with his nephew of the same name whose *Study of History* became a much debated treatment of world civilisations). In a posthumously published and much read lecture of 1884, Toynbee argued that the Industrial Revolution had transformed Britain at the beginning of the nineteenth century and created a modern, class-based society.[57] This indictment was to be explored in depth thereafter.

The Industrial Revolution itself was central to understanding the foundations of Victorian Britain. One of the key works of the post-war period was by the American economist W.W. Rostow, who popularised the notion of 'take off into self-sustained growth', which posited, following his work on the British Industrial Revolution, a series of preconditions necessary for industrial development.[58] Nineteenth-century Britain's industrial past could be considered a guide to how societies industrialise and modernise. This imbued modern British history with an additional importance in the developing world. Britain provided a model of what to expect, what to do and what to avoid. Rostow drew up a much debated 'social tension chart' in which he mapped the development of social protest onto the level of wheat prices, demonstrating the material base behind the development of radicalism; hunger caused disorder.[59] In retrospect, much of the social history devoted to the nineteenth century reflected the worries sparked by post-war economic growth. Many historians suggested that growth could have severe social consequences. Debates over whether the Industrial Revolution caused the standard of living of workers to improve or decline also reflected Cold War concerns. At stake was the morality and legitimacy of capitalism itself. The response to the Victorians was, therefore, not a trivial matter.

Although economic historians in recent decades have taken a step back from seeing the development of Britain's industrial base as truly revolutionary by exploring continuities with earlier centuries and highlighting the gradual nature of industrial development, debates in the early post-war years focused on the dramatic effects of industrial change on society. Marxist historians, such as Eric Hobsbawm, were pessimists (holding that standards of living declined) while others, such as T.S. Ashton or R.M. Hartwell, were optimists believing that industrial production ultimately improved conditions for the workers.[60] Some of the key figures, such as Hobsbawm and E.P. Thompson, had been members of the Communist Party His-torians Group, but they were not so much Marxists as scholars engaged in a critical dialogue with Marx. Whilst emphasising issues relating to class, they eschewed reductive Marxist approaches, which assumed that politics could easily be reduced to economic forces. However, at least as important were non-Marxist historians, such as George Kitson Clark, Harold Perkin and Asa Briggs.[61] Even non-Marxists agreed with the Marxists about the importance of class and about some of the key moments of change that distinguished the early, mid- and late Victorian periods, a form of periodisation that now became widely accepted.[62] Few committed conservatives wrote Victorian social history, with the exception of W.L. Burn, author of *The Age of Equipoise*.[63]

Marxism as a system of thought always stressed the interconnectedness of knowledge. Thus there were strong links between the members of the Communist Party Historians Group and figures such as Richard Hoggart and Raymond Williams in Literature, Stuart Hall in Sociology and a range of scholars in the growing discipline of Cultural Studies, which many of the above helped to create. But interdisciplinarity did not stop there. This was also a time when social historians, such as the leading early modernist Keith Thomas, were urging a greater attentiveness to work in Anthropology.[64] E.P. Thompson was a distinctive advocate of an anthropological approach, which can be detected in *The Making of the English Working Class* and which explains his concern with popular rituals, traditions and indeed with the whole concept of 'culture'.[65] Economic history also boomed; cliometrics were the order of the day, meaning that historians had to become statistically and quantitatively literate. A feeling for literature was also important. Asa Briggs wrote his pioneering article about the medical history behind *Middlemarch* as early as 1948, part of the rediscovery of George Eliot that characterised the immediate post-war period. Even at this early stage, Briggs felt able to commence his article by reminding readers that 'Victorian novels have long been accepted as useful source-books for the social historian'.[66] Indeed, it became accepted that the Victorian novel offered a form of social history in itself. The call to interdisciplinarity was an established feature of intellectual discussion well before the late twentieth century.

This was very much a generation. Hobsbawm was born in 1917, Briggs in 1921, Thompson in 1924 and Perkin in 1926. They were the children of Victorians.[67] Generations of course do not always understand one another but there was a certain familiarity with the Victorian mindset in their work if only because it remained so pervasive in the world into which they were born. It should also be said that this was a generation that grew up in the 1930s; it was formed by the experiences both of economic depression and then of total war (in which they participated in various ways).[68] Their commitment to understanding the Victorians, however, was always provisional. They were really more concerned with the category of the 'nineteenth century'; indeed, most of them argued that the key moments of historical change (the Industrial Revolution and the struggle over political reform in 1830–2) occurred before Queen Victoria ascended the throne. E.P. Thompson's magisterial study, *The Making of the English Working Class*, was devoted entirely to the pre-Victorian years, 1780–1830 (although it shaped much of the debate about the Victorians). Even Asa Briggs' influential textbook, *The Age of Improvement*, devoted much of its length to the pre-Victorian period.[69] The left-wing orientation of these historians was significant not only in the way that they wrote history but also in the complex attitude to the Victorians that they exhibited. The high-mindedness of the Victorians and their concern to develop strong civic institutions, abolish slavery and confront social evils resonated with the younger generation for all their criticism of the effects of nineteenth-century capitalism. Significantly, few historians chose to write in a dismissive, Stracheyan mode about Victorian lives.

The 1960s and 1970s saw a concentrated effort to recover Victorian movements and individuals whose efforts had not been wholly successful, but whose actions illustrated the struggles between different groups. The Society for the Study of Labour History was founded in 1960. Chartism was rehabilitated from a failed movement to one that played a vital role in the political education of the working class.[70] Another debate concerned the failure of working-class people to remain radical after the collapse of Chartism in 1848, focusing on the role of the labour aristocracy.[71] Hobsbawm and George Rudé recaptured the world of the Captain Swing rioters in 1830 and their Luddite-style revolt in southeast England against the introduction of new threshing machinery. They demanded the labouring poor be viewed as employing custom and ritual to protest on behalf of their livelihoods.[72] Crime and disorder were probed for their social implications, while leisure was interpreted as a site of conflict between those who wished to relax and those who wished to maintain a degree of control over the working classes.[73]

The new wave of social historians did not simply look at the working classes. F.M.L. Thompson investigated the way in which landed society operated.[74] He suggested it shifted its economic power from agriculture to expand its income from urban rents and investment abroad. In one of the most ambitious treatments, Harold Perkin (the first Professor of Social History in Britain) explored the basic forces that sustained nineteenth-century society. He argued that Britain experienced a 'more than industrial revolution' in the early nineteenth century that transformed social relations. Britain had previously been governed by an aristocratic ethos that pervaded society at all levels. In the 1830s an 'entrepreneurial ideal' emerged as the values of the middle class began to dominate the common sense of local and national government and as the middle classes began to remodel society in their own image. Perkin argued that in the 1880s this was replaced by what he called the 'professional ideal' whereby society was dominated by the assumptions of middle-class professionals (such as doctors, lawyers and social workers). Perkin and Asa Briggs were relatively unusual at this time in thinking seriously about the middle classes.[75]

Many of the most important statements about the Victorians were by scholars in Literature. F.R. Leavis (who helped establish literary criticism as a morally serious and rigorous pursuit) considered certain Victorian novelists as part of a 'great tradition' in literature and his worldwide influence encouraged a more rigorous approach to nineteenth-century literature. Powerful as the Leavisite moment was, many literary critics moved away from Leavis in that they not only wanted to understand the Victorian novel or poem on its own terms but also wanted to understand (in Walter Houghton's words) 'the Victorian frame of mind' or (in Jerome Buckley's) 'the Victorian temper'.[76] Critics detected that the extraordinary burst of creativity that shaped Victorian literature was the result of the paradoxes of a period that was torn between confidence and doubt, materialism and spirituality, conformity and individualism.[77]

Literary critic Raymond Williams's *Culture and Society*, although not confined to the Victorian period, shaped the interdisciplinary atmosphere of Victorian studies.[78] He uncovered the way in which a set of key words such as 'class', 'art' and 'culture' acquired their current meanings in the late eighteenth century, thereby helping introduce the modern world. This provided him with a basis to investigate some of the leading writers and artists since 1780. By interrogating links between politics, society, economics, literature and art, he laid the foundation for the discipline of cultural history. His focus on the word 'culture' provided a space that scholars in many different disciplines could rally around. Moreover, his investigation of the enduring romantic critique of capitalism made sense of many Victorian writers. Williams wrote as a socialist who wanted to explore literature in the context of the prevailing ideologies of the period (what he famously called 'structures of feeling'). For Williams, the early to mid-nineteenth century marked a turning point and established a political agenda around class and capitalism that radicals in his own day were still dealing with. A foundation text for the discipline of Cultural Studies, *Culture and Society* initiated a greater interest in the sociology of litera-ture and of communications in the nineteenth century, which Williams followed up in *The Long Revolution* (1961). Francis Klingender accomplished something similar within art history. His *Art and the Industrial Revolution* interpreted painting and illustration in a wider economic context and laid the basis for a Marxist art history of the nineteenth century.[79]

Scholarly interest in the Victorians was not confined to Britain. The United States and Australia, among other countries, produced important work.[80] Figures such as Richard Altick and R.K. Webb in the United States wrote pioneering accounts of working-class consumption of fiction.[81] The journal *Victorian Studies* was founded at Indiana University in 1957 and established itself as an interdisciplinary publication. In its early days it would not accept an article unless it clearly drew on at least two disciplines (although this boldness was later modified to a belief that interdisciplinarity should be an 'aspiration').[82] Other projects that developed at the time included the *Wellesley Index to Victorian Periodicals*.[83] One of the great problems scholars encountered was that most articles in nineteenth-century periodicals were unsigned (despite in some cases having illustrious authors, such as John Stuart Mill or Gladstone). This multi-volume work sent scholars into publishers' archives to uncover the names of the authors of articles in a range of influential Victorian periodicals. The tradition of anonymous publication was breached and now it became clear who had authored individual articles, allowing for a more illuminating engagement with contemporary intellectual debates. Jonathan Miller described it as 'a Mount Palomar telescope through which the night sky of Victorian thought can appear as a majestic panorama of genius and error'.[84]

There were no frontiers on this map of learning as curiosity moved outside the public sphere and into the private. One member of staff at Indiana University had a major effect on the way the Victorians were remembered even though he was a zoologist; this was Alfred Kinsey. His investigations of sexuality based on interviewing ordinary people about their sex lives had an enormous impact when they were published in Eisenhower's America. Before the Kinsey Report Americans considered themselves heirs to a parallel repressive Victorianism that had flourished in the United States. All this seemed to be challenged by Kinsey's revelations about the variety of sexual practices among his interviewees. The Kinsey Institute set out to document sexuality in all cultures, assembling sexual materials from all over the world. One of the key books to emerge on British Victorian sexuality was partly researched at the Kinsey Institute. This was Stephen Marcus's *The Other Victorians*, a study of what ought to have been a contradiction in terms: Victorian pornography. Marcus was a literary scholar but his work doubled as a form of social history and was discussed as such.[85] It acknowledged that the Victorians had not only created the modern economy but had also established the basis of modern sexual culture with its reticence and codes of silence about the body. Marcus employed pornography and medical texts to break the silences around sexuality. He turned William Acton, the surgeon who claimed that women lacked sexual feelings, into an eminent (or, at least, an iconic) Victorian. He did much the same thing with the anonymous 'Walter', author of the pornographic work, *My Secret Life*, which Marcus took seriously as a form of autobiography. His reading of Victorian sexuality was subsequently absorbed by Michel Foucault in his history of sexuality. Marcus's book was very much part of the taboo-busting rejection of Victorian hypocrisies that became part of the 1960s' cultural revolution. A more populist treatment of the same theme by Ronald Pearsall, *The Worm in the Bud* (1971), made such an impact that spicy extracts were serialised in the *News of the World*. No one could deny that Victorian history mattered.

The serious spirit of post-war academic evaluation of the Victorians continued in the 1970s. However, there was one very important development that began to change perceptions of the Victorians. Women's history grew directly out of feminism's dissatisfaction with histories (including many left-wing histories) that simply concentrated on men and ignored women's lives. The interdisciplinary nature of this was clear in Martha Vicinus's pioneering collection *Suffer and Be Still* (1973) which brought together social historians, literary critics and art historians to suggest new ways of reading Victorian women's lives.[86] It is significant that the first tranche of Barbara Kanner's massive bibliography of sources on Victorian women also appeared here, spurring much new research.[87] The challenge for women's historians was to uncover sources about women when female experience had so often not been recorded. They proved that it was possible to write about women by discovering new sources and rereading conventional sources to uncover evidence about women that had previously been ignored. Victorian women's history initially concentrated on campaigns for women's enfranchisement, wider education, property rights, the removal of civil disabilities, and the influence of women novelists on the Victorian cultural world. Pioneering studies uncovered the realities of the lives of pit-brow lasses, domestic servants, nurses, political hostesses and others. In this sense it replicated the approach of social and labour history. It soon expanded, however, to explore how Victorian women grappled with the way patriarchal assumptions structured their lives. Recovering the lives of campaigners against female oppression teased out new ideas about women's roles in society.[88] Thus the campaign against the Contagious Diseases Acts acquired a new importance in the literature. Not only was it interpreted as a protest against the state's intrusion into private lives but it also became a critique of the problem of hegemonic male sexuality and a transforming moment in the history of feminism.[89]

A similar movement was taking place within Victorian Literature, as feminists challenged the prevailing methodological procedures and demanded a revision of the canon. There was nothing new about interest in female writers but **Elaine Showalter** (who had contributed to *Suffer and Be Still*) insisted that there was a distinctive female tradition of writing and interpreted the work of women novelists as a form of negotiation with a male-dominated society and with what was expected of a 'feminine' novel. Notoriously, a number of women (for example, George Eliot (Mary Anne Evans)) had employed male pseudonyms. Showalter dealt with the problems of learning to speak as a woman in a patriarchal society.[90] Two years after Showalter came Sandra Gilbert and Susan Gubar's *The Madwoman in the Attic* (1979) which read a variety of female texts as forms of subversion of patriarchal authority and described the peculiarities of the way that women struggled both to find a voice and to achieve growth when female creativity was so often not valued. By the end of the 1970s, women were truly on the agenda.

This period was a foundational moment when Victorian Studies really emerged as a serious discipline. It aimed for an interdisciplinary approach although this often really meant the juxtaposition of different approaches rather than a true cross-fertilisation of methodologies.[91] The most significant theme was the rise of a society based on class, but in the 1970s this was extended to include a concern with women's lives. Above all, social history inspired a focus on the material base of society. The key category was that of experience and, in particular, the lived experience of the whole of Victorian society and not just the elite. The focus of history had dramatically widened. This period was characterised not only by a serious and systematic evaluation of the Victorian world but also by locating the Victorians as a source of debate that frequently reflected contemporary politics. Some of the themes that emerged continued thereafter to hold good. However, from the end of the 1970s the premises of this wave of Victorian history were seriously challenged.

The Victorians since 1980: the 'Age of Representations'

Identity, performance and the self

In or about 1980, Victorian Studies entered a new phase that we call here the 'Age of Representations'. This captures the flavour of some of the most influential developments in the period covered by this book. In using this term we mean a number of things. It refers to the way critical theory (primarily literary and social theory) raised questions about the production of knowledge and meaning in all societies. The use of theory was not a new development. Marxist theories had shaped much of the debate about the Victorians, as we have seen, even though many historians disdained theory, preferring an empirical approach. From the late 1970s, new forms of critical theory (such as post-structuralism) drew attention to the importance of language and discourse. Rather than representing a pre-existing material reality, it was argued that language constructs how reality is perceived. This tendency became known as the 'linguistic turn'.

The 'Age of Representations' is also intended to convey the shift that took place in the late twentieth century from social history to a new interdisciplinary cultural history, which placed less emphasis on social structure.[92] Instead it considered the importance of symbols, rituals, ceremonial, print culture and other representations in binding together the Victorian world. Representations, it was argued, were not trivial; they actually created the whole idea of 'society' and performed what came to be called 'ideological work'.[93] There was also a focus on the ways in which personal identities were constructed. Cultural history considered a wide range of mentalities, attitudes and behaviour, including those that appear irrational to the modern mind. Categories such as 'theatricality' and 'performativity' became important because scholars considered the ways that people spoke and the ways they presented themselves to others (and to themselves) as forms of performance. These approaches are sometimes labelled 'postmodern' (an unsatisfactory term that refers to a number of different things).[94] They challenged the way History was written but also traditional forms of literary scholarship and most other forms of knowledge.

However, it should be said that there was as much continuity as change in the kinds of scholarship produced. Many scholars resisted or ignored the theoretical debates that flourished across the humanities. Empirically minded historians often found postmodernist insights not so much challenging as lacking in interest. Moreover, postmodernism was not by itself responsible for the new subjects that gained increasing attention such as race, empire, science and geography. Nor was it responsible for the new work in economic history that began to make us think about the nineteenth century in new ways and to challenge the most basic assumptions that had been held about it. Pure critical theory remained very much a minority pursuit but it did shape the climate in which these subjects were discussed and stimulated new views of the Victorians.

The 1980s was a time of political and intellectual ferment. At the beginning of the decade the Keynesian social democratic settlement that existed in the developed world was torn apart. Manufacturing increasingly shifted out of Western countries. Britain, and much of the West, began to become post-industrial societies, characterised by the growth of knowledge and service industries. National boundaries became more complex in an age of globalisation. Issues around the consumption of goods seemed to matter as much as their production. Above all, the world that drew its inspiration from Karl Marx began to collapse.

Just as Victorian Studies in the 'Age of Evaluation' reflected the post-war social democratic consensus, the New Victorian Studies in the 'Age of Representations' was also the product of its age. The context was now not just Thatcherism and Reaganism but also an agnosticism about what the progressive alternative on economic policy should be. Critical theory tended (with some exceptions) to be left wing in orientation and yet in the late twentieth century the political left everywhere was in retreat. This led to an increasing focus on the histories of identity and the private sphere. The Readings in this book demonstrate the shift away from class and industrialisation as the major themes. The personal was political. The shift towards interrogating Victorian views of the self mirrored an age in which there were major debates about the legitimacy of state and collective provision. As scholars traced the Victorian histories of shopping, financial capital, gay subcultures, democracy and the claims of science, they were expressing the opportunities, dilemmas and passions of their own times.

The 'Age of Evaluation' had defined its modernity by employing forms of social science, which allowed society to be seen as a whole. The postmodernist impulse was suspicious of these kinds of approaches and opted for complexity, arguing that human identities were far less stable and more diverse than they appeared in the post-war period. Victorian versions of the self became more complex. Even the notion of 'society' could not be taken for granted. It was no longer viewed as an objective reality but as the product of a particular form of knowledge and view of the world that emerged in the eighteenth-century Enlightenment.

Just as the influence of Marx shaped the Humanities in the post-war period, the most influential theorist after 1980 was probably the French philosopher Michel Foucault (who wrote about nineteenth-century Britain in a number of works). Foucault raised questions about the production of knowledge and the politics of information in societies. He argued that the categories employed to define and classify people contained a power of their own. In his wake, historians began to discuss how language, knowledge and specific institutions shaped human behaviour, emotions and manners in the nineteenth century. Much of Victorian Studies has developed a Foucauldian line (sometimes unconsciously so), focusing on the ways in which the nineteenth century produced new categories and ways of ordering knowledge with vast implications for how people saw themselves, their bodies and their world. 'Soft' versions of Foucault have been employed to think about the role of the state, law, race, gender and sexuality in shaping the Victorian world.[95]

The category of 'experience', which once seemed so straightforward in the days when scholars were rallying to E.P. Thompson's standard, came to be seen as extremely problematic.[96] The aim of post-war social history was to allow people from the past to speak for themselves and about their experiences; thus there was a focus on oral history and on the uncovering of working-class autobiographies so that the poor could be given a voice.[97] In the 1990s, the emphasis shifted in a different direction. Critical theory suggested that the way people talk about themselves is never simple or straightforward. Rather, people employ different kinds of images and forms of metaphor that circulate in the culture. The purpose of the scholar was to tease out (or 'deconstruct') these forms of representation. Hence the notion of simply recovering the voices of the past was considered naive or, at least, inadequate. Popular memory is a complex text.

The category of 'culture' was also rethought. It had come into wide use in the 1950s and 1960s to mean a way of life that reflected the material base of society. In the 1980s, 'culture' came to enjoy an agency of its own as something that was often independent of economic and material forces but nevertheless remained a key factor shaping a society. It was also redefined to mean the vast network of images and representations in circulation at any given time.

This broader cultural history (evident as much in Literature and History of Art as in History departments) was characterised by a reinvigorated call for a new kind of interdisciplinarity. Not all scholars responded to this clarion call to dissolve academic boundaries, but it became a distinctive feature of scholarly life among Victorianists.[98] Interdisciplinarity promised ways of thinking that were wider in scope than those of a single discipline. The hope was to create a transformative cross-fertilisation of disciplines, although this outcome remained elusive. Much current research continues to simply juxtapose different approaches rather than to create new ways of thinking.[99] In *The Victorian Studies Reader* we have tended to concentrate on historical works that are characterised by an interdisciplinary sensibility. These studies achieve this aim with varying degrees of success but express the increasingly sophisticated arguments about the Victorians that characterise our time.

As we have seen, there is nothing new about this. However, the characteristic of interdisciplinarity in the 'Age of Representations' is that it was propelled particularly by Literature scholars. Literary forms of analysis rather than sociological or anthropological theories set the pace for academic discussion. Much of this was inspired by scholars who subscribed to the 'New Historicism' in Literature, which demanded that texts be understood in the context of their moment of creation or consumption, rather than as individual works of genius.[100] For the New Historicist, words or 'discourses' became vehicles of power that circulated within the culture and shaped how people saw and related to the world around them. Significantly, many of the most important ways of thinking about the Victorians came from North America. This transatlantic connection in Victorian Studies was longstanding but much of the sustained engagement with theory emerged from North American Literature and History departments after 1980, which also gained from having a critical distance from British culture.[101] Out of this climate emerged the new kinds of Victorian Studies documented in this book.

Literary scholars began to look at sources of Victorian life that had previously been off limits for them. Statistics, science, legal discourse and medical texts joined more traditional texts, such as novels, drama and poetry, as worthy of study. A typical example is the 'Law and Literature' movement, which often focused on Victorian texts, but has done something far more ambitious than simply examine lawyers in fiction. It has unravelled the narratives and forms of emplotment on which the law is based, comparing the evidentiary strategies employed both in the courtroom and the novel. Law, it argues, is based around a series of narratives and stories (the use of evidence, the precedents of the common law) that are sometimes surprisingly similar to those in fiction. After reading this work, neither the Victorian legal system nor the Victorian novel looks quite the same.[102] Both were arenas where the Victorians tried to understand something about themselves.

Issues about class did not disappear after 1980 but there appeared new concerns about gender, national identity, imperialism, science and consumerism. In the 'Age of Evaluation', the key figures included the self-taught labour aristocrat, the feminist demanding a voice, or the businessman organising municipal reform. In the 'Age of Representations', the iconic figures included the black Victorian, the *flâneur* (a sophisticated man about town and observer of metropolitan life) and the deferential worker. These figures had been on the fringes of earlier studies, considered marginal (black or Asian Britons wrongly not being considered much of a presence until the mid-twentieth century), problematic (the ogling *flâneur*), or shameful (the mixed-up deferential worker who failed to recognise where his true class interests lay).[103] The *flâneur* fascinated because he offered a way of thinking about uses of public and private space and the importance of the male gaze in structuring the spectacles that the city offered.

Another context for the New Victorian Studies was the political climate. The election of Margaret Thatcher as Conservative Prime Minister in 1979 commenced a new era. Despite being born in the twentieth century, she instinctively harked back to the Victorian period in her rhetoric. During the General Election of 1983, she was asked about the values that inspired her and, in a famous statement, described them as 'Victorian values', invoking her childhood as a grocer's daughter in Grantham:

> We were taught to work jolly hard. We were taught to prove yourself [*sic*]; we were taught self-reliance; we were taught to live within our income. You were taught that cleanliness is next to godliness. You were taught self-respect. You were taught to give a hand to your neighbour. You were taught tremendous pride in your country. All of these things are Victorian values. They are also perennial values.[104]

Although Margaret Thatcher of course was not speaking about the nineteenth century at all (she was really recalling Britain between the wars), it was clear that she was invoking the Victorian era as a time of national greatness and moral certainty while identifying post-war Britain as a nation gone astray and in decline. In the same spirit, her Education Secretary, Sir Keith Joseph (who had largely developed Thatcherism as an economic doctrine), wrote the introduction to a new edition of Samuel Smiles' best-seller, *Self-Help* (a hymn to the values of hard work, good character, thrift and duty) and proclaimed it 'a book for *our* times'.[105]

The invocation of Victorian values by Margaret Thatcher was a call to arms for historians on both sides of the political spectrum and on both sides of the Atlantic. A number of books were published that explored Victorian values.[106] The Left had tended to associate the Victorians with poverty, squalor and the workhouse. A group of historians associated with the socialist History Workshop produced a special supplement on 'Victorian Values' in *The New Statesman* recalling the crime, misery, class differences and gender repression of the period.[107] On the Right, the American intellectual historian **Gertrude Himmelfarb** sought to rescue the Victorians from conventional charges of hypocrisy. She agreed that hypocrisy existed but claimed that the Victorians were aware of this and deliberately failed to publicise double standards because of the importance of clinging to basic rules about decency (something that the modern world had apparently forgotten to do). Himmelfarb celebrated the prevailing belief in virtues that were handed down to children and, in an elaborate two-volume study of poverty, found much to praise in Victorian attitudes to the poor (based on philanthropy and self-help) that did not depend on the assistance of the modern welfare state.[108] She believed Americans could learn from Victorian Britain. These kinds of views had been anathema to progressive thinking during the building of the welfare state.

After 1989, figures on the British Left began to think about which Victorian values they could appropriate, such as the importance of civic pride, the dignity of public service and local democracy. As socialism went into decline after the Berlin Wall came down in 1989 and the Soviet Union collapsed, Victorian liberalism and radicalism were increasingly scrutinised as the basis for a new progressive politics.[109] The Victorians retained their relevance in the age of Tony Blair and Gordon Brown even though the 'New Labour' project of the 1990s disliked looking back to the past.

The political struggles of the late twentieth century renewed interest in the Victorian state and economy. A shift to a more laissez-faire approach in modern politics meant the great Victorian age of laissez-faire needed further consideration. How did a laissez-faire state work? Was a polity where government prided itself (at least much of the time) on not intervening either in the economy or society at large a desirable thing? Was the Victorian state weak or strong?[110] There was nothing new in the interest in the great Victorian political philosophy, Liberalism, but the renewed focus on its political complexities took shape in the shadow of Thatcherism.

It was not only the Victorian state but also the Victorian economy that was rethought. Old orthodoxies were challenged. The first was the assumption that Victorian Britain was the product of the Industrial Revolution. Some scholars began to ask if the latter had ever taken place.[111] Figures showed that economic growth in the early nineteenth century was confined to a small number of industries. Despite the lengthy discussions of the 'factory question' in early Victorian Britain by contemporaries, factories were relatively unusual. Most production in 1850 still went on in small-scale workshops.[112] There were suggestions that the Industrial Revolution was a myth and that the nineteenth century had more in common with the century that preceded it than with the modernity of the twentieth century that it was always held to prefigure. At best what took place was an 'industrial evolution'.[113] This was a major reversal in thinking and a different, more complex nineteenth century began to emerge.

A second orthodoxy that was overturned was the assumption that the middle class took over the running of Victorian Britain during the early Victorian decades, ushering in a bourgeois age. The conventional wisdom held that the 1832 Reform Act not only gave the bourgeoisie the vote but a stake in the political system. With the repeal of the Corn Laws in 1846 and the development of free trade, the state was won over to a broadly middle-class, liberal outlook. By contrast, it became increasingly common to point out that the old aristocratic elite survived the 1832 Reform Act and dominated both national and local government right up to the end of the century.[114] This was not a wholly new argument but it certainly challenged glib assumptions about the rise of the middle class.

A third orthodoxy that ran into trouble concerned the nature of Victorian capitalism itself. It had been assumed that the leading sector in the accumulation of wealth was manufacturing. However, W.D. Rubinstein's research on wealth holding suggested that fortunes derived from the financial sector such as banking and insurance were always greater than those made through industry.[115] Serious money was made not so much by a new elite in the North of England as by the old elite based in the South. **Cain and Hopkins** brought this all together in their work on 'Gentlemanly Capitalism' (that is, wealth derived from land and financial capital). They argued that Britain's world domination was not so much a by-product of industrial power as the skill in investment by aristocrats and financiers. Britain's ruling elite not only survived in Victorian Britain, but it managed to tame newer forms of capitalism and shape the global economy. **Martin Wiener** had earlier argued that this deference towards tradition and the values of the public school gentlemen carried the seeds of economic British decline, impeding modernisation.[116] Therefore, the middle class had never quite made it in Britain. Aristocratic values taught them to despise trade (the very source of their wealth); and hence they lost their capitalist killer instinct and modernisation was impeded. Wiener's work on British decline was probably the most widely debated of all the studies in this book, taken up by Thatcherites as an example of what they were fighting against but also by the Left as an example of how British culture was suffused by traditional and old-fashioned values. In retrospect, it marked a coming of age for cultural history. Wiener demonstrated how culture could shape the economy rather than the other way round.

As a whole, these debates reflected the atmosphere of the 1980s when much of British industry went to the wall but the financial sector did extremely well. Historians demonstrated that this reliance on the financial sector was long standing and that British capitalism had always been divided. The Victorians entered the twenty-first century with their significance up for grabs. Oddly, the revisionist work on the Industrial Revolution had an unintended consequence. Traditional economic history, with its focus on industry and production, seemed to lose some of its authority when it came to explaining the Victorians. Instead, new fields such as the history of consumption became more important.

The new intellectual atmosphere had consequences for the great theme of post-war social history: class. There had been a broad consensus, even among non-Marxists, that class had shaped identity in the nineteenth century. In the 'Age of Representations', class became less an objective reality than a story that people told about themselves to make sense of the social order, but it was noted that they also employed other narratives as well, defining themselves frequently in gendered, racial or religious terms. To establish the contrast, let us take Asa Briggs' famous article from 1960 about class. Briggs demonstrated how the language of 'class' (based on the metaphor of classes in a school) replaced an earlier language of social description based on 'ranks' and orders' in the later eighteenth century.[117] Briggs' assumption was that this shift was a reflection of the making of a new industrial society where class differences were being thrown into sharp relief by the new stage of capitalist production caused by the Industrial Revolution. In contrast, in 1995 Dror Wahrman investigated the language used to describe the middle classes and argued that the term 'middle class' emerged in the 1790s, not as an objective form of social description but for political reasons. In the age of the French Revolution, the authorities needed to describe a class of 'middling' people to offset arguments about the gulf between the rich and the poor.[118] This differed from earlier approaches based on sociology.

Wahrman's was a political rather than a social interpretation, part of a moment when political history was reappraised. Having been unfashionable for a long time, it sprang into new life as a way of thinking seriously about the operation of power in society. There was a feeling that the social history of the previous generation had been weakened by the failure to take the contingencies and complexities of the political process seriously.[119] Moments like the 1867 Reform Act were rethought. No longer could it be seen simply in terms of the growth of democracy and the emergence of mass political parties; it was also necessary to recognise its base in a particular view of manhood and of racial superiority.[120] More than anyone else, **Gareth Stedman Jones**' work inspired arguments based around the 'relative autonomy of politics' and its complex links to the social order.[121] He argued that social history could not fully account for the language and ideology of movements such as Chartism. Instead he employed the resources of intellectual and political history to raise questions about the extent to which Chartism embodied a form of class-consciousness. Social historians had failed to take the politics of the Chartists seriously enough. The ideology of Chartism could not be reduced easily to questions of class, an argument that shocked many labour historians.

Another change in the discussion of class was the shift from talking about the 'working class' in the singular. Historians of social structure came to argue that these terms covered such a diverse group of people that it was more appropriate to talk of the 'working classes' (the same is true of the middle class). Class continues to be a feature of debates but it is viewed in a more complex way than it used to be.[122] The context for these debates was the decline of class politics in Britain (and elsewhere) in the later twentieth century. This had been much discussed since the 1950s when it became clear that appeals to class loyalty and solidarities in the form of trade union activity had less impact than they had. Significantly, the middle classes began to receive more historical discussion than they had in the 1960s, when the Marxist assumption had been that the working class was the agent of historical change and therefore needed examination through labour history.

There were fewer concerns with the moments of social conflict that had invited earlier historians to focus particularly on the early Victorian decades. Instead there was a greater concentration on the mid-Victorian period and more generally on the sources of social and political consensus, which explained why the social order had not broken down despite massive poverty.[123] Interest in the rise of socialism and the more organised labour movement in the late Victorian period also ebbed. Scholars began to focus on identities that were not based on class. **Patrick Joyce** argued that the language of 'class' co-existed with other, vaguer, but still meaningful, identities, such as the 'people', with its patriotic resonance; he described this as an ideology of 'populism', which he considered more helpful for understanding nineteenth-century mentalities.[124] Joyce argued that not only was 'class' an invented identity in the nineteenth century but that historians also needed to think about the ways in which such categories as 'selfhood', 'democracy', 'society' and 'the social' came into use. These were not objective terms that were just there in nature. They had to be actively constructed in the nineteenth century and implied a particular viewpoint based on the values of liberalism and modern understandings about the ability of the state to control and direct people's lives and even their bodies.[125]

In the later twentieth century, nation mattered as much as class. The conservatism of the 1980s was reflected in a greater interest in issues of national identity, patriotism, Englishness, heritage and the Victorian celebration of the past. Nations were no longer seen as existing in any objective sense, but as 'imagined communities' that had to be constructed through the rhetoric of political leaders, intellectuals and others.[126] These intellectuals included the great historians of the age such as Macaulay and Seeley who were retrieved as important thinkers as well as custodians of the national memory. They developed what has since been termed the 'whig interpretation of history', which defined national identity in terms of progress.[127] Part of this national identity, it was observed, was an obsession with antiquity and history. For example, the Victorians attempted to revive the age of chivalry, part of the code of the English gentleman. Celebrations of mediaeval knights, the Arthurian legends and romantic accounts of Jacobitism were common currency from Walter Scott to Tennyson. They reached their risible but magnificent height in the Eglinton Tournament (1839), a quixotic attempt to recreate mediaeval jousting, that was rained off.[128] Perhaps more crucially they made up the bulk of imaginative literature available to all classes from the 'penny dreadful' or boys' story paper to the Sunday school prize volume.[129] The most important book about national identity was Linda Colley's *Britons* (technically, a pre-Victorian study), which suggested that what was formed in the early nineteenth century was not just a class system but a distinctive national identity based on the values of Protestantism.[130]

In the same spirit, monarchy (the emblem of national identity) became important once more (see **John Plunkett**'s Reading). It had been fashionable in the 1960s and 1970s to despise the kind of history that was made up solely of kings and queens. Although royal biography had never gone away, after the success of Elizabeth II's Silver Jubilee in 1977, followed by the cult of Princess Diana after 1981, historians were impelled to take popular monarchism more seriously. Queen Victoria was examined in terms of her gender (she was even reclaimed for women's history), her role as an imperial symbol, her influence on family structures and her reinvention of the constitutional monarchy as acceptable, indeed preferable, to other types of heads of state. Above all, there was a concern with the evolution of the institution of monarchy although the resurgence of republicanism in the late 1990s was reflected in new studies of the republican tradition in Victorian Britain.[131] It was established that patriotism was never simply the preserve of the political Right. In the nineteenth century, it had also been an element in Victorian radicalism; an example of the importance but also the complexity of national identity.[132]

Women's history (which had been characterised by the desire to put women back into the historical record) was itself challenged. A new kind of gender history insisted that it was no longer enough simply to reconstruct the lives of women; instead, it was important to think about how gender was an important form of social organisation that determined people's lives every bit as much as the economy did.[133] All subjects needed to be rethought in terms of the way gender assumptions structured existence. Where Chartism was seen as heroic in the 1960s, it was now suggested that it actually expressed a very masculine view of politics and economy. It was reinterpreted by **Anna Clark** as a movement structured by patriarchal assumptions, where men's jobs were seen as under threat from female labour; thus its mentality led it to progressively exclude women. Gender mattered as much as class.

Leonore Davidoff and **Catherine Hall**'s *Family Fortunes* (1987) demonstrated the interpenetration of gender and class. In their view, the middle class was not just the product of the fortunes made during the Industrial Revolution or Harold Perkin's 'entrepreneurial ideal'. It also owed much to a gender system that had become widespread: separate spheres. The public sphere was the world of work but middle-class women came to be exclusively associated with the home and there emerged an ideology of domesticity that profoundly shaped women's lives (as well as men's). There was nothing new about separate spheres but it did mark a departure from an earlier world where men and women had often worked together on the land.

In Victorian Britain there was enormous pressure to get women out of the workplace, partly to shield them from the operation of the market but more profoundly because of prevailing cultural assumptions that a woman's place was in the home (or the private sphere). Working women and men also found themselves increasingly segregated in the workplace. Women never left the workforce, but the stress on respectability meant a greater compulsion to conform to prevailing expectations about gender. Thus society expected young women to work until they had children, while men were eager to attain the 'breadwinner wage' (sufficient to allow their wives and children to remain at home and not work). However, few Victorian working-class families ever obtained the breadwinner wage. In other words, women's history demanded historians re-examine something as familiar as industrialisation in a new way. It also led to a greater appreciation of the crucial role that women had played as the foot soldiers of the Industrial Revolution, being drawn in as cheap labour that could be discarded as the market contracted or shifted. In many ways, women were the archetypal proletarians of industrial Britain. This contrasted with the older labour history which mainly concentrated on male workers.[134]

A history of masculinity began to emerge for the first time. While most history up to the 1970s had been about men, as we have seen, it did not take masculinity seriously as a problem. A new men's history emerged shaped by the view that masculinity (and femininity) are not universal categories but change historically. The attributes of manliness and masculinity were in flux during the course of the nineteenth century.[135] The new historians of masculinity showed how masculinity varied in different contexts according to class but also explored it in an imperial and racial context as well.[136] The key figure in making us think seriously about masculinity has been **John Tosh**. He has focused particularly on the way men interacted with their families, demonstrating how that icon of Victorian life, the paterfamilias, changed during the period. Gender has been re-established as one of the most important elements to constitute identity rather than an attribute so obvious it is invisible.

Victorianists have increasingly turned their attention to empire in the 'Age of Representation'. There had, of course, been a flourishing discipline of imperial history, but British and imperial historians rarely had much to do with each other. With the rise of Post-Colonial Studies, British historians began to think further about the Empire and its impact on Britain. There emerged in the 1980s an understanding that the Empire needed to be brought back into domestic history, provoking new questions. First of all, it was necessary to explore the impact of Empire on the average Victorian. Some historians have argued that the bulk of the population had little knowledge of the Empire and only remembered it when required on celebratory occasions.[137] But this ignores the extent to which Britain's economy was enmeshed in world trade. The cotton workers of Manchester were engaged in a business that encompassed India as well as Britain; other workers also interacted with raw and finished goods from foreign shores. Assessing the extent of Victorian knowledge of Empire involved examining representations of military campaigns, music hall songs and juvenile literature where Empire was a constant theme.[138] This ubiquity of Empire in popular culture (particularly in the late Victorian period) had implications for the development of British attitudes towards peoples of the Empire, which has had long-lasting effects. Popular culture taught ideas of racial superiority to white Victorians of all classes.

This brings us to the other half of the imperial equation: how the subjects of British imperialism interacted with the Victorian Empire. If modern racial tensions were to be understood, then it was necessary to think about the role of the British in the system of slavery and its abolition, and of the impact of Empire on racial attitudes.[139] Although mass migration from the periphery to the metropolis is generally seen to be a twentieth-century phenomenon, it is clear that people of all ethnic backgrounds were present in Victoria's Britain. These included immigrants from Ireland after the famine, German radicals relocating after 1848 (most famously, Karl Marx), and Jews fleeing pogroms in the 1880s and 1890s. All of these 'races', and many others, settled in Victorian Britain, which was in many ways a multicultural society. Its strong economy and relatively open society made it attractive to many. Most were economic migrants; all were seen as 'foreign'. The term 'race' was used in a relatively indiscriminate way to indicate people of other nationalities and ethnic groups. Their presence challenged and broadened national identity.[140] Modern writing about race usually denies its objective existence; the notion of racial difference is not recognised by today's scientists. Race therefore is a cultural construction, a way in which people are taught to classify and react to other people of different ethnic backgrounds. How people view other so-called races varies historically. The nineteenth century is significant because 'scientific' ideas about racial difference became stronger from mid-century, drawing on Darwin, supporting the alleged superiority of the white Anglo-Saxon races and laying the basis for future forms of racism down to the present. The increasing prominence of race in discussion of the Victorians reflected Britain's multicultural identity and the rise of Post-Colonial Studies.

The study of Victorian science has also become more important, not least because of the way it promoted new views of the self (most notably through Darwinian evolution). To understand the Victorians, it was clear that it was necessary to engage with the ways that technology transformed time and space while the natural sciences challenged the nature of identity. In the past the role of Darwinian ideas had dominated this type of analysis. Now a wider range of scientific ideas came to be explored through a cultural history approach. The Victorians were associated with the application of science and technology to everyday life, but their definition of what constituted a science was very broad. On the one hand it included geology and biology, but the Victorians also deliberated on mesmerism and phrenology. There was a greater emphasis on the 'false starts' in science, the roads not taken and pseudo-sciences, such as forms of quack medicine. Victorian science has become the site of a quite remarkable interdisciplinary exchange between historians, scientists and figures in literary criticism.[141] Science was re-conceived not so much as a search for objective truth but as a discipline that answered the needs of society at a particular time or that embodied prevailing concerns within the culture. The influence of Thomas Kuhn's *The Structure of Scientific Revolutions* (1961) was powerful here as it argued that changes in scientific thinking were generally mired in a specific world-view, until a new idea suddenly made everyone see things in a completely different light. Kuhn termed this a 'paradigm shift' and the Victorians were witness to a gigantic one (evolution) in the way they viewed science but additionally in the way they understood the self. The debates over Darwinian evolution were rethought. Earlier works that anticipated Darwin such as Robert Chambers' *Vestiges of the Natural History of Creation* (1844) were analysed in order to reconstruct the rich dialogue of ideas in which Darwin produced his theory.[142]

Finally, the turn towards cultural history led to a greater interest in Victorian performativity and theatricality (see the Readings by **Breward** and **Winter**). This did not necessarily mean more work on the theatre (although a richer theatrical history did develop during the period) but a focus on how theatrical images began to shape language and the ways that people saw the world and themselves.[143] If there was no such thing as a true self, then identity was a matter of a profusion of selves that were performed in different contexts according to different needs and requirements.

The dominant form of theatre in the nineteenth century was melodrama. Scholars in a variety of disciplines experienced a 'melodramatic turn' as they explored how the themes of the stage structured not only other arts but also language and the way in which people perceived reality and themselves.[144] This was a remarkable shift because one of the features of twentieth-century moderns had been a disdain for melodrama with its ludicrous coincidence-driven plots, ham acting, moustache-twirling villains, loveable yokels, nautical spectacles, talented dogs, and women tethered to the railway track before an oncoming train (although the cinema appropriated most of these elements). In the 'Age of Representations', melodrama was taken more seriously both because of its popularity and because it was a key to the Victorian frame of mind. Melodrama was, in the words of literary critic Peter Brooks, a 'sense-making system'. It offered a way of maintaining the rigours of traditional morality in the wake of the French Revolution when new values were emerging and a more secular world (a 'post-sacred order') was coming into being.[145] In the works of a number of scholars, it became common to argue that melodrama could not be confined by the proscenium arch and began to organise reality for people at all levels of society.[146] Women were frequently seen within the framework of melodrama. They could be viewed as intrinsically good and requiring protection by men (as in the virginal heroines of the stage) or alternatively as evil (particularly in the form of the femme fatale, popular in the later nineteenth century). Shaped around binary opposites, melodrama did not allow any moral complexity (which is why the intelligentsia disliked it). Melodrama also colluded in the Victorian tendency to label women as inherently hysterical and prone to emotions they could not control.[147] In the 'Age of Evaluation', social reporters, such as Henry Mayhew, were reclaimed for the way they gave voice to people whose lives would have been otherwise unrecorded, thereby creating an early form of sociology.[148] In the 'Age of Representations', scholars considered how Mayhew's way of looking was shaped by cultural assumptions, including a tendency to 'melodramatise' the lives of Victorian prostitutes.[149] Similarly, politicians, lawyers, campaigners and journalists were reassessed for the way they presented information through the conventions of the stage both as a way of explaining human motivations and as a way of moving audiences. For the modern generation of scholars, melodrama was not a trivial piece of Victorian kitsch but a part of the making of the modern world that has had consequences both in popular culture and in assumptions about the self.

We still live in the 'Age of Representations' and most of the tendencies we have described are central to current studies as they unpick the complexities of race, gender, class, religion, politics, economics, the Empire and many other topics. The necessity of reading texts, images, events and activities from a variety of perspectives will remain crucial as students of the Victorian period continue to uncover the ever shifting identities of their subjects and their implications for economic production and consumption, political behaviour, educational experiences and philosophical debates.

Whither Victorian Studies?

The year 2001 was a crucial moment in Victorian Studies as it marked the centenary of Queen Victoria's death. The occasion was marked by a number of exhibitions, books and conferences. Once more the Victorian inheritance provided an occasion for stocktaking — and yet there was a difference. Unlike the experience of the generation who had built Victorian Studies in the 1950s and 1960s, the Victorians were now a lot further away. They could no longer be referred to as 'the last century'. Moreover, historians have begun to focus less on the nineteenth century and more on the centuries either side. Yet the potential of the Victorians to shock and surprise remained. Matthew Sweet was able to commence his book debunking the myths that had circulated about Victorian Puritanism by saying: 'Suppose that everything we think we know about the Victorians is wrong.'[150] Sweet's Victorians were strikingly modern in their views. 'Exposed: The Victorian Nude', an exhibition at Tate Britain in 2001, told a different story about the Victorians from the one that existed in the popular imagination. Rather than fearing the body, it became obvious that many Victorians (including Victoria and Albert) relished representations of the nude. The Victorians enjoyed a more complex sexual culture than many had thought. Similarly, Sarah Waters enjoyed enormous success with a series of novels featuring Victorian lesbians. Her first, *Tipping the Velvet*, was filmed by the BBC deliberately as a way of doing something different with the classic serial format. Waters's fiction built on queer theory and the kind of feminist approaches to Victorian life and literature that had been developed during the 'Age of Representations' and introduced them to a wider audience, not only in her exploration of lesbian romances but her enthusiasm for the mid-Victorian sensation novel which had become the focus of renewed scholarly interest in the 1990s.

Another surprising way in which the Victorians have returned to screens is through several reality television series that successfully exploited an interest in the past. In the 1999 series, *The 1900 House*, a modern family was filmed as they lived in a recreation of a Victorian home. They had to cope without modern-day appliances and had to negotiate the different social expectations of the time. It was more than an exercise in fancy dress; it allowed the present to comment on the Victorians and vice versa.[151] It was soon joined by further series about the Edwardian and the Regency country house, though these were less successful in finding participants to replicate class relationships between masters and servants.

It seems likely that the Victorians will remain relevant in the new century. The general public frequently takes comfort in Victoriana and representations of the nineteenth-century past. Scholars still find it a source of questions that need answering. Indeed, it seems reasonable to expect that we are on the crest of a new wave of Victorian Studies. Speculation on the ways that the world of the Victorians may be reconfigured in the years ahead is a dangerous proposition. There may, however, be a few clues if we consider the logic of our times. The historians of the 1950s (and Margaret Thatcher) were essentially writing about their parents and grandparents and were making sense of what many presumably felt was a Victorian upbringing. The scholars represented in this collection, however, are generally younger; they represent a generation for whom the Victorians are much further away. The probable focus for the New Victorian Studies will, therefore, be shaped by the distance of the Victorians from ourselves. What is becoming clear is the strangeness of the Victorians, a strangeness that is only accentuated when we think about how they look superficially similar.

Moving further away from the Victorians means that scholars may be less concerned with constructing the Victorians as a path to modernity, but instead will look at the Victorians in terms of the eighteenth century. This is the significance of **Richard Price**'s challenge to orthodox forms of periodisation. The 'long eighteenth century' is likely to make a great deal of difference to the writing of Victorian history. Nineteenth-century historians are now as likely to talk of continuity as change. The challenge for the new generation will be to revisit the question of whether the 1830s and 1840s marked a turning point in British history. Martin Hewitt encourages us to focus on the new ways of looking at, and the understanding of, time and space that emerged in the early Victorian years.[152] This, he argues, means that the notion of a decisive Victorian break with the past can remain, but in a different way from that of the Asa Briggs' generation. Literary scholars point to the early Victorian decades as a moment of rising literacy and hence greater access to books and newspapers. In other words, the Victorians were distinctive because they presided over a cultural revolution in which knowledge was democratised.[153]

While some scholars will want to discuss continuity, others will want to discuss change. The meaning of 'the modern' or 'modernity' (which are in themselves extremely complex terms) meant something slightly different for scholars writing in the 1950s from what it means today. For them 'the modern' signified a world of industry and mass production, much of which was still based in Britain. We have now allegedly entered an age of post-industrialism (at least in the West). This could of course make the steam-driven world of the Victorians appear less relevant in an age when modernity is often defined by digital forms of communication. On the other hand, as Tom Standage's study of the early years of the telegraph (with its eye-catching title, *The Victorian Internet*) makes clear, we can discover in the Victorians the basis not only of modern technology but also of ways of thinking and communicating that are not entirely foreign to ourselves.[154] Scholars working on the emergence of cinema and its predecessors in the nineteenth century have already made us think about the sensations and modern structures of feeling that new technologies could produce.[155] It has become increasingly common to argue that cinema was essentially an outgrowth of Victorian culture with its demand for ever increasing realism in representation, rather than simply a scientific breakthrough.[156] We need to think about the modern in new ways.

One characteristic of the literature on the Victorians since 1980 is that it has resisted easy synthesis. The clarity of the 1950s generation with its emphasis on industrialisation and class is no more. The 'Age of Representations' has been suspicious of the totalising grand narratives of the earlier generation (a hallmark of postmodernism). This means that the overall shape of the nineteenth century, the patterns that we find in the past to explain it, are once more in contention. The challenge of our times will be to establish new forms of periodisation and redefine old ones.

Another way in which Victorian Studies will be reconfigured is the continuing role of interdisciplinarity. We live at a time when Victorian history is as likely to be taught in Literature or History of Art as in History departments. A good example of this would be the recent work by literary scholar **Mary Poovey**. Well-known for her early studies of gender and Victorian literature, she has increasingly focused on the cultural politics of information and the construction of the idea of 'society'. Since then she has gone on to investigate the way in which the financial system worked in Victorian Britain (something that would once have been the preserve of economic historians).[157]

National identity is likely to remain a feature of Victorian Studies but national boundaries will continue to be breached. There will be greater focus on the international dimensions of Victorian culture. Rethinking Victorian history and culture in the light of the Empire remains a task that still has a long way to go. The role of the British Empire in shaping globalisation and modernity means that this is an issue that will concern people all over the world. But there are other international issues. We need to think more about Britain as a European nation. How did European cultures shape the trajectory of the Victorians? This was a great age of liberal internationalism that was defined by the transformations taking place in Europe.[158] Victorian Britain was also part of a larger trans-Atlantic world, defined by its cultural, economic and intellectual links with North America. There are good reasons why the culture of the United States in the nineteenth century is identified as 'Victorian', but this requires further exploration. It is also clear that we need to proceed further with a genuinely British (as opposed to English) history that incorporates all four nations of the United Kingdom.

Moreover, different aspects of Victorian life have come to the fore, which continue to relate to the world in which we live. With so much of the production of goods based elsewhere in the world, we need to continue thinking more about the creation of the globalised market place (which certainly did not originate in the nineteenth century but which became far more integrated in the Victorian age).[159] The Victorians will also continue to be studied because environmental issues are likely to dominate the political agenda of the twenty-first century. As the peoples of the Earth continue to deal with the problems of climate change, there will certainly be interest in the moment when the planet started to get warmer. This began to happen in the second half of the nineteenth century and can be linked to the rise of modern industry in Victorian Britain and the adoption of this form of production on a global scale. Finally, as issues of imperialism and rights of interference in other countries continue to dominate international relations in the twenty-first century, it is likely that the Victorians will be most remembered for their empire and their ability to govern other peoples.[160]

The argument of this chapter has been that academic discussion has never been totally unrelated to the wider public interest in the Victorians. It is therefore reasonable to expect that Victorian Studies will be shaped, to some extent, by the interest in the Victorians in society in general. Scholars will interrogate nineteenth-century lives as long as people collect Victorian bric-à-brac, preserve steam engines, restore Victorian fittings in their homes, cherish Victorian pubs, seek out Victorian haunts and engage with Victorian fantasies and nightmares in the fiction that they enjoy. The nineteenth century is currently alive and well and living on the Internet.[161] These 'theatres of memory' continue to shape the twenty-first-century imagination.[162] Moreover, if we are to proclaim the values of democracy and citizenship, we will need to continue pondering how Victorian Britain became, in fits and starts, a kind of democracy. Even now, the Chartists and other champions of democratic rights do not have the prominence in British or international collective memory that they ought to have.

The Victorians are likely to continue to fascinate us because they created us. The ways in which they did this are complex and we are likely to continue finding new ways of understanding the Victorian past. Every time we think we understand the Victorians, a new work comes along to show how much more we have still to learn.

Notes

1   Edwin Paxton Hood, *The Age and its Architects* (London: Charles Gilpin, 1850), 71.
2   Walter Bagehot, *The English Constitution*, edited by Miles Taylor (Oxford: Oxford University Press, 2001 [1867]), 7.
3   Ezra Pound, 'Lytton Strachey on Left Over Celebrity', *The Future* (October 1918), 265.
4   This genre was inspired particularly by John Fowles, *The French Lieutenant's Woman* (London: Cape, 1969). Good examples of pastiche Victorian novels would be: Phillip Pullman, *The Ruby in the Smoke* (Oxford: Oxford University Press, 1985); Charles Palliser, *The Quincunx* (London: Canongate, 1989); Margaret Atwood, *Alias Grace*

(London: Bloomsbury, 1996); James Wilson, *The Dark Clue* (London: Faber, 2001); Michael Faber, *The Crimson Petal and the White* (Edinburgh: Canongate, 2002); Sarah Waters, *Fingersmith* (London: Virago, 2002); D.J. Taylor, *Kept: A Victorian Mystery* (London: Chatto & Windus, 2006). A.S. Byatt's *Possession* (London: Chatto & Windus, 1990), with its long pastiches of Victorian poetry, should be included in this list despite its largely contemporary setting.

5   On twentieth-century Victorianism, see: Gary Day (ed.), *Varieties of Victorianism: The Uses of a Past* (Basingstoke: Macmillan, 1998); John Kucich and Dianne F. Sadoff (eds), *Victorian Afterlife: Postmodern Culture Rewrites the Nineteenth Century* (Minneapolis, MN: University of Minnesota Press, 2000); John Gardiner, *The Victorians: An Age in Retrospect* (London: Hambledon & London, 2002); Christine L. Krueger (ed.), *Functions of Victorian Culture at the Present Time* (Athens, OH: Ohio University Press, 2002); Miles Taylor and Michael Wolff (eds), *The Victorians since 1901* (Manchester: Manchester University Press, 2004).

6   For a useful discussion of the problems of thinking about historical periods, see Penelope J. Corfield, *Naming the Age: History, Historians and Time* (Egham: Royal Holloway, 1996); see also her *Time and the Shape of History* (London: Yale University Press, 2007).

7   Compare the dates of Sir Ernest Llewellyn Woodward's *The Age of Reform, 1815–1870* (Oxford: Clarendon Press, 1962) with the more recent collection edited by Arthur Burns and Joanna Innes, *Rethinking the Age of Reform: Britain, 1780–1850* (Cambridge: Cambridge University Press, 2003).

8   Richard Price, *British Society, 1680–1880: Dynamism, Containment and Change* (Cambridge: Cambridge University Press, 1999).

9   See the debate on periodisation in *Journal of Victorian Culture*, 11(1) (2006), 146–79 and 11(2) (2006), 316–48.

10   J.L. Hammond and Barbara Hammond, *The Bleak Age* (London: Longman, 1934).

11   Asa Briggs, *The Age of Improvement* (London: Longman, 1959); Geoffrey Best, *Mid-Victorian Britain, 1851–1875* (London: Weidenfeld & Nicolson, 1971); K. Theodore Hoppen, *The Mid-Victorian Generation, 1846–1886* (Oxford: Clarendon Press, 1998).

12   W.L. Burn, *The Age of Equipoise: A Study of the Mid-Victorian Generation* (London: George Allen & Unwin, 1964).

13   José Harris, *Private Lives, Public Spirit: A Social History of Britain, 1870–1914* (Oxford: Oxford University Press, 1993).

14   F.M.L. Thompson, *The Rise of Respectable Society: A Social History of Victorian Britain, 1830–1900* (London: Fontana, 1988).

15   Peter Gay, *Schnitzler's Century: The Making of Middle-Class Culture, 1815–1914* (London: Allen Lane, 2001), a companion to Gay's larger work on European Victorianism, *The Bourgeois Experience: From Victoria to Freud* (5 vols, New York: Oxford University Press, 1984–98). On American Victorianism, see the special issue 'Victorian Culture in America', *American Quarterly*, 27 (1975), 507–625.

16   On interdisciplinarity, see Joe Moran, *Interdisciplinarity* (London: Routledge, 2001). For reflections on interdisciplinarity and Victorian Studies, see: Martin J. Wiener, 'Treating "Historical" Sources as Literary Texts: Literary Historicism and Modern British History', *Journal of Modern History*, 70 (1998), 619–38; Kucich and Sadoff (eds), *Victorian Afterlife*; Martin Hewitt, 'Victorian Studies: Problems and Prospects', *Journal of Victorian Culture*, 6(1) (2001), 137–61; Krueger (ed.), *Functions of Victorian Culture at the Present Time*; Helen Rogers, 'Victorian Studies in the UK' in Taylor and Wolff (eds), *The Victorians since 1901*, 244–59.

17   Hewitt, 'Victorian Studies', esp. 145.

18   Moran, *Interdisciplinarity*, 16.

19   It should be said that Gosse's portrait of his father is in many ways an attractive one. Philip Gosse emerges as a loving parent (and a remarkable scientist) who was concerned for the soul of his son. See Edmund Gosse, *Father and Son: A Study of Two Temperaments* (London: Heinemann, 1907).

20   One of the key works shaping this mythology of the *fin de siècle* was Holbrook Jackson, *The Eighteen Nineties: A Review of Art and Ideas at the Close of the Nineteenth Century* (London: Grant Richards, 1913). In a subsequent edition published in 1927, he reflected that although 'the period reviewed in this book closed less than thirty years ago it had become as legendary as the Shakespearian or Johnsonian eras' (p. 11).

21   Élie Halévy, *La formation du radicalisme philosophique* (3 vols, Paris: F. Alcan, 1901–4), in English as *The Growth of Philosophic Radicalism* (London: Faber, 1928). Halévy was not the only French scholar of this period interested in nineteenth-century British social history; see also Edouard Dolléans, *Le Chartisme, 1831–1848* (Paris: H. Floury, 1912). French literary critics at this time also helped shape criticism of the Victorian novel and place it in a social context; see Louis Cazamian, *Le roman social en Angleterre, 1830–1850* (Paris: Société nouvelle de librairie et d'édition, 1904).

22   Élie Halévy, *Histoire du peuple anglais au XIXe siècle* (4 vols, Paris: 1912–47), in English as *A History of the English People in the Nineteenth Century* (6 vols, London: Ernest Benn, 1949–52).

23   An account of the years between was later incorporated into the *History* derived from Halévy's other writings.

24   For example: J.L. Hammond and Barbara Hammond, *The Village Labourer, 1760–1832: A Study in the Government of England before the Great Reform Bill* (London: Longman, 1911); Sidney Webb and Beatrice Webb, *The History of Trade Unionism* (London: Longman, 1894); G.D.H. Cole, *A Short History of the British Working Class Movement, 1789–1925* (London: George Allen & Unwin, 1932). On this wave of historiography, see: Rohan McWilliam, *Popular Politics in Nineteenth-Century England* (London: Routledge, 1998); Stuart Weaver, *The Hammonds: A Marriage in History* (Stanford, CA: Stanford University Press, 1997).

25   Lytton Strachey, *Eminent Victorians* (London: Penguin, 1975 [1918]), 1.

26   Virgina Woolf, 'Mr Bennett and Mrs Brown' (1924), in her *Collected Essays: Volume 1*, edited by Leonard Woolf (London: Hogarth Press, 1966), 320.

27   Virginia Woolf, *Moments of Being* (London: Chatto & Windus/Sussex University Press, 1976), 173–4.

28   Rohan McWilliam, 'Elsa Lanchester and Bohemian London in the Early Twentieth Century' (forthcoming).

29   Margaret Barton and Osbert Sitwell (eds), *Victoriana: A Symposium of Victorian Wisdom* (London: Duckworth, 1931), 12, 16, 46.

30   Richard Altick, 'Victorians on the Move; Or, 'Tis Forty Years Since', *Dickens Studies Annual*, 10 (1982), 3.

31   'One of the Old Brigade' [i.e. Donald Shaw], *London in the Sixties* (London: Everett, 1908).

32   Ralph Nevill, *The Gay Victorians* (London: Nash & Grayson, 1930), 1. Dora, the Defence of the Realm Act (introduced in 1914), contained new licencing laws, which shortened pub hours and cut the potency of drink.

33   Arthur Machen, *Dog and Duck: A London Calendar et Cetera* (London: Jonathan Cape, 1924), 134–5.

34   L.E. Jones and E.T. Williams, 'Young, George Malcolm (1882–1959)' in *Oxford Dictionary of National Biography*, 60 (Oxford: Oxford University Press, 2004), 904.

35   Miles Taylor, 'G.M. Young and the Victorian Revival' in Taylor and Wolff (eds), *The Victorians since 1901*, 81.

36   G.M. Young, *Early Victorian England, 1830–1865* (Oxford: Oxford University Press, 1934). 'Portrait of an Age' was later published separately (with revisions that extended the essay's coverage beyond 1865) and remains in print.

37   It is significant that cinematic representations of Sherlock Holmes almost always presented him in modern dress in the inter-war years; it was only after the Second World War that it became unthinkable to present Holmes as anything other than a

quintessential Victorian figure. The final Sherlock Holmes story was published in 1927, so the inter-war setting is not so far-fetched.

38   Humphrey House, *The Dickens World* (Oxford: Oxford University Press, 1941).

39   Basil Willey, 'Ideas and Beliefs of the Victorians', *Radio Times* (30 January 1948), 3.

40   *Ideas and Beliefs of the Victorians: An Historic Revaluation of the Victorian Age* (London: Sylvan Press, 1949), 455.

41   *Ideas and Beliefs of the Victorians,* 11; see also James Thompson, 'The BBC and the Victorians' in Taylor and Wolff (eds), *The Victorians since 1901,* 150–66.

42   Becky Conekin, *The Autobiography of a Nation: The 1951 Festival of Britain* (Manchester: Manchester University Press, 2003); Becky Conekin, '"No Glorious Assurance": The 1951 Festival of Britain Looks at the Victorian Past' in Taylor and Wolff (eds), *The Victorians since 1901,* 138–49.

43   Michael Newton, *Kind Hearts and Coronets* (London: British Film Institute, 2003), 50–4.

44   Raphael Samuel, *Theatres of Memory* (London: Verso, 1994), 96.

45   Mark Connelly, *The Charge of the Light Brigade* (London: I.B. Tauris, 2003).

46   John Gardiner, 'Theme-park Victoriana' in Taylor and Wolff (eds), *The Victorians since 1901,* 167–80.

47   Patrick Wright, *On Living in an Old Country: The National Past in Contemporary Britain* (London: Verso, 1985); Robert Hewison, *The Heritage Industry: Britain in a Climate of Decline* (London: Methuen, 1987); David Cannadine, 'The Past in the Present' in Lesley M. Smith (ed.), *The Making of Britain: Echoes of Greatness* (London: Channel 4/Macmillan, 1988), 4–20; Raphael Samuel, *Theatres of Memory*.

48   For example: Norman Gash, *Politics in the Age of Peel: A Study in the Technique of Parliamentary Representation, 1830–1850* (London: Longman, 1953); Robert Blake, *The Conservative Party from Peel to Churchill* (London: Eyre & Spottiswoode, 1970); Maurice Cowling, *1867: Disraeli, Gladstone and Revolution: The Passing of the Second Reform Bill* (London: Cambridge University Press, 1967).

49   Oliver MacDonagh, *Early Victorian Government, 1830–1870* (London: Weidenfeld & Nicolson, 1977); Brian Simon, *Studies in the History of Education, 1780–1870* (London: Lawrence & Wishart, 1960); Brian Simon, *Studies in the History of Education: Education and the Labour Movement, 1870–1920* (London: Lawrence and Wishart, 1974); David Roberts, *Victorian Origins of the Welfare State* (New Haven, CT: Yale University Press, 1960); Derek Fraser, *The Evolution of the British Welfare State: A History of Social Policy since the Industrial Revolution* (London: Macmillan, 1973).

50   Harold Perkin, 'Individualism versus Collectivism in Nineteenth Century Britain: A False Antithesis' in Harold Perkin, *The Structured Crowd: Essays in Social History* (Brighton: Harvester, 1981), 57–69.

51   Robert Blake, *Disraeli* (London: Eyre & Spottiswoode, 1966).

52   George Kitson Clark, *The Making of Victorian England: Being the Ford Lectures delivered before the University of Oxford* (London: Methuen, 1962).

53   Jim Obelkevich, 'New Developments in History in the 1950s and 1960s', *Contemporary British History*, 14(4) (2000), 125–67.

54   Asa Briggs, *Victorian Cities* (London: Odhams, 1963). David Cannadine hails Briggs as the great historian of the 'white heat of technology' era: see 'Welfare State History' in David Cannadine, *The Pleasures of the Past* (London: Fontana, 1990), 172–83.

55   John R. Vincent, *The Formation of the Liberal Party, 1857–1868* (London: Constable, 1966); H.J. Hanham, *Elections and Party Management: Politics in the Time of Disraeli and Gladstone* (London: Longman, 1959); P.F. Clarke, *Lancashire and the New Liberalism* (London: Cambridge University Press, 1971). On the 'electoral sociology' school, see Jon Lawrence and Miles Taylor (eds), *Party, State and Society: Electoral Behaviour since 1820* (Aldershot: Scolar Press, 1997).

56   Michael Wolff, 'Victorian Study: An Interdisciplinary Essay', *Victorian Studies*, 8(1) (1964), 61.

57 Arnold Toynbee, *Lectures on the Industrial Revolution in England* (London: Rivingtons, 1884).

58 W.W. Rostow, *The Process of Economic Growth* (Oxford: Clarendon Press, 1953), 102–5; W.W. Rostow, 'The Take-Off into Self-Sustained Growth', *Economic Journal*, 66 (1956), 25–48.

59 W.W. Rostow, *British Economy of the Nineteenth Century* (Oxford: Clarendon Press, 1948), 123–5; for a critique of Rostow's 'social tension chart', see E.P. Thompson, *The Making of the English Working Class* (London: Pelican, 1968 [1963]), esp. p. 214.

60 Arthur J. Taylor (ed.), *The Standard of Living in Britain in the Industrial Revolution* (London: Methuen, 1975); see also David Cannadine, 'The Past and the Present in the English Industrial Revolution, 1880–1980', *Past and Present*, no. 103 (1984), 131–72.

61 Miles Taylor, 'The Beginnings of Modern British Social History?' *History Workshop Journal*, 43 (1997), 155–76.

62 See J.F.C. Harrison, *Early Victorian Britain, 1832–51* (London: Fontana, 1979); Geoffrey Best, *Mid-Victorian Britain, 1851–75* (London: Weidenfeld & Nicolson, 1971).

63 W.L. Burn, *The Age of Equipoise*. On Burn, see Martin Hewitt, 'Prologue: Reassessing *The Age of Equipoise*' in Martin Hewitt (ed.), *An Age of Equipoise?: Reassessing Mid-Victorian Britain* (Aldershot: Ashgate, 2000), 1–38; Martin Hewitt, 'Culture or Society?: Victorian Studies, 1951–64' in Taylor and Michael (eds), *The Victorians since 1901*, 90–104.

64 Keith Thomas, 'History and Anthropology', *Past and Present*, no. 24 (1963), 3–24; Keith Thomas, 'The Tools and the Job', *Times Literary Supplement* (7 April 1966), 275–6; see also Peter Burke, Brian Harrison and Paul Slack, 'Keith Thomas' in Peter Burke, Brian Harrison and Paul Slack (eds), *Civil Histories: Essays Presented to Sir Keith Thomas* (Oxford: Oxford University Press, 2000), 8–10.

65 E.P. Thompson, *The Making of the English Working Class*; see also E.P. Thompson, 'Anthropology and the Discipline of Historical Context', *Midland History*, 1 (1972), 341–55.

66 Asa Briggs, '*Middlemarch* and the Doctors', *The Cambridge Journal* (1948), 749.

67 Hobsbawm was not born in Britain but in Egypt (to an English father) and spent his childhood in Europe before coming to Britain. See his autobiography, *Interesting Times: A Twentieth-Century Life* (London: Allen Lane, 1992). Edward Thompson's father was a missionary in India, which possibly explains the consciousness of Empire that is present in some of his work: see his *Alien Homage: Edward Thompson and Rabindranath Tagore* (Delhi: Oxford University Press, 1993).

68 William Palmer, *Engagement with the Past: The Lives and Works of the World War II Generation of Historians* (Lexington, KY: University Press of Kentucky, 2001).

69 E.P. Thompson, *The Making of the English Working Class*; Asa Briggs, *The Age of Improvement* (London: Longman, 1959).

70 Asa Briggs (ed.), *Chartist Studies* (London: Macmillan, 1959).

71 Eric Hobsbawm, *Labouring Men: Studies in the History of Labour* (London: Weidenfeld & Nicolson, 1968); Robert Gray, *The Labour Aristocracy in Victorian Edinburgh* (Oxford: Clarendon Press, 1976); Robert Gray, *The Aristocracy of Labour in Nineteenth-Century Britain, c.1850–1900* (London: Macmillan, 1981); John Foster, *Class Struggle and the Industrial Revolution: Early Industrial Capitalism in Three English Towns* (London: Weidenfeld & Nicolson, 1974); Geoffrey Crossick, *An Artisan Elite in Victorian Society: Kentish London, 1840–1880* (London: Croom Helm, 1978); see also Rohan McWilliam, *Popular Politics in Nineteenth-Century England*, 24–5.

72 Eric Hobsbawm and George Rudé, *Captain Swing* (London: Lawrence & Wishart, 1969).

73 Robert W. Malcolmson, *Popular Recreations in English Society, 1700–1850* (Cambridge: Cambridge University Press, 1973); A.P. Donajgrodzki (ed.), *Social Control in Nineteenth-Century Britain* (London: Croom Helm, 1977); Peter Bailey, *Leisure*

and Class in Victorian Britain: Rational Recreation and the Contest for Control, 1830–1885 (London: Routledge & Kegan Paul, 1978). For critiques of the idea of social control, see: Gareth Stedman Jones, 'Class Expression *versus* Social Control', *History Workshop Journal*, 4 (1977), 162–70; F.M.L. Thompson, 'Social Control in Victorian Britain', *Economic History Review*, 2nd series, 34 (1981), 189–208.

74 F.M.L Thompson, *English Landed Society in the Nineteenth Century* (London: Routledge & Kegan Paul, 1963).

75 Harold Perkin, *The Origins of Modern English Society* (London: Routledge and Kegan Paul, 1969); Asa Briggs,'Middle-class Consciousness in English Politics, 1780–1846', *Past and Present*, no. 9 (1956), 65–74.

76 Walter E. Houghton, *The Victorian Frame of Mind, 1830–1870* (Oxford: Oxford University Press, 1957); Jerome H. Buckley, *The Victorian Temper: A Study in Literary Culture* (London: George Allen & Unwin, 1952).

77 Buckley, *The Victorian Temper*, 2.

78 Raymond Williams, *Culture and Society, 1780–1950* (London: Chatto & Windus, 1958).

79 Francis Klingender, *Art and the Industrial Revolution* (London: Noel Carrington, 1947). Klingender exemplified the new interdisiplinarity. He was an economist and sociologist who became an expert in art history as well. On Klingender, see Tim Barringer, *Men at Work: Art and Labour in Victorian Britain* (New Haven, CT, and London: Yale University Press, 2005), 12.

80 Christopher Kent, 'Victorian Studies in North America' and Miles Fairbairn, 'The State of Victorian Studies in Australia and New Zealand' both in Taylor and Wolff (eds), *The Victorians since 1901*, 215–29, 230–43.

81 R.K. Webb, *The British Working Class Reader, 1790–1848: Literacy and Social Tension* (London: Allen & Unwin, 1955); Richard Altick, *The English Common Reader: A Social History of the Mass Reading Public, 1800–1900* (Chicago, IL: Chicago University Press, 1957). In Britain, Louis James was working along parallel lines: *Fiction for the Working Man, 1830–1850: A Study of the Literature Produced for the Working Classes in Early Victorian Urban England* (London: Oxford University Press, 1963).

82 Michael Wolff, 'Preface' in Taylor and Wolff (eds), *The Victorians since 1901*, x–xv. See also Michael Wolff, 'Victorian Study'.

83 *The Wellesley Index to Victorian Periodicals, 1824–1900*, edited by Walter Houghton (4 vols, London: Routledge & Kegan Paul, 1966–79).

84 Jonathan Miller, 'Mesmerism', *The Listener* (22 November 1973), 686.

85 Steven Marcus, *The Other Victorians: A Study of Sexuality and Pornography in mid-19th Century England* (London: Weidenfeld & Nicolson, 1966). See also Brian Harrison's response, 'Underneath the Victorians', *Victorian Studies*, 10 (1966), 239–62.

86 Martha Vicinus, *Suffer and Be Still: Women in the Victorian Age* (Bloomington, IN: Indiana University Press, 1973).

87 S. Barbara Kanner, 'The Women of England in a Century of Social Change, 1815–1914: A Select Bibliography', in Vicinus, *Suffer and Be Still*, 173–206. This was later published in a more developed form: Barbara Kanner, *Women in English Social History, 1800–1914* (New York: Garland, 1988).

88 Angela John, *By the Sweat of their Brow: Women Workers at Victorian Coal Mines* (London: Croom Helm, 1979); Anne Summers, *Angels and Citizens: British Women as Military Nurses, 1854–1914* (London: Routledge & Kegan Paul, 1988).

89 Judith R. Walkowitz, *Prostitution and Victorian Society: Women, Class and the State* (Cambridge: Cambridge University Press, 1980); Paul McHugh, *Prostitution and Victorian Social Reform* (London: Croom Helm, 1980); Lucy Bland, *Banishing the Beast: English Feminism and Sexual Morality, 1885–1914* (London: Penguin, 1995).

90 Elaine Showalter, *A Literature of Their Own: British Women Novelists from Brontë to Lessing* (Princeton, NJ: Princeton University Press, 1977).

91   Martin Hewitt, 'Victorian Studies'.

92   As early as 1964, Michael Wolff predicted that interdisciplinarity would inevitably draw Victorianists towards cultural history: see his 'Victorian Study', 70. The changes in cultural history are best caught in Lynn Hunt (ed.), *The New Cultural History* (Berkeley, CA: University of California Press, 1989).

93   For example, Mary Poovey, *Uneven Developments: The Ideological Work of Gender in mid-Victorian England* (London: Virago, 1989).

94   Callum G. Brown, *Postmodernism for Historians* (Harlow: Longman, 2005) is a useful and student-friendly introduction.

95   Christopher Kent, 'Victorian Social History: Post-Thompson, Post-Foucault, Post-modern', *Victorian Studies*, 40 (1996), 97–133. Other theorists who were influential included Louis Althusser, Antonio Gramsci, Edward Said and Hayden White. Among the many Foucault-influenced works in Victorian Studies, see the Readings by Joyce, Poovey and Walkowitz in this volume. See also Frank Mort, *Dangerous Sexualities: Medico-Moral Politics in England since 1830* (London: Routledge, 2000 [1987]).

96   Joan Scott, 'The Evidence of Experience', *Critical Inquiry*, 17 (1991), 773–97.

97   For example: Paul Thompson, 'Voices from Within' in H.J. Dyos and Michael Wolff (eds), *The Victorian City: Images and Realities* (2 vols, London: Routledge & Kegan Paul, 1973), 1: 59–80; John Burnett, *Destiny Obscure: Autobiographies of Childhood, Education and Family from the 1820s to the 1920s* (London: Allen Lane, 1982).

98   Journals such as *The Journal of Victorian Culture*, *Victorian Contexts* and *Victorian Studies* proclaim their attachment to interdisciplinary dialogue, which has also been a feature of conferences organised by the British Association of Victorian Studies and the North American Victorian Studies Association.

99   Martin Hewitt, 'Victorian Studies'.

100 For the Victorian period, the most influential New Historicist text was Catherine Gallagher, *The Industrial Reformation of English Fiction: Social Discourse and Narrative Form* (Chicago, IL: University of Chicago Press, 1985). See also Catherine Gallagher and Stephen Greenblatt, *Practicing New Historicism* (Chicago, IL: University of Chicago Press, 2001).

101 Christopher Kent, 'Victorian Studies in North America'.

102 See, for example: Alexander Welsh, *Strong Representations: Narrative and Circum-stantial Evidence in England* (Baltimore, MD: Johns Hopkins University Press, 1992); Jan-Melissa Schramm, *Testimony and Advocacy in Victorian Law, Literature, and Theology* (Cambridge: Cambridge University Press, 2000); Jonathan Grossman, *The Art of Alibi: English Law Courts and the Novel* (Baltimore, MD: Johns Hopkins University Press, 2002); for a discussion of recent approaches to Victorian law, see Margot Finn, 'Victorian Law, Literature and History: Three Ships Passing in the Night', *Journal of Victorian Culture*, 7(1) (2002), 134–46.

103 On Black Victorians see Gretchen Gerzina (ed.), *Black Victorians/Black Victoriana* (New Brunswick, NJ: Rutgers University Press, 2003); on the *flâneur*, see Keith Tester (ed.), *The Flâneur* (London: Routledge, 1994); on the deferential worker, see Patrick Joyce, *Work, Society and Politics: The Culture of the Factory in Later Victorian England* (Brighton: Harvester, 1980).

104 *Evening Standard* (15 April 1983).

105 Keith Joseph, 'Introduction' in Samuel Smiles, *Self-Help* (London: Penguin, 1986), 16.

106 Eric M. Sigsworth, *In Search of Victorian Values* (Manchester: Manchester University Press, 1988); Gordon Marsden (ed.), *Victorian Values: Personalities and Perspectives in Nineteenth-Century Society* (London: Longman, 1990); T.C. Smout (ed.), *Victorian Values* (Oxford: Oxford University Press, 1992).

107 *New Statesman* (27 May 1983, supplement on 'Victorian values').

108 Gertrude Himmelfarb, *The Idea of Poverty* (London: Faber 1984); Gertrude Himmelfarb, *Poverty and Compassion: The Moral Imagination of the late Victorians* (New York: Knopf, 1991); Gertrude Himmelfarb, *The De-Moralization of Society: From Victorian Virtues to Modern Values* (New York: Knopf, 1995).

109   'A Prophet for the Left', *The Economist* (18 April 1992), 11–12; Peter Mandler and
      Susan Pedersen (eds), *After the Victorians: Private Conscience and Public Duty in
      Modern Britain* (London: Routledge, 1994); Andrew Marr, 'Blair's Big Secret: He's
      a Liberal', *Observer* (26 July 1998), 21; Tristram Hunt, *Building Jerusalem: The Rise
      and Fall of the Victorian City* (London: Weidenfeld & Nicolson, 2004); Tristram Hunt,
      'It wasn't all Mills and Morals', *Guardian* (22 May 2004); David Marquand, *Decline
      of the Public: The Hollowing-out of Citizenship* (Cambridge: Polity, 2004).

110   Peter Mandler (ed.), *Liberty and Authority in Victorian Britain* (Oxford: Oxford
      University Press, 2006).

111   N.F.R.L. Crafts, *British Economic Growth during the Industrial Revolution* (Oxford:
      Clarendon Press, 1981); Pat Hudson (ed.), *Regions and Industries: A Perspective on
      the Industrial Revolution* (Cambridge: Cambridge University Press, 1989); Patrick
      O'Brien and Roland Quinault (eds), *The Industrial Revolution and British Society*
      (Cambridge: Cambridge University Press, 1993).

112   Raphael Samuel, 'The Workshop of the World: Steam Power and Hand Technology
      in mid-Victorian Britain', *History Workshop Journal*, no. 3 (1977), 6–72; N.F.R.
      Crafts, *British Economic Growth during the Industrial Revolution*.

113   Michael Fores, 'The Myth of the British Industrial Revolution', *History*, 66 (1981),
      181–98. Pat Hudson, *The Industrial Revolution* (London: Arnold, 1992) is a good
      treatment of these recent debates.

114   David Cannadine, *The Decline and Fall of the British Aristocracy* (New Haven, CT:
      Yale University Press, 1990); Matthew Cragoe, *An Anglican Aristocracy: The Moral
      Economy of the Landed Estate in Carmarthenshire, 1832–1895* (Oxford: Clarendon
      Press, 1996).

115   W.D. Rubinstein, *Elites and the Wealthy in Modern British History: Essays in Social
      and Economic History* (Brighton: Harvester, 1981).

116   Martin Wiener, *English Culture and the Decline of the Industrial Spirit* (Cambridge:
      Cambridge University Press, 1981).

117   Asa Briggs 'The Language of Class in Early Nineteenth Century England' in Asa Briggs
      and John Saville (eds), *Essays in Labour History* (Basingstoke: Macmillan, 1967
      [1960]), 43–73.

118   Dror Wahrman, *Imagining the Middle Class: The Political Representation of Class in
      Britain, c.1780–1840* (Cambridge: Cambridge University Press, 1995).

119   Adrian Wilson (ed.), *Rethinking Social History: English Society, 1570–1920, and its
      Interpretation* (Manchester: Manchester University Press, 1993).

120   Catherine Hall, Keith McClelland and Jane Rendall, *Defining the Victorian Nation:
      Class, Race, Gender and the British Reform Act of 1867* (Cambridge: Cambridge
      University Press, 2000).

121   Gareth Stedman Jones, *Languages of Class: Studies in English Working-Class History,
      1832–1982* (Cambridge: Cambridge University Press, 1983).

122   David Cannadine, *Class in Britain* (New Haven, CT: Yale University Press, 1998).

123   Studies of the mid-Victorian period were not new (see W.L. Burn, *The Age of Equipoise*).
      However, before 1980 there had been a concentration on the first half of the nineteenth
      century and its end which goes all the way back to Halévy.

124   Patrick Joyce, *Visions of the People: Industrial England and the Question of Class,
      1840–1914* (Cambridge: Cambridge University Press, 1991).

125   Patrick Joyce, *The Rule of Freedom: Liberalism and the Modern City* (London: Verso,
      2003).

126   Benedict Anderson, *Imagined Communities: Reflections on the Origins and Spread of
      Nationalism* (London: Verso, 1983).

127   John Burrow, *A Liberal Descent: Victorian Historians and the English Past* (Cambridge:
      Cambridge University Press, 1981).

128   Mark Girouard, *The Return to Camelot: Chivalry and the English Gentleman* (New
      Haven, CT: Yale University Press, 1981); Stephanie Barczewski, *Myth and National*

Identity in Nineteenth-Century Britain: The Legends of King Arthur and Robin Hood (Oxford: Oxford University Press, 2000); Rosemary Mitchell, Picturing the Past: English History in Text and Image, 1830–1870 (Oxford: Oxford University Press, 2000); Peter Mandler, History and National Life (London: Profile Books, 2002), Ch. 2; Billie Melman, The Culture of History: English Uses of the Past, 1800–1953 (Oxford: Oxford University Press, 2006).

129   Kelly Boyd, Manliness and the Boys' Story Paper: A Cultural History, 1855–1940 (London: Palgrave, 2003).

130   Linda Colley, Britons: Forging the Nation, 1707–1837 (New Haven, CT: Yale University Press, 1991).

131   David Cannadine, '"The Context, Performance and Meaning of Ritual: The British Monarchy and the "Invention of Tradition", c.1820–1977' in Eric Hobsbawm and Terence Ranger (eds), The Invention of Tradition (Cambridge: Cambridge University Press, 1983), 101–64; Dorothy Thompson, Queen Victoria: Gender and Power (London: Virago, 1990); Margaret Homans, Royal Representations: Queen Victoria and British Culture, 1837–1876 (Chicago, IL: University of Chicago Press, 1998); Lynn Valone, Becoming Victoria (New Haven, CT: Yale University Press, 2001); David Nash and Antony Taylor (eds), Republicanism in Victorian Society (Stroud: Sutton, 2000).

132   Hugh Cunningham, 'The Language of Patriotism, 1750–1914', History Workshop Journal, 12 (1981), 8–33; Raphael Samuel (ed.), Patriotism: The Making and Unmaking of British National Identity (3 vols, London: Routledge, 1989).

133   Joan Wallach Scott, Gender and the Politics of History (New York: Columbia University Press, 1988); Denise Riley, 'Am I That Name': Feminism and the Category of 'Woman' in History (Minneapolis, MN: University of Minneapolis Press, 1988).

134   Jane Rendall, Women in an Industrializing Society: England, 1750–1880 (Oxford: Basil Blackwell, 1990); Deborah Valenze, The First Industrial Woman (New York: Oxford University Press, 1995); Carol E. Morgan, 'The Domestic Image and Factory Culture: The Cotton District in mid-Nineteenth-Century England', International Labor and Working-Class History, no. 49 (Spring 1996), 26–46; Jane Lewis, 'Sexual Divisions: Women's Work in late Nineteenth-Century England' in S.J. Kleinberg (ed.), Retrieving Women's History: Changing Perceptions of the Role of Women in Politics and Society (Oxford: Berg, 1988), 148–65; Sonya Rose, Limited Livelihoods: Gender and Class in Nineteenth-Century England (London: Routledge, 1992); Maxine Berg, 'What Difference did Women's Work Make to the Industrial Revolution?', History Workshop Journal, 35 (1993), 22–44.

135   J.A. Mangan and James Walvin (eds), Manliness and Morality: Middle-Class Masculinity in Britain and America, 1800–1940 (Manchester: Manchester University Press, 1987); Michael Roper and John Tosh, (eds), Manful Assertions: Masculinities in Britain since 1800 (London: Routledge, 1991).

136   Mrinalini Sinha, Colonial Masculinity: The 'Manly Englishman' and the 'Effeminate Bengali' in the Late Nineteenth Century (Manchester: Manchester University Press, 1995).

137   Bernard Porter, The Absent-Minded Imperialists: Empire, Society and Culture in Britain (Oxford: Oxford University Press, 2004).

138   John M. McKenzie, Propaganda and Empire: The Manipulation of British Public Opinion, 1880–1960 (Manchester: Manchester University Press, 1984).

139   Catherine Hall, White, Male and Middle-Class: Explorations in Feminism and History (Cambridge: Polity, 1992); David Cannadine, Ornamentalism: How the British Saw their Empire (London: Allen Lane, 2001).

140   David Feldman, Englishmen and Jews: Social Relations and Political Culture, 1840–1914 (New Haven, CT: Yale University Press, 1994).

141   Gillian Beer, Darwin's Plots: Evolutionary Narrative in Darwin, George Eliot and Nineteenth Century Fiction (London: Routledge, 1983; Cambridge: Cambridge University Press, 2001).

142 James Secord, *Victorian Sensation: The Extraordinary Publication, Reception, and Secret Authorship of 'Vestiges of the Natural History of Creation'* (Chicago, IL: University of Chicago Press, 2000).

143 Among the sophisticated theatrical histories of this period, see: Tracy C. Davis, *Actresses as Working Women: Their Social Identity in Victorian Culture* (London: Routledge, 1991); Nina Auerbach, *Private Theatricals: The Lives of the Victorians* (Cambridge, MA: Harvard University Press, 1990); Jane Moody, *Illegitimate Theatre in London, 1770–1840* (London: Cambridge University Press, 2000).

144 On the 'melodramatic turn', see Rohan McWilliam, 'Melodrama and the Historians', *Radical History Review*, 78 (2000), 57–84; see also Rohan McWilliam, *The Tichborne Claimant: A Victorian Sensation* (London: Hambledon Continuum, 2007), Ch. 13.

145 Peter Brooks, *The Melodramatic Imagination: Balzac, Henry James, Melodrama and the Mode of Excess* (New Haven, CT: Yale University Press, 1976).

146 Examples would include: Mary Poovey, *Uneven Developments*; Judith Walkowitz, *City of Dreadful Delight: Narratives of Sexual Danger in Late Victorian London* (London: Virago, 1992).

147 Elaine Showalter, *The Female Malady: Women, Madness and Culture in England, 1830–1980* (London: Virago, 1987).

148 E.P. Thompson and Eileen Yeo (eds), *The Unknown Mayhew: Selections from the 'Morning Chronicle', 1849–50* (London: Penguin, 1973).

149 McWilliam, 'Melodrama and the Historians'.

150 Matthew Sweet, *Inventing the Victorians* (London: Faber, 2001).

151 Mark McCrum and Matthew Sturgis, *1900 House* (London: Channel 4/Macmillan, 1999).

152 Martin Hewitt 'Why the Notion of Victorian Britain Does Make Sense', *Victorian Studies*, 48(3) (2006), 395–438.

153 Juliet John and Alice Jenkins, 'Introduction' in Juliet John and Alice Jenkins (eds), *Rethinking Victorian Culture* (Basingstoke: Macmillan, 2000), 2–3.

154 Tom Standage, *The Victorian Internet: The Remarkable Story of the Telegraph and the Nineteenth-Century Online Pioneers* (London: Weidenfeld & Nicolson, 1998).

155 Leo Charney and Vanessa R. Schwartz (eds), *Cinema and the Invention of Modern Life* (Berkeley, CA: University of California Press, 1995). This is very much a transnational collection covering the United States, Britain and Europe with a strong interdisciplinary focus.

156 Rohan McWilliam, 'The Licensed Stare: Melodrama and the Culture of Spectacle', *Nineteenth-Century Studies*, 13 (1999), 153–75; see also Alexander Nicholas Vardac, *Stage to Screen: Theatrical Method from Garrick to Griffith* (Cambridge, MA: Harvard University Press, 1949); Ben Brewster and Lea Jacobs, *Theatre to Cinema: Stage Pictorialism and the Early Feature Film* (Oxford: Oxford University Press, 1997); Grahame Smith, *Dickens and the Dream of Cinema* (Manchester: Manchester University Press, 2003).

157 Mary Poovey, *A History of the Modern Fact: Problems of Knowledge in the Sciences of Wealth and Society* (Chicago, IL: University of Chicago Press, 1998); Mary Poovey (ed.), *The Financial System in Mid-Nineteenth-Century Britain* (Oxford: Oxford University Press, 2003). Other examples of literary scholars using ostensibly non-literary materials include: Regenia Gagnier, *The Insatiability of Human Wants: Economics and Aesthetics in Market Society* (Chicago, IL: University of Chicago Press, 2000); Catherine Gallagher, *The Body Economic: Life, Death and Sensation in Political Economy and the Victorian Novel* (Princeton, NJ: Princeton University Press, 2006).

158 Margot Finn, *After Chartism: Class and Nation in English Radical Politics, 1848–74* (Cambridge: Cambridge University Press, 1993). Eugenio Biagini, *Gladstone* (Basingstoke: Macmillan, 2000) reclaims the European vision of the Victorian statesman.

159 C.A. Bayley, *The Birth of the Modern World, 1780–1914: Global Connections and Comparisons* (Oxford: Basil Blackwell, 2003).

160   Niall Ferguson, *Empire: How Britain made the Modern World* (London: Allen Lane, 2003); Niall Ferguson, *Colossus: The Price of America's Empire* (London: Penguin, 2004).

161   Patrick Leary, 'Victorian Studies in the Digital Age' in Taylor and Wolff (eds), *The Victorians since 1901*, 201–14; Patrick Leary, 'Googling the Victorians', *Journal of Victorian Culture*, 10(1) (2005), 72–86.

162   Raphael Samuel, *Theatres of Memory*.

PART 1

Periodisation

Richard Price

SHOULD WE ABANDON THE IDEA OF THE VICTORIAN PERIOD?

'Historiography, Narrative and the Nineteenth Century', *Journal of British Studies*, 35 (April 1996), 220–33, 240–56.

We commence the *Victorian Studies Reader* with the issue that has challenged most profoundly the way we see the Victorians in recent years. As discussed in the Introduction, Victorian Britain was usually held to be a departure from previous forms of society because of the transformation brought about by the Industrial Revolution and the distinctive class society that emerged, in which the middle classes became the dominant grouping. This approach was challenged during the 1980s by a wave of revisionist writings in economic history that contested the figures for economic growth during the period 1780–1850. It was argued that there was no substantial industrial take-off, that growth was limited to a certain number of, admittedly leading, industries such as cotton textiles, and that the notion of an 'Industrial Revolution' was not warranted. Moreover, research on eighteenth-century society (which had not been much studied before the mid-1970s) revealed a dynamic, commercial society characterised by the growth of cities and entrepreneurialism and torn apart by anxieties about the treatment of the poor and the fear of social conflict; in other words, a society that sounded very like what Britain was assumed to be in the *nineteenth* century. It became increasingly common to talk of a 'long eighteenth century' lasting up to at least 1832, implying that the allegedly modern society of the early nineteenth century had far more in common with the previous century than with the factory-based world of mass production that really only became mature in the 1880s. What then was distinctive about the world of the Victorians?

The historian who has done most to rethink conventional forms of periodisation is **Richard Price**. Previously he enjoyed a reputation as an historian of Victorian labour. He commenced his study of periodisation with a provocative essay entitled 'Does the Notion of Victorian Britain Still Make Sense?'. The following Reading comes from a more developed article where he urged nineteenth-century historians to come to terms with the continuities from the earlier period. We present a shortened version of this piece (the original contains discussions of the historiography and an important critique of some aspects of the 'linguistic turn' which are not reproduced here). Price argues that a distinctive political and social settlement emerged after the 'Glorious Revolution' of 1688 that continued to exist until at least the 1880s. In other words, the coming of the Victorians was not the rupture that previous historians had claimed. This challenging revisionist argument, which emphasises continuity rather than change, was subsequently articulated in its fullest form in his book *British Society 1680–1880* (1999). All Victorian specialists will in future need to deal with the challenge that Richard Price has issued to the conventional wisdom.

Richard Price is Professor of History at the University of Maryland, College Park. He is the author of several books on British social and labour history, including *British Society 1680–1880: Dynamism, Containment and Change* (1999). He is currently completing a book on the history of the encounter between the British and the Xhosa peoples of southern Africa in the early nineteenth century.

———————

THE LATE SEVENTEENTH CENTURY to the late nineteenth century constituted a "stage" in the history of modern Britain that can be usefully demarcated and discussed as a unit. Throughout this period the basic structures of society operated within contexts whose boundaries, scripts, tensions, and instabilities are visible by the late seventeenth century and are only decisively disrupted into new arenas of engagement two hundred years later. It is not particularly helpful to see the period as marked by ruptures and transformative change. Indeed, it is a mistake to privilege either continuity or change as the overriding category of the period; it is rather more useful to see them as both operating within borders whose limits were subject to greater or lesser pressures throughout the period, but which generally held firm. How they were challenged — along class, sectional, regional, and gender lines — and why they held firm must be major questions for historians to explore. And in doing so, they will explore what we call "change." No justice can be done here to the complexities and nuances of the argument that would have to be made to sustain these contentions; that must await another place. The best that can be done is to describe in bald design the architecture of such an argument and categories used to support it.

I start with the themes of economic history simply because they are a starting point, not necessarily *the* starting point and because I am not concerned in this piece with causation, only with presenting a series of associations that can be seen to fall within similar general narrative lines. In addition, the patterns of economic history in this period that illustrate the argument may be quickly and easily explained; they are such an obvious part of the historiographical landscape that I can confine myself to making some fairly simple remarks.

In the first place, it is clear from statistical and other evidence that economic growth was largely a continuous process, that "new" elements appeared much earlier than the late eighteenth century and "old" elements remained central much later, and that Britain's economy possessed a significant manufacturing component by the late seventeenth century. By the mid-eighteenth century, at least most labor was occupied outside the agricultural sector. Equally, the intensification of production in the early nineteenth century was as much a function of the "traditional" sectors of production as of the factory, and as late as 1860 around 50 percent of productivity growth came from the nonmechanized sectors of the economy. Steam power did not displace water power in manufacturing or sail on the ocean until the 1860s.[1]

In the second place, it is important to note that this emphasis on continuity does not deny the significance or importance of economic growth in this period. Abandoning the term "industrial revolution" does not mean decentering the significance of economic growth. Although there will continue to be debate over the measurement of economic indices, the perspective that fits best within a total societal context seems to be the historiographical stance of J.U. Nef and J.H. Clapham, whose careful and qualified histories suggested that "industrialization" was not something that happened once but was a process that accompanied the different phases and stages of capitalist growth from the sixteenth century onward. Perhaps the most notable aspect of economic growth was regional concentration around particular industries. The phenomenal growth of textiles in the northeast in the late eighteenth century was part of a process of regional variation and relocation that first appeared in the sixteenth-century expansion of the coal industry.[2]

Accompanying this was the progression of economic change through the vast expansion of traditional modes of production. This was a familiar pattern from the past and at this moment reflected the many routes to mass production apart from the factory. The economic structure in the period of industrialization was, and remained, highly variegated, but the fluctuating intensity and pace of economic change operated within a workshop-dominated economic structure. Thus, while there will probably continue to be dispute over the measurement of the economic indices, the effect of this "revolution" in social terms seems to have been manifested not through exposure to new technologies or modes of working. If foreign trade statistics provide evidence for "takeoff" in the 1780s, the actual structures of production and distribution that lay behind that growth experienced expansion rather than alteration. The experience of this particular phase of economic growth was represented by the intensified intrusion of market forces into the structures of everyday life; a keyword of the period for both the political economists and their opponents is "competition." And, thus, neither urbanism nor the factory defined this period of economic change more than the destruction of wage and apprenticeship standards or the redivision of labor.[3]

But by most comparative indices, Britain's economic growth has been extremely slow over the past three hundred years. And this suggests how its economic success lay less in manufacturing prowess and more in commerce and trade, which is a third aspect of economic structure that needs to be highlighted in any new narrative of British history. If by the mid-nineteenth century Britain was the workshop of the world, it had self-consciously sought to be the world's warehouse since the seventeenth-century struggles against the Dutch — whose own experience provided the model for Britain's imperial dreams and fiscal innovations. The "commercial revolution" was not a preparation for industrialization but an abiding and determining feature of Britain's political economy. Indeed, the secret of Britain's economic success lay primarily in the network of international trade, commerce, and financial systems and services that came to center on London from the late seventeenth century. Britain was the facilitator of trade services and a great entrepôt for world trade (thus the competition with the Dutch who had first charted this map of economic growth); it does not become an export economy until the mid-nineteenth century. The history of reexports (which made up over 30 percent of all exports in the eighteenth century), for example, is likely to prove the great untold story of British trade policy and economic growth in this period.

This network was a central concern of state policy from the 1650s, and a major theme of economic policy was how best to protect and expand its reach. Simply put, this priority forged the tight relationship between the state and finance capital that until the middle of the nineteenth century remained the unchallenged nexus of economic policy making. The idea that free trade was a nineteenth-century invention reflecting the priorities of the industrial sector of capital is quite wrong. Indeed, industry, like finance, was divided on the advantages of free trade whose hold over the world of business was much more fragile than historians have appreciated. In any case, at no point in the nineteenth century did the priorities of the industrial sector displace those of the alliance between landed and commercial interests that has been termed "gentlemanly capitalism."[4]

Thus, to place commerce and finance at the heart of the economic process and to make it predominant in the political economy enables us to interpret economic and imperial history more meaningfully than a perspective that accords prime attention to industrial capital. It also conforms with what we know about the relationship between social class and political power during the period. The distinguishing mark of the British landed classes was their unequivocally capitalist character, as revealed by their key role as agricultural, industrial, and adventuring entrepreneurs. In this period, the most important pole of economic and political power was that modus vivendi forged between the landed and the "monied" interests during the financial revolution of the 1690s that allowed the mobilization of landed (and other) surplus capital by the Bank of England and other financial institutions in the City.

The history of British capitalism in this period was essentially the story of this configuration, its internal struggles and changes, and its response to changing international and domestic circumstances. It was a south of England formation: most commercial wealth circulated there, most imperial investment seems to have been generated there (at least in the later nineteenth century), and London was its particular center of activity.

This system produced a set of mutually beneficial interconnections and the most powerful political field of force in Britain's domestic and imperial political economy. Its various elements, of course, had diverse interests and priorities — as is illustrated by the struggle within the City over whether to adopt free trade in the period ca.1820 to the 1840s.[5] But it tied together the key elements of the social, political, and commercial elites within an arena of self-interest that focused on the generation of imperial trade and power. The great trading companies with their close ties to government finances were one facet of this many-sided prism; the Bank of England was another; what John Brewer has called the "fiscal-military" state was a third;[6]

and the corporate relationship between these institutions gave rise to the appellation of "old corruption" — which was another way to express its power.

London was the center of the system, reinforcing the existing fault lines in the distribution of power and influence between capital and province. And the London middle classes who staffed the commercial and financial services possessed an economic and political power that far outstripped that of the provinces. Indeed, W.D. Rubinstein has estimated that for much of the nineteenth century the income generated by the London middle classes was 50 percent of the national income for the whole of the middle class. That fact reflected the modest wealth of the industrial middle classes compared to the magnates of land or trade. The wealthiest businessman in the nineteenth century left only £6 million at his death — less than one half of the estate wealth of the richest landowner. Such well-known figures as John Bright and Joseph Chamberlain possessed quite modest fortunes.[7]

It no longer makes sense, therefore, to privilege the industrial middle class as the dynamic group in the nineteenth century as the older historiography tended to do. Until the later part of the century, for example, the greatest champions and initiators of "reform" were to be found in segments of the landed classes. In the post-Napoleonic period and during the Whig governments of the 1830s in particular it was the inheritors of the Foxite tradition within the aristocracy who provided the leadership in dismantling the "fiscal-military" state. Furthermore, and even more important, the industrial middle class was only one segment of the complex and changing social stratum that constituted the middle orders of society whose social and political presence was not to be calibrated to the rise of industry or the language of evangelicalism.[8]

There are important lines of continuity within the key features of urban middle-class social and political life between the eighteenth and nineteenth centuries. Thus, struggles between the various groups of the middle station, their overall relationship to the landowning elites, and the central question of how they were to represent and exercise their power were all dominant throughout the period from the late seventeenth century. The central elements that we take to define provincial middle-class civic life in the nineteenth century emerge and develop throughout the eighteenth century — the concept of "improvement," for example, and the networks of professional and voluntary associations that served as agents of integration for the fragmented social structure of both the eighteenth and the nineteenth centuries. Thus, the origins of a middle-class provincial consciousness and assertive influence lay essentially in the eighteenth century. The shape and contours of this middle class clearly changed over time; as the nineteenth century wore on, for example, factory owners replaced "middle men" as the characteristic representatives of the industrial middle classes. But the questions of how to establish and realize its political identity were part of a much longer continuum.

Middle classness, however, more than all other class identities, was a gendered concept. As both working- and middle-class women were excluded from the public (economic) sphere, a powerful patriarchially based ideology brokered the division between private and public spheres and the definition of the family. Working women experienced this largely in the labor market, where they were decisively separated from higher-paid and status-ranked jobs. Middle-class women experienced it through their relegation to the privacy of the drawing room and the "nonwork" of running the household. Gender roles were separated into female private and male public spheres, mediated by the power of evangelical religion. In both the traditional and revisionist feminist scholarship, this process is located in the notion of a great transformation in the late eighteenth and early nineteenth centuries, but in fact it may be pushed back much earlier. By the end of the seventeenth century, patriarchalism was becoming much less a foundation of political order and hierarchy and more an ideology for the private sphere. Significantly, it was at this time that the development of a public space that was specifically identified as middle class emerged. How men and women fit into the functioning of that space was an inseparable part of this process.[9]

Separate spheres and domestic ideology were, therefore, clearly visible one hundred years before "Victorian" England. The combined exclusion of middle-class women from a public business role in the early nineteenth century and their private centrality to middle-class economic life that is described in Leonore Davidoff and Catherine Hall's *Family Fortunes* may be replicated almost exactly in the account of early eighteenth-century middle-class life in London given by Peter Earle — which in its turn confirms the arguments of Alice Clark for the seventeenth century. Similarly, the arguments of domestic ideology and separate spheres were formulated at this moment, from Rousseau to less important thinkers like James Fordyce, an eighteenth-century nonconformist minister whose sermons prefigured Ruskin's doctrine of the "angel in the home": "there is an Empire which belongs to you . . . . . I mean what has the heart for its object and is secured by meekness and modesty, by soft attraction and virtuous love."[10]

This foreshortening of the historical process is further confused by the way the argument relies on a particular view of evangelical religion to define "middle class" and to explain the evolution of this family ideology. It is worth noting that this version of "middle class" (characteristic of both traditional and revisionist historiography) conflates the evangelical middle classes with the whole in an act of borrowing that writes the version of history concocted by the evangelical middle classes themselves. Evangelicalism as a source of middle-class self-definition and morality did not issue newborn out of the mouths and minds of the Clapham Sect, although it was given greater urgency in the age of the French revolution. It belonged to a preexisting tradition that assumed its characteristically "Victorian" form in the 1690s with the formation of various reformation societies whose purpose was to enforce an evangelical morality in public and private. They did so using the principles of voluntary association and private prosecution that later became the characteristic weapons of Victorian reformers. When William Wilberforce established his Society for the Suppression of Vice in 1804, the model was the evangelical societies of the 1690s.[11]

But as the history of philanthropy in this whole period illustrates, the separate spheres were inherently unstable, and there was constant tension around their borders as women pressed into the forbidden public sphere. This was as true of the eighteenth century as it was of the nineteenth, although the particular forms of contestation might be different. Sexual politics was a fiercely contested terrain in the 1760s and 1770s, revolving around the right of women to engage in public organization of patriotic politics. Hannah More's resolution of this tension was not unlike that of Florence Nightingale one hundred years later: to behave in ways that transgressed those boundaries quite decisively while publicly accepting the strict observance of the separate spheres. Although the case of Hannah More illustrates quite nicely how it is impossible to separate class from this process, it also suggests how the use of the language and ideology of patriarchy to open certain spaces for middling-class women was not peculiar to Victorian times. Similarly, the Queen Caroline affair served to mobilize women against the double standard and in that respect presaged the campaign against Contagious Diseases Acts in the 1860s and 1870s. In short, both the formation of, and the contestation around, the domestic ideology of Victorian times belongs to a longer continuum in the history of patriarchy and gender relations than one that begins with the evangelical reaction to the French and industrial revolutions. Throughout the period I am proposing, the practice and operation of domestic ideology remained confined within the same gendered boundaries; it stayed within clearly defined class limits; and it also generally remained behind the same political limits that excluded women. The first suggestion of a challenge to those limits that would redefine the question of gender relations comes in the 1860s with the creation of local suffrage committees.[12]

Conceptualizing the late seventeenth to the late nineteenth centuries as a distinct period also allows us to make better sense of lower-class social relations. Organizing this period around the "making" of an English working class turns out to be somewhat misleading because the main economic, social, and political formations of plebeian culture remain constant. Workshop production ranging from artisanal through family forms of organization dominated the economic foundations of lower-class life. Social customs like wife selling and the charivari of rough music, which first appeared around the 1670s, tended to go underground in response to the pressure of evangelical attack from around the 1780s, but they did not die out until the 1870s-80s. Popular political consciousness continued to be expressed in the languages of the "moral" political economy. The case of the Tichborne Claimant, for example, was the last social movement that would have been understood by John Wilkes. Its language was the language of popular constitutionalism against the corruption of vested interests; its leadership was patrician — at least in appearance if not in lineage; it appealed to the deeply rooted suspicion of the centralizing tendencies of the state (opposition to the income tax was a part of its campaign); and in its search for legitimation it skipped over Chartism to appeal to the tradition of the Commonwealth radicals and the Magna Charta for the "fair play" and virtue it found absent in the current political system's treatment of the claimant.[13]

E.P. Thompson's work on the "making of the working class" was framed in a theoretical stance that assumed the nineteenth century was the moment when the twentieth-century working class emerged. But to see that period as marked by the erosion of a political economy of (essentially) artisanal workshop production rather than the creation of a working class makes much better sense of the evidence than looking for signs of modern class politics. The response to this decay occurred within the framework of notions of a "moral economy" that protested the replacement of "custom" as the determination of economic rights by the capricious will of an abstract "market." But even if only a cruel parody, the workshop economy of artisanal independence persisted into mid-Victorian Britain with enough vitality to allow echoes of this *mentalité*, in what Joyce terms the "moral discourses of labour," to continue to shape the vocabulary of employer-worker relations.[14]

Social relations can only reflect the possibilities of the time as they are structured materially and imagined, and to expect twentieth-century forms of social organization to describe the class relations of this period is anachronistic. The ideological vibrancy of the period from 1790 to the 1840s in which certain prefigurative ideas in socialism and feminism broke through the restraints of culture reflected the way times of generalized crisis provide opportunities for widespread reconsideration of political and social conventions. But ultimately, this swirl of ideas and proposals remained moored in the language and concepts of the eighteenth, rather than the twentieth, century. The organizational forms that represented plebeian social and political aspirations in this period were, therefore, qualitatively different from those that emerged after the 1870s, when collective organization came to provide the arena of mediation between social interests and groups. And this, it seems to me, is the key to evaluating and categorizing class relations. Trade unions are the obvious example. Where trade unions existed, they did so not as proto-twentieth-century formations but as expressions of the independence of the mainly artisan members. Collective bargaining was no more on their agenda than it was in the vision of the employers. But, as Joyce suggests, the problem is largely one of chronology, and if we want to talk of a making of the working class in the sense of the emergence of a class identity in the Thompsonian sense (and I still think this is useful), we have to postdate it by seventy years or so.[15]

In this context, too, the language of paternalism becomes more than just a refutation of class: it becomes the ambivalent, elusive, and reciprocal vocabulary that expressed the patrician and paternal styles of social relations. The structuring of relationships around paternal styles provided an arena for mediation that was markedly different from that which developed once collective organization was allowed. The paternal style was more than a matter of language, however, it was primarily about behavior that, if it served to mask certain realities of class power, also allowed social relations to be expressed in ways that legitimated both patrician rule and plebeian presence. Following a well-established historical pattern, such modes of expressing social relations were revitalized in the accelerated economic change in the late eighteenth and early nineteenth centuries as they met the need to assert patrician authority in the face of destabilizing forces. Here, too, there was constant tension around defining the proper boundaries of this relationship, of what described the duties of patricians and the rights of plebeians — and vice versa. Thus, the supreme importance of the law in the eighteenth century as one of the fields where this contest was played out.

In a similar way, the poor law was a site of frequent tension because it was the place where the paternal contract was most visibly expressed and where the pressure of costs put it under the most severe strain. In the 1840s, when the mask of paternalism had almost slipped completely off, coal owners like the third marquis of Londonderry tried to push it back with Chadwickian social engineering projects to keep his workers loyal. This strategy was, perhaps, more visible at the local, personal level than in state policy. But even there, one of the strands that fed into the "reforms" of the 1830s and 1840s was the necessity to restore the ties of connection between the classes. All of this makes sense in the context of the economic change described above. Not only were paternal styles a valid historical experience to call on, but they fit well with broad-based notions of "independence" from the tyranny of collective organization.[16]

There were strong similarities between the world of popular culture and the structures of popular public politics. Both contained large portions of symbolic theatrical and rowdy assertions of popular rights. The rituals of popular politics revolved around the claims of the excluded to a place in the processes of electoral choice and patrician genuflection to this "right." As O'Gorman has explained, these forms of popular politics emerged after 1688 in the party competition of the period until the 1720s and proved impossible to shut off as elections became fewer in number. The agitations from the 1760s through the 1780s injected new life into the practices, and its forms continued to infuse popular politics until the 1860s. It would be a mistake to romanticize the opportunities this system provided for popular participation, but it did represent a political system that was peculiar and distinct to the period ca.1690–ca.1880.[17]

This was true also of the more formal parts of the political structure, whose key theme from the Restoration through the mid-nineteenth century was the establishment and maintenance of landowner, aristocratic control. Until 1867 the major change was, not the Reform Bill of 1832, but the tendency to greater partisanship in electoral behavior that begins in the 1770s. This hardly signified an "inexorable movement towards parliamentary democracy" as John Phillips claims (against the burden of his evidence) but, rather, a clever and effective defense against admitting the possibility that electoral politics should be democratized. There was no systematic and progressive march toward greater democracy: reform was designed not to chart that route but rather to close it off. After 1832, patronage and influence remained, as did the proprietary borough, and over sixty members continued to owe their return to the influence of great landowners. The weakened informal structures of authority actually encouraged corruption — the importance of which (according to Charles Seymour) cannot be overstated — following 1832 until its final eradication in the 1880s. Registration did make a real difference, but not enough to redefine the political world or to alter the central question of political identity in the period: where to fix the boundaries of the political nation?[18]

The answer to that question remained consistent — around property and gender, although the definition of the former was uncertain and, as we have seen, the boundaries of the latter were in constant dispute. It is impossible to assess the expansions or contractions of participation in the governing process. There were many opportunities in the eighteenth century for quite modest people to become involved in the many functions of government. And it is quite possible — though by no means certain — that these opportunities diminished until the party organizations of the late nineteenth century opened different kinds of channels to participation. But we do know (because Sidney Webb and Beatrice Webb told us) that fewer householders had the vestry franchise by the early nineteenth century than at the end of the seventeenth century.[19] There were many different qualifications for participation in the governing functions of the country in the eighteenth century. And even if these were not always strictly observed (as Vernon has noted of the vestry franchises), the fact remains that the tendency over time was to raise ever higher the amount of property it took to become a member of parliament, justice of the peace, turnpike, or improvement commissioner.

The proper level of property qualification was a continual issue for debate from the 1690s and a perpetual source of tension between and within the middling, urban, and landed elites as attempts were made to balance the values of different kinds of property. By the mid-eighteenth century the tension between real and personal property, or monied or landed wealth, had been effectively resolved — although resonances continued well into the early nineteenth century. And it was never the case that franchises were confined entirely to landed property. But the decisive admission of the urban middling classes came in the early 1800s, when vestry franchises were put on a ratepayer basis, thus removing them from the influence of "corrupt" popular control. This became the model for the local government franchise in the 1830s, which, like 1832, was not necessarily the precedent for an expanding franchise. The boundaries of the political nation held firm under the pressures of the 1760s and post-Napoleonic agitations and were not decisively challenged until the 1880s, when the unintended logic of 1867, the growing presence of labor as a collective entity, and the continuing struggle over gender exclusion drew in faint but distinct lines of relief the bare outlines of a new political world.[20]

Both revisionist and traditionalist scholarship tends to treat the early nineteenth century as a ceasura in state formation. But from the perspective of 1870 or 1900 it looks more like a culmination and a continuity. The structures of the state that were "reformed" in the 1830s had been under increasing pressure for the previous sixty years, sometimes longer. It had been Wilkes who first put parliamentary reform on the public political agenda, and that cat was never rebagged. The debate over the poor law was a quintessential eighteenth-century debate. In its essentials — how to control costs, what were the duties of the rich to the poor, and what were the moral responsibilities of the poor — the debate from the 1790s replayed the debate of a century before that had culminated in the establishment of a workhouse and union-based system of poor relief in the Act of 1723. The same was true of the municipal corporations that for a hundred years or more had been the target of complaints about oligarchical control, the site of middling-class struggles for power, and the place where civic improvements had been installed. And if the debate over these issues came right out of the eighteenth century, so, too, did the core of the "reform" solution: rate-payer democracy.[21]

Thus, although the 1830s are conventionally seen as introducing a new tendency to centralization in the balance of power between the center and the localities, it is not clear that these changes amounted to a revolution in government. Parliament in the eighteenth century was the place where the power and rights of local authorities to do things was secured and protected — just as it had been in the seventeenth century — and the arena where national interest groups mediated their disputes. And this was still largely true in the mid-nineteenth century. Although it is possible to detect a change from enabling legislation to prescriptive legislation in the 1830s and 1840s, this merely served to heighten local resistance to central encroachments on local prerogatives — as the well-known struggle over the police bill in 1854–56 illustrated. Indeed, the net effect of the reforming legislation on municipal government and the poor law in the thirties and forties was to reinforce local authority rather than to diminish it. And it remained true that the machinery of central government to assist local authorities and enforce standards remained extremely rudimentary. The frontier between central and local power remained in basically the same place that it had been throughout the eighteenth century until the 1870s. After that date, we can detect a partial and hesitant but decisive movement in favor of central government driven by changes in tax policy, a growing attention to social policy issues that resisted local emollients, and the resultant increased bureaucratization.[22]

This shift was paralleled, and partly related to, a restructuring of the realms of the public and private. I have already indicated above how it is more appropriate to see Victorian struggles around gender boundaries as part of this broader period rather than as prefiguring twentieth-century feminism. One further aspect of the public-private divide is the naming of sin. Since the 1690s, definitions of morality and the work of reformation had been actively propagated through private associations, using what law stood to hand with what support could be mustered from local magistrates and the like. During the early eighteenth century, it was difficult to secure patrician backing for these efforts, but by the early nineteenth century a solid phalanx of elite approval stood behind moral reformation. It remained true, however, at that time that the state was not much involved in the regulation of morality. Frontiers began to be breached in this regard, too, from the 1880s, ironically as a follow-through to the libertarian protests against the Contagious Diseases Acts of the 1860s. Local governments were pressed by organized social purity campaigns to regulate brothels, prostitution, soliciting, and other, more benign matters like theater performances. More dramatically, by legislation in 1885 male homosexuality was distinguished from the more varied practice of buggery, was precisely defined for the first time both as a social and medical problem, and was subjected to criminal penalties. In the Empire, too, private sexuality came under increased scrutiny, and regulation from the 1870s led to the legislated end of cross-race liaisons, a stricter separation of the races, and an official code of sexual purity. At home, state regulation of key aspects of family life crossed a previously established boundary as it began to assume the responsibility of protecting wives and children against certain abuses by husbands and parents. Many other examples could be cited from the field of social policy — especially at the local level — which, of course, had changed direction almost entirely by the time of the famous reforms of the 1906 Liberal government.[23]

This, then, is the outline of a narrative I would propose to replace those that currently frame "Victorian" Britain. [. . .] It enables us to bridge the traditional and ahistorical gap between the eighteenth and nineteenth centuries by linking them together in ways that illuminate both. [. . .] [I]t proposes a framework of organizing principles that focuses on the interactive nature of the various spheres of society. My emphasis here has been on how those spheres conjoined; how the political, economic structures, for example, can be described as operating in mutually reinforcing ways. This is not to make any judgment about determination; it is purely a descriptive statement that proposes a way of seeing a particular period.

Further reading

Richard Price developed his ideas about periodisation more fully in his *British Society, 1680–1880: Dynamism, Containment and Change* (Cambridge: Cambridge University Press, 1999). For responses to Price, see the 'Roundtable on *British Society, 1680–1880*' in *Journal of Victorian Culture* 11(1) (2006), 146–79; and Martin Hewitt, 'Why the Notion of Victorian Britain Does Make Sense', *Victorian Studies*, 48 (2006), 395–438.

Notes

1   See N.F.R. Crafts, *British Economic Growth during the Industrial Revolution* (Oxford, 1985), pp. 42, 45–47, 61, 63, 66, 87; essays by C.H. Feinstein and Donald McCloskey in *The Economic History of Britain since 1700*, vol. 1, ed. Roderick Floud and Donald McCloskey (Cambridge, 1981); C. Knick Harley, "British Industrialisation before 1841: Evidence of Slower Growth during the Industrial Revolution," *Journal of Economic History* 42, no. 5 (1982): 267, 276–77; Dolores Greenberg, "Power Patterns of the Industrial Revolution," *American Historical Review* 87, no. 2 (1982): 1237–61. The growth rate reached 3 percent — the rate recognized to be the signal of an industrializing economy — only in the 1830s and 1840s.

2   On the historiography of the Industrial Revolution and its relationship to contemporary economic moods, see David Cannadine, "The Past and the Present in the English Industrial Revolution, 1880–1980," *Past and Present*, no. 103 (May 1984): 131–72. See also J.U. Nef, *The Rise of the British Coal Industry* (London, 1932), vol. 1, pt. 2; and J.H. Clapham, *An Economic History of Modern Britain: The Early Railway Age, 1820–1850* (Cambridge, 1926). Pat Hudson has recently reemphasized the importance of regional growth for the idea of an industrial revolution in *The Industrial Revolution* (London, 1992). See Maxine Berg's book *The Age of Manufactures* (London, 1984) for a good statement of the variegated and uneven process of this phase of economic growth.

3   See Jonathan Zeitlin and Charles Sabel, "Historical Alternatives to Mass Production: Politics, Markets and Technology in Nineteenth Century Industrialisation," *Past and Present*, no. 108 (August 1985): 133–76. It is worth noting that Toynbee saw the essence of the Industrial Revolution as "the substitution of competition for the medieval regulations which had previously controlled the production and distribution of wealth"; Arnold Toynbee, *The Industrial Revolution* (Boston, 1956), p. 84. See Maxine Berg, "What Difference Did Women's Work Make to the Industrial Revolution?" *History Workshop Journal* 35 (Spring 1993): 22–44, for the key role that female labor played in the growth industries. See also Javier Cuenca Esteban, "British Textile Prices, 1770–1831," *Economic History Review* 48, no. 1 (February 1994): 66–105.

4   Charles Wilson, *England's Apprenticeship, 1603–1763*, 2d ed. (London, 1984), esp. chap. 8; François Crouzet, "Toward an Export Economy: British Exports during the Industrial Revolution," *Explorations in Economic History* 17 (1980): 48–93; Jacob Price, "What Did Merchants Do? Reflections on British Overseas Trade, 1660–1790," *Journal of Economic History* 49, no. 2 (June 1989): 267–84. See also C.H. Lee, *The British Economy since 1700: A Macroeconomic Perspective* (Cambridge, 1986), pp. 3–23, 271–74; and W.D. Rubinstein, *Capitalism, Culture and Decline in Britain, 1750–1990* (London, 1993); P.J. Cain and A.G. Hopkins, *British Imperialism: Innovation and Expansion, 1688–1914* (London, 1992).

5   See Anthony Webster, "The Political Economy of Trade Liberalization: The East India Company Charter Act of 1813," *Economic History Review* 43, no. 3 (1990): 404–19; A.C. Howe, "Free Trade and the City of London c.1820–1870," *History* 77, no. 251 (October 1992): 391–410.

6   John Brewer, *The Sinews of Power: War, Money, and the English State, 1688–1783* (London, 1988).

7   W.D. Rubinstein, "The Size and Distribution of the English Middle Classes in 1860," *Historical Research* 61, no. 144 (February 1988): 65–89; Cain and Hopkins, *British Imperialism*, pp. 53–104.

8   See Philip Harling and Peter Mandler, "From 'Fiscal-Military' State to Laissez-Faire State, 1760–1850," *Journal of British Studies* 32, no. 1 (January 1993): 46–47, 61–66; P.J. Cain and A.G. Hopkins, "Gentlemanly Capitalism and British Expansion Overseas: Part I. The Old Colonial System, 1688–1850," *Economic History Review* 39, no. 4 (1986):

501–25. Even within the industrial towns of the nineteenth century (as Morris and Koditschek among others have demonstrated), the segmentation and fractionalization within the myriad professional, commercial, and bureaucratic elements that made up the middling groups make any valid generalizations difficult. See R.J. Morris, *Class, Sect and Party: The Making of the British Middle Class, Leeds, 1820–1850* (Manchester, 1990); and Theodore Koditschek, *Class Formation and Urban Industrial Society* (Cambridge, 1990).

9   On the process of the gendering of politics and the way the definition of middle-classness itself is intricately related to politics, see Dror Wahrman, "'Middle Class' Domesticity Goes Public: Gender, Class, and Politics from Queen Caroline to Queen Victoria," *Journal of British Studies* 32, no. 4 (October 1993): 396–432. For the most complete statement of this argument, see Leonore Davidoff and Catherine Hall, *Family Fortunes* (London, 1988); and various articles such as Catherine Hall, "The Early Formation of Victorian Domestic Ideology," in *Fit Work for Women*, ed. Sandra Burman (London, 1979), pp. 15–31. See also Susan Dwyer Amussen, *An Ordered Society: Gender and Class in Early Modern England* (Oxford, 1988). On the notion of the public and private spaces as part of the emergence of bourgeois politics and identity, see, of course, Jurgen Habermas, *The Structural Transformation of the Public Sphere*, trans. Thomas Burger (Cambridge, Mass., 1989).

10 See Davidoff and Hall; Peter Earle, *The Making of the English Middle Class: Business, Society and Family Life in London, 1660–1730* (London, 1989), pp. 160–74; Alice Clark, *The Working Life of Women in the Seventeenth Century*, 2d ed. (London, 1982). Fordyce is quoted in Paul Langford, *A Polite and Commercial People: England, 1727–1783* (Oxford, 1989), p. 606.

11 Wahrman, pp. 402–3; T.A. Curtis and W.A. Speck, "The Societies for the Reformation of Manners: A Case Study in the Theory and Practice of Moral Reform," *Literature and History* 3 (March 1976): 45–64.

12 On eighteenth-century gender politics, see Langford, *A Polite and Commercial People*, pp. 110–11, 112, 602–3, 606–7; Linda Colley, *Britons: Forging the Nation, 1707–1832* (New Haven, Conn., 1992), pp. 237–81. On Nightingale, see Mary Poovey, *Uneven Developments: The Ideological Work of Gender in Mid-Victorian England* (Chicago, 1988), pp. 164–66 passim; and Martha Vicinus and Bea Nergaard, *Ever Yours, Florence Nightingale: Selected Letters* (Cambridge, Mass., 1990). On the colonization of philanthropy by women in the mid-nineteenth century, see Frank Prochaska, *Women and Philanthropy in Nineteenth Century England* (Oxford, 1980). On the suffrage and mid-Victorian feminists, see Philippa Levine, *Victorian Feminism, 1850–1900* (Talla-hassee, Fla., 1987), chap. 3. Obviously, the suffrage situation was different in the mid-nineteenth century — in some ways more confusing — with some openings in the local government franchise, but the agitation for a parliamentary franchise — on a class basis — was only just beginning to emerge.

13 See E.P. Thompson, *Customs in Common* (New York, 1993), pp. 1–15, on the way "custom" underlay the plebian political consciousness of the eighteenth century, and pp. 410–11, 442, 451–53, 456, 476–77, 505, 511, 517–18, 528–29, on the chronology of wife sales and rough music. Also see Rohan McWilliam, "Radicalism and Popular Culture: The Tichborne Case and the Politics of Fair Play, 1867–1886," in *Currents of Radicalism: Popular Radicalism, Organised Labour and Party Politics in Britain, 1850–1914*, ed. Eugenio Biagini and Alastair Reid (Cambridge, 1991), pp. 44–64.

14 See Joyce's use of the term in his *Visions of the People: Industrial England and the Question of Class, 1840–1914* (Cambridge, 1991), pp. 87–113, Also see Raphael Samuel, "The Workshop of the World: Steam Power and Hand Technology in Mid-Victorian Britain," *History Workshop Journal* 3 (Spring 1977): 6–72. Joyce's *Visions of the People* is an excellent description of the persistence of the languages of moral economy in mid-nineteenth-century social relations.

15   Barbara Taylor, "'The men are as bad as the masters . . . ': Socialism, Feminism and Sexual Antagonism in the London Tailoring Trade in the 1830s," in *Sex and Class in Women's History*, ed. Judith L. Newton, Mary P. Ryan, and Judith Walkowitz (London, 1983). Although this is not the main point of Gregory Claeys's work on Robert Owen, there is much support for this argument in his *Machinery, Money and the Millenium: From Moral Economy to Socialism, 1815–1860* (Cambridge, 1987), pp. 189, 192–94, and even more in his *Citizens and Saints: Politics and Anti-Politics in Early British Socialism* (Cambridge, 1989), esp. pp. 7, 14–15, 25–29, and 329, where the main argument is the continuities between eighteenth- and nineteenth-century social thought. See Joyce, *Visions of the People*, p. 4.

16   See E.P. Thompson, "Patrician Society, Plebeian Culture," *Journal of Social History* 7, no. 4 (Summer 1974): 382–405, and "Eighteenth-Century English Society: Class Society without Class," *Social History* 3, no. 2 (May 1978): 133–66; David Levine and Keith Wrightson, *The Making of an Industrial Society: Whickham, 1560–1765* (Oxford, 1991), pp. 356–60, 378–81; Peter Dunkley, "Paternalism, the Magistracy and Poor Relief in England, 1795–1834," *International Review of Social History* 24, no. 3 (1979): 371–97; and Peter Mandler, *Aristocratic Government in the Age of Reform: Whigs and Liberals, 1830–1852* (Oxford, 1990) for the coexistence of paternalist and individualist tendencies in Whig ideology.

17   Frank O'Gorman, *Voters, Patrons and Parties: The Unreformed Electorate of Hanoverian England, 1734–1832* (Cambridge, 1989); Frank O'Gorman, "Campaign Rituals and Ceremonies: The Social Meaning of Elections in England, 1780–1860," *Past and Present*, no. 135 (May 1992): 79–115; and James Vernon, *Politics and the People: A Study in English Political Culture, 1815–1867* (Cambridge, 1993).

18   See Charles Seymour, *Electoral Reform in England and Wales* (Archon reprint, New Hamden, Conn., 1970), p. 193, for corruption. Seymour fully recognized the way 1832 changed little in the operation of politics, and his findings have been confirmed by Gash and others. But Seymour's work is marred by the framing of the issue of political reform as one of aristocracy versus middle class. See also, of course, Norman Gash, *Politics in the Age of Peel*, 2d ed. (Hassocks, 1976); John A. Phillips, *The Great Reform Bill in the Boroughs: English Electoral Behaviour, 1818–1841* (Oxford, 1992), quote on p. 303, and also his *Electoral Behaviour in Unreformed England: Plumpers, Splitters and Straights* (Princeton, N.J., 1982), pp. 306–7.

19   Sydney Webb and Beatrice Webb, *English Local Government from the Revolution to the Municipal Corporations Act: The Parish and the County* (London, 1906), pp. 146–72.

20   Vernon, *Politics and the People*, pp. 16–22; and Webb and Webb. On 1867, see the very important article by John Davis, "Slums and the Vote, 1867–1890," *Historical Research* 64, no. 155 (October 1991): 375–88.

21   On the poor law in this period, see Tim Hitchcock, "Paupers and Preachers: The SPCK and the Parochial Workhouse Movement," in *Stilling the Grumbling Hive: The Response to Social and Economic Problems in England, 1689–1750*, ed. Lee Davison (New York, 1992), pp. 145–47. The major and important difference between this effort and the successful replay a hundred years earlier was that in the early eighteenth century this policy flowed not from the state but from the Society for the Propagation of Christian Knowledge (SPCK) and was taken up by parishes. The 1723 workhouse act was an enabling bill, not a prescriptive one. But there were interesting similarities; thus, at both periods the magistrates were suspicious of the workhouse policy, preferring the system of outrelief. For towns, see Penelope Corfield, The *Impact of English Towns, 1700–1800* (Oxford, 1982), pp. 154–56; and Peter Borsay, ed., *The Eighteenth Century English Town: A Reader in Urban History, 1688–1828* (London, 1990).

22   The opening chapter of Oliver Macdonagh, *Early Victorian Government, 1830–1870* (London, 1977), pp. 1–21, is a good example of the internal inconsistencies in the revolution in government thesis by its leading proponent. See also Christine Bellamy, *Administering Central-Local Relations, 1871–1919* (Manchester, 1988); W.L. Burn, *Age*

of Equipoise (London, 1964), pp. 167–76; Jennifer Hart, "The County and Borough Police Act, 1856," *Public Administration* 34 (1956): 405–17; Carolyn Steedman, *Policing the Victorian Community: The Formation of English Provincial Police Forces, 1856–1880* (London, 1984), pp. 25–32.

23   Jeffrey Weeks, *Sex, Politics and Society: The Regulation of Sexuality since 1800* (London, 1981); Judith Walkowitz, *Prostitution and Victorian Society: Women, Class and the State* (Cambridge, 1980); George Behmer, *Child Abuse and Moral Reform in England, 1870–1914* (Palo Alto, Calif., 1982); Ronald Hyam, *Empire and Sexuality: The British Experience* (Manchester, 1991), chaps. 4–6.

PART 2

Economy

SINCE SIR JOHN CLAPHAM'S WORK in the inter-war period, some of the earliest and most valuable studies of the nineteenth century have come from economic historians who sought to explain Britain's industrial transformation but who have been equally attentive to the fact that Britain was a predominantly rural nation until at least the mid-nineteenth century. In other words, economic history shaped the paradigms around which the Victorian world was understood. One group of questions revolved around whether the Industrial Revolution was really a revolution at all, as it had taken such a long time to be completed. A second question concerned regions. Did economic change affect *all* of Britain, or was it a phenomenon of the North, while the South remained predominantly agricultural? Did standards of living rise or fall for the working class during the Industrial Revolution? Other historians focused on the question of the success of British entrepreneurs in creating factories and developing markets. Historians of the later nineteenth century were preoccupied with the question of whether the economy failed in the later nineteenth century. A range of explanations have been offered to explain this apparent failure, ranging from the fact that Britain had the first industrial revolution (which allowed other nations to learn from its record), to the poor quality of technical education, to an overcommitment to the staple industries of the Industrial Revolution (cotton textiles, iron, steel and shipbuilding). Some revisionists have suggested that Britain did not fail, and that the economy was working well up to 1914. It suffered a relative decline only when measured against the record of the United States and Germany in the later nineteenth century, when it could no longer dominate the world's markets.

The following two Readings are both influential works that require us to view the world's first industrial nation in new ways. Each offers a cultural explanation for the path the British economy took and suggests the continued dominance of elite classes was due to their ability to mould the economy so their way of life would not be threatened. In the long run this would mean an economy more dependent on certain types of overseas investment than on technological and manufacturing innovation at home.

Martin Wiener

CAN CULTURE EXPLAIN ECONOMIC DECLINE?

English Culture and the Decline of the Industrial Spirit, 1850–1980 (Cambridge: Cambridge University Press, 1981), 11–22.

Martin Wiener's *English Culture and the Decline of the Industrial Spirit, 1850–1980* (1981) offers a cultural explanation for Britain's industrial decline. He argues that in the later nineteenth century the elite successfully maintained a vision of Britain as a place where old and tested values predominated, allowing it to maintain its dominance while incorporating the new middle classes into its vision of the country. There was, in cultural terms, a reaction against industrial growth and a deference to pre-industrial values which came to characterise national identity. Wiener draws on a range of sources to demonstrate how an 'English way of life' was constructed that emphasised the nation's rural identity and minimised the importance of industrial progress. Wiener describes the role of the public school in the creation and main- tenance of an elite class, which perpetuated a contempt for applied sciences and manufacturing. In other words, middle-class children were taught to disdain the source of their wealth. Gentrification damaged the construction of an enterprise culture. Economic decline was inevitable because the English never adopted the correct mindset. The industrial spirit was tamed by English culture with its love of tradition, antiquity, the countryside and deference to the elite. Wiener traces such changes into the twentieth century and presents a seductive explanation about economic decline. The extract below sets out this central argument, but other chapters in Wiener's book develop the ideas in more depth.

On publication, Wiener's ideas prompted a debate about the extent to which cultural explanations could explain economic decline and spawned some important responses (see Further reading). *British Culture and Economic Decline* (1990), edited by Bruce Collins and Keith Robbins, offered a range of essays challenging Wiener's various points and providing a more positive assessment of economic development. A parallel response might be seen in *Englishness: Politics and Culture, 1880–1920* (1986), edited by Robert Colls and Philip Dodd, which explored the increasing focus on a romantic vision of Englishness based around the Home Counties in the late nineteenth century. The Wiener thesis inspired wide discussion by politicians and policy makers as it arrived at the moment when the collapse of old industries was in the news and Thatcherism was challenging the way Britain was run. It also inspired reflection on the continuing role of the class system and the feeling that Britain was an 'old country' in love with a glorified past and therefore at odds with modernisation.

Martin Wiener holds the Mary Gibbs Jones Chair in History at Rice University. He published *Reconstructing the Criminal: Culture, Law and Policy in England 1830–1914* in 1990 and *Men of Blood: Violence, Manliness and Criminal Justice in Victorian England* in 2004. He is currently writing a book on *Violence, Race and Authority in the British Empire, c.1880–1930*.

> England . . . owes her great influence not to military successes, but to her commanding position in the arena of industry and commerce. If she forgets this, she is lost.
> — *Annual Register* (1867)

> Sixty-four years that favored property, and had made the upper middle class; buttressed, chiselled, polished it; till it was almost undistinguishable in manners, morals, speech, appearance, habit, and soul from the nobility.
> — John Galsworthy, *The Forsyte Saga* (1922)

"**NINE ENGLISH TRADITIONS** out of ten," an old don in a C.P. Snow novel says, "date from the latter half of the nineteenth century."[1] This period saw the recasting of British life. Modern British political, commercial, and social institutions are predominantly the creation of Victorian reform and accommodation. Similarly, twentieth-century social values bear the imprint of Victorian arguments. Much of the criticism of mid-Victorian Britain by men like Mill, Arnold, Ruskin, and Dickens, for example, was amplified by social trends under way, and helped shape the outlook of succeeding generations of educated opinion. A distinctive English world view was being formed in the crucible of the mid-Victorian ferment of social ideas. It proved highly suitable to the new upper stratum taking shape at the same time, a stratum produced by the coming together of businessmen, the rapidly expanding professional and bureaucratic classes, and the older gentry and aristocracy. The central institution of the consolidation, the public school, came into its own in this period. From the eighteen-forties, old schools were revived, new schools were founded, and a common ethos began to crystallize. It was an ethos that readily absorbed one side of mid-Victorian social thought, institutionalized it, and propagated it. By Victoria's death, her nation possessed a remarkably homogeneous and cohesive elite, sharing to a high degree a common education and a common outlook and set of values. This shared outlook represented an adaptation by the traditional landed ruling class (as was widely noted at the time), but it also marked a crucial rebuff for the social revolution begun by industrialization.

A re-formed elite

The early years of Victoria's reign were widely thought at the time to be bringing about the triumph of the middle classes. It was frequently claimed that the parliamentary reform in 1832 and the repeal of the Corn Laws in 1846 were pulling out the props from the political and economic supremacy of the landed aristocracy. Marx and Engels went so far as to assert in 1850 that "the only remaining aristocracy is the bourgeoisie."[2] Was, in fact, the death knell tolling for the English aristocracy as a ruling class? In the long view, no doubt. Yet not before the aristocracy had succeeded in both prolonging its reign and educating its successors in its world view.[3] Power was peacefully yielded in return for time and for the acceptance of many aristocratic values by the new members of the elite. Hostility on both sides began to wane. After 1846 the interests of landlords were no longer clearly opposed to those of industry or capital: The greater landlords drew an increasing proportion of their incomes from railways, canals, mines, and urban property, and the growing scale of business organization was producing a new class of big businessmen, wealthier than their predecessors yet less directly involved in management and enterprise. For men of these groups, the old class antagonisms meant less and less, and a process of mutual accommodation was soon under way. In 1850 the *Economist* had criticized capitalists who advertised in the newspapers their desire to purchase land in order to acquire status. By 1870 it had changed its tune, observing that:

> Social consideration is a great and legitimate object of desire, and so great is the effect of this visibility of wealth upon social consideration that it would pay a millionaire in England to sink half his fortune in buying 10,000 acres of land to return a shilling percent, and live upon the remainder, rather than to live upon the whole without land. He would be a greater person in the eyes of more people.[4]

English history's normal pattern of ready absorption of new into old wealth, broken in the late eighteenth century by the explosive growth of geographically and religously isolated industrial wealth, resumed with a vengeance. In such Establishment spheres of activity as "society," the military (particularly the Volunteers), the Church of England, and the public schools and universities, the process of accommodation and absorption accelerated in the second half of the century. As Harold Perkin has noted, "the seeds of many of the aristocratic directorships of late Victorian England — in 1896 167 noblemen, a quarter of the peerage, were directors of companies — were no doubt sown on the playing fields of mid-Victorian public schools."[5]

The children of businessmen were admitted to full membership in the upper class, at the price of discarding the distinctive, production-oriented culture shaped during the century of relative isolation. "The main point about landowners — in England at least — is that they did not acquire their land in order to develop it, but in order to enjoy it," observed H.J. Habbakuk.[6] The adoption of a culture of enjoyment by new landowners and aspiring landowners meant the dissipation of a set of values that had projected their fathers as a class to the economic heights, and the nation to world predominance. In its place, they took up a new ideal — that of the gentleman.[7] This new ideal was in its essentials the older aristocratic ideal purged of its grosser elements by the nineteenth-century religious revival. Indeed, Bertrand Russell—himself a hereditary peer — was to suggest that "the concept of the gentleman was invented by the aristocracy to keep the middle classes in order."[8]

And so, in a sense, it did. Through these mechanisms of social absorption, the zeal for work, inventiveness, material production, and money making gave way within the capitalist class to the more aristocratic interests of cultivated style, the pursuits of leisure, and political service. Similarly, the modern industrial town was abandoned, whenever the means existed, in favor of a rural, preferably historic, home. The sons of the enormously successful mill owner John Marshall, for instance, let the business slide and became country gentlemen in the Lake District.[9] Fledgling gentry, F.M.L.Thompson observed, "could be more aristocratic than the aristocrats in their anxiety to conform to the rules of country life."[10] The London merchant banker Baron von Schroeder (to take one instance of many) bought a country house in Cheshire about 1868, became a magistrate in 1876, and was high sheriff and returning officer at the time of the first county council elections in January 1889. He was a well-known follower of the Cheshire hounds. In Cheshire, as elsewhere, it was increasingly difficult to distinguish between the habits of a banker, like "Fitz" Brocklehurst, a Liberal and a Unitarian, who insisted on spending three months in every year shooting in Scotland, and those of the aristocracy. Several generations would complete the transformation. J.M. Lee, examining the Cheshire elite, instructively compared the careers of James Watts, born in 1804, and his grandson, James Watts, born in 1878: The former was a Manchester businessman, possessed of only the most rudimentary education. A Congregationalist and an active participant in Liberal politics, he became mayor of Manchester during the eighteen-fifties. From the huge profits of a warehouse trade in fancy goods, he built an impressive country house, Abney Hall. His grandson was sent to Winchester and New College, Oxford, rowed for his college at Henley, and followed all the fashions of his generation, "even to the extent of taking an American wife!"[11]

The peculiar flexibility of the English aristocracy snatched a class victory from the brink of defeat, and helped alter the course of national development. At the moment of its triumph, the entrepreneurial class turned its energies to reshaping itself in the image of the class it was supplanting. That self-conscious spokesman of a bourgeois revolution, Richard Cobden (1804–65), watched with dismay his troops deserting the cause:

> We have [he complained to a friend in 1863] the spirit of feudalism rife and rampant in the midst of the antagonistic development of the age of Watt, Arkwright and Stephenson! Nay, feudalism is every day more and more in the ascendant in political and social life. So great is its power

and prestige that it draws to it the support and homage of even those who are the natural leaders of the newer and better civilisation. Manufacturers and merchants as a rule seem only to desire riches that they may be enabled to prostrate themselves at the feet of feudalism. How is this to end?[12]

As capitalists became landed gentlemen, JPs, and men of breeding, the radical ideal of active capital was submerged in the conservative ideal of passive property, and the urge to enterprise faded beneath the preference for stability.

The gentrification of the Victorian middle classes proceeded as well through a second social trend of the period: the rise of the modern professions. Professional men — lawyers, doctors, public officials, journalists, professors, and men of letters — came into their own during the reign of Victoria. They grew numerous and distinct enough to be considered a class, or more strictly speaking, a subclass, with an influence on English opinion and culture far out of proportion to its size. By the second half of the nineteenth century there was a professional upper middle class in Britain alongside the capitalist class.

Throughout the century, old professions like law and medicine restructured themselves to emphasize expertise, expanded in numbers, and achieved enhanced status. Even the clergy followed a similar pattern. At the same time, new professions proliferated. The establishment of the Royal College of Surgeons in 1800, the British Medical Association in 1856, and the Law Society in 1825 placed the traditional secular professions on a new footing of secure respectability.[13] One after another, new professions, greatly influenced by the model of the older ones, began to detach themselves from the world of business and organize themselves — civil engineers in 1818, architects in 1834, pharmacists in 1841, actuaries in 1848, and so on, all revealing an aspiration to use their claims of expertise and integrity to rise above the rule of the marketplace. Between 1841 and 1881, the nation's population rose by 60 percent, whereas the seventeen main professional occupations increased their numbers by 150 percent, thereby coming to constitute a substantial portion of the middle class.[14]

The growth of the professions bolstered the emerging cultural containment of industrial capitalism. Professional men as a class were characterized by their comparative aloofness from the struggle for income. The scale of professional prestige was largely determined by distance from flagrant "money grubbing." T.H.S. Escott (1844–1924), author of the most informative contemporary survey of late-Victorian Britain, explained that GPs and solicitors had lower occupational status than barristers and clergymen partly because the former had to undergo the "vulgar" commercial process of receiving money directly from their clients.[15] Professional aloofness was of course partly a myth. Individuals often competed for clients, and the maintenance of high professional standards also served to limit entry and thus bolster incomes. Nevertheless, as Harold Perkin argued, "once established, the professional man could generally rely on a steady income not subject to the same mutual competition as rent, profits and wages. To a certain extent, then, he was above the economic battle."[16] Furthermore, professionals valued services and intangible goods such as those they provided higher than the material goods whose production was the concern of much of the nonprofessional middle class and working class. This bias toward services, together with the independence of their status from the vagaries of the market, served to detach professional men from the mental and emotional world of the industrial capitalist.

Of course, professionalization also carried other values more attuned to an industrial world view: the career open to talent and effort, specialization, and efficiency. But these values were not as encouraged in English society as they were, for example, in America.[17] Professionalization did not have a single, universal meaning: Its actual forms derived from the interaction between its multiple tendencies and its social environment. The English environment magnified the older gentry face of professionalization at the expense of its newer bourgeois one.[18] The very modes by which an English profession typically defined itself set its members off from the world of capitalism. As one historian observed:

> The process of incorporation, acquisition of an expensive and palatial headquarters in central London, establishment of an apprenticeship system, limitations on entries, and scheduling of fees, are all manifestly designed to "gentrify" the profession and make it acceptable to society. This aspect of professionalization is profoundly anticapitalist, and hence at odds with much of the rest of nineteenth-century British society.[19]

The existence of a powerful aristocracy in Britain reinforced the anticapitalist tendencies within professionalization. Here, consequently, more than elsewhere, the development of the professions was separating many of the most able men from the world of commerce and industry. A perceptive contemporary pointed this out: Matthew Arnold, poet and school inspector, observed in 1868 that professional men, admitted to an education with aristocrats, tended to model themselves on the aristocracy. Consequently, Arnold claimed, "in no country . . . do the professions so naturally and generally share the cast of ideas of the aristocracy as in England." In England the professions, including the emerging civil service, were "separate, to a degree unknown on the Continent, from the commercial and industrial class with which in social standing they are naturally on a level." The result was the spectacle of

> a middle class cut in two and in a way unexampled anywhere else; of a professional class brought up on the first plane, with fine and governing qualities, but without the idea of science; while that immense business class, which is becoming so important a power in all countries, on which the future so much depends . . . is in England brought up on the second plane, but cut off from the aristocracy and professions, and without governing qualities.[20]

The shaping of a gentleman

Ironically, the educational system that Arnold's father did so much to shape played a leading role in fixing this separation, and the attitude and values that went with it, upon English society. The public school was of particular importance, for this "peculiar institution" unique to England had become by the end of Victoria's reign the shared formative experience of most members of the English elite. For all their vaunted independence, the public schools, through new institutions like Headmasters' Conference, converged on a common model. Despite the absence of state direction, they came to constitute a system,[21] one that separated the next generation of the upper class from the bases of Britain's world position — technology and business.

The decade of the eighteen-sixties had seemed to be destined to be a time of sweeping reform in secondary education. A spreading awareness of the need to modernize the unsupervised hodgepodge of existing schools led to the creation of two royal commissions. The Clarendon [Public Schools] Commission, appointed in 1861, was to examine the nine most prestigious endowed schools, and the Taunton [Schools Inquiry] Commission, created three years later, was to look at all the other endowed schools. Their reports did indeed lead to acts of Parliament, but the thrust for fundamental reform was deflected. The main effect of the prolonged attention was to establish the nine ancient public schools, more or less as they were, as *the* model of secondary education for all who aspired to rise in English society. After examining in detail the faults of the public schools, the Clarendon Commission turned to their greater merit:

> These schools have been the chief nurseries of our statesmen; in them, and in schools modelled after them, men of all the various classes that make up English society, destined for every profession and career, have been brought up on a footing of social equality, and have contracted the most enduring friendships, and some of the ruling habits of their lives; and they have had perhaps the largest share in moulding the character of an English Gentleman.[22]

There was change — new schools appeared, new subjects were introduced, improvements in physical facilities and innovations in school procedures were made — but only the minimum necessary to preserve and extend the social dominance of the public school pattern. This aim was attained: In the later nineteenth century the sons of the middle classes flocked in increasing numbers into schools modeling themselves upon the "Clarendon nine." What was usually desired was expressed in a fictional parent's enthusiasm for the reinvigorated Shrewsbury: "Just the very place: new buildings, old traditions. What could possibly be better?"[23]

The most obvious example of the public schools' detachment from the modern world was the virtual absence of science of any sort from their curricula. In the teaching of science the public schools lagged far behind schools of lesser social standing. It was first taught in private and Dissenting academies in the eighteenth century, and by Victoria's accession it was a normal part of the curriculum in most such schools, and in many grammar schools.[24] Yet it did not penetrate the schools of the upper class for some years thereafter, and then only over determined obstruction.

At Rugby, the pioneer of public school science instruction, the first science teachers were barely tolerated. J.M. Wilson, an astronomer, was allowed after 1859 to offer four hours a week of "natural philosophy" as long as it did not interfere with the fourteen hours he put in on algebra, geometry, and trigonometry. For this science instruction no room could be found on the premises at Rugby, and "the experiments were performed out of sight, in the cloakroom of the Town Hall a hundred yards away down the road from the school, with the apparatus locked up in two cases so that the townspeople could use the space for other purposes at night."[25] This was the situation the Public Schools Commission found at the most scientifically minded of the leading schools! Even after the commission urged the development of science instruction, the pace of change was slow. Graham Wallas (1858–1932), at Shrewsbury between 1871 and 1877, later recalled that "we had no laboratory of any kind, and I never heard in my time of any Shrewsbury boy receiving a science lesson."[26]

This neglect of science rested on an educational ideology. Its positive face was exaltation of the Greek and Roman classics as the basis of any liberal education. Its negative side was a fear of science as antireligious, which sharply waned as the century drew on, and an association of science with vulgar industry, artisans, and commercial utility, which did not diminish so readily. Headmasters, more or less equating the classics (together with Christianity, of course) with civilization and ideal mental training, were eloquent in defense of a purely classical curriculum, and they were backed up by most educated persons of note. No less a figure than Gladstone added his views: "What I feel is, that the relation of pure science, natural science, modern languages, modern history and the rest to the old classical training, ought to be founded on a principle . . . I deny their right to a parallel or equal position; their true position is ancillary, and as ancillary it ought to be limited and restrained without scruples."[27]

Most significant for the future, science was linked in the public mind with industry, and this damaged its respectability in upper-class eyes. Industry meant an uncomfortable closeness to working with one's hands, not to mention an all-too-direct earning of money. The question of science teaching was enmeshed in the class system: Despite the tradition of Hooke, Boyle, and their contemporaries of the great days of the Royal Society, it was not until the twentieth century that experimental science was fully accepted again in England as a fit occupation for a gentleman. The fact that the classics were a mark of social class worked to prevent the application of parental pressure for "modern" instruction. As the Taunton Commission concluded in 1868:

> They [the great majority of professional men and poor gentry] would, no doubt, in most instances be glad to secure something more than classics and mathematics. But they value these highly for their own sake, and perhaps even more for the value at present assigned to them in English society. They have nothing to look to but education to keep their sons on a high social level. And they would not wish to have what might be more readily converted into money, if in any degree it tended to let their children sink in the social scale.[28]

Although argument raged in the reviews over the nation's need for education in science, when it came down to the crucial question of one's own sons, the modernists rarely pushed principle to the point of practice. Isambard Kingdom Brunel (1806–59), the greatest engineer of his generation, sent two sons to Harrow, where they were hardly likely to follow their father's profession; T.H. Huxley (1825–95) sent a son to University College School; Lyon Playfair (1818–98), another leading critic of outdated public school curricula, sent one to Cheltenham; and so on.[29] When science teaching finally arrived in the public schools, it came late, marked by a social stigma and a bias against those aspects that bordered on engineering.

Similarly, the public schools resisted calls for particular training to prepare boys for the expanding professions. Vocational preparation — for law, medicine, or any newer profession — carried the stigma of utility. Edward Thring (1821–87), of Uppingham, a highly successful headmaster, found it "absolutely impossible to direct the studies of a great school to this end [professional education] beyond a certain degree, without destroying the object of a great school, which is, mental and bodily training in the best way, apart from immediate gain."[30] Thring was stating a platitude against which it was extremely difficult for gentlemen to take a stand. One exception was Dean Farrar (1831–1903), who observed that a scientific education would be useful.

> And no sooner [Farrar wrote] have I uttered the word "useful" than I imagine the hideous noise which will environ me, and amid the hubbub I faintly distinguish the words, vulgar, utilitarian, mechanical . . . Well, before this storm of customary and traditional clamour I bow my head, and when it is over, I meekly repeat that it would be *more useful* — more rich in practical advantages, more directly available for health, for happiness, for success in the great battle of life. I for one am tired of this "worship of inutility." One would really think it was a crime to aim at the material happiness of the human race.[31]

Thring's view remained pedagogical gospel. The weight of prejudice was heavily against the compatibility of liberal education (increasingly *the* mark of a gentleman) and utility. Yet if the public school produced exceedingly few scientists, and even fewer engineers, they did send forth increasing recruits to the growing ranks of professional men. As landed society entered its decline, and public schools expanded and increased in number, they became the nursery of professionals. Their disparagement of specialized and practical studies reinforced the traditional content of the professional ideal — the imitation of the leisured landed gentleman — at the expense of the modern role of the professional as expert.

If the technical skills necessary for professionalism were discouraged at public school, the world of business was openly disparaged. Pre-Victorian public schools had been little more than finishing schools for sons of the landed gentry, with an admixture of farmers' sons and a few town boys. Aristocratic values were unchallenged, and trade despised. Arnoldian reforms retained — even deepened — the low valuation of commerce. In *Tom Brown's Schooldays,* that testament of gratitude to Dr. Arnold, Thomas Hughes spoke scornfully of England's previous "twenty years of buying cheap and selling dear." When Tom Brown, son of an idealized country squire, wishes upon leaving Rugby to "be at work in the world, and not dawdling away three years at Oxford," he is set straight by a master. Nothing was a greater vice to Arnold or Hughes than "dawdling," but there was work and there was work:

> You talk of "working to get your living" and "doing some real good in the world" in the same breath. Now, you may be getting a very good

living in a profession, and yet doing no good at all in the world, but quite the contrary, at the same time. Keep the latter before you as your only object, and you will be right, whether you make a living or not; but if you dwell on the other, you'll very likely drop into mere money-making.[32]

Despite Thomas Hughes's assertion of the sovereignty of individual character "apart from clothes, rank, fortune, and all externals whatsoever,"[33] no children of businessmen were in evidence at Tom Brown's Rugby, and none of the characters so much as contemplated a commercial career. In a later and very popular novel about Harrow, Horace Vachell's *The Hill* (1905), a businessman's child arrives at school, but under a cloud of suspicion. Though rising by ability to captain of the cricket team, he remains an outsider, and ends by being expelled for dishonesty. "One is sometimes reminded," another boy typically comments, "that he is the son of a Liverpool merchant, born in or about the docks."[34] Given this stigma, it is hardly surprising that one of the most successful means of resisting the introduction of modern subjects was to associate them with the world of business. When the Taunton Commission was told by the inspector of schools for London that "I have been assured by several men of business that few things would please them better than a successful attack upon classical studies," a potent weapon was handed to the opponents of curricular change.[35]

The public schools gradually relaxed their entrance barriers. Boys from commercial and industrial families, however, were admitted only if they disavowed their backgrounds and their class. However many businessmen's sons entered, few future businessmen emerged from these schools, and those who did were "civilized"; that is, detached from the single-minded pursuit of production and profit.[36] "Somehow or other," the zealous founder of public schools, Nathaniel Woodard (1811–91), had written the bishop of Manchester in 1871, "we must get possession of the Middle Classes . . . and how can we so well do this as through Public Schools?"[37] Although Woodard's ambitious scheme for a vast network of boarding schools to embrace the entire middle class did not go far, the success of the public schools on a more modest and indirect scale gave a new lease on life to traditional social values. Their very physical environment held the urban industrial world at arm's length, and evoked the life of the old landed gentry. Disproportionately, whether new or ancient, they were distant from cities and industrial regions. Southern England had a very high proportion of the most prestigious public schools.[38] New schools were placed, whenever possible, deep in the countryside. Older schools sited in the cities moved out, like Charterhouse to the Surrey Hills. Every public school acquired, or sought to acquire, an estate to ensure its undisturbed rural character.[39] In this endeavor they were ironically assisted by the economic difficulties of the landed aristocracy; particularly after the First World War many large country houses were taken over by old and new public schools.[40]

The ethos of the schools, in keeping with their surroundings, exalted the careers colored by the aristocratic ideals of honor and public leadership — the military, politics, the civil service, and the higher professions. Public school boys made excellent administrators of a far-flung empire, but the training so admirably suited for that task ill fitted them for economic leadership.[41] The public schools nurtured the future elite's political, not economic, abilities, and a desire to maintain stability and order far outweighed the desire to maximize individual or national wealth.

During the second half of the nineteenth century the public schools took a central place in the life of the English upper classes. More than this, although less than one in twenty Englishmen ever passed through them, they became an archetypal national institution. "When we are criticizing its products," noted a typical defender in 1929, "whether by way of praise or blame, it is really to a great extent the English character that we are criticizing."[42] The public schools, observed Roy Lewis and Angus Maude (not unsympathetically) as late as 1949, enjoyed an "invisible empire" among the middle classes, who avidly read the new genre of public school literature.[43] Those who could afford it, sent their sons; those who could not, sought a grammar school as close as possible to the public school model. This latter quest was made easier after 1902, as a state system of secondary education was developed by public school men committed to public school ideals. Soon after it was established in 1899, the secondary school section of the Board of Education came under the control of the Headmasters' Conference.[44] Public school standards became the standards of the section and its officials. The chief official, Sir Robert Morant (1863–1920), who wrote and administered the Education Act of 1902 (for a prime minister with two public school headmasters in his family), "believed," a critic complained in Parliament many years later, "that the best form of education was that which had been given to him at Winchester," and consequently sought to replicate that education as far as practicable throughout the upper reaches of the state system.[45] Supported by nearly all the civil servants involved, this effort succeeded, and the new secondary schools developed a curriculum, an outlook, and forms of organization in line with the ideals of the education of the gentry. This molding of state education, affecting every inhabitant of Britain in one way or another, was a legacy equal in importance to the continued direct education in public schools of the bulk of the country's elite.[46] Through one or the other route, the late-Victorian public school outlook continued to shape British attitudes and values in the twentieth century.

Further reading

Martin Wiener's book was heavily debated. Among the works which contain responses to Wiener, see: Simon Gunn, 'The "Failure" of the Victorian Middle Class: A Critique' in Janet Wolff and John Seed (eds), *The Culture of Capital: Art, Power and the Nineteenth Century Middle Class* (Manchester: Manchester University Press, 1988), 17–43; Bruce Collins and Keith Robbins (eds), *British Culture and Economic Decline* (London: Weidenfeld & Nicolson, 1990); W.D. Rubinstein, *Capitalism, Culture, and Decline in Britain, 1750–1990* (London: Routledge 1993); Peter Mandler, 'Against Englishness: English Culture and the Limits to Rural Nostalgia, 1850–1940', *Transactions of the Royal Historical Society*, 6th series 7 (1997), 155–75; Richard English and Michael Kenny (eds), *Rethinking British Decline* (Basingstoke: Macmillan, 2000); F.M.L. Thompson, *Gentrification and the Enterprise Culture: Britain, 1780–1980* (Oxford: Oxford University Press, 2001). The revised edition of Wiener's book that appeared in 2004 contains some reflections on the debate around his book. For Victorian economic history more generally, see the first two volumes of Roderick Floud and Paul Johnson (eds), *The Cambridge Economic History of Modern Britain* (Cambridge: Cambridge University Press, 2004). A good starting point for students is Roderick Floud, *The People and the British Economy, 1830–1914* (Oxford: Oxford University Press, 1997).

Notes

1   C.P. Snow, *The Masters* (New York, 1951), 349.
2   Quoted in George Lichtheim, *Marxism* (New York, 1961), 136.
3   See W.L. Guttsman, *The British Political Elite* (London, 1963); Walter Arnstein, "The Survival of the Victorian Aristocracy," in *The Rich, the Well Born, and the Powerful*, ed. F.C. Jaher (New York, 1973), 203–57; and F.M.L. Thompson, "Britain," in *European Landed Elites in the Nineteenth Century*, ed. David Spring (Baltimore, Md., 1977), 22–44.
4   *Economist*, 29 June 1850 and 16 July 1879; quoted in F.M.L. Thompson, "Britain," 29.
5   Harold Perkin, *The Origins of Modern English Society, 1780–1880* (London, 1969), 435. Richard Helmstadter has described the parallel absorption of Nonconformity in *The Conscience of the Victorian State*, ed. Peter Marsh (Syracuse, N.Y., 1979), 162–4.
6   "Economic Functions of English Landowners in the 17th and 18th Centuries," in *Explorations in Enterprise*, ed. H.G.J. Aitken (Cambridge, Mass., 1965), 339. This is not to say that there were not many individual cases of development-minded aristocrats, and even peers very interested in industrial enterprise. See *Land and Industry: The Landed Estate and the Industrial Revolution*, ed. J.T. Ward and R.G. Wilson (Newton Abbot, Devon, 1971); and Michael W. McCahill, "Peers, Patronage, and the Industrial Revolution 1760–1800," *Journal of British Studies* 16, no. 1 (Fall, 1976), 84–107. Ward and Wilson, in particular, stress the keen interest of the landed proprietors in new sources of income, and their importance in the industrial revolution. Yet one can accept the economic vitality of the landed elite and still argue for their long-run inhibiting effect on the national economy: If the landed families had consistently held themselves aloof from the new economic currents, they would have been swept aside. Instead, they were economically aggressive enough to preserve their predominance without abandoning their distinctive set of values and style of life, to which the new businessmen and industrialists came to aspire.
7   The appeal of the gentlemanly ideal was well-nigh irresistible. Even the most well-known ideologist of industrial capitalism, Samuel Smiles, sought to appropriate it. In the final chapter of *Self-Help* (entitled "The True Gentleman"), he took the gentleman as his standard, seeking to strip him only of his outward, class-bound associations. Gentility, for Smiles, was the ultimate crown to be worn by those who had helped themselves.
8   Cited by Alan Brien, *Sunday Times* (London), 1 August 1971.
9   See W.G. Rimmer, *Marshalls of Leeds* (Cambridge, 1960), 276–303. Mark Girouard (*The Victorian Country House* [Oxford, 1971]) has shown how this social fusion shaped mid- and late-nineteenth-century country house architecture. William Thomas (*The Philosophic Radicals* [Oxford, 1979], 449) has noted how "the rage for titles and pedigrees, for heraldic pomp and castellated architecture" overtook even some radical politicians: "One of the most sustained attempts to create a medieval setting which would reinforce his social pretensions was the rebuilding, or rather smothering in gothic additions, of Bayons Manor, by Charles Tennyson, radical M.P. for Southwark."
10   Thompson, "Britain," 30.
11   *Social Leaders and Public Persons: A Study of County Government in Cheshire since 1888* (Oxford, 1963), 36.

12 Quoted in John Morley, *Life of Richard Cobden* (London, 1881), II, 481–2. This attitude became more entrenched with time. Friedrich Engels (who in 1850 had announced the triumph of the bourgeoisie) observed in 1892, with a mixture of bewilderment and contempt, that "the English bourgeoisie are, up to the present day, so deeply penetrated by a sense of their inferiority that they keep up at their expense and that of the nation, an ornamental caste of drones to represent the nation worthily at all state functions; and they considered themselves highly honoured, whenever one of themselves is found worthy of admission into this selected and privileged body, manufactured, after all, by themselves" (*Socialism, Utopian and Scientific* [New York, 1935], 26).

13 See Brian Heeney, *A Different Kind of Gentleman: Parish Clergy as Professional Men in Early and Mid-Victorian England* (Hamden, Conn., 1976).

14 W.J. Reader, *Professional Men* (New York, 1966), 211 and *passim*.

15 *England: Her People, Polity and Pursuits* (London, 1885), 355–6.

16 Perkin, *Origins of Modern English Society*, 256.

17 For an American contrast, see Burton Bledstein, *The Culture of Professionalism* (New York, 1976).

18 Magali Sarfatti Larson, *The Rise of Professionalism: A Sociological Analysis* (Berkeley, CA 1977), concludes (103) that "the English case shows with clarity that the internal characteristics of professionalization and of the professional model are subordinate to broader social and economic structures." Using Philip Elliot's distinction (in *The Sociology of the Professions* [London, 1972]) between "status professionalism" and "occupational professionalism," we can see that the transition from the first to the second form was less complete in Britain than, for example, in America. The most valuable discussion of the English nineteenth-century professional outlook is in Reader, *Professional Men;* see also Sheldon Rothblatt, *The Revolution of the Dons* (London, 1968), 90–2; G. Kitson Clark, *The Making of Victorian England* (Cambridge, Mass., 1962), 258–74; W.L. Burn, *The Age of Equipoise* (London, 1964), 253–67.

19 W.D. Rubinstein, "Wealth, Elites and Class Structure in Britain," *Past and Present*, no. 76 (August, 1977), 1220.

20 *Schools and Universities on the Continent* [1868], ed. R.H. Super (Ann Arbor, Mich., 1964), 308–9.

21 For a detailed substantiation of this claim, see J.R. de S. Honey, *Tom Brown's Universe: The Development of the Victorian Public School* (London, 1977), ch. 4.

22 *Parl. Papers 1864 20, Report of H.M. Commissioners appointed to inquire into the Revenues and management of certain Colleges and Schools and the Studies pursued and instruction given therein* [hereafter called *Public Schools Commission*] I, 56. As the novelist and translator Rex Warner, himself a schoolmaster, observed in a brief popular account, the Clarendon report "is evidence of the complete acceptance of the public school system as the best possible means of education for those who were to be leaders of the country in peace or war." (Rex Warner, *English Public Schools* [London, 1945], 30).

23 Quoted in T.W. Bamford, *The Rise of the Public Schools* (London, 1967), 15.

24 See J.H. Plumb, "The New World of Childhood in the Eighteenth Century," *Past and Present*, no. 67 (May, 1975), 64–95; and Bamford, *Rise of the Public Schools*, 87, 97.

25 Bamford, *Rise of the Public Schools*, 88.

26 Quoted in Martin J. Wiener, *Between Two Worlds: The Political Thought of Graham Wallas* (Oxford, 1971), 6.

27 *Public Schools Commission* 2,42. J.R. de S. Honey concluded (*Tom Brown's Universe*, 128), "The position of the classics, public schools and in English education in general, was if anything more powerful at the end of the nineteenth century then it had been at the beginning."

28 *Parl. Papers 1868 28, Report of the Schools Inquiry Commission 1*, 17–18.

29 See Bamford, *Rise of the Public Schools*, 105.

30 *Education and School* (1864), quoted in Reader, *Professional Men*, 108.

31   F.W. Farrar, "Public School Education," *Fortnightly Review 3* (new series) (March, 1868), 239–40.

32   Thomas Hughes, *Tom Brown's School Days* [1857] (New York, 1968), 46, 276–7. The dean of Lincoln, addressing Wellington College on its fiftieth anniversary, typically described the school as a place where the young might "learn to put honour before gain, duty before pleasure, the public good before private advantage" (*Wellington College Year Book,* 1909, quoted in David Ward, "The Public Schools and Industry in Britain After 1870," *Journal of Contemporary History* 2, no. 3 [July, 1967], 49).

33   Hughes, *Tom Brown*, 54.

34   Quoted in Ward, "Public Schools and Industry," 38.

35   *Schools Inquiry Commission 1*, 18. See E.C. Mack, *Public Schools and British Opinion, 1780–1860* (New York, 1938), 391.

36   See, for example, Rupert Wilkinson and T.J.H. Bishop, *Winchester and the Public School Elite* (London, 1967), *passim*.

37   Sir John Otter, *Nathaniel Woodard: A Memoir of His Life* (London, 1925), 240. Woodard, a High Church clergyman, was the son of a country gentleman of modest means. See Honey's account of Woodard's and others' efforts to provide public schools for a wider section of the middle classes (*Tom Brown's Universe*, ch. 2).

38   See Honey, ibid., 286.

39   See Bamford, *Rise of the Public Schools*, 16. When cities threatened to encroach, as at Eton and Harrow, expensive defensive measures were taken: Both schools, in effect, sealed off their buildings with a green belt. Harrow's land purchases between 1885 and 1898 were described at the time as a necessary preservative of the invaluable "beauty and dignity" of the school's "rural" setting, upon which "the romantic affection which gathers round an ancient public school" would soon erode (C. Colbeck, quoted in E.W. Henson and G.T. Warner, *Harrow School* [London, 1898], 155).

40   See W.H.G. Armytage, *Four Hundred Years of English Education* (London, 1970), 232.

41   Foreign imitations of the public schools, developing in different societies, moved in different directions. Wilkinson and Bishop, for example, found that comparing their subject, Winchester, with the most fashionable boarding schools in the eastern United States brought out all the more clearly "how often the public schoolboy's outlook on careers resisted the pull of private money-making": "Although the founders of Groton and St. Paul's tried sincerely to emulate the public school way, it has been estimated that the major American boarding schools have sent less than one percent of their boys into government since 1900" — a vastly lower proportion than that at Winchester (Wilkinson and Bishop, *Winchester and the Public School Elite*, 72).

42   Bernard Darwin, *The English Public School* (London, 1929), 28.

43   Roy Lewis and Angus Maude, *The English Middle Classes* (London, 1949), 22, 232.

44   See Brian Simon, "Introduction," in *The Victorian Public School*, ed. Brian Simon and Ian Bradley (London, 1975), 16–17.

45   Chuter Ede, in Parliament, 4 February 1943; quoted in Bamford, *Rise of the Public Schools*, 260.

46   One effect was, in Bamford's view, to delay "lower-class (elementary school) aspirations . . . for a generation and more. With those aspirations went any hope of a massive development of technical and scientific education that the scientists and industrialists had been urging for half a century" (*Rise of the Public Schools*, 261).

P.J. Cain and A.G. Hopkins

GENTLEMANLY CAPITALISM

'Gentlemanly Capitalism and British Expansion Overseas I: The Old Colonial System, 1688–1850', *Economic History Review*, 39 (1986), 501–10, 525.

In this extract **Peter Cain** and **Anthony Hopkins** trace the growth of what they term 'gentlemanly capitalism' in the eighteenth and nineteenth centuries. By 'gentlemanly capitalism', they mean the dynamic relationship between the aristocracy and the financial and commercial sectors, which shaped the development of the British economy and the Empire. In their view, industrial wealth was less the driving force than the capitalist-minded elite who derived their wealth from land and farming. The elite's alliance with financial capital (wealth derived from banking and insurance services) and the service sector not only shaped Britain's development but also the character of the Empire. Cain and Hopkins draw attention to *rentier* forms of capitalism (wealth derived from property or investment). Britain's capitalist class was geared towards investment abroad. The necessity of retaining the social attributes of the gentleman led aristocratic investors to prefer agriculture or rents to industry. In imperial terms, this meant investment in plantations and raw materials. Gentlemanly capitalism was not only the dynamic force behind the growth of Empire but it also helped to create the international trading system with the City of London and Sterling at its centre; hence the thesis has been widely discussed by scholars dealing with international relations. Cain and Hopkins emphasise the way new groups were incorporated into the category of gentleman through social networks, patronage and the subtle differentiation of the gentlemanly merchant prince and the less eligible captain of industry who operated too closely to the actual point of manufacture to be considered quite of a superior class. The Cain and Hopkins thesis therefore integrates domestic and imperial history and is another example of the way the

Empire has been brought back into British history (see Part 14, on 'Race, Empire and national identity'). Their emphasis on continuities within British capitalism is comparable to that of **Richard Price** and (in a very different way) to **Martin Wiener**'s exploration of the negative influences of the cult of the gentleman and the decline of the industrial spirit. Cain and Hopkins also confirm W.D. Rubinstein's work on the capital accumulation of British elites in which he demonstrates the greater wealth and profitability of men who worked with Britain's invisible exports of capital and investment in the City.

This Reading is made up of an extract from the article where they originally presented their thesis. We present it as a portrait of 'gentlemanly capitalism', although it is mainly focused on the domestic rather than the imperial consequences of this economic development. The Cain and Hopkins thesis was subsequently developed into a two-volume work: *British Imperialism: Innovation and Expansion, 1688–1914* and *British Imperialism: Crisis and Deconstruction, 1914–1990* (2001). As this extract suggests, they strongly disagree with theories about the connection between British imperial growth and Britain's industrial strength.

Peter Cain is Research Professor in History at Sheffield Hallam University. In recent years he has published on aspects of British imperial thought including: *Hobson and Imperialism: Radicalism, New Liberalism and Finance, 1887–1938* (2002); and 'Character and Imperialism: The British Financial Administration of Egypt, 1878–1914', *Journal of Imperial and Commonwealth History*, 34(2) (June 2006). Forthcoming articles include: 'Empire and the Languages of Character and Virtue in Late Victorian and Edwardian England' which will be published in *Modern Intellectual History*, 4(3) (November 2007); and 'Capitalism, Aristocracy and Empire: Some "Classical" Theories of Imperialism Revisited' which will appear in the *Journal of Imperial and Commonwealth History*.

A.G. Hopkins, formerly Smuts Professor of Commonwealth History at Cambridge University, is now the Walter Prescott Webb Professor of History in the University of Texas at Austin. He is currently working on two related themes: the history of globalisation, and a comparison of British and American empires. An edited book on the first topic was published in October 2006 under the title *Global History: Interactions between the Universal and the Local*; essays on the second theme will appear in the *Journal of Imperial & Commonwealth History* in 2007.

"The first of all the English games is making money."

Ruskin, 'Work' (1865)

IN AN EARLIER SURVEY of the history of British imperialism we suggested that closer attention should be given to the connexions between the slow and uncertain development of British industry and the pace and direction of overseas expansion.[1] We also argued that insufficient regard had been paid to the influence of non-industrial forms of capitalism on both overseas development and imperial policy. In the course of that survey, the former problem was dealt with in some detail, whereas the latter was treated briefly and tentatively. The purpose of the present article is to correct this deficiency and to advance a new perspective on British imperialism for the period between the Glorious Revolution and the Second World War.

We begin by emphasizing that, despite their many differences, Marxist and non-Marxist historians share a conception of imperialism which is derived from certain broad assumptions about the place of the industrial revolution in modern British history. These assumptions are made explicit in Marxist theories, which attempt to relate empire building to stages in the evolution of industrial capitalism. They also underlie the leading non-Marxist explanations, which emphasize the diverse commercial, political, and cultural forces brought to the fore by industrial progress. Thus, Gallagher and Robinson, though concerned to refute Marxist claims and to avoid charges of economic determinism, nevertheless started from the position that "British industrialization caused an ever-extending and intensifying development of overseas regions", and they proceeded to interpret the rise of free trade and the growth of informal empire from this standpoint.[2] The implications of this common approach, based on the story of the "triumph of industry", extend well beyond the boundaries of the nineteenth century. Historians as far apart ideologically as Harlow and Wallerstein have agreed that 1763 is a watershed between a "mercantilist" empire and the start of a new type of imperialism which owes its unity to the development of industrial capitalism.[3] Similarly, whether historians date the beginnings of imperial decline from about 1870 or after 1914, they associate it almost exclusively with the steady erosion of Britain's industrial supremacy.[4]

We believe that this approach is seriously at variance with what is now known about British economic history during this period. In particular, it draws upon a generalized and somewhat stereotyped view of the industrial revolution which has failed to resolve central questions of causation and periodization in the study of overseas expansion. If the case for reconsidering the current formulation is compelling, the obstacles to constructing an alternative are formidable. The exercise which follows is revisionist in intent, but also exploratory in execution.[5]

Since the historiography of this subject has been strongly influenced by the definition of terms, and particularly by their imprecision, it is necessary to begin by stating what it is that needs to be explained. The problem is not only to account for the existence of a vast formal empire but also to understand the presence of imperialist, that is hegemonic, impulses in the wider world. Economic imperialism did not follow automatically from economic dependence. What mattered was whether, and to what degree, a foreign country became an "organic portion"[6] of Britain's international economic system, and how far its political and indeed cultural independence were compromised by this relationship. Evidently, a spectrum of possibilities can be envisaged: the United States and parts of western Europe were economically dependent on Britain at various times; republics in South America were sometimes subject to economic imperialism; China experienced imperialist intentions but few of the results. Our aim in this article is to show that the impulses making for imperialism, within the formal empire or outside it, and whether successful or not, cannot be grasped without first comprehending the interaction between economic development and political authority in the metropole.

The only ready-made alternative to the view that the link between the metropolitan economy and imperialism was forged by the industrial revolution lies in Schumpeter's and Veblen's theories that imperialism was the product of pre-capitalist, especially aristocratic, forces which mobilized the wealth produced by capitalist industry for militarist and imperialist ends.[7] This interpretation is interesting because it avoids the assumption that imperialism is a necessary function of industrial capitalism. But it is correspondingly weak in accounting for imperialist drives in societies which were not directed by pre-capitalist aristocracies. Moreover, both Schumpeter and Veblen were concerned mainly to explain German expansion after 1870, an example which cannot readily be tailored to fit the British case.[8] The view of British history advanced by Anderson and Nairn certainly emphasizes the adaptability of the aristocracy in forestalling a bourgeois revolution;[9] and Wiener's contribution also concentrates on the way in which a patrician order, suspicious of capitalist values, tamed an emerging industrial middle class.[10] However, these arguments, like Schumpeter's, are predicated on the notion that capitalism has an ideal growth path which is determined by its own laws of development. It follows from this assumption that the main purpose of historical enquiry is to account for deviations from the perceived norm, such as the atavistic exploits of aristocratic imperialists and the failure of a permanently aspiring middle class to rise to power. But, as we shall now try to show, modern British history is not simply the story of a feudal order adapting to an industrial bourgeois one, or of the industrial bourgeoisie's adjustment to traditionalism; nor is there any compelling reason why it should be.

The argument we wish to advance begins with the observation that modern British history is bound up with the evolution of several separate but interacting forms of capitalist enterprise — agricultural, commercial, and financial, as well as industrial. This initial statement is not designed to point towards a naive multicausal interpretation which includes everything and therefore explains nothing; nor is it intended to promote a new, albeit broadly based, form of economic determinism. It is indeed hard to avoid that most difficult of terms, capitalism, which — like the Loch Ness monster — is frequently hunted yet is hard to describe and impossible to capture. But if we adopt a wide and non-ideological usage, the term can be given specific historical content without presuming either that it is synonymous with the process of industrialization or that it is driven by an inner logic which treats history as a branch of applied metaphysics.[11]

This approach involves discarding the assumption that non-industrial forms of capitalist wealth were either mere predecessors of the industrial revolution and were then subsumed by it, or were subservient by-products of one of its subsequent developmental stages. It runs against both an older, heroic, conception of the industrial revolution and a newer, growth-oriented, historiography which tends to equate development with industrialization. Our aim is not to deny what is irrefutable, namely that Britain industrialized, but rather to suggest that non-industrial, though still capitalist, activities were much more important immediately before, during, and after the industrial revolution than standard interpretations of economic and imperial history allow. The problem is not how to rewrite the history of industrial-ization so that it covers still larger stretches of imperial history, but how to fit the industrial revolution into other vigorous types of capitalist enterprise which merit greater emphasis than they have received hitherto. In this context it is not just landed wealth which must be taken into account. The service sector occupied a far larger and more independent place in the economy than has customarily been acknowledged, and specific forms of "service capitalism" had attributes of status and leisure which allowed privileged access to political authority as well as to economic power.[12]

Initially, however, the most important form of capitalist wealth in Britain was the rentier capitalism which arose from the ownership of land by a numerically small elite. By the close of the seventeenth century the landed magnates had ceased to be a feudal aristocracy and were ready to embrace a market philosophy. Nonetheless, they were still the heirs of a feudal tradition; and the landed capitalism which evolved in Britain after the Stuarts was heavily influenced by pre-capitalist notions of order, authority and status. Hence the emphasis which continued to be placed on land as an inalienable asset to be passed on intact, as far as possible, through the generations; the assumed primacy of relations, even economic ones, based upon personal loyalties and family connexions; the "studied opposition to the matter-of-fact attitude and business routine";[13] the contempt for the everyday world of wealth creation and of the profit motive as the chief goal of activity; and the stress laid on the link between heredity and leadership. Since the prestige of birth, together with independent means, allowed an unusual degree of freedom of action, the landed élite had an authority "beyond any precise professional or functional limits". The "cult of the amateur", so familiar until recent times in every sphere of life from sport to politics had its origins in this "distinctive — because innate, hereditary and hence general — character of aristocratic power".[14]

The peculiar character of the modern British aristocracy was initially shaped by merging its pre-capitalist heritage with incomes derived from commercial agriculture. The landed class controlled the traditional means of authority and was also the most successful element within emergent capitalism. What we call "gentlemanly capitalism" was, therefore, a formidable mix of the venerable and the new: it became the touchstone by which all other economic activities were judged. The more an occupation or a source of income allowed for a life-style which was similar to that of the landed classes, the higher the prestige it carried and the greater the power it conferred. Just as landed capitalism in Britain in the eighteenth century evolved slowly out of pre-capitalist hierarchies and status structures and was modified by them, so too the newer forms of economic activity in services and industry adapted themselves to the ideals of gentlemanly conduct.[15]

The gentlemanly capitalist had a clear understanding of the market economy and knew how to benefit from it; at the same time, he kept his distance from the everyday and demeaning world of work. In an order dominated by gentlemanly norms, production was held in low repute. Working for money, as opposed to making it, was associated with dependence and cultural inferiority. Writing well after modern industry had become an accepted feature of life in Europe and America, Veblen observed that:

> there are few of the better class who are not possessed of an instinctive repugnance for the vulgar forms of labour . . . and vulgarly productive occupations are unhesitatingly condemned and avoided . . . . From the

days of the Greek philosophers to the present, a degree of leisure and
of exemption from contact with such industrial processes as serve the
immediate everyday purposes of human life has ever been recognized by
thoughtful men as a pre-requisite to a worthy or beautiful, or even a
blameless, human life.[16]

Industrialists who traced their descent from yeomen or gentry referred to
themselves in the nineteenth century as "gentleman manufacturers", but the claim,
however authentic, was also contradictory because full-time involvement in industry
was incompatible with the gentlemanly ideal. The contradiction is seen most clearly
in the political sphere. Politically speaking, the trouble with capitalist manufacturing
was that it left no time for leadership and for the social activities which were essential
to success in public life. Long before the industrial revolution, Harrington commented
in *Oceana* that "mechanics" had neither the leisure nor the qualities needed for
politics;[17] some time after the event Oscar Wilde observed that socialism would
never be achieved in Britain because "it takes too many evenings".[18]

The division between gentlemanly and ungentlemanly occupations and forms
of wealth is similar to Weber's distinction between "propertied" wealth on the one
hand and "acquisitive" or "entrepreneurial" wealth on the other.[19] The first implies
a rentier interest, not just in land but in other forms of property, while the second
involves active participation in the market and in the creation of goods and services.
Weber recognized the generally higher status accorded to propertied wealth and
the greater power and authority which it commanded.[20] In the present context,
however, Weber's categories need modifying to allow for the fact that some forms
of "entrepreneurial" wealth were closer to the gentlemanly ideal than others. A line
has to be drawn not just between rentiers and entrepreneurs but also, among the
latter, between those whose relationship with the productive process was direct and
those whose involvement was only indirect. Manufacturing was less eligible than
the service sector: even at the highest levels, captains of industry could not command
as much prestige as bankers in the City.[21]

Capitalists could remain (or become) gentlemen if they derived incomes from
agricultural or urban property or if they were rentiers drawing on other types of
investment, whether public or private. Some non-industrial occupations, because
of their remoteness from the world of everyday work and their ability to generate
high incomes, also came nearer to the gentlemanly ideal than did the "vile and
mechanical"[22] world of manufacturing. The higher reaches of the law, the upper
echelons of the Church, and the officer class of the armed services all offered
opportunities for attaining a gentlemanly life-style. Even the gentleman's gentleman,
further down the hierarchy, gained prestige by reflecting the lustre of those he served.
And it is worth stressing at this point that, throughout the period under review,
British administrators and civil servants were drawn largely from the ranks of those
whose economic ties were with landed, rentier or service-sector wealth, rather than
with industry. Their social origin and education gave them an extraordinarily high
degree of coherence which makes it possible to speak even today of "family life in
the Treasury or village life in Whitehall", where "mutual trust is a pervasive bond"
and where business takes place "in the market place exchange of an agreed culture"[23]
— albeit a culture remote from the world of industrial capitalism and often hostile
to it.

High status could also be achieved by those who were "something in the City" or who, as large merchants, managed to distance themselves from the "shopocracy" of the nation. In view of the prominent position occupied by the financial and commercial activities of the City of London in the ensuing argument, it is important for us to stress that, although the City was a centre of "entrepreneurial" activity in Weber's sense, it rapidly became, in its higher reaches, a branch of gentlemanly capitalism and, as such, exercised a disproportionate influence on British economic life and economic policymaking. Bankers and financiers often rose to prominence in societies dominated by aristocrats because the aristocracy's propensity for "generosity" promoted indebtedness.[24] And, as will become clear in the following section, the fate of the City was entwined with that of the aristocracy in Britain after 1688 with all the expected consequences in terms of wealth, prestige and incorporation into the body politic.[25] The great businesses of the City — private and merchant banking, insurance, broking and acceptance, the activities of the Stock Exchange — generated fortunes which were much greater than those acquired in industry before the twentieth century. These businesses were conducted upon principles which were much closer to the ideals of gentlemanly capitalism fostered by the landed class and their supporters than to the mores of manufacturing, even before mechanization.

The City began as, and remained, an extended network of personal contacts based on mutual trust and concepts of honour which were closer to the culture of the country house circuit or the London club than they were to the more impersonal world inhabited by industrialists.[26] Moreover, the confidence inspired by reputable bankers or financial intermediaries, such as large merchants, gave them a virtual monopoly of the business of their clients. As Bagehot put it: "an old established bank has a 'prestige', which amounts to a 'privileged opportunity'; though no exclusive right is given by law, a peculiar power is given it by opinion". And he emphasized the fact that "the 'credit' of a person — that is the reliance which may be placed on his pecuniary fidelity — is a different thing from his property".[27] Consequently, bankers were able to handle vast amounts of other people's money, while putting relatively small amounts of their own capital into their businesses, with the result that the most successful could earn profits which were immense by the standards of industrial capitalism even in the days of its greatest success after 1815.[28] City activities not only generated large incomes for the established and the lucky, but were also, generally speaking, simple businesses to operate in comparison with industrial organizations.[29] The City élites therefore enjoyed greater freedom from daily cares, higher prestige and better openings for political careers, public activities and the exercise of power than leaders of industry;[30] and, to a lesser degree, the same was true of their financial and commercial imitators in the great outports of the kingdom such as Liverpool.

This combination of high profitability, small-firm structure and the gentlemanly nature of the business also meant that City firms provided the most successful and long-running examples of "family capitalism" well into the twentieth century. Moreover, the club-like atmosphere within which City business was transacted ensured that decisions were likely to be taken "on the basis of particularist and moralistic" assumptions to a greater degree than was the case in industry.[31] Gentlemanly capitalism did not hold sway to the same extent in the joint stock banks which developed in the nineteenth century.[32] Nevertheless, directors of joint stock banks enjoyed high prestige; and the boards of these banks were often dominated by City gentlemen.[33]

Bankers, financiers and others in the commercial world also shared with the landed interest and the more prestigious members of the service sector a relative immunity from the stresses of class conflict in the nineteenth and twentieth centuries. Industrialists were the shock troops of capitalism, and the hostility which they generated from the late eighteenth century onward undermined some of the authority which wealth would otherwise have given them. However antagonistic they might have been to the landed magnates and their associates, the pressures of class conflict often forced industrialists to come to terms with gentlemanly capitalism to create a broad front of propertied interests. Given their indirect relationship with the productive process, and their paternalist relations with their own more fragmented and less class-conscious workforce, gentlemanly capitalists could present themselves more easily as "natural" leaders, while also benefiting from developments in which industrial capitalism was the most visible agent of change.[34] Indeed, British industrialists were constantly trapped between a gentlemanly culture, which flourished upon capitalist wealth but derided the technology upon which that wealth depended, and radical trades unionism and other working men's associations, which exalted production but attacked the profit motive.

The gentleman capitalist was not a paradox: on the contrary, his ethics assisted his enterprise, which was concerned with managing men rather than machines. Tom Paine's jibe that the nobility were men of no ability is not lacking in illustrious examples;[35] but the feudal remnants, and the tendency for aristocrats and gentlemen to behave in an "economically irrational" manner,[36] could be useful assets in occupations which placed a premium on organizing men and information rather than on processing raw materials. High finance, like high farming, called for leadership from "opinion-makers" and trust from associates and dependants. A gentleman possessed the qualities needed to inspire confidence; and because his word was his bond transactions were both informal and efficient. Shared values, nurtured by a common education and religion, provided a blueprint for social and business behaviour. The country house led to the counting house; the public school fed the service sector; the London club supported the City. Gentlemanly enterprise was strongly personal, and was sustained by a social network which, in turn, was held together by the leisure needed to cultivate it. The predominance of in-group marriage, like the elaboration of techniques of heirship to entail property, was not a gesture to traditionalism, but a strategy to reinforce group solidarity, to create economic efficiency and political stability, and to take out an option on the future by ensuring dynastic continuity. Social proximity was aided by geographical concentration; both came together in London, the focal point of the gentleman and his activities. In this world conspicuous consumption was not merely wasteful; it was a public manifestation of substance, a refined advertisement which used hospitality to sustain goodwill, to generate new connexions and to exclude those of low income or low repute.[37]

In describing how ethics fit actions, our aim has been to establish the characteristics of gentlemanly capitalism, not to pass judgement on it. We have deliberately avoided adopting the radical distinction between productive and unproductive labour, for instance, not only because it is hedged with difficulties of definition but also because it does not recognize the capitalist qualities of the activities we have identified or any interaction between gentlemanly enterprise and industry.[38] What can be said, however, is that the bias of incomes and status favoured gentlemanly occupations to a much greater extent than standard accounts of British economic history allow, and that the attributes of the leisured amateur, though highly effective in his own sphere of enterprise, were not well suited to the needs of "scientific rationalism".[39]

Cobdenite entrepreneurial ideologies which stressed the need for a social revolution to place the industrial bourgeoisie at the centre of the social and political stage faced formidable barriers, even at the high point of the industrial revolution.[40] The impressive success of gentlemanly capitalism in its landed form until 1850 and the growing wealth and power of service capitalism after that date meant that manufacturers who sought prestige and authority often had to adapt to gentlemanly ideals. And players could become gentlemen only by abandoning the attitudes or even the occupations which had brought them their original success.[41] The industrial revolution emerged out of an already highly successful capitalist system, and it took place without any fundamental transformation of property ownership. The benefits of the dynamic growth of manufacturing, whether via the division of labour or through the advent of machinery, were bound to lead, in these circumstances, to a large proportion of the gains accruing to non-industrial forms of property.[42]

One result of this development was that, in a society which was only slowly becoming democratic even in the early twentieth century,[43] and where power was concentrated in the hands of wealthy élites, manufacturers neither owned enough "top wealth" nor made it in a sufficiently acceptable way to be able to impose their will on the political system. In the nineteenth century the industrial bourgeoisie in Britain was forced to come to terms with gentlemanly capitalism: it modified rather than superseded it, and in turn felt the weight of its compelling influence. Marx's assumption that industrial capitalism was the *dominant* force after 1850 and that the "moneyed interests" were subservient to it[44] is overdrawn, as we shall see.

Rather than distinguishing between mercantile and industrial phases of overseas expansion or contrasting formal and informal techniques of control, we suggest that British imperialism is best understood by relating it to two broad phases in the development of gentlemanly capitalism. Between 1688 and 1850 the dominant element was the landed interest: after 1850 it was succeeded by the financial and commercial magnates of the City and the wealthiest and most influential elements arising from the growth of services in the south-east of England. As we shall try to demonstrate, these two phases of gentlemanly capitalism and the transition between them left an enduring mark on Britain's presence abroad. [. . .]

The main purpose of this article has been to establish a connexion between gentlemanly capitalism based on landed wealth and overseas expansion, particularly in its imperialist forms, between 1688 and 1850. After 1850, free trade destroyed the old colonial system and, in combination with the rise of new wealth, ensured the gradual demise of the landed aristocracy, thus bringing one phase in the history of gentlemanly capitalism to an end. But the new economic and political structures which arose — and the imperialism which flowed from them — were not dominated by industrial capitalism. From the middle of the nineteenth century the major area of growth was the service sector, and the most rapidly developing region was the south-east. The City was at the heart of both. London stood at the centre of a well-developed network of international services, and these were destined to expand rapidly as world trade increased in the second half of the nineteenth century. Even before 1850, financial flows from the City were a major determinant of the rhythm of development in the colonies.[45] Beyond formal empire, London's influence as the main source of long-term international finance had begun to spread to Europe and north America after 1815 and was poised to increase dramatically after 1850, as the age of the steamship and railway began.[46] The service sector and the City supported the introduction of free trade and proved, during the next seventy years, to be its chief beneficiaries. They also carried into free-trade Britain many of the cultural values acquired in the course of their long apprenticeship to the landed aristocracy. After 1850, as one form of gentlemanly capitalism began to fail, another arose to take its place.

Further reading

The Cain and Hopkins thesis was fully explored in their book, *British Imperialism* (2 vols, London: Longman, 1993). This was reissued in a single volume, revised form as *British Imperialism, 1688–2000* (London: Longman, 2001), which contained a new Foreword in which Cain and Hopkins considered the responses to the first edition of their book. Such was the interest in the thesis that it inspired two books of responses: see Raymond E. Dumett (ed.), *Gentlemanly Capitalism and British Imperialism: The New Debate on Empire* (London: Longman, 1999); and Shigeru Akita (ed.), *Gentlemanly Capitalism, Imperialism and Global History* (Basingstoke: Macmillan, 2002). Both contain replies by Cain and Hopkins. A useful review of Cain and Hopkins can be found in: David Cannadine, 'The Empire Strikes Back', *Past and Present*, no. 147 (1995), 180–94. This was reprinted in a revised form in the chapter entitled 'Empire' in David Cannadine's *History in Our Time* (New Haven, CT: Yale University Press, 1998), 143–54. Among other works on 'Gentlemanly Capitalism', see: W.D. Rubinstein, *Elites and the Wealthy in Modern British History* (Brighton: Harvester, 1987); Martin Daunton, '"Gentlemanly Capitalism" and British Industry, 1820–1914', *Past and Present*, no. 122 (1989), 115–58.

Notes

1   P.J. Cain and A.G. Hopkins, 'The Political Economy of British Expansion Overseas, 1750–1914', *Economic History Review*, 2nd ser. XXXIII (1980), pp. 463–90.

2   J. Gallagher and R. Robinson, 'The Imperialism of Free Trade, 1815–1914', *Econ. Hist. Rev.* 2nd ser. VI (1953), p. 5. Gallagher and Robinson were of course also concerned to show that 'phases of imperialism' did not 'correspond directly to phases in the economic growth of the metropolitan economy'. Ibid. p. 6.

3   V.T. Harlow, *The Founding of the Second British Empire, 1763–1793*, I, *Discovery and Revolution* (1952), pp. 10–1, 64, 166, 593; I. Wallerstein, *The Modern World System*, II. *Mercantilism and the Consolidation of the European World Economy, 1600–1750* (New York, 1980), p. 258.

4   1870 is the turning point preferred by B. Porter, following Robinson and Gallagher's lead: *The Lion's Share: A Short History of British Imperialism, 1850–1970* (1975), p. XI. A case for both dates is made by Ronald Hyam, *Britain's Imperial Century* (1976), p. 377.

5   It will no doubt be apparent that this is a compressed statement of a much larger work. In selecting from many possible references we have sought to acknowledge particular debts, to document the more contentious claims, and to refer to very recent publications.

6   L.H. Jenks, *The Migration of British Capital to 1875* (1927, reprinted 1963), p. 197.

7   J.A. Schumpeter, *Imperialism and the Social Classes* (New York, 1951); T. Veblen, *Imperial Germany and the Industrial Revolution* (New York, 1915).

8   For an interesting attempt to apply a Schumpeterian analysis to pre-First World War Europe as a whole see A. Mayer, *The Persistence of the Old Régime* (1981).

9   P. Anderson, 'Origins of the Present Crisis', *New Left Review* 23 (1964), pp. 26–53; T. Nairn, *The Break-up of Britain* (2nd ed. 1981); also E.P. Thompson, 'The Peculiarities of the English', in ibid., *The Poverty of Theory and Other Essays* (1978), pp. 35–91.

10 M. Wiener, *English Culture and the Decline of the Industrial Spirit, 1850–1980* (Cambridge, 1981). For a summary of the main issues in this debate see P. Warwick, 'Did Britain Change? An Inquiry into the Causes of National Decline', *Journal of Contemporary History*, 20 (1985), pp. 99–533.

11 We refer to the pursuit of private profit by rational means which raise productivity and incomes through increased specialization, improved technology, and the postponement of present consumption for the sake of future returns.

12 We hope to substantiate this claim in the present article, but we also wish to emphasize the need for further historical research on this complex and neglected subject. For an interesting discussion of the conceptual issues see J. Bhagwati, 'Splintering and Disembodiment of Services and Developing Nations', in Bhagwati, *Essays in Development Economics*, I (Oxford, 1985), pp. 92–103.

13 R. Bendix, *Max Weber* (1966 ed.), p. 366.

14 The quotations are taken from J. Powis, *Aristocracy* (1984), pp. 88–9. In thinking about the relations between land, economy and power we have also benefited from reading: P. Mason, *The English Gentleman: The Rise and Fall of an Ideal* (1982) and M. Girouard, *The Return of Camelot: Chivalry and the English Gentleman* (Yale, 1981). Apart from Powis — and, unfortunately, not cited by him — by far the best introductions to this subject can be found in Schumpeter, 'The Rise and Fall of Whole Classes', in his *Imperialism and the Social Classes*, and in J. Scott, *The Upper Classes: Property and Privilege in Britain* (1982).

15 In *Max Weber* (1982), p. 96, F. Parkin argues persuasively that a capitalist system is compatible with a variety of political and social frameworks and that, rather than reshaping them, as Marx implied, capitalism actually adapts itself to these pre-existent frameworks: 'it is less active than acted upon by existing forms of social stratification'.

16 T. Veblen, *The Theory of the Leisure Class: An Economic Study of Institutions* (1924 ed.), pp. 37–8.

17 J. Harrington, *The Model of the Commonwealth of Oceana* (1656), in J.G.A. Pocock, ed. *The Political Works of James Harrington* (Cambridge, 1977), pp. 257–62.

18 Different implications of this observation are discussed by A.O. Hirschman, *Shifting Involvements: Private Interest and Public Action* (Princeton, NJ, 1982), and A. Ryan, *Property and Political Theory* (Oxford, 1984), ch. 7.

19 M. Weber, *Economy and Society: An Outline of Interpretive Sociology*, ed. G. Roth and C. Wittich (1978), ch. IV: 'Status Groups and Classes'. The word "acquisitive" is used instead of "entrepreneurial" or "commercial" in A.M. Henderson and T. Parson's translation of M. Weber, *The Theory of Social and Economic Organization* (New York, 1947), pp. 424–9. Works we have found useful in helping us to understand both Weber's sociology and how to use it for our purposes include: Parkin, *Max Weber*;

Bendix, *Max Weber*; S.M. Lipset, 'Social Stratification and Social Class', *International Encyclopaedia of the Social Sciences*, 15 (1968), pp. 296–316; and the same author's 'Values, Patterns, Class and the Democratic Polity: The United States and Great Britain', in R. Bendix and S.M. Lipset, eds *Class, Status and Power: Social Stratification in Comparative Perspective* (2nd ed. 1967), pp. 161–71; T. Parsons, 'The Professions and Social Structure', in Parsons, *Essays in Sociological Theory: Pure and Applied* (Glencoe, Ill., 1949), pp. 185–99; J. Rex, 'Capitalism, Elites and the Ruling Class', in P. Stanworth and A. Giddens, eds *Elites and Power in British Society* (Cambridge, 1974), pp. 212–19.

20   Weber, *Economy and Society*, p. 307.

21   This idea is, to some extent, the result of reading D. Lockwood, *The Black Coated Worker: A Study in Class Consciousness* (1958), esp. pp. 202 ff.; and W.G. Runciman, *Social Science and Political Theory* (Cambridge, 1965), pp. 137–8. There are also some suggestive comments in G. Ingham, *Capitalism Divided? The City and Industry in British Social Development* (1984), pp. 240–3, which we read after our own ideas had been formulated.

22   Powis, *Aristocracy*, p. 10.

23   H. Heclo and A. Wildavsky, *The Private Government of Public Money* (2nd edn. 1981), pp. 2–3.

24   Powis, *Aristocracy*, esp. pp. 511–13.

25   P.J. Cain and A.G. Hopkins, 'Gentlemanly Capitalism and British Overseas Expansion', *Economic History Review* 39/4 (1986), 511–3.

26   For an engaging introduction to City life from the vantage point of the twentieth century see R. Palin, *Rothschild Relish* (1971). See also S. Chapman, *The Rise of Merchant Banking* (1984), p. 169.

27   W. Bagehot, 'Lombard Street', in N. St. John-Stevas, ed. *Collected Works*, (1978), IX, pp. 171, 191.

28   Ibid. pp. 171–2.

29   Ibid. pp. 171–2, 177.

30   Note the comment of Sir Clinton Dawkins in 1900 after moving from the Colonial Civil Service into the City: "I am happy enough in the City but there is *not* enough to do there, and I feel the want of handling big questions again". Quoted in Chapman, *Merchant Banking*, p. 169.

31   M. Lisle-Williams, 'Beyond the Market: The Survival of Family Capitalism in the English Merchant Banks', *British Journal of Sociology*, XXXV (1984), p. 241.

32   Their vast size, and the technical and rather impersonal nature of the business in the nineteenth century, meant that the managers who were "tied to the business" and "devoted to it" were put on a par, socially speaking, with the managers of industrial concerns. See Bagehot, *Lombard Street*, p. 188. See also M. de Cecco, 'The Last of the Romans', in R. Skidelsky, ed. *The End of the Keynesian Era* (1977), p, 20.

33   On this relationship in the late nineteenth and early twentieth centuries see Y. Cassis, *Les banquiers de la City à l'époque édouardienne, 1890–1914* (Geneva, 1984). For a different approach to the question of City power and influence see G. Ingham, 'Divisions within the Dominant Class and British "Exceptionalism"' in A. Giddens and G. Mackenzie, eds *Social Class and the Division of Labour: Essays in Honour of Ilya Neustadt* (Cambridge, 1982), pp. 209–27.

34   Weber, *Economy and Society*, pp. 931–2.

35   T. Paine, *Rights of Man*, in *The Political and Miscellaneous Works of Thomas Paine* (1819), I, p. 75.

36   Weber, *Economy and Society*, p. 307.

37   See the very interesting recent attempt to employ Veblen's concept of conspicuous consumption in an historical context by R.S. Mason, *Conspicuous Consumption: A Study of Exceptional Consumer Behaviour* (1981). Conspicuous consumption and intermarriage

are examples of what Weber called "social closure", a phenomenon recently examined in F. Parkin, *Marxism and Class Theory: A Bourgeois Critique* (1979).

38   For a brief look at the radical argument in the context of Hobson's theory of finance capitalism, see P.J. Cain, 'Hobson, Wilshire and the Capitalist Theory of Capitalist Imperialism', *History of Political Economy*, 17 (1985), pp. 455–60.

39   This theme is discussed in D.C. North, *Structure and Change in Economic History* (Toronto, 1981), chs. 12–13.

40   See P.J. Cain, 'Capitalism, War and Internationalism in the Thought of Richard Cobden', *British Journal of International Studies*, v (5979), pp. 229–48.

41   D.C. Coleman, 'Gentlemen and Players', *Econ. Hist. Rev.* 2nd ser. (1973), pp. 92–116.

42   W.D. Rubinstein, 'Entrepreneurial Effort and Entrepreneurial Success: Peak Wealth Holding in Three Societies, 1850–1930', *Business History*, XXV (1983), p. 57.

43   It is worth remembering that in 1914 Hungary was the only other European country which shared with the United Kingdom the dubious distinction of not having manhood suffrage. The vote "was still something dependent on a successful claim to possession" and "a privilege purchased through property". See H.C.G. Matthew, R.I. McKibbin and J.A. Kay, 'The Franchise Factor in the Rise of the Labour Party', *English Historical Review*, XCI (1976), pp. 723–6.

44   'The complete rule of industrial capital was not acknowledged by English merchants' capital and moneyed interests until after the abolition of the duties on corn, etc.', K. Marx, *Capital*, III (1909 ed.), p. 385 n. 47. Ch. 38 and p. 385 ff. are also of great interest in this context.

45   See especially here H.J. Habakkuk, 'Free Trade and Commercial Expansion, 1853–70', *Cambridge History of the British Empire, II* (1940), pp. 798–9. For examples of networks of trade and factor movement connecting the City with colonies, see F.J.A. Broeze, 'Private Enterprise and the Peopling of Australia, 1831–50', *Econ. Hist. Rev.* 2nd ser. XXXV (1982), pp. 235–51; and W.E. Cheong, *Mandarins and Merchants. Jardine Matheson and Co., a China Agency of the Early Nineteenth Century* (Malmo and London, 1978), chs. 6 and 7.

46   For some insights into the growth of British overseas credit operations and investments see D.C.M. Platt, *Foreign Finance in Continental Europe and the U.S.A., 1815–70: Quantities, Origins, Functions and Distributions* (1984). Platt has argued here and in 'British Portfolio Investment Before 1870: Some Doubts', *Econ. Hist. Rev.* 2nd ser. XXXIII (1980), pp. 1–16, that the amount of British investment has been over-estimated. But see the review of 'Foreign Finance' by M. Edelstein in *Econ. Hist. Rev.* 2nd ser. XXXVIII (1985), pp. 485–6.

PART 3

Consumerism and material culture

ECONOMIC HISTORY USED TO FOCUS mainly on the way goods and services were produced. For the Victorian period, the role of consuming had generally been ignored as historians preferred to concentrate on the way new markets overseas were conquered, how technical advances spurred the Industrial Revolution, and how the economy had been export-driven. The period since 1980 has seen an increased interest in how objects were acquired and used. Eighteenth-century historians began the trend by looking at how luxury items helped to drive certain parts of the British economy; for example the need for fine china as a marker of class status. Increasingly, consumption and material culture have become vital fields for exploring Victorian Britain, which has been re-conceived as an embryonic consumer society. The most influential statement about consumption has been the American Thorstein Veblen's *The Theory of the Leisure Class* (1908), which holds that modern societies are glued together by emulation. People lower down the social order attempt or aspire to emulate the lifestyles and tastes of those higher up. This perspective has shaped much, though not all, of the literature and has proved attractive to social historians.

Cultural, gender, fashion and design history have begun to explore how and why people bought things. A defining work in the recent literature came (not for the first time) from Asa Briggs with his *Victorian Things* (1988), which examined the Victorian fascination with objects, while Thomas Richards' *The Commodity Culture of Victorian England: Advertising and Spectacle, 1851–1914* (1990) showed how things were sold. The relationship to goods became a way into the Victorian home and understanding household management. Shopping was not a Victorian invention but it became a vital part of the metropolitan experience especially as standards of living and wages rose in the second half of the century. There was an incredible surge in items to buy in these years and, although the poorest in society seldom had much disposable income, the respectable working class, the middle class and the elite loved to shop. Goods (in the form of clothes, food, furniture, domestic fittings and much else) offered a form of status as well as of satisfaction. The retail revolution created the basis of the modern consumer society. The extracts here deal with two different types of consumer.

Erika Rappaport

WOMEN AND THE DEPARTMENT STORE

Shopping for Pleasure: Women in the Making of London's West End (Princeton, NJ: Princeton University Press, 2000), 18–19, 29–33, 36–7, 39–40.

In this extract from *Shopping for Pleasure* (2000), **Erika Rappaport**'s study of women's shopping habits and their impact on consumer culture, the British economy and female autonomy, the focus is on the birth of the department store and its multiple meanings. William Whiteley's 'Universal Provider' opened in 1863 as a draper's shop, but quickly expanded to include all types of goods, and eventually foodstuffs. It was located in the new London suburb of Westgrove Terrace, or Bayswater, in Paddington which was typical of recently-established shopping districts emerging in the latest suburban developments around the edges of central London. These areas were created for a new middle class although they seldom attained the type of social homogeneity claimed by estate agents. These neighbourhoods were often viewed as primarily female spaces during the daytime, after men had departed for work on the increasingly available railways, omnibuses and underground trains. Whiteley was one of the most successful entrepreneurs to rise to prominence in this period and his establishment served as a model for other merchants. Prior to the arrival of Gordon Selfridge at the turn of the century, Whiteley's store defined the British department store.

This extract looks specifically at the debates aroused when Whiteley and other retailers applied for licences to serve alcohol on the premises. The applicants deployed a language of gentility and the creation of protected female spaces, while opponents (usually local publicans, but sometimes other commentators) raised fears of secret assignations and women's activities extending well beyond the private sphere. Rappaport demonstrates that shoppers venturing beyond their own neighbourhoods was a recent occurrence and illuminates how women's emergence into the public sphere through shopping was perceived as a modern phenomenon. In this she enters into debates about the role of women in the public sphere that reach beyond the political and into the economic life of the modern city. The debates should also be seen in the context of elevated state regulation of the drink trade in the 1870s and publicans' efforts to maintain their business, which they perceived to be under threat from the Liberals led by Gladstone. Furthermore, Rappaport illustrates the breadth of this debate as other respectable businesses, such as hotels located near the newly established rail termini like Paddington, sought to create a more respectable environment for provincial shoppers eager to come to London, but wary of the city itself. Whiteley's arguments were echoed, Rappaport shows, by a wide range of businessmen and women seeking to establish innovative modes of trade. By the end of the century, they had been accepted and women's right to shop both near and far from home had been confirmed.

Erika Rappaport is Associate Professor of History at the University of California, Santa Barbara. She has been working on several projects exploring the connections between imperialism and consumerism in nineteenth- and twentieth-century Britain. These include a study of urban redevelopment in London, imperial family/consumer cultures, and a book on tea, which charts the globalisation of British imperial culture, provisionally entitled 'Tea Parties: Britishness, Global Cultures and Imperial Legacies'.

———————

BETWEEN THE 1860S AND 1880S, the Universal Provider [*William Whiteley*] and the shopping district in and around Westbourne Grove symbolized the mass culture and economy that were becoming visible throughout the West End of London. During those years, transformations in retailing, catering, entertainment, publishing, and transportation produced public spaces that were identified with a new type of mass public. Large hotels and theaters, restaurants and department stores grew by selling diverse commodities and services to a clientele that could not be easily categorized. This mass market was not a synonym for either a working-class or a bourgeois public. Rather, it implied heterogeneity.

As Mary Poovey has explained, by the 1860s new technologies of representation along with material innovations "brought groups that had rarely mixed into physical proximity with each other and represented them as belonging to the same, increasingly undifferentiated whole."[1] Although society was also perceived as segregated by class, in certain locations it appeared as a mass aggregate. While Poovey emphasized how novel methods of quantification and social investigation represented this aggregate, others have observed that public transportation also constituted society in this way. In his work on public amenities in New York City, William Taylor pointed out that with the expansion of mass transit "the public" came to be perceived as a "mobile and embodied mass."[2] Taylor observed that in America the railway helped transform the political public into an embodied mass. This public was conceptualized as a mass market made up of, as Wolfgang Schivelbusch perceived it, "parcels" not unlike other goods circulating in the economy.[3]

There were in fact several competing notions of "the public" and "the masses" in mid- and late-Victorian London.[4] These constructs were both gendered and varied in meaning as particular groups attempted to legitimize their understanding of politics, urban space, and economic activities. At times the public was conceived as a male and political entity, but it equally could become a feminine body of consumers. While few understood how it would act, where it belonged, and what it wanted, virtually all agreed that the consuming public was primarily, if not wholly, a feminine entity. Between the 1860s and 1914, the shopping public also looked like a mobile crowd, a group of traveling suburban and provincial women who were defined by their presence outside of the domestic sphere. The mass press, large shops, and crowded shopping streets of the Victorian West End made this public manifest. Yet such entities could not have existed independent of the idea of this feminine public. The shopping public and London's commercial spaces were quite simply mutually constitutive. Throughout this book we will see many individuals and groups attempting to understand, perceive, and define the shopping public. This study traces how the emergence of this public was born at the intersection of social, economic, and cultural contests over new forms of retailing, communication, and urban space.

The shopping public was an integral part of urban and economic change in the late-nineteenth century, yet its feminine and amorphous nature challenged bourgeois gender ideology, which had long characterized public spaces and the more abstract public sphere as masculine. Not surprisingly, the implications of a female consuming crowd were fiercely contested. Shopkeepers, shoppers, social reformers, government officials, feminists, and journalists debated several related questions. To what extent did the presence of this crowd in London's streets spell social collapse or improvement? What type of pleasure did the city legitimately offer this public? What was the relationship between shopping, conceived as the public face of consumption, and what was perceived as the private sphere of the family and the self? Though the participants in and the terms of this discussion would shift over the course of the next fifty years, these questions would never entirely disappear. The attempt to find answers produced new social identities based upon notions of pleasure and consumption. Consumer practices such as shopping thus fashioned identities by disrupting and reconstituting social categories and their perceived relationship to public and private spaces.[5] [. . .]

"When Ladies Go 'Shopping'"

Early department stores such as Whiteley's emerged within a culture that was profoundly equivocal about consumption and the urban crowd. Such ambivalence shaped the history of the department store because opponents charged Whiteley with having committed a variety of social and moral crimes, including turning ordinary suburban ladies into jezebels. While historians have noted how similar criticisms were leveled at French and American department stores during these years, these charges did not simply grow from the public nature of female shopping crowds or from long-standing associations between markets and excess. Rather, many enemies of the department store wanted to find a way to regulate market growth and protect their own financial and social status without denouncing the much-cherished ideals of free trade. One convenient way to do this was to suggest that the number of department stores had to be limited not because they fostered unfair competition but because they encouraged immoral female behaviors.

By the early 1870s, Whiteley's neighbors began to perceive that he was embarking on a new type of retailing in which diverse goods were being vended to a heterogenous urban crowd. They regarded this style of doing business as essentially immoral, threatening their trade and their values. Most troubling of all, they suggested, was that Whiteley's shop lured women into the city to engage in unhealthy pleasures.

[. . .] Although not consistently organized, retailers in Whiteley's shadow vented their frustration in the streets, in the press, and on local government committees. [. . .] Instead of deploring the economic impact of large-scale trading on the retail community, they typically condemned the negative social and cultural consequences for consumers, especially female shoppers. They particularly "exposed" the almost pathological behaviors that such enterprises supposedly encouraged. Whiteley's enemies charged that by selling an array of commodities, services, and pleasures to a mixed shopping crowd, he had disorganized class, gender, moral, and aesthetic categories. By ignoring the cherished boundaries between public and private spheres, the Universal Provider denied the essential distinction between respectable and immoral women. Specialized shopkeepers thus deployed bourgeois gender ideology to defend their economic position against the threat of large-scale retailers.

[. . .] [*William Whitely*] legitimized his own institution by arguing that the shopper was a respectable, rational individual whose home was the public spaces of the metropolis. If his opponents portrayed shoppers as immoral and disorderly, Whiteley presented them as a sign of improvement. A debate about gender and consumption developed, then, from the social and economic struggle between retailers.

[. . .] During his first ten years, Whiteley had relentlessly acquired leases, renovated interiors, and opened up new departments. In 1872 he began selling entirely new types of commodities when he opened a house agency, a cleaning and dyeing service, and a small refreshment room.[6] The public attacks began with this latest "innovation." Opponents charged that Whiteley was selling more than just goods; he was now vending new identities. In the next decade many West End drapers would add dining facilities, reading and writing rooms, entertainments, lavatories, and a host of other amenities to their stores. Luxurious interiors and graceful exteriors may have made shopping comfortable and amusing, something apart from the everyday, but when amenities were first introduced in the early seventies, they sparked a great deal of anger and frustration. Even small lunchrooms aroused fears about the morality of consumption and the instability of urban class and gender identities.

The furor against Whiteley and the selling of conveniences first erupted in 1872 when Whiteley applied for a liquor license to serve wine and beer in his new refreshment room. At the general licensing meeting, the magistrates listened to Whiteley and his lawyer's arguments, they read an endorsing petition from several local religious and medical men, but in the end they refused Whiteley's application. [. . .]

All those involved in the debate viewed shopping as an inherently female and amusing activity. The disagreement arose over whether this pleasure was healthy and profitable or socially and economically destructive.[7] At the licensing meeting, Mr. W. Wright argued the case against Whiteley by linking economic expansion with the decline of female morality. [. . .] He posited that Mr. Whiteley must have not read the recent article in the *Saturday Review*, which warned that drinking was "on the increase amongst ladies," or he would not wish "to offer them a facility for indulging in that propensity." Assailing the character of Whiteley's customers still further, Wright implied that the provision of alcoholic beverages might transform "respectable" ladies into prostitutes and drunkards. Although he apologetically stated that he had no intention of "questioning the respectability of Mr. Whiteley or his customers," he felt that as many of the shoppers "might be ladies or females dressed to represent them . . . the place might be made a place of assignation." Therefore, Wright urged that "in the interest of morality the application would be refused." Wright argued that the sale of alcohol transformed a glorified linen draper's into a brothel filled with females "dressed to represent" ladies.[8]

Wright knew that women who drank in public were assumed to be prostitutes.[9] This assumption was underscored by a disquieting geographical correlation between the West End clothing and sexual markets.[10] The most fashionable West End shopping areas, such as Regent Street and the Burlington Arcade, were also the most well-known prostitute haunts in London. Even in Bayswater it was not at all clear what pleasures certain shops sold. For example, the owners of the innocent-sounding "Westbourne Grove Coffee and Dining Rooms," known to regulars as "The Drum and the Monkey," were convicted of running a "disorderly house" in March of 1872.[11] Brothels commonly disguised themselves as coffeehouses and temperance hotels so that when Whiteley's began to serve food and drink, residents could easily have been confused about what type of institution he was creating.[12] Whiteley's "innovation" therefore had raised concerns that this rapidly expanding, prosperous inner suburb would soon suffer from the ills as well as the benefits associated with urban life.

While opposing Whiteley, Wright raised the specter of the "Great Social Evil" because no other issue so directly touched upon the apprehension sparked by rapid urbanization, commercial growth, and women's place in this process. While the prostitute could symbolize the problems associated with urban life, she could also represent the fate of the individual-turned-commodity in a consumer society. As Walter Benjamin later wrote, "In the prostitution of the metropolis the woman herself becomes an article that is mass-produced."[13] The fallen woman could also, according to Amanda Anderson, personify the "predicaments of agency and uncertainties about the nature of selfhood, character, and society."[14] The shopper-turned-prostitute thus perfectly represented bourgeois angst that all those involved in market society were losing their agency, morality, independence, and reason.

Like other critics of market culture, Wright drew upon and furthered the perceived relationship between prostitution and women engaged in consumer activities. By collapsing the distinction between women buying and selling pleasure, Wright invoked the theme of Eliza Linton's notorious article "The Girl of the Period," published anonymously in 1868 in the *Saturday Review*. Linton had accused modern English girls, particularly those living in "Bayswater and Belgravia," of boldly imitating the ways of the prostitute. Dyeing their hair, painting their faces, and wearing the latest fashions, she warned, led to the use of "slang, bold talk, and fastness; to the love of pleasure and indifference to duty." To support these consumer desires such a young woman, Linton believed, would sell herself to a wealthy husband. Her marriage was then simply "the legal barter of herself for so much money."[15] Linton feared that young women's participation in an urban commercial culture of style and display encouraged sexual, moral, and social disorder. By entering the market as consumers, these girls ruined themselves in the public sphere and brought market relations into the sacred space of the private home.

The reactions to Whiteley's reflected specific local economic and political grievances and more general apprehension that urban commercial change had afforded women indulgent freedoms and improper powers. Critics contended that the "powerful fascination in shopping to most women" came from the "endless possibilities of indulgence which belonged to it." In the 1875 *Saturday Review* article "The Philosophy of Shopping," the author, probably Linton, wrote that in "its mystical feminine meaning, to shop is to pass so many hours in a shop on the mere chance of buying something . . . . [It] springs immediately from a taste for novel and various entertainment . . . [and] seems to be undertaken for the pure love of the occupation." This lengthy article concluded that the real pleasure associated with shopping came from the experience of being served. While shopping, "the dethroned mistress . . . trodden under foot in her own house," had the authority of "an Oriental potentate." Being patiently served by the "assiduous shopman" afforded "mothers and daughters" the opportunity to "luxuriate" in a deep and intense "sense of power."[16]

For others the problem with shopping was not that it granted women illegitimate powers, but that it represented the new, inauthentic, and vulgar suburban world that now ringed London. Although satirizing Linton's essay, the authors of the humor magazine *The Girl of the Period Miscellany* shared her belief that when "girls" participated in commercial culture, they acquired ugly, tasteless characteristics. In the sardonic essay, "Girls at the West End," Tyburnian girls were particularly lambasted for spending their days shopping and flirting in Westbourne Grove, lacking "*le style*," and possessing a certain "metropolitan provincialism."[17] This humorous essay played upon the same misgivings that surfaced with Whiteley's lunchroom. In all of these portraits of shopping, young middle-class women appear to be out of their place, out of control, and willingly engaging in a sensuous and potentially sexual public culture. Disputes over large-scale retailing, then, were also debates about acceptable feminine spaces and behaviors outside the private home and family circle.

In order to gain acceptance from the local authorities and potential customers, Whiteley challenged these pervasive images of a passionate public sphere filled with disorderly women. He rejected the immoral associations attached to public amusements and attempted to create an acceptable public femininity. Charles Mills Roche, Whiteley's solicitor and a prominent local politician, argued for the license and the concept of Universal Providing by refusing to use the moral language established by his opposition. He first addressed the retailers' economic concerns. Roche professed that far from ruining the business of local traders, Whiteley had brought new wealth to the neighborhood. As he now occupied ten separate shops, and employed 622 individuals on the premises and another thousand out-of-doors, Roche stated that "Mr. Whiteley has been the making of Westbourne Grove." He then confidently asserted that drink was neither a physical nor social pleasure, but merely "a great public convenience."[18]

When questioned, Whiteley similarly defended large-scale retailing and cast himself as a benefit to the neighborhood, a provider of necessities, not a stimulator of desires. He pleaded that nearly a quarter of the four thousand customers who visited his establishment each day were country folk who stayed in his store from "ten o-clock in the morning until five o-clock in the afternoon." These provincial visitors, Whiteley asserted, had actually asked him "for a glass of wine and a biscuit." Whiteley thereby presented himself as merely responding to consumer demand, serving a public necessity. He defined drink as a "convenience," not as a luxury or indulgence to dispel the perception of moral danger with which it was associated. "There was not the shadow of foundation," Whiteley concluded, "that if he obtained a license his establishment would become a place of assignation." He further implied that the lunchroom would moralize the Grove, since female shoppers would not be forced to enter places of ill repute to have a drink or other refreshment. The magistrates refused to buy this argument, however. They resolutely denied the application with the suggestion that Mr. Whiteley "had enough to do in looking after his present establishment."[19]

[. . .] Henry Walker, the editor of the *Bayswater Chronicle,* fully supported this limitation on trade, but turned the event into a meditation on the morality and pleasures of shopping. After the license had been blocked, he quipped, "Shopping has sufficient charm in itself to prevent [customers] swooning."[20] An avowed proponent of women's emancipation, Walker nonetheless did not share Whiteley's image of women in public life. Instead, he sounded remarkably similar to the conservative moralist Eliza Linton, since Whiteley's thirsty shopper was something other than the productive, rational woman envisioned by early feminists. Whiteley's critics thus came from both ends of the political spectrum. Conservatives and liberals alike found fault with his large shop and the new women he apparently had created. [. . .]

Elements of the Angel in the House, the ideal of bourgeois womanhood, were also imbricated with their vision of economic woman. Just as this Angel could signify a virtuous middle-class home and society, she could also manifest a virtuous economy and city. This was a difficult argument to make, since the essential characteristic of the Victorian Angel was that she remained "in the house." Nevertheless, traders such as Whiteley identified their "houses" with respectable women and suggested that when they did so, they transformed the urban center into a chaste space. In a subtle way, then, domesticity and political economy competed and merged to develop a shopper who seemed both independent from the household and "at home" in the urban marketplace. Her liberty in the city and its shops also ideally enabled this shopping Angel to create a comfortable, pleasurable private realm. In this view the public and private were seen as overlapping and interconnected territories held together by a rational and moral female shopper. This image stood in opposition to the irrational and sensual shopper constructed by a range of different critics. These two views of the shopper circulated widely in the culture and were by no means restricted to local government committees.

The periodical, trade, and local presses relied upon similar images of the disorderly and rational shopper when reporting on the machinations of the Universal Provider. For example, the first issue of a national draper's trade journal began an article on Whiteley by describing his refreshment room as one of the many "new ideas" of this "enterprising man." Believing that the law of supply and demand would determine the value of the lunchroom, the editor wrote, "We offer no opinion on the absolute propriety of such an arrangement. Experience will soon show whether the innovation is acceptable to the visitors and advantageous to trade." His hope for its success was clear, however, for he believed that "[a] Day's Shopping is one of the most agreeable occupations a Lady can devise, but pleasure is toil without agreeable relaxation and rest." Although "wine may not be desirable," he felt sure that a "bun, ice or refreshing fruit beverage," if "attainable in the ladies' room," would enable the "varied attractions" of the dress, millinery, and other departments to be "better appreciated."[21] [. . .]

Walker, Flood, and several vestrymen may have resented Whiteley's spectacular shopkeeping, but they were not enemies of women's urban freedoms. [. . .] [T]he vestry was in the midst of debating whether and how they should provide amenities for female residents, workers, and visitors. Feminist groups such as the Ladies Sanitary Association and individual feminists, including Emily Faithfull, supported Flood's vision of government-provided recreations and pleasures. In doing so, they began to articulate a critique of the commercial emancipation promoted by Whiteley and others.

As we have seen, Whiteley's critics came from diverse social and political groups. They included moralists like Linton, conservative publicans, upper-class magistrates, liberal journalists and politicians, feminists and shopkeepers. These commentators similarly painted the department store as the "halls of temptation." In their attacks, the department store was described as a threatening place that seduced women, encouraged shopping orgies, and introduced dangerous French, Oriental, and American influences into the heart of British bourgeois life. Marketplaces have been described in such terms in the past, but these images were developed by particular individuals for the specific purpose of market and moral control. Some used the spectacle of the sensuous bazaar to represent and contain the unruly nature of nineteenth-century capitalism, urban growth, and female independence. Others did so to promote an alternative vision of women's emancipation. Whiteley and his fellow merchants decried these portraits and championed the natural workings of an amoral market.

Large-scale retailers like the Universal Provider thus encouraged consumption by cleansing public amusements of their immoral image. They licensed consumer desires by theoretically separating the pleasures of shopping from other forms of physical desire and gender interactions. As this idea became more accepted by the late 1870s and 1880s, Whiteley's critics began to talk about department stores as bringing a delightful cosmopolitanism to suburban hinterlands, even suggesting that Whiteley's had single-handedly made Westbourne Grove into a cosmopolitan pleasure center. Together, the store, street, and shopping crowd were described as a glittering show, a symbol of prosperity and modernity. This is precisely the "Westbournia" that Sala witnessed in 1879 and that articles such as "Young London" also helped create. This narrative facilitated the expansion of the department store, London's commercial districts, and the production of new ideals of bourgeois femininity.

Further reading

Other works on shopping and consumerism include: Rachel Bowlby, *Just Looking: Consumer Culture in Dreiser, Gissing and Zola* (London: Methuen, 1985); Thomas Richards, *The Commodity Culture of Victorian Britain: Advertising and Spectacle, 1851–1914* (London: Verso, 1991); Lori Ann Loeb, *Consuming Angels: Advertising and Victorian Women* (Oxford: Oxford University Press, 1994); Bill Lancaster, *The Department Store: A Social History* (Leicester: Leicester University Press, 1995); Geoffrey Crossick and Serge Jaumain (eds), *Cathedrals of Consumption: The European Department Store, 1850–1939* (Aldershot: Ashgate, 1939). Another nineteenth-century (but pre-Victorian) study that discusses shopping is Amanda Vickery, *The Gentleman's Daughter: Women's Lives in Georgian England* (New Haven, CT: Yale University Press, 1993). For Victorian material culture, see: Asa Briggs, *Victorian Things* (London: Batsford, 1988); Thad Logan, *The Victorian Parlour* (Cambridge: Cambridge University Press, 2001); Deborah Cohen, *Household Gods: The British and their Possessions* (New Haven, CT: Yale University Press, 2006).

Notes

1   Mary Poovey, *Making a Social Body: British Cultural Formation, 1830–1864* (Chicago: University of Chicago Press, 1995), 4. Asa Briggs argued that during the 1890s the term "the masses" shifted from meaning a threatening crowd to a consuming public. Asa Briggs, *Victorian Cities* (Berkeley: University of California Press, 1993 [1963]), 49; and "The Human Aggregate," in *The Victorian City: Images and Realities* (London: Routledge and Kegan Paul, 1973), 1:83–104. Both marketing and sociological investigation developed in part to be able to quantify, see, and control the masses. Indeed, marketing grew out of the turn-of-the-century poverty studies. See T.A.B. Corley's work on Seebohm Rowntree's social investigations and the marketing of his family's cocoa in "Consumer Marketing in Britain, 1914–1960," *Business History* 29 (October 1987): 69; Francis Goodall, "Marketing Consumer Products before 1914: Rowntrees and Elect Cocoa," in *Markets and Bagmen: Studies in the History of Marketing and British Industrial Performance, 1830–1939*, ed. R.P.T. Davenport-Hines (Aldershot: Gower, 1986), 16–56; and Robert Fitzgerald, *Rowntree and the Marketing Revolution, 1862–1962* (Cambridge: Cambridge University Press, 1995).

2   William Taylor, "The Evolution of Public Space in New York City: The Commercial Showcase of America," in *Consuming Visions: Accumulation and Display of Goods in America, 1880–1920*, ed. Simon J. Bronner (New York: W.W. Norton, 1989), 291, 300.

3   Wolfgang Schivelbusch, *The Railway Journey: The Industrialization of Time and Space in the Nineteenth Century* (Berkeley: University of California Press, 1986), 54.

4   Geoff Eley has argued that since the inception of the public sphere in the eighteenth century, there have been many "competing publics." "Nations, Publics, and Political Cultures: Placing Habermas in the Nineteenth Century," in *Habermas and the Public Sphere*, ed. Craig Calhoun (Cambridge: MIT Press, 1992), 306.

5   Sociologists and anthropologists have spent a good deal of effort delineating the relationship between consumer practices and social identities. See, for example, Thorstein Veblen, *The Theory of the Leisure Class* (London: Penguin, 1994 [1899]); Pierre Bourdieu, *Outline of a Theory of Practice*, trans. Richard Nice (Cambridge: Cambridge University Press, 1977); and *Distinction: A Social Critique of the Judgement*

of Taste, trans. Richard Nice (Cambridge: Harvard University Press, 1984); Mary Douglas and Baron Isherwood, The World of Goods (New York: Basic Books, 1979); Arjun Appadurai, ed., The Social Life of Things: Commodities in Cultural Perspective (Cambridge: Cambridge University Press, 1986); Daniel Miller, Material Culture and Mass Consumption (Oxford: Basil Blackwell, 1987).

6   In 1867 Whiteley's included the following departments: Silks, Dresses, Linens, Drapery, Mantles, Millinery, Ladies' Outfitting, Haberdashery, Trimming, Gloves, Hosiery, Ribbons, Fancy Goods, Jewellery, Lace, Umbrellas, Furs, and Artificial Flowers. Gross profits were estimated to be around £4,500 for that year. Soon thereafter Whiteley added a dressmaking service, men's outfitting, and a furnishing drapery. Richard S. Lambert, The Universal Provider: A Study of William Whiteley and the Rise of the London Department Store (London: George G. Harrap, 1938), 67–72. Traders believed that competition was intensifying in these years, but if anything grocers faced greater competition than drapers did. In 1872 the Warehousemen and Draper's Trade Journal (hereafter WDTJ) reported that there were 1,200 drapers and 2,500 retail grocers in London. This may explain why Whiteley inspired the greatest hostility when he moved into the food trades. "Malthusian Trading — The Surplus Shopkeeper," WDTJ, December 14, 1872, 447–48.

7   This question was a prominent theme in nearly all texts that depicted shopping in this period. See Drapier and Clothier 1 (July 1859); Henry Mayhew, ed., The Shops and Companies of London and the Trades and Manufactories of Great Britain (London: 1865), 5, 86; "Shopping without Money," Leisure Hour (1865): 110–12; "Going a Shopping," Leisure Hour (1866): 198–200; "The Philosophy of Shopping," Saturday Review, October 16, 1875, 488–89; "Ladies Shopping," WDTJ, July 12, 1873, 374.

8   Bayswater Chronicle (hereafter BC), March 23, 1872. This strategy for limiting trade was an old one. In 1816 West End shopkeepers complained to Parliament that among "the numerous evils" associated with bazaars was the way they increased "places of public promenade [and] intrigue." Like those who opposed the department stores, however, these traders helped construct the perception that all women in public were prostitutes. Gary R. Dyer, "'The Vanity Fair' of Nineteenth-Century England: Commerce, Women, and the East in the Ladies Bazaar," Nineteenth-Century Literature 46, no. 2 (September 1991): 205.

9   Robert Thorne, "Places of Refreshment in the Nineteenth-Century City", in Buildings and Society: Essays on the Social Development of the Built Environment, ed. Anthony D. King (London: Routledge and Kegan Paul, 1980), 235. Descriptions of West End nightlife nearly always characterize the women who drink, dance, and dine in public as prostitutes. See, for example, J. Ewing Ritchie, The Night Side of London (London: William Tweedle, 1857); Stephen Fiske, English Photographs (London: Tinsley Brothers, 1869); Donald Shaw, London in the Sixties (London: Everett and Co., 1908); Ivan Bloch, Sexual Life in England Past and Present, trans. William Forstern (London: Francis Aldor, 1938); and Henry Mayhew, London's Underworld, ed. Peter Quennell (1862; reprint, London: Bracken Books, 1983), 121–27.

10   Tracy Davis, Actresses as Working Women: Their Social Identity in Victorian Culture (London: Routledge, 1991), 139–45; Judith R. Walkowitz, City of Dreadful Delight: Narratives of Sexual Danger in Late-Victorian London (Chicago: University of Chicago Press, 1992), 50–52. In his detailed description of West End prostitution Henry Mayhew portrayed its streets and shops as both commercial and sexual marketplaces. He also identified milliners, dressmakers, servants, those who served at bazaars, and "frequenters of fairs" as especially prone to entering the illicit trade. Mayhew, London's Underworld, 38.

11   Paddington Times, March 30, 1872.

12   Brian Harrison, Drink and the Victorians: The Temperance Question in England 1815–1872 (Pittsburgh: University of Pittsburgh Press, 1971), 303.

13   Walter Benjamin, "Central Park," trans. Lloyd Spencer, *New German Critique* 34 (Winter 1985): 40. Also see Susan Buck-Morss's analysis of Benjamin's treatment of the prostitute as commodity, "The Flâneur, the Sandwichman, and the Whore: The Politics of Loitering," *New German Critique* 39 (Fall 1986): 99–140; and her longer study, *The Dialectics of Seeing: Walter Benjamin and the Arcades Project* (Cambridge: MIT Press, 1989).

14   Amanda Anderson, *Tainted Souls and Painted Faces: The Rhetoric of Fallenness in Victorian Culture* (Ithaca: Cornell University Press, 1993), 2. Also see, Judith R. Walkowitz, *Prostitution and Victorian Society: Women, Class, and the State* (Cambridge: Cambridge University Press, 1980) and *City of Dreadful Delight*; Lynda Nead, *Myths of Sexuality: Representations of Women in Victorian Britain* (Oxford: Basil Blackwell, 1988), 110–35; Elizabeth Wilson, *The Sphinx in the City: Urban Life, the Control of Disorder, and Women* (Berkeley: University of California Press, 1991), 55–57; Kathy Peiss, "Making Up, Making Over: Cosmetics, Consumer Culture, and Women's Identity," in Victoria de Grazia with Ellen Furlough, eds, *The Sex of Things: Gender and Consumption in Historical Perspective* (Berkeley: University of California, 1996), 315; Christine Buci-Glucksmann, "Catastrophic Utopia: The Feminine as Allegory of the Modern," *Representations* 14 (Spring 1986): 220–29; Laurie Teal, "The Hollow Women: Modernism, the Prostitute, and Commodity Aesthetics," *Differences: A Journal of Feminist Cultural Studies* 7, no. 3 (Fall 1995): 80–108; Mariana Valverde, "The Love of Finery: Fashion and the Fallen Woman in Nineteenth-Century Social Discourse," *Victorian Studies* 32, no. 2 (Winter 1989): 169–88; Daniel A. Cohen, "The Murder of Maria Bickford: Fashion, Passion, and the Birth of a Consumer Culture," *American Studies* 31, no. 2 (Fall 1990): 5–30. Also see the editorial on crime and the love of "dress" among male and female shop assistants, *BC*'s February 10, 1872; and Arthur Sherwell, *Life in West London: A Study and a Contrast* (London: Methuen, 1897), 145–48.

15   "The Girl of the Period," *Saturday Review*, March 14, 1868, 339–40. On the reaction to Linton's *Saturday Review* essays, see Nancy Fix Anderson, *Woman against Women in Victorian England: A Life of Eliza Lynn Linton* (Bloomington: Indiana University Press, 1987), 117–36. Also see Herbert Van Thal, *Eliza Lynn Linton, the Girl of the Period: A Biography* (London: George Allen and Unwin, 1979).

16   *Saturday Review*, October 16, 1875, 488.

17   "London Girls of the Period: The West End Girl," *Girl of the Period Miscellany* 1, no. 3 (May 1869): 92.

18   *BC*, March 23, 1872. Spencer, Turner and Boldero in Lisson Grove was even larger, however, with its approximately one thousand employees. *WDTJ*, December 21, 1872, 643.

19   *BC*, March 23, 1872. Whiteley made a similar argument about customers' "convenience" in "How to Succeed as a Shopkeeper: A Practical Article by William Whiteley," *London Magazine*, newspaper clipping, Whiteley's Archive, Westminster City Archives.

20   *BC*, March 23, 1872.

21   *WDTJ*, April 15, 1872, 4. For a slightly different formulation of these oppositional portraits of the consumer, see Rachel Bowlby, *Shopping with Freud* (London: Routledge, 1993), 3.

Christopher Breward

CLOTHING THE MIDDLE-CLASS MALE

The Hidden Consumer: Masculinities, Fashion and City Life, 1860–1914 (Manchester: Manchester University Press, 1999), 54–60, 75–84, 86–8.

In this extract from *The Hidden Consumer* (1999), a monograph on male consumerism in urban Britain, fashion historian **Christopher Breward** focuses on the way clothes helped to structure status across the middle class. Taking an interdisciplinary approach, he draws from literature, theatre studies and social history to navigate the complex system of signs embodied in Victorian male clothing.

He argues that fashion is not simply imposed from the top down, but has a fluidity that offers a complex system of stylistic changes and finely tuned gradations to the observer. Breward thinks this was particularly important in a period when the 'gentleman' was an expanding category, as more of the middle classes reached positions of authority. He calls attention to the work of **Cain and Hopkins** and **Martin Wiener** (also in this volume) and their arguments about the influence of the gentleman on capitalism and culture. For all classes, clothing immediately marked out a man's place on the social scale. Not included here is Breward's examination of how aristocratic dress, personified in the short-lived Duke of Clarence, helped to set fashion trends and represent 'glamour'. The elite of society spent an inordinate amount of time and money on their apparel, which Breward suggests was in lieu of having other masculine traits, such as muscularity, to display. He explores the depth of their wardrobe because gentlemen were expected to change clothes several times a day, each different activity demanding a particular mode of dress. The assistance of a personal servant was required to deal with the dozens of items of clothing needing constant attention in a time before technology made the care of clothing easier. Also not included here is Breward's discussion of working-class men who, if respectable, struggled to look neat and clean, and descended into raggedness when poverty intensified. This extract begins with Breward's discussion of the overall scene in late Victorian London and his method of extracting meaning from it before moving on to a specific examination of middle-class male clothing. He pays special attention to the challenges to men of the lower middle class in maintaining a proper wardrobe and their precarious steps up the social scale. This reading is also important because it represents the more complex arguments that are currently being put forward about social class and the increasingly sophisticated work being undertaken in fashion history.

Christopher Breward is Deputy Head of Research at the Victoria & Albert Museum, London, and a Professorial Fellow at London College of Fashion, University of the Arts, London. He has published widely on the cultural history of fashion and on the relationship between the production and consumption of clothing and space in London. His current research interests are focused on the role of dress in nineteenth-century theatre.

It was such a sight — civilization in a nutshell — that was what made me pause. I was a part of it, and Apollo was taking a peep at his own legs . . . What a scene! The Exchange I had just left, with its groups of millionaires gossiping, Baghdad and the Irawaddy, Chicago and the Cape; dividend day over at the bank yonder, and the well known sight of the Blessed going to take their quarterly reward; a sheriff's coach turning the angle of the mansion House (breakfast to an African pro-consul I believe), a vanishing splendour of satin and plush and gold; dandy clerks making for Birch's with the sure and certain hope of a partnership in their early grace; shabby clerks making for the bun shops; spry brokers going to take the odds against Egyptians, and with an appropriate horsiness of air, a parson . . . itinerant salesmen of studs, pocket combs and universal watch keys; flower girls at the foot of the statue, a patch of colour; beggar at the foot of the steps, another patch, the red shirt beautifully toned down in wear . . . eruption of noisy crowd from the Cornhill corner (East End marching West to demonstrate for the right to a day's toil for a day's crust); thieves and bludgeon men, and stone men in attendance on demonstration; detectives in attendance on thieves; shutters up at the Jeweller's as they pass . . . And, for background, the nondescript thousands in black and brown and russet and every neutral hue, with the sun over all, and between the sun and the thousands the London mist. It was something as a picture, but so much more as a thought. What a wonder of parts and whole! What a bit of machinery! The beggars and occasionally the stock jobbers and the nondescripts to go wrong; the policeman to take them up; the parson to show the way of repentance; and the sheriff to hang them, if need be, when all was done. With this, the dandies to adorn the scene — myself not altogether unornamental — the merchants, the clerks, and the dividend takers, all but cog and fly and crank of the same general scene. What a bit of machinery![1]

IN 1888 THE SOCIALIST-REALIST writer Richard Whiteing published a novel *The Island: Or an Adventure of a Person of Quality* that presaged many of the concerns that would engulf cultural debate during the following decade. The title suggests common concerns with that genre of literature produced around 1900 by authors including Rudyard Kipling, Rider Haggard and H.G. Wells. These were explicitly romance epics offering spectacular yet safely removed geographical and psychic spaces for the negotiation of pressing or taboo contemporary subjects, particularly those concerning developing sexual and social identities. What is significant . . . , however, is the contrived familiarity of Whiteing's opening paragraph, which, in its vivid portrayal of the hub of London's financial district, offers a more commonplace, 'democratic' setting than the tailoring journal or the etiquette guide, for those themes of tradition and modernity which underpinned the development of masculine fashionable style [. . .]. I wish to examine here how that rather abstract, stylistic history related to the experience and representation of the urban everyday and to the formation of distinct sartorial identities.

In their orientation towards specific social contexts, the fashionable ideals promoted by the clothing trade shared a common language with other more imaginative texts, in which the identification and assessment of urban 'types' through visual codings was of central importance. This is a connection which has been utilised to great effect by Daniel Roche in his recent account of French fashion systems in the eighteenth century. He has shown how the textual communication of status and character in the novel can be of enormous use to the fashion historian seeking opinions and attitudes which may have been obscured by the partial or 'functional' nature of documentary and 'official' archival sources. As he states

the novelist provides information about ways of life because he places objects in a context, so conferring on them a different truth from that discovered by the deciphering of archives . . . fiction achieves authentic effects both by the truth of the descriptions and by their location within a story which reveals forms of reasoning and structures of the imagination of an age. In the amicable quarrel over the use of texts between literary scholars and historians, this median position must be retained.[2]

Literary scholar Lynn Hapgood alludes to Whiteing's espousal of a process that she defines as 'textual disorientation' in his proto-cinematic and self-consciously sublime introductory passage. This pivotal narrative moment, when the author looks back from his island refuge to the day of his decision to leave the corruption of the City, achieves through the staccato register of reportage and the glancing imagery of impressionism a complex sense of distance through geographical and chronological space. What is not distanced, according to Hapgood, is the psychic impact of the experience, though the two are closely implicated with each other. She goes on to argue that

> Whiteing suggests that topographical viewpoint — from where one looks — is inseparable from mental viewpoint — what one is open to seeing . . . This symbiotic relationship between the physical eye and the inner eye gives sharpness and precision to the concept of social determinism and reveals both the collective nature of social experience and the struggle of individuals to transcend it.[3]

In this sense, and following Roche's suggestive method, though the provenance of the passage belongs to the imaginative world of the novelist, its descriptions offer a privileged view of the manner in which the social spectrum and psychological make-up of late Victorian society might have been perceived. Furthermore, its self-conscious debt to the new traditions of 'objective' journalism and its avant-garde control of the authorial voice provide a more nuanced reading of sartorial image 'in motion' than the more cloistered writer on trade, modes or manners. All was disorientating in Whiteing's London at the close of the nineteenth century. The ordered commercial machine of empire barely containing those notes of social unrest and moral apprehensiveness evidenced through the ever shifting direction of the crowd and the world-weary ennui of the narrator. Yet at the same time the characters isolated in its mêlée were fixed in a precise hierarchy, marked by an outward appearance that confirmed the spectator's preconceptions of class. The year 1888 may have been the time of 'dittos' for the masses and 'subdued checks' for the aristocracy in *The Tailor and Cutter*,[4] but Whiteing captured in stereotypes the repercussions of such style dictates, from their reflection in the gossiping groups of millionaires and spry brokers, their approximation in the figures of dandy and shabby clerks and their refraction in the red shifts and russet suits of beggars and hooligans. As the historian of theatrical performance J.S. Bratton has shown, such stereotyping offers a useful, if conceptually problematic, means of assessing historical attitudes to social (and racial) hierarchies and relationships. These might be extended beyond the stage to encompass the communication of class positions through clothing in the 'performances' offered and recorded by popular literature and social reportage:

> Important to the function of theatre in negotiating identity . . . is the formalization and conventionalizing of the concept of character, via the mechanism of the stereotype. Stereotyping is a mental activity condemned by . . . moralizing modern critical arguments, as the root of almost all the evils of . . . injustice and oppression from which we suffer . . . The difficulty is that without the mental activity of discrimination of which stereotyping is the first tool we learn, we would be without any sense of a real self with which to begin . . . Performance offers audiences . . . a rich assortment of stereotypes and a locus for relating to them which has greatly varied potential. The emotional response elicited may be blindly, pathologically crude, or, at the other extreme, the complexities

of the performance may offer a unique opportunity for the individual to become aware of stereotyping as a mental activity rather than a reflection of reality, and so to acquire the beginnings of detachment and understanding.[5]

By drawing on the power of discursive fictions such as stereotyping to explain the organisation of social relations, art historians and literary scholars contradict recent readings of nineteenth-century class formations by social and economic historians. These have stressed a greater fluidity between and within supposed class groupings than was previously acknowledged. From an emphasis on 'top down' coercion and subordination accepted in the early phases of social history in the 1960s, historians now prioritise a diversity of competing 'popular identities'. Alastair Reid usefully identifies 'the inadequacy of simple horizontal divisions . . . and an emphasis instead on the importance of vertical divisions within both the ruling classes and the working classes: between branches of economic activity, between regions, and between religious and political affiliations'. The outcome of such a shift has, inevitably, moved discussion towards the nature of social difference, for, as Reid continues: 'Perhaps a society held together by coercion or control would become more homogenous under pressure from above, but one held together mainly by consent is likely to contain a variety of popular identities.'[6] On this basis the circulation of widely recognised class stereotypes represents not so much a reductive framework for understanding the 'frozen' structures of society but an acknowledgement of a constantly shifting interplay of role models, types and identities. The figures I introduce in this chapter, should therefore be seen not simply as all-embracing representations of lived experience but as indicative of the several ways in which consumers were encouraged to imagine, identify and interpret a range of social models.

[. . .] The categorisation of dress employed here has more in common with current debates concerning the nature of class definition and social mobility than the totalising interpretations of dress adopted by recent fashion history texts which have taken masculinity as their subject.[7] In the latter it has been taken for granted that aristocratic dress codes provided an all-encompassing gentlemanly template against which other men could arrive at an approximation of fashionable taste. To be fashionable, in other words, was to adopt the sartorial rules of the social and economic elite. Such a reading assumes a coherent interpretation of the aristocracy as a single social grouping and a clear, unchanging relationship between that group and its supposed imitators (also defined as fixed in their self-image and aspirations). As Reid's comments have illustrated, in both methodological and historiographical terms such assumptions no longer convince. The economic historians Andrew Miles and David Vincent, for example, have shown how even arriving at a common definition of class is not straightforward:

> In both the conceptual and technical senses there are essentially two approaches to the construction of occupationally based classification schemes. While virtually all students . . . start from Sorokin's premise that 'any organised social group is always a stratified social body', they then separate into those who view society as either class or status based.

The former assume fundamental lines of division in society based on Marxist distinctions concerning the differing relationships of groups to the means of production, or, adopting a Weberian model, on their work and market positions. The latter conceive of the social spectrum as an ascending ladder, or seamless continuum, of ever more prestigious occupations, unbroken by any marked distinction.[8]

To speak of a seamless continuum suggests more than an appropriate metaphor for fashion historians, for it is undoubtedly in this context that the unchanging, undemonstrative and undifferentiated nature of male dress has been conceived, explained through recourse to a prevailing hegemony of 'gentlemanliness' propagated by the landed classes.[9] Contemporary rhetoric appears to uphold such readings. Commentators from *The Tailor and Cutter* through to George Fox presented the consumption habits of the 'upper ten' as an appropriate model for emulation, and on one level Whiteing's conception of the City posits a familiar metaphor of smoothly functioning machinery, an 'ascending' ladder linking the occupations of millionaire and beggar in the same mutually beneficial configuration. However, Whiteing's position was heavily imbued with the perspective of the critic: the socially variegated crowd that he described was also a harbinger of moral unease and signified the recognition of difference in a more problematic sense. New work on class formations has begun to unpack the manner in which seemingly powerless or disregarded social groups refuted the stereotypes set up for them in such representations, choosing instead to establish cultural forms and practices that related more closely to their own set of economic, political or moral circumstances. G. Crossick and H.G. Haupt note that

> as we turn from contemporary novels and cartoons to the image in historical writings, we find the petit bourgeoisie presented as an essentially imitative social group . . . It is a powerful image, with small businessmen, minor civil servants and office workers driven by a combination of anxiety and aspirations to imitate a bourgeois culture whose substance they could barely grasp . . . The . . . image is nonetheless more difficult to sustain once we explore the realities of petit bourgeois life.[10]

This recognition of the tension between stereotype and 'reality' implies that a more robust playing off of contradictory images, role models, aspirations and boundaries took place through processes of self-presentation than the stricter parameters of more didactic texts allow.

In a related vein, the easy association between power, money and lineage that underpinned the social system was also yielding to increasing pressure for change by the closing decades of the century, further undermining any simple reading of the stereotype as a stable hegemonic cipher. Recent studies of the aristocracy have taught us that such associations can never be taken as given. Economic historians Cain and Hopkins characterise the period as 'one of precarious equipoise, when the power of finance, growing increasingly cosmopolitan, reached a transitory equality with that of land, whose agricultural base was being slowly undermined by the free trade internationalism on which the City flourished'.[11] In a controversial thesis

Martin Wiener has translated this economic shift into a cultural equation whereby aristocratic traditions in institutionalised forms maintained a symbolic hold over government, education, finance and industry, ensuring in the process that progressive commercial and technological imperatives in Britain remained safely in check.[12] Seen in this light, the English gentleman's sartorial image becomes not so much a badge of unchanging social stability but rather a contested site for the playing out of struggles for pre-eminence between waning and rising social groups and outlooks.[13] That forms of self-presentation for men seemed to remain largely static over the period does not necessarily suggest a consensus in these matters, but offers room for debate 'about whether the continued prominence of the landed elite reflected a real aristocratic dominance or whether aristocratic government and cultural norms were merely convenient veils behind which the "bourgeoisie" could work its will undisturbed'.[14] The fact that these tensions were communicated through the medium of popular literature, personal testimony and journalistic observation means that a closer scrutiny of the ways in which class positions and sartorial presentations interrelated should be attempted. Only by acknowledging the fluid manner of their operation is it possible to arrive at a clearer view of the varied meanings attached to men's clothing, its complex systems of stylistic change and finely tuned gradations during the late nineteenth and early twentieth centuries. [. . .]

Whatever the parameters for contesting the ownership and meaning of the image of the English gentleman during the period, there is no doubt that the material accoutrements of such an ensemble cost a great deal of money and were engineered to communicate that fact. As power passed from the old order to the new, sartorial display retained an important sociological function. [. . .]

The performance of professionalism

If [. . .] the evidence of tailoring journals and etiquette guides concurred closely with the fashionable choices of the aristocratic elite, then the clothing consumption of middle-class men and those below them offered more scope for the contesting of sartorial identities — a sign perhaps of the greater fluidity and lack of consensus afforded descriptions of social rank below the upper ten. Whereas the construction of aristocratic modes of fashionable taste implied assurances of quality and expense and an unquestioning assumption of control, the clothing of the professional or middle-class man was suggestive of more paranoid attempts to access some of those qualities while carefully distancing the bourgeois image from the excesses of those sartorial stereotypes that abutted it. [. . .]

Recent studies of the middle classes, by social and economic historians reliant on Marxist interpretations of class relationships, have retained scant sympathy for exploring the internal aspirations and imaginative culture of a broad swathe of the English population. Such a lack of analysis concurs with MacQueen Pope's self-serving assertion that

The middle class has always been inarticulate, it has never been very interested in itself, its members have been known to disown it. But there it was — a most important section of the community — working, playing, marrying, dying . . . paying its rates and taxes and always supplying that great gift of balance, common sense and respectability which kept the prosperity of the country on an even keel.[15]

Unsurprisingly, more effort has been directed at arriving at objective definitions of the strata of a silent majority resting between the ruling classes and the proletariat. Ownership of property, occupation and proximity to the labour market have been the most common features used to identify class position in a bewildering array of possibilities.[16] This rather reductive approach, while useful in supplying a loose framework for the positioning of particular occupations, offers few clues to the sense of self engendered by an outlook supposedly dogged by 'a sense of precariousness, of contingency . . . of life as struggle . . . menaced from above and below'.[17] In its insistence on viewing the middle classes only in relation to those 'above and below' in an assumed ranking, of finding evidence for 'false consciousness' and 'class traitorship', this is a position in danger of losing sight of the specific qualities that identified people as belonging to a particular grouping in the first place. Clothing and the maintenance of a public persona were one area of 'cultural' production much less fixed and far more subjective than those fields associated with property or employment, yet central to the definition of social standing across the middle-class spectrum from shopkeeper to stockbroker, [. . .] The sartorial presentation of self allowed for a negotiation with those more static class indicators, providing the possibility of movement from, or acquiescence with, the prevailing social stereotypes of what it meant to be middle-class. A central tenet in that construction of the male middle-class ideal, across all its strata, was the notion of professionalism. While the aristocratic image presumed a natural propensity towards social supremacy and its attendant responsibilities, manifested through the military bearing of morning dress or the material and visual credentials of land ownership (from the tweed shooting jacket to the pink melton hunting coat), professional standing was presented as a position to be striven for and earned. The onus on duty and respectability that it entailed ensured a greater concentration on the correctness of its physical manifestations. [. . .]

Contingent on the development of professional models, the increasing attention paid to the economic rewards of business by the late nineteenth century saw an uneasy fusing of aristocratic and middle-class models, the arising tensions of which commentators observed in the material trappings of upper-middle-class life. T.H. Escott, writing in 1885, reserved particular admiration for 'the great merchant or banker of today . . . an English gentleman of a finished type':

> If he is not a peer, the chances are that he is a member of the House of Commons. He is a man of wide culture, an authority upon paintings, or china, or black-letter books, upon some branch of natural science, upon the politics of Europe . . . he goes into the City as punctually as his junior clerks; and when he returns from the City he drops for a few minutes into the most exclusive of West End clubs. His grandfather would have lived with his family above the counting house and regarded a trip to Hyde park as a summer day's journey. As for the descendant, his

town house is in Belgravia or Mayfair. He occupies it for little more than six months out of the twelve, and during the rest of the year lives in his palace in the country . . . There is in fact, but one standard of 'social position' in England, and it is that which is formed by a blending of the plutocratic and aristocratic elements.[18]

This meeting of duty, self-improvement and moral display was rooted in a form of long-established gentlemanly mercantilism that stood in stark contrast to the showier pretensions of those whose fortunes derived from more recent excursions in the money markets, whose social backgrounds displayed a wider range of origins than those whose wealth depended on the more gradual attainment of 'good connections' or a thorough training in the traditions of trade or the professions. As Escott noted

There is a rush now equally on the part of patrician and plebeian parents to get their sons into business, and noblemen with illustrious titles . . . eagerly embrace any good opening in the City . . . It is perhaps the younger son of an earl or a duke who sees you when you call on your broker to transact business; it may be the heir to a peerage himself who is head partner in the firm which supplies the middle class household with tea, puts a ring fence around the park of the Yorkshire squire, or erects a trim conservatory in one of the villa gardens of suburban Surrey.[19]

Between the two models, merchant and stockbroker, status was seen to be either deserved and refined in character or fortuitous and over-opulent 'the life of the ideal stockbroker is one of display, that of the ideal merchant, one of dignified grandeur'.[20] Positioning oneself publicly between these extremes through the consumption of commodities ranging from furniture through literature or leisure to clothing was therefore a precarious act, one that relied increasingly on precisely the sort of professional discretion that underpinned the boundaries of the class in the first place. [. . .]

In sartorial terms, contemporary observers translated professional discretion into an overriding obsession with 'good form' in middle-class male dress. The columns of family journals and popular novels resound with discussions of fashionable faux-pas, recollections of instances where the fraudulently respectable betrayed their ulterior motives through a doubtful haircut, inappropriate trousers or a too perfect demeanour. 'Keeping up appearances' was a recurring concern of the humorist Reginald Smith, who published his 'Londoner's Log Book' at the turn of the century in *The Cornhill Magazine*. Purporting to relay the domestic experiences of a young couple in Bayswater, it provided an upper middle class equivalent of the Grossmith brothers' more frequently quoted *Diary of a Nobody*[21] and maintained a focused interest in the idiosyncrasies of male dress:

Last month I ventured to express dislike of the epithet 'well groomed' as applied by Pennialinus to the young Tories in the House of Commons, and I affirmed . . . that it meant nothing more than 'well dressed'. But the editor of 'Hiccadocius' in a letter which bears the Cambridge postmark, takes me to task, and says 'The odious expression in my mind, implies also that particular neatness and glossiness of hair which you notice in A D C's, Guardsmen, 10th Hussars, and a few of the younger nobility and Eton boys . . . I therefore retire from a conflict for which I am imperfectly equipped and concede my critic's proposition that well groomed involves a well brushed head as well as a well cut coat and well creased trousers and well varnished boots. I turn from the abstract to the concrete, and ask myself and my wife whether we can lay our finger on a well groomed man in stuccovia . . . It is sometimes easiest to illustrate one's meaning by negative examples, and our excellent MP, Mr Barrington Bounderly, whom I have just met in Stucco Gardens (Progressive Conservative) is neither well dressed nor even well groomed. He wears a turned down collar of the new type, much too high for his short neck, and a red tie in a sailor's knot. He has celebrated the return of Spring by putting on a white waistcoat and brown boots; but as the air is chilly, he wears a great coat with a fur collar, and thick trousers of a conspicuous check. I protest that I would rather be apparelled like our curate, young Bumpstead, whom I saw returning from his Easter Monday trip in a college 'blazer', a Roman collar, grey knickerbockers, and a straw hat.[22]

'Good form' for Smith erred on the side of a manly negligence or sporty simplicity, eschewing the more polished glamour of aristocratic swagger. The ridiculous inappropriateness of Piccadilly fashion-plate dressing was thrown into sharper relief in a later discussion of the curate's sartorial transformation at the hands of his new fiancée:

His hair, which aforetime looked as if he had been dragged through a quickset hedge backwards is now carefully parted and smoothly brushed, while a faint odour of lime juice glycerine pervades the boudoir in which he spends most of his time. His hands . . . I fancy, have been submitted to a process of manicure and are thrust, all unwillingly into gants de suede. He has discarded the greased shooting boots . . . in favour of buttoned elegancies from the Burlington Arcade; and I have even heard rumours of possible developments in the way of patent leather. The shapeless jacket . . . is now reserved for parochial visitation. When he comes to see Bertha he wears a well cut frock coat with braided edgings . . . The whole edifice is crowned by a 'topper' of unusual brilliancy, and a neatly folded umbrella with a hooked handle of bamboo completes the transformation.[23]

This aping of aristocratic trappings commonly formed the focus for the invective of conservative social commentators, including T.W.H. Crosland, who in his *The Wicked Life* of 1905 displayed an uncritical admiration for the 'discretion' of the landed rich while exposing a deep-rooted prejudice against the conspicuous consumption associated with an increasingly commercial society. The middle class, incorporating 'the successful traders, the stockbrokers, the company promoters, the insurers and financiers, snobbish doctors and solicitors, strutting actors and music hall agents, and retired brewers and tailors', he claimed, 'knows nothing about noblesse oblige, having no noblesse to oblige, he has money without position, land without ancestry, servants without authority, lust without discrimination, ice in his champagne, college colours on his hand bags'.[24] Economic historians have identified the last quarter of the nineteenth century as a period of falling prices accompanied by higher living standards, temporary for the working classes but maintained into the opening years of the twentieth century by professional and entrepreneurial groups whose salaries remained constant.[25] Paradoxically, rather than engendering a sense of ease with regard to appropriate levels of consumption and the fluidity of social status, this climate encouraged precisely the kind of paranoid jeremiads which Crosland's writing typifies. Those at the precarious borders between the working and lower middle classes, the shopkeepers and small businessmen, were hit by the fierce competition of department stores and co-operative movements, while also benefiting from the increased custom of the affluent group above them. The fear of bankruptcy and attendant social ruin epidemic amongst the petit bourgeoisie also infected the professional classes, who as Harold Perkin points out were dangerously under insured during the period, preferring to devote their income and savings to outward show.[26] The only outright winners in a situation marked by a lack of financial confidence alongside a headlong rush to prove status through spending were those plutocrats, the owners of the shopping emporia, stock companies, comestible factories and leisure outfits whose products fuelled that competition.[. . .]

How then did the middle classes articulate social position through clothing in such a fraught arena? And is it even possible to define an encompassing middle-class manner of dressing in the face of such conflicting social pressures? It would seem appropriate here to present the constraints, financial and material, within which such practices could take place. *The Cornhill Magazine* budgets of 1901 offered a range of representative examples of which G. Colmore's 'Eight Hundred a Year' presented the benchmark for a comfortable middle-class lifestyle:

> To the toiling clerk it seems unbounded wealth; to the woman of fashion a poor thing in pin-money; to those who usually start marriage on such an income, the professional man, or the younger son with a narrow berth in the Civil Service, it is a sum upon which the two ends can be made to meet with comfortable success or inconvenient uncertainty, according to the requirements and habits of the people who have the spending of it.[27]

Setting aside expenditure on rent, taxes, food and servants' wages, the husband's allowance was set at £70 a year, of which £40 was reserved for clothing bills. Of greater concern to Colmore than the necessary payments to the tailor was the consumption of commodities that suggested status in a rather more reckless manner 'which means wine and tobacco'. [. . .] G.S. Layard in his description of the minimum expenditure of households earning 'A Hundred and Fifty a Year', isolated those occupations most readily associated with the 'uneasy stratum':

> certain skilled mechanics; bank clerks; managing clerks to solicitors; teachers in the London Board Schools; the younger reporters on the

best metropolitan papers; the senior reporters on the best local papers; second division clerks in the Colonial, Home and India Offices; senior telegraphists; sanitary inspectors; relieving officers; clerks under the County Councils; many vestry officials; police inspectors; barristers' clerks, organists, and curates in priest's orders.[28]

He drew attention to the greater concentration paid to the clothing of male members of these households with respect to their standing in the community and the demands of their employers:

> The unit of the class with which we are concerning ourselves is in a very different position from the skilled mechanic who may be earning a like income. It is more and more recognized as an axiom in those businesses and professions which are in immediate touch with the client, that the employees, whether they be salesmen in shops or clerks in banks or offices, must be habited in what may be called a decent professional garb. The bank clerk who looks needy, or the solicitor's clerk who is out at elbows, will find that he has little chance of retaining his position. Here he is clearly at a disadvantage compared with the man who works with his hands and who has only to keep a black coat for high days and holidays. Thus the 'lower middle' bread-winner is forced into an extravagance in the matter of clothes out of all proportion to his income.[29]

The relationship between remuneration, expenditure and outward show among the lower middle classes was the focus of much discussion and dissent during this transitional period. The limits imposed by tight wages and prescriptions of appropriate behaviour by employers and social peers set the parameters for the kind of moral position and sartorial image the clerk, the teacher or the shopworker was expected to achieve and sometimes wished to transcend. These influences certainly bore more direct, practical relation to the circumstances of lower-middle-class life than tales of aristocratic excess. A growing tension between the falling salaries associated with over-expanding employment sectors such as banking or retail, a seeming rise in living standards elsewhere and the stress on 'respectability' demanded by moral and religious teaching, led to significant pressures. J.A. Banks notes that men of the middle and lower middle classes were marrying at an increasingly late age after 1840, simply in order to achieve the kind of position and income that would bear the expense of running a 'respectable' household.[30] [. . .]

Of more concern to the philanthropist were those who 'still are not in society, place little value on gloves, lunch in the office on bread and cheese, clean their own boots, and are not alarmed by the prospect of doing without a servant when married, of lighting the fire each morning before they go out, and of never entering a theatre or buying a bottle of wine'.[31] Men of this calibre, on £80 a year, made up the majority of the clerking workforce. Their predicament informed those familiar descriptions of genteel poverty, narrow vision and desire for propriety which characterised the lower middle classes for writers such as H.G. Wells and E.M. Forster. Historians from Carey[32] to Crossick and Haupt[33] have condemned these literary representations as 'unflattering' and prone to 'distortion', and have used their hostility as proof of a barely disguised disgust for the class among the intellectual elite. Yet while the caricatured descriptions put forward by novelists and playwrights probably did incorporate these tendencies, such representations also offered creative mirror images in which the clerk class could recognise and concur with depictions of their own kind, however slanted. As Michael Hayes suggests, the young male working- and lower-middle-class population of the period immediately preceding the First World War provided a foundation for the huge expansion of popular reading that took place during the interwar years.[34] Their custom was vitally important to publishers, who could not afford to alienate them completely with overly disparaging or unrealistic portraits. St John Adcock, a less well-remembered novelist belonging to the 'cockney school' of self-conscious social realism, delineated the pathetic figure of Andrew Jessop in his 1898 melodrama, *In the Image of God — A Tale of Lower London*, as an example of the penury incurred by a constant drive towards professional respectability. His sympathetic pen portrait must have elicited a resigned recognition from his intended readership:

> He made his daily journeys to and from the City afoot with a view to economy; he lived sparely and dressed shabbily, indulging at long intervals in a new coat, which was threadbare before he could supplement it with new trousers, which in turn were worn to shabbiness before another new coat was attainable . . . There was nothing striking about his features . . . One does not grow spirited on insufficient nutriment, or healthy by leaning over a desk all day in a close back office, and spending one's leisure exclusively in the half basement and pinched attic of a shabby genteel house in the densest quarter of Camden Town.[35] [. . .]

Published autobiographies provide a further perspective on the material 'stuff' of middle- and lower-middle-class male fashionable taste. Frederick Willis and W. MacQueen Pope both published in 1948 accounts of their lives in London at the turn of the century. The anecdotal tone of their texts, and the clear subjective positions which the authors took in a bid to compare the gentle rhythms of the past with a post-war modernity that they may have found alienating, position such narratives on the very peripheries of 'objective' historical method. Yet to dismiss their recollections as unreliable overlooks the value to be gained from descriptions of the ephemeral nature of social life that carry a heavy personal and emotional commitment lacking in more quantified forms of documentary evidence. More than any other source (in the absence of an oral history record for the period), these texts constitute the language and prejudices that built up middle- and lower-middle-class lifestyles and consequently offer a privileged view of their physical manifestations. Willis was a silk hatter in the West End with a heightened memory for the idiosyncrasies of dress, as well as the reassurance to be gained from its function as a social marker. 'It was an age when everyone made the best of his appearance. No proper clerk would dare to appear at the office without the official black coat and vest and pin stripe trousers. Bank and similar clerks wore silk hats. People were expected to dress in clothes suitable to their calling.'[36] Any attempt to disguise, or get beyond, that calling sartorially was remembered by Willis with contempt. The marker of a 'respectable' wardrobe for him was the time lavished on its maintenance, its strict adherence to an ordered neatness and the uncomfortable weight of a necessary formality:

Stiff white shirts and collars . . . were indispensable. On Saturday afternoons and evenings children could be seen in every street carrying home the weekly white shirt and collars from the laundry . . . He who could not afford the dignity of a white shirt, carefully built up the illusion of one by covering his chest with a dicky and pinning stiff white cuffs to the wrist bands of his plebeian Oxford shirt. Further economy was effected by those who were a nick or two higher in the social scale. They had a white shirt but the cuffs and front were removable so that the shirt, which had to last a week, could be renewed and refreshed in the middle of this period with clean cuffs and front . . . Some people were so lost in moral darkness that they wore ready made clothes and rubber collars . . . an abomination of the period with a rubber foundation and a white shining surface like the tiles in a public lavatory . . . At the best, a rubber collar looked like a dead collar that had been embalmed for centuries, and I only resurrect it as being a curious faux-pas in an otherwise immaculate period.[37]

MacQueen Pope made a more direct association between the restrained and heavy appearance of middle-class, middle-aged respectability and the pecuniary comfort enjoyed by that stratum. Good cloth and the morally assertive display of gold accessories went beyond symbolism to constitute the very substance of bourgeois confidence: 'The watch chain, the watch and the sovereign purse were the outward and visible signs of solvency. You pulled out your purse, flicked it open, slipped out your sovereign, and there you were. You could not carry many sovereigns that way, but there was no need, so great was its purchasing power.'[38] Here is the essence of the middle-class stereotype. Aristocratic forms of dressing directed all economic energy into the fine distinction that a Savile Row tailor could bestow, pursuing shifting templates of fashionable taste that dictated a spectacularly fugitive approximation of modish gentlemanliness. In the centred dependability of the watch chain and the sovereign purse, or the static functionalism of the business suit, the successful bourgeois found an image that fixed an otherwise precarious existence with remarkable symbolic clout. This had nothing to do with an evangelical rejection of luxury, but was intimately bound up with the optimism of a newly discovered authority.

Further reading

See also Breward's 'Fashion and the Man, From Suburb to City Street: The Cultural Geography of Masculine Consumption, 1870–1914', *New Formations*, 37 (Spring, 1999), 47–70. Other studies of men and clothing include: John Harvey, *Men in Black* (London: Reaktion, 1997); David Kuchta, *The Three-Piece Suit and Modern Masculinity: England, 1550–1850* (Berkeley, CA: University of California Press, 2002); and Brent Shannon, *The Cut of His Coat: Men, Dress and Consumer Culture in Britain, 1860–1914* (Athens, OH: Ohio University Press, 2006). The figure of the *flâneur* is best approached through Keith Tester (ed.), *The Flâneur* (London: Routledge, 1994).

Notes

1   R. Whiteing, *The Island: Or an Adventure of a Person of Quality* (London: Longman, 1888), p. 1.

2   D. Roche, *The Culture of Clothing: Dress and Fashion in the Ancien Regime* (Cambridge: Cambridge University Press, 1996), pp. 18–49.

3   L. Hapgood, 'Regaining a Focus — New Perspectives on the Novels of Richard Whiteing' in N. Le Manos and M.J. Rochelson (eds), *Transforming Genres: New Approaches to British Fiction of the 1890s* (London: Macmillan, 1994), pp. 178–84.

4   *The Tailor and Cutter*, 19 April 1888, p. 215.

5   J.S. Bratton, *Acts of Supremacy: The British Empire and the Stage 1790–1930* (Manchester: Manchester University Press, 1991), pp. 7–9.

6   A.J. Reid, *Social Classes and Social Relations in Britain 1850–1914* (London: Macmillan, 1992), pp. 60–1.

7   F. Chenoune, *A History of Men's Fashion* (Paris: Flammanion, 1993); D. DeMany, *Fashion for Men* (London: Batsford, 1985); P. Byrde, *The Male Image: Men's Fashion in Britain 1300–1970* (London: Batsford, 1979).

8   A. Miles and D. Vincent, *Building European Society: Occupational Change and Social Mobility in Europe, 1840–1940* (Manchester: Manchester University Press, 1993), p. 3.

9   P. Mason, *The English Gentleman, The Rise and Fall of an Ideal* (London: Deutsch, 1982); M. Girouard, *The Return to Camelot: Chivalry and the English Gentleman* (New Haven: Yale University Press, 1981).

10   G. Crossick and H.G. Haupt, *The Petit Bourgeoisie in Europe, 1780–1914* (London: Routledge, 1995), p. 191.

11   P.J. Cain and A.G. Hopkins, *British Imperialism: Innovation and Expansion 1688–1914* (London: Longman, 1993), p. 131; W.D. Rubinstein, *Men of Property: The Very Wealthy in Britain since the Industrial Revolution* (London: Croom Helm, 1981); W.D. Rubinstein, *Elites and the Wealthy in Modern British History* (Brighton: Harvester, 1987).

12   M. Wiener, *English Culture and the Decline of the Industrial Spirit, 1850–1980* (Harmondsworth: Penguin, 1981).

13   S. Gunn, 'The Failure of the Victorian Middle Class: A Critique' in J. Wolff and J. Seed (eds) *The Culture of Capital: Art, Power and the Nineteenth Century Middle Class* (Manchester: Manchester University Press, 1988), pp. 17–39.

14   Cain and Hopkins, *British Imperialism*, p. 116.

15   W. MacQueen Pope, *Twenty Shillings in the Pound* (London: Hutchinson & Co., 1948), p. 9.

16   F. Bechofer and B. Elliott, *The Petit Bourgeoisie: Comparative Studies of the Uneasy Stratum* (London: Macmillan, 1981), p. 182.

17   Bechofer and Elliott, p. 184.

18   T.H.S. Escott, *England: Its People, Polity, and Pursuits* (London: Chapman & Hall, 1885), p. 315.

19   Escott, p. 315.

20   Escott, pp. 332–3.

21   G. and W. Grossmith, *The Diary of a Nobody* (Harmondsworth: Penguin, 1979).

22   R. Smith, *A Londoner's Log Book 1901–1902: Reprinted from the Cornhill Magazine* (London: Smith, Elder & Co., 1902), pp. 54–8.

23   Smith, pp. 290–1.

24   J. Camplin, *The Rise of the Plutocrats: Wealth and Power in Edwardian England* (London: Constable, 1978), p. 149.

25   J. Harris, *Private Lives, Public Spirit 1870–1914* (Harmondsworth: Penguin, 1993).

26   H. Perkin, *The Rise of Professional Society: England since 1880* (London: Routledge, 1989), p. 95.

27   G. Colmore, 'Eight Hundred a Year', *Cornhill Magazine*, June 1901 quoted in E. Royston Pike, *Human Documents of the Age of the Forsytes* (London: Allen & Unwin, 1969), p. 165.

28   G.S. Layard, 'A Hundred and Fifty a Year', quoted in Pike, *Human Documents of the Age of the Forsytes*, p. 161.
29   Layard, pp. 162–3.
30   J.A. Banks, *Prosperity and Parenthood: A Study of Family Planning among the Victorian Middle Classes* (London: Routledge, Kegan & Paul, 1954), p. 48.
31   B.J. Orchard, *The Clerks of Liverpool* (Liverpool: J. Collinson, 1871), p. 63.
32   J. Carey, *The Intellectuals and the Masses: Pride and Prejudice among the Literary Intelligentsia 1880–1939* (London: Faber, 1992).
33   Crossick and Haupt, *Petit Bourgeoisie*, p. 1.
34   M. Hayes, 'Popular Fiction and Middle Brow Taste' in C. Bloom (ed.), *Literature and Culture in Modern Britain, Vol. 1. 1900–1929* (London: Longman, 1993), pp. 80–1.
35   A. St John Adcock, *In the Image of God — A Tale of Lower London* (London: Skeffington & Son, 1898), p. 125.
36   F. Willis, *101 Jubilee Road: A Book of London Yesterdays* (London: Phoenix House, 1948), p. 20.
37   Willis, p. 70. and p. 127.
38   MacQueen Pope, *Twenty Shillings*, p. 19.

PART 4

Society and class

THE EXPANSION OF SOCIAL HISTORY after the Second World War was propelled by the need to include the whole of society rather than simply the actions of monarchs and statesmen. It suited a more democratic and egalitarian age. 'History from Below' was the product of left-wing or progressive politics, developing more inclusive forms of history. Where previously it had been assumed that histories of women or the working classes could not be written because there were no sources, social historians proved that this was not the case. They found new sources but also interpreted conventional sources (such as Parliamentary Papers) in new ways. For the first time it was possible to write a history of everyday life and to give ordinary people back their history. The great theme for social historians of the nineteenth century was the rise of class-based society and the emergence of a powerful middle class that had shaped the values of Victorian Britain (although the middle class was not heavily studied in the 1960s). E.P Thompson's emphasis on the importance of experience (that we need to be true to the lived experience of people in the past, whether we sympathise with them or not) struck a powerful chord, which endowed social history with a crusading quality.

While much social history continues to be written in this vein (using historical records to reconstruct the quality of past experiences), the procedures of social history have come under attack. Arguments derived from literary studies and post-structuralism have raised questions about whether we can simply reconstruct past experiences in an unproblematic way. All we have are a series of accounts of the past (newspaper articles, census data, memoirs, etc.) but these sources do not represent the past in an objective way. They are all shaped by particular kinds of knowledge and language that determined the way contemporary life was viewed and the way people spoke about the world in which they lived. In other words, it has been argued that all we can do is reconstruct these knowledge systems that shaped Victorian realities. This involves a cultural history of the systems of representations, knowledge and language and a belief that any attempt to simply reconstruct past societies is naive. This focus on language is often called the 'linguistic turn'. We include Readings by two powerful critics of conventional social history, the historian **Patrick Joyce** and the literary critic **Mary Poovey**, to demonstrate the ways in which Victorian social history has now become a contested area.

Patrick Joyce

THE FALL OF CLASS

Democratic Subjects: The Self and the Social in Nineteenth-Century England
(Cambridge: Cambridge University Press, 1994), 1–7.

Among Victorian historians, the scholar who has done most to critique conventional forms of social history and to embrace postmodernist ideas is **Patrick Joyce**. One abiding theme of Joyce's work is that he has always been more interested in the history of consensus than that of social conflict. Joyce's early work concerned the culture of the factory in Lancashire. In *Work, Society and Politics* (1980), Joyce studied popular Toryism and the factory paternalism and deferential workers of towns such as Blackburn. Joyce subsequently went on to argue that conventional social histories in the Marxist mould had overemphasised the language of class and ignored the complex social relations of everyday life in Victorian Britain. In *Visions of the People* (1991), he began to embrace postmodernism (with its suspicion of grand theories such as Marxism) and the linguistic turn (with its proposition that language constructs reality). He argued that 'populism' and the ambiguous but resonant language of 'the people' (with its nationalistic and romantic overtones) were more important in structuring popular politics than the language of class. The following Reading comes from his subsequent book, *Democratic Subjects* (1994), where he continues the critique of class but also develops a Foucault-inspired investigation about the invention of modern notions of 'the self' and 'the social' in Victorian Britain. His approach is not dissimilar to that of **Mary Poovey**. In his more recent book, *The Rule of Freedom* (2003), Joyce has examined the ways in which Liberalism represented not so much a political and economic doctrine as a way of structuring knowledge and a way of seeing the extent to which Liberalism governed the construction of the Victorian urban environment.

Democratic Subjects is structured around case studies of the working-class poet Edwin Waugh and the great Liberal statesman John Bright. The writings of both reveal forms of identity that are more complex than a narrow focus on class would allow. Along with a third essay on 'democratic romances', Joyce's theme is the role of narrative in shaping how people see 'the self' and 'the social'. The latter are not categories that exist in nature but have to be constructed by the culture through language and through the powerful stories that people tell to make sense of their world. This explains why Victorian radicalism was shaped as much by discussions about the English constitution as by economic questions. The following extract comes from the Introduction to the book and has been chosen because it features Joyce's critique of the idea of 'class' and his advocacy of a postmodernist position which questions ideas of 'the real' (something that is a cultural construction). Joyce does not deny the existence of economic inequality but he argues that we have to take seriously the way that inequality was perceived and expressed. This frequently took the form of language and thought that was not class-based. Joyce's work is symptomatic of the shift away from class as the major theme of Victorian social history. In his emphasis on language and discourse, he is a product of the 'Age of Representations' that we identify in the Introduction.

Patrick Joyce is Professor of Modern History, Manchester University, and Visiting Professor of Sociology at the London School of Economics, 2006–9. He has published widely on the history of class, work, politics, and the city, his most recent books being *The Social in Question* (2002) and *The Rule of Freedom* (2003). He is also interested in questions of historiography, history and theory, and social theory. His current work is a book on the nature of the British state, with the working title 'The Soul of Leviathan: Making the British Technostate'. He is a research convener with The Centre for the Study of Sociocultural Change (CRESC/ESRC).

THIS HISTORY IS THE STORY of two men [*Edwin Waugh and John Bright*], and of the stories they and others told in order that it might be known who they were. It is a history of identity, about 'the self' and about 'the social', the latter in the sense of collective identities, and the contexts in which these were set. The quotation marks signal that these terms have significance in so far as their meanings are made by us, and not found by us in a world beyond this assignation of meaning. In thinking about identities in the past, whether of the 'self' or of the collective, class has, until recently, occupied a very considerable role among social historians, especially those of the nineteenth century. The sorrows of Edwin Waugh, and the measured certainties of John Bright, serve to question this dominance, as do the democratic romances that gave shape to the social and political imagination of millions of their contemporaries. Other forms of the self and of collective identity emerge, long obscured by the concentration on class. And class itself, like any other collective 'social' subject, is seen to be an imagined form, not something given in a 'real' world beyond this form.

All three accounts involve looking at subjectivities, at the subject as a self and as an imagined collectivity. The two are seen to be inextricably connected. The 'social' or collective selves, that arguably had more significance than class at the time, were represented by terms like 'the people', 'humanity', 'mankind', 'the Million', and so on, selves that went to make up the sense of what it meant to live in a democratic polity, but also in a society and a culture that were also felt to be 'democratic' (or felt *not* to be democratic). The pun in my title [*Democratic Subjects*] points therefore to these linked subjectivities, to a subject as a person and as a subject of democracy.

The social subjects I describe, and the narratives that gave them meaning, are seen to be the means by which contemporaries named, and hence lived, the 'social relations' of their day. The inclusions and exclusions these subjects and narratives enforced are understood to have often been more important than class, though in their turn these distinctions were classifications of another kind. Many of them have been hidden from view because they have been naturalised, or reified, taken in a 'common-sense' way to exist beyond our naming of them: 'man' and 'woman' are good examples, as well as 'humanity' and the others. The aim of this book is to subvert perhaps the central distinction which enacts this naturalisation of the social and its categories, that between representation and the real.

The subject of class has become a matter for disputation among historians. The opening statement of the position taken here may itself seem disputatious to some of these. I had originally called this book *The Fall of Class*, hardly a neutral title. There is a powerful sense in which class may be said to have 'fallen'. Instead of being a master category of historical explanation, it has become one term among many, sharing a rough equality with these others (which is what I meant by the 'fall' of class). The reasons for this are not hard to find. In Britain, economic decline and restructuring have led to the disintegration of the old manual sector of employment, and of what was, mistakenly, seen to be a 'traditional' working class.[1] The rise of the right from the 1970s, and the decline of the left, together with that of the trade unions, pointed in a similar direction to that of economic change, towards a loosening of the hold class and work-based categories had, not only on the academic mind, but also on a wider public. Changes going on in Britain were mirrored elsewhere, but the greatest change of all was the disintegration of world communism, and with it the retreat of intellectual Marxism.

Feminism represented another current of change, one also combining social and intellectual elements: it presented a new object of analysis, gender, and problematised our understanding of identity itself. Allied to feminism, though of enormous significance in itself, post-structuralist thought led in a similar direction: an understanding of identity as radically de-centred and unstable could hardly be without consequences for the concept of class. The term 'post-structuralism' does not do justice to the range of what has been a fundamental rethinking of Western traditions: the term 'post-modernism' has often, and somewhat confusingly, been used to describe this range. Behind this rethinking, and behind all the other transformations so far described, may be said to emerge a new condition of society itself, the condition of post-modernity. Partly in the form of the so-called 'new cultural history' these currents have coalesced for historians in what has come to be known as the 'linguistic turn'. It is within this 'turn' that I would situate my own work.

Whether class has fallen quite so far as some think is another matter: the hold of older categories is still strong in labour and social history, both in Britain and the

US, for liberal as well as for left historians. Among the former, if the accent on conflict is not so marked, then whole histories are narrativised around the collective subjects of classes: classes become the actors around which explanations of social change take place, and whole swathes of human behaviour are cast in the roles of these actors (such as 'working-class culture', or the 'pastimes of the working class').[2] This applies even when these same historians imagine they are not writing under the sign of class. In its historical origins, as will be evident in these studies, class was as much a product of the liberal, as of the Marxist, mind. One manifestation of the latter, in the form of the influence of E.P. Thompson, is still immense (and beyond historians too, a recent sociology textbook on 'current debates' on class seeing fit to cite Thompson as the only historical work worthy of note).[3] So, there are still arguments to be had, though as will become apparent class is more the occasion than the cause of such arguments.

By way of providing, first of all, a theoretical and historiographical context for the three studies that follow, and then a historical context, I will identify the position from which this book is written by means of a couple of quotations, the first from E.P. Thompson. Thompson's famous words from the opening of *The Making of the English Working Class* go as follows,

> And class happens when some men, as a result of common experiences (inherited or shared), feel and articulate the identity of their interests as between themselves, and as against other men whose interests are different from (and usually opposed to) theirs. The class experience is largely determined by the productive relations into which men are born — or enter voluntarily. Class consciousness is the way in which these experiences are handled in cultural terms: embodied in traditions, value systems, ideas and institutional forms. If the experience appears as determined, class consciousness does not.[4]

The familiar formula is apparent, one that has charmed a generation. Productive relations, themselves beyond discourse, are primary, despite the qualification. These then give rise to an 'experience' which itself seemingly floats free of 'culture'. 'Experience' is then acted upon by values, traditions, and so on. Despite the emphasis on culture it quite clearly comes at the end of things, not the beginning. What vast assumptions are made about people and knowledge in this contraption of causes and stages! Once this machine is set in motion it turns out a 'class consciousness' which then becomes both a class made and a class self-making as it progresses through history. Class has become the — unacknowledged — leading player around which the drama of history is then written.

A different understanding is possible when we begin to put 'culture' at the beginning of our thinking, not at the end, when we become aware that 'experience' and 'productive relations' cannot be understood outside discourse and the 'imaginary' to which it gives rise. This is Cornelius Castoriadis writing about the 'imaginary institution of society',[5]

> Those who speak of 'imaginary', understanding by this the 'specular', the reflection of the 'fictive', do no more than repeat, usually without realising it, the affirmation that has for all time chained them to the

underground of the famous cave: it is necessary that this world be an image *of* something. The imaginary of which I am speaking is not an image *of*. It is the unceasing and essentially *undetermined* (social, historical and physical) creation of figures/forms/images, on the basis of which alone there can ever be a question *of* 'something'. What we call 'reality' and 'rationality' are its works.

In this book I am concerned with an imaginary that is not the image *of* something else, but without which there cannot be something else. In the understanding of Castoriadis, and of myself, society and 'the social' are the outcome of this 'imaginary'.

I frequently employ the terms 'social imaginary' and 'democratic imaginary' in what follows. By using the former I point to the countless, and relatively uncharted forms in which 'society' has been understood. As well as the forms of its understanding I also include the ways in which these forms are produced. 'Society' is therefore itself an historical construct, one we might best approach through an etymology of the term.[6] The idea that 'society' comprised a *system*, was one particular manifestation of this much larger history of 'society', a manifestation taking clearer form in the eighteenth century. It was, however, a manifestation the people I write about in this book were not usually in tune with, though it has since grown to be a major part of our thinking.

I employ the term 'democratic imaginary' as one manifestation of this protean social imaginary, in the Victorian period a new and overwhelmingly important one. I might more correctly have used the term 'demotic imaginary', for, in order that a democracy could be imagined at all (and hence realised in practice), it was first necessary that a subject, and hence a cause and justification of this democracy, be imagined in the shape of demos. So that a democratic polity might be thought about, demos had first to be born, and in these studies it is the shapes of demos that are traced ('the people', 'mankind', and so on). They were indispensable to the feeling of living in a democratic culture and society, as well as a polity; the stability of the polity itself resting on these broader foundations of what was felt to be democratic. None the less, I have stuck with the term 'democratic imaginary' because so much of my attention is given to politics, and because I want to indicate how these different aspects were always in practice linked together (a 'demotic' reading 'public' say, with a democratic polity). These demotic identities, often formed outside and prior to politics, as it were, I consider to circulate within the 'political unconscious', a term I use in the study of narratives below. My use of this term is metaphoric not analytic, designed as it is not to denote an unconscious, but to signpost the significance of the proto-political, imagined forms of power and the social order which were articulated by formal politics.

In thinking about the shapes of demos I am interested in the 'soft, sticky, lumpenanalytical' notions Baudrillard describes:[7]

> The term 'mass' is not a concept. It is a leitmotif of political demagogy, a soft, sticky lumpenanalytical notion. A good sociology would attempt to surpass it with 'more subtle' categories: socio-professional ones, categories of class, cultural status etc. Wrong: it is by prowling around these soft and acritical notions . . . that one can go further than intelligent critical sociology.

I, too, want to prowl around these soft and acritical notions, this time those of demos in the nineteenth century.

When we look closer, as Baudrillard also says, the seeming hardness of 'more subtle' categories dissolves (categories like 'class', 'status'). It is necessary to pursue something of this history of the softness and hardness of concepts. The notion that some knowledge is 'hard' is inseparable from the idea that there is somewhere a basis or origin for it which sanctions this hardness, this certitude. Such modes of thought have been called 'essentialist' or 'foundationalist'. It is the immensely liberating, but immensely troubling, message of post-modernist thought that this is not so, that there is no 'centre' which will serve as a fixed point for knowledge and action. This is the burden of post-structuralism also of course, but I prefer the broader term, which speaks about the dissolution of centres in a post-modern condition of society as well as a post-modern condition of knowledge.[8]

This 'essentialist' mode of thinking, this idea that there is a 'bottom line' which serves as an epistemological foundation, has been attacked from many quarters, and not least by historians. Here the work of feminist historians has been inspirational, drawing heavily as it has upon post-structuralism. There is no more important figure than Joan W. Scott. Most recently the foundation she has challenged has been 'experience', a category central to earlier thinking about the social order, especially, as we have seen, that of E.P. Thompson.[9] Scott's one-time collaborator, Denise Riley, has been equally innovative in releasing us from the naturalised, 'essentialised' categories of 'man' and 'woman'.[10] A now enormous history of medicine and the body has similarly shaken the idea that the body itself is a foundation for knowledge and truth.[11] In historicising 'science' this new history has also undermined what was once a pillar of 'the real'. The category of 'the social' is similarly shaken, as will already be apparent, not least the idea of class itself, which has been a founding concept for 'social history' in Britain and the US. A history of class has emerged which has questioned the earlier ontological certitudes surrounding the concept,[12] and as a consequence of this a new questioning of social history has begun to emerge.[13]

Most of the forms of this philosophical foundationalism are related to ideas about 'the real'. The 'real' is the hard, the imaginary the soft. Concepts and procedures gain hardness, and hence credence, as they approach it. 'The real' is the ultimate guarantee that there is a centre or foundation to knowledge. 'Representation' rests upon its firm foundations, reflecting it in the secondary domain of the imaginary. It is the aim of these studies to question these distinctions, distinctions that are as firmly entrenched in history as elsewhere, perhaps more entrenched, as history has been particularly impervious to the intellectual ferment of the last quarter of a century, at least in Britain. The impact of what has come to be called 'post-modernism' has been registered as an attack on history itself, 'history' here becoming privileged as the beleaguered guardian of the real.

Further reading

For responses to *Democratic Subjects*, see Anne Humphreys, James Epstein and Patrick Joyce, 'Roundtable on Patrick Joyce's *Democratic Subjects*', *Journal of Victorian Culture*, 1 (1996), 318–39. For further critiques of traditional social history, Joyce's other works should be consulted, especially: *Visions of the People:*

Industrial England and the Question of Class, 1840–1914 (Cambridge: Cambridge University Press, 1991); and *The Rule of Freedom: Liberalism and the Modern City* (London: Verso, 2003). Comparable work in a postmodernist vein has been undertaken by Joyce's former student, James Vernon. See his *Politics and the People: A Study in English Political Culture, c.1815–1867* (Cambridge: Cambridge University Press, 1993).

Notes

1   On another level, a new gradualist reading of the 'Industrial Revolution' in Britain has removed a good deal of the ground from under the feet of the class idea. For an account see Patrick Joyce, 'Work', in F.M.L. Thompson (ed.), *The Cambridge Social History of Britain 1750–1950*, (Cambridge 1990), 3 vols, II.

2   For a typical example, see F.M.L. Thompson, *The Rise of Respectable Society: A Social History of Victorian Britain, 1830–1900* (1988).

3   Rosemary Crompton, *Class and Stratification: An Introduction to Current Debates* (Cambridge 1993).

4   E.P. Thompson, *The Making of the English Working Class* (1968), pp. 9–10. This is not at variance with Thompson's later formulation, E.P. Thompson, 'Eighteenth-Century English Society: Class Struggle Without Class?', *Social History*, 3:2 (May 1978), esp. 146–50.

5   Cornelius Castoriadis, *The Imaginary Institution of the Social* (1975; translated by Kathleen Blaney, 1987), p. 3. See also 'The Imaginary: Creation in the Social Historical Domain', in L. Appignanesi (ed.), *The Real Me: Post-Modernism and the Question of Identity*, (1987).

6   Raymond Williams, 'Society', in *Keywords: a Vocabulary of Culture and Society* (1976).

7   Jean Baudrillard, *In the Shadow of the Silent Majorities, or, The End of the Social and Other Essays* (New York 1983), p. 3.

8   Zygmunt Bauman has been a crucially important figure in the field of sociology, looking at once for a sociology of the post-modern condition and a post-modern sociology, Zygmunt Bauman, *Intimations of Postmodernity* (1992), chaps. 4, 9.

9   Joan W.Scott, 'The evidence of "experience"', *Critical Inquiry* 17 (Summer 1991).

10   Denise Riley, *'Am I That Name': Feminism and the Category of 'Women' in History* (1988).

11   On the body and foundationalist thinking see the remarks of Judith Butler, 'Contingent Foundations: Feminism and the Question of "Postmodernism"', in Judith Butler and Joan W. Scott (eds), *Feminists Theorise the Political* (1992).

12   See for example Gareth Stedman Jones, *Languages of Class: Studies in English Working-Class History 1832–1982* (Cambridge 1983); Joan W. Scott, *Gender and the Politics of History* (1988); Patrick Joyce, *Visions of the People: Industrial England and the Question of Class, 1840–1914* (Cambridge 1991). See also Patrick Joyce, *Class: A Reader* (Oxford, 1995).

13   David Mayfield and Susan Thorne, 'Social History and its Discontents: Gareth Stedman Jones and the Politics of Language', *Social History*, 17:2 (May 1992); Jon Lawrence and Miles Taylor, 'The Poverty of Protest: Gareth Stedman Jones and the Politics of Language — a Reply', *Social History*, 18:1 (January 1993); Patrick Joyce, 'The Imaginary Discontents of Social History: a Note of Response . . . ', ibid.; D. Mayfield and S. Thorne, 'Reply', *Social History*, 18:2 (May 1993); James Vernon, 'Who's Afraid of the Linguistic Turn? The Politics of Social History and its Discontents', *Social History* 19:1 (January 1994).

Mary Poovey

REPRESENTING THE
MANCHESTER IRISH

Making a Social Body: British Cultural Formation, 1830–1864 (Chicago, IL: University of Chicago Press, 1995), 55–6, 63–72.

Some of the most innovative social history today is being written by scholars in Literature departments who have promoted interdisciplinarity by using their skills in textual analysis to decode the narratives, assumptions and forms of knowledge that are employed in the recording of social information. The best example of this approach would be **Mary Poovey**. She became well known for her book, *Uneven Developments* (1988), which examined the 'ideological work' of gender, not only in a number of literary texts such as *David Copperfield* but also in sensational court cases such as that of Caroline Norton for custody of her children. Poovey epitomises the modern notion that the whole world is a text that requires decoding, a position that has affinities with traditional social history but differs in its suspicion of a purely materialist analysis.

The following Reading comes from Poovey's pioneering book, *Making a Social Body* (1995), where she interrogates the ways in which the idea of 'the social' emerged. She does not see this as unproblematic in the way that earlier social historians would have done; instead, she views it as a distinctive form of knowledge that emerged in the early nineteenth century. After this book, Poovey followed through the logic of her enquiry by going on to look at the means by which the science of statistics emerged as a way of knowing and governing society (the influence of Foucault is evident in her work). This was part of her study of the idea of the 'fact'. She has since examined another allegedly non-literary topic, the role of finance and money in Victorian Britain, which produced a particular kind of knowledge that shaped the social.

In this Reading, Poovey takes the treatment of the Irish in Manchester in 1842 and tries to reconstruct, not their social experience, but the ways in which they were represented by the doctor, and educational and social reformer, James Kay (later Kay-Shuttleworth, 1804–77), in his influential pamphlet on working-class conditions. Poovey describes how state formation in the nineteenth century was shaped by the construction of an idea of the 'social body' in which national identity and race played a part. The Irish in Manchester were imagined by Kay as 'the other'. Cholera in particular was integral to the building of the British state as repeated outbreaks spurred the formation of a public health movement to demand sanitary reform. Poovey's deep reading of Kay's pamphlet on the Manchester working class allows her to probe the mentality of early Victorian social reform. In the first part of the chapter from which this excerpt is taken, but not included here, Poovey examines Kay's autobiography (composed in 1877) and notes the emphasis he places on three things he sees as key to understanding the plight of the Manchester labouring class. First, there was 'the chronic social and moral woes that afflicted the laboring population — their lack of education, their poverty, and their lax morality'. Poovey shows how these relate to Malthusian ideas about the failure of the working class to practice sexual self-control. Second, there was political turmoil, especially the conflict over Catholic Emancipation in 1829 and Parliamentary Reform before 1832. Finally, there was the importance of Asiatic cholera's continuing presence from 1832 onwards. From this Poovey moves to Kay's transference of these problems to the Irish population to explore the way discourses on race might be utilised to drive forward Kay's plan of social reform.

Mary Poovey is Samuel Rudin University Professor of the Humanities and founding Director of the Institute for the History of the Production of Knowledge at New York University. She is the author of four books on eighteenth- and nineteenth-century British literature and culture, including the award-winning *A History of the Modern Fact* (1998). She is currently completing a volume on the relationship between literature, economics, and money.

––––––––––––

The consolidation of a national identity or national character is necessarily a protracted and uneven process, just as its maintenance is always precarious and imperfect. These generalizations rest upon two assumptions, which constitute the theoretical bedrock of my argument in this essay. My first assumption is that national identity — like nationalism, the movement by which such identity is politicized — only becomes available as a salient cultural concept at certain historical conjunctures. Such historical moments are sometimes marked by explicit conflict with another country or by enhanced imperial ambitions, and they are generally characterized by a widespread perception that not everyone who lives in the country embodies its national virtues. My second assumption is that such differentiation within the nation is repeated within individuals or groups that seem united by a single interest. That is, the process by which individuals or groups embrace the concept of the nation as the most meaningful context for self-definition necessarily involves temporarily marginalizing other categories that could also provide a sense of identity. Because other categories and interests persist even in periods of nationalistic fervor, however, and because they often compete with or even contradict national values, national identity is always a precarious formulation for every individual who shares the nationalist sentiment as well as for the nation as a whole.[1]

The process by which a national identity is consolidated and maintained is therefore one of differentiation and displacement — the differentiation of the national *us* from aliens within and without, and the displacement of other interests from consciousness. Because the consolidation of any national identity occurs over time and therefore in the midst of changing historical circumstances, moreover, this process may also involve alternative inclusions and exclusions of the *same* group from the idea of the nation. Such alternations are partly signs of the persistent competition of categories and interests to which I have just alluded. Partly, they reflect the fact that the consolidation of national identity does not always take center stage in a national or individual agenda. That is, sometimes the idea of a national identity is deployed to support another political or social campaign; sometimes an apparently unrelated political or social cause may also contribute to the formation of national values.

In this essay I offer a detailed analysis of this dynamic as James Phillips Kay described it in his 1832 pamphlet, *The Moral and Physical Condition of the Working Classes in . . . Manchester*. (Page references to this work are cited parenthetically in the text.) My justification for such radical selectivity is that Kay's text materially influenced how what Carlyle was to call the "condition of England" was conceptualized by Whig ministers and their publicists in the 1830s and 1840s. My rationale for the method of this essay — close textual and historical analysis — is two-fold. First, I suggest that the narrative logic of this text — its contradictions and ostentatious omissions as well as its explicit argument — exposes the cultural logic by which certain attitudes and habits that we associate with the middle class were successfully elevated over other concerns as *the* characteristic values of the English. Second, I suggest that the complex conjuncture of issues in Kay's text provides an example of how thoroughly imbued with its immediate historical context is every text or event that is retrospectively assimilated to nationalism. Detailed analyses of symptomatic texts and events should remind us that the consolidation of nationalism and the construction of national identities are marked at every moment by competing currents whose energy derives from — and might return to — interests only incidentally related to the nation or national issues. [. . .]

Kay's analysis of the destructive role that "abnormal" domestic relations play in vitiating the health of the social body was to influence not only fellow bureaucrats like Edwin Chadwick and Hector Gavin but also aristocratic M.P.s like Viscount Ashley, Seventh Earl of Shaftesbury, who spent much of his rhetorical capital supporting factory legislation by melodramatizing the plight of unmothered infants.[2] Whereas similar analyses of the condition of England written only a few years later tended to emphasize the class-specific nature of domestic impropriety, Kay reads domestic disorder not primarily in the context of class (which could exacerbate social conflict) but in relation to his foundational metaphor (which emphasized harmony or health). Like other maladies of the social body, that is, domestic disorder could be cured if noxious elements, of "accidental and remote origin," were removed from working-class neighborhoods. Kay's brief history of England's cotton industry makes it perfectly clear that although injudicious legislation now retards his country's recovery, the ills that afflict England originated in another country — Ireland.

> The rapid growth of the cotton manufacture has attracted hither operatives from every part of the kingdom, and Ireland has poured forth the most destitute of her hordes to supply the constantly increasing demand for labour. This immigration has been, in one important respect, a serious evil. The Irish have taught the labouring classes of this country a pernicious lesson. The system of cottier farming, the demoralization and barbarism of the people, and the general use of the potato as the chief article of food, have encouraged the population in Ireland more rapidly than the *available* means of subsistence have been increased. Debased alike by ignorance and pauperism, they have discovered, with the savage, what is the minimum of the means of life, upon which existence may be prolonged. The paucity of the amount of means and comforts *necessary for the mere support of life*, is not known by a more civilized population, and this secret has been taught the labourers of this country by the Irish. As competition and the restrictions and burdens of trade diminished the profits of capital, and consequently reduced the price of labour, the contagious example of ignorance and a barbarous disregard of forethought and economy, exhibited by the Irish, spread. The colonization of savage tribes has ever been attended with effects on civilizations as fatal as those which have marked the progress of the sand flood over the fertile plains of Egypt. Instructed in the fatal secret of subsisting on what is barely necessary to life — yielding partly to necessity, and partly to example, — the labouring classes have ceased to entertain a laudable pride in furnishing their houses, and in multiplying the decent comforts which minister to happiness. What is superfluous to the mere exigencies of nature, is too often expended at the tavern, and for the provision of old age and infirmity, they too frequently trust either to charity, to the support of their children, or to the protection of the poor laws.
>
> (pp. 20–22)

The domestic theme in this passage is both manifest and latent. If one explicit effect of the Irish invasion has been the loss of English "pride in furnishing their houses," then this failure of English pride has implicitly been caused by the increase in the Irish population, which drives the Irish to subsist on the potato and to cultivate other "barbarous" habits. The sexual profligacy behind this population explosion is elided in Kay's description, although the awkward syntax of his allusion to it suggests what is missing ("The system of cottier farming, the demoralization and barbarism of the people, and the general use of the potato as the chief article of food, have encouraged the population in Ireland [to reproduce] more rapidly than the *available* means of subsistence have been increased"). Because of this Irish profligacy, Kay suggests, the English working classes now fail to multiply the decent comforts of domesticity and threaten instead to multiply indecently, like the Irish — to bear more children than they, or the nation as a whole, can feed.

As this passage makes clear, Kay's image of a healthy social body cannot accommodate the Irish, because — especially in their domestic habits — they are not human. In his climactic description of the Irish, Kay explicitly presents them as a cross between matter and beast: the Irish are a "mass of animal organization" whose "savage habits" counteract any short-term gain they might bring to the unwitting employer.

> The introduction of an uncivilized race does not tend even primarily to increase the power of producing wealth, in a ratio by any means commensurate with the cheapness of its labour, and may ultimately retard the increase of the fund for the maintenance of that labour. Such a race is useful only as a mass of animal organization, which consumes the smallest amount of wages. The low price of the labour of such people depends, however, on the paucity of their wants, and their savage habits. When they assist the production of wealth, therefore, their barbarous habits and consequent moral depression must form a part of the equation. They are only necessary to a state of commerce *inconsistent* with such a reward for labour as is calculated to maintain the standard of civilization. A few years pass, and they become burdens to a community whose morals and physical power they have depressed; and dissipate wealth which they did not accumulate.
>
> (pp. 82–83)

Throughout his pamphlet, Kay associates every English problem with the Irish. The poverty and ignorance from which the English workers suffer, for example, is typified by the condition of Irish houses (pp. 32, 34–35, 38). He depicts the poor laws, which "pauperize" the English poor and oppress the respectable classes, as disproportionately devoted to relieving Irish immigrants (pp. 53, 55, 56), and this is true partly because the Irish, more than any other group, have suffered from the introduction of machinery, especially the power loom (p. 44). Taverns, which Kay connects explicitly to intemperance and crime, he implicitly associates with the Irish (p. 22). Kay does not specify the Irish when he laments the working class's lack of religion, but Catholicism, which was practiced by most Irish immigrants after 1810, was thought by many of the English to be worse than no religion at all, Finally, Kay depicts the strikes and trade unionism that he holds responsible for so much of the English problem as exacerbated by the Irish — both because, according to Kay, English strikes necessitated the importation of these workers (p. 110) and because, once in England, Irish workers have driven wages down, thereby increasing English workers' discontent (p. 80).

Kay's denigration of the Irish obviously draws upon a long tradition of English prejudice against them, which by the 1830s could target both the "racial" difference between the two peoples[3] and their religious differences.[4] Such prejudices were not always articulated in the same terms, however, nor were they always more prominent than the concern for national well-being. In Kay's treatment of the Irish, we see a particularly complex example of the way that a proponent of one set of issues — in this case, social reform at the national level — mobilized prejudices against a particular group of people by constructing an image of the nation that excluded this group. The complexities in Kay's treatment arise from the fact that, even though the Irish could be so vilified in 1832 because they did occupy slum dwellings in Manchester, they were also necessary to the prosperity and security of England. Indeed, by 1832, the Irish were the beneficiaries of three decades of legislation that had explicitly included them in the kingdom of Great Britain. For James Kay, then, the Irish were available *both* as a scapegoat for national woes and as a resource to be exploited when needed. To trace the intricacies of Kay's representation, we must review briefly some aspects of the turbulent relationship between England and Ireland.

What most of the English in the early nineteenth century saw as the self-evident racial differences between the Anglo-Saxons and the Celts seemed to coincide with and be reinforced by the difference between the Protestant and Catholic religions. The latter was mapped onto national identity when England broke from Rome in the sixteenth century; it was reinscribed in the early eighteenth century when England levied the repressive penal codes against Irish Catholics as punishment for the 1641 Ulster uprising, the Catholic rebellion against Protestant incursions during the first decades of the century. Paradoxically, however, the penal codes, which, among other restrictions, denied Catholics the right to own land, served to drive Irish Catholics into trade and therefore eventually into increased prosperity. By the late eighteenth century, Irish Catholics as a whole constituted a creditor class, in stark contrast to the debtor class of Irish Protestants. Meanwhile, the relationship between the two countries, which had been one of colonial occupation, had also become more complex. By the late 1770s, it had become clear to many English legislators that it was more important to forestall an Irish move toward independence and to consolidate Great Britain by securing its Celtic fringes than to enforce the penal code. As the conflict between England and France persisted, then, restrictions against the Catholics' right to own property were eased. In 1793, Irish Catholic forty-shilling freeholders were enfranchised in a further move to keep Ireland part of Great Britain and to counteract Ireland's susceptibility to France. In 1800, Ireland was drawn even closer to England by the Act of Union, which established the United Kingdom of Great Britain and Ireland. The Act of Union was passed for security reasons on both sides: international security was at stake for England; domestic security was the concern of the Protestant Anglo-Irish Ascendancy, which, while politically dominant, constituted a distinct and embattled minority within Ireland. By this time, of course, the identity of England had been further complicated by the 1707 amalgamation of Scotland. Within the resulting Great Britain, differences of "race," religion, diet, habit, and even time (before the railways managed to standardize Greenwich mean time in the 1840s) continued to render the representation of the nation problematic and highly various, depending on where one lived, one's party alliance, and the importance of local concerns in relation to national interests.[5]

If the 1801 Union promised to solve the problem of Ireland, however, it actually exacerbated both the religious and political differences that still divided the two parts of the kingdom. Because Irish representatives constituted an unassimilated minority in Parliament, their very presence and political isolation there kept the issue of Catholic emancipation alive. By the 1820s, in the midst of widespread agrarian violence, the issue of emancipation had become so pressing that the Duke of Wellington capitulated to the cause. Without emancipation, Wellington argued, Ireland was rushing headlong toward civil war. Equally frightening, of course, were the possibilities that, without some remedy for the uneasy alliance of Ireland and England, either Ireland would secede from the Union or else the British people would urge more sweeping parliamentary reforms.[6] Wellington and Peel therefore supported the Catholic Emancipation Act of 1829 — with its freehold wing that raised the Catholic voting qualification from forty shillings to ten pounds.[7] Their support split the Tory party and, to compound the paradox, helped pave the way for the very parliamentary reforms Wellington and Peel sought to foreclose.

The complex series of concessions and alliances that culminated in Catholic Emancipation in 1829 and the qualified triumph of the Whigs in 1830 constitute the backdrop to Kay's pamphlet. Equally important, however, is the extent to which his pamphlet repeats — and therefore exposes — the tensions that characterized these events. Just as various groups of English legislators with their own (often party) interests in mind had alternately invoked the innate differences between the Irish and the English to authorize keeping the Catholics subordinate (the official Tory position) and emphasized the two peoples' commonalities to advocate legislative programs of social reform (the Whig position), so Kay alternately insists that the Irish are unlike the English *and* suggests that the two populations have become alike, because of the "contagious example" of the Irish. This textual alternation does not simply reflect the contentious context of party politics, however, with Kay taking first one position, then the other. Instead, Kay's representation constitutes an attempt to advance the basic program of the Whigs without allowing it to be taken — as popular agitation and some Whig radicals were trying to do — to its logical extreme. As part of his effacement of any specifically *political* formulation of a cure, that is, Kay's contradictory representation of the relation between the English and the Irish functions to advance social reform while keeping parliamentary representation out of working-class hands.

Kay's insistence that the Irish are different from the English is explicit and adamant. The Irish are not only "debased," according to Kay; they are "savage." As such, they cannot be reformed, but must be sent back to Ireland, where Kay is apparently unconcerned about their fate. Indeed, in contrast to his multifaceted program for curing English maladies, his only suggestion for alleviating Irish distress is to levy "an impost on the rental of Ireland" — a suggestion that obscures what was, in many ways, *the* problem of Ireland, the problem of the land.[8]

Kay's blurring of the distinctions between the two populations is less explicit but no less pervasive. Partly, the difference between the two groups dissolves through the metaphor with which he repeatedly characterizes their relationship. If the Irish constitute a "contagious example," after all, the differences between the original carrier of the disease and its victims soon disappear. More striking, perhaps is the way that Kay's discursive treatments of the Irish so often simply evolve, without transition, into descriptions of English workers. So, for example, Kay's primary diagnosis of the Irish problem, which begins on page 21, blends into his discussions of the domestic chaos generated by women working and the demoralizing effects of long hours, poor diet, and domestic overcrowding. These last problems are clearly shared by English and Irish workers, and Kay's use of generic nouns and pronouns conflates the two groups into a single "population." Only when this section culminates six pages later does the difference between the two groups surface again.

If English politicians' anxieties about party and revolution led even some Tory stalwarts like Wellington to shift positions on Catholic emancipation in 1829, then

Kay's repetition of this alternation addresses the political results *of* emancipation. That is, prior to the Emancipation Act, the identity of the English could be more securely tied to the differences that the Tories represented as paramount: the innate differences between a tolerant Protestant Anglo-Saxon Establishment and a tyrannical Catholic Celtic fringe. Never mind that these oppositions were already blurred by the existence of the Anglo-Irish Ascendancy and by a small Catholic minority in England, or that both radicals and Foxite Whigs were beginning to say that the English government could be a tyrant too. Before 1829, the Tory position seemed less like a party position than simple common sense, and distrust of the Catholic French fueled widespread suspicion that all Catholics were enemies. With Emancipation, however, the traditional bases of the English identity clearly demanded reformulation. After 1829, the decisive diacritical mark that separated "us" from "them" was no longer race or religion, nor could "us" mean simply the English. Instead, with the appending of the freehold wing to the Emancipation Act, the diacritical mark of Britishness (not Englishness) became a certain level of property ownership. If a man met the £10 qualification, even if he was a Catholic, he belonged to the kingdom of Great Britain in a way that he did not if he failed to meet it.

The foundation for reformulating British identity had already been laid by the time cholera invaded Manchester in June of 1832. Kay's insistence that because the Irish epitomize and cause the English problem, they should be sent home, to their own country, is clearly one response to this situation; Kay's program is to reinforce the health of the English workers and the autonomy of the English nation by getting rid of foreign agents. When he also blurs the boundary between the Irish and the English, however, Kay simultaneously acknowledges that a new mark of difference has been instigated by Emancipation and suggests that it must be reinforced if it is to work as effectively as the old. That is, only if English workers are in some way *like* the Irish workers is it clear why the former (who are, by nature, human) should be denied political representation when all of the latter (who are, by nature, animals) are not.

In order to ground property ownership in some legitimating discourse, so that it can seem as unobjectionable a basis for British identity as religion and race had seemed for Englishness, Kay links certain *attitudes* toward property with certain domestic behaviors, which he has already linked to the Irish. By implication, of course, this grounds British respectability not in class but in "nature" — the natural morality of sexual self-control, cleanliness, forethought, and health — all of which are implicitly the domain of women. Kay, however, is less interested in assigning women the responsibility for upholding this ideal than in arguing that the "contagious example" of the Irish has infected English workers with domestic (especially reproductive) improvidence. In his climactic description of a Malthusian degeneration of the race of workers, Kay elides the difference between the English and the Irish once more.

> Want of cleanliness, of forethought, and economy, are found in almost invariable alliance with dissipation, reckless habits, and disease. The population gradually becomes physically less efficient as the producers of wealth — morally so from idleness — politically *worthless* as having few desires to satisfy, and *noxious* as dissipators of capital accumulated. Were such manners to prevail, the horrors of pauperism would

accumulate. A debilitated race would be rapidly multiplied. Morality would afford no check to the increase of the population: crime and disease would be its only obstacles — the licentiousness which indulges its capricious appetite, till it exhausts its power — and the disease which, at the same moment, punishes crime, and sweeps away a hecatomb of its victims. A dense mass, impotent alike of great moral or physical efforts, would accumulate. . . . They would drag on an unhappy existence, vibrating between the pangs of hunger and the delirium of dissipation. . . . Destitution would now prey on their strength, and then the short madness of debauchery would consummate its ruin.

(pp. 81–82)

Because the entire working population exhibits a "want of cleanliness, of forethought, and economy," English workers are more like Irish workers than they are like their English betters, who are immune to the "contagious example" the Irish present because they do embody these virtues.

Such passages function not just to secure the likeness among all workers, but also to consolidate that group to which they are opposed — the class of (male) British property owners, which is characterized not by birth or by the kind of property they own but by their *attitude toward* property and the domestic sphere. In arguing that the working class is "politically *worthless*" because their domestic improvidence leaves them responsive to "emissaries of every faction," Kay is also arguing, by extension, that those who incarnate domestic virtues are politically *valuable* because their material and psychological investment in property makes them impervious to bad influence. Kay does not make this specifically *political* argument in his pamphlet because he wants to efface all traces of the political case being made in 1831 and 1832; he wants to do this because only the most radical Whigs were willing to advocate dramatically extending the franchise.[9] Despite Kay's silence on this issue, however, the economic argument that he makes implies this political component, just as his allusions to the economically motivated Peterloo and Swing riots also refer to the reform riots of 1831. Instead of emphasizing a political solution, however, Kay focuses on removing the other accidental interference to English well being — the Corn Laws.

Repealing the Corn Laws, Kay promises his readers, will bring England both economic and moral reform. "Unrestricted commerce," Kay explains, " . . . would rapidly promote the advance of civilization, by cultivating the physical and mental power of individuals and nations to multiply the amount of natural products, and to create those artificial staple commodities, by the barter of which they acquire the riches of other regions" (pp. 85–86). This economic improvement will foster individual improvement because it will increase the time available for education: "Were an unlimited exchange permitted to commerce, the hours of labour might be reduced, and more afforded for the education and religious and moral instruction of the people" (p. 88). Free trade will also purge England of the Irish, for once English workers work without costly trade unions, English manufacturing will no longer require cheap Irish labor.

In 1832, it could hardly have seemed plausible that the Corn Laws, which explicitly protected (upper-class) land owners, not (middle-class) manufacturers, would be repealed unless parliamentary reform gave political representation to at least some segments of the middle classes.[10] When the visitation of cholera interrupted Kay's work on behalf of this reform, then, his attention turned to disease in the context of politics — or, phrased differently, to the kind of political reform that would facilitate the economic power of manufacturers *in the context* of a program of social reform that was acceptable to the newly ascendant Whigs.[11] Cholera proved the perfect vehicle for Kay's position because it enabled him to harness one kind of "remote and accidental" affliction (the Corn Laws) to another (the Irish) and to propose the removal of both as a cure for all of England's ills, including cholera. What Kay's formulation reveals but does not acknowledge is that in each case the metaphor derived from cholera also provides an interpretation of the way the emergent social domain should be understood. That is, just as the invasion of cholera has enabled Kay to formulate the economic problems of the poor *in bodily and then domestic terms*, so using the metaphor of a foreign disease to describe Irish immigration constitutes as "other" a group once assumed to be essential to both British security and prosperity. Just as the Union was critical in consolidating Britain's immunity to France, in other words so the existence of Irish labor, investment capital, and uncompetitive markets had been critical to the consolidation of Britain's international superiority. Only because Ireland was also part of Great Britain was English manufacturing now strong enough to profit from free trade.[12]

The cure Kay suggests for the maladies of society therefore reinscribes the contradiction that pervaded England's relationship to Ireland throughout these decades. Just as he alternately insists upon and obscures the characteristics that distinguish the Irish from the English, so too does Kay implicitly argue for both the divorce of the two nations and a continuation of their unhappy marriage. On the one hand, Ireland must remain another country; otherwise, the chronic poverty that continued to cripple Ireland would necessitate much larger expenditures of British poor relief and increase the national debt. On the other hand, however, like a good wife or sister, Ireland must remain sufficiently accessible to the needs of English manufacturers to provide cheap labor when world demand is high, and non-competitive markets when world demand falls.

Kay's argument that England was a nation sufficiently consolidated to engage in and profit from free trade depended on constituting the Irish economy as neither autonomous nor free and as simultaneously separable from and dependent on the English economy.[13] Emphasizing cholera is part of this argument, because cholera, as Kay described it, was an ill that conflated physical disease with moral failings epitomized by domestic improvidence; as such, cholera, like immorality, could be cured. That Kay's solution implied but did not explicitly include political reform helped restrict the terms in which the maladies of society — and the social domain more generally — were formulated, and at the same time made this reform the necessary basis of Great Britain's health. If the Catholic Emancipation Act had jeopardized the traditional foundation of English identity, Kay's cure promised to give the nation a new foundation not simply, as disgruntled Tories imagined, by marshalling a majority of newly enfranchised Protestants against Irish Catholics, but by equating national well-being with the economic health of a newly politicized, respectable middle class. This physic, which was liberally administered in England during the next two decades, did at least temporarily enshrine domestic virtues as distinctively English at the same time that it authorized the government apparatus epitomized by the New Poor Law and the Board of Health. In Ireland of course,

Kay's cure proved bitter medicine indeed. Appropriately, perhaps, its legacy was not an embrace of English respectability but the growth of an increasingly militant Irish nationalism.

Further reading

For responses to Poovey, see Ian Burney, Regenia Gagnier, Joseph Melling and Mary Poovey, 'Roundtable on *Making a Social Body*', *Journal of Victorian Culture*, 4 (1999), 104–39. Readers should also consult Poovey's subsequent book, *A History of the Modern Fact: Problems of Knowledge in the Sciences of Wealth and Society* (Chicago, IL: University of Chicago Press, 1998). Some comparable themes to Poovey's are discussed in Robert Gray, *The Factory Question and Industrial England, 1830–1860* (Cambridge: Cambridge University Press, 1996) and Pamela Gilbert, *Mapping the Victorian Social Body* (Albany, NY: State University of New York Press, 2004).

Notes

1   Catherine Hall also notes that nationalism is always crosscut and undercut by axes of gender, racial, and political identities. See "Missionary Stories: Gender and Ethnicity in England in the 1830s and 1840s," *White, Male and Middle Class: Explorations in Feminism and History* (Cambridge: Polity Press, 1992), pp. 205–54.

2   For a discussion of Chadwick's assumptions about domesticity, see Mary Poovey, "Domesticity and Class Formation: Chadwick's 1842 *Sanitary Report*," in her *Making a Social Body* ch. 6. The relevant text by Hector Gavin is his *Sanitary Ramblings . . .* (1848; facsimile ed., London: Frank Cass, 1971). For typical speeches by Shaftesbury, see *Hansard's Parliamentary Debates*, 3d ser. vol. 73: March 15, 1844, c.1073–1155; March 22, 1844, c.1376–1387. It should be noted that Shaftesbury was a Tory, but found his own party "ten times more hostile to my views" than the Whigs (quoted in Mandler, *Aristocratic Government*, p. 82).

3   The transitional nature of the term *race* in the 1830s led writers such as Kay to conflate biological with cultural or ethnic characteristics. According to George W. Stocking, Jr., "Given the belief that the habitual behavior of human groups or different environments might become part of their hereditary physical makeup, cultural phenomenon were readily translatable into 'racial' tendencies" (*Victorian Anthropology* [New York: Free Press, 1987], p. 64). The "distinctly racial meaning," which *Anglo-Saxon* had taken on by the nineteenth century, emphasized the orderly, mature, disciplined, and devout nature of this group. By contrast, the Celts were held to be lawless, childlike, indolent, and superstitious. See Stocking, *Victorian Anthropology*, pp. 62–63; Richard Ned Lebow, *White Britain and Black Ireland: The Influence of Stereotypes on Colonial Policy* (Philadelphia, PA: Institute for the Study of Human Issues, 1976), chapter 5; and Lynn Hollen Lees, *Exiles of Erin: Irish Migrants in Victorian London* (Ithaca, NY: Cornell University Press, 1979), especially pp. 136–37. Lees argues that the widespread assumption that the Irish population increased more rapidly (and recklessly) than the English was inaccurate.

4   Some English writers did acknowledge the fact that different Irishmen and women had different religious faiths. Most often, predictably, these religious differences were mapped onto the "character" differences that corresponded to "race." Here, for example, is Nassau Senior, writing of the "two Irelands": "One is chiefly Protestant,

the other is chiefly Roman Catholic . . . . The population of one is labourious but prodigal; no fatigue repels them — no amusement diverts them from the business of providing the means of subsistence and of enjoyment . . . . that of the other is indolent but parsimonious" (quoted in Richard Ned Lebow, "British Images of Poverty in Pre-Famine Ireland," in *Views of the Irish Peasantry, 1800–1916*, ed. Daniel J. Casey and Robert E. Rhodes [Hamden, Conn.: Archon Books, 1977], p. 73). Lebow discusses the various tensions and paradoxes of the English views of the Irish in this essay. One of his conclusions is that "the real distinction in Ireland was not between Saxon and Celt or between Protestant and Catholic but between those Irishmen protected by custom and law and those exposed to the arbitrary power of the landlords" (p. 72).

5   Mandler argues that one of the principal distinctions of the Whig party was that it was cosmopolitan, emphasizing national over local interests. See *Aristocratic Government*, p. 6.

6   By the 1840s, these two dangers came together in the Irish campaign to repeal the Act of Union. The connection between the agitation of Irish Catholics and more sweeping parliamentary reforms was identified by Isaac Butt in 1843. Butt, who later invented Home Rule, objected to repeal because of its democratic implications. "Repeal [is] revolution . . . . The proposition [is] not to return to any state of things which had previously existed in Ireland — not to adopt the constitution of any European state — but to enter on an untried and wild system of democracy" (quoted in Oliver MacDonagh, *States of Mind: A study of Anglo Irish conflict, 1780 1980* (London: George Allen and Unwin, 1983), p. 57).

7   See McDonagh, *States of Mind*, pp. 105–7.

8   Here is Kay's suggestion in full: "We believe, however, that an impost on the rental of Ireland, might be applied with advantage in employing the redundant labour in great public works — such as draining bogs, making public roads, canals, harbours, & c., by which the entire available capital of the country would be increased, and the people would be trained in industrious habits, and more civilized manners. England would then cease to be, to the same extent as at present, the receptacle of the most demoralized and worthless hordes of the sister country" (p. 84). Notice that Kay devotes far more attention here to the improvements that could result from this tax revenue than to how it might be raised. Given the assumption held by many nineteenth-century English people that most of the Irish land was owned by absentee landlords, Kay probably intends for the tax to be imposed on this group. His solution, however, does not even address the land owned by resident landlords, nor does it take into consideration the fact that many landowners were also in debt — often to Catholics. Kay also leaves unspecified how this tax was to be collected or disbursed, and who is to oversee the public works projects — not to mention how the transition to this idealized state of public works is to be achieved, especially since Kay specifically argues against instituting an "unmodified" poor law in Ireland (p. 83).

The Irish "land question," which Kay sidesteps here, and which was to gain urgency during the course of the century, was partly at least a result of the relationship between England and Ireland. At the turn of the eighteenth century, the populations of the two countries held very different attitudes toward property. Whereas the three English "revolutions" had generated a model of property that depicted land as an individual possession that entailed absolute rights as well as responsibilities, the Irish experience had produced a competing image — of land as a communal trust whose ownership conferred obligations. The Act of Union subjected Ireland to the English assumption and policies, and the first decades of the century witnessed efforts by Irish landowners to extract rents from their tenants commensurate with these assumptions — despite, and often in bitter confrontation with, the claims of the latter.

For discussions of the Irish land question, see MacDonagh, *States of Mind*, pp. 34–41; Richard Ned Lebow, "Introduction" to *J.S. Mill and the Irish Land Question* (Philadelphia, PA: Institute for the Study of Human Issues, 1979), pp. 3–12.; Lebow,

White Britain, chapter 4; and Michael J.Winstanley, *Ireland and the Land Question, 1800–1922* (London and New York: Methuen, 1984), pp. 1–27.

9   Among the most radical Whigs on this position was Poulett Thomson, for whom Kay campaigned in his successful run for Parliament in 1832.

10   Like many Liberal Tories, some moderate landed Whigs did think that repeal was inevitable, but they never saw it as a panacea. Whigs characteristically supported government noninterference in the economic sphere — laissez-rester — rather than the implicitly more dynamic, because permissive, laissez-faire. See Mandler, *Aristocratic Government*, p. 98.

11   Kay's position is closest to that of the Reverend Thomas Chalmers. Chalmers was the Professor of Moral Philosophy at St. Andrews and was called the "McCulloch of Malthusianism" and "greatest preacher of his age." Kay agreed with Chalmers's condemnation of Speenhamland, his support for abolishing the Corn Laws, and his advocacy of improved morality as the most effective cure for poverty; however, Kay did not oppose reform, as Chalmers did. On Chalmers, see Boyd Hilton, *The Age of Atonement: The Influence of Evangelicalism on Social and Economic Thought, 1785–1865* (Oxford: Clarendon Press, 1988), especially chapter 2.

12   See Boyd Hilton, *Corn, Cash, Commerce: The Economic Policies of the Tory Government, 1815–1830* (Oxford: Clarendon Press, 1977), chapter 1.

13   The inequality of these two parts of Great Britain was also clear in the legislative reforms of the nineteenth century. The Reform Act of 1832, for example, did not reform Irish representation in Parliament or eliminate Ireland's rotten and pocket boroughs. State-aided elementary education was instituted in Ireland in 1831, with the explicit goal of combatting Irish "disorder." The police and new poor law seemed similar in the two countries, but "the Irish police constituted . . . a paramilitary force, while the Irish poor law could never attempt to deal with such questions as unemployment" (MacDonagh, *States of Mind*, p. 53). MacDonagh's summary comment is that "the same body controlled the legislative process for both, but in the case of Ireland its fundamental object was the maintenance of imperial control" (p. 54).

PART 5

Space

Simon Gunn

PUBLIC SPACES IN THE VICTORIAN CITY

The Public Culture of the Victorian Middle Class: Ritual and Authority and the English Industrial City, 1840–1914 (Manchester: Manchester University Press, 2000), 60–71, 78.

One of the most recent developments in Victorian Studies has been the 'spatial turn'. After considering issues such as class and gender, scholars have begun to think seriously about the uses of space in Victorian Britain and the ways that this made certain identities and means of behaviour possible. Maps and mapping, for example, have been rethought, not as objective records of the world, but as forms of knowledge that organise space and legitimate power. People behave differently in different kinds of space (most obviously, when they are in public places and when they are in the home). The city was usually seen as a different kind of space from the countryside, making possible new kinds of association, identities and work patterns. Specific districts in cities were constructed as spaces for different classes to exist in. Following on from this, it is obvious that spaces can be gendered (there are places where women can go and places where they cannot; see **Erika Rappaport**'s Reading for this). Centres of political power and administration were constructed as spaces for men. Taking space seriously means that even as basic a function as walking becomes a complex activity. Men were more often able to walk around unaccompanied and therefore had a different relationship to space from that of women. The 'walker' who has occupied most scholarly attention has been the *flâneur* (the elite man about town) who has the time and leisure to walk around by himself and to enjoy metropolitan life as a form of spectacle. Shops and arcades were shaped by the gaze of the *flâneur*, catering to his need for new entertainment and diversion. These are not trivial issues but fundamental to understanding how society functions.

Space as a category has made possible interdisciplinary exchange in which, amongst others, geographers make a great contribution.

The following Reading is an extract from **Simon Gunn**'s study of the Victorian middle class, *The Public Culture of the Victorian Middle Class* (2000). Simon Gunn has been an important figure in the development of urban history and the different kinds of identities that Victorian urban life made possible. Examining Birmingham, Leeds and Manchester, Gunn traces the way that the urban middle classes created distinctive institutions and a civic culture that reflected their authority and power. He is concerned with the cultural meaning of city centres that remain a vital legacy derived from Victorian Britain. These were not just important in architectural terms but, as he demonstrates, made possible new kinds of identity and social classification. This reinforces **Christopher Breward**'s analysis of clothing and fashion elsewhere in this volume.

Simon Gunn is Professor of Urban History at the University of Leicester. He is the author of *The Public Culture of the Victorian Middle Class: Ritual and Authority and the English Industrial City, 1840–1914* (2000) and a wider study (with Rachel Bell), *The Middle Classes: Their Rise and Sprawl* (2002) that accompanied a BBC television series of the same name. His most recent book is *History and Cultural Theory* (2006). He is currently studying issues of cultural identity and urban place in post-1945 English industrial cities.

———————————

THE REBUILDING OF THE CITY CENTRE in Birmingham, Leeds and Manchester had significant consequences for the spatial organisation of urban populations and for their representation. One effect of emptying the centre of its inhabitants and recreating it as a monumental space was to throw into relief the identities of the different social groups that entered it. Who people were and how they were socially positioned became an issue of vital interest. In London as well as in the industrial cities, the decades between the 1840s and the 1880s saw an extraordinary attention to the minute detailing of matters such as appearance, dress and behaviour on the street.[1] This social phenomenology was not neutral. Implicit in it was the consistent, if indefinite, idea of a threat posed by certain groups to the social order in the double sense of the term, both hierarchical and regulatory. In London the fault-line of concern took spatial form in the division between a proletarian East End and a fashionable West End. In the industrial cities, however, attention was directed to the central zone itself, together with the slums and workers' districts immediately bordering it. Between the 1840s and the 1880s these areas of the industrial cities became a highly sensitised testing-ground, not only for new efforts at policing and moral regulation, but also for new forms of social identity and ways of representing authority.

The reconstruction of the industrial cities therefore raised a series of questions in sharp and immediate ways. Who was to have access to the centre and on what terms? How were social identities and relationships to be handled in the newly created environment of the city? The idea of the city centre as a space designed to represent morality and power indicates some of the ways middle-class commentators envisioned the new urban 'design'. But it does not specify with any precision how the centre was used by different sections of the population: men, women, workers, employers, the urban poor. In practice as well as at the level of representation the idea of the 'moral city' was inseparable from its designation as a space of physical and moral danger. For groups such as middle-class women, appearance in the city centre raised in acute form issues of security and identity. Recent critics have followed contemporaries like Engels in viewing the nineteenth-century metropolis as a whirlpool or vortex in which the individual was caught in a bewildering spiral of sense impressions. In this context, the experience of the centre betokened not so much a recovery of moral order as disorientation and even temporary loss of identity.[2]

For these reasons, how the city centre was to be regulated and how appearance and social interaction were to be managed were perceived by mid-Victorian observers to be important issues. This chapter will specify these concerns as they were articulated in Birmingham, Leeds and Manchester from the 1840s onwards. The vicissitudes of the streets and the threat to social identity that they posed to contemporaries can be exaggerated. Historians have rightly pointed to the varied strategies by which migrants and workers handled the pressured conditions of city life, and the resilient vitality of urban popular cultures.[3] The wealthier, suburbanised sections of local society equally devised their own strategies for negotiating the city centre and for representing status and hierarchy on the streets. Principal among these were the description and classification of social 'types' and the regular enactment of what I shall term 'ritualised performances' at the heart of the city. Both of these strategies operated with the idea of the city centre as a stage for the display of social identity and difference, and worked to stabilise and limit the democratic flux of city life.

The perils of the streets

The perception of the city as physically and morally dangerous was not new in the mid-nineteenth century. It was a significant theme in Henry Fielding's descriptions of eighteenth-century London as the home of the idle, profligate and debauched, as also in William Cobbett's well-known denunciation of the capital and the new industrial centres as 'wens'.[4] But the residential withdrawal of the wealthy from the industrial city to suburbs like Victoria Park, Edgbaston and Woodhouse in the 1830s and 1840s intensified the idea of a collapse of moral authority at its centre at times when a middle class was absent, at night and weekends. Leon Faucher articulated the idea powerfully in his description of Manchester in 1844: 'At the very moment when the engines are stopped, and the counting-houses closed, everything which was the thought — the authority — the impulsive force — the moral order of this immense industrial combination, flies from the town and disappears in an instant'.[5] The idea that the centre became, at certain times, a moral vacuum was a staple and more or less constant observation in all the provincial cities between the 1840s and the 1880s. 'We must not measure the civilisation of Leeds by what we see in Park Row, Bond Street, Commercial Street, Briggate and Boar Lane during the day time', a local journalist warned in 1883; 'our streets in the dark and lonesome hours of midnight and early morning also bear witness to the social cancers which may be covered up, but never healed'.[6] From the last decades of the nineteenth century many commentators looked back nostalgically to a golden age of urban community, located vaguely in the early 1800s, when different classes were seen to have harmoniously inhabited adjacent streets in the old centre.[7] Yet the representations of the industrial city as dangerous and as romantic were not antithetical or contradictory; in the mid-Victorian decades the idea of the centre as a space of danger became part of its romance.

In Birmingham, Leeds and Manchester the dangers of the city had a specific socio-spatial location in the slums and workers districts that bordered on the central area. The city centre was portrayed as an island surrounded by a sea of crime and immorality. 'The town is encircled by a huge cordon of beastliness and filth, enough to strike fear into the heart of every civilised inhabitant', a Manchester journal proclaimed in 1870. In similar vein, visitors to Birmingham were advised that if they stepped 'outside the magic circle' of the central area they would immediately encounter squalor, stench and the 'rookeries of vice'.[8] Streets on the fringes of the commercial district were identified as especially dangerous for respectable passers-by; they included parts of Deansgate and Oldham Road in Manchester, Thomas Street in Birmingham and York Street in Leeds. As late as 1892, when fears of violent crime were subsiding in many cities, the Chief Constable of Leeds warned of the dangers of entering the Dark Arches, Swinegate and Whitehall Road, in which prostitution, assault and larceny were seen as rife.[9] Where the new police led, journalists followed. The reports of Angus Bethune Reach on the slums of Angel Meadow, Manchester in the 1850s, were succeeded by a stream of accounts in the press of the industrial cities, describing drunkenness, violence and immoral behaviour in a style which mixed the frankly censorious with the slyly picaresque.[10] In this way, not only was suburban respectability alerted to the dangers lurking at the edges of the city centre, but the city itself was subjected to a detailed moral mapping, from the level of districts down to that of specific streets, markets and pubs.

Particular concern was voiced at moments when social and spatial boundaries appeared to break and the population of the slums and worker's districts spilled on to the main city streets, principally at night and weekends. In the 1870s and early 1880s the Birmingham press complained vociferously at the 'drink-delirium' which overtook the working population on Saturday nights, creating 'disgraceful scenes at the very heart of the town'. Similarly, the *Leeds Mercury* bemoaned the 'crowds of men and women drunk, surging up and down the streets' on Saturday nights, and 'the disgusting immorality, the ribald jesting, the cursing and profanity' which accompanied these occasions. In Manchester, considerable attention was given to the popular promenade in Oldham Street on Sunday evenings, a 'surging mass of human beings overflowing from the broad pavement into the roadway', from Ancoats into Market Street and Piccadilly.[11] What was at issue here was not simply the perception of immorality on show. It was also the perceived transgression of the social and spatial boundaries of the mid-Victorian city, the outflow from the slums into the symbolic centre of bourgeois authority. Such occasions were seen as incarnating the idea of disorder on the 'principal thoroughfares' and of the dangers of the streets.

Fears about the permeability of the boundaries between slums and centre led to concerns about crime and violence on the city streets. In the 1840s and 1850s much attention was given to crimes against property. Following Engels, commentators noted the elaborate use of iron plates and shutters to protect shops and warehouses in Manchester; theft from workshops in the metal trades was viewed as a serious social problem in mid nineteenth-century Birmingham.[12] But from the 1860s there was a discernible shift in all three cities to a focus on crimes against the person carried out in the central streets. There were fears of a crime epidemic in Manchester, set off by the Deansgate 'garotting panic' of 1862–63 and evidence of rising numbers of arrests. In Leeds there was similar anxiety about the rising crime rate, perpetuated by a number of well-publicised attacks on notable local figures; in 1882, for example, the painter Atkinson Grimshaw was reported to have been assaulted in a 'moonlight outrage' in Kirkgate.[13] However, statistical evidence does not suggest an increase in crime in the central areas of the city, even allowing for the problems of interpreting police statistics. The police returns for Manchester, for example, show an absolute decline in the number of arrests in the central wards of Exchange and St Ann's between 1847 and 1865. Arrests for crimes committed in each ward were most numerous, and increased most rapidly, in working-class areas such as Ancoats, Angel Meadow and Deansgate.[14] But neither this evidence, nor the efforts to distinguish the 'dangerous' and 'criminal' classes from 'upright' workers, appeared to reassure propertied opinion before the 1890s. The high-profile reporting of murder, assault and theft meant that the centre, and areas immediately bordering it, continued to be represented as the site of criminality and random violence, especially 'out of hours'.

More insidious, however, and in many ways more alarming to respectable opinion since it was pervasive and hard to regulate, was prostitution, 'the great sin of great cities' as a Birmingham periodical termed it.[15] In Leeds, police reports indicated that there were one hundred and fifty prostitutes in 1852, mainly gathered in brothels off Kirkgate. The figures for Manchester were between five hundred and a thousand at any time between the 1840s and the 1880s.[16] These numbers were relatively small by comparison with port cities like Liverpool, but they underestimated the scale of the phenomenon since they failed to take into account the numbers of women using prostitution as a form of casual work to supplement wages.[17] Official attitudes were ambiguous, the police in Leeds, for example, tolerating prostitution where it was restricted in fixed brothels. But the concern of the police and the press escalated when prostitutes were seen to enter the central streets and squares. In 1844 Faucher estimated that there were over five hundred prostitutes in the vicinity of the Manchester Exchange at dusk, and the opening up of the city at night with improved lighting and commercialised entertainment enhanced public awareness of prostitution. In 1882 a woman contributor to a Leeds journal commented that 'it is impossible to walk along [Boar Lane] after nightfall without observing the large number of very young girls', while in 1877 a Birmingham periodical cryptically noted the 'stream of gaily-dressed women' who gathered outside the Midland Hotel 'as soon as the theatres closed'.[18]

The presence of prostitutes on the streets of the city centre, rather than in enclosed brothels on its fringes, was seen as destabilising for a number of reasons. Firstly, it brought into the open the association between prostitution and middle-class youths and businessmen who made up an important part of the clientele, thus exposing men's 'double standard'. Secondly, prostitutes were seen not only to flout codes of femininity and public morality, but also to permeate 'society' occasions such as concerts, balls and soirées. At the Annual Ball of the Lancashire Artillery Volunteers, a Manchester journalist professed shock at the number of prostitutes present who, in the quadrilles, 'would have to take the hands of the wives, sisters and sweethearts of the members of the gallant L.A.V!'.[19] Thirdly, as this suggests, the presence of prostitutes was seen to compromise the respectability of middle-class women in public places. 'Nearly every respectable woman who may be out after dusk', a Leeds correspondent complained, 'knows that if she is compelled to stand or loiter for a single moment she is addressed by some man or other'.[20] The issue of prostitution therefore displaced on to women as a whole responsibility for men's sexual behaviour. At the same time, the prostitute was cast as the transgressive figure *par excellence*, capable of moving across established boundaries of space and class in ways which disrupted bourgeois notions of respectability and social order.

The idea of the city centre as a moral space, then, coexisted with its representation as a space of danger. From the later 1850s there is evidence that police strategy turned to moral regulation of street behaviour in the forms of drunkenness, prostitution and begging. It was these offences which largely accounted for the increase in arrests between the 1860s and the 1880s in cities such as Manchester and Leeds.[21] Yet from their formation in the 1830s until at least the 1880s, the new police were consistently perceived by propertied opinion as ineffective. In the 1830s and 1840s opposition could be put down to urban Tory hostility to Liberal reforms, but from the 1850s it was general. 'The fact must be confessed that during the still hours of every night and day our streets are insufficiently protected' a Birmingham journal lamented in the 1880s, while in Leeds the police were depicted as incompetent as they were autocratic.[22] Consequently, there was little middle-class confidence in the police's ability to protect either person or property before the late 1880s, when crime rates began to decline and observers perceived cities like Manchester to be safer than at an earlier period.[23] Means other than policing were necessary to bring a sense of order and stability to the city streets.

Within the ranks of the middle classes, the city centre was used and experienced differentially. Age was one factor here, the centre being strongly identified in reportage with the 'gilded youth' of both sexes as a focus for courtship, consumption and fashionable display. Equally, there were specific problems for middle-class women in entering the central area. The volume of traffic, mud on the streets and the unwanted attentions of male 'pests' were among the difficulties which had to be negotiated. While men might benefit from the opening up of the city at night and find in its streets a new freedom, the spatial and temporal liberties of women were restricted by the sense of danger lurking at the city's edge and the heightened visibility of prostitution.[24] Yet if women faced in particularly acute form the 'perils of the streets', the experience of the city raised problems of status and authority for middle-class populations as a whole, men as well as women. Centrally important here was the issue of appearance on the street, of how a sense of hierarchy and social order were to be upheld in an urban society characterised by fluidity, democratic mixing and a weakening of the traditional markers of social distinction.

Appearance, street philosophy and social 'types'

Appearance on the street, and how one appeared to others, was of vital importance to the mid-Victorian middle class. It had to signal distinction, respectability
and authority in an anonymous social context where personal or social recognition
was far from automatic, and where an aristocratic display of conspicuous wealth
was likely to be frowned upon, to be seen as out of place. Changes in fashion
from the 1860s, notably the production of cheap crinolines and ready-made suits,
meant that dress itself no longer served as a reliable index of a person's class or
status.[25] Yet, paradoxically, dress and appearance became more important as a guide
to who someone was. For the critic Thomas Carlyle, clothes might be 'despicable'
but they were also 'unspeakably significant' since they provided clues to a person's
identity at a period when a conventional sign-system of appearance was disintegrating.
As Elizabeth Wilson suggests, 'it became essential to read character and proclivity
from details that were immediately perceived, for in the metropolis everyone was
in disguise, incognito, and yet at the same time an individual more and more was
what he [or she] wore'.[26]

These concerns about appearance and status, of course, were not novel. The
comedy of manners attendant upon social pretension and mobility was a staple
subject of eighteenth-century depictions of Bath and London. However, the
transformation of the industrial towns into provincial metropolises, and the recreation
of the city centre as a form of monumental stage-set, meant that concerns about
appearance intensified. Indeed, evidence from the provincial cities reveals something
akin to a crisis of representation in this respect between the 1860s and the 1880s.
The crisis was characterised by a series of oppositions in bourgeois representations of the public self, between concealment and disclosure, between conformity
and individualism, and, above all, between authenticity and pretence. In Manchester,
it was asserted in 1871, wealthy men and women out in public 'have determined
to convert themselves into clothes-screens'. Changing male fashions since the
1830s were perceived to conceal men's figures in loose-fitting suits and their faces
behind beards. Black frock coats and trousers were adopted as a uniform, giving
mid-Victorian men an aspect of funereal conformity at a point when 'individualism'
was assumed to be on the ascendant in other domains of social and economic life.[27]
The provincial satirical press, meanwhile, provided a running critique of social
pretension, contrasted with an always elusive ideal of authenticity: 'We too constantly
sail under false colours, travel under false pretences amongst our fellow men; in
short, perpetually perpetrate upon them a contemptible programme of social
humbug'.[28]

Respectable appearance was therefore crucially important and problematic for
those assuming middle-class status. This duality related to a basic contradiction in
social perception. On the one hand, it was desired that class or status should be
immediately recognisable, to spring automatically from an authentically 'classed'
self on the other, respectable appearance was seen to be contrived, something that
required mastery of complex social codes. Difficulties were compounded by the
reconstruction of the city centre itself. Whereas in the suburbs, roles and identities
were clearly defined, and it was generally known who individuals were, in the centre
the lines of identity were prone to dissolve. The city centre was characterised not
only by anonymity in social relationships, but also by its conceptualisation as a social

stage. It was here, as Judith Walkowitz has noted, that 'new social actors' first made their appearance, the 'new woman' and the 'swell', in the 1880s.[29]

These issues took shape in specific, and often gendered, ways. Respectable 'ladies' were confronted by the difficult task of conforming to the dictates of femininity and fashion while establishing a clear visual demarcation from increasingly public, well-dressed prostitutes. Significantly, in Leeds during the 1880s a Rational Dress Society worked to dispense advice to women on appropriate dress in public.[30] But the problems of appearance affected all sections of the middle class, men as well as women. The figure of the 'gentleman' was seen as continuously threatened by counterfeits, the 'mashers' and 'counter-jumpers' whose true identity the satirical press delighted in exposing. Thus a Birmingham journal rejoiced in the tale of a tram passenger 'who had the appearance of a gentleman, but soon showed himself that contemptible creature, a masher'.[31] Respectable appearance was especially important for those on the fringes of gentility, such as clerks. Ironically, however, it was precisely these occupational groups which were most often identified by the local press as dressing 'above their station'.[32]

A central concern for those with a claim to middle-class status, therefore, was to establish recognisable lines between different social groups and to sustain an idea of hierarchy in appearance on the street. At a general level, novelists like Dickens, George Eliot and Charlotte Brontë, were useful guides to these issues. In their works such novelists paid detailed attention to dress and appearance. Their particular skill, as John Harvey has noted, was to interpret the 'inner meaning of externals'.[33] But of more specific importance at the local level was the periodical press, which provided a running commentary on social life in provincial cities like Birmingham, Leeds and Manchester. A key figure in these accounts was the 'street philosopher' whose pleasure, as one such put it, was 'to watch the passers by, to speculate on character from a chance expression, and an occupation from the cut of a coat or the shape of a pair of boots'.[34] For the street philosopher, the city appeared as a 'living panorama', a 'vast museum', from which general truths could be deduced about human character: 'What a world of speculation lies open to the man who, himself placid and unmoved in the strife, attentively regards his fellow man, and what golden lessons are to be derived by one who indulges in such contemplation'. The new industrial cities were regarded as especially favourable terrain for such speculation compared to older urban centres, as one commentator explained: 'In a large manufacturing town, [there] is more room for the display of the ever shifting chances and changes of life'.[35]

This 'gastronomy of the eye', Richard Sennett has suggested, was a feature of urban bourgeois perception in the mid- and later nineteenth century, in France as well as in England.[36] But if the city was seen as a spectacle, it was not an undifferentiated one. Through the figure of the street philosopher the periodical press engaged in a systematic process of categorising and classifying individuals as 'social types', providing a sociological guide to the streets and restoring order to the confusion of sense impressions.

Much of this social description was concerned with specifying occupational and status differences within a propertied population. W.H. Mills recalled the 'type' of the Manchester man of the 1870s, generally a large employer, identified by the panoply of horses, carriages and grooms.[37] In the early 1880s a Leeds journal noted the increasing 'grandeur and sublimity of the word professional', identified with the law, medicine and the clergy, but now aspired to by accountants and architects. Here, as in other literary genres, the gentleman represented the apogee of masculine status. The same Leeds journal dwelt lovingly on the details of old-fashioned gentle-manly appearance encountered in a Headingley tram: 'a moustache, a pair of dog-shin gloves, two and a half inches of wrist linen, a pair of gaiters, a bull-dog's head pin, a circumference of stiff collar, and a circuitous hat'.[38] Gentlemanliness represented the yardstick by which all other forms of masculine appearance were judged. In Birmingham in the late 1870s the *Owl* ran a series of articles entitled 'People One Doesn't Care to Meet', male 'types' encountered at the social club or at church whose behaviour failed to live up to the standards expected of the 'true' gentleman.[39] But most ire was expended on 'swells', 'mashers', 'cads' and 'counter-jumpers', young men associated with marginal status, such as warehouse clerks and shop assistants: 'He is the man who during the week consents to appear in the seediest and most threadbare garments, but on Sundays emerges in all the glories of gaiters, "masher" collars [and] a crutch stick'.[40] It was predominantly men who were depicted as 'social types' in this manner, but observation was not restricted to them. Women in public were classified, for instance, according to 'types of beauty' — the 'languishing', the 'dressy', the 'genteel', and so on —, while a sense of social hierarchy was provided by the portrayal of 'shopping ladies', 'showy shopgirls' and barmaids as distinct species of femininity.[41]

This brand of journalistic caricature was used to reinforce particular notations of gender and sexuality, which themselves helped to underwrite the perception of social difference. As an expert in appearances, the street philosopher was skilled in deciphering the prostitute from the 'true' lady. The former could be identified by details of style or gesture: 'Mark how she struts and stalks along, thinking that she is gracing the room with an elegant and refined style of locomotion'. 'Ladies' were distinguished by naturalness of appearance and manners, which were invariably seen as artificial and contrived in prostitutes, even of the most fashionable kind.[42] Equally, an over-attention to dress among 'swells' and 'mashers' disqualified them from gentlemanliness; as a Leeds journal put it, by their appearance and behaviour such 'types' forfeited 'any claim to be considered *men* in the ordinary and best acceptation [*sic*] of the term'.[43] Indeed, anxiety about the sexual as well as the social identity of young men was a repeated motif in the periodical press of the 1880s. The association of 'mashers' with prostitutes was seen to compromise not only their moral standing but also their masculinity; both groups were identified with surface and illusion as against substance and 'character'. In Birmingham the presence of Oscar Wilde impersonators in New Street and transvestites in Aston Lower Grounds, alluded to in the press, was connected with a larger trend in which a younger generation of men was seen as corrupted and 'feminised'.[44] Such concerns focused on groups who could themselves be regarded as new social actors in the 1870s and 1880s: the sons of established middle-class families yet to acquire a responsible position in business or the professions and young white-collar males whose social status was inherently precarious. Representations of sexuality were thus entwined with perceptions of class and status, moral and social qualities complimenting one another at each point in a hierarchy of respectability.

Social 'types' were also categorised according to specific locations in and around the city. A Birmingham commentator satirised Edgbaston as the home of the 'wretched rich' whose 'miserable conditions' were related to the number of 'at homes' and dinner-parties such families were forced to hold. A series on 'types' observed on Leeds tram routes allowed for disquisition on the different social character of suburbs: 'Chapeltown Varieties', 'the Perambulatory Gallery of Mixture' (Headingley), 'Humanity in the Rough' (Hunslet).[45] In Leeds, in particular, the connotations of individual streets or districts were brought out by means of visual and literary caricature, the prosperous Jew representing the Leylands, a fashionable woman and chaperone Commercial Street, a female factory worker Hunslet Lane, and so on.[46] Such descriptions rendered the city knowable in a way that differed from statistical investigation and abstract maps. They both reflected local knowledge and re-constituted that knowledge by depicting in specific and increasingly stereotyped ways an image of the city as socially zoned. While presenting the city as a 'living panorama', they sharpened the idea of bounded social differences coexisting in a seemingly unchanging social order.

As Pierre Bourdieu has argued, such classificatory schemes are part of a practical knowledge of the social world, organising that knowledge on the principles of 'vision and division'.[47] The visual and literary representation of the social order conveyed by the periodical press in Birmingham, Leeds and Manchester was essentially harmonious and hierarchical; its predominant tone was comic or ironic rather than contestatory or overtly class-based. Nevertheless, it organised local society in a manner which was implicitly classed. The higher echelons were seen as graded by a series of coteries and status divisions. In the old days, a Birmingham correspondent lamented, dances were a 'merry meeting' of young people; but from the 1850s they had become fashionable events where 'to have anything to do with a partner outside the correct "set", is a thing not to be thought of'.[48] By contrast, little direct attention was given in the periodical press to workers or the poor as part of urban society. While Jews, street arabs and factory workers were identified in passing, they were conventionally described only in relation to the presence of the well-to-do. Moreover, by contrast with statistical surveys there was limited attempt at hierarchisation and division within or between elements of the 'lower classes' and little or no refer-ence to the 'intelligent artisan' or to the distinction between the 'rough' and the 'respectable' found in other forms of contemporary literature.[49] Where such groups were described, it was generally in the visceral terms noted earlier: beggars who 'follow you with their whining appeals' and 'clutch you by the coat-sleeve', or workers in the trams whose presence was registered by the smell of 'the rough cut and the shag'.[50] Thus, the society of the well-to-do was presented as complex and finely graded, that of workers and the poor as comparatively simple and uniform.

Ostensibly hierarchical, the view of the social order projected in the periodical press was intrinsically dichotomous. It was predicated on an implicit division between a population whose resources derived from 'non-manual' occupations, the families of clerks as well as of employers, and the bulk of the urban population dependent on physical labour of different kinds. This division was reproduced in a multiplicity of forms: between those with legitimate access to the city centre and others whose presence was viewed as threatening and transgressive; between consumers as 'subjects' and those who were represented as 'objects' of the largesse of the well-to-do; between those identified as possessing education and culture and the 'Great Unwashed' upon whom the benefits of education were wasted.[51] At its most fundamental, the division between mental and manual labour was rooted in analogies between the human and the social body. In 1892 the president of the Birmingham and Edgbaston Debating Society defined the aristocracy, the middle class and the working class as respectively 'the belly, the brain and the bone of modern society'. In the periodical press the well-to-do were identified by the outward signs of mental discernment, taste and refinement. By contrast, workers and the poor were distinguished by their physicality, by sensual excess, as in the figure of the prostitute, or by bodily grossness, as in the caricatures of 'Smowler', the eponymous 'working-man's candidate'.[52] In these ways, the seemingly diverse and hierarchical representation of social 'types' developed between the 1860s and the 1890s turned on a latent dichotomy between mental and manual categories which was to continue to be a staple element in the representation of class and the social order into the twentieth century.[53] [. . .]

The heyday of the portrayal of middle-class 'types' and rituals was the years between 1860 and 1890. From the later date they ceased to be so prominent in descriptions of life in the provincial cities. In part, this reflected the decline of the periodical press. Many of the satirical journals had closed down by 1890 and were not replaced by equivalent journals as at an earlier period.[54] Where such journals did continue, they increasingly submitted to commercial pressures, carrying advertisements for shops and businesses in the form of descriptive articles and reports of mass spectator sports such as cricket and football.[55] But the decline of the particular types of representation and modes of behaviour described here can also be connected to a number of more general factors. Firstly, it occurred simultaneously with the waning of civic ceremonial and processions, and of journalistic interest in them, from the later 1880s. [. . .] In this sense, it was linked to a wider decline of ritual expression among the middle classes in the industrial cities. Secondly, if a literature of social 'types' and ritual performance were related to fears of crime and social mixing in the city centre, then one would expect them to diminish in importance once these fears abated. The reduction of crime rates in the provincial cities by the 1890s, noted earlier, together with the development of a more self-sufficient and commercialised workers' culture from the 1880s, suggests that the need to intervene, practically or symbolically, in the city centre was commensurately less pressing.[56] Finally, there was a tendency among all social groups in the last decades of the century to move from outdoor forms of leisure to those pursued indoors or in enclosed spaces. In popular culture these forms comprised the music hall, professional sport and the pub; in bourgeois culture they included the concert hall and the social club. By the 1890s the street was no longer so significant a site of leisure and display as it had been in earlier decades. [. . .]

Further reading

Key writings on space in a Victorian context include: Deborah Epstein Nord, *Walking the Victorian Streets: Women, Representation and the City* (Ithaca, NY: Cornell University Press, 1995); Lynda Nead, *Victorian Babylon: People, Streets and Images in Nineteenth-Century London* (New Haven, CT: Yale University Press, 2000); Patrick Joyce, *The Rule of Freedom: Liberalism and the Modern City* (London: Verso, 2003); Pamela Gilbert, *Mapping the Victorian Social Body* (Albany, NY: State University of New York Press, 2004). For a recent discussion of Victorian cities see Tristram Hunt, *Building Jerusalem: The Rise and Fall of the Victorian City* (London: Weidenfeld & Nicolson, 2004). The Victorian middle class has received far more attention in recent years. Alongside Simon Gunn's work, see: Janet Wolff and John Seed (eds), *The Culture of Capital: Art, Power and the Nineteenth-Century Middle Class* (Manchester: Manchester University Press, 1988); Theodore Koditschek, *Class Formation and Urban-Industrial Society: Bradford, 1750–1850* (Cambridge: Cambridge University Press, 1990); R.J. Morris, *Class, Sect and Party: The Making of the British Middle Class, Leeds, 1820–1850* (Manchester: Manchester University Press, 1990); Dror Wahrman, *Imagining the Middle Class: The Political Representation of Class in Britain, 1780–1840* (Cambridge: Cambridge University Press, 1995); Martin Hewitt, *The Emergence of Stability in the Industrial City: Manchester, 1832–1867* (Aldershot: Scolar, 1996); Alan J. Kidd and David Nicholls (eds), *Gender, Civic Culture and Consumerism: Middle-Class Identity in Britain, 1800–1940* (Manchester: Manchester University Press, 1999). For more general study of spatial issues, see Simon Gunn and Robert J. Morris (eds), *Identities in Space: Contested Terrains in the Western City since 1850* (Aldershot: Ashgate, 2001), especially Gunn's introduction ('The Spatial Turn'), pp. 1–14.

Notes

1　The best-known example is Henry Mayhew's *London Labour and the London Poor* (London, 1851), but intense and detailed speculation on the appearance and conditions of urban populations was a feature of fiction, the press and medical and statistical reports.

2　These issues are discussed variously in the following: M. Berman, *All That Is Solid Melts into Air* (London: Verso, 1984); R. Fishman, *Bourgeois Utopias: The Rise and Fall of Suburbia* (New York: Basic Books, 1987); S. Marcus, *Engels, Manchester and the Working Class* (London: Weidenfeld and Nicholson, 1974); M. Nava, 'Modernity's disavowal: women, the city and department store' in M. Nava and A. O'Shea (eds), *Modern Times: Reflections on a Century of English Modernity* (London: Routledge, 1996); R. Sennett, *The Fall of Public Man* (London: Faber, 1993).

3　The literature is extensive but see in particular P. Bailey, *Leisure and Class in Victorian England* (London: Routledge, 1978); M. Hewitt, *The Emergence of Stability in the Industrial City* (Aldershot: Scolar Press, 1996); P. Joyce, *Visions of the People: Industrial England and the Question of Class, 1840–1914* (Cambridge: Cambridge University Press, 1991).

4　R. Williams, *The Country and the City* (St Albans: Paladin, 1975), pp. 178–80.

5　L. Faucher, *Manchester in 1844* (London, 1844), p. 26.

6　'Leeds at night', *Toby the Yorkshire Tyke*, 17 November 1883.

7　For examples of such literature see J.T. Slugg, *Reminiscences of Manchester Fifty Years Ago* (Manchester, 1881); T. Swindells, *Manchester Streets and Manchester Men* (Manchester, 1889).

8　'Manchester slums', *Freelance*, 12 March 1870; 'Improved Birmingham', *Owl*, 29 September 1882.

9　E.W. Clay, *The Leeds Police, 1836–1974* (Leeds: Leeds City Police, 1975), pp. 59–60.

10　C. Emsley, *Crime and Society in England 1750–1900* (Harlow: Longman, 1996), p. 70. For examples of this type of reportage in the three cities see the *Owl*, 20 October, 1882; 'A Deansgate tragedy', *Freelance*, 20 April 1867; 'Leeds at night', *Toby the Yorkshire Tyke*, 17 November 1883.

11 'The ruins of Birmingham', *Owl*, 3 November 1882; 'Birmingham cribs', *Lion*, 7 June 1877; *Leeds Mercury*, 16 July 1863; 'A Sunday promenade', *City Lantern*, 6 August 1874; 'Oldham Street on a Sunday night', *Freelance*, 6 August 1870.

12 F. Engels, *The Condition of the Working Class in England* (London, 1844); *The Builder*, vol. xxiv (1866), p. 292; Emsley, *Crime and Society*, p. 103.

13 S.J. Davies, 'Classes and police in Manchester 1829–1880' in A.J. Kidd and K.W. Roberts (eds), *City, Class and Culture: Studies of Cultural Production and Social Policy in Victorian Manchester* (Manchester: Manchester University Press, 1985), pp. 36–8; Clay, *Leeds Police*, pp. 39–40; *Yorkshire Busy Bee*, 1 April 1882, p. 297.

14 'Manchester police returns, 1847–65', Manchester Central Library Archives Department. For studies of Birmingham and Leeds see D. Philips, *Crime and Authority in Victorian England* (London: Croom Helm, 1977) and Clay, *Leeds Police*.

15 'Birmingham cribs', *Lion*, 10 May 1877.

16 S. Burt and K. Grady, *The Illustrated History of Leeds* (Derby: Breedon Books, 1994), p. 169; D. Jones, *Crime, Protest, Community and Police in Nineteenth-Century Britain* (London: Routledge, 1982), pp. 164–5.

17 J.R. Walkowitz, *Prostitution and Victorian Society* (Cambridge: Cambridge University Press, 1980).

18 'Boar Lane', *Yorkshire Busy Bee*, 7 October 1882; 'Birmingham cribs', *Lion*, 17 May 1877.

19 'At the Volunteer ball', *Freelance*, 8 January 1875. On the identification of prostitutes with fashionable middle-class youth in Birmingham see the series on 'cribs' in the *Lion*, April-May 1877; in Leeds see *Yorkshire Busy Bee*, 27 January 1883, p. 52.

20 'Social laxity', *Toby the Yorkshire Tyke*, 1 December 1883.

21 Jones, *Crime, Protest, Community and Police*, pp. 161–7; Davies, 'Classes and police', pp. 36–40; Clay, *Leeds Police*, pp. 39–40.

22 'Hoots', *Owl*, 29 September 1882; 'Policemen', *Toby the Yorkshire Tyke*, 17 November 1883.

23 Jones, *Crime, Protest, Community and Police*, p. 167; C. Rowley, *Fifty Years of Ancoats* (Manchester, 1899), p. 15.

24 The issue of whether the modern city expanded or contracted opportunities for women's involvement in public life in the nineteenth century has been debated by feminist historians. For a classic statement of the pessimistic view see J. Wolff, 'The invisible *flâneuse*: women and the literature of modernity' in Wolff, *Feminine Sentences* (Cambridge: Cambridge University Press, 1990). For more optimistic (and plausible) views of the increasing participation of middle-class women, especially from the 1880s, see Nava, 'Modernity's disavowal' and J.R. Walkowitz, *City of Dreadful Delight: Narratives of Sexual Danger in Later Victorian London* (London: Virago, 1992).

25 C. Breward, *The Culture of Fashion* (Manchester: Manchester University Press, 1995), pp. 156–61, 174–5.

26 Carlyle cited in Sennett, *Fall of Public Man*, p. 153; E. Wilson, *Adorned in Dreams* (London: Virago, 1985), p. 137.

27 'The Botanical', *Freelance*, 27 May 1871; Slugg, *Reminiscences of Manchester*, p. 316; J. Harvey, *Men in Black* (London: Reaktion, 1997), pp. 24–7.

28 'Social humbug', *Yorkshire Busy Bee*, 3 February, 1883.

29 Walkowitz, *City of Dreadful Delight*, ch. 2.

30 'Feminine apparel', *Yorkshire Busy Bee*, 24 February, 1883.

31 'A masher routed', *Owl*, 15 October 1884.

32 H. Taylor, *Our Clerks* (Manchester, 1874); J. Tomlinson, *Some Interesting Yorkshire Scenes* (London, 1865), p. 22; G. Anderson, *Victorian Clerks* (Manchester: Manchester University Press, 1976).

33 Harvey, *Men in Black*, p. 19.

34 'In City Road', *City Lantern*, 21 May 1875.

35 'Phases of "life" in Manchester', *Comus*, 13 December 1877; 'Leeds shop windows', *Yorkshire Busy Bee*, 10 December 1881; 'From my window', *Yorkshire Busy Bee*, 18 February 1882; 'In City Road'.

36 Sennet, *Fall of Public Man*, p. 160.

37 Mills, *Sir Charles W. Macara, Bart.: A Study in Modern Lancashire* (Manchester, 1917), p. 25.

38 'The professional man', *Yorkshire Busy Bee*, 7 April 1883; 'Riding in the trams', *Yorkshire Busy Bee*, 22 April 1882.

39 See the *Owl*, 29 May and 5 June 1879.

40 'Mis-spent Sundays', *Yorkshire Busy Bee*, 28 April 1883. For descriptions of such 'types' in Manchester and Birmingham see *inter alia* 'Manchester swells', *City Lantern*, 11 February 1876; 'The natural history of the cad', *Dart*, 31 March 1877.

41 'Types of beauty', *Yorkshire Busy Bee*, 21 January 1882.

42 'A midnight dance', *Comus*, 17 January 1878; 'Birmingham cribs', *Lion*, 19 April 1878.

43 'A word to the young', *Town Crier*, January 1884; 'Respectable black-guardism', *Yorkshire Busy Bee*, 10 March 1883.

44 'The "club"', *Lion*, 5 April 1877; 'Talking of Oscar', *Owl*, 8 September 1882; 'Chilli Chutnee', *Owl*, 6 October 1882. For more general comments of lower middle-class 'manliness' see A.J. Hammerton, 'The English weakness?' in A.J. Kidd and D. Nicholls (eds), *Gender, Civic Culture and Consumerism: Middle Class Identity in Britain 1800–1940* (Manchester: Manchester University Press, 1999).

45 'The wretched rich', *Town Crier*, February 1884; 'Riding in the trams', *Yorkshire Busy Bee*, 14 January and 11 February 1882.

46 See, for example, 'Studies from the streets' and 'Leeds street types', *Yorkshire Busy Bee*, 28 January and 18 March 1882.

47 Bourdieu, *Distinction: A Social Critique of the Judgement of Taste* (London: Routledge, 1992), p. 467; *Practical Reason* (Cambridge: Polity, 1998), ch. 1.

48 T. Wemyss Reid, *A Memoir of John Deakin Heaton* (London, 1883), p. 157; 'A word to the young'.

49 See, for example, the discussions in F.M.L. Thompson, *The Rise of Respectable Society* (London: Fontana, 1988), pp. 181–2; N. Kirk, *Change, Continuity and Class* (Manchester: Manchester University Press, 1998), pp. 115–37.

50 *Yorkshire Busy Bee*, 27 January 1883, p. 51; 'Riding in the trams', *Yorkshire Busy Bee*, 14 January 1882.

51 'Ladies public houses', *Owl*, 10 April 1879; 'The pursuit of literature', *Yorkshire Busy Bee*, 15 April 1882.

52 J. Lloyd, 'Errors of civilisation from a medical standpoint' [1892], *Birmingham and Edgbaston Society Addresses 1877–1927* (Birmingham, 1927), p. 11. For the figure of Smowler see 'A tavern parliament', *The Lion*, 11 January 1877; *Owl*, 4 June 1884.

53 B. Waites, *A Class Society at War* (Leamington Spa: Berg, 1987), esp. ch. 2; G. Stedman Jones, *Languages of Class* (Cambridge: Cambridge University Press, 1983), ch. 5.

54 In Manchester, for example, the *Freelance*, *City Lantern* and *Momus* had all disappeared by 1890.

55 See, for example, the *Owl* in the mid-1890s.

56 For the development of a commercialised working-class culture in the later nineteenth century see E.J. Hobsbawm, 'The making of the working class, 1870–1914' in *Worlds of Labour* (London: Weidenfeld and Nicholson, 1984); G. Stedman Jones, 'Working-class culture and working-class politics in London, 1870–1900' in *Languages of Class*; C. Waters, *British Socialists and the Politics of Popular Culture, 1884–1914* (Manchester: Manchester University Press, 1992).

PART 6

Politics high and low

IN THE 'AGE OF EVALUATION' (1945–80), political history flourished and was widely taught despite the ascendancy of social history. The main tendency was to view politics as a matter of political manoeuvres rather than as being centred on ideas or ideology. In his great work, *The Formation of the British Liberal Party, 1857–1868* (1966), John Vincent held that the Liberal party was made up of a constellation of 'single issue' pressure groups, who only maintained coherence and unity through the charisma of William Gladstone. In Maurice Cowling's *1867* (1967), the Second Reform Act was passed, not through ideological conviction or pressure from below, but because of a struggle between groups within parliament to gain the upper hand. Despite Cowling, it was clear that politics was not confined to Westminster. The study of popular politics was undertaken by social historians, many of whom were inspired by E.P. Thompson's *The Making of the English Working Class* (1963). Thompson demonstrated how a working-class consciousness and political movement emerged during the Industrial Revolution. He rescued a wide range of political figures from obscurity and 'the enormous condescension of posterity'. These included the Luddites and the hand-loom weavers. Thompson argued that by 1830 a working-class political movement had emerged and was the single most important presence in Britain. Much of the literature thereafter evaluated why this working-class movement was so unsuccessful and why it failed to become revolutionary. In general, political history was characterised by the need to explain how the modern political process had emerged, studying the expansion of the franchise and the emergence of organised political parties.

During the 1980s political history was renewed in a dramatic way. First of all, a younger generation of historians began to argue that ideas and political philosophy were important at all levels of society. Newer political histories were characterised by a greater respect for ideas (often apparent in the deployment of approaches derived from intellectual history). Rather than tracing back modern politics to its nineteenth-century roots, the new focus was on looking at Victorian politics within the preoccupations and context of their times, to explore the way in which political ideas were different from our own. In other words, there was a concern to abandon the Whig interpretation of history, whereby history is written with one eye on the present day and with a narrative based around ideas of 'progress'. This, it was felt, led to distortions of the historical record. Second, historians increasingly argued for the 'relative autonomy of the political'. Attempts to argue that political language and identities were merely expressions of social or material interests (such as class) were viewed as reductionist. What should one make of Liberalism, which proved to be attractive across all classes? What should one make of working-class conservatism, which ought (from a Marxist point of view) to have been a contradiction in terms? What should one make of issues that cannot be reduced to simple class questions, for example, foreign policy? The development of political identities and languages was a more complex matter. Third, there was a concern that, by failing to take politics seriously, social historians had weakened themselves. The nature of state formation was extremely important in shaping and controlling the political agenda; so were the contingencies of the political process (such as the make-up of a cabinet or the effectiveness of a government in passing legislation). The formation of political parties was viewed as more complex than before. Rather than reflecting clear social constituencies, there was a greater focus on how complex and drawn out the creation of political parties was and the ways in which parties constructed rather than reflected constituencies. Finally, there was a concern to not only write women back into political history (their lack of a vote had previously meant they could be safely ignored) but also to reconsider politics in gendered terms.

The Readings that follow demonstrate the shape of the 'new political history'. Each of these works is boldly revisionist, reshaping how we should view Victorian politics.

Jonathan Parry

LIBERALISM AND GOVERNMENT

The Rise and Fall of Liberal Government in Victorian Britain (New Haven, CT, and London: Yale University Press, 1993), 1–7, 17–20.

One of the hallmarks of the new Victorian political history has been a fascination with Liberalism as a social and political philosophy. Liberalism is often difficult to define because it meant different things to different people. It stood for free trade, free markets, careers open to talent, anti-slavery, individualism and opposition to state intervention (and yet Liberals could often foster interventionism when circumstances dictated). Whigs and Liberals dominated the political agenda of Victorian Britain to a remarkable extent. **Jonathan Parry** has been a key historian of Victorian high politics. He began his career with a major study of the Gladstonian Liberal party, which restored the theological dimensions of political thought after the Second Reform Act. Politics, he showed, was not simply a secular activity, explaining why religious issues dominated the political agenda and why apparently secular issues often had a religious dimension. Parry is significant also because he takes political ideas seriously (which contrasts with earlier political historians who wrote about politics in terms of strategy, tactics and manoeuverings in the corridors of power and ignored the role of ideology). The following Reading is made up of two extracts from the Introduction to his second study, *The Rise and Fall of Liberal Government in Victorian Britain* (1993), where he examined the Whig-Liberal governing tradition as a whole from the 1820s through to its dissolution in the 1880s. This Reading is included as an example of the history of Victorian high politics that aims to restore its proper context and reveal its complexities. Parry's approach reminds us how important the Whigs (with their distinctive aristocratic viewpoint) were in shaping the Victorian political agenda.

Jonathan Parry is Reader in Modern British History at the University of Cambridge and Fellow of Pembroke College. His latest book, *The Politics of Patriotism: English Liberalism, National Identity, and Europe, 1830–1886* (2006) examines the roles of European issues and national identity concerns in nineteenth-century Liberal politics. His short life of Disraeli is also being published in 2007.

LIBERALISM WAS THE DOMINANT political force of Victorian Britain. Gladstone, looking back in 1884, maintained that since the 1830s it had been 'the solid permanent conviction of the nation'.[1] Between 1830 and 1886, a coalition of anti-Conservatives known at various times as Whigs, Reformers and Liberals was out of office for scarcely a dozen years and lost only two of fourteen general elections.[2] They claimed that only they understood how to govern a nation experiencing rapid and unsettling growth and traditionally intolerant of strong central government rule.

This book aims, first and foremost, to be a general account of parliamentary Liberalism during its nineteenth-century heyday. On the face of it, it is astonishing that no satisfactory account exists.[3] The contrast with the Conservatives is striking.[4] Yet the Conservative party was always a more coherent force, more homogeneous, less independently-minded, and usually more amenable to central direction and organisation. Those who define the existence of political parties in terms of a nationwide structure would be hard put to identify a Liberal party until the 1860s (the Liberal Registration Association was founded in 1860) or even 1870s. It was difficult to discipline MPs in the 1840s and 1850s, leading many historians to argue that the Liberal party was not formed until 1859. But discipline hardly became less difficult in the 1860s and 1870s; Gladstone regarded MPs as unleadable in 1867–8, as did Hartington in 1874, and in that year Cardwell wrote that the Liberals had 'never been a party, except *ad hoc*, for some special purpose'.[5] The lack of formal organisation, the exuberance and independence of grassroots Liberals, the variety of local factors behind Liberal electoral success, all these elements make a useful general history of the nineteenth-century Liberal movement almost impossible. One might write a casserole of a book, anxiously including something on every aspect of the Liberal experience. But this would be an indigestible dish, of incompatible ingredients. Far better, then, to accept that there are many valid ways of tackling such diversity and that any coherent one must be partial in scope.

This book is about government and leadership. It examines the ideas and strategies by which the most important Liberal politicians attempted to lead the people, and it discusses the obstacles and crises which frustrated many of their aspirations. So it complements, rather than contributes to, the large amount of recent work which has investigated aspects of Victorian *popular* politics.

Leadership was a particular problem for nineteenth-century politicians. The variety, extent, and fervour of public expectations of central government became altogether novel after about 1800 — as did the legislative ambitions of the governing elite itself. The root problem was unprecedentedly rapid economic development, which heightened social tensions and political awareness at the same time as it eroded the capacity of local hierarchies to restrain discontent and discipline opinion. The pace of European economic and political change from the late eighteenth century onwards threw up a public opinion much larger, more mobile, more politically sophisticated and, it seemed, infinitely more restless than any previous one. The British population rose from 10.69 million to 16.37 million between 1801 and 1831; food imports tripled between the 1770s and the 1820s; there was a great migration of labour to new urban settlements where traditional structures of government were minimal or inappropriate, and overpopulation on the land made paupers of many who could or would not migrate, creating the conditions for rural social tension. The regular recurrence of severe economic depressions intensified the threat to order. Most industry was dependent on volatile but limited home demand, and on fragile credit mechanisms. The cotton industry, the basis of British export strength, relied on foreign raw material and on exports to countries which might well find cheaper supplies in the long run. Until about 1850, the economy, and the social order which depended on it, seemed highly vulnerable, or 'artificial'.[6] Rapid economic and population growth made it essential to discipline the people into an understanding of the benefits and fairness of law, taxation, religious establishment and constitutional arrangements. But it also increased public pressure on government. Lop-sided economic development was bound to create grievances among individuals about exploitation or oppression of various sorts — in factories, on the land, and in tax and poor rate burdens — and a demand that they should be rectified. Meanwhile, the feeling that political leaders had a duty to promote the *moral* reformation of society was encouraged by the shock-waves emanating from continental revolutions, by prosperity and broader horizons among the farming, commercial and professional middle classes, and by the spread of evangelical religious fervour which accompanied economic and political ferment. Central government, local magistrates and other professional agencies were impelled to action, partly by fear of losing their authority and partly by a late-eighteenth-century confidence in the power of human intelligence, detailed knowledge and propertied benevolence to dominate nature and to improve society.

This book argues that the whig and Liberal governments in power from 1830 had a more or less coherent response to this situation. Liberals saw government as a matter of integrating and harmonising different classes and interest groups within the political nation. To them, good government involved guiding the people so as to strengthen their attachment to the state and to the firm, fair rule of law, and using policy to shape individual character constructively. Disunity among the diverse individuals, groups and classes which constituted the nation was a worry for them because it heightened the prospect of unrest and perhaps revolution, but also because it failed to realise the potential of man as a communal animal; it encouraged apathy and discouraged the productive application of God-given human energies. Liberals claimed that animosities between land and trade, Church and Dissent, or Protestant and Catholic were not only crippling but unnatural. If nineteenth-century Liberalism meant anything, it meant a political system in which a large number of potentially incompatible interests — whether nationalities, classes, or sects — were mature enough to accept an over-arching code of law which guaranteed each a wide variety of liberties. To accept the rule of law in this way was to demonstrate character, fitness for citizenship. By the 1850s and 1860s, Liberals were confident that their creed was making progress in three senses. The duties and rewards of citizenship were being appreciated by more and more elements of British society; the remit of character-forming law was being extended to more and more aspects of national life; and ever-larger areas of the globe were adopting at least some of the Liberal world-view. The Liberal ideal was to bring as many people as possible under the rule of those principles. This meant binding Scotland, Wales and especially Ireland within a genuinely United Kingdom, spreading progressive commercial and constitutional values internationally, and entrenching those values particularly firmly in the empire. It follows from this that Liberalism should not be confused with nationalism, the principle of national separateness and division. In the Liberal model, self-government for particular geographical regions was to be limited according to the level of citizenship reached by the inhabitants. Their willingness voluntarily to live by Liberal principles would determine the amount of power that could safely be devolved to them.

These assumptions made the Liberal party distinctive in a number of ways from the 1830s onwards. First, whereas the Conservative party was always essentially *English*, the Liberals were a *British* party, a genuinely *unionist* force committed to the integration of all parts of the United Kingdom. Second, whereas the Conservative party remained preoccupied with the defence of government authority, and innately suspicious of popular political activity, the Liberals were committed to open politics, anxious to demonstrate a willingness to respond to popular grievances. Third, whereas the Conservative party never broke free of landed influence, the Liberals were much happier with arguments drawn from political economy, arguments that stressed that different social groups had *common*, not clashing, economic interests. And fourth, whereas the Conservatives remained specifically an Anglican party, Liberals sought to rally public opinion behind a notion of religion as a broad, modern and essentially undogmatic creed, capable of speaking to and uniting the whole nation. Dogmatic differences between sects were to be tolerated, and would naturally diminish as man's understanding of real religion improved. Though Irish Catholic sensitivities often prevented Liberals from making the point quite as explicitly as they might have liked, in general they presented themselves as the party of Protestantism and pluralism, and their faith in the progress of human reason allowed them to deny any incompatibility between the two.

Most of all, Liberals were united by the powerful myth that tories, or Conservatives, offered rule by 'vested interests' — by the aristocracy, the Anglican church, colonial trading interests, local corporations, and sinecure-hunters. The tories seemed a landed, stupid rump incapable of providing government to the general benefit. Liberals defined themselves as opponents of government by class, sect or interest. This was crucial — much more so than historians have tended to recognise. It meant that, while the Conservatives might with justice be called a landed or church party between the 1830s and 1870s, Liberals could not be labelled an urban or Dissenting party in the same way. Liberals' ingrained mythology required them to believe that they offered national, not class, government. Of course individual Liberal leaders had their own prejudices and political requirements, and of course they were often capable of manipulating the political situation to suit them. But the need to appear 'disinterested' still affected their behaviour fundamentally. Much of the most valuable historical work on nineteenth-century Britain published in the last twenty years has emphasised the defensive determination of propertied Victorians to protect their privileges from lower-class attack. To some extent, this insight can be applied to nineteenth-century Liberals. But it needs to be qualified. Liberal leadership strategy must not be reduced to a 'conservative' or 'concessionary' mindset, a negative outlook which was primarily anxious to assert 'social control'. All strategies are by definition conservative of something, but political leadership also always involves movement, participation, invigoration and reconciliation. It is about coalition-building, about forming alliances between as many different kinds of passions, principles and interests as possible. This was particularly true of Liberals in our period. It is, for example, unfortunate that the most popular explanation of the 1832 Reform Act presents Liberal leaders as reluctant barterers of small chunks of 'power' to some defined 'middle-class' group outside their narrow charmed circle.[7] In fact [. . .] , liberals dealing with parliamentary reform were usually more interested in the distribution of parliamentary seats than in the question of who should vote, and their main concern in discussing the franchise was that defined interests should not appear *excluded* from the constitution. As the composition of the politically-aware nation changed, Liberals altered their perception accordingly. For instance, Lord John Russell equated the 'people' with the 'middle classes' in 1831, but by 1861 he was defining them as the 'working classes'.[8]

To argue this is not to say that Liberal leaders were 'classless' in a late twentieth-century sense. All the party leaders discussed in the text believed that the possession of property, character and wisdom was an invaluable asset in leadership, both nationally and locally. All of them shared the standard nineteenth-century belief that civilisation depended on the maintenance of social ranks. They encouraged individual self-improvement *within* all classes not least because of their ingrained assumption that the class structure was preordained and that men of property were society's natural leaders.

Liberals' distinctiveness came in not believing that possession of property alone made a leader. They assumed that rule by the landed interest, acting as an interest, would almost certainly become selfish, complacent and sectional. Good political leadership required other qualities: breadth of popular sympathy, self-confidence, courage and disinterestedness, and a cultured understanding of the relation between the present and the past, developed through the study of history, literature, theology and perhaps science.[9] In particular, the good leader needed to be able to respond to social and intellectual change. Liberals believed that politics could not dominate society, which was an immensely complex entity directed by the interaction of millions of wills. The politician needed to understand the intellectual and spiritual drift of national life, so that he could reconcile social evolution with institutional forms. The effective exercise of judgment was his most basic task. All abstract theories of government were too rigid and simplistic to fit the human personality; a flexibility of approach was necessary in order to formulate acceptable laws. Good law regulated passion, suppressed barbarism and encouraged the development of human character; it bolstered true liberty. But legislation which was unsuited or repulsive to the people would, at best, be unable to stimulate their energies, and, at worst, foment class or sectional division in the country because it seemed to favour some group over another. Struck by the force of public opinion, Liberals dismissed out of hand the notion that unpopular law could permanently 'control or govern the people'.[10] Popular acquiescence in legislation was necessary. As Russell wrote in 1839, 'laws and institutions must act gradually and generally in order to be beneficial . . . laws must be respected as well as enacted; the minds of men must be engaged to a willing conformity with the new order of the State'.[11] As more and more social groups came to be included within the loose structure of the Liberal party, it was forced to take account of public opinion all the more assiduously. For example, the speed with which it responded to provincial clamour for Corn Law reform in the winter of 1838–9 is remarkable.

The Liberal party which developed from the 1830s was therefore a different animal from anything which had preceded it in British politics. But it was not born in a vacuum. It owed a lot to the thinking of the whig opposition of the years before 1830. But it was also indebted to the initiatives undertaken by the tory governments of the 1820s [. . .]. The emergence of a vociferous public opinion after 1800 forced the tories of the 1820s to make signicant changes in the substance and presentation of politics. These changes were particularly associated with Foreign Secretary Canning, who was primarily responsible for establishing the word 'liberal' as British political currency. He claimed that 'liberal' government meant a willingness to listen to public opinion, and that the result was reduced taxes, a more open commercial policy and the encouragement of constitutional principles abroad. However, in practice the 'liberal toryism' of the 1820s was as much tory as liberal. In particular, the bulk of the tory party remained resistant to parliamentary reform and Catholic emancipation. In a sense, this resistance led to the fall of tory government in 1830, when faced with an unusual degree of public clamour. But this book is at pains to stress that the events of 1830 did not mean that the political nation was as advanced as the incoming whig government on the two issues of Reform and Ireland. Indeed the whig/Liberal governments of the 1830s eventually foundered because the electorate distrusted their over-responsiveness to popular pressure in general, and Irish Catholicism in particular. Their electoral defeat in 1841 revealed that Liberals had not succeeded in winning the voters who mattered round to their own conception of politics.

It was only after 1846 that Liberals were able to do this. Their strongest weapons were free trade, Protestantism and foreign policy — and Palmerston, who crafted out of them an uplifting vision of national purpose and identity. British prosperity seemed to vindicate Liberals' claim to be able to cater for all major economic interests, while political stability appeared to testify to the superiority of her constitutional settlement. The result was general contentment with Liberal government. Between the 1850s and 1880s, the Liberal coalition spanned an astonishing range of classes and groups, from aristocrats to artisans, industrial magnates to labour activists, and zealous Anglican high churchmen to nonconformists and aggressive free-thinkers. It was strong among merchants and shopkeepers in the large towns of the midlands and north; it relied on the enthusiasm of the Dissenting chapels and the trades unions. Yet it also had a power base in traditional county and market towns, in the literary, legal and academic intelligentsia, and among an important minority of Anglican aristocrats and country gentlemen who not only supplied the party with its parliamentary leadership and its social centres (London salons and country houses) but also influenced the return of MPs for a large proportion of small boroughs and a significant number of county seats. At parliamentary level, it was a loose body of men sitting for a great variety of seats, most of whom stood on their dignity as independent and propertied representatives. [. . .]

Approaches

The over-arching theme of this book is that, in the half-century after 1830, there was a coherent Liberal approach to politics, which previous literature has failed to stress. Though nuances obviously changed over time, reflecting altered political circumstances, there was continuity in fundamental principles. It was an approach which owed most to the whig tradition, but which was influenced also by Canning and the liberal tories of the 1820s. The Liberal constitution aimed to integrate the four countries of the kingdom into a harmonious whole; it allowed parliamentary reform within a carefully-defined framework; and it marginalised those, like Chartists or Irish Nationalists, who complained that the 'parliamentary government' which it offered was repressive (Liberals assumed that critics of the principle of 'parliamentary government' must, by definition, be reactionaries or anarchists). Liberals attempted, by recasting political structures, to supply 'disinterested' and respected rule by a propertied, civilised governing class: by aristocrats and university-educated gentlemen at the centre, by assiduous landowners in the counties, and by the most cultured and respectable merchants in the towns. The leadership offered by this governing class was to be primarily administrative. At the centre, it would check sectional lobbying and corruption in favour of firm economy, yet it would defend Britain's real interests as a modernising commercial, imperial and international power. Legislative reform would allow reinvigorated local elites to practise rational social administration, while representative local government would prevent central dictation and encourage pluralism and regulated political participation. Parliament would not be force-fed with legislative programmes inspired by a party machine or faddist sectional pressures. The Liberal governments of 1830–86 implemented a great deal of legislation, but they did so as part of a strategy, acceptable to most propertied opinion, to use the power of government to strengthen particular moral values in society: hence the importance of economic, religious and Irish measures. So the Liberal political system was didactic, yet also pluralist. It reflected well the dominant culture of the Victorian prosperous classes, bourgeois, manly, individualist, consumerist, Protestant, rational. It appealed to a very wide political constituency. And, by the 1880s, most Liberals had no doubt that fifty years of their rule had assisted enormously in the material and moral development of the nation.[12]

By stressing the power and continuity of Liberal values, this book adopts a different perspective from that in which nineteenth-century Liberalism is normally viewed. Liberal historiography has always been dominated by the figure of Gladstone, and the period of his leadership, from 1868 to 1894, is usually regarded as the climax of Liberal politics. Traditionally, pre-Gladstonian Liberalism is seen as 'whiggism', socially narrow, philosophically ill-defined and politically slippery. Professor Gash criticises Liberals of the 1830s and 1840s for lacking a firm policy.[13] Few historians have much time for Lord John Russell, while hardly anyone has written successfully about Palmerston as a domestic Liberal leader.[14] The standard assumption is that the party was always divided between exclusive 'whigs' and aggressive 'radicals', and that the former's role was increasingly to make 'concessions' to the latter (who are broadly equated with the party rank-and-file). Professor Newbould has criticised Liberal parliamentary leaders of the 1830s for their lack of interest in professional provincial party organisation, because it threatened to increase the power of those 'radicals'.[15] In their classic works on mid-Victorian Liberalism, Professors Vincent and Shannon tend to define party primarily in extra-parliamentary terms and so see the 'Liberal party' maturing only when grass-roots enthusiasm was mobilised on a national basis in the 1860s and 1870s.[16] Professor Hamer, the only writer recently to attempt a synthetic history of Liberalism after 1867, asserts that 'Liberals were not held together by any strong sense of common purpose', and places his major emphasis on constituency-based 'faddists' who advocated particular 'sectional policies'.[17] In contrast, this book asserts that the *parliamentary* whig-Liberal tradition was central to British politics, that it was much more fertile than undisciplined radicalism, and that the lack of a professional national organisation added to its flexibility rather than hindering it. Distinctions between 'whigs' and 'radicals' were employed very loosely, and all Liberals worked from within a common tradition. Despite tensions, only a few radicals wished to set up as a political force separate from landed Liberals; conversely, any Liberal from a whig landed family who hoped for a serious political career knew that he had to work with rather than against MPs from the industrial centres. It was an essential part of the Liberal myth that by joint action each group fertilised the other: 'The process of permeation is reciprocal in its character . . . The Radical is permeated no less than the Whig, as we believe to the great advantage of them both'.[18] The principal problem on the 'left' in the nineteenth century was not conservatism and social exclusiveness on the part of the whig leaders, but the difficulty of rousing the country behind a coherent progressive programme. Liberal leaders were much more adventurous than the political nation. The conservatism of the electorate posed a serious problem in the late 1830s and for most of the 1850s, 1860s and 1870s. The challenges of self-appointed radical firebrands Cobden, Bright and Chamberlain foundered on this apathy.

[. . .] Victorian politics has fallen out of favour with historians, and is thought to be difficult to comprehend and teach. But it is misleading conceptions founded on social class, big bills and the role of popular political organisation which have created that difficulty. If nineteenth-century politics is a giant jigsaw puzzle, the Liberal creed examined in this book is its large central piece. [. . .]

Further reading

Other major recent works on Victorian Liberalism include: Jonathan P. Parry, *Democracy and Religion: Gladstone and the Liberal Party, 1867–75* (Cambridge: Cambridge University Press, 1986); Eugenio Biagini, *Liberty, Retrenchment and Reform: Popular Liberalism in the Age of Gladstone, 1860–1880* (Cambridge: Cambridge University Press, 1992); Terry Jenkins, *The Liberal Ascendancy, 1830–1886* (Basingstoke: Macmillan, 1994); H.C.G. Matthew, *Gladstone, 1809–1898* (Oxford: Clarendon Press, 1997).

Notes

1   J. Morley, *The life of William Ewart Gladstone* (3 vols, 1903), I, 128.

2   For most of this period, 'whig' and 'Liberal' were both used to describe the party, but I have used 'Liberal' from 1835 [. . .] . I have usually referred to it before 1835 as 'whig', though I have called the government of 1830–4 a 'Reform' government, following contemporary practice. From mid-century onwards, if not before, 'whig' was used principally to distinguish particular tendencies within the party, such as a special attachment to the party's traditions, or membership of the Liberal aristocracy and gentry. I have aimed to use it in these senses from 1835. It is important to note that there was no agreement on what a 'whig' was, and that the 'whigs' were at no time a discrete and easily identifiable section of the party. I have often needed a term to describe the middle ground of the parliamentary party and its propertied extra-parliamentary supporters. I have sometimes employed 'whig' and sometimes other phrases — 'moderate', 'propertied' or 'traditional' Liberal, or 'whig-Liberal' — depending on context or whim.

3   Only two modern books even approximate to this description, and both are avowedly thematic: D. Southgate, *The passing of the whigs, 1832–1886* (1962); I. Bradley, *The optimists: themes and personalities in Victorian Liberalism* (1980). R.B. McCallum, *The Liberal party from Earl Grey to Asquith* (1963) is thin.

4   See R. Blake, *The Conservative party from Peel to Churchill* (1970); *The Conservative leadership 1832–1932*, ed. D. Southgate (1974); N. Gash, D. Southgate, D. Dilks and J. Ramsden, *The Conservatives: a history from their origins to 1965* (1977) and B. Coleman, *Conservatism and the Conservative party in nineteenth-century Britain* (1988).

5   T.A. Jenkins, *Gladstone, whiggery and the Liberal party 1874–1886* (Oxford, 1988), p. 40.

6   For Peel's use of this phrase, see e.g. B. Hilton, 'Peel; a reappraisal', *H[istorical] J[ournal]*, XXII (1979), 601.

7   There is a good short summary of the historiographical debate about the 1832 Act in J. Milton-Smith, 'Earl Grey's cabinet and the objects of parliamentary reform', *H.J.*, XV (1972), 55–7. See also R.W. Davis, 'The whigs and the idea of electoral deference: some further thoughts on the Great Reform Act', *Durham University Journal*, LXVII (1974–5), 79–91.

8   *Times* 24 July 1861, p. 10.

9   There was a long whig/Liberal tradition of familiarity with intellectual, scientific and theological thinking and literary and historical culture. The whig salon Holland House, in its heyday in the 1810s and 1820s, brought politicians, and men of letters together. Successive generations of leading Liberal politicians patronized worthy debating bodies such as the Society for the Diffusion of Useful Knowledge, the British Association for the Advancement of Science and the Social Science Association. Russell and Gladstone, among Liberal Prime Ministers, were particularly widely-read and prolific authors.

10 Lord J. Russell, *Hansard['s parliamentary debates, 3rd series]*, III, 802, 22 March 1831. All references to *Hansard* debates in these notes are to the 3rd series unless indicated.

11 Lord J. Russell, *Letter to the electors of Stroud, on the principles of the Reform Act* (1839), p. 29.

12 This was true even of Gladstone, who was unusually aware of the burden of sin in the world. See his 'Locksley Hall and the jubilee', *Nineteenth Century*, XXI (Jan.–June 1887), 1–18, and 'Universitas Hominum: or, the unity of history', *North American Review*, CXLV (1887), 589–602.

13 N. Gash, *Reaction and reconstruction in English politics 1832–1852* (Oxford, 1965), pp. 199–200.

14 An interesting exception is P.M. Gurowich, 'The continuation of war by other means: party and politics, 1855–1865', *H.J.*, XXVII (1984), 603–31.

15 I. Newbould, 'Whiggery and the growth of party 1830–1841: organization and the challenge of Reform', *Parliamentary History*, IV (1985). See also Matthew in *Gladstone diaries*, X, li.

16 J.R. Vincent, *The formation of the Liberal party, 1857–1868* (1966); R.T. Shannon, *Gladstone and the Bulgarian agitation, 1876* (1963).

17 D.A. Hamer, *Liberal politics in the age of Gladstone and Rosebery: a study in leadership and policy* (Oxford, 1972), esp. p. xi.

18 A. Elliot, 'Three Reform bills', *Edinburgh Review*, CLXI (Apr. 1885), 582.

Gareth Stedman Jones

RADICALISM, LANGUAGE AND CLASS

'The Language of Chartism' in James Epstein and Dorothy Thompson (eds), *The Chartist Experience: Studies in Working-Class Radicalism and Culture* (London: Macmillan, 1982), 3–16.

After 1980, the most discussed and influential work in the field of Victorian political history was undoubtedly **Gareth Stedman Jones**' article, 'The Language of Chartism', later published in an extended version as 'Rethinking Chartism' in his collection *Languages of Class* (1983). Gareth Stedman Jones has been one of the leading Marxist historians of the nineteenth century. His book, *Outcast London* (1971) was a major study of the social structure of later Victorian London containing a strong emphasis on class and economic relationships. From the late 1970s, Stedman Jones became a prominent left-wing figure devoted to rethinking the premises of Marxism and critiquing Marxist approaches to the nineteenth century (for example, the idea of 'social control'). He also became more open to the work of intellectual historians and scholars who were thinking about the determining role of language.

Chartism was the leading popular agitation of the 1830s and 1840s. It was based around the People's Charter and demanded that parliament introduce universal manhood suffrage among other democratic reforms. Three petitions were presented to parliament (in 1839, 1842 and 1848), all of which were rejected. The movement, however, played a vital role in the political education of the working class. Stedman Jones' 'The Language of Chartism' (and subsequently 'Rethinking Chartism') questioned the notion that the radical movement of the 1830s and 1840s represented a new stage of class consciousness (which many labour historians had held it to be). If this was so, why were the six points of the People's Charter all political (as opposed to economic) demands? He argued that social historians had ignored the peculiarities of the political identity of the Chartists; instead it was important to take seriously what they actually said and wrote. Rather than representing a new stage in radicalism, the Chartists were better understood as the continuation of an older radical tradition going back to the 1770s. Social historians, such as Asa Briggs, had argued in the 1960s that Chartism varied in form from one locality to another; by contrast, Stedman Jones contends that we need to think more about how Chartism was a national movement with a programme that commanded wide agreement. This article was heavily debated, both in terms of what it had to say about class but also about the uses of language. Stedman Jones was associated (not quite accurately) with the ideas of post-structuralism. In the wake of the article, a large number of revisionist historians have been inspired by Stedman Jones to write histories of Victorian popular politics that reconstruct the peculiarities of political languages, ideas and identities and have demonstrated that these older forms of radicalism retained their appeal up to the late nineteenth century (see Biagini and Reid (eds), *Currents of Radicalism*). Whereas social history often ignored politics, there was a new focus on the contingencies of the political process and on the way in which the changing structure of the British state helped shape the wider political agenda.

In this extract, we reprint the opening passages of Stedman Jones' article where he challenges the prevailing historiography and insists on the essentially political nature of Chartism. In the rest of the article he demonstrates that the Chartists' attitude to class (and the middle class in particular) was more complex than was assumed in the 1960s and 1970s. Class was defined as much in political as economic terms. He also argues that Peel's reforms of the 1840s (especially the repeal of the Corn Laws in 1846) meant that the state could not be seen as the preserve of one class, as some Chartists had maintained, leading to the ideological undermining of the movement. This contrasted with earlier views which suggested that Chartism failed because of state repression or because economic improvements reduced social tension. Stedman Jones' article is important because he demonstrates the possibilities of a linguistic and political, as opposed to a social, interpretation of the Chartists.

Gareth Stedman Jones is Professor of Political Science in the History Faculty, Director of the Centre for History and Economics, and Fellow of King's College, Cambridge University. In addition to the works mentioned above, his recent publications include *An End to Poverty* (2004) and the introduction to a new edition of *The Communist Manifesto* (2002).

———————

WHO WERE THE CHARTISTS? The Chartists' own view was stated by Thomas Duncombe, introducing the 1842 Petition: 'those who were originally called radicals and afterwards reformers, are called Chartists'.[1] But this was never accepted by the great bulk of contemporary opinion. From the moment that Chartism first emerged as a public movement, what seized the imagination of contemporaries were not the formally radical aims and rhetoric of its spokesmen, but the novel and threatening social character of the movement. A nation-wide independent movement of the 'working classes' brandishing pikes in torchlight meetings in pursuit of its 'rights' was an unprecedented event, and whatever Chartism's official self-identity, contemporary observers could not refrain from projecting onto it deeper unavowed motives and sentiments. Thomas Carlyle's distinction between the 'distracted incoherent embodiment of Chartism' and its 'living essence' . . . 'the bitter discontent grown fierce and mad, the wrong condition therefore or the wrong disposition, of the Working Classes of England', with its implied gulf between the real and formal definition of Chartism, set the terms of the predominant response, whatever the precise definition given to these terms.[2] Chartists in vain protested their respect for property.[3] Macaulay, debating the 1842 Petition, deduced the Chartist position on property from the social composition of its constituency. To accept the petition would be to commit government to a class which would be induced 'to commit great and systematic inroads against the security of property'. 'How is it possible that according to the principles of human nature, if you give them this power, it would not be used to its fullest extent?'[4] Even the more sympathetic middle-class observers virtually ignored the political case of the Chartists. Mrs Gaskell's novel, *Mary Barton*, for instance, analysed Chartism solely in terms of anger, distress and the breakdown of social relationships. Thus, from the beginning, there was virtual unanimity among outside observers that Chartism was to be understood, not as a political movement, but as a social phenomenon.

From the continental Communist left, the young Engels, also deeply impressed by Carlyle's depiction of the condition of England's problem, made a similar assumption. 'The middle class and property are dominant; the poor man has no rights, is oppressed and fleeced, the constitution repudiates him and the law mistreats him'. Thus, in Engels's view, the form of democracy represented by Chartism was not that 'of the French Revolution whose antithesis was monarchy and feudalism, but *the* democracy whose antithesis is the middle class and property' . . . 'The struggle of democracy against aristocracy in England is the struggle of the poor against the rich. The democracy towards which England is moving is a *social democracy*'.[5] Engels's picture of Chartism, developed in *The Condition of the English Working Class in 1844*, was seen retrospectively as a major empirical confirmation of the later Marxist conception of 'class consciousness', elaborated in such works as the *German Ideology*, the *Poverty of Philosophy* and the *Communist Manifesto*. The premises of this position was, in Marx's words, that 'the struggle' against capital in its developed modern form, in its decisive aspect is 'the struggle of the industrial wage worker against the industrial bourgeois'.[6] Thus, applied to Chartism, whatever its formal professions, its living essence was that of a class movement of the proletariat born of the new relations of production engendered by modern industry. Its real enemy was the bourgeoisie and the revolution it would have to effect would amount to the overthrow of this class. As Chartism disencumbered itself from its middle-class allies — a process which Engels considered to have culminated in 1842[7] — the proletarian character of the struggle would assume an ever more conscious form.

While Engels's optimistic conclusions have, for obvious reasons, not been accepted, many of his basic ways of seeing this period have been incorporated into the subsequent historiography of Chartism. The relationship between Chartism, modern industry and class consciousness has remained a prominent theme of labour and socialist historians. His contrast between Manchester and Birmingham, between the class relations of the factory town and that of a city of small workshops, has been amply developed by social historians and sociologists. But it is important to insist that Engels's emphasis upon the social character of Chartism, however brilliantly argued, was — as the testimony of Carlyle and Macaulay suggests — in no sense the peculiar property of a proto-Marxist position. The social interpretation represented the predominant approach of contemporaries. The analysis of the young Engels represented one particular variant of it — that which interpreted Chartism as the political expression of the new industrial proletariat. Another variant, elements of which could also be traced back to liberal commentators at the time, has been equally, if not more influential in the subsequent historiography of Chartism: that which locates Chartism, not as the expression of modern factory workers, but of handloom weavers and other declining 'pre-industrial' groups. The period since the Second World War has yielded further and equally distinct variants of the social approach — the correlation between Chartism and the trade cycle, associated with Rostow, and the identification of Chartism with atavistic responses to modernisation, associated with Smelser.[8] Indeed in nearly all writings on Chartism, except that of Chartists themselves, it has been the movement's class character, social composition or more simply the hunger and distress of which it was thought to be the manifestation, rather than its platform or programme which have formed the focal point of enquiry.

It is not surprising that historians have placed these themes at the centre of their studies of Chartism. But it is surprising that there has not been more recognition of the interpretative costs of such an approach. Generally doubts that have been expressed about particular versions of a social approach have not extended to the limitations of the social approach as such. The prevalent mode of criticism has been as resolutely social in its assumptions as that of the interpretation to be opposed. Critical discussion has mainly clustered around such questions as the exploitative character of industrialisation itself, the reality of the threat to living standards and the real extent or depth of class hostilities. The difficulty of this form of criticism is that pressed to its conclusions, it makes the very existence of a combative mass movement difficult to explain, irrespective of its precise character. Far more problematic, yet barely touched upon by the critics of the various social interpretations of Chartism, is the general neglect of the specific political and ideological form within which this mass discontent was expressed and the consequent tendency to elide the Chartist language of class with a range of Marxist or sociological notions of class consciousness. What has not been sufficiently questioned is whether this language can simply be analysed in terms of its expression of, or correspondence to, the putative consciousness of a particular class or social or occupational group. If an analysis of this language does not confirm such a relation of direct manifestation or correspondence, what implication does this have for the interpretation of Chartism as a whole? The language itself has seldom been subjected to detailed examination.[9] But even in cases where it has, the gravitational pull exercised by the social interpretation has generally been powerful enough to inhibit any major revision of the conventional picture of the movement.

The intention of this essay is to suggest the rudiments of such a reinterpretation. In contrast to the prevalent social-historical approach to Chartism, whose starting-point is some conception of class or occupational consciousness, it argues that the ideology of Chartism cannot be constructed in abstraction from its linguistic form.

An analysis of Chartist ideology must start from what Chartists actually said or wrote, the terms in which they addressed each other or their opponents. It cannot simply be inferred — with the aid of decontextualised quotation — from the supposed exigencies, however plausible, of the material situation of a particular class or social group. Nor is it adequate, as an alternative, to adopt a more subjective approach and to treat Chartist language as a more or less immediate rendition of experience into words. This way of interpreting Chartism possesses the virtue of paying more serious attention to what Chartists said. But it too ultimately resolves problems posed by the form of Chartism into problems of its supposed content. Against this approach, it is suggested that the analysis of the language itself precludes such a directly referential theory of meaning. What is proposed instead is an approach which attempts to identify and situate the place of language and form, and which resists the temptation to collapse questions posed by the form of Chartism into questions of its assumed substance. It is argued that if the interpretation of the language and politics is freed from *a priori* social inferences, it then becomes possible to establish a far closer and more precise relationship between ideology and activity than is conveyed in the standard picture of the movement.

In adopting this approach, however, it is not intended to imply that the analysis of language can provide an exhaustive account of Chartism. Or that the social conditions of existence of this language were arbitrary.[10] It is not a question of replacing a social interpretation by a linguistic interpretation, it is how the two relate, that must be rethought. Abstractly the matter determines the possibility of the form, but the form conditions the development of the matter. Historically, there are good reasons for thinking that Chartism could not have been a movement except of the working class, for the discontents which the movement addressed were overwhelmingly, if not exclusively, those of wage-earners, and the solidarities upon which the movement counted were in fact also those between wage-earners. But the form in which these discontents were addressed cannot be understood in terms of the consciousness of a particular social class, since the form pre-existed any independent action by such a class and did not significantly change in response to it. Moreover, the form was not, as is sometimes implied in the social interpretation, a mere shell within which a class movement developed. For it was what informed the political activity of the movement, it defined the terms in which oppression was understood and it was what provided the vision of an alternative. It was further what defined the *political* crisis from which Chartism emerged and it fashioned the political means by which that crisis was resolved. The type of explanation which ascribes the movement to distress or the social changes accompanying the industrial revolution, never confronts the fact that the growth and decline of Chartism was a function of its capacity to persuade its constituency to interpret their distress or discontent within the terms of its political language. Chartism was a political movement and political movements cannot satisfactorily be defined in terms of the anger and disgruntlement of disaffected social groups or even the consciousness of a particular class. A political movement is not simply a manifestation of distress and pain, its existence is distinguished by a shared conviction articulating a political solution to distress and a political diagnosis of its causes. To be successful, that is to embed itself in the assumptions of masses of people, a particular political vocabulary must convey a practicable hope of a general alternative and a believable means of realising it, such that potential recruits can think within its terms. It must be sufficiently broad and appropriate to enable its adherents to inhabit its language in confronting day-to-day problems of political and social experience, to elaborate tactics and slogans upon its basis, and to resist the attempts of opposing movements to encroach upon, reinterpret or replace it. Thus the history of Chartism cannot satisfactorily be written in terms of the social and economic grievances of which it is argued to be the expression. Such an approach does not explain why these discontents should have taken a Chartist form, nor why Chartism should not have continued to express the changing fears and aspirations of its social constituency in new circumstances. It is with these questions that this essay is concerned. But before embarking upon such a discussion, we must first attempt to demonstrate more concretely what the interpretative costs of the social approach have been.

One major consequence of the social interpretation of Chartism is that when the actual demands of the movement have been discussed, they have been treated more as a legacy from its prehistory than as a real focal point of activity. Given the assumption that Chartism represented the first manifestation of a modern working-class movement, there has appeared something paradoxical in the fact that such a movement could have come together behind a series of radical constitutional demands first put forward over half a century before. But even in works in which no strong assumptions are made about the modernity or class character of Chartism, little effort is made to explain why distress and unemployment should find expression in a movement for universal suffrage rather than more immediate pressure for relief from the state. Instead, ever since 1913 when Edouard Dolléans first suggested that the cause of Chartism was to be discovered in the working-class reaction against the industrial revolution,[11] historians have tended to downplay the political programme of the Chartists as merely expressive of discontents whose true sources and remedies lay elsewhere.

Such an approach has been compounded by another emphasis in Chartist historiography, originally unconnected to the social interpretation, but which in the course of the twentieth century has increasingly coalesced with it. From the time when Chartism first began to be written about, attention was focused on the divided nature of the movement. The first generation of Chartist historians, embittered ex-Chartists like Gammage, Lovett and Cooper, concentrated disproportionately upon rifts in organisation and the angry and divisive battles between leading personalities.[12] In subsequent historiography, concentration upon the social character of the movement lent itself easily to the analysis of these divisions in social and economic terms. Divergencies of personality and cultural formation were now made to correspond to divergencies of economic situation and locality. The antagonism between Lovett and O'Connor was given a sociological coloration. It became a symbol of the supposed incompatibility between the non-industrialised constitutionally minded artisans of London and Birmingham — followers of Lovett, Attwood and Sturge, inclined to class alliance and moral force — and northern factory workers or declining handloom weavers, followers of O'Connor, hostile to the middle class, ill-educated and quasi-insurrectionary.[13] Later and more sophisticated versions of this approach, freed from some of the Fabian assumptions which had originally structured it, shifted arguments about Chartism even further from the battles and ideas of the leaders to the differing social textures of protest in different regions, and these regions themselves were arranged along a scale of progressive class polarisation determined in the extent of industrialisation.[14] Such polarities, however, have been weakened by more recent research. Despite Birmingham's well-publicised reputation for harmonious inter-class radicalism in the nineteenth century, its Chartists rejected the Birmingham Political Union leadership and for four years after 1838 looked mainly to O'Connor and stressed class independence.[15] It has similarly been shown that London Chartism in the 1840s was neither particularly weak, nor particularly moderate, as the old interpretation supposed. By 1848 it had become one of Chartism's most militant centres.[16] Conversely factory and heavy industrial areas like south Lancashire and the north east, distinctly militant centres in the early years of Chartism, were far less prominent in 1848.[17] Moreover recent occupational analysis of Chartist adherence in its early years appears to suggest that the extent to which certain trades were disproportionately represented — shoemakers or handloom weavers, for instance — has been exaggerated and that Chartism attracted a more representative cross-section of the main trades in each locality than has usually been assumed.[18] If this is the case, it implies that too much attention to local or occupational peculiarities can obscure the extent to which Chartism was *not* a local or sectional movement. Chartism was a national movement. Yet this more surprising phenomenon — the extent of unity in the early Chartist Movement and the enduring loyalty of a sizeable minority over more than a decade to the remedies of the Charter, despite all disagreement and difference — has been left in the realm of commonsense assumption.

Thus the stress upon division and local differences has tended to accentuate the weak points in the social interpretation of Chartism: its tendency to neglect the political form of the movement and thus to render obscure and inconsequential the reasoning that underlay the demand for the Charter. Mark Hovell, still perhaps the most influential historian of Chartism, set the terms of the predominant approach when he argued that 'by 1838 the Radical Programme was recognised no longer as an end in itself, but as the means to an end, and the end was the social and economic regeneration of society'. This was a seemingly unexceptionable statement and something like it had been said on occasion by Chartists themselves. But Hovell's amplification of it betrayed a basic misunderstanding, which rendered the Charter an oddity and the 'end' incoherent. 'The most optimistic of Chartist enthusiasts', he wrote, 'could hardly have believed that a new heaven and a new earth would be brought about by mere improvements of political machinery'. But, he continued, 'social Chartism was a protest against what existed, not a reasoned policy to set up anything in its place. Apart from machinery, Chartism was largely a passionate negation'.[19] Subsequent landmarks in the historiography of Chartism have, if anything, only strengthened the impression of incoherence at the core of the movement. For G.D.H. Cole, 'the Chartist movement was essentially an economic movement with a purely political programme'. 'A common idea might have held them together; the Charter, a mere common programme, was not enough to prevent them from giving their mutual dislikes free rein'.[20] For Asa Briggs, writing in *Chartist Studies* in 1959, the Charter was not so much a focus as 'a symbol of unity'. But 'it concealed as much as it proclaimed — the diversity of local social pressures, the variety of local leaderships, the relative sense of urgency among different people and different groups'.[21]

In the face of this interpretative consensus, it is worth citing the position of the first historian of Chartism, R.G. Gammage, writing in 1854. Gammage certainly did not deny the social origins of political discontent in the sense that 'in times of prosperity there is scarce a ripple to be observed on the ocean of politics'. Nor did he deny that the people, once victorious, would adopt 'social measures' to improve their condition. But significantly, he does not talk of 'political machinery', 'a mere common programme' or 'a symbol'. He states, on the contrary, that it is the existence of great social wrongs which principally teaches the masses the value of political rights; and his explanation of the thinking behind the Charter places the emphasis quite differently from Hovell and the historians who have followed him. In a 'period of adversity', he wrote,

> The masses look on the enfranchised classes, whom they behold reposing on their couch of opulence, and contrast that opulence with the misery of their own condition. Reasoning from effect to cause there is no marvel that they arrive at the conclusion — that their exclusion from political power is the cause of our social anomalies.[22]

Political Power is the cause. *Opulence* is the effect. But to subsequent historians whether liberal, social democrat or Marxist, it has been axiomatic that economic power is the cause, political power the effect. If this axiom is read back into the political programme of the Chartists, there is no marvel that that programme should have appeared incoherent.

Not all historians have assumed that Chartists must have meant the economic and social, when they spoke about the political. The under-estimation of the political character and context of the popular struggles in the pre-Chartist period has been magnificently remedied by Edward Thompson's *Making of the English Working Class*. As he demonstrates, the experience of the plebeian movement between 1780 and 1830 was not simply that of intensified economic exploitation, but also of sharp and semi-permanent political repression. Moreover, the attitude of the government and the unreformed Parliament to customary trade practices often seemed yet more cavalier than that to be found in the localities. Thus he can argue with some force that 'the line from 1832 to Chartism is not a haphazard pendulum alternation of "political" and "economic" agitation, but a direct progression, in which simultaneous and related movements converge towards a single point. This point was the vote'.[23]

The great achievement of Thompson's book is to have freed the concept of class consciousness from any simple reduction to the development of productive forces measured by the progress of large-scale industry and to have linked it to the development of a political movement which cannot be reduced to the terminology of incoherent protest. To have established this connection is a vital advance. But we must go further. Thompson's concept of class consciousness still assumes a relatively direct relationship between 'social being' and 'social consciousness' which leaves little independent space for the ideological context within which the coherence of a particular language of class can be reconstituted. A simple dialectic between consciousness and experience cannot explain the precise form assumed by Chartist ideology. A highlighting of the experience of exploitation and political oppression, would not in itself account for Gammage's statement. It was not simply experience, but rather a particular linguistic ordering of experience which could lead the masses to believe that 'their exclusion from political power is the cause of our social anomalies' and that 'political power' was the cause of 'opulence'. Consciousness cannot be related to experience except through the interposition of a particular language which organises the understanding of experience, and it is important to stress that more than one language is capable of articulating the same set of experiences. The language of class was not simply a verbalisation of perception or the rising of consciousness of an existential face, as Marxist and sociological traditions have assumed. But neither was it simply the articulation of a cumulative experience of a particular form of class relations. It was constructed and inscribed within a complex rhetoric of metaphorical association, causal inference and imaginative construction. Class consciousness — 'a consciousness of identity of interests between working men of the most diverse occupations and levels of attainment' and 'consciousness of the identity of interests of the working class or productive classes as against those of other classes', as Thompson defines it[24] — formed part of a language whose systematic linkages were supplied by the assumptions of radicalism: a vision and analysis of social and political evils which certainly long predated the advent of class consciousness, however defined.

In England radicalism first surfaced as a coherent programme in the 1770s, and first became a vehicle of plebeian political aspirations from the 1790s. Its strength, indeed its definition, was a critique of the corrupting effects of the concentration of political power and its corrosive influence upon a society deprived of proper means of political representation. As such, in variant forms, it could provide the vocabulary of grievance to a succession of political and social groups. Elements of this vocabulary went back to the seventeenth-century revolutions and were reforged by those who felt excluded by the settlements of 1688 or 1714 or by the so-called 'country party' during the years of Walpolean or Pelhamite dominance. The particular resonance, still alive in the Chartist period, of words like 'patriot' or 'independent' and the demonological associations of fundholding and stock-jobbing dated back to this time. From the 1760s the tenancy of this language tended to pass from right to left. Country toryism receded — though it never disappeared — in the face of radical Whiggery. New components of the vocabulary were added by the Americans and their English supporters, and echoes of a less decorous seventeenth-century radicalism could again be detected. With the Wilkesite controversy, a radical movement in a full sense began. The focus was no longer simply upon court and city coteries and the corruption of patronage and place, but more consistently and determinedly upon the constitution and the means of representation. The unbalanced and disordered constitution could only be restored to health by drawing upon the 'people', and at the same time the definition of the people was widened, with a shift of emphasis from property to person. In the 1790s radicalism became plebeian and democratic, and successes in America, Ireland and above all, France, lent it a revolutionary edge. It was accordingly repressed, a condition which, given its survival, bestowed upon it a yet more intransigent sense of its righteousness and the accuracy of its diagnosis. In the post-war situation radicalism found itself forced to stretch its vocabulary to encompass new sources of distress and discontent within its terms. For not only did it find itself confronted by a new economic situation but also it found its nostrums challenged, though in quite different ways, by the novel emphases of political economy and Owenism, both of which cut across its premises. In response, radicalism attributed a growing number of economic evils to a political source and in the following thirty years managed to withstand these rival analyses with some success. It accommodated many of the preoccupations of the Owenites, while rejecting with less and less equivocation any compromise with political economy.

The cost of this process was an increasing distance from the bulk of its former middle-class constituency. But however much radicalism extended its scope during this period, it could never be the ideology of a specific class. It was first and foremost a vocabulary of political exclusion; whatever the social character of those excluded. Thus, if it *de facto* became the more and more exclusive property of the 'working classes' in the 1830s and 40s, this did not lead to a basic restructuring of the ideology itself. The self-identity of radicalism was not that of any specific group, but of the 'People' or the 'nation' against the monopolisers of political representation and power *and hence* financial or economic power.

It is in this sense that the growing political hostility between the middle and working classes after 1832 must be understood. In radical terms, in 1832 the 'people' became the 'working classes'. Explaining the emergence of Chartism in 1838, for instance, the *Northern Star* considered:

> The attention of the labouring classes — the real 'people' — has been successively (and yet to a certain degree simultaneously) aroused by the injuries they have sustained by the operation of a corrupt system of patronage hanging around their necks a host of locusts, in the shape of idle and useless pensioners and a warm of hornets, in the form of mischievous placemen and commissioners to support whom they are weighed to the earth by the pressures of taxation; by the operation of the Corn Laws which made rents high and bread dear; by the iniquitous protection of the fundholders which made money dear and labour cheap; by the horrors of the factory system which immolates their progeny and coins the blood of their children into gold, for merciless grasping ruffians and by the abominations of the poor law act which virtually and practically denies them the right to live. All these and one hundred minor grievances, subservient to the same grand end (of making the working classes beasts of burden — hewers of wood and drawers of water — to the artistocracy, Jewocracy, Millocracy, Shopocracy, and every other Ocracy which feeds on human vitals) have roused the feelings of the people and prompted the respective parties to seek a remedy for the smarting of their wounds.[25]

By the same token, as a group, the middle classes had ceased to be part of the 'people'. For they had joined the system of oppressors and were henceforth answerable for the actions of the legislature. Indeed rigorously speaking, government now became that of the 'middle classes'. Speaking of the Reform Bill, the *Poor Man's Guardian* wrote a year later:

> By that Bill, the government of the country is essentially lodged in the hands of the middle classes; we say the middle classes — for though the aristocracy have their share of authority, it is virtually absorbed in that of the middlemen who form the great majority of the constituency.[26]

Now, if it is true that the language of class — at least in its usage by the popular movement — was the language of radicalism, then a number of consequences follow. The most obvious one is that the political demands of the popular movement should be placed at the centre of the story of Chartism, rather than treated as symbolic or anachronistic; and not only the demands, but also the presuppositions which underlay them. For these were neither the superficial encasement of proletarian class consciousness, nor a simple medium of translation between experience and programme. If the history of Chartism is re-analysed in this manner, then the chronology of its rise and decline can be made more precise. The central tenet of radicalism — the attribution of evil and misery to a political source — clearly differentiated it both from a Malthusian-based popular political economy which placed the source of dissonance in nature itself and from Owenite socialism which located evil in false ideas which dominated State and civil society alike. But it also suggested that the success of radicalism as the ideology of a mass movement would depend upon specific conditions, those in which the State and the propertied classes in their *political and legal capacity* could be perceived as the source of all oppression. The programme of Chartism remained believable so long as unemployment, low wages, economic insecurity and other material afflictions could convincingly be assigned political causes. If, for instance, lack of political representation and a corrupt system of power rather than economic phenomena were responsible for the misery of the working classes, then it followed from this that partial reforms like the ten hours bill or the repeal of the Corn Law, could not bring real improvement, indeed were more likely to hasten deterioration, since they left the system intact. Nor could trade unionism be thought a realistic alternative since, if the labour market was politically determined, then differences of bargaining power between different groups within the working classes were largely illusory. So long as the empirical forecasts which followed from radical premises appeared to be borne out, Chartists had little reason to expect widespread defections from their ranks. Once, however, the evidence suggested that real reform was possible within the unreformed system, that the State did not wholly correspond to the radical picture and conditions changed in such a way that differences in the fortunes of various trades became clearly visible, despite the identity of their political situation, then radical ideology could be expected to lose purchase over large parts of its mass following. Such an approach suggests a different way of looking at the period of mid-Victorian stabilisation, from that prevalent among social historians.[27] In radical ideology the dividing line between classes was not that between employer and employed, but that between the represented and the unrepresented. Thus hostility to the middle classes was not ascribed to their role in production, but to their participation in a corrupt and unrepresentative political system, and it was through this political system that the producers of wealth were conceived to be deprived of the fruits of their labour. Once therefore the conviction of the totally evil character of the political system itself began to fade and distress became less pervasive, there was no independent rationale within radical ideology for antagonism towards the middle class as such. If this is the case, there is then little need to introduce ambitious sociological explanations, such as the emergence of a labour aristocracy, co-option by the middle class or the invention of new and subtle means of social control to explain the disappearance of Chartism. Such approaches ignore the more elementary point that as a system of beliefs, Chartism began to fail, when a gulf opened up between its premises and the perception of its constituency. Local and everyday awareness of differences of social position, of course, remained but it was no longer linked across the country through the language of radicalism to a shared conviction of a realisable institutional and political alternative. Thus if expressed hostility to the middle classes declined, despite the continuation of capitalist relations of production, this should be no occasion for surprise. For it was the product of the decline of a political movement whose expressed reasons for hostility to the middle class had had little to do with the character of the productive system in itself.

Further reading

This article is available in its fullest form as 'Rethinking Chartism' in Gareth Stedman Jones, *Languages of Class: Studies in English Working-Class History, 1832–1982* (Cambridge: Cambridge University Press, 1983), 90–178. Stedman Jones' subsequent works should be consulted, especially his very important introduction to Karl Marx and Frederick Engels, *The Communist Manifesto* (London: Penguin, 2002) and his *An End to Poverty?: A Historical Debate* (London: Profile, 2004).

The article reprinted here elicited a series of important responses and critiques from historians, which focused particularly on Stedman Jones' discussion of class. Among these, see especially: Robert Gray, 'The Deconstructing of the English Working Class', *Social History*, 11 (1986), 363–73; Neville Kirk, 'In Defence of Class: A Critique of Recent Revisionist Writings upon the Nineteenth-Century English Working Class', *International Review of Social History*, 32 (1987), 2–47; James Epstein, 'Rethinking the Categories of Working-Class History' in his *In Practice: Studies in the Language and Culture of Popular Politics in Modern Britain* (Stanford, CA: Stanford University Press, 2003), 15–33. Another set of responses were concerned with Stedman Jones' methodology. See the debate that took place in *Social History*, begun by David Mayfield and Susan Thorne, 'Social History and its Discontents: Gareth Stedman Jones and the Politics of Language', *Social History*, 17 (1992), 165–88. This led to an extensive debate about postmodernism and history. Stedman Jones' influence on the history of popular politics is particularly evident in Eugenio Biagini and Alastair Reid (eds), *Currents of Radicalism: Popular Radicalism, Organized Labour and Party Politics in Britain, 1850–1914* (Cambridge: Cambridge University Press, 1991). For further discussion of Stedman Jones and Chartism, see: Miles Taylor, 'Rethinking the Chartists: Searching for Synthesis in the Historiography of Chartism', *Historical Journal*, 39 (1996), 479–95; Rohan McWilliam, *Popular Politics in Nineteenth-Century England* (London: Routledge, 1998). The standard work on Chartism itself is Dorothy Thompson, *The Chartists* (Hounslow: Temple Smith, 1984).

Notes

1   *Hansard*, 3rd series, vol. LXIII, 13–91; cf. [*Feargus*] O'Connor's observation: 'The movement party was known, had become strong and united under the political term Radical, when, lo! - and to shew there is much in a name, our political opponents rebaptised us, giving us the name of Chartists. Now although there was no earthly difference between the principles of a Radical and of a Chartist, yet did the press of both parties . . . contrive to alarm the prejudices of the weak, the timid and the unsuspecting, until at length they accomplished their desired object — a split between parties seeking one and the same end.' (*The Trial of Feargus O'Connor* (1843) p. ix.).

The left wing of the movement tended to describe itself as 'democrat' rather than 'radical'.

2   T. Carlyle, *Chartism* (1839), ch. I.

3   'MR DOUBTFUL: But where is the clause for the redistribution of property? Have you forgotten that?
RADICAL: That is a base and slanderous calumny, which those who profit by things as they are have forged to damage our cause. There never was the slightest foundation for such a charge, although judges on the benches and parsons in the pulpit have not scrupled to give currency to the falsehood.'

'The Question "What is a Chartist?" Answered' (Finsbury Tract Society, 1839) reprinted in D. Thompson (ed.) *The Early Chartists* (1971) p. 92. Given the Chartist definition of property, however, it is not surprising that the propertied classes should feel threatened.

4   *Hansard*, 3rd series, vol. LXIII, 13–91

5   F. Engels, 'The Condition of England, the English Constitution', Karl Marx, Frederick Engels, *Collected Works* (1973) vol. 3, p. 513.

6   K. Marx, 'The Class Struggles in France, 1848 to 1850', *Collected Works*, vol. 10, p. 57.

7   F. Engels, 'The Condition of the Working-Class in England', *Collected Works*, vol. 4, p. 523.

8   W.W. Rostow, *British Economy of the 19th Century* (Oxford, 1948); N.J. Smelser, *Social Change in the Industrial Revolution* (London, 1959).

9   For two analyses which do illuminatingly focus upon the language and politics of radicalism during this period, see T.M. Parssinen, 'Association, Convention and Anti-Parliament in British Radical Politics, 1771–1848', *English Historical Review*, LXXXVII (1973); I. Prothero, 'William Benbow and the Concept of the "General Strike"', *Past & Present* 63 (1974).

10 Nor is it intended to suggest that what is being offered here is an exhaustive analysis of the language of Chartism. The language analysed here is largely taken from radical literature and speeches reported in the radical press. Quite apart from the fact that such reported speech took no account of accent or dialect, it is not suggested that this is the only language Chartists employed. What is examined here is only the public political language of the movement. Much further research would be required before a full account of the language of Chartism could be produced.

11 E. Dolléans, *Le Chartisme, 1831–1848* (rev. edn, Paris, 1949) p. 319 and ch. 1.

12 R.G. Gammage, *The History of the Chartist Movement* (London, 1855); W. Lovett, *Life and Struggles of William Lovett, in his pursuit of Bread, Knowledge and Freedom* (London, 1876); T. Cooper, *Life of Thomas Cooper, Written by Himself* (London, 1872).

13 See in particular M. Hovell, *The Chartist Movement* (Manchester, 1918).

14 See for instance A. Briggs, 'The Local Background of Chartism', in Briggs (ed.), *Chartist Studies* (London, 1959).

15 See C. Behagg, 'An Alliance with the Middle Class: The Birmingham Political Union and Early Chartism' in J. Epstein and D. Thompson (eds), *The Chartist Experience* (London 1982); see also T. Tholfson, 'The Chartist Crisis in Birmingham', *International Review of Social History* vol. III (1958).

16 See I. Prothero, 'Chartism in London', *Past and Present* 44 (1969); D. Goodway, 'Chartism in London', *Bulletin of the Society for the Study of Labour History*, 20 (1970).

17 On the north-east, see W.H. Maehl, 'Chartist Disturbances in Northeastern England, 1839', *International Review of Social History* VIII (1963); on south Lancashire, see R. Sykes, 'Early Chartism and Trade Unionism in South-East Lancashire' in J. Epstein and D. Thompson (eds), *The Chartist Experience* (London, 1982); see also J. Foster, *Class Struggle and the Industrial Revolution, Early Industrial Capitalism in three English Towns* (London, 1974); P. Joyce, *Work, Society and Politics* (Brighton, 1980).

18 D. Thompson, 'The Geography of Chartism' (unpublished MS); see also her remarks on this in the Introduction to Thompson (ed.), *The Early Chartists*.

19 Hovell, *The Chartist Movement* (1970 edn) p. 7; ibid. p. 303.

20 G.D.H. Cole, *A Short History of the British Working Class Movement, 1789–1947* (London, 1948), p. 94; ibid. p. 120.

21 Briggs, *Chartist Studies*, p. 26.

22 Gammage, *History of the Chartist Movement* (facsimile reprint of 1894 edn., London, 1976) p. 9.

23 E.P. Thompson, *The Making of the English Working Class* (London, 1963) p. 826.

24 Ibid., p. 807.

25 *Northern Star*, 4 August 1838.

26 *Poor Man's Guardian*, 17 August 1833.

27 See for example H.J. Perkin, *The Origins of Modern English Society, 1780–1880* (London, 1969); Smelser, *Social Change;* Tholfson, *Working Class Radicalism in Mid-Victorian England* (London, 1979); Foster, *Class Struggle*.

Anna Clark

GENDER AND RADICALISM

Anna Clark, *The Struggle for the Breeches: Gender and the Making of the British Working Class* (London: Rivers Oram, 1995), 220–32.

Following **Gareth Stedman Jones**'s Reading, we offer another rethinking of Chartism but from a different perspective: gender. The new wave of women's history from the 1970s onwards was heavily influenced by E.P. Thompson's *The Making of the English Working Class* (1963), specifically his passion for giving a voice to working-class people and his insistence that they had agency (i.e. that they were not simply acted upon by impersonal economic forces but created rituals, language and institutions that were empowering). In that spirit, there was a determination that women should no longer be 'hidden from history' (in Sheila Rowbotham's phrase). However, the inclusion of the categories of 'woman' and 'gender' were extremely challenging to conventional political history. This was particularly true of Chartism — usually seen by social historians as an essentially heroic moment of working-class struggle. **Anna Clark** offered a feminist approach to the movement. This extract comes from her book *The Struggle for the Breeches* (1995), which re-imagines the territory that E.P. Thompson discussed (working-class formation during the early Industrial Revolution) from the point of view of gender. In terms of Chartism, Clark not only seeks to reinstate the role of women but she demonstrates that Chartism was a masculine and patriarchal movement whose terms of reference served progressively to exclude women as the agitation went on. Clark's Reading is therefore very different from the type of work produced in the Chartist histories of the 1950s and 1960s, reflecting the gender politics of the later twentieth century and, in particular, the view that the personal is political. This Reading should also be read alongside other works in this volume, particularly **Leonore Davidoff** and **Catherine**

Hall on the significance of separate spheres in patterning social life in the nineteenth century and John Tosh on masculinity.

Anna Clark is Professor of History at the University of Minnesota, where she holds the Samuel Russell Chair in the Humanities (2005–8), and she is currently editor of the *Journal of British Studies*. Her latest book is *Scandal: The Sexual Politics of the British Constitution* (2004) and she has also published several articles on the poor law in England and Ireland in the nineteenth century.

IN 1837 AND 1838 RADICALS began to rally working-class people to demand the "People's Charter": a call for universal manhood suffrage, annual Parliaments, the ballot, and other political reforms.[1] Like the Painites of the 1790s, the Chartists believed that citizenship was a "universal political right of every human being" rather than a privilege of property, and a few women took this philosophy to justify female suffrage.[2] Furthermore, Chartism was a mass movement, in which working men *and* women drew upon their plebeian heritage of community mobilization to meet on moonlit moors, petition Parliament, and riot for their rights.

Yet this wider vision of the working class ultimately narrowed. Most Chartist women defined themselves as wives and mothers, auxiliaries to their husbands and fathers, and eventually retreated from activism.[3] Chartist men pushed to exclude women from the factory system and even hoped to "protect" them from wage labor altogether. By the late 1840s, they seemed to understand working-class consciousness as representing the political and economic concerns only of skilled men.[4] Why did Chartism lose its egalitarian potential and adopt a restrictive rhetoric of domesticity? The answer lies in the fact that domesticity helped Chartists address two tasks: first, to resolve sexual antagonism among working people; and, second, to refute claims that working people were immoral, undeserving of both family life and political rights.

Chartists tried to create a positive class identity for working people, uniting diverse elements into an "imagined community" through political organization and rhetoric.[5] They wished to draw upon working people's heritage of tumultuous community action but also strove to overcome the indiscipline and sexual antagonism that had plagued plebeian cultures. Since the Chartists lacked political power, they had to mobilize the power of numbers, appealing to women as well as men. Chartism therefore built on the experiences of the anti-Poor Law and factory struggles to define working-class interests as encompassing those of impoverished mothers and wan factory girls as well as proud artisans. Chartists tried to transform the old masculine plebeian public of beershops and workshops into a more integrated, disciplined public sphere.[6] They organized female powerloom weavers of Lancashire, Glasgow housewives, and London schoolteachers alongside male cotton spinners, handloom weavers, and shoemakers, inviting them all to mass meetings and genteel soirees.[7] This was very different from the middle-class public sphere, where men associated together to discuss politics and economics, relegating family issues to the private realm.

Yet, with few exceptions, Chartists were not willing or able to articulate the practice of organizing women along with men into a principle of gender equality. A possible precedent, Owenite feminism, had seemed to divide the working class at a time when unity was needed, for it exposed the festering sore of sexual antagonism and demanded concessions men were not willing to make. Working men instead often defined their fight for the vote as a struggle for manhood, using highly gendered language that would make egalitarianism impossible to consider.

The most important reason why Chartists turned to domesticity, however, has to do with the movement's second, and crucial, task: to defend working people against attacks on their family morality and to assert that they deserved political rights. For instance, some opponents of a wider suffrage denied working men the vote by claiming that they were not good husbands and fathers. In the conservative *Blackwood's Edinburgh Magazine*, Archibald Alison, the sheriff of Glasgow, contrasted the middle-class man's "self-denial" in supporting his family with the "sensual indulgence" of excessive drinking, bastardy, and desertion of wives allegedly prevalent among working men.[8] Chartist men, in response, blamed capitalism and governmental oppression for the misery of their families, and they manipulated the ideology of separate spheres to claim that domesticity was a privilege all, not just the middle class, should enjoy. Domesticity provided a way of both defending working-class families and appealing to women without threatening men.

Manhood, domesticity, and melodrama

Chartists often spoke of domesticity in melodramatic terms, for melodrama provided a vision of a golden past spoiled by aristocratic exploitation and reclaimed by heroic working-class manhood. It spoke to working people's experience of domestic misery and promised to cure it, and it enabled working men and women to stretch and debate domesticity to define political identities for themselves. Chartist rhetoric did not create a consistent, coherent political philosophy, but mingled Painite radicalism, constitutionalism, and Owenite socialism with Scripture and dialect literature. Similarly, Chartists used the rhetoric of domesticity to serve several functions and convey several meanings.[9]

Chartist domesticity echoed middle-class moralists but twisted their sentimentality into melodramatic tropes. In Evangelical narratives, individual sin, especially feminine indiscipline, poisoned the happy home.[10] But melodrama blamed familial disruption on an outside villain — the aristocratic libertine.[11] Gerald Massey, a Chartist working-class poet, encapsulated the domestic melodramatic narrative neatly in verse:

> Our Fathers are Praying for Pauper Pay
> Our Mothers with Death's Kiss are white;
> Our Sons are the Rich Man's Serfs by day,
> And our Daughters his Slaves by night.[12]

But, as Massey proclaimed in another poem, "The Chivalry of Labor," "We'll win the golden age again."[13]

Melodramatic domesticity appealed to working people whose families were disrupted by industrialization, urbanization, and unemployment. The vision of the golden age enabled Chartist orators to condense the disparate family experiences of artisans, factory workers, and laborers into one potent narrative of a past golden age, present domestic misery, a wicked villain, rescue by heroic Chartist manhood, and a future of domesticity brought about through manhood suffrage.[14] For many textile workers, domesticity originally meant domestic industry, when families worked together under one roof. In an era of factory labor, it had become a nostalgic vision of independence.[15] For London artisans, however, domesticity meant that a man deserved a breadwinner wage.[16] The vague, symbolic narrative of melodrama enabled Chartists to evoke a vision of domesticity that attracted all these disparate workers.

By using even fragmentary melodramatic motifs in their speeches, Chartists increased the emotional power and accessibility of their rhetoric.[17] For instance, individual Chartists disagreed on whether economic, ideological, or political oppression was more important. But if orators wove their political analyses into a melodramatic narrative, audiences could simply identify the upper-class villain as the enemy. One Chartist speaker attributed working people's woes to mill owners, asking a meeting, "Who are compelling women and tender babes to procure the means of subsistence in the cotton factories — to be nipt in the bud, to be sacrificed at the shrine of Moloch? They are the rich, the capitalists."[18] George Harney blamed Malthusianism: "A pretended philosophy . . . [that] crushes, through the bitter privations it inflicts upon us, the energies of our manhood, making our hearths desolate, our homes wretched, inflicting upon our heart's companions an eternal round of sorrow and despair."[19] And Scottish Chartist Mr. MacFarlane pointed the finger at Toryism: "Toryism just means ignorant children in rags, a drunken husband, and an unhappy wife."[20]

Melodramatic narratives gave working people "a moral purpose and a sense of agency" — in other words, a political identity.[21] The Tory paternalists used melodrama to express the melancholy of a lost paternalist past, but working men wanted to be the heroes of their own dramas, not impotent victims. To the pathos of melodrama's images of broken homes, they added a new vision of domesticity redeemed by working-class manhood. Chartist Thomas Ainge Devyr firmly believed melodramatic romances would inspire men to chivalrous deeds against aristocratic tyrants in order to win "woman's smile."[22] In using melodrama to portray manhood in opposition to childhood, Chartists also repudiated the paternalism of Tory radical leaders such as Richard Oastler.

While melodrama provided a tragic vision of the past and a promise of heroic rescue, Chartists also discussed domesticity as a hopeful dream of future family life. They tried to create a new ideal of working-class manhood, in part to attract women alienated from the masculinity of previous trade union movements. For instance, when a southern orator proclaimed at a Newcastle meeting, "If I had a wife I would fight for her, I would die for her," a working-class woman in the audience muttered to her neighbor, "He disen't [sic] say he would work for her."[23] By promising women that Chartism would transform their husbands from drunken louts into responsible breadwinners, radicals overcame women's suspicion of the movement. For instance, Mr. Macfarlane of Glasgow proclaimed, "Instead of the old Tory system of the husband coming home drunk to his family, we will have him sober, contented, and happy."[24]

Two years later, the Scottish *Chartist Circular* detected that the promise of domesticity was being fulfilled: "our fair countrywomen . . . acknowledged the change for the better in the 'guidman,' as he comes home on the Saturday evening to read his *Circular*, and watches over the interests of his family."[25]

Chartists desired women's support because they feared that if women remained uneducated they would deter their husbands from participating in politics or would even drag down the movement. The East London Mental Improvement Association declared that "in the absence of knowledge [wives] are the most formidable obstacles to a man's patriotic exertions, as, imbued with it, they will prove his greatest auxiliaries."[26] Apparently wives often saw Chartist meetings as just another excuse for men to go to the pub.[27] A fictitious Stockport couple in a Chartist magazine "spent a very fractious and uncomfortable life, since that plaguey Charter, as Betsy termed it, came up."[28]

In Chartists' promise to transform the old marital misery into happy domesticity, temperance played a major role, for it was crucial to solving the problems of working-class marriage. Looking at temperance in this way makes it clear that it was not an emulation of false middle-class ideals of respectability but a practical response to the ravages alcoholism made on the ability of men to be good husbands and good Chartists.[29] This was a change from the old trade-union response to accusations of domestic mistreatment: that a working man's private life was not a political issue.[30] While plebeian ballads told the wives of drunken husbands to "whack them with a rolling pin" or admonished them to forgive, temperance Chartists sympathized with the women's plight and promised a solution. The complaints women had been making for decades finally acquired a political context: the taxes the government extracted for liquor and the demoralization of the working-class cause.[31] Robert Lowery declared, "I hate a pot-house politician, who, to satisfy his own desires, robs his wife and family of those comforts he ought to administer to them; such are not the men on whom we must depend."[32] A writer observed in the Chartist *Lifeboat* that drunken men who were brutal to their wives did not deserve the name of Chartist.[33]

The precise nature of Chartist manhood, however, became entangled in Chartist debates over whether "physical force" or "moral force" would be most effective in obtaining the vote. Should the Chartist patriarch protect his family by instructing them at home, or by fighting in the streets to defend them? The mainstream majority of the movement were willing to consider physical force as the ultimate resistance to state repression, and in the first two years of Chartism some, especially in Lancashire, in fact engaged in arming and drilling.[34] Their motto was "peaceably if we can, forcibly if we must." Moral-force Chartists demanded that the movement utterly repudiate any possibility of violence and rely totally on persuading middle-class allies and Parliament that they were respectable enough to deserve the vote. Although the older historiography viewed physical-force Chartists as "irrational," degraded, and deskilled factory workers who discredited Chartism by their threats of violence,[35] more recent historians have pointed out that the divisions could not be broken down sociologically on occupational lines. Physical-force Chartists considered violence as a last resort and preferred to concentrate on building communities through moral reform.[36] Nonetheless, the physical-moral division *was* a major focus of debate in the first two years of Chartism, especially in Scotland.[37]

There, intense controversy broke out when the Reverend Patrick Brewster of Paisley insisted that his fellow Chartists follow him in repudiating physical force, only to be defeated as a delegate to the 1839 convention and defied by Paisley workers who armed themselves.[38]

While both sides agreed on the prevalence of domestic misery among working people, and the necessity of gaining the vote in order to ameliorate it, they differed in their visions of the source of masculine authority. The moral-force Chartists never gained the adherence of more than a minority, partially because in order to gain middle-class support they regarded suffrage not as a right but as a privilege that had to be earned by proving moral virtue. The moral-force London Working Men's Association admitted as members only those men who "possess the attributes and characters of men; and little worthy of the name are those who . . . forgetful of their duties as fathers, husbands, and brothers . . . drown their intellect amid the drunken revelry of the pot house."[39] William Lovett's vision was closer to the middle-class sentimental ideal of domesticity, for he blamed working people for their own familial misery. His notion of masculinity was middle-class as well, for he stressed a masculinity based on rationality and self-control, rather than the "pugilistic skill" on which many working-class men still based their honor.[40]

Not surprisingly, Lovett's opponents complained that he was too beholden to middle-class men such as Edward Swaine, an anti-Corn Law activist who told working-class men, "If you are careless of personal decency and domestic comfort, you cannot be believed, if you profess concern about national improvement."[41] Mainstream Chartists argued that they did not want to wait to persuade the middle class that they deserved the vote. The only power working men had, they argued, was that of numbers — and without the vote, they could exercise that power only by threatening physical force as a last resort if moral force failed. They scorned the moral-force men as toadies to the middle class. Physical-force men vaunted the vigorous, even violent, manhood that had its roots in pugilist and pub culture.[42] They took over meetings of the Anti-Corn Law League by force of fisticuffs to declare that the Charter was the first political priority, to be taken up before any other cause.[43]

The physical-force *London Democrat* often referred to the "manly virtues" of working men and opposed the *Charter* newspaper because its "dandy cockney politician" editor did "not represent the straightforward, manly political sentiments of the working men of this country."[44] They insulted their moral-force opponents with such epithets as "old women" and "kitchen maids."[45] As David Goodway writes, "By 1839, the capital was firmly physical force," with the militant London Democratic Association claiming far more adherents than Lovett's London Working Men's Association.[46] The London Democratic Association allied itself with the physical-force movement of the north, which was rooted in the anti-Poor Law and factory system struggles. Physical-force Chartists eschewed Lovett's sentimental, self-blaming domesticity, espousing instead a melodramatic and biblical narrative that blamed familial misery on the forces of evil — capitalism, the New Poor Law, and the aristocracy. When Lovett and his colleagues later repudiated the "foolish displays and gaudy trappings" of early Chartism, Trowbridge Chartists wrote that this "passionate invective . . . first aroused [many working men] to a sense of their degradation, their rights, and their strength."[47]

Working men often felt that oppression had robbed them of their masculinity. They were especially enraged at their loss of control over women, as the Rev. J.R. Stephens made clear when he proclaimed to a meeting, "God cursed woman as well as man . . . that she should be in subjection to her own husband, her desire should be unto her husband, and he should rule over her (hear hear) and not the millowners (tremendous cheering) nor the coal pit masters (continuous cheering) — not the Poor Law Commissioners."[48] Stalybridge Chartist Mr. Deegan echoed this sentiment when he argued that English men wanted their wives and children in happy cottages, not "polluted by lickspittles" in the mines and factories.[49] Stephens explicitly linked physical force to familial issues when he proclaimed, "If society cannot be renovated . . . [so that] every industrious, virtuous man should have a home, and the blessings of home . . . then, I say, 'Cry havoc, and let slip the dogs of war!' (Loud cheers) Revolution by force — revolution by blood!"[50]

The favorite slogan of Stephens's followers was "For child and wife, / We will war to the knife!"[51] Their claim was that they wished to exclude women from the workplace in order to protect and support them.[52] This tactic had, of course, long been an issue in the northern factory movement, but the problem of women's work affected London as well. Silk weavers, hatters, shoemakers, and tailors were disproportionately involved in Chartism, and all were trades whose unions had had to cope with the threat of undercutting by cheap female labor.[53] Yet Stephens's supporters were not simply motivated by a desire to regain patriarchal authority. Rather, they were following a new rhetorical strategy which united their diverse experiences and transformed sexual antagonism into chivalry. As a result, they gained the support of many women in their communities. Despite its belligerent masculinity, the London Democratic Association was rooted in a Painite radicalism which opened up possibilities for women's independent participation. It was allied with the London Female Democratic Association, whose women declared, "We assert in accordance with the rights of all, and acknowledging the sovereignty of the people as our right, as free women (or women determined to be free) to rule ourselves."[54]

Women's activism in the Chartist movement

In the north, women continued their tradition of supporting community uprisings as Lancashire workers in many localities made pikes and even bought revolvers in expectation that the government would use violence to repress a planned general strike.[55] Lancashire women purchased pikes for their men, and one young mother, a framework knitter, was arrested for marching in a Chartist demonstration carrying a revolver and ammunition.[56] In Dunfermline, Scotland, a Mrs. Collie incited a physical-force meeting to defy the government: she sang,

> The time draws nigh, and is at hand,
> When females will with courage stand!
> Each heart united will decree,
> We'll have our rights, we will be free!
> We'll sever ne'er, but steadfast be!
> We'll die to have our liberty![57]

The men of Dunfermline believed that women could defy the government: the government had imprisoned three hundred men, but they would never dare to jail hundreds of females.[58] Sketching the dire consequences of an insurrection in Birmingham or Glasgow, Alexander Somerville anticipated fierce participation by women: in his imagined scenario, the wife of a "fustian-jacketed pikeman" who was wrestling with a policeman sprang to her husband's aid "like a tigress." Admonishing her neighbor Peggy to "break their heads with the axe, or the poker, or the tongs," she "laid on the shoulder of a policeman most prodigiously, with a sawyer's handspoke." For the rather moderate Somerville, however, such female ferocity was just another reason to avoid violence.[59] The violence of physical-force Chartism, however, was more often rhetorical than real, intimidating opponents and inciting the fervor of its adherents with a "language of menace."[60]

In late 1839, the failure of the planned general strike and insurrectionary plots turned the movement in a new direction. Despairing of revolutionary tactics, Chartists renewed their interest in temperance, education, and radical religion.[61] That move also enabled them to gain greater female support, for only the most militant women would risk their family's safety by advocating arming. Chartists did not need women's support only in the home. They also needed women in mass demonstrations; gathering signatures on petitions; striking; and exclusive dealing, that is, boycotting shopkeepers who refused to support Chartists.

Yet male Chartists expressed ambivalence about women's activities. In 1839 the radical *Scottish Patriot* lauded the new Gorbals Female Universal Suffrage organization for supporting their brothers and husbands, but noted, "We lament the necessity that exists for drawing the female mind from employment more congenial to the close and retiring habits of the women of this country, than the arena of politics."[62] A Leeds speaker declared that women must "take the part of men" in the Chartist struggle, but also hoped they would remain delicate and domestic.[63] They preferred females to act as decorative symbols of working-class virtue. When militant Chartist Mary Anne Walker spoke at length before a mixed meeting, the *Northern Star* reporter rhapsodized about her "very graceful bust" before alluding to her political views.[64] In Scotland, one Dunfermline radical, observing many women present at a political meeting, grumbled, "A lecture on domestic economy would perhaps be more suitable for them." In response, the militant women there formed their own association.[65] Yet Chartist men usually defined women's role initially in subordinate terms and in many areas they controlled women's meetings tightly, taking up the time with long speeches by male visitors.

Nonetheless, Chartist women organized themselves, even if only as supportive auxiliaries. Women formed over a hundred and fifty flourishing female Chartist associations in England, and at least twenty-three in Scotland.[66] They extended the activist tradition of women in textile communities into Chartism. Women were particularly involved in Chartism in "centres of decaying industry," such as Lancashire handloom weaving communities, and in industrial towns such as Stockport, where there were high concentrations of women workers.[67] In Bradford, center of the woolen industry, the Female Radical Association was a "quasi-autonomous group of five branches with six hundred members."[68] In Scotland, female Chartist associations flourished in the textile districts of Aberdeen and in the factory villages of Bridgeton, Calton, Mile End, and the Gorbals, near Glasgow.[69] Although we know the occupations of only a few Glasgow female Chartists, Robert Duncan states that most female Chartists in Aberdeen were mill workers.[70] In 1839, the largest contributions to the Chartist Defense Fund by factories in Bridgeton came from the women of Stephen's Factory and Humphrey's Mill.[71] The more articulate women in Chartist meetings, however, probably came from politically active artisan families.[72]

Chartist women fashioned a political identity for themselves as mothers, workers, and activists which differed in important ways both from the middle-class ideal of domesticity and from male Chartists' notions of women's role.[73] They developed what I would call a "militant domesticity," justifying their actions in stepping outside the home by defining the responsibilities of motherhood not just as nurturing children in the home but as laboring to feed them and organizing to better their lives.[74] Mrs. Lapworth, a Birmingham reformer, compared the hunger she suffered after childbirth with the luxury of "hundreds around her, of her own sex, who had never labored, and did not know how to labor, and were enjoying all the comforts of life."[75] The female Chartists of Manchester maintained "we have a right to struggle to gain for ourselves, our husbands, brothers and children, suitable houses, proper clothing and good food."[76]

Women's own addresses differed subtly from the flowery rhetoric of the Chartist men who objected to female factory labor. For instance, Ashton's Rev. J.R. Stephens presented a lurid picture of female mill workers who "don't care whether their children live or not — when they don't care whether they have husbands or not."[77] Stephens was admittedly extremely popular among Chartist women and counterbalanced his criticism of mill workers by blaming their faults on the system. Yet when the Ashton female Chartists wrote their own address in the same month, they presented themselves as griefstricken, rather than indifferent, at the "desolat[ion]" of their homes. Instead of depicting factory girls as immoral, they declared that "our daughters, are considered, by haughty and iniquitous capitalists, as only created to satisfy their wicked desires." And, in contrast to Stephens's patriarchalism, they demanded the franchise for themselves as well as for men.[78]

In contrast to Lovett's paternalist view of marriage, an anonymous author in the *National Association Gazette* declared, "Woman stands in the same relationship to a man, as the subject of a despotic government to his monarch."[79] Some Scottish women called for their sisters to "enlarge their thoughts beyond the domestic circle."[80] Other Chartists claimed that factory labor deprived women of the education that would enable them to be active beyond "the dull round of their household duties."[81]

As they became more deeply involved in Chartism, some women changed their political identities from passive spectators to outspoken activists. Since it was more difficult for women to claim a public political role, most Chartist women initially defined themselves as auxiliaries in the struggle for the rights of their husbands and brothers. It must be acknowledged, however, that the women's stress on domesticity was in part a rhetorical gesture to answer vitriolic attacks made on their activities by the middle-class press.[82] The Scottish Chartist women of Glasgow initially spoke with great hesitance and modesty, but they soon became more militant, defining themselves as heroines and not just as victims. They "improved their habits of thought" by reading and by writing essays on various topics.[83] Their spokeswoman Agnes Muir at first apologized for her oratorical inadequacies, but soon refuted the notion that it was indelicate for a "starving woman to say she is in want." She cited a long list of heroines for Chartist women to take as precedents.[84] A Miss M'Kay went even further when she declared, "I offer no apology for appearing before you this evening, nor do I require to prove to you that the sex to which I belong has rights, and that these rights have been unlawfully taken from us as from the other sex."[85] The women of Dunfermline defended themselves against criticism for organizing a meeting by declaring that "until woman becomes an independent creature, not the subservient slave of man, but a fit companion and assistant in all his undertakings," the Constitution could never be reformed.[86]

A few women demanded the vote for themselves on the basis of natural rights, and a few men supported them.[87] A "plain working woman" of Glasgow, a weaver, argued in 1838 that women could reason as well as men and therefore deserved the vote.[88] The *National Association Gazette* accused opponents of female suffrage of hypocrisy for "contradicting the Chartist profession of universal justice."[89] After all, according to Chartist logic there was no reason women should not have the vote. Because working men lacked property and, often, households, Chartists could not demand the vote on the Lockean basis of the male householder, but instead resorted to the Painite tradition of the inherent individual right to representation. For instance, Ashton women argued, "intelligence [being] the necessary qualification for voting," women should "enjoy the elective franchise along with our kinsmen."[90] But female suffrage was difficult to reconcile with domesticity. For instance, R.J. Richardson in his pamphlet *The Rights of Women* used a Painite language of rights and citizenship to show that women, because they were subjected to the laws of the state, paid taxes, and worked, should participate in political affairs. Yet Richardson also proclaimed that women were formed to "temper man" and should "return to [their] domestic circles and cultivate [their] finer feelings for the benefit of their offspring."[91] He attempted to resolve these contradictions by advocating suffrage only for single women and widows; married women were to be represented by their husbands. However, radicals were somewhat uncomfortable with the notion of independent political spinsters. At a Southwark reform meeting, D.W. Harvey, a radical publisher and member of Parliament, admitted that spinsters who kept shops and acted as churchwardens logically deserved the vote. But he then elicited laughter from the audience, jovially dismissing women's claims and ridiculing their independence by alluding to the punishment of female scolds in the stocks.[92] Only the Owenites consistently supported female suffrage.[93] When an Owenite tried to raise the question of female suffrage at an 1842 meeting in Shoreditch, a poor East End district, he was laughed down by the audience.[94] These arguments continued through 1846 and 1847, as Owenites supported female suffrage but the majority opposed it as creating "domestic unhappiness."[95]

Yet opponents of universal manhood suffrage used the argument for women's votes as a reductio ad absurdum; if everyone had the inherent natural right to vote, they asked scornfully, why not women? Commenting on the 1842 debates in the House of Commons over Sharman Crawford's motion to extend the suffrage, the *Times* noted, "Were they consistent with themselves, they must at least give the franchise to women."[96] Chartists could only answer lamely that it was "paltry twaddle" to argue that working men should be denied the vote unless women were included as well.[97] By subsuming women under their husbands, the rationale for universal suffrage as a natural right was lost.

One alternative was household suffrage, descended from eighteenth-century versions of civic humanism that defined the citizen as the property-owning heads of households.[98] Advocates of household suffrage believed that the role of male head of household proved a man's stability and responsibility, even without property. *Northern Star* editorials denounced household suffrage because it would subsume radical sons' views under conservative fathers' votes, but they did not see any contradiction in excluding wives from the vote in order to "preserve harmony" in the family.[99] Feargus O'Connor, for instance, on this ground opposed the vote for any woman, thundering that "it would lead to family dissensions."[100]

Conclusion

The Chartists adopted the rhetoric of domesticity, in part, to address this problem of "family dissensions." By promising women better husbands, who would actually bring home the bacon rather than drinking up their wages at the pub, Chartists gained women's support for the movement. At the same time, men believed domesticity would give them back their masculine self-respect through the breadwinner wage, and hoped the vote would help them attain that wage. Yet the image of the delicate wife sheltering at home while her brave husband strove forth into the world to protect her was always an ideal rather than a reality for working people — and for the movement. Chartists did not only need women's passive support at home, they needed their active participation in the movement, which had grown out of traditions of community mobilization where women workers struggled alongside men.

As Chartism matured, it became more and more difficult to balance egalitarianism and domesticity, to draw upon the strength of women's activism while depicting them as helpless creatures in need of male protection. Like the radicals of the 1790s, Chartist men could not accept the full implications of Painite egalitarianism because their notion of citizenship was so bound up with masculinity.

Further reading

Anna Clark developed some of her themes about gender and politics in her book *Scandal: The Sexual Politics of the British Constitution* (Princeton, NJ: Princeton University Press, 2004). Important discussions of gender and Chartism can also be found in: Dorothy Thompson, *The Chartists* (Hounslow: Temple Smith, 1984); Jutta Schwarzkopf, *Women in the Chartist Movement* (London: Macmillan, 1991); Helen Rogers, *Women and the People: Authority, Authorship and the Radical Tradition in Nineteenth-Century England* (Aldershot: Ashgate, 2000). Another important study of women and politics in the early Victorian age is Barbara Taylor, *Eve and the New Jerusalem: Socialism and Feminism in the Nineteenth Century* (London: Virago, 1983).

Notes

1 Dorothy Thompson, *The Chartists: Popular Politics in the Industrial Revolution* (Aldershot: Wildwood House, 1986), is a good overview.

2 "Petition Adopted at the Crown and Anchor Meeting," 1838, in Dorothy Thompson, ed., *The Early Chartists* (Columbia: University of South Carolina Press, 1971), p. 62; James Epstein, "The Constitutional Idiom: Radical Reasoning, Rhetoric, and Action in Early Nineteenth Century England," *Journal of Social History* 23 (1990): 565.

3 Joan Scott, "On Language, Gender and Working-Class History," in her *Gender and the Politics of History* (New York: Columbia University Press, 1988), p. 53.

4 Sally Alexander, "Women, Class and Sexual Difference in the 1830s and the 1840s: Some Reflections on the Writing of a Feminist History," *History Workshop Journal* 17 (1984): 125–49. My analysis owes a great deal to Sally Alexander for her recognition of sexual antagonism in the working class. See also Ruth L. Smith and Deborah M. Valenze, "Mutuality and Marginality: Liberal Moral Theory and Working-Class Women in Nineteenth Century England," *Signs* 13 (1988): 288.

5 Benedict Anderson, *Imagined Communities* (London: Verso, 1983), applying his discussion of nationalism to class. Gareth Stedman Jones, "Rethinking Chartism," in his *Languages of Class: Studies in English Working Class History 1832–1982* (Cambridge: Cambridge University Press, 1983), pp. 90–95. For a recent critique of his methodology, see David Mayfield and Susan Thorne, "Social History and Its Discontents: Gareth Stedman Jones and the Politics of Language," *Social History* 17 (1992): 165–69. See also Theodore Koditschek, *Class Formation and Urban Industrial Society: Bradford, 1750–1850* (Cambridge: Cambridge University Press, 1990), pp. 484–93. Even if Chartists did not use socialist rhetoric, they defined themselves as a working-class movement. See James Epstein, "Rethinking the Categories of Working-Class History," *Labour/Le Travailleur* 18 (1986): 202; Neville Kirk, "In Defense of Class: A Critique of Gareth Stedman Jones," *International Review of Social History* 32 (1987): 5; John Belchem, "Radical Language and Ideology in Early Nineteenth-Century England: The Challenge of the Platform," *Albion* 20 (1988): 258. Paul Pickering, "Class Without Words: Symbolic Communication in the Chartist Movement," *Past and Present* 112 (1986): 160, points out that Chartist leader Feargus O'Connor, while upper-class in origin, wore a fustian jacket to symbolize his identification with the workers. For a biography of O'Connor, see James Epstein, *The Lion of Freedom: Feargus O'Connor and the Chartist Movement* (London: Croom Helm, 1982), p. 239.

6 For the working-class public sphere, see Geoff Eley, "Rethinking the Political: Social History and Political Culture in Eighteenth and Nineteenth Century Britain," *Archiv für Sozialgeschischte* 32 (1981): 451.

7 James Epstein, "Some Organisational and Cultural Aspects of the Chartist Movement in Nottingham," in James Epstein and Dorothy Thompson, eds, *The Chartist Experience: Studies in Working-Class Radicalism and Culture, 1830–1860* (London: Macmillan, 1982), pp. 221–68; James D. Young, *The Rousing of the Scottish Working Class* (London: Croom Helm, 1979), p. 73.

8 Archibald Alison, "The Chartists and Universal Suffrage," *Blackwood's Edinburgh Magazine* 187 (1839): 296–97.

9 Belchem, "Radical Language and Ideology," p. 257; Robert Gray, "The Deconstructing of the English Working Class," *Social History* 11 (1986): 363–73; James Epstein, "Understanding the Cap of Liberty: Symbolic Practice and Social Conflict in Early Nineteenth Century England," *Past and Present* 122 (1989): 75–118; Koditschek, *Class Formation*, p. 503; Eileen Yeo, "Christianity and Chartist Struggle," *Past and Present* 91 (1981): 109–39; and Eileen Yeo, "Chartist Religious Belief and the Theology of Liberation," in James Obelkevich, Lyndal Roper, and Raphael Samuel, eds, *Disciplines of Faith: Studies in Religion, Politics and Patriarchy* (London: Routledge and Kegan Paul, 1987), pp. 410–20.

10   Nancy Armstrong, *Desire and Domestic Fiction: A Political History of the Novel* (Oxford: Oxford University Press, 1987), p. 252.

11   This plot acquired radical connotations in Jacobin novels of the 1790s: see Marilyn Butler, *Jane Austen and the War of Ideas* (Oxford: Clarendon Press, 1975), pp. 29–50, and Gary Kelly, *The English Jacobin Novel* (Oxford: Clarendon Press, 1976). For melodrama, which originated as a theatrical form during the French Revolution and then became a working-class popular genre in Great Britain, see James C. Smith, *Victorian Melodrama* (London: J.M. Dent, 1976); Louis James, *Fiction for the Working Man* (Harmondsworth: Penguin, 1974), pp. 171–72; Peter Brooks, *The Melodramatic Imagination* (New Haven: Yale University Press, 1976), p. 44; Martha Vicinus, "Helpless and Unfriended: Nineteenth Century Domestic Melodrama," *New Literary History* 13 (1981): 143; Anna Clark, "The Politics of Seduction in English Popular Culture, 1784–1848," in Jean Radford, ed., *The Progress of Romance* (London: Routledge and Kegan Paul, 1986), pp. 47–72.

12   Gerald Massey, *Poems and Ballads* (New York, 1854), p. 147. Another classic narrative is found in a tale, "English Life," from the *Northern Star* of 5 June 1847, in which a happy family is evicted from a cottage and must move to a factory town. The son is crippled in the army, and the beautiful daughter is seduced by the factory master, deserted, becomes a prostitute, and dies.

13   Massey, *Poems and Ballads*, p. 76. For other examples of golden age rhetoric, see *Northern Star*, 16 May 1840, letter by Feargus O'Connor; 13 June 1840, address from J. Lomax; 9 Jan. 1841, poem by William Hick, "My Five-Acre Cottage That Stands by the Green."

14   For examples of this rhetoric, see *Northern Star*, 7 April 1838; *Scots Times*, 27 Jan. 1841; *Bronterre's National Reformer*, 21 Jan. 1837; *McDouall's Journal*, 3 April 1841, quoted in Kirk, "In Defense of Class," p. 21; and see David Jones, *Chartism and the Chartists* (New York: St. Martin's Press, 1975), p. 113 for this motif in Chartist poetry.

15   On domesticity as independence, see Deborah Valenze, *Prophetic Sons and Daughters: Female Preaching and Popular Religion in Industrial England* (Princeton: Princeton University Press, 1985), p. 211.

16   *English Chartist Circular* 2 (1842): 5.

17   Victor Turner, "Social Dramas and Stories About Them," *Critical Inquiry* 7 (1980): 144. Turner notes that in social dramas, unlike fiction, the narrative structure is implicit and often alluded to in terms of metaphorical threads which connect the drama with the social situation. For more examples of melodramatic rhetoric, see *Southern Star*, 19 Jan. 1840, and the similar motif in the anonymous poem *The Doom of Toil* (Sunderland, 1841), p. 10. Cf. the contrast of upper-class immorality with the virtue of the poor in *Northern Star*, 27 Jan. 1838, speech by Mr. William Thornton at Halifax anti-Poor Law meeting. Also *Northern Star*, 6 Oct. 1838; a similar speech in *Northern Star*, 29 Sept. 1838, by Mr. Beal, at a Sheffield demonstration; and an editorial in the *Northern Star*, 17 Feb. 1838.

18   *Northern Star*, 1 June 1839.

19   *Northern Star*, 13 Oct. 1838.

20   *Scottish Patriot*, 14 Dec. 1839.

21   James Vernon, *Politics and the People: A Study in English Political Culture 1815–1867* (Cambridge: Cambridge University Press, 1993), p. 389. [. . .]

22   Thomas Ainge Devyr, *The Odd Book of the 19th Century; Or, Chivalry in Modern Days* (New York, 1882), p. 40. Devyr emigrated to America in 1840 to escape prosecution for Chartist activity: Thompson, *Chartists*, p. 271.

23   "Autobiography," in *Robert Lowery, Radical and Chartist*, ed. Brian Harrison and Patricia Hollis (London: Europa Publications, 1979), p. 141.

24   *Scottish Patriot*, 14 Dec. 1839.

25   *Chartist Circular*, 18 Sept. 1841, p. 433.

26   London, British Library, Place Coll., Set 56, July–December 1838.

27   Thompson, *Chartists*, p. 144.

28   O'Connor and Ernest Jones, eds, *The Labourer* (Manchester, 1847), vol. 1, pp. 44–49.

29   John Foster, *Class Struggle and the Industrial Revolution* (New York: St. Martin's Press, 1974), p. 221, tends to portray temperance as part of "liberalization" and the cooptation of the working class. For another view, see Brian Harrison, "Teetotal Chartism," *History* 58 (1973): 193–203. Temperance had been advocated in the 1820s for political reasons by trade unionist John Gast; see Iorwerth Prothero, *Artisans and Politics in Early Nineteenth Century London* (London: Methuen, 1981), p. 216.

30   *Trades' Newspaper*, 30 Oct., 28 Aug. 1825, on domestic mistreatment.

31   Harrison, "Teetotal Chartism," p. 194.

32   *Carlisle Journal*, 6 Oct. 1838, quoted in *Robert Lowery*, p. 33.

33   *Lifeboat*, 9 Dec. 1843 (Westport, Ct.: Garland, 1972).

34   Renee Sofer, "Attitudes and Allegiances in the Unskilled North," *International Review of Social History* 10 (1965): 429–54.

35   This originated with R.G. Gammage, *History of the Chartist Movement 1837–1854* (New York; Augustus M. Kelley, 1969 [1894]); J.T. Ward, *Chartism* (New York: Harper and Row, 1973), pp. 111–42.

36   Clive Behagg, *Politics and Production in the Early Nineteenth Century* (London: Routledge, 1990), p. 212; Thompson, *Chartists*, p. 58; Epstein, *Lion of Freedom*, p. 239. Robert Sykes points out that there was an overlap in tactics between the two wings. "Physical Force Chartism: The Cotton District and the Chartist Crisis of 1839," *International Review of Social History* 30 (1985): 211.

37   For evidence of this debate, see *Northern Star*, 27 Jan., 24 March, 23 June, 7 July, 28 Sept., 13 Oct., 3 Nov., 17 Nov., 22 Dec., 29 Dec. 1838, While the Scottish Chartist movement has often been described as inclining more toward moral force, other historians have pointed out that proponents of physical force were strong, especially in Glasgow. Leslie C. Wright, *Scottish Chartism* (Edinburgh: Oliver and Boyd, 1953), p. 45; Alexander Wilson, *The Chartist Movement in Scotland* (New York: Augustus M. Kelley, 1970), p. 101; Young, *Rousing*, p. 82.

38   Tony Clarke, "Early Chartism in Scotland: A Moral Force Movement?" in T.M. Devine, ed., *Conflict and Stability in Scottish Society 1700–1850* (Edinburgh: John Donald, 1990), pp. 111, 114. In another book, Clarke points out that this debate was also complicated by ethnic divisions, for Daniel O'Connell, who opposed physical-force Chartism, won the allegiance of the Glasgow Irish, who often violently disrupted O'Connorite meetings that refused to denounce physical force: *Scottish Capitalism: Class, State and Nation from Before the Union to the Present* (London: Lawrence and Wishart, 1980), p. 205.

39   *Address and Rules of the Working Men Association, for Benefitting Politically, Socially, and Morally the Useful Classes* (London, 1836), p. 2.

40   William Lovett, *Social and Political Morality* (London, 1853), p. 83.

41   Edward Swaine, *The Political Franchise a Public Trust, Demanding an Intelligent and Virtuous Care for the Public Good* (London, n.d.), p. 28.

42   This form of rough yet radical manhood is discussed by Iain MacCalman in *Radical Underworld: Prophets, Revolutionaries and Pornographers in London, 1795–1840* (Cambridge: Cambridge University Press, 1988), p. 149.

43   David Goodway, *London Chartism* (Cambridge: Cambridge University Press, 1982), p. 45; Christopher Godfrey, *Chartist Lives: The Anatomy of a Working-Class Movement* (Westport, Ct.: Garland, 1987), p. 119, for disruption of an anti-Poor Law meeting; and *Glasgow Constitutional*, 7 Nov. 1840, for disruption of a meeting about a house of refuge; 5 Dec. 1840, for a meeting to celebrate the queen's birthday; 25 Dec. 1839, interrupting an anti-Corn Law meeting.

44   *London Democrat*, 11 May 1839.

45   *Northern Star*, 16 Oct., 22 Dec. 1838.

46 Goodway, *London Chartism*, p. 25; Jennifer Bennett, "The London Democratic Association 1837–41: A Study in London Radicalism," in Epstein and Thompson, eds, *Chartist Experience*, pp. 87–119.

47 *Northern Star*, 1 May 1841, in the context of Lovett and Collins's "New Move," which broke away from Feargus O'Connor and the National Charter Association.

48 Speech at Wigan Chartist meeting reported in *Northern Star*, 17 Nov. 1838; see also Jones, *Chartism*, p. 115.

49 *Northern Star*, 1 June 1839.

50 *Northern Star*, 18 May 1839. While Stephens's support of universal suffrage was ephemeral, fading by 1840, he had very strong support among the Chartists in the first years of Chartism. Thompson, *Chartists*, p. 265.

51 *Northern Star*, 18 May 1839.

52 *English Chartist Circular* 1 (1841): 166.

53 Goodway, *London Chartism*, p. 16.

54 *Northern Star*, 11 May 1839.

55 Sykes, "Physical Force Chartism," p. 213; Goodway, *London Chartism*, p. 34.

56 Thompson, *Chartists*, p. 141; also Wright, *Scottish Chartism*, pp. 105, 148.

57 *Scots Times*, 11 Nov. 1840.

58 *True Scotsman*, 28 Nov. 1840.

59 Alexander Somerville, *Dissuasive Warnings to the People on Street Warfare* (London, 1839), letter 5, p. 5.

60 Thomas Milton Kremitz, "Approaches to the Chartist Movement: Feargus O'Connor and Chartist Strategy," *Albion* 5 (1973): 57–73; William Henry Maehl, Jr., "The Dynamics of Violence in Chartism: A Case Study in North-East England," *Albion* 7 (1975): 102.

61 Thompson, *Chartists*, p. 259.

62 *Scottish Patriot*, 14 Sept. 1839.

63 *Northern Star*, 9 June 1838.

64 *Northern Star*, 10 Dec. 1842.

65 Wright, *Scottish Chartism*, p. 43.

66 Jutta Schwarzkopf, *Women in the Chartist Movement* (London: Macmillan, 1991), p. 199; for Scotland, Wilson, *Chartist Movement*, p. 273, lists twenty; cf., for Barrhead and Paisley, *Scottish Patriot*, 27 July 1839; for Campsie, *Scots Times*, 27 Jan. 1841; for Dundee, *True Scotsman*, 8 Feb. 1840. Also see David Jones, "Women and Chartism," *History* 68 (1983): 1–21; Jutta Schwarzkopf, "The Sexual Division in the Chartist Family," *British Society for the Study of Labor History Bulletin* 54 (1989): 12–14.

67 Schwarzkopf, *Women in the Chartist Movement*, pp. 80–81; Thompson, *Chartists*, p. 62.

68 Koditschek, *Class Formation*, p. 504.

69 Wilson, *Chartist Movement*, p. 273.

70 Robert Duncan, "Artisans and Proletarians: Chartism and Working-Class Allegiance in Aberdeen, 1838–42," *Northern Scotland* 4 (1981): 56.

71 *Scottish Patriot*, 19 Oct. 1839.

72 Thompson, *Chartists*, p. 144.

73 Catherine Hall, "The Tale of Samuel and Jemima: Gender and Working-Class Culture in Early Nineteenth-Century England," in her *White, Male and Middle Class: Explorations in Feminism and History* (Cambridge: Polity, 1992), pp. 124–50.

74 This vision is similar to that of the "republican motherhood" of the American Revolution. See Linda K. Kerber, *Women of the Republic: Intellect and Ideology in Revolutionary America* (Chapel Hill: University of North Carolina Press, 1980).

75 *Birmingham Journal*, 18 July 1838, in London, British Library, Place Coll., Set 56, July-December 1838; for very similar sentiments see also the London Female Democratic Association, reported in the *Northern Star*, 11 May 1839.

76 *Northern Star*, 24 July 1841, quoted in Ruth Frow and Edmund Frow, eds, *Political Women 1800–1850* (London: Pluto, 1989), pp. 199–200.

77   *Northern Star*, 16 Feb. 1839.

78   *Northern Star*, 2 Feb. 1839.

79   The pages of the *National Association Gazette* contained both such bitter feminism and celebrations of domesticity, sometimes in the same article. Cf. 30 April and 5 Feb. 1842.

80   *True Scotsman*, 20 Oct. 1839.

81   *Scottish Patriot*, 21 Dec. 1839; cf. the similar sentiment in *Scots Times*, 13 March 1840.

82   Epstein, "Understanding the Cap of Liberty," p. 103.

83   *Scots Times*, 1 May 1840.

84   *Scots Times*, 18 Nov. 1840.

85   *Scots Times*, 30 Dec. 1840.

86   *True Scotsman*, 22 Dec. 1838.

87   Jones, "Women and Chartism," pp. 2–3; Thompson, *Chartists*, p. 126; Schwarzkopf, *Women in the Chartist Movement*, p. 59.

88   *Northern Star*, 23 June 1838.

89   Quoted in Schwarzkopf, *Women in the Chartist Movement*, p. 62; Thompson, *Chartists*, p. 124.

90   *Northern Star*, 2 Feb. 1839.

91   R.J. Richardson, *The Rights of Woman* (1840), in Thompson, ed., *Early Chartists*, pp. 115–27; cf. Barbara Taylor, *Eve and the New Jerusalem: Socialism and Feminism in the Nineteenth Century* (New York: Pantheon, 1983), p. 269.

92   *London Dispatch*, 11 Feb. 1838.

93   Schwarzkopf, *Women in the Chartist Movement*, p. 63.

94   Taylor, *Eve and the New Jerusalem*, p. 270.

95   *Northern Star*, 26 Oct. 1846, 30 Oct. 1847.

96   Quoted in *National Association Gazette*, 30 April 1842, p. 141.

97   *Scottish Patriot*, 3 Aug. 1839. The *Southern Star*, 19 Jan. 1840, quoted Cobbett as saying that women's feminine duties disqualified them.

98   See Anna Clark, *The Struggle for the Breeches: Gender and the Making of the British Working Class* (London: Rivers Oram, 1995), ch. 8.

99   *Northern Star*, 19 Sept. 1840, 2 Jan. 1841.

100 Quoted (in all capital letters) in Taylor, *Eve and the New Jerusalem*, p. 271; cf. pp. 270–72; also Thompson, *Chartists*, p. 126.

PART 7

Morality

Gertrude Himmelfarb

IN DEFENCE OF THE VICTORIANS

Gertrude Himmelfarb, *The De-Moralization of Society: From Victorian Virtues to Modern Values* (New York: Knopf, 1995), 21–36.

No issue has done more to ensure the Victorians have received a bad press than the issue of morality. Invocations of the Victorians are often accompanied by the word 'hypocrisy', a characteristic that, as we saw in the Introduction, defined twentieth-century anti-Victorianism. The Victorians professed a rigorous code of morality in public while prostitution and poverty were rampant. Any reappraisal of Victorianism therefore requires a new look at the nature of morality. Revisionists have noted that the Victorians themselves were tormented by the distance between their public morality and the sordidness of much private life. More recently, the American historian **Gertrude Himmelfarb** has confronted the question of morality as a way of restoring the Victorian vision.

Gertrude Himmelfarb is a leading intellectual historian who has investigated the work of John Stuart Mill, Charles Darwin and Lord Acton among other important Victorian thinkers. A significant figure on the American Right, she has insisted that the Victorians accomplished much to inspire the present day. In an ambitious two-volume study, she examined nineteenth-century approaches to poverty, developing a sophisticated approach to reportage, political writings and fiction. She acclaimed the role of individualism and philanthropy that made up the Victorian world-view, but was more critical of Fabian approaches that began to move towards a welfare state, something that, she argued, created a dependency culture. The current Reading is an extract from her book *The De-Moralization of Society* (1995), in which she argues that Victorian society was structured by a belief in virtues and a vigorous and nourishing public morality, which contrasts with post-1945 Britain and the

United States with its belief in rights (as opposed to duties) and with a relativist indifference to private behaviour. Himmelfarb's work should be seen as consonant with Margaret Thatcher's attempt to reclaim Victorian values. This Reading is an extract from her chapter on 'Manners and Morals' in which she argues that the Victorian values of hard work, sexual respectability and cleanliness were widely diffused throughout society and were not imposed on the working classes through middle-class 'social control'. Hers is a more optimistic and positive account of Victorian lives than is found in the pages of many social historians. The fact that modern political arguments in both Britain and the United States can still require discussion of Victorian Britain demonstrates its enduring importance as a contested issue. This Reading can be profitably read alongside those by **Stefan Collini** and **Michael Mason**.

Gertrude Himmelfarb is Professor Emeritus at the Graduate School of the City University of New York. Her most recent books are *The Moral Imagination* (2006) and *The Roads to Modernity: The British, French, and American Enlightenments* (2004). She is currently editing a volume of essays by eminent Victorians.

"**MANNERS AND MORALS**" — the expression is unmistakably Victorian. Not "manners" alone: Lord Chesterfield in the eighteenth century was fond of discoursing to his son on the supreme importance of manners, as distinct from morals. And not "morals" alone: philosophers had always taken this as their special province; some had made it so elevated a subject that it had little to do with anything as mundane as manners.

It was the Victorians who combined those words so that they came trippingly off the tongue, as if they were one word.[1] Yet in this, as in so much else, they were drawing on a long intellectual heritage. When William of Wykeham, bishop of Winchester and chancellor of England, founded New College, Oxford, in the late fourteenth century, he took as its motto "Manners Makyth the Man," meaning by manners something very nearly indistinguishable from morals. So too John Milton in the seventeenth century, when he defended freedom of the press except for "that which is impious or evil absolutely either against faith or manners."[2] Or Thomas Hobbes shortly afterward: "By manners I mean not here, decency of behavior; as how one man should salute another, or how a man should wash his mouth, or pick his teeth before company, and such other points of the *small morals*; but those qualities of mankind, that concern their living together in peace and unity."[3]

If the Victorians were concerned with the "small morals" of life — table manners, toilet habits, conventions of dress, appearance, conversation, greeting, and all the other "decencies" of behavior — it was because they saw them as the harbingers of morals writ large, the civilities of private life that were the corollaries of civilized social life. It was this conjunction of "small morals" and large that made Victorian society so moralistic, in aspiration at least, if not always in achievement. When William Thackeray protested, "It is not learning, it is not virtue, about which people inquire in society; it is manners,"[4] he was speaking of "society" and "manners" in their trivial senses: the high society of *le beau monde* and the genteel manners of the drawing room. For manners and society in their larger senses he had the greatest concern, which is why he was so distressed by their trivialization.

Margaret Thatcher is reported as saying that she would be pleased to restore all Victorian values, with the exception of hypocrisy. If she did say that, she could only have been thinking of the familiar sense of hypocrisy, the deliberate living of a lie, professing beliefs one does not have and acting in such a way as to belie those beliefs. There was, no doubt, a fair amount of this kind of hypocrisy in Victorian times —although it hardly qualifies as a "Victorian value."[5] But there was another kind of hypocrisy that was more in keeping with Victorian values, and that Mrs. Thatcher might well find tolerable. This was the hypocrisy that La Rochefoucauld commended in his famous adage, "Hypocrisy is the homage that vice pays to virtue." It is also the homage that manners pay to morals. The Victorians thought it no small virtue to maintain the appearance, the manners, of good conduct even while violating some moral principle, for in their demeanor they affirmed the legitimacy of the principle itself.

This was, in fact, what many eminent Victorians did when they felt obliged to commit some transgression. They did not flout conventional morality; on the contrary, they tried to observe at least the manner of it because they truly believed in the substance of it. George Eliot, living with a man whom she could not marry because he could not legally be divorced from his wife, reproduced in their relationship all the forms of propriety. They lived together in perfect domesticity and monogamy, quite as if they were married. She called herself, and asked others to call her, "Mrs. Lewes," and had the satisfaction of hearing the real Mrs. Lewes voluntarily address her that way. And when Mr. Lewes died, after twenty-four years of this pseudo-marriage (one can hardly call it an affair), she almost immediately took the occasion to enter a real, a legal marriage with John Cross, with all the appurtenances thereof: a proper trousseau, a formal wedding in church, and a honeymoon. A recent biographer praises Eliot for her perfect freedom, the freedom from conventionality and from the "burdens of respectability."[6] But she did not seek that freedom; she wanted to be married and respectable, and if she was content with her situation, it was because she assumed the forms and manners of marriage and respectability.

So too with other notorious "irregularities," as the Victorians delicately put it: extramarital relationships (like that of John Stuart Mill and Harriet Taylor), or marriages that were unconsummated (the Carlyles and Ruskins), or longstanding but discreet affairs (Dickens and Ellen Ternan), or homosexual relationships (at least until the Oscar Wilde affair toward the end of the century). Those caught up in such an irregularity tried, as far as was humanly possible, to "regularize" it, to contain it within conventional limits, to domesticate and normalize it. And when they succeeded in doing so, they agonized over it in diaries, memoirs, and letters — which they carefully preserved, and which is why we now know so much about these scandals. Like the "fastidious assassin" in Albert Camus' *The Rebel*, who deliberately gives up his own life when he takes the tyrant's life, so these Victorians insisted upon paying for their indiscretions. They tormented themselves, one has the impression, more than they enjoyed themselves.

William Gladstone, the most eminent of Victorian statesmen (so eminent one can hardly call him a politician), was the perfect example of the fastidious immoralist

— except that his immoralities, by any standards except his own, were more infirmities than vices. Like a recent American president, he lusted in his heart; and when he could not contain his desires, he indulged them in solitude. When his diaries were published a century later, reviewers greeted them as the ultimate in Victorian hypocrisy, the revelation of sexual fantasies and practices that exposed the fraudulence of the Grand Old Man who posed as the Grand Old Moralist. One of the volumes opens with the verse: "He spake no word, he thought no thought / Save by the steadfast rule of Ought."[7] That volume, like the others, records his painful struggles to abide by that rule and his frequent yielding to what he called his "besetting sins": masturbation, pornography, and an obsession with prostitutes.

By the norms of later generations (or of his own predecessors like Lord Melbourne or Lord Palmerston), these were surely venial sins. If Gladstone gave way to masturbation, it was perhaps because of the periods of abstinence resulting from the nine pregnancies of his wife in fifteen years. (The convention of the time was to abstain from sexual intercourse during pregnancy and nursing.) The pornography for which he so bitterly castigated himself was of an elevated kind: rakish passages in Petronius or bawdy Restoration poems. And he never, so far as is known, actually slept with the prostitutes he picked up; he preached at them in the street or brought them home, where he and his wife plied them with hot chocolate and tried to persuade them of the errors of their ways. (Before his death, he assured his son, who was also his pastor, that he had never been guilty of "infidelity to the marriage bed," and there is no reason to doubt his word.)[8] He did not conceal these forays in the streets from the public; he immediately informed the police of one blackmail attempt and took the case to the courts. But neither did he conceal from himself, or excuse in himself, the "courting of evil" or "filthiness of spirit" that provoked them. Instead he punished himself by flagellation (marked in the diaries by the symbol of a whip) — an act that he and most of his contemporaries thought of as chastisement but that we, in a more sophisticated age, believe to be yet another form of sexual perversion (*le vice anglais*, as the French dubbed it).[9]

Gladstone's diaries are titillating; one's eyes are inevitably drawn to those whip symbols and the little *x*'s that signified encounters with prostitutes or impure thoughts. But the diaries are also (like Carlyle's memoirs, or Mill's autobiography, or Eliot's letters) sobering. For they remind us that the eminent Victorians were not only eminently human, with all the failings and frailties of the species, but also eminently moral. They did not take sin lightly — their own sins or anyone else's. If they were censorious of others, they were also guilt-ridden about themselves. They were not hypocrites in the sense of pretending to be more virtuous than they were. On the contrary, they deliberately, even obsessively, confessed to their sins. If they did not all punish themselves quite in the manner of Gladstone, they did suffer in private and behave as best they could in public. They affirmed, in effect, the principles of morality even if they could not always act in accordance with those principles.

Indeed, they affirmed moral principles all the more strongly as the religious basis of those principles seemed to be disintegrating. There were dire predictions, after the publication of Charles Darwin's *Origin of Species* in 1859, that the theory of evolution, and the progress of science in general, would undermine not only religion but morality as well. What happened instead was that morality became, in a sense, a surrogate for religion. For many Victorians, the loss of religious faith inspired a renewed and heightened moral zeal. Darwin himself, asked about the implications of his theory for religion and morality, replied that while the idea of God was "beyond the scope of man's intellect," man's moral obligations were what they had always been: to "do his duty."[10] Leslie Stephen, after abandoning the effort to derive an ethic from Darwinism, finally confessed: "I now believe in nothing, but I do not the less believe in morality."[11] George Eliot uttered the classic statement of this secular ethic when she said that God was "inconceivable," immortality "unbelievable," but duty nonetheless "peremptory and absolute."[12]

The religious census of 1851 was generally interpreted as evidence of the decline of religious faith even before Darwinism appeared on the scene; on the Sunday of the census only half of those able to go to church did so. By Victorian standards, that number was disappointing; by modern standards it is impressive. On that same date, over two million children attended (or at least were enrolled in) Sunday schools — over half of all the children aged five to fifteen and three-quarters of the working-class children of that age group. And the Sunday schools were perhaps a more significant institution than even the churches in the social, moral, and religious life of the Victorians — and more particularly, in developing the ethos of respectability that became so prominent a part of working-class life.[13]

By comparison with other countries, the English were notably pious. The French writer Hippolyte Taine, visiting England several years later, went to two churches and was surprised to find them full of middle-class worshippers and, more surprisingly, with as many men as women, and many of them "gentlemen" — "very different," he commented, "from our own congregations of women, aged dyspeptics, servants, working-class people." Returning to his hotel, he read in his newspaper a proclamation of the Queen affirming her duty "to maintain and augment the service of Almighty God, as also to discourage and suppress all Vice, profane practice, debauchery and immorality." To ensure the strict observance of the Sabbath, she prohibited the playing of cards or any other games in public or private, forbade the sale of liquor or the presence of guests in taverns during services, and commanded "each and every one . . . to attend, with decency and reverence, at Divine Service on every Lord's Day." The proclamation, Taine soon discovered, was not strictly enforced; one could have a drink in the back room of a tavern. Nevertheless a sophisticated Frenchman was shocked by that "vestige of former Puritanism."[14]

It is interesting that even in issuing the command to attend church and observe the Sabbath, the Queen invoked not only the name of God but also the duty to "discourage and suppress all vice, profane practice, debauchery and immorality"; the moral imperative was at least as prominent as the religious one. Taine remarked upon this moral preoccupation of the English. In English sermons, he observed, dogma always takes a "back seat" to the "good life," and religion as such "is hardly more than the poetry which informs ethics or a background to morality." He quoted Thomas Arnold, the famous headmaster of Rugby (now more famous as the father of Matthew Arnold), who advised a man tormented by religious doubts: "Begin by looking at everything from the moral point of view, and you will end by believing in God."[15] (Arnold himself was no passionate believer in God; his faith — "Muscular Christianity," as it was dubbed — resided not so much in God as in a national church that promoted ethical and civic virtues more than dogmas or rituals. But he was a passionate believer in virtue.)

A visiting Frenchman might be astonished by the English predilection for morality without doubting it in the least. Some recent historians are more skeptical. They charge those middle-class moralists with hypocrisy — indeed, of a double hypocrisy, paying lip service to values that they violated in their personal lives, and compounding their offense by imposing those values on the lower classes for their own ulterior motives.

This view is often advanced by historians who claim to be writing "history from below," history as experienced by the ordinary people, the working classes or "anonymous masses." From this perspective, "Victorian values" are seen not as generically Victorian but as specifically middle-class values, values that were alien to the working classes and that the middle classes sought to instill in them for purposes of "social control." This canon of values included not only the familiar ones of work, thrift, cleanliness, temperance, honesty, self-help, but also less obvious ones that were crucial to the "work ethic": promptness, regularity, conformity, rationality. It is this work ethic that is said to have been the crucial instrument of capitalism, the means by which the ruling class transformed the agricultural laborers into an industrial proletariat and exercised its "hegemony" over a docile workforce and citizenry.[16] This "social control" thesis has been applied to manners as well — what Thomas Hobbes called "small morals" and what we call "etiquette." The ritual order of etiquette, by sternly guarding against slips in bodily and emotional control, assured the individual's deferential participation in the dominant social order. Instead of allowing any outward relaxation, bourgeois etiquette drove the tensions back within the individual self, providing ritual support for the psychological defense mechanisms of repression, displacement, and denial necessary to cope with the anxieties of the urban capitalist order.[17]

One of the paradoxes of this "social control" thesis is that it professes to celebrate the working classes — to rescue them from "the enormous condescension of posterity"[18] — while demeaning them as the unwitting victims of "false consciousness." Unable to perceive their own "indigenous" values, the argument goes, Victorian workers were all too easily persuaded to accept the values of their oppressors, to be "moralized" and "socialized" against their own best interests. But is it not more condescending to attribute to these workers a "false consciousness" than to credit them, as most Victorians did, with a true consciousness of their values? Is it not more respectful to think of them not as gullible victims or dupes but as rational people acting in their own interests and pursuing their own values? If they often failed to abide by those values, is it not less patronizing and more humane to assume that that was because of the difficult circumstances of their lives and the natural weaknesses of human beings?

And if these were middle-class values, what were the indigenous working-class values? One historian has said that the reformers' schemes to inculcate the principle of self-help can be understood only through the "distorting lens of middle-class aspirations to gentility."[19] Does this mean that self-help, or independence, was alien to the working classes, in which case are we to understand that dependency was more congenial to them? Or that they were, by nature and preference, indolent rather than industrious, profligate rather than frugal, dirty rather than clean, drunk rather than sober, dishonest rather than honest?

In fact, these Victorian values were as much those of the working classes as of the middle classes. And they were the values not only of the artisan class (the so-called "labor aristocracy") but of the overwhelming majority of the working classes and even of the very poor. Describing the primitive, overcrowded cottages in some rural areas, one historian observed: "One is continually struck, when reading nineteenth-century reports of housing conditions, by the extent to which the poor strove in the almost impossible circumstances of their lives, to conform to middle-class standards of morality."[20] This was especially true in the latter part of the century, as the less skilled and unskilled workers benefited from the expanding economy, the availability of consumer goods, the growth of literacy, and the greater mobility within the working classes — the latter facilitated by the dissemination of precisely these Victorian values. Indeed, toward the end of the century, the working classes became more puritanical and moralistic as the middle classes became more relaxed and permissive.

These values were summed up in the idea of "respectability." Today this word is suspect, redolent of "Victorianism" at its worst. To some historians, it is also redolent of the middle classes at their worst.[21] [. . .] Yet the word was used as much by the working classes as by the middle classes, and while it meant somewhat different things to each of them, it was equally important for both. What it did not mean for most of the working classes (except for a small portion of the artisan class) was any desire to emulate the middle classes or to aspire to that status.[22] For them, respectability was a "value" that was thoroughly "indigenous." It did not even necessarily imply "bettering" themselves, although that was often its effect. More often it simply meant being respected by themselves and by others in their own community.

Indeed, within the working classes, among laborers and factory workers as much as artisans, the division between the "respectable" and the "rough" amounted almost to a class distinction. And that distinction was moral rather than economic. In terms of income, some "roughs" might actually belong to a higher "class" than other workers. But in terms of behavior — drunk, dirty, disorderly — they were viewed by other workers as of a distinctly lower order. This is not to say that the respectable were paragons of virtue; they were quite capable of getting drunk on occasion or of spending money wastefully, even of lapsing for a time into the condition of the rough. For some it was a constant struggle to maintain their respectability. But it was a struggle most of them waged, often against great odds, precisely because they valued respectability. It was, in fact, the poorer workers who valued it most, because they were the most vulnerable without it.

Respectability was a function of character. And "character" had not only the meaning it has today — the moral and social attributes of a person — but a more specific meaning as well. It was a written testimony by an employer of the qualities and habits of his employee — his industriousness, honesty, punctuality, sobriety. Today we would call it a "reference," thus obscuring its specifically moral connotation. Moreover, it was not addressed and sent to a prospective future employer but remained in the possession of the worker, often carried in his pocket so that he could read it for his own satisfaction and produce it if required. He knew what his "character" said — and what his character was.

Working-class memoirs and the evidence of oral history testify poignantly to the efforts to remain respectable, to have a good character (in both senses of that word), in spite of all the difficulties and temptations to the contrary. For men it meant having a job, however lowly, and not being habitually drunk; for women, managing a clean, orderly, and thrifty household; for children, being obedient at home and school, doing chores and contributing, if possible, to the family income.

For the family as a whole, it meant staying "out of the house" (the workhouse) and off the dole, belonging to a burial club or Friendly Society so as to be spared the ignominy of a pauper's burial, having a "clean" (paid up) rent book, wearing clean if shabby clothes and, for special occasions, "Sunday best," and giving no cause for disgrace (such as being arrested for drunkenness or having an illegitimate child).

In this panoply of values, cleanliness is the one that is most difficult to credit, in view of the lack of running water and sewage systems, the dirty and foul-smelling streets, the crowded houses, and the overworked men and women (women particularly, whose job it was to keep the family clean). We envisage Victorian children as begrimed and ragged, looking like chimney sweeps fresh from their jobs. One historian, mocking Margaret Thatcher's invocation of the "cleanliness is next to godliness" adage, said that it was "so much pious nonsense" in Mrs. Thatcher's youth, let alone in Victorian England: "a dirty, smelly age in which a largely dirty, smelly population was sorely afflicted by all manner of diseases rooted in a chronic lack of hygiene at all levels." How could even the middle classes be clean, this critic asks, sweating in all those layers of thick, dark clothing and "without much in the way of regular dry cleaning!" or with all those heavy, cluttered furnishings in "the pre-vacuum cleaner age"?[23]

If anyone is guilty of imposing middle-class values upon the Victorian poor — and late-twentieth-century values at that — it is surely a historian who cannot conceive of cleanliness, either as a value or as a reality, in the absence of dry-cleaning and vacuum cleaners. (It was not Mrs. Thatcher but John Wesley who coined the motto "Cleanliness is next to godliness," more than two centuries earlier, at a time when sanitary conditions were even more primitive.) Of course, the Victorian working classes were dirty and smelly by our standards, as the early Victorians were by the standards of the late Victorians.[24] But what is impressive in reading their memoirs is the enormous effort made by the working classes to be clean as well as to be seen to be clean: the scouring of scullery floors and doorsteps and the black leading of stoves and grates; the ritual of weekly baths (carefully planned so that girls and boys could be bathed separately in a tub in the kitchen); the washing of clothes and linens (which involved heating the water on the stove, transferring it in buckets to the tub, scrubbing the clothes, emptying the buckets, refilling and reheating them for the rinse, wringing out the clothes, sometimes with the help of a mangle, drying them on lines in the yard or, when it rained, as it frequently did, in the kitchen, and finally ironing them).

Even more impressive is the spirit in which these tedious, backbreaking tasks were recalled. There was no minimizing of the hardship, but there was far less resentment than one might expect, and sometimes there was positive pride. A typical recollection is that of a woman whose chore it was, as a young girl, to do the steps:

> You sort of had to wash your step, then wet . . . the sandstone, like you do a pumice stone style, sand it along right on the edge and then you had to get your fingers and go nice and smooth. . . . [I] used to love scouring those steps. It's a work of art, you know.[25]

Foreigners regarded this obsession with cleanliness as yet another English eccentricity. It was not entirely in admiration that the German historian Heinrich Treitschke observed: "The English think soap is civilisation."[26] If cleanliness was next to godliness, work was godliness itself — or so it seemed to Thomas Carlyle:

> *Laborare est Orare*, Work is Worship. . . . All true Work is sacred; in all true Work, were it but true hand-labour, there is something of divineness. . . . No man has worked, or can work, except religiously; not even the poor day-labourer, the weaver of your coat, the sewer of your shoes.[27]

Carlyle, of course, can be dismissed as yet another middle-class preacher. But it is not so easy to dismiss the overwhelming testimony of workers who believed that work, if not sacred, was essential not only to their sustenance but to their self-respect. They could, in fact, have had sustenance without work — in the poorhouse, or on the dole, or from charity. But that would have put them in a condition of "dependency," which was repellent to the respectable working classes, for it was precisely their "independence" that defined their "respectability,"

One of the surprising things about the working-class memoirs of the period is the extent to which children shared this work ethic. They respected their parents' work and thought it perfectly natural that they themselves should work, first by helping in the house, then by earning small sums running errands or doing chores for neighbors, finally by getting a regular job. They took satisfaction in being able to contribute to the family income and seemed not to resent giving their earnings to their mothers. (The fact that their fathers also turned over their wage packets made this a manly thing to do.) "If you could earn a copper anytime," one man recalled of his youth, "then you ought to earn a copper, and of course when you came home you turned it up."[28] Part of the ethos of work was the pride of growing up, assuming the mantle of adulthood, and with it of work. But part of it was also a sense of responsibility to the family and, beyond this, a sense that work itself was something to be proud of; a source of self-respect and the respect of others.

It is at this point that "family values" and "Victorian values" merge, for the work ethic, like so many of the other values encompassed in the idea of respectability — cleanliness, orderliness, obedience, thrift, sexual propriety — centered in the family. "Respectability," one historian observes, "became a family enterprise; its achievement depended upon cooperation from the entire membership and an understanding that collective reputation took precedence over personal preference."[29]

Further reading

See also Gertrude Himmelfarb's studies of Victorian approaches to poverty: *The Idea of Poverty: England in the Early Industrial Age* (London: Faber, 1984); *Poverty and Compassion: The Moral Imagination of the Late Victorians* (New York: Knopf, 1991). Victorian morality is dealt with in: F.M.L. Thompson, *The Rise of Respectable Society: A Social History of Victorian Britain, 1830–1900* (London: Fontana, 1988); Matthew Sweet, *Inventing the Victorians* (London: Faber, 2001); Boyd Hilton, 'Moral Disciplines' in Peter Mandler (ed.), *Liberty and Authority in Victorian Britain* (Oxford: Oxford University Press, 2006), 224–46. A discussion of Himmelfarb's *De-Moralization of Society* can be found in Stefan Collini, 'Speaking with Authority: The Historian as Social Critic' in his *English Pasts: Essays in History and Culture* (Oxford: Oxford University Press, 1999), 85–102.

Notes

1   In France, of course, they were one word: "*moeurs*," as Montesquieu used it, meaning both morals and manners.
2   John Milton, *Areopagitica* (1644), in *The Prose of John Milton*, ed. J. Max Patrick (New York, 1968), p. 272.
3   Thomas Hobbes, *Leviathan* (1651), (Everyman ed., London, 1943), p. 49.
4   William Makepeace Thackeray, 'On Tailoring — and Toilets in General," in *The Four Georges [and] Sketches and Travels in London* (Boston, 1891), p. 148.
5   No satirist could have invented a character so consummately hypocritical as Dr. Pritchard, who, a few hours after poisoning his wife in March 1865 (having poisoned his mother-in-law the previous month), recorded her death in his diary: 18 Saturday — Died here at 1 am. Mary Jane, my own beloved wife, aged 38 years — no torment surrounded her bedside — but like a calm peaceful lamb of God passed Minnie away. May God and Jesus, Holy Gh. — one in three — welcome Minnie. Prayer on prayer till mine be o'er, everlasting love. Save us, Lord, for thy dear Son. W.L. Burn, *The Age of Equipoise: A Study of the Mid Victorian Generation* (London, 1964), p. 44.
6   Phyllis Rose, *Parallel Lives: Five Victorian Marriages* (New York, 1983), p. 221.
7   *The Gladstone Diaries*, ed. H.C.G. Matthew (Oxford, 1982), VIII, 163. One of the few sympathetic accounts of the diaries is Barbara C. Malament, "W.E. Gladstone: An Other Victorian?" *British Studies Monitor*, Winter 1978, pp. 22–38.
8   Ibid., III, xlvi-vii.
9   The editor of his diaries suggests that the idea of flagellation may have come to him from John Henry Newman, who used it himself and who described it graphically in his novel *Loss and Gain*, published in 1848. Gladstone had followed, with great interest and sympathy, Newman's involvement in the Oxford Movement, which sought to restore the high-church practices of the earlier Anglican Church, and was much distressed when Newman converted to Roman Catholicism. (*The Gladstone Diaries*, p. xlvii.)
10   *Life and Letters of Charles Darwin*, ed. Francis Darwin (London, 1887), I, 307 (April 2, 1873).
11   *Life and Letters of Leslie Stephen*, ed. F.W. Maitland (London, 1906), pp. 144–45.
12   Gordon S. Haight, *George Eliot: A Biography* (Oxford, 1968), p. 464.
13   See Thomas Walter Laqueur, *Religion and Respectability: Sunday Schools and Working Class Culture, 1780–1850* (New Haven, 1976).
14   Hippolyte Taine, *Notes on England*, trans. Edward Hyams (London, 1957 [1st French ed., 1860–70]), pp. 11–12.
15   Ibid., pp. 157, 276.
16   The most sophisticated forms of this thesis are modeled on Michel Foucault's *Discipline and Punish: The Birth of the Prison*, trans. Alan Sheridan (New York, 1977). Some examples of the theory applied to Victorian England are A.P. Donajgrodzki, ed., *Social Control in Nineteenth Century Britain* (Totowa, N.J., 1977); Phillip McCann, *Popular Education and Socialization in the Nineteenth Century* (London, 1979); Peter Bailey, *Leisure and Class in Victorian England: Rational Recreation and the Contest for Control, 1830–1885* (London, 1987); Paul Johnson, "Class Law in Victorian England," *Past and Present*, November 1993. For critical discussions of this theory and additional bibliography, see Gertrude Himmelfarb, *The Idea of Poverty: England in the Early Industrial Age* (New York, 1983), pp. 29, 41, 59, 178, 537, n. 18, 553, n. 2; Himmelfarb, *Poverty and Compassion: The Moral Imagination of the Late Victorians* (New York, 1991),

200–1, 431–32, n. 52; F.M.L. Thompson, "Social Control in Victorian Britain," *Economic History Review*, May 1981; Thomas L. Haskell, "Capitalism and the Origins of the Humanitarian Sensibility," *The American Historical Review*, April 1985; "Humanitarianism or Control: A Symposium on Aspects of Nineteenth-Century Social Reform in Britain and America," *Rice University Studies*, Winter 1981; Martin Wiener, "Social Control in Nineteenth Century Britain," *Journal of Social History*, 1978–79.

17 John F. Kasson, *Rudeness and Civility: Manners in Nineteenth-Century Urban America* (New York, 1990), p. 165.

18 E.P. Thompson, *The Making of the English Working Class* (New York, 1964), p. 12.

19 Gareth Stedman Jones, *Outcast London: A Study in the Relationship Between Classes in Victorian Society* (Oxford, 1971), p. 196.

20 Enid Gauldie, *Cruel Habitations: A History of Working-Class Housing, 1780–1918* (London, 1974), p. 22.

21 See note 16 above. Some historians have recently begun to speak more respectfully of respectability. The word even appears in the titles of books and articles: F.M.L. Thompson, *The Rise of Respectable Society: A Social History of Victorian Britain, 1830–1900* (Cambridge, Mass., 1988); Laqueur, *Religion and Respectability*; P. Bailey, " 'Will the Real Bill Banks Please Stand Up?' Towards a Role Analysis of Mid-Victorian Working-Class Respectability," *Journal of Social History*, 1978–79, p. 343. See also Brian Harrison, *Peaceable Kingdom: Stability and Change in Modern Britain* (Oxford, 1982), pp. 157 ff.; Elizabeth Roberts, *A Woman's Place: An Oral History of Working-Class Women, 1890–1940* (Oxford, 1984), passim; Michael J. Childs, *Labour's Apprentices: Working-Class Lads in Late Victorian and Edwardian England* (Montreal, 1992), passim.

22 This mistaken idea is encapsulated in the title of a recent essay, "How to Join the Middle Classes: With the Help of Dr. Smiles and Mrs. Beeton," by Christopher Clausen, *American Scholar*, Summer 1993.

23 Eric M. Sigsmouth, ed., *In Search of Victorian Values: Aspects of Nineteenth-Century Thought and Society* (Manchester, 1988), p. 2.

24 The situation improved greatly in the latter half of the century. The water supply became more plentiful as well as more potable; bathhouses were available in the towns, and many working-class houses acquired running water; sewage and sanitary conditions vastly improved; soap was cheaper and cotton fabric was increasingly used for clothing, which greatly facilitated washing.

25 Standish Meacham, *A Life Apart: The English Working Class, 1890–1914* (Cambridge. Mass., 1977), p. 89. See also Roberts, *A Woman's Place*, for abundant evidence to the same effect.

26 Jeffrey Richards, "Victorian Values Revisited," *Encounter*, March 1987.

27 Thomas Carlyle, *Past and Present* (Everyman ed., London, n.d.), pp. 193–99.

28 Childs, *Labour's Apprentices*, p. 15.

29 Meacham, *A Life Apart*, p. 27.

PART 8

Intellectual history

Stefan Collini

CHARACTER AND THE
VICTORIAN MIND

Stefan Collini, *Public Moralists: Political Thought and Intellectual Life in Britain, 1850–1930* (Oxford: Clarendon Press, 1991), 104–13.

Covering the age of Carlyle, Mill and Ruskin, the field of Victorian intellectual history has always been vigorous. During the 1980s, the discipline acquired new importance through its openness to arguments about language and linguistic analysis. Increasingly, the procedures of intellectual history were employed by scholars such as **Gareth Stedman Jones** (see his Reading, pp. 177–90) in order to explain wider currents of social and political thought. The history of ideas has therefore played a major role in the development of interdisciplinarity. Following the pioneering work of J.G.A. Pocock and Quentin Skinner (who study earlier periods), there has been a shift away from examining ideas through the academic conversation of a small number of great thinkers and towards a reconstruction of the linguistic and discursive fields that make new ideas possible (including forms of rhetoric) as well as a greater sensitivity to wider cultural contexts. There has also been a renewed focus on reading texts in depth to establish the interplay of different traditions and styles in Victorian thought and so reconstruct its peculiarities. However, the fundamental achievement of modern intellectual history (not just of the Victorians) is to establish that ideas matter and have consequences.

One of the leading Victorian intellectual historians has been **Stefan Collini**. Like fellow historians John Burrow and Donald Winch (sometimes referred to as the 'Sussex school' as they were all at one time based at the University of Sussex), he has produced rigorous studies of Victorian political thought, whose impulses, he demonstrates, are often foreign to the twentieth-century mind.

In this extract from *Public Moralists* (1991), Stefan Collini uses his skills as an intellectual historian to interrogate a term which is not peculiar to the Victorians, but which has resonated differently over many eras. The concept of 'character', however, took on a particular significance for the Victorians as a touchstone for the age. Collini is not merely tracing a 'mutation' of a term, but one that became (in his words) the 'chief structuring vocabulary of the political reflection of the age'. Thus, 'character' is what Raymond Williams would have termed a 'key word', and it helped inform the Victorian world-view.

Collini explores the way character as a concept underpinned different ideas of behaviour in a variety of realms, from the political, to the religious, to the behavioural. He traces its use by different groups to underpin their analysis of the problems of Victorian society. For example, the economist Alfred Marshall and the social reformer Helen Bosanquet both saw character as the force that shaped how individuals responded to the challenges of their lives, while socialists worried that individualism was undermining character. Samuel Smiles entitled one of his books *Character* (1871) and in it emphasised the sense of duty that men of character happily took on as part of worldly success. In this Reading, Collini demonstrates how the term has a complex set of meanings. Elsewhere he considers the means by which character was instilled in Victorian society, particularly through the public schools and their celebration of manliness. Collini's contribution is to bring together a variety of approaches in order to expose how one concept shaped many areas of Victorian life and politics.

Stefan Collini is Professor of Intellectual History and English Literature in the Faculty of English at the University of Cambridge. His most recent book is *Absent Minds: Intellectuals in Britain* (2006).

T RACING THE AETIOLOGY of this idea of character and the cluster of values it embraced, and, what might be of greater interest, charting the ways in which concepts long available came to acquire a new prominence and resonance, partly in response to the rise of new political preoccupations, would require a major effort of intellectual history which will be a constitutive part of the task facing any future historian of the Making of the English Respectable Class. But even the much more limited enterprise of identifying the place of this idea in the political thinking of Victorian intellectuals demands that we have an eye to the more general intellectual currents of which it was a part, to moral and social developments which may be regarded as preconditions rather than sources. One could not, for example, go very far into this subject without mentioning the wider cultural impact of Evangelical Christianity, though it must be said that the most directly relevant feature of that legacy — the vision of life as a perpetual struggle in which one's ability to resist temptation and overcome obstacles needed to be subject to constant scrutiny —

was, with only minor changes of emphasis, a feature shared by otherwise theologically diverse groups who also left their mark on the early Victorian educated classes, such as the Tractarians and the Arnoldians.[1] Of particular consequence for the present theme was the way in which an essentially Evangelical moral psychology penetrated the discussion of economic life early in the century. [. . .] In Evangelical social thought economic activity was portrayed as a proving-ground of moral discipline where the existence of the possibility of debt and bankruptcy, or, lower down the social scale, of unemployment and destitution, operated as a check on that financial imprudence which was only the outward sign of moral failure.[2] [. . .]

In exploring this issue, we also need to note a significant shift away from eighteenth-century ideas of the moral and cultural primacy of leisure. For the Georgian gentleman, and thus for all those who aspired to that status, the most prized human qualities could only be developed in the enjoyment of 'society' in the older meaning of the term; mechanics were rude and scholars monkish precisely because, whether from necessity or choice, they spent so little time cultivating the virtues of sociability.[3] By contrast, for the respectable Victorian — who might, of course, belong to a much larger and less leisurely class — work was the chief sphere in which moral worth was developed and displayed. It is not hard to see, for example, how the virtues of character spoke to the economic experience of those groups who made up the urban middling rank. That experience was above all of individual ventures under conditions of uncertainty with no financial safety-net. Stories of businesses which had 'gone down' and of modest fortunes lost in speculations which were imprudent or worse furnished the moralist with particularly telling illustrations. It was, at all levels, an economic world in which reputation played a powerful part: to be known as a man of character was to possess the moral collateral which would reassure potential business associates or employers. Victorian lexicographers, assigned a correspondingly prominent place to reputation in their definitions of character: 'good qualities or the reputation of possessing them' was how *The Century Dictionary* (1889) laconically and revealing put it, while the *OED* suggested 'the estimate formed of a person's qualities; reputation when used without qualifying epithet, implying "favourable estimate, good repute"'. (A less inhibited commentator on the language observed: 'Character is like an inward spiritual grace of which reputation is, or should be, the outward and visible sign.'[4] Although the classic scenes of character-testing are essentially private — facing the discouragement of an empty order-book, coping with the failure of one's inventions and projects, studying deep into the night to acquire by hard labour what seemed to come so easily to the expensively educated — it was also true that character was an ascribed quality, possessed and enjoyed in public view.

The increased circulation of the language of character also represented part of a wider reaction against the alleged vices and indulgences of the territorial aristocracy, especially in their metropolitan form. At its most general this involved a revolt against convention, artificiality, and mere outward polish, a post-Romantic assertion of authenticity as well as a puritan taste for austerity. More specifically, this repudiation of the ethics of the salon fed into a protest against the politics of patronage, in which the long-celebrated value of 'independence' acquired a new force. It is noticeable how often — Smiles could again be called to the witness-stand — but so could many others — the mid-Victorian panegyrics on character occur in the context of homilies on how true worth is unrelated to social position, or, conversely, how the justifiable pride of the man of noble character is contrasted with, even provides the criterion for criticism of the tawdriness of wealth and station and the snobbery of that sham gentility which pretended to them. Here we are beginning to back into the larger question of the sources of Victorian liberalism, for accompanying the self-assertion of new groups in the political nation there developed something of a vogue for candour and manliness, a revulsion from the degrading nature of dependence and the social pretences which dependence, demanded.

I shall return to the political form taken by these emotions, but first want to draw attention to a very different strand in the fabric, to a tradition of political reflection in which the relevant contrast to talk of 'character' was not a moral posture of dependence or inauthenticity, or even just a state of chronic weakness of will, but such terms as 'political machinery' and 'paper constitutions'. It was, that is to say, part of a vocabulary of political analysis, with a very wide currency among the educated classes in post-Napoleonic Britain, which insisted on the inadequacy of merely constitutional or legal changes when unaccompanied by the necessary qualities and habits in the people. In practice, this usually slid into a celebration of England's good fortune by contrast to the unhappy experiences of politically less gifted nations (the French, needless to say, provided the main source of cautionary tales), and there was certainly a congratulatory element in the way 'national character' acted as the chief explanatory concept in these meditations on comparative political fortunes.[5] Such assumptions were not confined to those who wished to conserve existing arrangements: by 1868 one also finds the likes of John Morley insisting that merely institutional change must be subordinate to 'the multiplication and elevation of types of virtuous character'.[6] Mill, in self-consciously scientific vein, maintained that 'the laws of national character are by far the most important class of sociological laws', even insisting that national character was 'the power by which all those of the circumstances in society which are artificial, laws and customs for instance, are altogether moulded'.[7] (It is worth noting that character is being regarded as the very bedrock of explanation when even 'customs' are classed as 'artificial'.) But Mill, too, raised his glass to that 'point of character which beyond any other, fits the people of *this* country for representative government', and Alfred Marshall was simply one of many who extended this analysis from political stability to economic prosperity: 'The same qualities which gave political freedom gave [the English] also free enterprise in industry and commerce'.[8]

We have here again that blending of descriptive and evaluative elements: progress is analysed in terms of the causal power of national character, and at the same time the development of a certain type of character, is itself an index of progress, a specification of modernity where what Bagehot described as the 'cake of custom' has been broken. Lecky generalized the point in a way which flattered the self-esteem of the political class: 'In the long run, the increasing or decreasing importance of character in public life is perhaps the best test of the progress or decline of nations.'[9] Progress, after all, was still regarded as a rarity in world history, a fragile achievement born of countless acts of initiative, acts which shape that character which in turn becomes the chief, perhaps the only, guarantee of future progress. Here is the anxiety about the long term once more. The fear of returning to a 'Chinese stationariness' was more than just a cultural cliché.

One way to bring out the distinctiveness and interdependence of the elements in the Victorian language of character is to contrast that language very briefly with comparable strands in the political discourse of the preceding century. The two strands that could most plausibly be seen as comparable are the language of virtue and the language of sociability or politeness, for unlike, say, political thinking which remained in the austere language of natural law or pressed one of the various radical or Utopian cases in the language of rights, these two dealt primarily with a comparable kind of concern and level of analysis — the moral qualities of the citizen and the habits and manners of a member of civil society. In making such a contrast, I do not mean to preclude the possibility of tracing survivals and mutations of these languages into the nineteenth century, but I take it that this is just what they would be — survivals and mutation rather than the chief structuring vocabularies of the political reflection of the age.

In both the language of virtue and the language of character there is a similar emphasis on the moral vigour of the citizens as the prime requirement for the health of the body politic, though the civic humanist tradition tended to portray this as instrumental to the maintenance of political liberty whereas in the nineteenth century the cultivation of character could more readily be represented as an end in itself.[10] But the simplest way to bring out the chief contrast between them is to look at their different visions of nemesis. Putting it in a single phrase, one might say that the politics of virtue was haunted by the fear of corruption, while it was stagnation that figured as the chief threat in the politics of character. As this suggests, the former was primarily concerned with maintaining an existing balance and was essentially backward-looking, in that it understood its political fate in terms of a well-established cycle, frequently enacted in the relevant ancient history, of liberty, opulence, corruption, loss of liberty; a cycle it was doomed to repeat if the valour and public spirit of its freeholding, militia-serving citizenry should once be sapped. By contrast, the striving, self-reliant, adaptable behaviour endorsed by the imperatives of character is inherently tied to movement and progress, to a future which must be regarded as to some extent open-ended (another point I shall return to below). Both, of course, are strenuous ideals, containing a generous dash of asceticism, yet they stand in an interestingly different relation to the private pursuit of wealth. In the civic humanist tradition, it is a precondition of political liberty that those classed as citizens should be able to devote their energies to participation in public affairs, and hence should be at least partly free of the need to engage directly in productive activity, while at the same time luxury is an agent of decay precisely because it diverts men's concerns from the public to the private sphere. In character-talk, the individual is not primarily regarded as a member of a political community, but as an already private (though not thereby selfish) moral agent whose mastering of his circumstances is indirectly a contribution to the vitality and prosperity of his society. Here, the getting of wealth, even in quite substantial quantities, is salutary moral experience, provided the emphasis is placed on the getting; the civic humanist ideal of an assured independence would from this perspective figure rather as a temptation to indulgence than as a guarantee of political commitment. Furthermore, for the civic humanist, uniformity of material conditions is conducive to the practice of virtue, whereas the growth of character is inherently tied to a situation of diversity. In both traditions there is an abhorrence of apathy: it is the obverse of their common strenuousness. But whereas in the civic humanist eschatology apathy is what leads to a decline from public to private, in Victorian individualism apathy, in the form of lack or weakness of character, is more likely to figure as the force propelling the otherwise self-maintaining individual into a state of dependence and in *that* sense into the public sphere.

Somewhat similar contrasts can be made between the eighteenth century language of politeness and sociability and the nineteenth-century language of character.[11] In this case we are dealing with a cultural or moral ideal which coloured political discussion without issuing in a systematic programme in the way that civic humanism did, but this arguably brings it nearer to the role of character in Victorian political thought. In general terms, of course, there is an obvious contrast between the emphasis the ideals of the two periods respectively placed on the outer and the inner man (though, as I have mentioned, character was also bound up with reputation). This is evident even where the same term is invoked, as in the praise for the way in which the founding of the Poker Club of Edinburgh in 1762 not only served 'national purposes' by bringing together representatives of different social groups, but also had 'Happy Effects on Private Character by Forming and polishing the Manners which are suitable to Civilis'd Society'.[12] Here, 'private' means 'individual' as contrasted with 'national', but it clearly involves social qualities far removed from character as the Victorians celebrated it. Where the autodidact, for example, was the archetypal Smilesian hero, Georgians deplored him as likely to be obtuse or crotchety, lacking the urbanity and moderation imparted by extensive experience of sociability. Similarly, where 'getting on' suggested to the Victorian the overcoming of adverse circumstances and engaging in wholesome competition, for the Georgian 'getting along' required more attention to the arts of winning esteem and cultivating connections. The Georgian fear of isolation or eccentricity as a sign of a rude, uncivilized way of life can be contrasted with the Victorian anxiety about the way in which the pressures of opinion in a commercial society made for conformity and lack of enterprise. 'Independence', to be sure, was highly valued in both traditions, but even here its ramifications differed somewhat. In eighteenth-century England, as one historian has well put it, 'the sinecure was, the favourite mode of achieving independence in the heyday of the patronage system',[13] whereas the holding of a 'place' came to be treated with opprobrium by Victorian moralists, scenting in the lack of fair competition damning evidence of both dependence and deceit.

These contrasts are clearly part of much larger developments: both of my chosen eighteenth-century languages were, for example, addressed to a smaller class than any nineteenth-century political idiom could plausibly be. Although none of these languages was exclusively the possession of a party, it is already evident that I am trenching on the larger question of the development of Whiggism into Liberalism.[14] The language of character encapsulated a substantial passage in this development. As a body of political thought, Whiggism had been formatively and enduringly shaped by a view about the nature, and certainly by a conviction about the importance, of the constitution, and in the course of the nineteenth century many of these matters inevitably lost their political immediacy. An increasingly attenuated Whiggism still spoke to the one great recurrent constitutional issue, namely the extension of the franchise, yet even here it is interesting to see that the language of 'interests' and 'balance', which still occupied the centre of the stage in 1832, had by 1867 ceded considerable ground to the language of character. Discussion of the Second Reform

Bill, both in and out of Parliament, turned to a considerable extent on the question of whether the moral qualities of the respectable urban artisan is such that he should be entrusted with the vote.[15] Proponents of reform argued that his exclusion could no longer be justified because he had revealed — whether in his regular contributions to Friendly Societies, or in what Gladstone termed 'that magnificent moral spectacle', his supposed support against his own economic interest of the North in the American Civil War — that he had now developed that strength of character which would prevent him from misusing the vote in recklessly short-sighted or self-interested ways.[16] 'Self-command and the power of endurance' had been among the desirable qualities of a potential elector enumerated by Mr Gladstone in the debate on Baines's Bill, and it is an indication of the hold of the language of character that so much of the discussion in 1867 was not about its respectable workman's rights but about his habits.

Approaching the same transition from a different angle, one of G.M. Young's remarks supplies, as so often, a helpful provocation to thought: the Whigs, he wrote, 'came from the eighteenth century where privilege was taken for granted'.[17] Although in the history of political thought Liberalism is mostly treated as a theory of the priority of liberty or of the defence of the rights of the individual, its expression in the political culture of mid-nineteenth-century England suggests that its fundamental emotional dynamic was something more like hostility to unreflective and unjustified privilege and a related hatred of being patronized. That somewhat prickly touchiness which characterized several leading Liberals — Bright is a particularly conspicuous example — was an expression of this resentment of unmerited superiority and a fear of being slighted. A generation ago we were persuasively urged to see a vehicle for the expression of such emotions in the electoral Liberalism of the bootmakers of Rochdale and the shipwrights of Whitby,[18] but something similar remains to be said, I think, due allowance being made for differences of register, about the theories of the likes of Spencer and Green. From one point of view, the lofty stoic ideal of self-command inculcated by the language of character may seem very far removed from that spirit of self-righteous, mean-minded *ressentiment* which marked much of provincial dissenting Liberalism. But for many of those who read Smiles and admired Bright the language of character could produce a certain *frisson*; it allowed a vicarious form of self-assertion, a public affirmation of one's own worth in the face of a daily experience of the condescension of the well-born and well-connected. Further up the social scale, the vogue among the professional and preaching classes for 'manliness' [. . .] expressed a not altogether dissimilar political aesthetic. That mingling of ethical and physiological properties which character-talk always involved was particularly pronounced here: bodily and moral vigour could be cultivated by the same means, expressed by the same actions. Weakness of will, of which sentimentalism was a variety, could be walked or climbed out of the system, an attitude which in many cases found expression in what, to coin a necessary label, can only be called 'Muscular Liberalism'.

Further reading

Useful starting points for Victorian intellectual history include: H.S. Jones, *Victorian Political Thought* (Basingstoke: Macmillan, 2000); Mark Francis and John Morrow,

A History of English Political Thought in the Nineteenth Century (London: Duckworth, 1994). Many of the leading strands in recent thinking can be followed in: Stefan Collini, Richard Whatmore and Brian Young (eds), *Economy, Polity and Society: British Intellectual History, 1750–1950* (Cambridge: Cambridge University Press, 2000); Stefan Collini, Richard Whatmore and Brian Young (eds), *History, Religion and Culture: British Intellectual History, 1750–1950* (Cambridge: Cambridge University Press, 2000). These foreground the work of the 'Sussex school', for whom see also: John Burrow, *A Liberal Descent: Victorian Historians and the English Past* (Cambridge: Cambridge University Press, 1981); Stefan Collini, Donald Winch and John Burrow, *That Noble Science of Politics: A Study in Nineteenth-Century Intellectual History* (Cambridge: Cambridge University Press, 1983). Noel Annan, *The Dons: Mentors, Eccentrics and Geniuses* (London: HarperCollins, 2000) contains portraits of Victorian as well as twentieth-century academics, but it should particularly be consulted for his famous article about the intellectual aristocracy (pp. 304–41).

Notes

1   For a general account, see the still useful Walter E. Houghton, *The Victorian Frame of Mind 1830–1870* (New Haven, Conn., 1957), esp. 233–4.

2   See the authoritative account by Boyd Hilton, *The Age of Atonement: The Influence of Evangelicalism on Social and Economic Thought 1795–1865* (Oxford, 1988).

3   For some perceptive remarks on this ideal, see Sheldon Rothblatt, *Tradition and Change in English Liberal Education: An Essay in History and Culture* (London, 1976), and Nicholas Phillipson, 'Culture and society in the eighteenth-century province: the case of Edinburgh and the Scottish Enlightenment', in Lawrence Stone (ed.), *The University in Society*, 2 vols (Princeton, NJ, 1975), ii. 407–48.

4   R.G. White, *Words and Their Uses* (London, 1870), 99.

5   For examples, see Collini, Winch, and Burrow, *That Noble Science of Politics*, 151–9, 170–4, 185–205, 317–29.

6   Quoted in Jeffrey von Arx, *Progress and Pessimism: Religion, Politics, and History in Late-Nineteenth-Century Britain* (Cambridge, Mass., 1985), 136.

7   Mill, *System of Logic*, CW, viii. 904–5.

8   John Stuart Mill, *Considerations on Representative Government* (1861), *CW*, xix. ii; Marshall, *Principles*, i. 744.

9   W.E.H. Lecky, *Democracy and Liberty*, 2 vols, (London, 1896), i. 370.

10   For my understanding of 'the language of virtue' I am primarily indebted to Pocock, *Machiavellian Moment*: for its relation, particularly relevant to my theme, to political economy, see Istvan Hont and Michael Ignatieff (eds), *Wealth and Virtue: The Shaping of Political Economy in the Scottish Enlightenment* (Cambridge, 1983), esp. the essays by Robertson and Pocock himself.

11   For 'the language of sociability' see the sources cited in n. 3 above, and Nicholas Phillipson, 'Adam Smith as civic moralist' in Hont and Ignatieff, *Wealth and Virtue*.

12   Quoted in Rothblatt, *Liberal Education*, 73.

13   Ibid. 28.

14   See the very perceptive treatment of this theme in J.W. Burrow, *Whigs and Liberals: Continuity and Change in English Political Thought* (Oxford, 1988).

15   For examples, see Stefan Collini, 'Political theory and the "science of society" in Victorian Britain', *Historical Journal*, 23 (1980), esp. 217.

16   Quoted in Ian Bradley, *The Optimists: Themes and Personalities in Victorian Liberalism* (London, 1980), 154–5. The fullest account of the educated classes' views of reform in 1867 is Christopher Harvie, *The Lights of Liberalism: University Liberty and the Challenge of Democracy 1860–1886* (London, 1976), but for some reservations about Harvie's interpretation see Collini, 'Political theory and the "science of society"', 212–18.

17   G.M. Young, *Victorian England: Portrait of an Age* (1936), annotated edn. by George Kitson Clark (London, 1977), 31.

18   John Vincent, *The Formation of the British Liberal Party 1857–1868* (London: 1966), and *Poll-Books: How Victorians Voted* (Cambridge, 1967).

PART 9

Religion

ONE OF THE CRITICISMS that was sometimes made of the 1960s generation of Victorian historians was that many of them (with their predominantly secular outlook) underplayed the importance of religion. While this is not entirely unfair, there has been a greater recognition in recent years that to ignore religion is to misunderstand the Victorian era completely. The nineteenth century was the last period in British history when Christianity was suffused into almost all aspects of life. Sermons could be best-sellers. Politics was intertwined with theology. National identity was shaped by a view of Britain as a Protestant nation. Britain was distinctive because of its established church but also because of the strength of nonconformity, which shaped the social and political outlook of the age. In the 1980s, historians began to focus on the way arguments about theology shaped apparently non-religious issues such as economic policy. Critics of Victorian literature were also impelled to evaluate the religious mind and the spirituality of many Victorian writers.

Religious controversies were a fault line in Victorian Britain. This was an age whose temper was defined by outstanding religious figures such as John Henry Newman, Thomas Chalmers and Charles Spurgeon. Even atheism, in the form of the Secularist movement, was proclaimed by its followers (such as the MP Charles Bradlaugh) with a religious fervour. The rupture within Anglicanism caused by the Oxford Movement, the impact of Evangelicalism and the ways in which the churches adjusted to urban Britain have been major themes of inquiry. The Roman Catholic Church was boosted by Emancipation in 1829, the restoration of its hierarchy in 1850 and the influx of Irish immigrants (who made their church into a major presence in the nation although anti-Catholicism was an intermittent feature of Victorian life). Religious historians in recent years have been particularly concerned with the variety of religious practice throughout the United Kingdom. The histories of faith in Scotland, Ireland and Wales differ in many respects from that of England. There has also been greater interest in other religions that were practised in Victorian Britain, such as Judaism, and in 'alternative' systems of belief such as theosophy. However, a great deal of religious history has been shaped by the fact that religious observance, particularly on the part of the working class, was on the decline. This was the shocking revelation of the 1851 religious census. The so-called secularisation thesis has shaped much of the way that Victorian religion is discussed. In recent years historians have pointed to the complexities of secularisation. Late Victorian Britain was a strongly religious nation. Jeffrey Cox and Sarah Williams have both employed a 'diffusionist' model to demonstrate that religion shaped the world-view and behaviour of most people even if they did not attend church. One of the reasons why the issue of religion has become more pressing is that it is a way of talking about *why* the Victorians are different in some respects from ourselves today.

Boyd Hilton

RELIGION, DOCTRINE AND PUBLIC POLICY

'From Retribution to Reform' in Lesley M. Smith (ed.), *The Making of Britain: The Age of Revolution* (Basingstoke: Macmillan Education, 1987), 37–49.

Boyd Hilton's *The Age of Atonement: The Influence of Evangelicalism on Social and Economic Thought, 1795–1865* (1988) has established itself as a classic work of intellectual, economic, political, scientific, literary and religious history. He draws on all these areas to demonstrate the ways in which Evangelicalism and its sober outlook underpinned the mind of Britain's elite in the first half of the nineteenth century. His book traces how this mentality, with its focus on Christ's atonement for humanity's sins, gave ground to a new, gentler conception of Christianity. This in turn had serious consequences for social policy, economic theory, and much else. The Reading that follows is derived from a television lecture in which Hilton presents his thesis in *The Age of Atonement*. It constitutes a vital argument for taking religion seriously as a key to the Victorian frame of mind.

Boyd Hilton is Reader in Modern History and Fellow of Trinity College at the University of Cambridge. His books include *Cash, Corn and Commerce: The Economic Policies of the Tory Governments, 1815–1830* (1977), and, more recently, *A Mad, Bad and Dangerous People?: England, 1783–1846* (2006).

IT IS COMMON NOWADAYS to talk about 'Victorian values', signifying thrift, hard work, independence, decency and respectability. Yet the concept is rather a surprising one since Queen Victoria reigned from 1837 until 1900, and it seems unlikely that in such a rapidly changing society as nineteenth-century Britain any single system of values could have persisted unchanged for so long. In fact, far from there having been any overall Victorian values, historians tend to distinguish between early, middle and late Victorian periods. This chapter considers the cultural revolution which occurred between the early Victorianism of the 1830s and 1840s and the mid Victorianism of the 1850s and 1860s, especially as it affected religious thought and social policy.

We often think of the 1850s and 1860s as an 'age of doubt' because of the well known 'crises of faith' which many members of the Victorian intelligentsia underwent at that time. It is well known that the truth of Genesis and other large tracts of the Bible was being called into question by geologists, biologists, literary critics and historians. However, we cannot understand the 'spirit of an age' by looking at what a handful of intellectuals thought, and what is clear is that, among the middle and upper classes at least, nineteenth-century British culture was (and remained) overwhelmingly religious.

However, to say that Victorian England was religious is not to say very much. Many societies are. The question is, in what way was it religious? The main characteristic of British people in the first half of the nineteenth century was their preoccupation with Providence — that is, with how God acts in the world. Take, for example, their response to what was undoubtedly one of the greatest natural disasters of the century — the Irish potato famine, which struck in 1845 and for the next four seasons and which killed more than a million Irishmen. The Great Famine is mainly remembered as a landmark in the development of Irish nationalism, but how about the reaction in the rest of Britain? Nearly everyone agreed that the event was providential. 'Here is a calamity *legibly* divine!' wrote Gladstone to his wife, meaning that one could read God's handwriting in it. 'There is', he went on, 'a total absence of secondary causes which might tempt us to explain it away', meaning that it must be a deliberate act of the Almighty and not merely the consequence of physical law, such as unfavourable weather patterns or backward methods of agriculture.[1] But what was the message? *Why* should God cause a million Irishmen to starve? For many Englishmen the answer was simple: God had turned on the Irish because of what the English had long considered to be their fecklessness and sloth, their neglect of so-called Victorian values. This was the view of Sir Charles Trevelyan, under-secretary of state in charge of famine relief, who did very little to help Ireland in the crisis because he was reluctant to interfere with market forces, believing as he (and many other people) did that market forces merely manifested God's moral providence. Others pointed to the British government's decision to increase the amount of state subsidy to the Roman Catholic College at Maynooth just months before the famine struck. God was of course assumed to be a Protestant, and many people thought that he must have been so angry at the government's concession to the Irish Catholics that he decided to blight the very next potato crop. But then there were others, less complacent, who feared that the warning must be pointed at England. Irishmen who starved were the lucky ones for they would be whisked to Paradise. It was the English, luxuriating in a railway boom and enjoying unexampled prosperity, who should tremble at what was obviously a warning to them to mend their ways. 'Ireland is the minister of God's retribution', said Gladstone — not the *object* but the *minister*; England was the *object* of God's wrath, and it was essential that Englishmen atone before it was too late.

This sense of retribution, propagated from pulpits up and down the land, also permeated the highest levels of government. Take the home secretary, Sir James Graham, Peel's right-hand man, whom we often think of as a cool and detached administrator. When the first intimations of famine came in October 1845, Graham wrote Peel a long and fairly humdrum letter about the reports he had received, and ended it with the following lament:

> It is awful to observe how the Almighty humbles the pride of nations. The Sword, the Pestilence, and Famine are the instruments of his displeasure; the Canker-worm and the Locust are his Armies; he gives his word; a single Crop is blighted, and we see a nation prostrate, and stretching out its Hands for Bread. These are solemn warnings, and they fill me with reverence; they proclaim with a voice not to be mistaken, that 'doubtless there is a God, who judgeth the earth'.[2]

Graham's view may seem wildly apocalyptic to us but at the time it was commonplace. Yet strangely, when — ten years later — the executors of Sir Robert Peel set about publishing that statesman's memoirs and correspondence, they came to Graham's letter and, after a great deal of agonising, decided not to print that concluding paragraph all about God's retribution. They felt that it would offend people's sensibilities to describe the Almighty as a vengeful Old Testament tyrant who would deliberately inflict pain to teach mankind a moral lesson. Reluctantly Graham agreed — which is why the passage has been omitted from the published version of the letter.[3]

For in the Church of England, that is in comfortable upper and middle-class circles, the image of God was changing — from that of a fierce headmaster proclaiming that vengeance was his — to that of a sort of Santa Claus. There was a famous incident in 1853 when Frederick Denison Maurice was dismissed from his professorship at King's College, London, for daring to suggest that there was no Hell, meaning no place where the damned were literally roasted and tormented for eternity. Twenty, even ten, years later he would have kept his job. By then it would have been widely accepted in Church of England circles that Hell was either a temporary reformatory — the place for a short sharp spiritual shock which would fit a sinner eventually for Heaven — or else a state of nothingness, a void. At the same time men's image of Heaven also turned about. Earlier it had been pictured in the same exaggerated way as Hell, as a place of jewelled pagodas and hallelujah choruses. But then, as the literal image of Hell receded, so Heaven began to be domesticated, came to be seen in terms of a cosy fireside where saints would be surrounded by their long-lost loved ones and by all mod cons and creature comforts. Instead of attempting to terrorise sinners into Heaven, Anglican ministers now placed more emphasis on trying to tempt them thither by promising them more of the good things which they had enjoyed throughout life.

Again, in the 1850s and 1860s people's idea of Jesus changed. In the first half of the nineteenth century it had been the bleeding lamb, the Atonement — Christ's death on the Cross — that signified, because it was believed that a person could enter Heaven *only* if he or she had faith that Jesus had died to save mankind. Mankind had sinned against God in the persons of Adam and Eve, and God had had to exact punishment for that offence, but he had sent his son to bear that punishment in man's place. The Atonement of Christ was therefore called 'the trick of redemption' or 'the scheme of salvation', because it was seen as a mechanism to get believers into heaven. So the divinity of Christ was the very centre-point of religious belief in the first half of the nineteenth century, and yet people were not actually very interested in what Christ had said and done while he was a man, or in his teaching as it is related in the New Testament.

All this changed in the middle of the century. There was a sudden surge of disgust at the very idea of Atonement, at the notion of a supposedly loving God inflicting pain on the innocent Christ merely in order to get his own back on wicked men. Instead people began to be fascinated with the *life* of Christ, as is clear from the thousands of biographies which began to be written after 1860. The parables as related by Christ, and his various other injunctions on how to behave, to turn the other cheek or love one's neighbour or be a Good Samaritan, all aspects of his ministry which had previously been played down, suddenly came into prominence. Anglican christianity now put over a more gentle, caring conception of the world, and Christmas — a festival celebrated so warmly in the novels of Dickens, for example — replaced Easter as the centre-point of the christian year. The Incarnation, or Christ's becoming man, rather than his death and Atonement, now seemed to be the important thing.

If we have to use labels — and they are always misleading — we would say that the religion of the first half of the century was predominantly 'evangelical'. It assumed that man is inherently sinful, in need of redemption, which is nevertheless open to him if he makes the right choice. The earth is a place of trial, in which God tempts us, tests us, and decides which of us will go to Heaven and which to Hell. God has no other interest in the world except as a sorting ground of future saints and sinners. The religion of the second half of the century, on the other hand, was of a predominantly 'liberal' New Testament sort. God wishes us to make earth as much like Heaven as possible, and so he sent Jesus down among us, not just to be a sacrificial offering but to guide and show us how to make a Heaven on earth. This is why Jesus came to be regarded by many members of the Labour movement in the later nineteenth century as 'the first socialist'.

So in all these ways the idea of a just but savage Jehovah was abandoned in favour of a God who was presumed to stand for gentleness and peace. There was a parallel development in the way in which scientific understanding of the universe changed at this time. During the first half of the nineteenth century scientific thought had been dominated by what we call 'catastrophism'. It derived partly from geology and palaeontology, which were extremely popular and fashionable sciences at the time. By banging around with their hammers, geologists had begun to discover an enormous catalogue of earth history — layers on layers of rock and fossil remains. Yet it was still assumed, on the basis of the Old Testament's genealogical lists, that the earth could only be a few thousand years old. They therefore needed a theory of the earth's formation whereby a great many events could be supposed to have occurred in a very short time-span, and that of course inclined them to believe in catastrophes — in sudden formations and changes — in volcanoes, earthquakes, floods (like Noah's Flood of the Bible), and miracles of that sort. This view of the physical world neatly complemented men's sense of an active God 'who judgeth the earth'.

But in the second half of the century, building on ideas which originated with Sir Charles Lyell, and freed from the constraints imposed by a biblical time-span, geologists came to accept that the earth had developed gradually and, as it were, gently over millions of years. The same applied to life itself, for developments in biological thought, particularly the rapid spread of evolutionary ideas in the mid century, ideas which we particularly associate with the name of Charles Darwin, paralleled the changes in geological thought. Life was no longer seen as arising from some mysterious force or ether which God had manufactured, but was rather the result of long organic development and fruition. Similar views revolutionised physics at the same time; an idea of the continuity or conservation of energy replaced the former notion which had seen the world as being held in equilibrium by external, divinely-ordained forces. In all these ways, men's understanding of the physical and organic world was revolutionised, at the same time as their conception of other-worldly matters was also overturned.

The difficult question is, how do these intellectual currents relate to the state of society and of men's perceptions of it? An obvious point to make about the first half of the century, when catastrophism dominated both science and religion, is that it was an age of revolutions: actual revolutions all over Europe and anticipated revolution here in Britain. This country might be wealthy as never before, but the price of that wealth was the creation of huge cities and a dangerous, downtrodden and explosive proletariat. Because of those insanitary cities it was also an age of epidemics, most notably the terrifying cholera which struck in 1831 and again in 1848. 1831 was just two years after the British Parliament had removed the constitutional restraints on Roman Catholics that went back to the Glorious Revolution of 1688, thereby making Catholics full citizens, and there were many observers who felt sure that the cholera must be a divine punishment for that piece of wickedness, just as there were many who later blamed the famine on the grant to the Catholics of Maynooth. Here is what an evangelical MP called Spencer Perceval (son of the prime minister of the same name) had to say about the cholera from his place in Parliament:

> Will ye not listen for a few moments to one who speaketh in the name of the Lord? I stand here to warn you of the righteous judgment of God, which is coming on you, and which is now near at hand. Ye have in the midst of you a scourge of pestilence, which has crossed the world to reach ye. Ye have mocked God and he will bring on ye fasting and humiliation, woe and sorrow, weeping and lamentation, flame and confusion, I tell ye that this land will soon be desolate: a little time and ye shall howl one and all in your streets.[4]

Perceval was undoubtedly at the extreme end of the evangelical spectrum, his language of lamentation far wilder than most public men would have indulged in, but his basic point — that public and private calamities are always sent by God for a purpose and a chastisement — was one which was very widely shared. After all, the most influential guru of the age was the country vicar Robert Malthus, who at the beginning of the century had prophesied an inevitable cycle of wars, famines and pestilence. This Malthusian prophecy hovered over the imagination of the age like a spectre and came to fulfilment in Ireland in 1845.

Yet with a suddenness that is difficult to explain, social pessimism evaporated in the 1850s. The ruling classes stopped worrying about revolution, confident that Britain's glorious constitution would satisfy working-class demands. Working men turned away from Chartism, the revolutionary movement of the 1840s, and seemed bent on self-improvement and the peaceful redress of grievances. Malthusian fears about famine suddenly disappeared also as people came to think that we could always import food from the Third World in return for the manufactured goods which we produced. Whereas the 1840s have often been referred to as 'the hungry forties', the fifties and sixties have been called by one famous historian the 'Age of Equipoise', for there was then a sense of calm and content, of improvement, expansion, satisfaction.[5] Perhaps the fact that Britain, alone of the major European nations, had escaped a revolution in the 'year of revolutions', 1848, did much to foster a sense of complacency. Providence was after all, perhaps, on Britain's side.

In terms of social policy too there was a move toward softness, to prevention in place of punishment. The treatment of deviants and social outcasts generally — the poor, the vagrant, the insane, the alcoholic, the child, eventually (though not at once) the criminal — became milder. A good example of this is the changing response to the cholera. In 1831 and 1848 it had seemed to many people impious to try to cure the insanitary condition of the cities. Men had hurried to the towns in search of higher wages, and the wages of their avariciousness had been disease. To try and prevent such providential maladies would be to disturb God's ecological mechanism whereby man was no doubt intended to be forced back to his natural habitat, the morally virtuous countryside. By the 1860s, however, God was no longer thought to operate in such a manner, and men had come to accept the inevitability and even the virtues of industrial life. So when cholera returned in 1866 the response was no longer prayer and fasting but — in Disraeli's phrase — *sanitas sanitatum, omnia sanitas* — the construction of drains and sewers. This was mirrored by changes in medical practice, as a concern for preventive medicine replaced the former cure-all preference for blood-letting, a catastrophic form of treatment which had dominated medical practice in the first part of the century. The most obvious development was in the treatment of the poor, however. The New Poor Law of 1834, with its workhouse test and abolition of outdoor relief, had in theory (though not always in practice) imposed a system of terror and deprivation on the unemployed; by the 1850s the institutions of the Poor Law were being widely used for more generous purposes, for medical and nursing provision and suchlike social kindnesses.

A striking example of this lurch into kindness was the Limited Liability legislation of 1856. It is fair to point out that if, in the first half of the century, the upper classes had treated the lower classes with harshness, they had at least applied a similar standard to themselves. Many enjoyed enormous wealth but, in that burgeoning capitalist society, much of that wealth was precarious. There were devastating financial collapses — 'commercial earthquakes' or 'mercantile seizures', as they were often called, thus pointing up the geological and medical parallels in 1825–6, 1837–9, 1847–8 and 1855, when many of the proud and prosperous were humbled overnight, and for such people there was little redress. Shareholders were held liable to their last penny if companies failed and the debtors' prison was to the middle classes what the workhouse was to the poor. It is clear from the novels of the period that the perils of bankruptcy dominated the imagination of the well-to-do.

But in the softer climate of the 1850s the well-to-do decided suddenly to lighten those fears. They allowed themselves to limit their liabilities for debt, so that they would lose only the amount of money which they had personally invested in a failed company. And in doing that, the upper classes chose to soften the capitalist system just at the point where it was hurting themselves. Where it had once seemed right and proper that capital should be spilled from the system every several years, with dire consequences for the victims, of course, just as doctors had thought it right to spill their patients' blood, now the investing upper and middle classes were being invited to seek what profits they might without having to suffer a commensurate penalty when things went wrong. The veteran Scottish political economist John McCulloch had no doubts that this soft-hearted approach to human affairs was an affront to God's righteousness:

> In the scheme laid down by Providence for the government of the world, there is no shifting or narrowing of responsibilities, every man being personally answerable to the utmost extent for all his actions. But the advocates of limited liability proclaim in their superior wisdom that the scheme of Providence may be advantageously modified, and that debts and contracts may be contracted which the debtors though they have the means, shall not be bound to discharge.[6]

There are obviously many reasons for the change in company law in the 1850s, and it would be silly to exaggerate the importance of this moralistic aspect. I would suggest, however, that the capitalist classes chose to soften the capitalist system because they could no longer bear the suspense which that system imposed upon themselves. But this limitation of liability, by making wealth no longer precarious also removed what had been one of the major justifications of the capitalist system, which was that the well-to-do gained the rewards but also ran the risks; for those among the well-to-do who were sincere and conscience-stricken, this in turn may have spurred them into taking an equally soft approach to the condition of the lower orders as well.

If this is so, it may provide a clue to what was happening to religion at the same time. It was the middle and upper classes in the established Church of England who decided to abolish Hell in the 1850s and 1860s, or at least to soften its terrors considerably. And of course it was they who had had most cause to be terrified. The poor had always been considered to be in a spiritual sense safe. Just like the Irishmen who starved in 1847, they could be supposed to be bound for Heaven, having suffered so much on earth. But the rich and mighty, those who had not suffered and who had probably succumbed to the tempting snares of earthly wealth, they it was who were mainly bound for that fiery workhouse in the bowels of the earth. The upper classes abolished Hell in the mid century because they could no longer bear the suspense of an evangelical 'scheme of salvation' in which their own chances of victory were meagre. Remember that sin had been thought of in terms of a *ransom* or *debt* which was owed to God and which must be paid if mankind was to be saved; that is why it had made sense to say that Jesus had *redeemed* mankind, for he had by his death and passion *discharged* the debt of sin. In that first capitalist age, it is probably not surprising that the relations between God and man should be conceived in terms of those between creditor and debtor. And that is why it was of central importance when Frederick Denison Maurice, who was, incidentally, a leading supporter of limited liability for investors, boldly denied the reality of Hell. He was (you might say) limiting the liability of sin.

It is impossible to exaggerate the relief which Maurice's new theology brought to the comfortable classes. There were thousands like the society lady whom we read about in the memoirs of Charlotte Williams-Wynn, who had suffered for many years from bouts of acute clinical depression. As Lady Charlotte wrote to Maurice in 1858:

> What religious teaching she had in her youth was of a so called evangelical nature. No sooner did affliction come upon her, than these teachers came about her, wrote, and in short, kept her in a state of high nervous excitement. This will not do for everyday 'wear and tear', and so, though she is loved by all who come near her, and devoted to her poor, she is thoroughly unhappy from the constant fear of the wrath of this inexorable Judge.[7]

But like many others among the ruling classes, this unfortunate lady was apparently cured by Maurice's preaching, in particular by his reassuring assertion 'that God is a God of love, and that He does not punish in anger'.

The point has been made that whereas the old evangelicals had hoped to terrify men into Heaven by threatening them with Hell and the wrath to come, the liberal theologians of the 1850s painted Heaven in a tempting light by domesticating it, so that it could be presented as a continuation of the good things to be enjoyed in life. Obviously, such a strategy could only succeed if life were indeed conceived to be a state of happiness. And this poses a difficulty, which is very common in the history of ideas and attitudes, that it is impossible to tell which came first, the chicken or the egg. Did mid-Victorians respond to social calm and economic prosperity by reorienting their notion of God? Or did a fashionable new system of theology in turn affect their outlook on the world, so that it came to seem a happier and more contented place? Either way, the shift that occurred in the mid century was a profound one indeed.

Further reading

The full version of this argument can be found in Boyd Hilton, *The Age of Atonement: The Influence of Evangelicalism on Social and Economic Thought, 1795–1865* (Oxford: Clarendon Press, 1988). On Victorian religion more generally, see the series of volumes edited by Gerald Parsons (volumes one to four) and James R. Moore (volume five), *Religion in Victorian Britain* (Manchester: Manchester University Press/Open University, 1988). Other important recent studies of Victorian religion include: Mark A. Smith, *Religion in Industrial Society: Oldham and Saddleworth, 1740–1865* (Oxford: Clarendon Press, 1994); S.J.D. Green, *Religion in the Age of Decline: Organization and Experience in Industrial Yorkshire, 1870–1920* (Cambridge: Cambridge University Press, 1996); Hugh McLeod, *Religion and Society in England, 1850–1914* (Basingstoke: Macmillan, 1996); R. Arthur Burns, *The Diocesan Revival in the Church of England, c.1800–1870* (Oxford: Clarendon Press, 1999); Joy Dixon, *Divine Feminine: Theosophy and Feminism in England* (Baltimore, MD: Johns Hopkins University Press, 2001).

Notes

1   W.E. Gladstone to his wife, 12 October 1845, *Correspondence on Church and Religion of William Ewart Gladstone*, ed. D.C. Lathbury (London, 1910), II: 266.
2   Graham to Peel, 18 October 1845, Peel Papers, British Library Add. MSS., 40451, ff.400–1.
3   *Memoirs by Sir Robert Peel*, ed. Earl Stanhope and Edward Cardwell (London, 1857), II: 125.
4   Perceval in House of Commons, 20 March 1832, *Hansard's Parliamentary Debates*, 3rd series XI, pp. 577–81.
5   W.L. Burn, *The Age of Equipoise: A study of the mid-Victorian generation* (London, 1964).
6   J.R. McCulloch, *Considerations on Partnerships with Limited Liability* (London, 1856), pp. 10–11.
7   Charlotte Williams-Wynn to Maurice, April 1858, *Memorials of Charlotte Williams-Wynn*, ed. her sister (London: 1877), pp. 246–7.

Callum Brown

HOW RELIGIOUS WAS
VICTORIAN BRITAIN?

'Did Urbanization Secularize Britain?', *Urban History Yearbook* (1988), 8–12.

The religious census of 1851 shocked the Victorians with its revelation that nonconformity was almost as strong as Anglicanism and that large parts of the working class did not attend church. The 'secularisation thesis' holds that religion's days were numbered after the eighteenth-century Enlightenment and the growth of urban, cosmopolitan society. Increasingly, new ways of life were emerging that simply did not refer to religion. However, **Callum Brown** has been a long-term sceptic of this interpretation. The following article is an early critique of his that deals with the secularisation thesis. It builds on Jeffrey Cox's influential argument that we need to examine further a 'diffusive Christianity' (informal religious beliefs that played a vital part in popular culture) if we are to understand the real impact of religion on everyday life and world-views. Brown's piece should be read alongside his more recent book, *The Death of Christian Britain* (2001), which demonstrates that Britain remained a distinctly religious society well into the 1950s. What undermined Christianity in Britain, according to Brown, was the cultural revolution of the 1960s. This was because, since the early nineteenth century, Christianity had been focused on female piety and women's duty to assist men who were too easily prone to sin. These kinds of assumptions could not survive the women's movement of the 1960s and its challenge to conventional views of femininity. In the extract included here, Brown employs a variety of data based on church-going in nineteenth-century Glasgow (a welcome balance to the English focus of many other Readings in this volume) and reinstates the essential strength of Victorian Christianity.

Callum Brown is currently Professor of Religious and Cultural History, University of Dundee. His more recent research has shifted the debates over secularisation away from urbanisation and the nineteenth century to the issues of gender and the 1960s' cultural revolution, notably in *The Death of Christian Britain* (2000) and *Religion and Society in Twentieth-Century Britain* (2006).

[. . .]

GIVEN THE DIRECTION of historiographical debate, social-composition analysis would seem to be a fundamental necessity in the study of cities and secularization. Yet, despite widespread reference to, and indeed assertion concerning the extent (or more precisely, in most cases, the absence) of working-class church attendance, there has been surprisingly little research on the issue.[1] Analysing the social make-up of congregations and religious voluntary organizations is an extremely time-consuming task, matching names from communicants lists, baptismal registers and so forth to occupations found in street directories or elsewhere. Ideally, the selection has to include a fairly large number of people from a given congregation, a reasonable cross-section of denominations, and a meaningful proportion of all the congregations within a given locality. The rewards seem small in relation to the hundreds of tedious research hours needed, and in point of fact the ideal has never been attained.

But the little research that has been conducted provides us with fairly clear-cut conclusions. [*The*] Table . . . summarizes the results of two of the largest studies — by [*A.D.*] Gilbert on English Dissent and [*Peter*] Hillis on Glasgow Presbyterians — and also provides an example drawn from one congregation. Despite the enormous problems of classifying occupations (between skilled and unskilled manual for instance), and despite variations in the classification systems used by researchers, it is clear that a significantly high proportion of churchgoers were composed of skilled working-class groups. However, as the results from John Street Church in Glasgow show, there could be significant changes in the composition of a given congregation over a relatively short period. This is an important phenomenon, and one little remarked upon in the literature. Nineteenth-century city dwellers were highly mobile both spatially and socially. Congregations of all denominations (but especially Dissent) were continuously moving to newer and more expensive churches as the wealth and status of their membership rose. Thus, in the 1830s, the Royal Commissioners on Religious Instruction in Scotland found that in Edinburgh and Glasgow usually a *minimum* of two-thirds, and in many cases the *total* membership of Dissenting congregations, together with normally one-half of Established Church congregations, were composed of 'the working classes and the poor'.[2] This was noted especially of two prominent denominations — the Relief Church and the Secession Church. However, 20 years after these denominations merged in 1847 to form the United Presbyterian Church, the congregations were renowned for their middle-class wealth. In 1871, for instance, the lowest rate of illiteracy amongst Scottish brides and grooms signing marriage registers was to be found in UP Churches.[3]

Table Social composition of church members

(Numbers)	Gilbert England c.1800–37		Hillis Glasgow		John Street Relief/United Presbyterian Church, Glasgow	
	Dissent	English society	Presbyt. dissent 1845–65	Ch. of Scot. 1855–65	1822–32	1853–57
(Numbers)	(10,997)	(n/a)	(2,397)	(1,269)	(161)	(148)
	%	%	%	%	%	%
1 Upper class/high status; aristocracy, merchants, manufact., professionals	2.2	3.6	19.1	12.8	6	10
2 Farmers	5.3	14.0				
Low status middle class			20.7	8.6	11	27
Tradesmen	7.1	6.2				
3 Skilled manual/artisans	59.4	23.5	48.0	54.2	75	50
4 Unskilled	17.4	19.5	12.3	24.2	9	13
5 Unclassified	8.6	33.2				
Total	100.0	100.0	100.0	100.0	101	100

Sources: A. D. Gilbert, *Religion and Society in Industrial England* (1976), 67; P. Hillis, 'Presbyterian and social class in mid-nineteenth century Glasgow: a study of nine churches', *Journal of Ecclesiastical History*, *32* (1981), 47–64; John Street Relief/UP Church, Glasgow, baptismal register, Scottish Record Office, CH3/806/12.

As churches moved up the social scale, and especially after 1850, so congregations commenced the massive evangelization schemes noted by all historians of the second half of the nineteenth century. These schemes invariably entailed a mission at which working-class adherents were encouraged to become self-financing congregations. Arguably, the vast bulk of new urban churches in the 1850s, 1860s and 1870s were formed in this manner. Thus, there was constant recruitment from the 'unchurched', predominantly upwardly-mobile members of the working classes.

To understand this operation, it seems crucial for historians of urban religion to consider the mechanism of in-migration to cities and how the churches coped with it. For most of the nineteenth century, more than half of all inhabitants in large cities were born elsewhere. This created a staggering logistical problem for the churches: to meet and recruit newcomers. The best known recruitment is probably that of Irish Catholic immigrants whose church could not keep pace with the number of in-migrants to British cities such as Liverpool and Glasgow until after 1850.[4] One of the few studies of Protestant migrants is that by Withers of Highland Presbyterians moving to Glasgow, Edinburgh and Aberdeen in the late eighteenth and early nineteenth centuries.[5] What studies of both Catholic and Protestant recruitment show is that the receiving congregations induced a social hierarchy with clergy and middle- or upper-working-class lay members socializing arriving migrants to the social mores and aspirations of city society. If the facilities for worship (church and mission halls, and prayer meetings in schools, houses and places of Sunday work) provided by religious voluntary organizations are added to the rising urban church accommodation of the second half of the century, then it seems inescapable that popular, working-class involvement in organized religion increased.

There are, of course, many writers who refer to contrary evidence.[6] The issue, though, is largely one of investigators' perception and methods. Those looking for non-churchgoing by the working classes will find it wherever they look, and can quite plausibly conclude that the majority of the working classes did not attend church either regularly or at all. But if research attempts to assess the proportion of churchgoers who came from the working classes, then it is becoming clearer that the answer is at least half — i.e. the majority.

This raises a whole series of questions about the extent of middle-class churchgoing which have really not been investigated.[7] In any event, the inevitable conclusion seems to be that we should not underestimate the extent of working-class religious observance in the nineteenth-century city. Chapel, church, religious and quasi-religious events (such as teetotal walks) sustained the role of religion in working-class communities. Though research has shown the importance of employers in supplying and controlling churches for their workers (especially in smaller industrial towns of the kind found in Lancashire and Lanarkshire),[8] considerable evidence has also been presented of proletarian self-management in religious organizations and activities for all periods in the nineteenth century.[9] Social control and class consciousness could co-exist within chapel, Sunday school and Rechabite tent. The divide in religious practice was thus not so much that between middle and working classes, but that *within* both classes.

Explaining how religion adapted to urban society in Glasgow is long and complex.[10] Much of the explanation is wrapped up in the story of church-building, which in turn relates to the timing and nature of social fragmentation in the industrializing city. Rising demand for church accommodation from middle-class and upper-working-class groups led initially in 1780–1830 to the progressive exclusion from existing Established Churches of the lower working classes and also of many artisan families. The mechanism for exclusion was the pew rent, which, while not a new phenomenon, nonetheless overtook pews set aside for paupers and 'the lower class of inhabitants'. Pew rents, rising rapidly on the supply-demand mechanism, prevented lower-income groups from being able to afford to attend church.[11] This led to waves of churchbuilding, first between 1790 and 1830 by Dissenters, followed in the 1830s by disenchanted lower-middle and upper-working-class groups *within* the Church of Scotland. The latter created 20 new evangelical congregations which laid the basis for the great Disruption of 18 May 1843 when, in Glasgow, over half the worshippers in the state Church (and 40–50 per cent in Scotland as a whole) walked out to form the Free Church of Scotland, commencing another wave of churchbuilding.

Throughout all these church extensions, the proportion of the population able to be accommodated in church was diminishing as the number of Glasgow's citizens doubled about every 20 years. The Catholic Church, for instance, had only three chapels in the city in 1840 to cater for up to 40,000 adherents. But after 1850, churchbuilding by all denominations rose in a frenzy of evangelizing recruitment, improving church accommodation for the population. Pew rents continued to be exacted in Scotland to a greater extent than in England, but in the mission stations and halls there was more often free access, permitting attendance by lower-income groups. However, the pew rent became the symbol of worldly and spiritual 'success', the gauge of economic and religious salvation. Working-class congregations were reported to be particularly keen on paying rents, and on setting the scale of rents by congregational vote.

Another part of the explanation is the evangelical 'home mission' — the evolution of new 'agencies' to recruit the non-churchgoing. This was where the adaptation to urban society was most apparent as the traditional urban paternalism of the early-modern period disintegrated. The first and always the largest agency was the Sunday school,[12] which by 1851 held more children than day schools. Sunday-school teachers — including significant numbers of future wealthy entrepreneurs — were the mainstay of the evangelical movement, undertaking home visitation to recruit children first for Sunday school and then, after 1840, for church day schools, Bands of Hope and other youth organizations. They were also important in the mission to adults, starting first with tract-distribution societies in the 1810s, but from the 1820s, they assisted 'home missionaries' (divinity students and, after 1850, young ministers). In the 1850s, 60s and 70s, it became *de rigeur* for fully sanctioned Protestant congregations to set up mission stations where fledgling working-class churches were nurtured to full status and financial self-reliance, and for congregational members to assist in large numbers as 'district visitors'. It was home visitation, which the non-churchgoing experienced at least three times a year in the 1850s and once a month by the 1880s, that contributed so much to the evangelical hegemony of 'respectable' popular culture and ideology in the second half of the century. Teetotalism and revivalism (in the mould established by visiting Americans such as Charles Finney, Edward Payson Hammond, Dwight Moody and Ira Sankey) were the two dominant themes after the 1860s. Many might and did reject the patronizing attitude of the evangelizers, but few could escape the ideas and influence of religion, so intense was the evangelizing of the city and so important was religion to organized leisure pursuits.

A third part of the explanation was the role of local government. In Glasgow as in many Victorian cities, outwardly secularized bodies like the Corporation, the poor-relief authority and (after 1872) the school board were dominated by church-men (laity and clergy) who pushed the evangelical agenda of social-reform issues (such as intemperance, immorality, irreligion and inadequate education) to the forefront of municipal politics. On the same agenda, of course, there also appeared 'secular' issues: municipalizing the gasworks and the trams, laying main sewers, bringing fresh water to the city, and doing something about insanitary and over-crowded housing. But these issues emanated from within the evangelical community. Evangelical councillors voted across party lines for such measures from as early as the 1830s, trying to use municipal collectivism to create the 'Godly Commonwealth'. Religious visions of 'democratic cities of God' were important to the advance of social welfare at local level in the nineteenth century, and churchmen organized religious campaigns for social reform. In Glasgow, the Rev. Robert Buchanan, a Free Church minister, marshalled his presbytery (the church court for the city) to stave off one of the periodic ratepayers' reactions to the cost of the mammoth Loch Katrine water project of the 1850s. The same minister's experience in evangelizing a city-centre slum inspired a co-partnery of 22 businessmen and councillors secretly to buy up large tracts of slum property. The intention of improving or replacing the housing proved too expensive, so councillors on the group (including six successive Lord Provosts) used their position to get the property bought by the Corporation under the Glasgow City Improvement Act of 1866. Again, during the fever epidemics of the 1860s, the Council's sanitary officers used congregational district-visiting societies to distribute leaflets giving advice on hygiene and counter-measures.

These kinds of linkages between municipal improvement schemes and the churches abounded with Glasgow being not unexceptional.[13] It helped to cement the ubiquity of the religious world view in civic life. Weekly church connection may have involved a minority of adults (though this may still admit of dispute), but it was a large minority that commanded the rules by which social mobility, economic success and 'respectability' were determined. Moreover, few could have been untouched at some point in their lives. In 1891, the number of enrolled Sunday-school scholars represented 65 per cent of Glasgow children aged 5–15 years. A census in Glasgow's adjoining industrial burgh of Clydebank in the same year showed that, despite rapid suburbanizing in-migration from Glasgow itself, 56 per cent of adults attended church one summer Sunday from amongst the 72 per cent who were church members.[14]

Late-Victorian society was thus very far from the irreligious state that many commentators both then and now would have us believe. It was arguably the point in British history when religion attained its greatest social significance. It did this not merely through churchgoing, but through a religious dominance of organized leisure (and leisure venues), social-policy formation and implementation, publishing, and many other facets of the nation's (urban) life. The fact that the majority of the population did not attend church on a given Sunday does not negate this. There were a whole host of levels of contact between individuals and religious activities and ideas. Glasgow was certainly an epicentre of evangelical innovation and enterprise; it was dubbed 'Gospel City' by one young churchman in the 1830s.[15] But it was not untypical of the progress of religion in other British cities, and was by no means the nation's 'most religious' urban community. Throughout the country, religion adapted to the new urban circumstances — at first rather slowly, but by the second half of the century with extraordinary skill and success.

Further reading

Callum Brown developed his discussion of secularisation in *The Decline of Christian Britain: Understanding Secularization, 1800–2000* (London: Routledge, 2001). Other works that cover the question of secularisation include: Jeffrey Cox, *The English Churches in a Secular Society: Lambeth, 1870–1930* (New York: Oxford University Press, 1982); Hugh McLeod, 'New Perspectives in Victorian Working-Class Religion: The Oral Evidence', *Oral History Journal*, 14 (1986), 31–49; Sarah C. Williams, *Religious Belief and Popular Culture in Southwark, c.1880–1939* (Oxford: Oxford University Press, 1999).

Notes

1   For a review of the literature, see H. McLeod, *Religion and the Working Class in Nineteenth-Century Britain* (1984).

2   Royal Commission on Religious Instruction, Scotland, First Report, PP, XXI (1837), 29. Second Report, PP, XXXII (1837–8), 17. For an English example of high religiosity amongst unskilled workers, see E. Hopkins, 'Religious dissent in Black Country industrial villages in the first half of the nineteenth century', *Journal of Ecclesiastical History*, *34* (1983).

3   C.G. Brown, *The Social History of Religion in Scotland since 1730* (1987), 151.

4   C. Johnson, *Developments in the Roman Catholic Church in Scotland 1789–1829* (1983); J E. Handley, *The Irish in Scotland 1798–1845* (1945) and *The Irish in Modern Scotland* (1947); L.H. Lees, *The Exiles of Erin: Irish Immigrants in Victorian London* (1979).

5   C.W.J. Withers, 'Kirk, club and culture change: Gaelic chapels, Highland societies and the urban Gaelic subculture in eighteenth-century Scotland', *Social History*, *10* (1985)

6   D.E.H. Mole, 'Challenge to the Church: Birmingham 1815–65', in H. Dyos and M. Wolff (eds), *The Victorian City*, vol. 2 (1973); T.C. Smout, *A Century of the Scottish People 1830–1950* (1986), 181–208.

7   But see H. Mailer, *Leisure and the Changing City, 1870–1914* (1976) on Bristol, and J. Kent, *Holding the Fort: Studies in Victorian Revivalism* (1978), which though misleading as to the middle-class monopoly of this socially widespread phenomenon, provides some useful perspectives.

8   P. Joyce, *Work, Society and Politics: The Culture of the Factory in Later Victorian England* (1980), and A.B. Campbell, *The Lanarkshire Miners 1775–1874* (1979).

9   T.W. Laqueur, *Religion and Respectability: Sunday Schools and Working Class Culture 1780–1850* (1976); A.J. Ainsworth, 'Religion in the working-class community and the evolution of socialism in late nineteenth-century Lancashire: a case of working-class consciousness', *Histoire Sociale*, *10* (1977).

10   C.G. Brown, 'Religion and the development of an urban society: Glasgow 1780–1914' (unpublished Ph.D. thesis, University of Glasgow, 1982).

11   C.G. Brown, 'The costs of pew-renting: church management, church-going and social class in nineteenth-century Glasgow', *Journal of Ecclesiastical History*, *38* (1987).

12   C.G. Brown, 'The Sunday-school movement in Scotland, 1780–1914', *Records of the Scottish Church History Society*, *21* (1981).

13   See for example E.P. Hennock, *Fit and Proper Persons: Ideal and Reality in Nineteenth century Urban Government* (1973), and R.V. Holt, *The Unitarian Contribution to Social Progress in England* (1938).

14   Figures calculated from *Glasgow Sabbath School Union*, *Annual Report* 1892, and *Clydebank and Renfrew Press*, 22 August 1891.

15   *Autobiography of a Scotch Lad* (1887), 30.

PART 10

Science

ONE OF THE MOST dynamic areas of research in recent years has been in the history of science, whether in the form of technological innovation or the ways in which science helped construct new forms of identity. The Victorian era was rocked by scientific discoveries, particularly by the publication of Charles Darwin's *Origin of Species* in 1859. However, the Victorians were also passionate about science. People at all social levels were interested in reading about new inventions and theories. Before 1900, the lay person could (up to a point) follow much of what was going on in science and the strict demarcation between the professional scientist and the ordinary person did not exist in quite the same way as in the twentieth century. Science was celebrated in popular periodicals, exhibitions (especially the Great Exhibition of 1851) and in *conversaziones* where people could examine the latest discoveries.

The defining feature of the modern history of Victorian science has been its anti-Whig character. It has not sought to tell the story of scientific progress in a linear way or to assume that scientific breakthroughs simply come from great minds in isolation making discoveries. Instead, historians have been interested in the way in which scientists have always been part of their culture. This has been typified by the extraordinary vitality of work on Charles Darwin and on the impact of evolution. Darwin is no longer viewed as a lone figure toiling in his study after his return from the Galapagos Islands. Rather, he has been portrayed by Adrian Desmond, James Moore and others as being part of a larger field of inquiry which was asking questions about evolution and natural science.

Alongside the study of Darwin and other theorists has arisen the study of the area now characterised as pseudo-science. This included discredited fields such as phrenology (the science of reading personality through the bumps on one's head), the theories of Cesare Lombroso who developed a 'scientific' typology of criminality, or the immensely influential eugenics movement, which sought to apply new ideas about genetics to the problem of 'degeneration' in the later nineteenth century.

Adrian Desmond

EVOLUTION BEFORE
DARWIN

The Politics of Evolution: Morphology, Medicine, and Reform in Radical London
(Chicago, IL: University of Chicago Press, 1989), 1–9, 20–4.

The following Reading comes from **Adrian Desmond's** agenda-setting introduction
to his *The Politics of Evolution* (1989). Desmond's theme is 'Darwinism before
Darwin'. For Desmond and some other scholars (such as James Secord), evolution
is not something that commenced with the publication of *The Origin of Species* in
1859. Rather, it was an integral part of scientific and popular debates during the
previous three decades (if not earlier). In Desmond's view, the debates on evolution
should not be viewed in a narrow, scientific context. Instead, he traces their roots
to the radical-Whig dissenting culture of the 1830s and suggests that evolution was
as much a struggle over the production of knowledge and scientific authority as it
was about developing a new theory. Evolutionary ideas emerged as much in a political
as a scientific context. Desmond studied London's medical schools in the 1830s,
which, as he shows, were caught up in and heavily divided by contemporary politics
and by views about evolution and comparative anatomy. Arguments about reform
in the political arena had a wider context in the scientific and medical communities.
We also reproduce the closing comments of the introduction where Desmond calls
for a new approach to the history of science.

Adrian Desmond is Honorary Research Fellow in the Department of Biology,
University College, London. Most recently he is the author of the two-volume
biography *Huxley* (1994–7), and now available in a single volume. He is currently

working with James Moore on a book on the anti-slavery underpinnings of Darwin's work on human evolution, and with Angela Darwin, on a four-volume edition of the Huxley family correspondence.

———————

THE "DARWINIAN REVOLUTION" — it is an evocative metaphor. So ingrained has the image become that we all take it for granted. Yet is it anything more than a consciousness-raising slogan bandied about by latter-day Darwinians? Does it really describe events surrounding the publication of the *Origin of Species* in 1859, or even the situation before the new Darwinian synthesis of the 1930s? There is no doubt that evolution became the stock-in-trade of biologists after Darwin published, and yet historians find little evidence of a mass switchover to Darwin's particular theory of natural selection in the nineteenth century.[1] If anything, in Britain Darwin's academic appeal was largely to a small group bent on professionalizing science — to men such as the pugnacious T.H. Huxley, outsiders intent on breaking the gentlemanly Oxbridge grip on natural history.[2]

And what of evolution before Darwin published? Was his a lone voice? Or was there already a "naturalistic" tradition in British society, with certain groups accepting a self-progressing natural organic world? On this question the recent shift among historians is quite evident; one even depicts Darwin's move as simply a "palace coup" among the elite, the final act in a long drama, with the real fight to establish a lawful, evolutionary worldview among the "people" taking place a generation earlier.[3]

But the "Darwin Industry" has hardly begun to acknowledge a naturalistic tradition in British biology. Why not? Perhaps because historians have been looking too closely at the gentlemen of science and their Anglican ministers. Among this governing class there was virtually no concession to evolution before 1859 (and not much to Darwin's brand after).[4] Darwin's book came as a bombshell (and, as this metaphor suggests, it was attacked by the dons and divines as an act of terrorism against the old wealthy elite). Just what was it about the old or aristocratic Anglicanism that made it so hostile to the progressive, natural, competitive, mobile view of life taught in more radical classrooms? Why did the squires of science consider it utterly irresponsible to view the world in this way?

The situation in the 1830s (when Darwin was secretly devising his theory) raises a whole new set of questions. Could it be that the sorts of evolutionary sciences openly imported from France into Britain at this time were not so much unworkable or old-fashioned (as the gentlemen — and later historians — maintained), but that they had disturbing social and political associations? Was it this that really made evolution unacceptable in the radical thirties? Remember that in 1830, at the time of the July Revolution in Paris, the Anglican elite in Britain was staving off concerted attacks by the radicals attempting to secularize and democratize their own society. Creationist politics were bound to be fierce in an age when French rationalist theories threatened the old subservience on which the ruling class's security depended. Was not France itself a cautionary tale? Had not the Parisian demagogues included Jean-Baptiste Lamarck's execrable evolutionary theory in their arsenal? The British gentry remained constitutionally suspicious of the republican rabble across the Channel, portraying them as the "national enemy."[5] And if France's periodic convulsions were fueled by poisonous, naturalistic, evolutionary philosophies, then the conservatives were determined to keep them off English soil.

This brings us to the "revolution" aspect of the Darwinian metaphor. It is an interesting label to pin on Darwin's particular theory. "Revolution" was no empty figure of speech in Darwin's younger days; it was a real political threat, with constant rounds of violence and repression in England between the time of the French Revolution of 1789 and the European uprisings of 1848. Darwin himself deplored the turbulence of the 1830s and shuddered at the mere mention of revolution. In his notebooks he actually talked of the natural, lawful processes of change in nature and society obviating the need for any sort of violent interruption [. . .]. Again, a growing number of historians tend to interpret Darwin's beliefs about legislated change and progress through competition not as revolutionary, but as stabilizing. Darwin's might not have been a "conservative revolution," but it did "ratify" the competitive, individualist Malthusian ideology of the arriviste merchants then acquiring a share of power.[6]

As a piece of "ratification," Darwin's book came rather late. In 1859, over twenty years after he conceived his theory, society was tranquil, the decades of mass unrest were past, and it was relatively safe to publish, even if he did have to be pushed into it. So what was happening in the meantime, while Darwin's theory was lying dormant in his private notebooks? What sciences were publicly serving a similar function: ratifying the change from the eighteenth-century world of nepotism, privilege, and aristocratic patronage to the more openly competitive, upwardly mobile Victorian society?

This is the cue for *The Politics of Evolution*. This volume surveys the vast social tracts ignored by the Darwin scholars studying the Oxbridge sporting gents. It makes contact with the radical social factions and identifies the audiences for the new dissident sciences. In short, it looks at the social context of public evolution and other naturalistic theories in the decades before Darwin published. But was there really any public support for evolution in the 1830s? Judging by the standard histories one might imagine not.[7] And yet if there was not, why the massive campaign to discredit it by the scientific gentry? Why did worried comparative anatomists and geologists tailor their major works to refute it? The problem, of course, has always been actually to locate it in context. The reason evolutionists have been hard to find is that historians have consistently looked in the wrong place. The curates' classrooms in Cambridge are hardly the best place to start; we need to insinuate ourselves deep into the radical underworld — to explore a totally different set of classrooms, in the secular anatomy schools and radical Nonconformist colleges. This is where we do our hunting. Hence this book is not about polite or "responsible" science — the sort promoted at Oxford or Cambridge — but about angry, dissident views. It is about science to change society.

Nor is it mainly about Darwin's Malthusian brand of evolution, but about a rival, flagrantly radical, anti-Malthusian sort. Darwin had applied the Rev. Thomas Malthus's analysis of society to nature. Malthus saw overpopulation lead to ruthless competition for resources. He believed that population growth would always outstrip food supply, making charity and welfare a waste of time. In 1834 the Whigs (who had Darwin's support) translated Malthus's program into action; they scrapped the old poor laws, ending outdoor relief for the destitute and forcing them either to compete in the labor market or face the workhouse. In 1838 Darwin read Malthus and applied this weak-to-the-wall image to nature, seeing species progress through savage struggle and the elimination of the unfit.[8]

At the other extreme, radical artisans abhorred Malthus's doctrines and the callous anti-working-class legislation passed in their name. By contrast, they envisaged society progressing through cooperation, education, emancipation, technological advance, and democratic participation. Their views of nature were equally distinct. Not for them the powerful and privileged surviving by exploiting and culling the weak, but an inexorable progress for all through harmony and cooperative striving. Cannibalized fragments of Lamarck's evolutionary biology — which provided a model of relentless ascent power-driven "from below" — turned up in the pauper press.[9] Lamarck's notion that an animal could, through its own exertions, transform itself into a higher being and pass on its gains — all without the aid of a deity — appealed to the insurrectionary working classes. His ideas were propagated in their illegal penny prints, where they mixed with demands for democracy and attacks on the clergy. Clearly Lamarckism had some disreputable associations. It was being exploited by extremists promoting the dissolution of Church and aristocracy, and calling for a new economic system. These atheists and socialists supported a brand of evolution quite unlike Darwin's. Moreover, theirs was evolution in a real "revolutionary" context; it grew out of a rival tradition in the 1820s and 1830s and was far more radical than anything Darwin envisaged.

Between the Malthusian Whigs and the socialist demagogues lies terra incognita. It is a territory that should be opened up. In this unexplored terrain all sorts of dissident knowledge flourished: not only varieties of evolution, but a swirling vortex of alternative economic, social, and biological sciences that threatened to wash away the pillars of the establishment edifice. Unlike the gentlemen's polished, expensive treatises, these sciences were spread through radical medical newspapers and inflammatory penny prints. They were not exercises in leisurely intellectual pursuit. Outside medicine, they were angry, working sciences, sometimes half articulated, often half taken for granted. Even inside radical medicine some theoretical sciences became highly speculative. As a result my technique for exploring them is unlike the Darwin scholars' textual analysis. By their very nature, these outcast forms of evolution require a social understanding. Nothing less can give us an insight into their meaning or hint at the reasons they were so attractive to aggrieved groups. We need to ask new sorts of questions. How could evolution have furthered a group's ends in a rapidly urbanizing, industrializing society? Once we start thinking of the downtrodden seeking greater recognition and challenging the authorities, a fascinating picture begins to emerge. The history of evolution in the past has been a pretty bloodless affair; we need to get some of the grit, humor, and suffering back into it. We need to restore the fine texture of social history and reestablish the proper context of early nineteenth-century scientific naturalism.[10]

A glimpse at the Edinburgh University medical graduates who accepted the natural birth of new species certainly suggests that a political connection must be made. Consider the personalities. That scourge of Oxford and orthodoxy, the rakish Robert Knox, never doubted the *consanguinité* of animal life and had only praise for the anticlerical French. The commercial tree cultivator Patrick Matthew, on hearing of the July Revolution, closed his *Naval Timber* mid-appendix (with its hodgepodge of calls for free trade, popular "self-government," and animal transmutation) to cheer on the republicans. The retiring Robert Grant made slashing attacks on corruption in medicine and society, and brought his evolutionary biology to London, where it was acclaimed by the ultraradicals. (He was actually the first in Britain to talk of animals having "evolved," using this word in 1826 to signify the transmutation of one species into another.)[11] The botanist Hewett Watson, who switched to evolution early in the 1830s, savaged the Tory old guard so viciously that he alienated even moderate reformers.[12]

The common denominator, of course, is that these were all political radicals and scientific materialists,[13] all committed to sweeping social reform. They were also atheists or deists. (Deists accepted God on rational grounds but rejected biblical revelation. Hence they tended to favor more lawful, deterministic explanations of nature.) And in a decade of radical demands for the separation (or "disestablishment") of the Church from the state, their venom was reserved for the Anglican placemen inside science and out. In this age of millennial expectations, all saw "a new state" of society "near at hand," in which the ancien régime injustices were to be swept away and a new democratic order instituted.[14]

We ignore these political aspects at our peril. Contemporary protagonists were quite aware of evolution's dark connotations. In pulpits and learned societies, artisans were warned to keep their place in society, and their bestial sciences were denounced for destroying the safeguards of the moral order. Some, like the reactionary country gentlemen, were appalled at the thought of the middle and lower orders laying their hands on any sort of science, let alone Lamarck's abomination. Science had to remain a prerogative of rank to preserve the chain of subordination, which was the "keystone" of government. Giving ordinary people a taste for it smacked of democracy, "for as distinctions in society arising from wealth & rank form the character of a monarchy, so is the doing away with such distinctions, or substituting talent or science in their place, the character of a democracy," and this would "plunge the country into irretrievable ruin and despair."[15] This was as much a warning to the professional middle classes hoping to establish a meritocracy as it was to the lower orders hoping for a revolution. But it is only when we consider the kinds of self-serving evolutionary sciences favored by many demagogues that the basis of such gentlemanly fears becomes starkly apparent.

So we shall be exploring the problem from an unashamedly political perspective. And, unlike the previous histories which focused on the country rectories and comfortable drawing rooms, our spotlight will be on the dirty dissecting theatres. We will examine the reasons why the radicals exploited the doctrines of nature's self-development and how these ideas served their democratic ends. (Why, in Matthew's words, the nobility, with its stultifying customs and "unnatural" privileges, had to yield to nature's law of competition and transformation or risk her revenge.) Ultimately, the radical's new society did not materialize, and the reforms of the 1830s were never enough to satisfy the diehards. As a result the 1840s were years of disillusionment for those teachers who had invested heavily in the cause. There was no payoff. Their letters and articles at this time tell of bitterness and recrimination. Knox and Watson were barred from academic chairs. Knox lost his teaching license and became an itinerant hack. An embittered Grant suffered a financial collapse. [*Patrick*] Matthew became a Chartist[16] before retiring in frustration to his farm. With the movements for democratic reform defeated, the sciences used to legitimate them receded too. In other words, radicalism's failure sealed the fate of the fiercer reductionist and evolutionary theories riding on its back. This kind of radical evolutionary science did not carry the day.

Of course, this is not the whole story. But the protest movement must be tackled if we are to understand the fluctuating fortunes of transmutation in Britain, at least in the two decades before 1844. In that year the situation changed markedly with the publication of the anonymous *Vestiges of the Natural History of Creation,* a best-selling popularization of a number of dissident sciences by Robert Chambers (a middle-brow publisher in Edinburgh). The book was more than a potboiler; it was a cleverly crafted work that took five years to finish. Chambers modified the view of evolution current in the medical schools and cunningly gave it a providential veneer. [. . .] He sold evolution — "development" he called it — as a case of Creation by lawful means. The introduction of new species and the ascent of life were controlled by a natural law preordained by God. In an age rejecting aristocratic intervention and whim and looking for constitutional means of change, Chambers deliberately remade God in the image of a benign Legislator. He dressed up the issue to appeal to the middle classes — those who looked to the law, not noble patronage, for their advancement (and the sort who were now buying educational magazines and novels hot off the press). It was a successful strategy; the book became the talk of the town, and in seven months *Vestiges* passed through four editions. As James Secord says, Chambers had finally domesticated the science of development and brought it "off the streets and into the home."[17]

The scientific context: the new philosophical anatomy

To reconnoiter this little-explored evolutionary territory, we must first understand the changing nature of biological theory at this time. And the best places to see the changes taking place are in London's and Edinburgh's cosmopolitan medical schools. Lamarckism actually attracted only limited support, and then mainly on the radical fringes. Far more important for a wide range of reformers was a comprehensive package imported from France in the 1820s known as "philosophical anatomy." This had a much larger medical following. And because it had a convoluted and often contested relationship to evolution, it is central to our story.

Philosophical or higher anatomy was based on the concept of "unity of composition" developed by the professor of zoology at the Muséum d'Histoire Naturelle in Paris, Etienne Geoffroy Saint-Hilaire. By 1830 Geoffroy and his disciples had come to accept a unitary composition for all animals. Not only were all vertebrates built to the same blueprint; in its most extreme formulation, the theory allowed insects, mollusks, and man to be reduced to common organ components. Animal life could therefore be strung into a continuous, related series — rather than broken into discrete "divisions," as Geoffroy's critic at the Museum, Georges Cuvier, demanded; and it was this that enhanced the prospect of evolution. The series could be used to show the "history" of each organ rising in complexity from snail to man, and that history could be given an evolutionary twist — it could be turned into a real ancestral bloodline. Inside the medical schools, discussions and disagreements broke out over the relationship between higher anatomy and evolution. Some philosophical anatomists (including Geoffroy himself) were transmutationists, and even Chambers's popular work was rooted in the science. So understanding the new anatomy and its supporters is the first step to assessing the place of evolution in the medical schools.

[. . .] Toby Appel, reappraising the French situation in *The Cuvier-Geoffroy Debate* (1987), demolishes the myth that Geoffroy was defeated during his famous confrontation with Cuvier at the Académie des Sciences in 1830. In reality he carried a bloc of republican sympathizers with him, and a younger generation of comparative anatomists went on to hammer out a compromise between his and Cuvier's extreme views. My conclusion here is broadly similar. The evidence shows that Geoffroy was far more influential in Britain in the 1830s than was previously realized. But again, it is no good searching among the clergy and gentlemen naturalists for his admirers; they detested Geoffroy's coldly deterministic views of animal form and evolution. Look in the medical schools, however, and a wholly different picture emerges. Geoffroy was immensely popular there. Innumerable courses started up, based on his science, after the 1820s, and many were taught by comparative anatomists who had studied in Paris and knew him personally.

[. . .] It must be said straightaway that I am not offering a deep internal study of Geoffroy's anatomy (which can be found elsewhere);[18] rather I am intrigued by the science's social appeal. I have tried to find out what made it attractive to specific medical groups in this period of professional upheaval.

Upheaval there certainly was. The 1830s saw a huge increase in the number of pressure groups demanding that the teachers and practitioners outside the traditional power structure had more say in the running of medicine. It is no coincidence that these marginal men were the staunchest supporters of Geoffroy's science. That there was such a plethora of lobbies, democratic groups, and dissident factions meant that philosophical anatomy spread far and quickly. Its effects were immediately apparent. I would go so far as to claim that the introduction of Geoffroy's controversial ideas and the conservative backlash caused the dramatic flowering of comparative anatomy in London in the 1830s. New teachers, new chairs, and new courses testified to a rapid growth of interest in the subject, which peaked (as did medical radicalism itself) in the mid-1830s. [. . .] The result of this struggle to support, refute, or modify Geoffroyism was that comparative anatomy went through one of its most productive phases. Courses at this time were much more varied in style and content than we ever realized. By mid-decade some two dozen teachers and writers were exploring a variety of approaches, ranging from the fiercely materialistic to the doggedly idealistic. [. . .]

A history of biology "from below" is long overdue. If we are to cease being "dazzled by the great,"[19] then we need to pry into those social worlds where the mass of people lived. The scientific gentry and Oxbridge clergy are now very familiar, but they typified only one "class" position on the historical stage. We have detailed accounts of the way they made establishment science a recipe for social stability and Anglican supremacy, We know their reaction to Lamarck's and Geoffroy's "dark school."[20] The expensive, ecclesiastically blessed Bridgewater Treatises, which dwelt on God's goodness deduced from nature, have been studied extensively. (We hear less of the fact that these "Bilgewater" books were pilloried in the radical press.)[21] Yet the radical protagonists of the Anglican dons seem to exist as shadows cast by actors standing offstage. There simply has not been much investigation of their mechanistic sciences which proved so terrifying, or of the extent to which they percolated through to the radical undermass. In the past it has even proved difficult for historians of some disciplines to get a handle on these post-Regency radicals.[22]

A good way to restore the balance is to look at lowlife in the medical schools. What the majority of students were taught in their comparative anatomy courses is hardly known at all. By ignoring the anatomical doctrines circulating among democrats, science history has fallen out of step with social history, where a flourishing tradition of radical studies exists.[23] The time is surely ripe to probe the radicals and their Lamarckian and Geoffroyan imports, sciences whose motif of self-advancement made them immensely attractive to the democrats. If we are not to see science as a monolithic creation of the conservative elite, then we must get this dissident dimension back into the picture. We need to appreciate why the Cambridge clerics projected a total social collapse following the rise of Lamarck's zoology. The medical schools provide our way into the anatomical underworld, where Lamarck's and Geoffroy's doctrines mingled with anti-Church-and-state propaganda. [. . .]

Sociology of knowledge

Although this is primarily a contextual study, using the methods of social history, I also exploit the sociology of knowledge (that is, the study of the social factors affecting the production, evaluation, and use of knowledge — in this case science). Such a mix of contextual and sociological approaches is necessary today more than ever. Few historians see their task any more as reconstructing a rational lineage of ideas through time, picking up gems of foreshadowed "truth" here, ignoring "deviant" approaches there — in short, tracing a path of progressive enlightenment. Nor do they have much truck with the old "internalists" who wrenched science from its social context and wrote ghostly histories of disembodied ideas. With sociologists and cognitive psychologists teaching that "reality" construction is an active, socially constrained process, they have started examining the network of interests that sustain each community's view of nature. This seachange in historical approach has profound implications. It raises fundamental questions about the status of science as transcendental knowledge whose "discovery" is unproblematic.

Just how problematic it really is becomes apparent as we look at a specific example later in the text: the rival interpretations of the celebrated Stonesfield fossil jaws. These tiny lower jaws, just over an inch long, were found in the Stonesfield slates in Oxford early last century. But there were angry disagreements over their nature. The gentlemen of geology accepted that they belonged to opossumlike marsupials. As such, they were evidence of the earliest known mammals, already living in the "Age of Reptiles." Others disputed this. Where Owen had seen typical marsupial features, Grant saw characteristic reptilian ones. This is the problem: How could two proficient comparative anatomists see the jaws so differently? How could each describe such distinct sets of features?

It would be naïve to cheer one and jeer the other, as if there were inherent rights and wrongs of the case. This would accept that one account was more "objective" because it coincided with our own today. But historians have long ceased reading history backward and assuming that the present explains the past. It does not apply here anyway, because neither diagnosis held up. According to Owen the animals were marsupials; Grant declared them to be reptiles. Thirty years later, however, they were categorized as early, generalized, "sub-marsupial" mammals of an entirely new order.

I have concentrated on the rival social, political, and religious interests of Owen's Anglican and Grant's radical factions. Then I have looked at how these led to diverging presuppositions about nature. And not merely pre-suppositions. These men represented bitterly antagonistic groups which actually saw the social and natural worlds quite differently. In other words, I am concerned with the way ideological factors influence not merely theories, but even the perception of nature. It has been said that the recent convulsions in the history of science have turned its practitioner "into something of an anthropologist, an explorer of alien cultures."[24] Because British culture during the Industrial Revolution is best treated as "alien," I have devoted a large amount of space to explaining the sectarian contexts in which these contrasting views of nature were held. [. . .] [The] clash over the fossil jaws [was] quite explicable in contemporary terms. The protagonists' supposedly objective descriptions of nature were in fact socially constrained interpretations. Both Grant and Owen were good comparative anatomists; the reason they came to opposing interpretations of the jaws was that their "good sciences" reflected the contrasting norms, expectations, and perceptions of their respective groups.

This of course raises all sorts of awkward questions about the truth content of science. If other societies are "different worlds," if their sciences make sense "from within," what then of objective knowledge? Does it make all knowledge culture-relative? Can we only talk of local truths?[25] I make no bones about taking a relativist approach here. I am not interested in the eternal verities, only the reasons why rival groups saw them so differently: why one sect's science was another's quackery. As a practical upshot I have looked at a larger number of social groups than is usual in histories of science. The Oxbridge clergyman is not studied exclusively because he was the guardian of "proper," responsible science; the artisan atheist is not ignored because he was writing in illegal penny newspapers. Each is assessed on his own terms; the context is used to elucidate the causes and the reasons why each held a particular view. This leads us back to the idea of Britain in the 1830s as a social patchwork. Once this social diversity and struggle are acknowledged by science historians, we can begin to understand the conflicting opinions over nature that were rife in the period.

I have also taken a largely "instrumental" approach to science, that is, I have looked at the context and uses of competing theories as a means of discerning their local meaning.[26] This can only be done by knowing a subject's social position and group interests precisely. The problem of course lies in detecting the links between someone's implicit social views and explicit polished science. This is one of the challenges still facing sociologists — to expose the "connections between the scientist's social situation and his intellectual output."[27] I have tried to meet this challenge by exploring the medical "class," religious, and occupational structures mediating between the content of comparative anatomy and its context of use. My overall conclusion is that the rival biological doctrines in the thirties were integrated into long-term commercial and political strategies, either to gain or to hold on to privileges. Hence the title of this volume — *Politics of Evolution* — is singularly appropriate: progressive evolutionary theories and related naturalistic sciences, according to this approach, served to legitimate the radicals' democratic convictions. They were adopted by outsider groups set on breaking the old religious authority and transferring its power to the secular state.[28] As these political strategies were designed to achieve a fundamental redistribution of power, the new sciences were obviously hotly contested. Geoffroy and Lamarck became symbols of resistance; they were the tricolor banners waved by the medical democrats massing outside the corporation porticos.

So my goal is to explain how Geoffroy's and Lamarck's doctrines fitted the reformers' needs. Comprehending the radical milieu is absolutely necessary. We must be sensitive to the new journals and institutions, and the social movements of which they were visible expressions. [. . .]

Further reading

Adrian Desmond went on to write a major biography, with James R. Moore, *Darwin* (London: Michael Joseph, 1991) and, by himself, a two-volume study of Darwin's champion, T.H. Huxley, *Huxley: The Devil's Disciple* (London: Michael Joseph, 1994) and *Huxley: Evolution's High Priest* (London: Michael Joseph, 1997). See also Lucy Hartley, Petro Corsi, Ted Benton, James Moore and Adrian Desmond, 'Roundtable on *Darwin*', *Journal of Victorian Culture*, 3 (1998), 123–68.

Notes

1   P.J. Bowler, *The Non-Darwinian Revolution: Reinterpretation of a Historical Myth* (Baltimore: Johns Hopkins University Press, 1988).

2   Adrian Desmond, *Archetypes and Ancestors: Palaeontology in Victorian London, 1850–1875* (London: Blond and Briggs, 1982).

3   James A. Secord, 'Behind the Veil: Robert Chambers and *Vestiges*', in James Moore, ed., *History, Humanity, and Evolution: Essays in Honor of John C. Greene*, (Cambridge: Cambridge University Press, 1989); Adrian Desmond, 'Artisan Resistance and Evolution in Britain, 1819–1848', *Osiris* 3 (1987): 77–110, on the artisan evolutionists.

4   P. Corsi, *Science and Religion: Baden Powell and the Anglican Debate, 1800–1860* (Cambridge: Cambridge University Press, 1988) on the exception that proves the rule: the Rev. Baden Powell, Savilian Professor of Geometry at Oxford. Powell became an extreme latitudinarian and even warmed hesitantly to evolution, but found himself increasingly isolated as a result.

5   Norman Gash, 'After Waterloo: British Society and the Legacy of the Napoleonic Wars', *Transactions of the Royal Historical Society* 28 (1978): 146.

6   James R. Moore, 'Crisis without Revolution: The Ideological Watershed in Victorian England', *Revue de Synthèse* 4 (1986): 58–59.

7   Even the older histories that did mention the "Minor Evolutionists" (L. Eiseley, *Darwin's Century: Evolution and the Men Who Discovered It* (New York: Anchor Books, 1961) did

not trouble themselves with questions of how, why, or where avant-garde biological views were adopted, being more concerned to ferret out Darwin's "forerunners." They paid no heed to the social context and thus were ill equipped to understand how evolution met the intellectual needs of specific groups.

8   D. Ospovat, *The Development of Darwin's Theory: Natural History, Natural Theology, and Natural Selection, 1838–1859* (Cambridge: Cambridge University Press, 1981): chap. 3; P.J. Bowler, 'E.W. MacBride's Lamarckian Eugenics and Its Implications for the Social Construction of Scientific Knowledge', *Annals of Science* 41 (1984): 96–99; M.J.S. Hodge and D. Kohn, 'The Immediate Origins of Natural Selection', in D. Kohn, ed., *The Darwinian Heritage* (Princeton: Princeton University Press, 1985): 192–93; R.M. Young, *Darwin's Metaphor: Nature's Place in Victorian Culture* (Cambridge: Cambridge University Press, 1985): chap. 2; James R. Moore, 'Socializing Darwin', in L. Levidow, ed., *Science as Politics* (London: Free Association Books, 1986).

9   Desmond, 'Artisan Resistance'; Edward Royle, *Victorian Infidels: The Origins of the British Secularist Movement, 1791–1866* (Manchester: Manchester University Press, 1974): 123–25.

10   A task already begun by Roger Cooter, *The Cultural Meanings of Popular Science: Phrenology and the Organization of Consent in Nineteenth-Century Britain* (Cambridge: Cambridge University Press, 1984); E. Richards, 'The "Moral Anatomy" of Robert Knox: A Case Study of the Interplay between Biological and Social Thought in Victorian Scientific Naturalism', *Journal of the History of Biology* 22 (1989): 373–436; and the various authors in Moore, ed., *History, Humanity and Evolution.*

11   R.E. Grant, 'Observations on the Nature and Importance of Geology', *Edinburgh New Philosophical Journal* 1 (1826): 297, 300, spoke of the spontaneous generation of worms and infusoria and of Lamarck's belief that "all other animals, by the operation of external circumstances, are evolved from these in a double series, and in a gradual manner." Previously the first such use of the word was attributed to the anti-Lamarckian geologist Charles Lyell in 1832 (P.J. Bowler, 'The Changing Meaning of "Evolution"', *Journal of the History of Ideas* 36 (1975): 100). First usages are, however, unimportant, for *transmutation, metamorphosis,* and (later) *generation* were much more common terms; I use them interchangeably throughout the text.

12   K.D. Wells, 'The Historical Context of Natural Selection: The Case of Patrick Matthew', *Journal of the History of Biology* 6 (1973): 225–58; W.J. Dempster, *Patrick Matthew and Natural Selection* (Edinburgh: Paul Harris, 1983): 98–99; E. Richards, 'Moral Anatomy', 1988; Adrian Desmond, 'Robert E. Grant: The Social Predicament of a Pre-Darwinian Transmutationist', *Journal of the History of Biology* 17 (1984); Adrian Desmond, 'Lamarckism and Democracy: Corporations, Corruption, and Comparative Anatomy in the 1830s', in Moore, ed., *History, Humanity and Evolution*; F.N. Egerton, 'Hewett C. Watson, Great Britain's First Phytogeographer', *Huntia* 3 (1979): 91–92.

13   Strictly speaking, *materialism* offered a worldview in which there were no spirits (or vital powers independent of matter) and in which the mind was inseparable from the brain; consciousness was simply neural matter in action. Nineteenth-century materialists also assumed that force was an inherent quality of matter. They argued that biological phenomena could be explained by the laws of physics and chemistry, and ultimately by the properties of the atoms themselves (this is *reductionism*).

In practice, however, the label was applied much more widely. Deists who expressed reductionist views were also called materialists, in spite of their belief in God. Some teachers therefore distinguished themselves as "physiological materialists": while they proposed a material explanation of biological, mental, and even moral phenomena, they claimed that it left their faith in God and the soul untouched. I follow this wider contemporary usage; it captures the feeling of the age and allows me to keep together groups (atheists, deists, radical Christians) that were linked in their struggle against "priestcraft." (Scientific or physiological materialism in these sects was always part of a political ideology; it cannot be dealt with as a philosophical abstraction.) In the text, therefore, *materialism* can signify either an atheistic strategy or a mechanistic explanation of the mind and body.

14   Matthew, reproduced in Dempster, *Patrick Matthew*: 99. While I concentrate in this book on the middle classes, social historians have more generally focused on the working-class atheists and their illegal newspapers (Joel H. Wiener, *The War of the Unstamped: The Movement to Repeal the British Newspaper Tax, 1830–1836* (Ithaca: Cornell University Press, 1969); Patricia Hollis, *The Pauper Press: A Study in Working-Class Radicalism of the 1830s* (Oxford: Oxford University Press, 1970); Royle, *Victorian Infidels*.

15   A Country Gentleman, *The Consequences of a Scientific Education to the Working Classes of the Country Pointed Out; and the Theories of Mr. Brougham on That Subject Confuted; in a Letter to the Marquess of Lansdown [sic]* (London: T. Cadell, 1826): 9, 15, 52–53. See B.T. Bradfield, 'Sir Richard Vyvyan and the Country Gentlemen, 1830–1834', *English Historical Review* 83 (1968): 729–743 on the country gentlemen as a political group.

16   Chartism was a mass movement originating in the late 1830s which loosely united large numbers of middle- and working-class radicals. The Charter proposals included universal suffrage by ballot, annual elections, and the removal of property qualifications for Members of Parliament (M.P.s), who were to be paid a salary.

17   Secord, 'Behind the Veil'.

18   T. Appel, *The Cuvier-Geoffroy Debate: French Biology in the Decades before Darwin* (Oxford: Oxford University Press, 1987).

19   D. Knight, 'Background and Foreground: Getting Things in Context', *British Journal of the History of Science* 20 (1987): 8.

20   J.W. Clark and T.M. Hughes, eds, *The Life and Letters of the Reverend Adam Sedgwick* (2 vols; Cambridge: Cambridge University Press, 1890): 2:86; J. Morrell and A. Thackray, *Gentlemen of Science: Early Years of the British Association for the Advancement of Science* (Oxford: Clarendon Press, 1981); S.F. Cannon, *Science in Culture: The Early Victorian Period* (New York: Dawson, 1978); M.M. Garland, *Cambridge before Darwin: The Ideal of a Liberal Education, 1800–1860* (Cambridge: Cambridge University Press, 1980).

21   C.C. Blake, 'The Life of Dr. Knox', *Journal of Anthropology* 1 (1870–71): 334; Rehbock, *Philosophical Naturalists*: 56; E. Richards, 'Moral Anatomy'; Desmond, 'Artisan Resistance': 87–88, 90. On Bridgewater science: C.C. Gillispie, *Genesis and Geology: A Study in the Relations of Scientific Thought, Natural Theology, and Social Opinion in Great Britain, 1790–1850* (New York: Harper, 1959): 209–16.

22   C.A. Russell, *Science and Social Change, 1700–1900* (London: Macmillan, 1983): chap. 8, has tried to locate them in the London Chemical Society, but without touching on the relationship between radicalism, secularism, and reductionist science.

23   This is not to deny the great strides made by scholars studying phrenology's impact in the 1830s; for more than a decade they have provided sophisticated analyses of the shopocracy's use of this particular self-help science. See especially Steven Shapin, 'Phrenological Knowledge and the Social Structure of Early Nineteenth-Century Edinburgh', *Annals of Science* 32 (1975); Steven Shapin, 'The Politics of Observation: Cerebral Anatomy and Social Interests in the Edinburgh Phrenology Disputes' in R. Wallis, ed., *On the Margins of Science: The Social Construction of Rejected Knowledge* (Keele: Staffordshire: Sociology Review Monograph No. 27, 1979), and Roger Cooter, 'The Power of the Body: The Early Nineteenth Century' in B. Barnes and Steven Shapin, eds, *Natural Order: Historical Studies of Scientific Culture* (London: Sage, 1979), and Cooter, *Cultural Meaning of Science*.

24   M. Hollis and S. Lukes, eds, *Rationality and Relativism* (Oxford: Blackwell, 1982): 1–13.

25   B. Barnes and D. Bloor, 'Relativism, Rationalism and the Sociology of Knowledge', in Hollis and Lukes, eds, *Rationality and Relativism*. K.M. Figlio, 'The Metaphor of

Organization; An Historiographical Perspective on the Bio-Medical Sciences of the Early Nineteenth Century', *History of Science* 16 (1976): 19, even talks of science as "a naturalized carrier of its context."

26   Steven Shapin, 'History of Science and Its Sociological Reconstructions', *History of Science* 20 (1982): 197; B. Barnes, *Interests and the Growth of Knowledge* (London: Routledge and Kegan Paul, 1977).

27   B. Norton, 'Review of *Statistics in Britain* by D. MacKenzie', *British Journal of the History of Science* 16 (1983): 305.

28   James Moore, 'Crisis without Revolution': 67; Desmond, 'Artisan Resistance'.

James A. Secord

DOMESTICATING EVOLUTION

'Behind the Veil: Robert Chambers and *Vestiges*' in James R. Moore (ed.), *History, Humanity and Evolution Essays for John C. Greene* (Cambridge: Cambridge University Press, 1989), 174–84, 186–7.

To complement the Reading from **Adrian Desmond**, we include another major interpretation of the evolution debate before Darwin began to set forth his ideas in 1859. One of the most popular versions of evolution was presented in the book, *Vestiges of the Natural History of Creation* that was anonymously published in 1844. An instant best-seller, it quickly ran into new (and constantly revised) editions. **James Secord** has detailed the publication history of this extraordinary book and its reception in *Victorian Sensation* (2000), a dazzling intermingling of scientific and cultural history. Darwin's status as a great scientist is not diminished, but it is changed by an understanding of the wider debate about natural science. This extract comes from an article that Secord wrote prior to publishing *Victorian Sensation*, in which he provides an assessment of *Vestiges* and its impact on the Victorian public.

Its analysis of creation in terms of 'transmutation' (another word for 'evolution') provoked a scandal and it was widely denounced. Evolutionary ideas were associated with atheism and revolution and the author had to remain anonymous to protect his family. Daring to talk about evolution and arguing for a developmental view of natural history in the 1840s was a dangerous business. The book claimed to be 'the first attempt to connect the natural sciences into a history of creation'. It presented a portrait of creation (including human life, animals, plants, the Earth, and the solar system) as developing from earlier forms. *Vestiges* argued that scientific laws were sufficient to explain the universe without recourse to explanations involving the intervention of a divine being (although God was behind all natural law). The book was so successful that a sequel, *Explanations*, was published in 1845. Both works paved the way for Darwin and introduced ideas about evolution to a wider public.

We now know that the author of *Vestiges* and its sequel was the Scottish writer and publisher Robert Chambers (1802–71), who, with his brother William, had begun a series of publications aimed at the broad reading public. Due to family setbacks, Robert's formal education ended at fourteen, but, as a voracious reader with access to books, he eventually established himself first as a bookseller and then as a writer, initially on Scottish themes. Despite his criticism of biblical accounts of the natural world, Chambers was a believing Christian. His identity as the author of *Vestiges* was not revealed until 1884, although many suspected that he was the author. In the twentieth century, *Vestiges* was often dismissed as a 'curious' precursor to Darwin. James Secord has succeeded in restoring *Vestiges* to its proper place as a landmark in the history of science.

In this Reading, Secord examines the shaping of Chambers's views on evolution. In passages not reproduced here, he discusses the widespread contemporary habit of anonymous publication (Sir Walter Scott's Waverly novels, for example, were anonymous initially). Secord notes that, before writing *Vestiges* when in his forties, Chambers had already been the editor of *Chambers' Edinburgh Journal*, which was aimed at a wide readership; *Vestiges* was intended for the same audience. Chambers was critical of the way that scientific thought was increasingly intended only for the specialist. Instead, he wrote for the general reader and his ideas were widely discussed. Secord also places Chambers's work in the context of his shift towards political liberalism (after 1832) and anti-clericalism (marking his shift from the Scottish Presbyterian to the Scottish Episcopal Church). Chambers's belief in models of scientific development mirrored his support for liberal reform. Additionally, Chambers was drawn to the new science of phrenology, especially its argument that different areas of the brain had different functions (phrenologists believed that human characteristics could be revealed by examining the shape of a person's head). All of this, Secord argues, was part of the background to Chambers's ideas about evolution, although not necessarily articulated directly in his writings. In this extract, Secord looks at the direct influences on *Vestiges*, which include recently-published anatomical texts, and also Chambers' own experiences of childbirth and development in his ever-expanding family.

James A. Secord is Professor in the Department of History and Philosophy of Science at Cambridge University, and Director of the Darwin Correspondence Project. His books include *Victorian Sensation: The Extraordinary Publication, Reception and Secret Authorship of 'Vestiges of the Natural History of Creation'* (2000). He is currently writing a study of science in the newspaper press in nineteenth-century New York, London and Paris.

BY THE MID-1830S Chambers had abandoned his purely antiquarian interests as products of his intellectual infancy. From the staunch Toryism of Walter Scott, he had turned to the advocacy of liberal (but always gradual) reform. He had left the Scottish Kirk and become a force to be reckoned with in the Edinburgh circle of George Combe. And, as evidenced by the children's book of 1836, [*Introduction to the Sciences*], he was beginning to evince an interest in science. It is not difficult to see how, having got this far, Chambers went on to write *Vestiges*. In 1824 the topic would have been abhorrent to him; by the mid-1830s, through a contingent series of circumstances, it was not. The rest of this essay will suggest how important aspects of the work were elaborated.

One point is clear. The idea of turning from the phrenological philosophy of mind to the entire natural world came from an exposure to the nebular hypothesis of the formation of the universe.[1] Here the direct influence of the author and lecturer John Pringle Nichol was critically important. The pages of the *Journal* indicate Chambers' intense enthusiasm for Nichol's *Views of the Architecture of the Heavens*. Published in 1837, this work described in vivid and accessible language the evolution of the universe and the formation of galaxies and stars. As the *Journal* said in a review, 'high and rational wonder has never been so delightfully associated with moral feeling'.[2] The very summer that the *Architecture of the Heavens* appeared, Chambers, Nichol and a number of their phrenological friends toured Ireland together for sixteen days; Anne Chambers jokingly warned her husband not to be carried away by his astronomical enthusiasm. What Chambers saw as Nichol's goal — to connect 'the mystical evolution of firmamental matter with the destinies of man' — became his own; he would carry the story further, into the living world of plants, animals and human origins.[3]

Once the nebular hypothesis had led Chambers to contemplate the application of a law of progress to the whole realm of nature, he rapidly began to explore other relevant sciences. Thus the day after Chambers returned from Ireland in the summer of 1837, he told a friend that he was 'in the commencement of a geology fever, and extremely anxious to make up a little collection of the appropriate objects'.[4] He began to explore not only the earth sciences but zoology and botany as well. Most pieces of the puzzle are evident in *Chambers's Edinburgh Journal*. There were essays on monstrosities, the progressive nature of the fossil record, the habits and instincts of animals, the learning abilities of dogs and pigs, the spontaneous generation of insects through electricity, and the effects of diet and exercise upon health.

As a result, a careful reader of the *Journal* would have been familiar with much of *Vestiges* well before it appeared. Especially striking was the large number of articles on the origins of races, nations, languages and civilizations. These elaborated a developmental model almost identical to that found in the chapter of *Vestiges* on the 'Early History of Mankind'. In the essay 'Gossip about Golf', Chambers even applied the model to his favourite sport, which he argued was an inevitable result of 'the existence of a certain peculiar waste ground called links'. Similarly, cricket was said to be a natural outcome of village greens in England.[5]

Comments in these essays indicate just how far Chambers had come from his High Tory antiquarianism. One article proclaimed that 'physiology alone could throw more light on the origin and progress of nations, within the bounds of one small volume, than could be done by a whole library of political history, or the united labours of a score of archaeological societies'.[6] This was a remarkable statement from an author whose best-known titles were *The Traditions of Edinburgh* and *A History of the Rebellions in Scotland*. Behind the wall of anonymity in the *Journal,* his volte-face was now complete: the new interest in science was now to be applied to history itself. Although he believed that scientific study of the past was just beginning, progress and physiology would ultimately subsume anecdote and antiquarianism.

As publication of *Vestiges* came closer, the *Journal* also featured articles on the aims and methods of natural science. There were comments on the fate of Galileo, the necessity of judging science by more than mere utility, and the benefits of speculation. It is hard not to see pieces like 'The Easily Convinced' of 1842 as attempts to soften the reception of the forthcoming bombshell:

> The constant cry is, give us facts and leave hypotheses alone. But it is not possible for any human being to go on constantly collecting dry unconnected facts. We require to be allowed a little generalisation by way of *bon-bons,* to encourage us in our tasks. And is not imagination often a means of leading on to fact? . . . And thus there is a utility and a final cause for even that mocked thing, credulity. The credulous are the nurses appointed for ideas in their nonage — which, if left to the tender feelings of the cautious alone, would for certain perish of cold and hunger, before ever they had shown their first teeth. The credulous catch them and foster them, and look out for their parishes, and get them comfortably brought on to their apprenticeships. By and by, they begin to kick about for themselves, and settle into respectable and useful members of society — but no thanks to the awful doctors who never have any thing to do with the intellectual bantlings that don't come into the world properly stamped and labelled.[7]

Well before he published, Chambers was acutely aware of the potential reception of his ideas, which were not at all 'properly stamped and labelled' by the standards of specialist Victorian science.[8] By this point the outline of a book had taken shape. It would, like his children's book, cover all aspects of the natural world from the formation of the Solar System to the origin of civilization, and it would do so from the standpoint of a law of development and progress.

The origin of animated tribes

How did Chambers come to incorporate organic evolution within his over-arching scheme? At one level, the answer seems obvious. For anyone anxious to replace divine intervention with law-like regularities, the origin of new organic beings needed an explanation. In 1837 Nichol had spoken of 'the germs, the producing powers of that LIFE, which in coming ages will bud and blossom', but had left the mechanism for an extension of natural law into the organic world to be inferred.[9] Chambers, in the excitement of reading the *Architecture of the Heavens,* believed that a gap had opened up between the planetary and the human realms, between the works of Nichol and the works of Combe. As the preface to the 1853 edition of

Vestiges explained, he 'first had his attention attracted to the early history of animated nature, on becoming acquainted with an outline of the Laplacian hypothesis of the solar system'.[10] Once Chambers accepted the need for a naturalistic explanation, generation from pre-existing species was by far the most obvious alternative.

The adoption of this view, however, demanded a radical shift in Chambers' attitude towards organic evolution — 'transmutation', as it was usually known. The transformation can be followed in the changing emphases of articles in the *Journal*. These are unsigned and at least some of them may not be by Chambers, but they had to pass his close editorial scrutiny. They are, in consequence, unlikely to deviate from a position he would have found acceptable.

In its early years the *Journal* firmly opposed organic evolution. The subject was first mentioned in an article of November 1832 entitled 'Natural History: Animals with a Backbone'. This attacked transmutation and those who upheld it in no uncertain terms. Ignorance of the facts and knowledge of the unity of organic types, it explained, had 'tempted many philosophers to hazard the absurd opinion that man had his beginning in a minute animalcule, and has attained his present perfect condition from progressive improvement by reproduction'. The article expressed 'astonishment' that learned men like Erasmus Darwin and Lord Monboddo had advocated such heresies. However, transmutation would never become popular: 'views like these can never be entertained by healthy minds, and it requires but little reflection to dispel such absurd theories'.[11]

A second essay appeared in September 1835, based on the discussion of Lamarck in the second volume of Charles Lyell's *Principles of Geology* of 1832. The article noted that some 'very eminent philosophers . . . have boldly asserted that all the varieties of plants and animals which abound in nature originally sprang from one individual specimen of organized life; in short, that man himself, Socrates, Shakespeare, and Newton, were merely zoophytes in a state of high improvement and cultivation!' As before, this idea was roundly condemned. The limits of variability, the sterility of mules, and a host of other evidences precluded any possibility of evolution. Lyell's demolition of Lamarck was 'so satisfactory as to require us to say nothing in addition'.[12] This continued to be the *Journal*'s editorial policy through 1838, as indicated by some brief comments on these 'most absurd notions' prefacing an extract from Dr Clarke Abel's description of the orang-utan.[13] Even if Chambers did not write all these articles (the second at least bears hallmarks of his style), his initial opposition to transmutation is obvious.

Conversely, after 1838, Chambers never came out publicly as an evolutionist; this would have been dangerous. With its audience among educated artisans and the middle class, the *Journal* could scarcely sanction a doctrine associated with revolutionaries, atheists and Frenchmen.[14] The opposition to evolution expressed in its early volumes was of a piece with its advocacy of political economy, self-help and Malthusian restraint among the working class. 'Moral affairs of this kind', the *Journal* noted in 1838, 'proceed with all the irresistible force of the great physical laws: as well try to give a check to the law of gravitation itself, as to counteract the principles which regulate the rise and fall of wages.'[15] Although Chambers came to believe that utilitarian economic and political doctrines were compatible with transmutation, its radical associations were simply too damaging to be embraced in public. After 1838, the *Journal* next spoke out on the subject in 1860, when Chambers reviewed the *Origin of Species*.[16]

Even leaving aside the political and religious dangers of transmutation, the topic could be discussed in detail only by revealing other more basic matters, which were usually kept veiled in a family paper like the *Journal*. In this forum, subjects unsuitable for women, children and workers could be mentioned only with the utmost discretion. Chambers explained the problem to Combe, who was revising some lectures for publication in the *Journal*:

> With regard to the duty of studying anatomy, I must really say that I fear considerably for the reception of that advice, and hope you will make every effort, in your contemplated alterations, to introduce and handle the subject in a manner so little startling as possible . . . . [F]or if they are told that one part of the sex has stood the supposed horror of the thing, and not been consequently looked upon as not comme il faut, they would see the less difficulty in their also doing it. At all events, pray try to make the passage as sweet as possible.[17]

When it came to sex and generation, the taboo was absolute. The *Journal* became a byword for chastity; as the London journalist Dudley Costello asked a later editor of the paper, Leitch Ritchie, 'How is the population of Scotland kept up? By immigration?'[18]

But during the late 1830s and 1840s, Chambers came as close as he could to discussing evolution in public. Articles on related topics such as progressionist geology could use language readily transferred to the terms of transmutation. Within a few years Chambers became more explicit. As he wrote in an 1842 piece on 'the educability of animals', 'We become more confident in the improvability of our own species, when we find that even the lower animals are capable of being improved, through a succession of generations, by the constant presence of a meliorating agency.'[19] The point was underlined by contemporary studies of the races of man. Instances of 'white negroes' demonstrated 'that the rise of the white races of men out of the black is within the range of possibility'.[20] Given the constraints on publishing on subjects relating to sex, it is not surprising that the *Journal* never spoke more directly. Of all the issues 'behind the veil', this was the most darkly hidden.

Because the *Journal* could not publish on sex, generation or embryology, we are thrown back upon *Vestiges* itself for indications of Chambers' inquiries into possible mechanisms for transmutation. In addition, the autobiographical preface to the 1853 edition makes it possible to link the public evidence into a more coherent account. Chambers noted how he commenced inquiry with the basic assumption that the '"fiats", "special miracles", "interferences", and other suggestions and figures of speech in vogue amongst geologists' would have to be rejected. With this starting point, he examined 'such treatises on physiology as had fallen in his way' for evidence of how species might have originated.[21]

In the late 1830s naturalistic physiological and anatomical doctrines were common currency among nonconformist medical men.[22] Chambers thus had a wide choice of works to consult. He relied especially on three works in transcendental anatomy by authors who had taught or been trained in Edinburgh. (His awareness of continental authors, such as E. Geoffroy St Hilaire, Lamarck, E. Serres, Friedrich Tiedemann and Karl Ernst von Baer, seems to have been entirely at second hand.) The first source, and probably the first to be consulted, was Perceval Lord's *Popular Physiology*

(1834).[23] This was an elementary manual published under the auspices of the Society for the Promotion of Christian Knowledge. Lord's anti-phrenological book is just the kind of test that Chambers would have encountered while researching his treatise on the philosophy of phrenology. Lord explained how the human embryo passed successively through stages resembling a fish, a reptile, a bird and a mammal; it then discussed how the human brain 'not only goes through the animal transmigrations we have mentioned, but successively represents the characters with which it is found in the Negro, Malay, American, and Mongolian nations'. This was the recapitulation doctrine that Chambers took as the heart of his hypothesis, expressed without qualification. *Vestiges* quoted these striking passages at length, turning Lord's argument to an evolutionary end.[24]

A second source for Chambers' theory was a much more reputable textbook, the Scottish medical lecturer John Fletcher's posthumous *Rudiments of Physiology* (1835–7). This work also contained sections critical of phrenology and discussed recapitulation at length. But Fletcher went further and cautioned against using it to support transmutation. The doctrine had 'nothing but the most vague and rambling presumptions in its favour', especially in the face of the functional integrity of each species. Individual organs, such as the brain, could form a perfect developmental series, but whole organisms could not. Differences in the timing of embryonic changes ruled this out.[25] Despite the denial of transmutation, Chambers must have been impressed. And although Fletcher rejected any simple Lamarckian series, he did range the entire animal kingdom in ascending order of complexity and degree of organization. Chambers found this list highly suggestive, especially when juxtaposed with an outline of the appearance of various species in the geological record. A chart illustrating this comparison became an important part of *Vestiges*.[26]

Both Fletcher and Lord presented the well-known doctrine of recapitulation. But Chambers was also aware of a rival, newer and more sophisticated embryology, which had been developed by Von Baer in Prussia. This argued that embryos do not pass through stages resembling the adult forms of simpler organisms; rather, the process is one of differentiation, with the embryo starting as a generalized form and gradually exhibiting the special characters of the adult species. As Chambers noted, 'the resemblance is not to the adult fish or the adult reptile, but to the fish and reptile at a certain point in their foetal progress'. This idea, known as 'Von Baer's law', was just becoming known in Great Britain in the later 1830s, particularly through a series of articles by Martin Barry. Chambers may have read these (he did cite Barry's essay on fissiparous generation), but his most obvious source was the second edition of William Carpenter's *Principles of General and Comparative Anatomy*, which appeared in 1841.[27] Chambers was aware of this work by the summer of 1844, and sent *Vestiges* to John Churchill partly because he had published it. Moreover, Carpenter was doing a considerable amount of writing for the Chambers firm in the early 1840s, including a *Rudiments of Zoology* for the *Educational Course* and articles for an expanded edition of *Chambers's Information for the People*. Neither of these primers discussed embryology, but in editing them Chambers was more likely to consult the textbook than would otherwise have been the case. A summary of Carpenter's presentation and a revised version of his diagram appeared in *Vestiges* without acknowledgement.[28]

The text of the first edition of *Vestiges* strongly suggests that there were two stages in the prepublication development of Chambers' ideas on an evolutionary mechanism. Von Baer's law differed fundamentally from the concept of recapitulation, but it appeared only as an inserted qualification and not as the primary definition of a mechanism. The first edition thus seemed contradictory to many readers, and within a few weeks Chambers altered his discussion of recapitulation to bring it closer to Von Baer. By the third edition of January 1845, all references to embryos passing through the 'permanent forms' of adult organisms had been excised. This shift towards Von Baer continued right through the tenth edition of 1853, although it was never complete.[29]

It would appear, then, that the transmutation theory of *Vestiges* was initially constructed around the traditional concept of recapitulation available in the works of Lord and Fletcher. Only afterwards did Chambers become aware of the alternative being imported into Britain by Carpenter, and he added it to his hypothesis at some point in the early 1840s. Far from being old-fashioned by advocating a linear progression, *Vestiges* served more than any other book to bring novel concepts of branching and differentiation to general notice.[30]

The domestication of development

Beyond the specific sources of Chambers' theory, however, lies the basic problem that transmutation was a radical doctrine. It had been ridiculed in the *Journal* and had few if any supporters in Edinburgh phrenological circles. Even after *Vestiges* was published, neither Combe nor Nichol advocated the idea. How could Chambers have become willing to consider a subject previously seen as dangerous and degrading?

Important clues are provided by the unusual circumstances in which the book was written. Chambers composed *Vestiges* in the early 1840s, when he had left the urban bustle of Edinburgh, and moved to St Andrews in Fife. This move has usually been seen as a way of avoiding prying eyes that might pin the authorship of *Vestiges* upon him. But this is simply a myth. In fact Chambers had suffered a mental breakdown, and the move was undertaken to aid his recovery. For a decade he had written the larger part of the weekly *Journal* single-handedly. The strain was simply too much, and in 1842 he collapsed. As Anne Chambers noted, 'incessant mental exertion' and 'intense mental action' had left him with a mind in an 'unsound, or partly in a *diseased* state'.[31] To escape, the family moved to a villa on the outskirts of St Andrews. Chambers took up golfing, participated in the local literary culture, and wrote occasionally for the *Journal*. In August 1842 Anne had a miscarriage and in 1843 his mother died, but for the most part the Chamberses found their stay pleasant and relaxing.[32] For the first time in ten years, Robert could turn his full attention to something other than his weekly essays. In this quiet family retreat, removed from controversy and potential critics, Chambers wrote *Vestiges*. The book was, as he said at its close, 'composed in solitude, and almost without the cognizance of a single human being'.[33]

Chambers, of course, was not alone in St Andrews; he brought with him a large and growing family. In many respects, his familiarity with everyday processes of birth and development was much more important for his theories than his exposure to technical treatments of embryology. Chambers was an occasional and desultory reader of physiology texts, but a full-time and enthusiastic father. By 1843 he had nine children (six girls and three boys), and watching them mature was a fundamental part of the experience that went into the making of *Vestiges*. Chambers was particularly moved by the birth of his eldest son, Robert, and published a signed poem, 'To a Little Boy', in *Blackwood's Magazine* for July 1835. 'The feelings there expressed', he told a friend two years later, 'have suffered no change, for he himself, in advancing out of childhood, has lost none of its endearing qualities. What a history, though an incommunicable one, resides in my mind respecting the aspects, talk, doings, and traits of progressive intelligence of this dear boy in the course of his brief existence.'[34] It may not be too much to say that this 'incommunicable history' was finally expressed in the cosmic story of *Vestiges,* which pictured all nature engaged in gestation and development.

Images of pregnancy, birth, childhood and the family were deeply embedded in the structure and language of the book. In explaining the evidence for the nebular hypothesis, Chambers immediately appealed to an analogy based on the familiar details of human growth. Stars were visible in every stage of development; 'it may be presumed that all these are but stages in a progress, just as if, seeing a child, a boy, a youth, a middle-aged, and an old man together, we might presume that the whole were only variations of one being'.[35] And the process applied not just to stars, but to our own Solar System. *Vestiges* quoted a passage from John Herschel's *Astronomy* to show how the planets were joined with all the mutual bonds of a Victorian family gathered around the hearth:

> When we contemplate the constituents of the planetary system from the point of view which this relation affords us, it is no longer mere analogy which strikes us, no longer a general resemblance among them, as individuals independent of each other, and circulating about the sun, each according to its own peculiar nature, and connected with it by its own peculiar tie. The resemblance is now perceived to be a true *family likeness*; they are bound up in one chain — interwoven in one web of mutual relation and harmonious agreement, subjected to one pervading influence which extends from the centre to the farthest limits of that great system, of which all of them, the earth included, must henceforth be regarded as members.[36]

This appearance of happy domesticity, Chambers went on to explain, could be taken in a literal sense, for the nebular hypothesis showed that the planets were 'children of the sun', generated from the stellar body according to the same universal law that had produced the galaxies. Language of this kind would have been familiar to Chambers from Nichol's *Architecture of the Heavens*, which spoke of 'nebulous parentage' and the 'inexhaustible womb of the future'.[37]

What Chambers did in *Vestiges* was to use these same generative images to bring the frightening notion of transmutation within the realm of the familiar. The production of new species, he wrote, 'has never been anything more than a new stage of progress in gestation, an event as simply natural, and attended as little by any circumstances of a wonderful or startling kind, as the silent advance of an ordinary mother from one week to another of her pregnancy'.[38] In other words, the birth of a new species was no more or less to be feared than the birth of a child. To disarm criticism, Chambers asked his readers what it would be like 'to be acquainted for the first time with the circumstances attending the production of an individual of our race'. Faced by the facts of sex and reproduction, 'we might equally think them degrading, and be eager to deny them and exclude them from the admitted truths of nature'. But these facts could not be denied by 'a healthy and natural mind'. Neither, by implication, could the analogous processes of gestation that gave birth to new species.[39]

Chambers, as much as any writer of his time, was aware of the expectations of his audience. For years he had spoken through his essays for the *Journal,* assuming the character of an 'intimate acquaintance or friend' on a weekly visit to his readers.[40] *Vestiges* was successful because it employed strategies learned during this long apprenticeship. The most touchy subject the book treated, the creation of new species by transmutation, had never been allowed into middle-class Victorian homes. But by building the generative model of *Vestiges* around images of pregnancy, childhood, the family and the hearth, Chambers was able to minimize the fears of his audience. Transmutation, which has been associated in the public mind with radical revolutionaries and dissolute foreigners, became infused with all the domestic virtues. With *Vestiges,* evolution quite literally moved off the streets and into the home.

It is worth noting that the domestic connections of a transmutation theory based on 'the universal gestation of nature' must have had great appeal for Chambers himself. In this lies the solution to what has always seemed a great paradox about *Vestiges:* how a respectable middle-class paterfamilias came to write on this subject at all. There is a great irony here, too; for it was ultimately because of his family that Chambers kept his authorship hidden for so many years. His son-in-law asked him directly about the reasons for remaining anonymous:

> I can easily understand now why Robert Chambers shrouded himself in impenetrable mystery. The veil was raised to me a few years after I married his daughter . . . . He and I had been out for a walk together, and as we were returning home I said to him, "Tell me why you have never acknowledged your greatest work." For all answer he pointed to his house, in which he had eleven children, and then slowly added, "I have eleven reasons."[41]

The authorship had to remain secret. The business might be damaged, the 'saints' might attack, but the greatest threat was that his growing family — especially his eight daughters — might be placed beyond the pale of respectability. Even Chambers' well-honed literary skills could not defuse the social threat of transmutation.

Chambers in context

Chambers had neither the secure position in society nor the scientific reputation that allowed Darwin to put his name on the title page of the *Origin of Species.* But there are at least a few parallels between the two authors. Not least, they were both middle-class family men who wrote their books in relative isolation. Darwin, plagued by a mysterious illness, retreated to the privacy of Down;[42] Chambers suffered a nervous collapse, withdrew into his domestic circle at St Andrews and produced a text that brought evolution into the middle-class homes of Victorian

England. Like the *Origin of Species,* however, *Vestiges* was not the product of one individual's idiosyncratic psychology. Rather, Chambers' use of his personal and domestic life can only be understood in the wider context of early Victorian religious, political and family history. He was well aware of his audience, especially the constraints that it imposed around public discussions of sex, development and transmutation. These limits created both opportunities and dangers, which he negotiated with considerable skill.

Vestiges, as we have seen, is most effectively viewed as the carefully crafted product of a leading journalist and author. A bestseller among the general public, the book was not always so successful in dealing with problems relating to specialist science. This aspect of the work has drawn particular attention from historians, who have often pictured Chambers as a bungling amateur naturalist, a failed Darwin.[43] The present essay has dealt at some length with the ways that Chambers may have elaborated his ideas relating to the organic world by using the specialist literature on embryology. In retrospect, these seem the most significant part of *Vestiges,* and even at the time transmutation created the most controversy. But problems in scientific physiology, like those relating to technical natural history, geology and astronomy, had only a minor part in the genesis of *Vestiges.*

Chambers' deployment of technical science, like his use of his domestic experience, can only be understood in relation to the wider context of the early Victorian era. In common with his associates Combe and Nichol, Chambers was intent upon using the natural sciences as part of a programme for gradual middle-class reform. The tendency of his book, despite its appeals to religion, was fundamentally secular. It advocated progress, hard work and the interests of the middle classes; it turned its back on antiquarian history, organized religion, conservative politics and the ancient universities. These were ideas and institutions that had been supported by science in the past. But in Chambers' view they had become barriers to progress, and needed to be replaced by a new order. In short, the natural sciences were being brought to the service of causes that Chambers had already advocated in hundreds of popular and readable essays. For that reason, the Reverend Adam Sedgwick of Cambridge was entirely correct to call *Vestiges* a 'rank pill of asafoetida and arsenic, covered with gold leaf'.[44] Thomas Henry Huxley hit the target even more precisely when he commented that *Vestiges* could have been written by anyone — anyone, that is, who was familiar with the contents of the most popular weekly periodical in the kingdom, *Chambers's Edinburgh Journal.*

Further reading

Readers should consult Secord's full treatment of Robert Chambers and *Vestiges* in *Victorian Sensation: The Extraordinary Publication Reception and Secret Authorship of 'Vestiges of the Natural History of Creation'* (Chicago, IL: University of Chicago Press, 2000) as well as his edition of *Vestiges* published by Chicago University Press in 1994. For a response to Secord, see Crosbie Smith, George Levine, David Vincent and James Secord, 'Roundtable on James Secord's *Victorian Sensation'*, *Journal of Victorian Culture*, 8 (2003), 119–50; and Michael Taylor, Evelleen Richards, Adrian Johns and James Secord, 'Review Symposium: Vestigial Sensations', *Metascience*, 11 (2002), 4–33.

Notes

1   [Chambers], *Vestiges* (10th edn, 1853), p. v; see also Marilyn Bailey Ogilvie, 'Robert Chambers and the Nebular Hypothesis', *British Journal for the History of Science*, 8 (1975), 214–32.

2   [Chambers], 'Professor Nichol's Views of the Architecture of the Heavens', *Chambers's Edinburgh Journal*, 6 (1837), 210–11.

3   As Simon Schaffer notes in 'The Nebular Hypothesis and the Science of Progress', in James R. Moore, ed., *History, Humanity and Evolution: Essays for John C. Greene* (Cambridge: Cambridge University Press, 1989), Nichol was often accused of authoring *Vestiges*, and privately he thought that Chambers had plagiarized from him. For Chambers' account of the Irish tour, see 'A Few More Days in Ireland', *Chambers's Edinburgh Journal*, 6 (1837), 289–90, 301–2, 309–10, 317–18, 325–6, 333–4.

4   Chambers to D.R. Rankine, 3 Sept. 1837, National Library of Scotland [hereafter NLS], Dep. 341/109/1.

5   [Chambers], 'Gossip about Golf', *Chambers's Edinburgh Journal*, 11 (1842), 297–8; also in Chambers, *Select Writings*, II, 313–24.

6   [Chambers], 'Thoughts on Nations and Civilisation', *Chambers's Edinburgh Journal*, 11 (1842), 137–8 (138).

7   [idem], 'The Easily Convinced', *Chambers's Edinburgh Journal*, 11 (1842), 185–6; also in Chambers, *Select Writings*, IV, 14–22.

8   For the problems Chambers faced in this area after publication, see especially Richard Yeo, 'Science and Intellectual Authority in Mid-nineteenth Century Britain: Robert Chambers and "Vestiges of the Natural History of Creation"', *Victorian Studies*, 28 (1984), pp. 5–31; Ogilvie, 'Robert Chambers and the Nebular Hypothesis'; and Schaffer.

9   John Pringle Nichol, *Views of the Architecture of the Heavens, in a Series of Letters to a Lady* (Edinburgh: William Tait, 1837), p. 127.

10 [Chambers], *Vestiges* (10th edn, 1853), p. v.

11 'Natural History: Animals with a Backbone', *Chambers's Edinburgh Journal*, 1 (1832), 337–8.

12 'Popular Information on Science: Transmutation of Species', *Chambers's Edinburgh Journal*, 4 (1835), 273–4.

13 'Sketches in Natural History: Monkeys', *Chambers's Edinburgh Journal*, 11 (1838), 251–2.

14 The dangerous associations of transmutation are well brought out in Adrian Desmond, 'Artisan Resistance and Evolution in Britain, 1819–1848', *Osiris*, 2nd ser., 3 (1987), 77–110; *idem*, 'Robert E. Grant: The Social Predicament of a Pre-Darwinian Transmutationist', *Journal of the History of Biology*, 17 (1984), 189–223; Michael Bartholomew, 'Lyell and Evolution: An Account of Lyell's Response to the Prospect of an Evolutionary Ancestry for Man', *British Journal for the History of Science*, 6 (1973), 276–303; and Pietro Corsi, 'The Importance of French Transformist Ideas for the Second Volume of Lyell's "Principles of Geology"', *British Journal for the History of Science*, 11 (1978), 221–44.

15 'Jealousies of the Employed against Employers', *Chambers's Edinburgh Journal*, 7 (1838), 41–2; for similar comments, see the speech by Chambers at the firm's annual soirée: 'Messrs Chambers's Soirée', *Chambers's Edinburgh Journal*, 12 (1843), 197–9.

16 In 1844 Chambers had tried to get his editorial assistant, David Page, to review *Vestiges*, but he refused; see *The Athenaeum*, no. 1414 (1854), 1463–4.

17 Chambers to Combe, 27 March 1834, NLS, MS. 7232, fos. 70–1. For Combe's own prudishness in phrenological discussions of sex, see Michael Shortland, 'Courting the Cerebellum: Early Organological and Phrenological Views of Sexuality', *British Journal for the History of Science*, 20 (1987), 173–99, esp. 187–9. Some of the effects of taboos

on discussions of sex in scientific work are brought out in John Farley, *Gametes & Spores: Ideas about Sexual Reproduction, 1750–1914* (Baltimore, Md.: Johns Hopkins University Press, 1982), pp. 110–28.

18   Cooney, 'Publishers for the People', p. 63.

19   [Chambers], 'Educability of Animals', *Chambers's Edinburgh Journal*, 22 (1842), 97–8; also in Chambers, *Select Writings*, IV, 154–62.

20   'Popular Information on Science: Effects of Climate, &c. on Human Beings', *Chambers's Edinburgh Journal*, 12 (1843), 346–7.

21   [Chambers], *Vestiges* (10th edn, 1853), pp. v-vi; see also Hodge, 'Universal Gestation'.

22   See Adrian Desmond, 'Lamarckism and Democracy: Corporations, Corruption and Comparative Anatomy in the 1830s', in Moore, ed., *History, Humanity and Evolution*, 99–130.

23   For example, Chambers' reference to Tiedemann in *Vestiges*, p. 201 is drawn directly from Lord, while his comments on Lamarck on pp. 230–1 imply no further knowledge than is available in Lyell's *Principles*.

24   *Vestiges*, pp. 200–1, quoting (with minor alterations) from Perceval B. Lord, *Popular Physiology: Being a Familiar Explanation of the Most Interesting Facts connected with the Structure and Functions of Animals, and Particularly of Man* (London: John W. Parker, 1834).

25   Desmond, 'Lamarckism and Democracy'; John Fletcher, *Rudiments of Physiology, in Three Parts* (Edinburgh: John Carfrae and Son, 1835–7), part i, esp. pp. 6–17.

26   *Vestiges*, pp. 226–7.

27   For these points, see the excellent discussion in Evelleen Richards, 'A Question of Property Rights: Richard Owen's Evolutionism Reassessed', *British Journal for the History of Science*, 20 (1987), 129–71 (133–9) and Dov Ospovat, 'The Influence of K.E. von Baer's Embryology, 1828–1859', *Journal of the History of Biology*, 9 (1976), 1–28.

28   *Vestiges*, p. 212. It is worth noting that the source was explicitly credited from the fifth edition of 1846, when Carpenter himself was actively contributing to the revision of *Vestiges*. For his participation in the other publications of the Chambers firm, see Cooney, 'Publishers for the People', p. 195.

29   Richards, 'Property Rights'. For examples of the revisions, see Marilyn Bailey Ogilvie, 'Robert Chambers and the Successive Revisions of the "Vestiges of the Natural History of Creation"' (Ph.D. dissertation, University of Oklahoma, 1973), esp. pp. 307–32.

30   Richards, 'Property Rights'; Ospovat, 'The Influence of K.E. von Baer's Embryology'. For an interpretation of Chambers that emphasizes the elements of linearity in the first edition, see Peter J. Bowler, *Fossils and Progress: Paleontology and the Idea of Progressive Evolution in the Nineteenth Century* (New York: Science History Publications, 1976), pp. 53–62. As Bowler has pointed out to me, *Vestiges* continued to use analogies with Babbage's calculating engine, which best fitted a linear model of progress, even after the embryological discussion had been revised to conform with Von Baer. Here, as in many other ways, Chambers was evidently more concerned with communicating a basic message about natural law than with analytical consistency. In fact, the embryology was revised towards Von Baer largely (although not entirely) because the physiologist Carpenter assisted in improving the later editions.

31   A. Chambers to W. Chambers, n.d., NLS, Dep. 341/82/31; R. Chambers to [A. Chambers], 23 Nov. 1842, NLS, Dep. 341/82/32. Another important event leading to the move may have been the death of a daughter, Margaret, from scarlet fever in March 1842. See [Chambers to Rankine], 14 Mar. 1842, NLS, Dep. 341/109/3. For the story that Chambers left St Andrews for secrecy, see Millhauser, *Just Before Darwin*, pp. 29–30.

32   [Chambers to Rankine], NLS, Dep. 341/109/5. For the death of Chambers' mother, see W. Chambers, *Memoir*, p. 243.

33   *Vestiges*, p. 387.

34   Chambers to Rankine, 3 Sept. 1837 NLS, Dep. 341/109/1. See also Chambers, 'To a Little Boy', *Blackwood's Edinburgh Magazine*, 38 (July 1835), 70. I am grateful to Mr A.S. Chambers for the following details concerning birth and death dates of the children of Anne and Robert Chambers: Jane (b. 1830), Robert (1832–88), Mary (b. 1833; unnamed twin died same day), Anne (b. 1835), Janet (1836–63), Eliza (1836–1909), Amelia (b. 1838), Margaret (1839–42), James (1841–1929), William (1842–3), William (b. 1843), Phoebe (1846–1918), Alice (1851–1925).

35   *Vestiges*, p. 8.

36   Ibid., pp. 11–12, quoting (with slight modifications) from John F.W. Herschel, *A Treatise on Astronomy* (London: Longman, Brown, Green and Longmans, 1830), p. 264. See the suggestive comments on this passage in Gillian Beer, *Darwin's Plots: Evolutionary Narrative in Darwin, George Eliot and Nineteenth-Century Fiction* (London: Routledge and Kegan Paul, 1983), p. 169.

37   Nichol, *Architecture*, pp. 194, 195.

38   *Vestiges*, p. 223.

39   Ibid., pp. 233–5. Because Chambers had prepared his readers so well, criticisms like those of Sedgwick tended to misfire.

40   Chambers to Combe, 17 Dec 1840, NLS, MS. 7254, fos. 1–6.

41   R.C. Lehmann, *Memories of Half a Century* (London: Smith, Elder, and Co., 1908), p. 7, quoting memoirs of Frederick Lehman, who married one of Chambers' daughters in 1852.

42   James R. Moore, 'Darwin of Down: The Evolutionist as Squarson-Naturalist', in David Kohn, ed., *The Darwinian Heritage* (Princeton, N.J.: Princeton University Press, 1985), pp. 435–81.

43   A.O. Lovejoy goes to the opposite extreme, making Chambers *successful* on what are essentially Darwin's terms. See Lovejoy, 'The Argument for Organic Evolution before the *Origin of Species*, 1830–1858', in Bentley Glass, Owsei Temkin and William L. Strauss, Jr, eds, *Forerunners of Darwin: 1745–1859* (Baltimore, Md.: Johns Hopkins Press, 1959), pp. 356–414. The dangers of these kinds of approaches were pointed out long ago in Hodge, 'Universal Gestation'.

44   A. Sedgwick to M. Napier, 10 April 1845, in Macvey Napier, ed., *Selections from the Correspondence of the Late Macvey Napier* (London: Macmillan, 1879), p. 492; [Thomas Henry Huxley], 'The Vestiges of Creation', *British and Foreign Medico-Chirurgical Review*, 13 (1854), 425–39 (438).

Gillian Beer

DARWIN'S IMAGINATION

Darwin's Plots: Evolutionary Narrative in Darwin, George Eliot and Nineteenth Century Fiction (Cambridge: Cambridge University Press, 2000 [1983]), 114–21.

Like so much of recent Victorian Studies, the study of Victorian science has been distinguished by its interdisciplinary ethos. Some important work has been done by figures in Literature, represented here by an extract from **Gillian Beer**'s extremely influential *Darwin's Plots*. Beer not only traces the impact of scientific discoveries on fiction (particularly George Eliot and Thomas Hardy) in the wake of the publication of *The Origin of Species* (1859), but employs the techniques of literary criticism to understand how science is itself a creative act that is structured by linguistic and cultural codes. Working in the context of literary debates about post-structuralism and the New Historicism, Gillian Beer undertook a study of Darwin's imagination. She explores Darwin's use of metaphor and allusion and his relationship to earlier stories and myths. His was a literary sensibility (he carried a copy of Milton with him on *The Beagle*) and Beer's investigation reveals Darwin as an artist, while respecting his credentials as a scientist. She does not argue that he simply 'made up' evolution, but that he developed his thesis employing the fictive elements that were common in the culture; she demonstrates that they were partly derived from Romanticism's structure of feeling. This view of Darwin as artist provides a major new insight and an opportunity for dialogue between science and literature. The following short extract reveals Beer's working method and her interpretation of Darwin in terms of the myths, story types and metaphors that were in circulation in Victorian Britain. Here she focuses on images of growth and abundance that helped create the 'Darwinian Romance'.

Dame Gillian Beer, Professor Emeritus at the University of Cambridge, is currently completing a study of Lewis Carroll's 'Alice' books in the context of Victorian intellectual controversies. She is also writing a number of essays on rhyming.

DARWIN'S THEORIES, with their emphasis on superabundance and extreme fecundity, reached out towards the grotesque. Nature was seen less as husbanding than as spending. Hyperproductivity authenticated the fantastic. In the following argument I shall illustrate some of the ways in which works of fantasy in the Victorian period fastened on problems *within* Darwinian ideas or on problems *revealed by* evolutionary theory in relation to older world orders. Writers could expand areas of difficulty while remaining secure within the provisionality of fantasy.

In *Orlando* (1928) Virginia Woolf characterises the Victorian age by rank profusion, prodigious growth, as well as by fulminating clouds: in a bravura passage she captures its oppressive fertility. Using hyperbole to mimic hyperbole she suggests the melancholy Romanticism, both rampant and dampened, of Victorian culture. Her memoir writer 'Eusebius Chubb' is overcome by this fertility:

> Innumerable leaves creaked and glistened above his head. He seemed to himself 'to crush the mould of a million more under his feet'. Thick smoke exuded from a damp bonfire at the end of the garden. He reflected that no fire on earth could ever hope to consume that vast vegetable encumbrance. Wherever he looked, vegetation was rampant. Cucumbers 'came scrolloping across the grass to his feet'. Giant cauliflowers towered deck above deck till they rivalled, to his disordered imagination, the elm trees themselves. Hens laid incessantly eggs of no special tint. Then, remembering with a sigh his own fecundity and his poor wife Jane, now in the throes of her fifteenth confinement indoors, how, he asked himself, could he blame the fowls?

Thus, she comments, 'through this alarming fertility' the British Empire came into existence 'for twins abounded'; 'and thus . . . sentences swelled, adjectives multiplied, lyrics became epics, and little trifles that had been essays a column long were now encyclopaedias in ten or twenty volumes'.[1] Darwin's 300-page *The Origin of Species,* as 'abstract' for his longer work, appears in this light as a triumph of compression.

The lush and menacing superfecundity of the earth and of living beings could appal as much as reassure. The argument about measure and the unmeasured is crucial to Victorian sensibility.

R.H. Hutton, reviewing Arnold's *Essays in Criticism,* comments on Arnold's love of measure, and contrasts it with 'that rampancy of insatiable unmeasured longing with which the intellect stands on no terms'. Darwin's theory of development depended to a large extent upon that 'rampancy of insatiable unmeasured longing', on the unassuageable passion of the sexes for each other, on the vigour of survival, on the profusion of production and on the insurgency of growth. To that extent his is a daemonic theory, emphasising drive, deviance and the will to power. It is not a theory which readily accords with ideas of measure or reason.

Tennyson was dismayed by the same problem:

> An omnipotent Creator who could make such a painful world is to me sometimes as hard to believe in as blind matter behind everything. The lavish profusion too in the natural world appals me, from the growths of the tropical forest to the capacity of man to multiply, the torrent of babies.[2]

To Darwin, in contrast, the tropical forest was the fullest type of natural beauty and the 'torrent of babies' simply a part of the general fructifying capacities of the natural order.

Whereas Malthus sought to curb and curtail human hyperproductivity, Darwin speaks of 'slow-breeding man'. In Kingsley's *The Water Babies* the shoals of babies are all the neglected, the unwanted, the superfluous, for which society found no love or use. They have returned to a foetal existence in the sea, relishing an oceanic abundance, as well as being chastened by the two moralistic sisters, the voluptuously maternal Mrs Doasyouwouldbedoneby and the hard-witted and censorious Mrs Bedonebyasyoudid.

Kingsley emphasised the fullness of the deeps, the play of life beyond use or number.[3] The terms of his allegory raise by implication a curious question present also in Darwin's theories. When did sexual distinction enter the economy of life?

In Darwin's own account of the primordial ancestor we hear always of 'one parent', an ungendered progenitor closely approximated to 'Nature'. His account of change and development (of the out-flaring and continuity of life on the earth, as well as its extinction) is an account of procreative energies. Indeed, evolutionary process relies on sexual division. But he never until *The Descent of Man* greatly emphasised sexual drive and choice. It is true that in chapter IV of *The Origin* he discusses sexual selection, which he describes as 'a struggle between the males for possession of the females' and of females (as in the case of bantams) 'selecting, during thousands of generations, the most melodious or beautiful males' (136–7). But the discussion occupies only two pages in a major account of natural selection to which at this stage in his thinking, he clearly gives prime importance. So the emphasis in Darwin's account is always upon productivity rather than on congress; on generation rather than on sexual desire. He is describing an entire economy of nature in which production may take many forms, and he inherits the romantic lyricism of his grandfather's work on *The Loves of the Plants,* without developing it further.[4] Nevertheless, style and theory both are lyrical and effusive, rather than sceptical and parsimonious.

His writing emphasises clutter and profusion. It relies on a nature which surges onward in hectic fecundity, a system both estranged and voluptuous in its relations to humanity. The organism — or the body — becomes the medium of transformation; engendering becomes the means of creating change. The physical is prolonged through generations. In the methodology of life proposed by Darwin, production, growth and decay are all equally needed for the continuance of life on earth.

The realisation that when organic form and life have gone the detritus of life becomes the ballast of the earth appealed to many Victorian writers as it had to Erasmus Darwin. Instead of the *memento mori* of the seventeenth-century skull, the geologist's hammer uncovers the surviving forms of the past. G.H. Lewes in *Studies in Animal Life* (London 1862) contrives to find reassurance in this image:

> Our very mother-earth is formed of the debris of life. Plants and animals which have been, build up its solid fabric. Ages ago these tiny architects secreted the tiny shells, which were their palaces; from the ruins of these palaces were built our Parthenons, our St Peters and our Louvres. So revolves the luminous orb of Life! Generations follow generations; and the Present becomes the matrix of the Future, as the Past was of the Present; the Life of one epoch forming the Prelude to a higher Life.[5]

This rather grandiose reading of the death cycle (all marble, no clunch) reinforces itself with Vico's image of cycle and spiral — an upward series of revolutions.

Exact responses and discrete relationships are necessary to the survival of the individual, for the continuance of the species, and even more for its adaptation to new conditions. But superabundance and waste are the primary conditions of such survival, and diversity is the medium of development. Darwin shared with Mill an emphasis on the creativity of *diversity*. Mill cites Darwin's much-loved Wilhelm von Humboldt at the beginning of *On Liberty*: 'The grand leading principle . . . is the absolute and essential importance of human development in its richest diversity.'[6] Remove the word 'human' and you have Darwin's enlarged and salient emphasis too.

The value of diversity is the new emphasis enforced by Darwin's thinking. Praise of hyperproductivity goes back much further. In Bernard Silvester's *Cosmographia* in the twelfth century, for example, we find:

> Cum morte invicti pugnant genialibus armis,
> naturam reparant perpetuantque genus.
> Non mortale mori, non quod cadit esse caducum,
> non a stirpe hominem deperiisse sinunt.

> (The unconquerable armies of procreation fight with death, renew nature, and perpetuate the species. They do not permit what is dying to die, what is falling to fall, nor do they allow mankind to perish from its stalk.)[7]

When Spenser described the Garden of Adonis in the third Book of *The Faerie Queene* he offered a world of cycle and of endless renewal: all plants, flowers, living beings pass forth out of the garden and 'returne backe' by the hinder gate. They take part in a replenishing cycle of fecundity:

> Infinite shapes of creatures there are bred,
> And uncouth formes, which none yet ever knew,
> And every sort is in a sundry bed
> Set by it selfe, and ranckt in comely rew:

> Some fit for reasonable soules t'indew,
> Some made for beasts, some made for birds to weare,
> And all the fruitfull spawne of fishes hew
> In endlesse rancks along enraunged were,
> That seem'd the *Ocean* could not containe them there.[8]

Yet the stock is never lessened 'but still remaines in everlasting store,/ As it at first created was of yore'.

Despite the cyclic nature of life, time in Spenser implies nihilistic destruction, because it implies the destruction of the individual. But in the Mutabilitie cantos he moves further towards the centre of the problem: Adonis is 'eterne in mutabilitie', and 'by succession made perpetuall'. Nature says that 'all things'

> by their change their being doe dilate;
> And turning to themselves at length againe,
> Doe worke their own perfection so by fate.[9]

Things through desire of change find constantly their own perfected form.

Mutability, to be bearable, must not include the idea of irreversible mutation. That was the new fear which natural selection enforced. In cycle or flux things may rediscover a persisting form, but not in mutation. In any transferred reading of evolutionary theory in human terms individualism is set under a new and almost intolerable tension by Darwin's emphasis on variability. All deviation, each individual, is potentially valuable as bearing the possibility of mutation and change. Yet many must founder and be squandered, leaving no mark nor consequence. At best, they may be recuperated as part of the unhistoric past: 'and that things are not so ill with you and me as they might have been, is half owing to the number who lived faithfully a hidden life, and rest in unvisited tombs'. (*Middlemarch*, Finale)

Evolutionary theory implied a new myth of the past: instead of the garden at the beginning, there was the sea and the swamp. Instead of man, emptiness — or the empire of molluscs. There was no way back to a previous paradise: the primordial was comfortless. Instead of fixed and perfect species, it showed forms in flux, and the earth in constant motion, drawing continents apart. This consciousness of the fluent, of the physical world as endless onward process, extended to an often pained awareness of human beings as slight elements within unstoppable motion and transformation. Nostalgia was disallowed, since no unrecapturable perfection preceded man's history. Ascent was also flight — a flight from the primitive and the barbaric which could never quite be left behind.

Further reading

For further discussion of *Darwin's Plots*, see Jenny Bourne Taylor, Harriet Ritvo and Gillian Beer, 'Roundtable on *Darwin's Plots*', *Journal of Victorian Culture*, 5 (2000), 129–45. Other studies in Victorian science and literature include James Paradis and Thomas Postlewait (eds), *Victorian Science and Victorian Values: Literary Perspectives* (New Brunswick, NJ: Rutgers University Press, 1981); Sally

Shuttleworth, *George Eliot and Nineteenth Century Science: The Make Believe of a Beginning* (Cambridge: Cambridge University Press, 1984); George Levine, *Darwin and the Novelists: Patterns of Science in Victorian Fiction* (Cambridge, MA: Harvard University Press, 1988); Gillian Beer, *Open Fields: Science in Cultural Encounter* (Oxford: Oxford University Press, 1996); Rebecca Stott, *Darwin and the Barnacle* (London: Faber, 2003).

Notes

1   *Orlando* (London, 1928): 208.
2   Hallam Tennyson, *Alfred Lord Tennyson* (London, 1897) 1:314.
3   See *Glaucus; or, The Wonders of the Shore* (London, 1855). The fashion for marine biology, recorded also in G.H. Lewes's *Seaside Studies* (London 1859) and George Eliot's Ilfracombe Journals owed much to the work of the naturalist Philip Gosse. See for example, *The Romance of Natural History* (1st and 2nd series) (London: 1860–1) with its emphasis on 'the emotions of the human mind, — surprise, wonder, terror, revulsion, admiration, love, desire . . . — which are made energetic by the contemplation of the creatures around him'. *Omphalos: An Attempt to Untie the Geological Knot* (London, 1857) set Gosse at odds with Kingsley. See Edmund Gosse, *Father and Son* (London, 1907) for the most authentic account of the relations between geology, biology and theology.
4   Erasmus Darwin, *The Loves of the Plants* (Lichfield, 1789–90). The running head for *The Temple of Nature* (London, 1803) was its subtitle 'The Origin of Society'. Darwin's title almost certainly alludes to his grandfather's, whose unashamed anthropomorphism envigorates his natural history. He emphasises profusion and destruction equally: 'the thick ranks of vegetable war' (41); 'births unnumber'd, ere the parents die,/ The hourly waste of lovely life supply' (341).
5   G.H. Lewes, *Studies in Animal Life* (London, 1862).
6   'During my last year at Cambridge I read with care and profound interest Humboldt's Personal Narrative. This work . . . stirred up in me a burning zeal to add even the most humble contribution to the noble structure of Natural life Science' (*Autobiography*: 38).
7   Cited in Brian Stock, *Myth and Science in the Twelfth Century: A Study of Bernard Silvester* (Princeton, 1972): 217–18. *Cosmographia* 2:14:162–5.
8   Edmund Spenser, *The Faerie Queene*, ed. J.C. Smith (Books 1–3) (Oxford, 1909): 428. First published 1590.
9   Spenser, *The Faerie Queene*, ed. Smith (Books 4–7): 455.

Chapter 19

Alison Winter

SCIENCE AND POPULAR CULTURE

Mesmerized: Powers of Mind in Victorian Britain (Chicago, IL: University of Chicago Press, 1998), 73–6, 81–93, 95–100.

Much recent research has been devoted to (so-called) pseudo-science, to the false starts in scientific work. This takes in the world of phrenology, quack medicine, spiritualism and herbalism, as well as discredited notions of racial science and eugenics. Victorian science has thus come to be viewed in a broader context and as something that was imagined within the contexts and needs of the prevailing culture. Perhaps the best example of this tendency is **Alison Winter**'s *Mesmerized* (1998), a rich study in cultural history that revives our interest in a neglected science that she never patronises but recovers in its complexity.

Mesmerism takes its name from the eighteenth-century German scientist, Franz Anton Mesmer, who drew on Newton to contend that a fluid existed in human beings that was linked to a void or spirit in the universe and that the fluid could link one person with an another. This invisible bodily fluid could be manipulated through magnetism or the touch of a trained practitioner; hence the process was known as Animal Magnetism (or 'mesmerism'). Discredited in France, mesmerism was briefly an object of interest in Britain in the 1780s but was then revived in early Victorian Britain as a form of fringe medicine that was regarded with suspicion by the medical establishment. At mesmeric séances or demonstrations, people became subject to fits and convulsions or entered trances that allowed them to act or speak in ways that they would not normally do, or to accept large amounts of pain without complaint. By allegedly restoring bodily harmony, it seemed to offer not only the possibility of new forms of medical treatment but also access to the universe in a deeper way and a new form of living. Mind could triumph over matter. Mesmerism has been seen in retrospect as an early attempt to explore hypnotism, spiritualism and what (after Freud) would be known as 'the unconscious', although Winter prefers the less anachronistic term 'altered states' to describe its effects. The Victorian revival of British mesmerism was led by the French physician, Baron Dupotet. In the following extract, Winter deals with Dupotet's English follower, Professor John Elliotson of University College London. Elliotson was a distinguished doctor who, among other accomplishments, was the first person to link hay fever with the weather and helped introduce the use of the stethoscope in England. In the 1830s he experimented with magnetic sleep by placing his patients in a trance in order to relieve illness (particularly epilepsy and hysteria). He believed that mesmerism could rid the world, not only of many illnesses, but also of crime hence producing a moral regeneration of society. The experiments turned Elliotson into a celebrity but, as Winter shows, accusations of deception led to his resignation from University College Hospital in 1838 (although this did not prevent him from continuing with mesmeric research). Notice how Winter uses ideas about class, millenarianism (belief in the second coming of Jesus Christ), theatricality and carnival to explain the extraordinary case of the O'Key sisters. Hers is also a form of medical history in which the patient matters as much as the doctor. At stake in this episode were both the cultural authority of the hospital as an institution and the notion of medical expertise.

In this Reading Winter explores the cultural resources the O'Key sisters might have called upon in constructing their mesmeric responses. Elizabeth and Jane O'Key were domestic servants aged sixteen and fifteen; they served as experimental subjects for Elliotson for eighteen months, residing during that time at University College Hospital. Contemporary medical theory saw the working class as the best subjects for study and experimentation as they were believed to have a weaker sense of self and to be closer to the primitive nature of man. In Elliotson's public experiments (often in scientific theatres that would also be used for surgical procedures) both sisters emerged from their usually servile demeanours and became cheeky, playful and demanding. In due course they were revealed to be fraudsters and for years to come their name remained shorthand in the medical profession for charismatic deceivers.

Alison Winter is Associate Professor of History at the University of Chicago. She is currently working on two projects relating to the cultural history of intellectual life since 1800. One is a study of the history of sciences of memory in America and Britain since the late nineteenth century. The other examines the representation of musical performance, and particularly the role of the orchestral conductor, in nineteenth-century Britain and Europe.

The mesmeric stage

O N 10 M A Y, [*John*] Elliotson held a nationally publicized demonstration in [*University College London*] hospital's theater. This was its architectural and intellectual center, scene of its most important and prestigious activities. Bringing a patient from the peripheral wards to this place announced the importance of the vicissitudes of her body and mind. Jeremy Bentham's corpse had been dissected here; Robert Grant's lectures on comparative anatomy were delivered to students in these banks of seats; the knife of the master of the surgical stage, Robert Liston, did its speedy work at its wooden table. [. . .] Audiences were placed in concentric semicircles to encourage the closest attention to the action on the stage, and the small size of the platform, coupled with the steep pitch of the rows of seats, placed observers within a few feet of the performers.

Among the hundreds who pressed into the theater's insufficient sitting room were several elite intellectual and medical figures, several members of Parliament, trustees on the UCL board, and prominent aristocratic figures.[1] Some of them, such as Dickens, Cruikshank, and Faraday, had been privy to Elliotson's private demonstrations. As for the rest, this was probably the first occasion on which they had assembled with the specific purpose of attending to the words and actions of a young working-class girl.

Elliotson chose only his most reliable and dramatic subject, Elizabeth O'Key, for this first public show. When she was carried on stage, she was already deep in the calm, sleeplike stage of the magnetic trance. With a few passes Elliotson brought her into the special state of "sleep-waking," or the artificial delirium, in which the magnetic phenomena appeared. At this point, according to the *Lancet,* her "dull and hippocratic" countenance changed to one of "mingled archness and simplicity." The most "accomplished actor that ever trod the stage," it concluded, "could not have presented the change with a truer show of reality."[2]

The delirium once established, O'Key displayed a number of striking phenomena. The ones that most impressed the *Lancet* were forms of "traction," produced when bodily movements by Elliotson and his assistant were made outside her field of vision. She echoed them in her own arms, legs, and face. At one point, "[t]he hands of the patient were then clasped, and she was told to keep them together, when the Doctor, from behind her, spread his arms, and, pointing to each elbow, drew his hands outwards and backwards from the body of the girl, who certainly did not see the process. After a few of these motions her arms attempted to follow, but the hands were firmly clasped. Gradually, however, her arms straightened, and the ends of her fingers, in keeping their hold, dug into the back of each hand."[3] As her hands moved apart, her "countenance [indicated] the greatest effort to prevent [their] separation." She even cried out, "[D]on't you; oh don't; pray don't," suggesting an opposition of body and mind that could only have heightened the drama of the situation.

O'Key's entranced mind contributed to the display in other ways, too. She directly engaged members of the audience in conversation and regaled them with jokes and songs — the latter despite Elliotson's instructions to the contrary.[4] Her interlocutors also included inanimate objects and parts of the body: boots, a wooden board, and her own hands. In the course of one experiment, a "mill board was . . . placed before her face for some experiment." She surprised the doctors by admonishing it. "Oh, you nasty boy," she said, "What a dirty black fellow you are."[5] However inexplicable this behavior may appear, the mesmeric literature did provide an explanation. French mesmerists had documented a phenomenon known as "transposition of the senses." During the magnetic trance, the action of certain sense organs would be displaced to other parts of the body. At times O'Key appeared to see or to hear with inappropriate bodily parts — the back of her hand, for instance, or her stomach. Confusing inanimate objects for people could be seen as a variation of a phenomenon involving changes in the geography of sensation, the difference being that this effect involved shifts in the object of sight and hearing, rather than the organ that perceived the object.[6] Accordingly, everything O'Key said and did was meticulously documented in the hope that it might be traced to the appropriate physiological cause.

Elliotson's ambition was not merely to develop plausible narrative explanations of these behaviors, but to use individual cases as a foundation for a quantitative science. At the end of the demonstration, he gave a preliminary example of how one might begin to quantify apparently qualitative effects, by counting the number of passes that were required to move his patient from one stage of the mesmeric phenomena to the next. Elliotson concluded that, eventually, one could calibrate the influence of "'mass.' or 'surface,' and in 'numbers'" by studying the relative contributions to the effects of the mass and the exposed surface area of the magnetizer's hand. This speculation was offered as a promissory note for future demonstrations. As Elliotson brought the demonstration to a close, he made it clear that this was just the beginning of what animal magnetism could do.

The public debut of Elliotson's "new science" would seem to have been a great success.[7] The only problem was that at the moment when everyone expected O'Key would awaken, Elliotson found that he could not rouse her. Some awkward moments passed for an audience who, after sitting still for hours, knew they could not leave their seats until the star performer had left the stage. All the ordinary means failed, until, in an unprecedented development, Elliotson asked his clinical clerk, Mr. Wood, to ask O'Key herself when she would awaken and what needed to be done to accomplish this. She replied that she would come awake

"In five minutes."
"Shall you awaken yourself?" — "No."
"How then?" — "You must wake me."
"In what way?" — "By rubbing my neck."[8]

Elliotson himself carried out this procedure but to no effect. The orders had been given to Wood, and only when *he* obeyed them did she emerge from the trance. This was the most dramatic obstacle that the entranced O'Key placed in Elliotson's way. As we shall see, it foreshadowed other, more spectacular actions.

When O'Key did awaken, she was transformed. The mischievous, playful, authoritative mesmeric subject was replaced by a shy servant girl. "No two manners," reported the *Lancet,* could have differed more than "her deportment now and that which she presented during the 'delirium.'" She had been strong and outgoing during the trance; now she was "downcast and reserved." She had been lively and playful; now she showed signs of "fatigue." As she left, the "throng of persons opened to let her pass," and "many gentlemen, won by her apparent amiability, shook hands with her." O'Key acknowledged their compliment "engagingly" with a "slight curtesy, seemingly greatly wearied, depressed, and much abashed at her situation."[9]

Modern readers may find it surprising that these events were recorded by the leading medical journal of the day as pathbreaking new medical discoveries. Many will find the mesmeric phenomena implausible. Rather than dismissing the London intelligentsia as credulous, however, it is more reasonable to see the divide between our notions of plausibility and theirs as growing out of more general differences between the Victorian period and the late twentieth century. These individuals lived in a world made up of very different mental, physiological, and natural possibilities, and if their skepticism was roused differently, this was not for lack of intelligence or a critical sensibility. [. . .]

The world of Elizabeth O'Key

The notion of the carnivalesque — of the world turned upside down — is a useful starting point for studying the experiments at University College Hospital (UCH), because carnivals traditionally disrupted or even temporarily inverted the social order. They could release tensions between different ranks and provide opportunities to air grievances, though they could also become truly insurrectionist.[10] By the nineteenth century, England did not have anything like the festival of carnival in the southern states of early modern Europe, but fairs and wakes contained some similar elements. On these occasions there was freedom to act out aggressions, abandonment of social restraint, familiarity between strangers, and above all, inversion of the normal rules of the social order, though these elements brought fairs under the criticism that they were demoralizing and subversive influences.[11] Descriptions of disorderly public revelry proliferated through the middle of the century.[12] But the notion of "carnival" is most useful in a looser, less literal sense. It provides a framework for understanding one part of the significance of what was going on during these experiments, and how the relationships among experimenter, experimental subject, and audience were changing over time. [. . .]

[. . .] Is there anything more we can learn about how [*Elizabeth O'Key*] herself understood these events? For those who did not believe that mesmeric subjects were mechanical beings with no intentions of their own, it would indeed seem that O'Key took a very different view of what she was doing on the stage of UCL from the perspective of her doctors and observers. Of course, we have no means of asking her directly, nor even indirectly in the way that historians consult the written records that people of greater means left behind (diaries, correspondence, and the like). But we are not completely without resources. We can reconstruct a number of contexts for O'Key's speech and action, each involving quite different definitions of authoritative public conduct and of theatricality. These will reveal the various ways one could make sense of her so-called nonsense.

Amid the publicity surrounding O'Key's case, there were claims that she was an active participant in apocalyptic forms of evangelical religion, specifically, in Edward Irving's chapel at Islington Green, where premillenarian ecstatics spoke in tongues and predicted the date of the Apocalypse. Whether and to what extent she was involved is difficult to judge. These statements appeared in hostile press reports, whose authors regarded such affiliation as a sign of bad faith or even madness. It would be possible to conclude from descriptions of O'Key's performances either that she was influenced by Irvingite religious practices or that observers merely associated her behavior with the so-called farce of the "unknown tongues."[13] However compromised the evidence may be, the possibility is nevertheless tempting as a way of illuminating O'Key's own sensibilities.

These claims of O'Key's millenarianism are informative regardless of her real religious affiliation. They reveal, for instance, that magnetic phenomena fit a contemporary Anglican representation of sectarianism: individuals laying claim to authority on the basis of their own psychic experiences, behaving with an explicit disregard for social hierarchy, and in so doing, mounting a democratic challenge to established religion. This characterization would fit Dissenters of many kinds, from Evangelicals to Quakers, all of whom had a heightened prominence in the wake of the repeal of religious disabilities legislation. The flurry of published attacks on Dissenters and Catholics, many of them associated with natural-magic literature, usually described mental phenomena and attitudes toward the mind that were to be understood as at best blasphemous and at worst demonic.[14] Whether or not such elaborate parallels were implicit in the attribution of O'Key's millenarianism, one thing is certainly clear: it was easier for skeptical doctors to diagnose O'Key's religious enthusiasm than to decide whether mesmerism itself was real.

What could the trance have meant to O'Key if she were an Irvingite devotee? Premillenarians claimed to pass into states of mind in which divine truths came to them as gifts from God. During these trances they were conduits, conveying this knowledge to other mortals. If O'Key borrowed conventions of authority from premillenarian ecstasy, she would have had a very different understanding from Elliotson of how one obtained knowledge from altered states of mind. These were states that revealed important truths, and they gave the possessed speaker the temporary power to reveal them. In short, the significance of the trance state would have been the *opposite* for O'Key of what it was for Elliotson. For him it was a state of utter submission not only to natural forces but to the mesmerist; for her, it would have offered a state of transient authority over all onlookers. Elliotson saw it as a means of dispelling superstition, and a confirmation of his materialist views. For O'Key, if she were an Irvingite, it would have provided direct knowledge of the will of God.

Another indication that O'Key might have had a supernatural, if not specifically Irvingite, understanding of the trance is that a weekly penny pamphlet circulating in London in 1837 was dominated by stories of supernatural states, influences, and healing powers with mesmeric associations: the king's touch, the evil eye, the cures of the seventeenth-century healer Valentine Greatrakes. [. . .] The series included several articles on mesmerism itself. They did not draw on the quasi-materialism of Elliotson, but on the immaterialist claims of J.C. Colquhoun and the German physiologist Jung-Stilling, both of whom located mesmerism not in the brain but in the immaterial mind and soul.[15] If O'Key or her friends had read such a work, or even glanced at the woodcuts, they would have taken away at least a general sense that mesmerism was an immaterial influence with divine associations.

There is a very different, but equally important, context in which we might understand O'Key's behavior: the theater. Working-class theatergoing involved the accepted notion that not only the official players but also the audience "performed" during the shows. In Covent Garden, working people formed a special section of the audience, and, according to contemporary reports, they rivaled stage actors in their entertainment value. They had their own idiosyncratic repertoire, and there was a regular give-and-take between them and the stage players, who accepted it as part of the show. The "stage" did not stop where the audience began, and it was not clear where "center stage" was, in the dialogues that developed between the "audiences" and the "actors."[16] Someone like O'Key might well have frequented early music halls and free-and-easies, since as many as a tenth of their clientele were younger than fifteen.[17]

During this period changes in the theater reflected shifting class relations. The ordering of seating and ticketing became increasingly hierarchical, marginalizing the plebeian members of the audience. [. . .] During this period the upper classes began to remove themselves entirely from theater like melodrama and pantomime, thus designating these kinds of theater "popular." These changes were part of a much broader and longer-term withdrawal of a self-conscious "elite" from common culture. The riots provoked by the changes in theatrical organization in the early nineteenth century may be seen, in part, as resistance to a denigrating process of distinction. Given the charged status of plebeian theater, it is striking that the UCH performances displayed a similar ambiguity about who was performing and who had authority, among the stage players and between them and the audience. An uninitiated observer would have concluded that the people involved in the UCH performances — the doctors, patients, and members of the audiences — acted according to conflicting views of how one should behave on stage, and where the center of the action lay.

There were more concrete similarities between O'Key's performances and one theatrical form that was becoming especially popular in London theater: pantomime. Pantomime has traditionally been a spectacle of defiance, disrespect, and contradiction, hence its most famous exchange ("Oh no it's not!" "Oh yes it is!"). Contradictions and insults are tossed back and forth in the dialogues of stage players and between them and the audience; the broad humor spares no one. O'Key's speeches on the UCH stage followed this pattern. They challenged the authoritative status of her interlocutors in astonishingly direct ways. Although she was relatively well spoken during her waking states, she uttered "vulgarisms" during the trance, and singled out various members of the audience to address them with "innocent familiarity." On one occasion, she remarked to the marquis of Anglesey, "Oh! How do ye? . . . White Trowsers. Dear! You do look so tidy, you do." She often mocked those around her, including Elliotson himself, telling him he was "silly" and "a fool."[18]

The published records of these speeches are careful to note that she never said such things "in her natural state."[19] Observers' confidence of the "innocence" of O'Key's "familiarity" therefore depended on their confidence in the trance. The following is a specimen exchange: "Dr. Elliotson having assured her that she had been asleep, she replied, 'Oh, Dr. Elliotson, you're mad; you're quite a baby; I haven't been to sleep; I wouldn't go to sleep in daylight; I'm going to make a parson now,' twirling her handkerchief; and before she could be prevented (a prelate and many reverend gentlemen being present) she had twisted it into a head and cassock."[20] O'Key was at liberty to speak crassly and to mock the man who was ostensibly manipulating her every state of mind and sensation, as a madman, a baby, and a fool. No one stepped in to stop her from caricaturing the aristocracy, the clergy, and the law.

The stakes were rising for Elliotson. It would be embarrassing enough to find he had been pursuing a false trail, especially now that he was so much in the public eye. It would be infinitely worse to be branded the dupe of a young servant girl, and to have been so badly deceived as to have solicited personal insults in the spectacular mistake of regarding them as valuable scientific phenomena. The likely implications of such an exposure were conjured up in a mesmeric warning, during the following exchange between Elliotson and his entranced star: "Relieved from [an] . . . experiment she placed her hands in her lap, and, leaning forward, said, with archness and good humour, amid abundant laughter, from the company seated around, which she did not at all notice, 'Poor Dr. Ellisson, would you like some sop, with some milk in it?' — 'No, for then I should be a milk-sop.'"[21] A "milksop" is an effeminate, ineffectual man,[22] and it was a striking term to use in relation to Elliotson himself. He walked a fine line between charismatic fashion and "dandyfication," and was known for his love of the latest fashions more generally: he rode the crest of all trends. First to wear trousers among his London acquaintance, first to dare new chemical treatments, first in the introduction of new instruments like the stethoscope, he cultivated a reputation for being socially and professionally intrepid. He ventured into situations that others shunned as compromising. In this case his risks were higher than ever. If O'Key were to be dismissed as a fraud and Elliotson her dupe, he would not only suffer professionally, but also risked his honor. He would become a milksop, an unmanned man.

The demonstration in which this exchange took place left its audience with another provocative term ringing in their ears. O'Key ended her performance with a song called "Jim Crow." During the 1830s the term "Jim Crow" was first becoming an adjective referring to policies of racial segregation in America. Jim Crow was also a new character in pantomime, and his song was only a few years old.[23] Jim Crow played the fiddle and danced a dazzling, heel-kicking dance [. . .]. This song had arrived in London only in 1836, but already there were several varieties of it, judging from the specimens that have survived in broadside collections. They ranged from the silly to the subversive, and it is striking that the particular version that provided O'Key's jibe involved a very particular kind of foolishness: a world turned upside down. This Jim Crow served up a crazily garbled Bible history. In his version of the Old Testament (or as he called it, his "almanack"),

> . . . Cane was de fust man,
> Juvcome Caesar was de oder,
> Dey put Adam on de treaden mill
> 'Case him kill him broder
>
> And den dat Mr. Sampson
> Was de man who built de ark,
> Mr. Jonas was de fisherman
> Who swallowed down de shark.[24]

As O'Key sang, she stopped in midverse "to ask Dr. Elliotson if *he* had also "come over from Kentucky," like Mr. Crow.[25] If he answered, there is no record of his reply. O'Key then "volunteered to 'wheel about, and turn about,'" but, as the *Lancet* recorded, she was prevented — "to the manifest disappointment of many spectators." UCL was not the only venue where one could hear "Jim Crow." At the Sadler's Wells Theatre across town, a few pennies bought admission to Jefferini's daily pantomime, where this song had become an important part of the act.[26] Hostile reports of the UCH experiments took delight in pointing out the similarity of the two theaters.[27]

O'Key's song and choice of a blackface character are suggestive. She would have been familiar with blackface from shows like Jefferini's; in fact, the novelty of the character and song suggest that she could have referred to them only after seeing the show or hearing a description of it from someone who had. Both blackface and "negro" entertainers performed in the metropolis during the early Victorian period. These performers straddled the domestic and the exotic, the authentic and the fraudulent. The Jim Crow blackface characters were soon followed by "nigger" minstrels, whose popular performances were constantly appraised for their "authenticity" as specimens of "negro" or "African" culture [. . .]. Popular caricatures supplied comical and dismissive representations of "Black" practices [. . .]; at the same time, reports also evaluated the extent to which these performers attained European ideals of dress, manners, and artistic performance.[28] The "truly" black minstrels had to strike what may have been an impossible balance between a performance that could be judged to be "truly" exotic and one that displayed an ability to meet European aesthetic expectations. Blackface, on the other hand, connoted foolishness, alienness, or inequality, depending on the mode of performance. Such a character could therefore be translated from one form of inequality (race) to another (class and gender) in a tailor-made spectacle of disrespect.

A nexus of racial difference and authority also figured in the sisters' explanation of how their extraordinary knowledge came to them. It involved a mysterious intermediary. They did not have direct sensory knowledge of future events, but learned of them from a spirit: their "Negro." He made his first appearance in mid-May when Jane O'Key fell ill. She reported on 14 May that a spirit of this name had told her during a recent experiment "that the attack in her side was a swelling, in consequence of her ribs being strained . . . in lifting weights." A fortnight later, Elliotson's assistant described a number of premonitions of Elizabeth O'Key, in which her "Negro" accurately predicted the timing, duration, and content of her delirium.[29] The following is a published account of a dialogue between O'Key and a house surgeon, in which she relayed instructions from this spirit for her treatment:

> Mr. Wood said to her, in the usual whisper,
> "O'Key, how do you do?"
> "I have violent pains in my head, and you will soon have to do something for it."
> "What is to be done?"
> "You will have to bleed me."
> "When?" (It was now about half-past five o'clock, P.M., Wednesday.)
> "I shall have this pain for twelve hours, and then it will be very violent, and I should be bled to stop it."[30]

The relation the "Negro" bore to the O'Key sisters paralleled their relation to medical observers. Both stood outside the social order, more knowledgeable yet less powerful than the observer to whom they conveyed information. This symmetry lends itself to the idea that the attributes of alienness and comparative weakness equipped one for being a medium or vehicle for the transmission of knowledge from somewhere else into a world to which one was only liminally connected.

I have discussed the religious and theatrical contexts for Elizabeth O'Key's behavior in the hope that they will illuminate the differences between her perceptions and those of her several audiences, and show how these differences rendered the interpretative context of the experimental trials increasingly unstable as the summer wore on. Whether or not the reports of O'Key's Irvingite past were true, they, along with the resonance between O'Key's behavior and popular theater, made it increasingly easy to construct accounts of her that differed from Elliotson's. As we shall see below, some accounts painted O'Key as a stereotypical prophetess, seductress, or actress. She turned the hospital around her into a chapel, a brothel, or a music hall. And her audiences became increasingly divided as to whether she was a physiological effect, a supernatural phenomenon, or a fraud. [. . .]

The collapse of Elliotson's project

During July and August, claims of mesmerism's fraudulence intensified. At the same time, people were beginning to ask about Elliotson's own mental state. To the most cynical skeptics, the mesmeric carnival had now turned the medical world completely upside down: Elizabeth O'Key was completely sane and sober; Elliotson, on the other hand, had developed a peculiar mental state in which his every professional thought was controlled by her. Ironically, those onlookers who thought O'Key was a fraud did believe her when she pronounced "Dr. Ellisson" a "fool."

The tide of medical opinion turned in mid-August, when Thomas Wakley staged a spectacular discreditation. Initially, Wakley had thrown the weight of his journal behind Elliotson's experiments, in part because he hoped they would make medicine more scientific and give doctors more authority. As the demonstrations progressed, however, it became clear that he thought animal magnetism produced the opposite of the quiescent, deferential patient of reformist medicine. The subjects, and possibly the would-be science that studied them, could not be controlled.

The fourth *Lancet* report, published in July 1838, warned that the phenomena "are not absolute, or certain." A number of mesmeric subjects — Ann Ross, Charlotte Bentley, and a few unnamed others — had confessed to pretending the mesmeric effects. While they did not have, individually, the significance of either of the O'Key sisters, a case of fraud necessarily raised questions about the whole enterprise.[31] It suggested that Elliotson was not fully in control of his experiments. The fifth report openly declared the *Lancet*'s suspicions. "A careful watching" of O'Key's "*character*" must be attempted, it warned, in order to ascertain whether her behavior was real. The journal apologized for not yet coming to a firm conclusion, but said that the character of the proceedings had made this impossible so far. The direction the trials had taken was frustrating because, it complained, "careful observers of facts" require "more exact and well-authenticated evidences" — that is, evidences for or against the O'Keys' authenticity. This was tantamount to claiming that Elliotson was incapable of controlling the experimental environment and enforcing the proper relationship between doctor and patient. The report refrained from dismissing the phenomena only because of their potentially enormous significance for that most important "department of medicine — the field of physiology."[32]

The matter was settled decisively when Elliotson agreed to bring the O'Key sisters to Thomas Wakley's home in Bedford Square for experiments. A trial was convened, its jury drawn (of course) from Elliotson's peers rather than the O'Keys'.

The girls would be judged by ten gentlemen, five chosen by Wakley and five by Elliotson. The state of forensic medicine at this time gave the arrangements a special significance. Wakley, Elliotson, and many of their reformist friends were deeply involved in establishing the field of medical jurisprudence. Their efforts relied upon, and in their turn encouraged, a public acceptance of doctors as expert, trustworthy authorities, at a time when the profession was in poor esteem. [. . .] When the passage of the controversial Medical Witnesses Act in 1836 gave doctors a new authoritative role in the courtroom, one might have imagined that it would make doctors less controversial as public arbitrators. Instead, public scrutiny of medical judgment intensified. The trials of animal magnetism therefore took place in a climate in which doctors, as much as the phenomena they were studying, were on trial in the public eye.

Before proceeding with the events of the "trial" itself, a brief word about the venue is in order. Wakley's house in Bedford Square, near the *Lancet*'s office, on the edge of a large constituency he wished to represent in Parliament, was the seat of powerful work in journalism and in politics.[33] Everything that happened there concerned medicine in some way, but Wakley would never have used his home for medical research or the training of students. The proper place for this was the hospital. He and his circle insisted, in the strongest terms, on its primacy in the making of medical knowledge. The medical school at UCH, especially, stood for a professionalizing shift away from an older patronage system, in which doctors had been taught by apprenticeship and studied illnesses in the homes of the ill. Hospitals made doctors into professionals and sick people into patients. Why, then, remove a patient from the wards? Because Wakley had already decided that O'Key was a fraud. She was not a proper hospital patient or a scientific apparatus. She was merely an impudent servant. There was no more appropriate place for her discipline than the parlor; no more appropriate parlor than one in a house that had become the hub of medical reform. In this context, a successful trial would be one that failed.[34]

On 16 August Elliotson brought Elizabeth and Jane O'Key to Wakley's home to test the mesmeric phenomena. Among these, there was one particularly contentious category of effects that on this occasion became a sort of "experimentum crucis." Recall that Elliotson wished to prove the physical character of the mesmeric influence in the same manner that other researchers were tracing the characteristics of electricity and magnetism, namely, by studying which minerals and metals conducted or resisted animal magnetism. Elliotson had accumulated a list of substances that could receive the mesmeric influence and then dispense it (water, for instance, could be mesmerized, and then entrance the individual who drank it). Of metals, nickel was thought to be receptive to the influence; lead was not. If Elliotson carried his point, he would have gone a long way to proving the reality of a physical force as the foundation of the effects. This line of research had been taken fifty years before, by a commission appointed by the Académie de Médecine in the 1780s (and composed of luminaries such as Antoine Lavoisier and Benjamin Franklin). The prestigious commission tested mesmerized water and mesmerized metals but could detect no sign of magnetism on their instruments. They then tricked patients into believing that they were being magnetized, at which point the patients duly displayed mesmeric effects. The commission concluded that the mesmeric effects were real, but that they were the result of the patients' imagination, rather than of any physical agent.[35]

Wakley's investigation followed the same pattern. Elizabeth O'Key and her sister were tested several times with mesmerized nickel and mesmerized lead. Elliotson and Wakley agreed that there were no definitive results. Then, unbeknownst to Elliotson, Wakley took aside a third party, James Fernandez Clarke, Wakley's deputy on the *Lancet* and author of some of the reports on animal magnetism. He had attended the trial at Elliotson's request, as one of his chosen witnesses. Wakley gave Clarke a sample of nickel that Elliotson had mesmerized, and told him to take it to the far end of the room while Wakley tested the effects of lead. He then approached O'Key with the lead, without identifying either to her or to Elliotson what kind of metal he was holding. By previous arrangement another bystander told him in a stage whisper not to "apply the nickel too strongly." He then applied the lead (which should have had negligible effects) to O'Key's skin. The results were dramatic: "Scarcely had these words escaped from his lips, when the face of the girl . . . became violently red; her eyes were fixed with an intense squint, she fell back in the chair, a more evident distortion of the body ensued than in the previous paroxysm, the contractions of the voluntary muscles were more strongly marked, producing a striking rigidity of the frame and limbs."[36] When Elliotson learned of the trick, he insisted on several more trials. All of them convinced Wakley of the absence of true effect; none of them convinced Elliotson. In each case, he claimed, the experiment had been compromised. Wakley had no such reservations.

Some historians have faulted the observers for not considering the possibility of "suggestion," in the modern sense of a physical response caused by anticipation. But such causal explanations did not exist at the time.[37] In fact, they came into being in consequence of experiments like this one, over the course of the next several decades. Even though the eighteenth-century committee of the Académie des Sciences had attributed mesmeric effects to the imagination rather than to fraud, this possibility was not considered in the 1830s debates. And if it had been, it probably would not have seemed to confer scientific reality to mesmeric phenomena. The significance of "imagination" as a legitimate cause of natural phenomena did not exist during the eighteenth-century trials (their conclusions amounted to a dismissal), and it was only now beginning to emerge. Witnesses had to choose between a capriciously acting physical force and a deceitful servant. Everyone present, with the outraged exception of Elliotson, found it easy to choose the latter.

The jury did not render a verdict only on O'Key but also on Elliotson. By the time the *Lancet*'s report of the "trial" appeared, Wakley announced that he had invited Elliotson to Bedford Square not to test "the reality of the phenomena displayed" but to demonstrate the phenomena before his colleagues and to examine "the real opinions of the Doctor."[38] Wakley claimed (in retrospect) that he was sure of O'Key's fraudulence before the test. The only remaining question was the state of mind of her doctor. Elliotson, not O'Key, was the real experimental subject. Wakley therefore deceived O'Key, whom he believed to be deceptive, and Elliotson, whom he suspected of being gullible to deception. The fact that Wakley's most convincing results came from deceiving Elliotson, as well as O'Key, implied that Elliotson was not capable of keeping his thoughts from her.

To Wakley's fury, Elliotson continued his work throughout the autumn. Matters reached a crisis in December with reports that the mesmerized O'Key had been taken through the male wards to diagnose patients. The *Lancet* reporter seemed particularly distraught that her visit took place "during the twilight hours" — an especially compromising time of day, it would seem, for a young clairvoyant to gaze upon the innards of a dying man. According to the report, she passed the beds one by one, when suddenly she cried out fearfully that she could see "Great Jackie," the angel of death, hovering over a bed. "Little Jackie" it seemed, could be seen above another patient. The first man died in the night, and the second had declined markedly by morning. The episode triggered furious disputes about the connection between O'Key and the fate of the two men. The calmest critics pointed out that O'Key could easily have identified likely candidates for the attentions of "Great Jackie" and "Little Jackie." But there was also talk that O'Key was possessed, and that the shock of hearing these pronouncements had killed one man outright and caused the "sinking" of another. Elliotson's explanation was to reiterate that the magnetic states made the senses "preternaturally acute." Morbid emanations informed her of their state of health, and she had expressed this knowledge by presenting herself with a sign of death that made sense to her.

The council decided that the best course was to expel Elizabeth O'Key and the other magnetic subjects. Elliotson submitted a letter of resignation in protest, hoping that pressure from the medical students would force the council to reinstate him. This seems to have been a possibility, because a majority vote by the student body urged the council to reject the letter, but moments before they read the results of the vote, they accepted his resignation.[39] If the long-term effects of the guilty verdict in Wakley's trial worked to the detriment of Elliotson and O'Key, they consolidated Wakley's authority. He was complimented by a wide spectrum of the London medical community, drawing grudging congratulations even from the rival journals. It is noteworthy, perhaps, that some months after his nationally publicized magnetic "trial," Wakley became coroner for Middlesex, securing his status as a power in the courts.[40]

Further reading

Other works on the impact of mesmerism in England include: Jonathan Miller, 'A Gower Street Scandal', *Journal of the Royal College of Physicians of London* 17(4) (1983), 179–91; Roy Porter, '"Under the Influence": Mesmerism in England', *History Today* 35 (September 1985), 22–9. Daniel Pick's *Svengali's Web: The Alien Enchanter in Modern Culture* (New Haven, CT: Yale University Press, 2000) considers the significance of mesmerism in European culture among other subjects. Literary dimensions of mesmerism are explored in: Martin Willis, *Mesmerists, Monsters and Machines: Science Fiction and the Cultures of Science in the Nineteenth Century* (Kent, OH: Kent State University Press, 2006); and Martin Willis and Catherine Wynne (eds), *Victorian Literary Mesmerism* (Amsterdam/New York: Rodopi, 2006). For 'unorthodox' forms of science, see: Roger Cooter, *The Cultural Meaning of Popular Science: Phrenology and the Organization of Consent in Nineteenth-Century Britain* (Cambridge: Cambridge University Press, 1984); Janet Oppenheim, *The Other World: Spiritualism and Psychical Research in England, 1850–1914* (Cambridge: Cambridge University Press, 1985); Logie Barrow, *Independent Spirits: Spiritualism and English Plebeians, 1850–1910* (London:

Routledge & Kegan Paul, 1986); Alex Owen, *The Darkened Room: Women, Power and Spiritualism in Late Victorian England* (London: Virago, 1989); Nadja Durbach, *Bodily Matters: The Anti-Vaccination Movement in England, 1853–1907* (Durham, NC: Duke University Press, 1995).

Notes

1   They included the marquis of Anglesey, Sir Charles Paget, the earl of Burlington, the duke of Roxburgh, Earl Wilton, Lord Dinorben, Dr. Michael Faraday, Sir Joseph De Courcy Laffan, and Sir J. South ("University College Hospital: Animal magnetism," *Lancet*, 26 May 1838, 282).

2   "University College Hospital: Animal magnetism," *Lancet*, 26 May 1838, 284. Fred Kaplan, in "'The Mesmeric mania': The Early Victorians and Animal Magnetism," *Journal for the History of Ideas* 35 (1974): 691–702, and his *Dickens and mesmerism: The Hidden Springs of Fiction* (Princeton: Princeton University Press, 1975) discusses the public demonstrations and the controversy attending them. The *Lancet* reports are reprinted in Fred Kaplan, ed., *John Elliotson on mesmerism*, (New York: Da Capo, 1982). An interesting point of comparison as to what the "most accomplished actor" might have been thought to accomplish in the way of an altered state of mind was the Irish actress Harriet Smithson, who was becoming wildly popular during these years for her portrayal of Ophelia (among other things; Hector Berlioz, *Memoirs of Hector Berlioz, including his Travels in Italy, Germany, Russia and England, 1803–1865* trans. D. Cairns (New York: Dover, 1969), 109–13). After seeing Smithson playing *Hamlet* for the first time, Berlioz developed a "nervous condition like a sickness, of which only a great writer on physiology could give an adequate idea. I lost the power of sleep, and with it all my former animation" (58).

3   "University College Hospital: Animal magnetism," *Lancet*, 26 May 1838, 285–86.

4   O'Key sang several psalms and "The green hills of Tyrol": "'Pray don't sing,' said the Doctor. 'Don't sing,' she replied; 'Where does sing live? I *may* sing 'Buy a Black Sheep,' for Mr. Wood told me so" ("University College Hospital: Animal magnetism," *Lancet*, 26 May 1838, 286).

5   "University College Hospital: Animal magnetism," *Lancet*, 26 May 1838, 286. Little historical attention has been given to portrayals of race in Britain during this period, and certainly too little to know whether and to what extent "Black" would have been a racially specific term for O'Key. Given the importance of the character of a "Negro" to the O'Key sisters soon after this experiment, I suspect that it was. This issue will be discussed below.

6   Mayo as quoted in "Animal magnetism," *Athenaeum*, 1838; "Animal magnetism," *Medico-Chirurgical Review*, 1 October 1838, 635. On France see Alan Gauld, *A History of Hypnotism* (Cambridge: Cambridge University Press, 1992).

7   The *Lancet* drily summed up the reactions of the nonmedical observers: "'Marvellous!' murmured the astonished commoners. 'Very odd concern,' observed the carriage company, who arrived by turns, and saw the phenomena by bits'" ("University College Hospital: Animal magnetism," *Lancet*, 26 May 1838, 286).

8   "University College Hospital: Animal magnetism," *Lancet*, 26 May 1838, 287–88.

9   "University College Hospital: Animal magnetism," *Lancet*, 26 May 1838.

10   Michel Bakhtin, *Rabelais and his world* (Cambridge: MIT Press, 1968); Peter Burke, *Popular culture in early modern Europe* (London: T. Smith, 1978), 192.

11   Douglas A. Reid, "Interpreting the festival calendar: Wakes and Fairs as Carnivals," in R.D. Storch, ed., *Popular Culture and Custom in Nineteenth-Century England* (London: Croom Helm, 1982), esp. 227ff.

12   R. and G. Cruikshank, "The grand carnival," in R. Egan, *Life in London* (1821). For a later example see "Carnival in Lewes" (*Illustrated London News*, no date [midcentury], on file under "Carnival" in Mary Evans Picture Library), in which top-hatted gentlemen and their ladies look on from the shadowy margins as night revelers with animal masks and torches sweep through the streets.

13   J.F. Clarke, *Autobiographical recollections of the medical profession* (London: J. and A. Churchill, 1874): 163–164 n: "She was, I believe, one of the foremost actors in the farce of the 'unknown tongues' . . . in the séances of that remarkable preacher Edward Irving" at Islington Green, after he left Hatton Garden. On Irving's meetings, see the (hostile) account by Robert Baxter, *Narrative of facts, characterizing the supernatural manifestations in members of Mr. Irving's congregation . . . and formerly in the writer himself* (London: J. Nisbet, 1833).

14   For instance, Baxter's *Narrative of facts*. The religious disabilities legislation, established in the Restoration, prevented non-Anglicans (Catholics and Dissenters) from participating in any office connected with the state.

15   G.E. Smith, *Legends and miracles of human nature* (London, 1837).

16   Marc Baer, *Theatre and disorder in late Georgian London* (Oxford: Clarendon, 1992): 166–88; Clive Barker, "The Chartists, theatre, reform and research," *Theatre Quarterly* 1 (1971): 3–10; Michael Booth, "East End and West End: Class and Audience in Victorian London," *Theatre Research International* 2 (1977): 98–103; Joyce Mekeel, "Social influence on changing audience behavior in the London theatre, 1830–1880" (Ph.D. thesis, Boston University, 1983).

17   Peter Bailey, "Custom, capital, and culture in the Victorian Music Hall," in Storch, *Popular Culture and Custom*, 180–208.

18   "University College Hospital: Animal magnetism," *Lancet*, 26 May 1838, 284–85.

19   At one point O'Key woke in a state of delirium from a deep sleep and, when asked, claimed she hadn't "been nowhere" ("University College Hospital: Animal magnetism: Second report," 381).

20   "University College Hospital: Animal magnetism: Second report," 381.

21   "University College Hospital: Animal magnetism," *Lancet*, 26 May 1838, 286–87.

22   *OED:* "an effeminate and spiritless man or youth; wanting in courage or manliness." For a contemporary usage, see "Noctes Ambrosianae," *Blackwood's Magazine* 32 (1832): 392: "This new dandyfied era of milksoppism."

23   "Jim Crow" was written by Thomas D. Rice in 1832, according to C. Vann Woodward, *Strange career of Jim Crow* (New York: Oxford University Press, 1955), 7 n.

24   "Jim Crow" (1836), Madden Collection of Broadsides, Cambridge University Library, 9:202.

25   "University College Hospital: Animal magnetism," *Lancet*, 26 May 1838, 286–87.

26   Presumably the dance O'Key offered to make figured in the popular pantomime routines of the late 1830s that used the character Jim Crow. On Jim Crow at Sadler's Wells see D. Salberg, *Once upon a pantomime* (Luton: Cortney, 1981): 15–16.

27   "Our weekly gossip," *Athenaeum* 569 (1838): 699: "Sadler's Wells is the only fit arena for a more protracted discussion; and heavily do we feel the loss of our old favourite Grimaldi, who would have been so admirable a professor to pit against the magnetists."

28   "Juba at Vauxhall," *Illustrated London News*, 1848, Mary Evans Picture Library; "The Ethiopian serenaders," *Illustrated London News*, 1848. "Juba at Vauxhall" evaluated this man's performances at the Vauxhall Gardens in 1848. The published sketch depicts him in a posture reminiscent of Jim Crow (suspended in the air, one knee bent). His was a "national dance" (i.e., a "Nigger dance") that "we can believe in" because it combined a dizzying speed and dexterity of movement that no European could match with the air of natural movement: "how could Juba enter into their wonderful complications so naturally?" The "Ethiopian serenaders," on the other hand, were more ambiguous. They dressed in "dandy costume, *á la Jullien*" and performed their

Western airs in so "grotesque" a manner that they cast doubt on the "authenticity" of the African airs.

29   See Kaplan, *Dickens and mesmerism*, 43, for further discussion.

30   "University College Hospital: Animal magnetism: Sixth report," 590.

31   "University College Hospital: Animal magnetism: Sixth report." See also John Leeson, "Objections to the reality of phenomenon in animal magnetism," *Lancet*, 18 August 1838, 727–28.

32   "University College Hospital: Animal magnetism: Fifth report."

33   See S.S. Sprigge, *The Life and times of Thomas Wakley, founder and first editor of "Lancet"* (London: Longman, Green and Co., 1897). Sprigge described Wakley's move to Bedford Square in 1828 as a triumphant conclusion to professional and personal struggles of the 1820s.

34   J.A. Secord, "Extraordinary experiment: Electricity and the Creation of Life in early Victorian England," in David Gooding, Trevor Pinch and Simon Shaffer, eds, *The Uses of Experiment* (Cambridge: Cambridge University Press, 1989): 337–83, has discussed a similar strategic discreditation of controversial experimental findings during this period, in the case of Andrew Crosse's electric production of life.

35   Robert Darnton, *Mesmerism and the end of the Enlightenment in France* (Cambridge: Cambridge University Press, 1968), 64–66.

36   "'Animal magnetism,' or 'Mesmerism:' Experiments performed on Elizabeth and Jane O'Key, at the House of Mr. Wakley, Bedford-Square, in August, 1838," *Lancet*, 1 September 1838, 806.

37   "Suggestion" was, however, an important term in the psychology of cognition as developed by Thomas Brown in 1820 (connoting a positive role for the imagination and intellectual faculties in changing the character of a sensation before it was presented to the conscious mind in the act of perception). While this was very different from suggestion in the hypnotic sense of the term (beginning in the 1840s), Brown's notion was an important contributor to its development.

38   "'Animal magnetism,' or 'Mesmerism,'" 805.

39   These events are chronicled in Kaplan's *Dickens and mesmerism*.

40   Wakley put on trial and condemned other doctors routinely. For a timely example of a case of alleged malpractice and alleged misrepresentation of what had transpired, see the editorial in the *Lancet*, 16 December 1837, a condemnation of Samuel Cooper of UCH, who was accused of causing a patient's death.

PART 11

Gender and
the family

G ENDER HAS BEEN AT THE CENTRE of the expansion of Victorian
Studies into new realms in the past quarter of a century. As a field it emerged
out of women's history in the 1970s, which demanded that women should be no
longer 'hidden from history'. While we now see that there was a flowering of women's
history in the inter-war period, through the work of people such as Ivy Pinchbeck,
the fact remains that most histories which purported to be about the whole of society
only looked at what men were doing. Women's history vastly expanded the range
of social history, investigating women as political, social, intellectual and cultural
beings. It was also heavily politicised, as many of its pioneers were also active in
the women's movement. Retrieving the lives of women helped explain the social
structure of the present. The Victorians were seen very much as the authors of the
modern phase of patriarchy and hence were extremely important. Much of the early
phase of research concerned feminist pioneers. For example, Barbara Taylor's *Eve
and the New Jerusalem* (1983) rediscovered the lives of women in the Owenite
socialist movement of the early Victorian years — women whose 'New Moral World'
offered a utopian vision of feminism. In particular, the lives of working-class women
were heavily studied, both in relation to the workplace and motherhood. The history
of the family was an essential part of understanding women's lives.

Feminist historians wanted to know how 'being' a woman helped to structure
female lives: the choices women could make, the paths they could follow. Eventually
this became the centre of what we term 'gender' history as it went beyond the
description of women's lives to the way a person's sex could shape her or his life.
Particularly controversial was the question of whether class or gender was the more
important in shaping people's lives. By the 1990s, it was common to argue that it
was not sufficient to add women to the historical account and proceed to write the
same kind of social history as before (the 'add gender and stir' approach). Joan

Scott, Denise Riley and others argued that the inclusion of 'gender' meant that we had to rethink the whole writing of history as it reveals different kinds of issues. This led to the question, which many thought too obvious to pose: how does being a man shape his life choices? The new men's history investigated male institutions (such as boys' schools, the military and the gentlemen's clubs, as well as trade unions and political organisations) to consider how men used institutions and cultural traditions to maintain their power in society. Along with race and class, gender became a cultural category that needed to be explored in order to understand the way Victorian society functioned.

It is impossible to consider the Victorian gender system without engaging at some point with the history of the family. The nineteenth century was characterised by its elaborate enthusiasm for family life across the classes. Historians usually argue that the modern nuclear family emerged from the earlier pattern of extended families in the eighteenth century. This accounts for the increasing concern with privacy, a great Victorian theme. The period after about 1750 also witnessed a clearer division of labour between men and women. Increasingly, the idea of a family or breadwinner wage emerged, in which men (considered heads of the household) would earn sufficient money to maintain their wives and children at home. However, this ideal was only enjoyed by the aristocracy, the middle classes and by some skilled workers. The modern idea of childhood as a time of innocence also began to emerge. By the time Victoria ascended the throne, family life was increasingly defined in terms of parents and children and happy family life was viewed as the basis for a healthy society. At one level family history has been shaped by demographers, who have produced statistics for birth, marriage, death and household size. However, social historians have also been concerned with class and regional variations in the nature of the family, as well as issues such as domestic discord or the relationship of outsiders (such as servants or friends) to families. All of the Readings in this section engage with the role of the family in shaping the Victorian gender system.

Leonore Davidoff and Catherine Hall

SEPARATE SPHERES

Family Fortunes: Men and Women of the English Middle Class, 1780–1850
(London: Hutchinson, 1987; revised edition: Routledge, 2002), 180–8.

The most important idea to shape the history of nineteenth-century gender relations has been that of 'separate spheres'. This holds that the characteristic of modern life has been the division of society into the world of the public sphere (principally the world of work and presumed to be dominated by men) and the private sphere (the home and the allotted place for women). Much of the debate within gender and women's history has been concerned with the applicability of this model.

The most influential statement of the separate spheres argument has been **Leonore Davidoff** and **Catherine Hall**'s *Family Fortunes* (1987). The authors argue that gender was integral to the making of the English middle class in the period 1780–1850. The division between home and work that accompanied industrialisation led to a belief that the home was the appropriate place for women. This view was particularly fostered by the role of Evangelical religion and (in the following extract) by authors of conduct manuals who developed the idea of separate spheres and helped turn it into a social norm. Davidoff and Hall insist that separate spheres evolved as a historical process. Although aspects of separate spheres can be found earlier, it became particularly rigid in the early nineteenth century and thereby came to shape Victorian life in an important way. Domestic life for Victorians was based around the ideal of the woman as the 'Angel in the House' (after a poem by Coventry Patmore). In the considerable debate about *Family Fortunes*, discussion focused on the ways in which consumerism empowered women by taking them out of the home and also whether conduct manuals are reliable guides to how people actually behaved.

Another line of discussion has concerned the applicability of the separate spheres model to the working classes.

Although *Family Fortunes* is often discussed as a work of women's history, it is in fact as much about men as it is about women. However, it demonstrated how women's history and the category of 'gender' could force a substantial rethink of what was at stake in the early industrial period (see also the Reading by **Anna Clark**, pp. 191–206). *Family Fortunes* was based around case studies of two localities (rural Essex/Suffolk and industrial Birmingham) so that middle-class life could be explored and compared in different contexts. Davidoff and Hall examine individual families, studying both their public and private lives. They trace the impact of the proponents of separate spheres such as Hannah More and William Cowper at the end of the eighteenth century. In the following Reading, the authors consider two influential writers of the early Victorian years who praised 'separate spheres' for different reasons: Sarah Stickney Ellis and Harriet Martineau. They expressed two views about the importance of domesticity and femininity that were powerful influences in Victorian Britain. Both were remarkable writers who used their public voices to celebrate the virtues of the private sphere. Sarah Ellis (1799–1872) was an educationist, novelist and author of the best-selling conduct manual, *The Women of England* (1839), as well as numerous works of morally improving fiction. Harriet Martineau (1802–76) was a leading reformer and journalist who championed anti-slavery, women's rights, mesmerism, political economy and the Utilitarian philosophy of Jeremy Bentham. In the original, but not included here, the authors also discuss a third writer, John Loudon (the landscape gardener), and his distinctive vision of suburban living.

Leonore Davidoff is Research Professor in the Department of Sociology at the University of Essex. Her current research is on kinship in the English nineteenth-century middle strata with a focus on sibling relationships. In addition to *Family Fortunes*, her books include *The Best Circles* (1973), *Worlds Between: Historical Perspectives on Gender and Class* (1995) and (with others) *The Family Story: Blood, Contract and Intimacy, 1830–1960* (1999).

Catherine Hall is Professor of Modern British Social and Cultural History at University College, London. Her current research interests focus on the ways in which nation and Empire were imagined and conceptualised in the nineteenth century, with a particular focus on the life and work of Thomas Babington Macaulay. In addition to *Family Fortunes*, her books on gender include *White, Male and Middle Class: Explorations in Feminism and History* (1992) and (edited with others) *Gendered Nations: Nationalisms and Gender Order in the Long Nineteenth Century* (2000).

THE WORK OF TRANSLATING the late eighteenth-century domestic utopias to a middle-class public was not confined to lesser known writers of the early part of the period. By the second quarter of the nineteenth century there were also major national figures who had taken the process further towards realization. Mrs [*Sarah Stickney*] Ellis [*and*] Harriet Martineau . . . in their very different ways were concerned with transforming the daily lives of middle-class families and finding ways to make domesticity a lived reality. [*Both*] were self-conscious idealogues, seeking to form taste and win others to their opinions. Speaking within established genres, they extended their meanings, offered new possibilities and reiterated pieties. Writing in the troubled decades of the 1830s and 1840s, when political and social unrest both at home and abroad was rife, they propagandized for the family as a repository of stability and firm values, just as [*William*] Cowper and [*Hannah*] More had done for the 1790s. At a time when some socialists and feminists were seeking new forms of marriage and new kinds of relations between men and women, these thinkers were arguing for a stable family as the way to achieve not only social harmony but also individual fulfilment. Just as in the 1790s, the debates over manliness, femininity, the family and home were constructed around an argument as to the meaning of sexual difference. Were women naturally subordinate to men? If so, what did spiritual equality really mean? Could women be equal to men? Did this mean that they had to behave like men? Was the domestic sphere the only proper place for women? Was it acceptable for women to be 'gainfully employed'?

Cowper and More both envisaged in their writing an organic society, based on the land, in which there would be no substantial separation between production, reproduction and consumption. The household was to unite within it the separate but complementary activities of the two sexes. By the 1830s and 1840s such a vision was no longer appropriate or possible. Middle-class families were increasingly living, or at least desiring to live, not on premises which combined workplace with living space but in homes which were separated from work, away from the pressures of business with the concomitant apprentices and employees.[1] Writers on domesticity by the 1830s and 1840s all assume that this separation has taken place, and that if it has not it is an unfortunate aberration.

Mrs Ellis, therefore, does not like More, write about a whole society peopled by both men and women. Her advice books and novels assume a world in which the domestic sphere is occupied by women, children and servants, with men as the absent presence, there to direct and command but physically occupied elsewhere for most of their time. Similarly, Harriet Martineau assumes a world divided between political economy and domestic economy [. . .]. It was recognized that men would be preoccupied with business, and domesticity had become the 'woman's sphere' rather than, as it is for Cowper, a way of living for both men and women.

A second major shift had occurred by the 1830s and 1840s. The original inspiration for new patterns of behaviour in the home and family lay with the religious revival of the late eighteenth century. First Cowper and More, then Isaac and Ann Taylor and their generation were converted in their adult lives and had all the enthusiasm of the new discoverers of truth. However, for many of the writers of the later period, religion was a given part of their intellectual framework but no longer occupied centre stage. Many of the public protagonists of domesticity still received their inspiration from 'real religion' but for others domestic life no longer had to be framed in predominantly Christian terms, no longer required the revolutionizing force of salvationist religion.

Ellis [*and*] Martineau [. . .] , from their very different backgrounds and preoccupations, all exemplify these shifts in the meanings of home and domesticity. [. . .] Mrs Sarah Stickney Ellis was probably the best-known idealogue of domesticity, one of a number of women writers in the genre in the second quarter of the nineteenth century. Indeed conservative thinkers were sometimes worried at the extent to which advice books were written by women. 'We doubt much', complained one critic, 'whether women are the best direct preceptors of women'.[2] Yet these women were tremendously popular.[3] Mrs Ellis, born in 1799, was a tenant farmer's daughter. Expected to contribute to the household from an early age, she divided her time between familial responsibilities and writing, from which, by the mid 1830s, she was making a precarious living. At the age of 37, she started to correspond with Mr Ellis, her husband-to-be who was then working for the London Missionary Society. Through her connection with him she became more seriously interested in religion and in 1837 she joined the Congregational church before marrying. She never had children of her own but took major responsibility for her step-brothers and sisters, her nieces and nephews and her three step-children. Her advice to women on childcare was based on long experience, though her insistence on the importance of maternal *instinct* is ironic in the context of her adopted mothering. After her marriage she continued to write prolifically and, furthermore, established a school in their home in the country in 1844 so that throughout her life she contributed economically to the household.[4]

Her best-known books were the series on the wives, mothers, daughters and women of England. Mrs Ellis will soon, commented one unsympathetic reviewer, 'have circumnavigated the female world; every variety of female condition will have had its separate book . . . .'.[5] Even in such potentially critical journals as *The Quarterly* she was well received, though her pompous tone and the 'magnificent catalogue of virtues' which she was attempting to inculcate were commented upon with amusement.[6] In more progressive circles there were doubts as to whether her view of women as 'relative creatures' was acceptable, but her general advice on educa-tion and household organization was welcomed.[7] What is significant is the extent to which Mrs Ellis's views were seen as a radical departure, an attempt to break with the unhappy state of affairs in the middle-class homes of England, where gentility had been winning too many victories over practicality.

Mrs Ellis was rooted in the middling ranks of the provincial middle class; her father a tenant farmer, her husband a minor professional, herself a struggling writer and teacher. Yet she addressed herself first and foremost to women who did not need to earn. This may have been more to do with her sense of a proper domestic ideal, than with her individual needs. Indeed, she clung with some guilt to her financial independence. 'The middle class' that she addressed represented for her 'the pillar of our nation's strength', renowned for their intelligence and moral power.[8]

She was particularly concerned with those families of traders, manufacturers and professionals where there were one to four servants, where there had been some kind of liberal education, and where there was no family rank. 'False notions of refinement', were rendering their women, 'less influential, less useful, and less happy than they were'. This was a moral crisis for the nation and her concern was to find ways of improving 'the minor morals of domestic life'.[9] Once again the family was to provide a secure basis for national stability. Men did not have the time; they were occupied in the world of business and politics. Women had both the time, the moral capacity and the influence to exercise real power in the domestic world. It was their responsibility to re-create society from below.

A tension between the notion of women as 'relative creatures' and a celebratory view of their potential power lies at the heart of Mrs Ellis's writing and helps to explain her popularity. Like Hannah More her belief in the separate spheres of men and women went together with a conviction that women's influence could be felt far beyond her own limited circle.[10] *Influence* was the secret of women's power and that influence, as wives and mothers, meant that they did not need to seek other kinds of legitimation. Having been criticized for placing women on too low a scale Mrs Ellis responded by arguing that,

> I still think that as a wife, woman should place herself, instead of running the risk of *being placed,* in a secondary position; as a mother, I do not see how it is possible for her to be too dignified, or to be treated with too much respect.[11]

The tension between subordination and influence, between moral power and political silence, was one which preoccupied all the protagonists of 'woman's mission'.[12] If the moral world was theirs, who needed the public world of business and politics? Women could find the true meaning of their lives in the family which was a woman's profession, the love that she would find there would answer her needs. For women, wrote Mrs Ellis, love was her very being 'In that *she* lives, or else *she* has no life', unlike a man who had his public character.[13] To love was woman's duty; to be beloved her reward. Women's aim should be to become better wives and mothers. However, much improved education for girls would be necessary for the natural maternal instinct needed training and support. Women should regard good domestic management not as degrading but as a moral task and abandon false notions of refinement, accepting that they had a vital job to do at home, just as their sons and husbands had to do at work. Wives and daughters, 'enclosed, as it were, in the home-garden', should practice the domestic virtues of making others happy.[14]

For herself, Mrs Ellis was never under the illusion that enclosure in the 'home-garden' was enough. She was well aware that in many middle-class households, as indeed in her own, women's financial contribution could make an essential difference. Women in the lower middle class, she argued, should be educated to be useful and active members of society. There was nothing degrading in women's employment if it were essential, and there were fields such as engraving and the drawing of patterns as well as the more common teaching and needlework.[15] But this was a small comment among volumes which argued that woman's place was in the home, and although she prefaced *The Women of England* with the proviso that it was written for those who did not have to work for money, her works, and those of others like her, were taken to apply far more generally. The moral panic engendered in the 1840s by the vision of women working in the mines, mills and factories of England was fuelled by the view that woman's duty was to care for home and children.

Mrs Ellis, whether she intended to do so or not, played a part in rigidifying existing views that it was not genteel for women to work. At the same time that she was writing *The Women of England,* she described in a letter the 'blessings of constant employment' her step-daughters, and indeed herself, enjoyed from their teaching as daily governesses.[16] But this also brought guilt and anxiety as to whether her work as a wife and mistress of a household was suffering. Like Mrs Gaskell she felt obliged to make sure that she never allowed those other responsibilities to be neglected.[17]

In some ways Mrs Ellis directly inherited the mantle of Hannah More. She had similar concerns about the nature of marriage, the importance of motherhood, the need for better education for women and the nurturing of their rationality, the advantages of rural life and suspicion of 'society'. But there were also significant differences between them. She did not share Hannah More's conservative politics for [. . .] she was attached publicly to progressive liberal causes and throughout her life remained sympathetic to the Quakers (whose faith she had known as a child) and their preoccupation with issues such as anti-slavery, peace, capital punishment and temperance. Furthermore, she was concerned to address a much wider audience than More had originally envisaged and to make domesticity a more available practice. All women could be mothers, she argued, and

> the heart of woman, in all her tenderest and holiest feelings, is the same beneath the shelter of a cottage, as under the canopy of a tree . . . .[18]

This democratization of domesticity was solidly rooted in the homes of the middle class and not in the country estates of the minor gentry. It was no longer tied to a desire for a retreat from the development of towns and industries and a return to a patriarchal rural idyll, but located in the towns and villages of England, among middling manufacturers, traders, professionals and farmers.

A second major difference between More and Ellis also played a vital part in making domesticity the practice of a class rather than of a particular religious group, for she was never evangelical in her religion, remaining within a generally Christian framework but without spiritual inspiration. Rather her primary concern was with morals. Hannah More would never have made this distinction between religion and morality. It was precisely the religious meaning of the minutiae of daily life that had led to More's insistence on rules of habit and behaviour, to the emphasis on every detail of private life and the necessary distinctions between the spheres and duties of men and women. For Mrs Ellis, however, women did not have to be seriously religious to follow her precepts. The loose Christian framework within which she placed her work, her characterization of religious influence or 'atmosphere' including those who 'did not want quite to give up the world, yet not quite to live without God' meant that it was acceptable to many.[19] The tone that Mrs Ellis achieved was precisely that of a respectable moralist with a 'Christian tint', that had come to dominate mid century England, enveloping the language of the proper relations between the sexes.[20]

Sarah Stickney Ellis developed the idea of female satisfaction being achieved through selflessness;[21] Harriet Martineau, from a different tradition, saw other advantages in domesticity. Born in Norwich in 1802, the daughter of a successful

Unitarian merchant and manufacturer, Martineau suffered an unhappy and frustrating childhood. Despite her intellectual interests and the relatively progressive position of Unitarians on female education, she was expected to settle into the life of a young lady at home. In an early article 'On Female Education' she refused the belief in the natural mental differentiation of the sexes, as Wollstonecraft had before her, and argued that women had the same mental endowment as men. But at the same time, she believed that the female mind was peculiarly susceptible to religion and virtue and dwelt on the importance of the personal and moral to women.[22] In 1829 the family business collapsed and for Harriet this turned out to be a blessing in disguise. Her surreptitious writing done before breakfast became a serious occupation and source of income.[23] Now, she commented thankfully, she won friends, independence, and an interesting life and was able to feel that she had 'truly lived'. Becoming increasingly interested in political economy, Martineau had the idea of writing tales to popularize the theories of Smith, Ricardo, Malthus and Bentham. Despite her difficulties in finding a publisher for this unlikely female enterprise, the venture was an immediate success with its simple language to explain such issues as the corn laws, the poor law and population. But how did Martineau weld together her newfound commitment to the Benthamites with her Unitarianism and belief in the equality of men and women?

Classical liberalism had been content to combine a belief in the individual rights of propertied men with an acceptance of sexual inequality within the family.[24] Building on this tradition, Bentham had little to say about either women or the family but when he did address himself to such matters he relied on customary morality. 'The sensibility of the female sex appears in general to be greater than that of the male', but women's sympathies went to individuals, not classes or divisions. They were modest, delicate and more superstitious than men, with stronger affections for children. Women, in short, occupied a smaller sphere than men. Finally, and most damning of all, women were less sympathetic to the principle of utility than were men. Bentham was happy to rest with custom when it came to relations between the sexes. Like Hobbes and Locke before him, he thought that marriage must be a contract but that powers would have to rest with the husband who would act as 'master' and 'guardian'.[25] For the most part the political economists were happy with a conventional view of the family as separate from the market and providing a haven from the competitive thrust of the economic world. Martineau recorded that Malthus came to see her after the publication of her tale on taxation:

> on purpose to thank me for a passage, or a chapter, (which has left no
> trace in my memory) on the glory and beauty of love and the blessedness
> of domestic life; and that others, called stern Benthamites, sent round
> messages to me to the same effect.[26]

It was ironic that this was the moment at which the 'stern Benthamites' thanked her — for a passage on the 'blessedness of domestic life' of which she had no recollection.

Martineau's experience of domestic life was mixed; a consistently difficult relationship with her mother, serious quarrels with most of her siblings, never interested in marriage and only in later life able to set up a household on her own terms. Why, then, did she feel the need to celebrate domesticity? Building as she did on the twin traditions of Utilitarianism and Unitarianism she took from them a powerful belief in individual rights and a commitment to rationality. All women should have the right to develop their full potential and she consistently opposed educational and economic discrimination. But arguments for better opportunities for women must be made from a spirit of rationality, not from passion and misery. Critical of [*early feminist Mary*] Wollstonecraft, who she saw as a poor victim of passion, Martineau's feminism was based on the need for self-control and self-discipline. The best friends of women's cause, she insisted, were happy wives and 'busy, cheerful, satisfied single women'.[27] Every woman who could think and speak wisely and bring up her children soundly was advancing the time when women's interests in society would be better represented.

But Martineau firmly believed also in the positive value of domestic life. 'No true woman', she wrote,

> married or single, *can* be happy without some sort of domestic life; — without having somebody's happiness dependent on her . . . .[28]

Her demand for women was for individual fulfilment. For married women this meant as wives and mothers. While recognizing the need for single women and working-class women, even those who were married, to work for pay, she saw home and family as the most satisfying site for married women of the middle class. Setting the path for John Stuart Mill, she never seriously queried the division of labour within the family.[29] But if the family was to be all that it could and should, women must be better educated to be good wives and mothers. The highest domestic enjoyment, she asserted, went with the best educated women. In *Household Education*, published in 1848, she argued that the most ignorant women she had known had also been the worst housekeepers. A woman of superior mind knew better than an ignorant one what to require of servants and how to deal with tradespeople.[30] 'Every woman ought to have that justice done to her faculties', she wrote, making the classic liberal feminist case,

> that she may possess herself in all the strength and clearness of an experienced and enlightened mind, and may have at command, for her subsistence, as much intellectual power and as many resources as education can furnish her with.[31]

Martineau saw the artisan household as providing a good model for the running of a household for there women necessarily had to be heavily involved themselves and could not leave the upbringing of the children and the management of the home to servants. The mother would take major responsibility for the children but the father would be involved when he came home in the evenings. The children would learn to help from the beginning and girls would learn domestic management the best possible way. Love was the right source of parental authority she thought, and she combined this with advice on breastfeeding, on fresh air and exercise, and the importance of cleanliness. Children should learn regularity and discipline and the importance of making good use of time. In this context Martineau strongly recommended the works of Mrs Ann Martin Taylor [*poet; the Taylor family of Essex are extensively discussed elsewhere in the book*].

Martineau's recommendation of Mrs Taylor (despite the latter's evangelicalism to which she was hostile), and her proximity in attitudes to some aspects of the thinking of More and Ellis, gives an indication of the pervasiveness of domesticity. The starting points of these writers were widely different. More and Ellis regarded domesticity as a moral imperative, Martineau argued for a good domestic life in terms of the needs of individuals for fulfilment. None of them wanted for themselves quite what they advised for others. Martineau was wedded to the life of an independent woman writer and determined to succeed in a male literary world. The costs of this included her steadfast refusal of her own sexuality and her labelling as 'eccentric'. More and Ellis also made ambitious claims for women, if on a different plane, and in their own ways advanced women's cause in their separate spheres. For all of them their versions of domesticity were to enhance women's status, not reduce it.

The tensions which were present in the writings of these authors, the contradictions between influence and the narrow sphere, fulfilment and domestic economy, often disappeared, however, in the popularizations of their work. The *Magazine of Domestic Economy*, for example, started in 1835, aimed at a middle-class audience, was priced at 6d and appeared monthly. Its motto read,

> We are born at home, we live at home, and we must die at home, so that the comfort and economy of home are of more deep, heartfelt, and personal interest to us, than the public affairs of all the nations in the world.

The aim of the journal, which the proprietors felt had been overlooked by other periodicals, was to explore 'the principle and practice of rendering the enjoyments of home more generally appreciated, and more habitually delightful'. The magazine dealt with domestic economy in its widest sense: the management of the household, the care of children, the fulfilment of social duties, the proper use of time and the management of income all came within its purview. They strongly recommended the 'excellent Miss Martineau' and much of their advice might have come straight from the pages of Mrs Taylor (bar the religion) or Mrs Ellis. But the tone was bland, the tension which informed the more creative writers missing. The magazine demonstrated an acceptance of separate spheres without any moral or political imperatives — it simply was the way to be. The province of men was to find the means to support a home, the province of women was to make the home enjoyable. It was wrong for women to seek to be active in men's sphere and women should not complain about the legal disabilities associated with marriage. 'A woman gives up her worldly possessions', they argued,

> in exchange for a determinate station; for protection, for support . . .
> she gains station . . . she gains protection . . . .

What else could she need?[32]

In 1852 Martineau wrote a series for *Household Words* based on her experiences in Birmingham during a long stay with her brother and his family. One concerned 'A New School for Wives', established through the efforts of a Unitarian led group of women, friends and admirers of Miss Martineau. The school aimed to educate married working women, of whom there were many in the Birmingham metal trades, in the arts of housewifery as well as the three Rs. It was an initiative which came out of the prevalent middle-class anxieties as to the nature of working-class family life and the deleterious effects of married women's employment. This particular school was a success for Unitarians had a genuine belief in the value of education, as well as a powerful desire to inculcate their own familial ideals.[33] But such ventures were frequently inspired by less sympathetic attitudes and it was no great leap from a dissatisfaction with the state of working-class homes to a wholesale disapproval of women's employment. The loss of the political and philosophical imperatives behind the arguments about separate spheres, whether in the form of a genuine belief in woman's influence or demand for individual fulfilment for women, and the common-sense reduction of those beliefs which took place, had very mixed effects for women by the middle of the nineteenth century.

Further reading

The 2002 edition of *Family Fortunes* should be consulted as it contains a response by the authors to the debate that the book created. The authors have also written about gender and domesticity elsewhere: see Catherine Hall, *White, Male and Middle Class: Explorations in Feminism and History* (Cambridge: Polity, 1992); Leonore Davidoff, *Worlds Between: Historical Perspectives on Gender and Class* (Cambridge: Polity, 1995). A more recent study of the middle-class family is R.J. Morris, *Men, Women and Property in England, 1780–1870: A Social and Economic History of Family Strategies amongst the Leeds Middle Classes* (Cambridge: Cambridge University Press, 2005). The 'separate spheres' model is discussed in Amanda Vickery, 'Golden Age to Separate Spheres?: A Review of the Categories and Chronology of English Women's History', *Historical Journal*, 36 (1993), 383–414. The most influential theoretical works about gender history are: Joan Scott, *Gender and the Politics of History* (New York: Columbia University Press, 1988); Denise Riley, '*Am I That Name'?: Feminism and the Category of 'Women' in History* (Basingstoke: Macmillan, 1988).

Notes

1   See Leonore Davidoff and Catherine Hall, *Family Fortunes: Men and Women of the English Middle Classes, 1780–1850* (rev. ed.: London: Routledge, 2002), ch. 8, especially 1851 census data.

2   Anon. 'Englishwomen of the seventeenth and nineteenth centuries', *English Review*, 12 (1847), p. 288.

3   Mrs Ellis's publishers had the inspired idea of re-issuing her *Wives of England* in a marriage-day edition bound in white morocco.

4   Mrs S. Stickney Ellis, *The Home Life and Letters of Mrs Ellis* (1893).

5   Anon. 'Englishwomen', p. 285.

6   A.W. Kinglake, 'The rights of women', *The Quarterly Review*, 75 (1844–5), p. 122.

7   Anon. review of *The Daughters of England* in *Congregational Magazine*, 25, 3rd series 6 (1842), p. 766.

8   Mrs S. Stickney Ellis, *The Women of England* (1839), p. 14.

9   Ellis, *Women of England*, p. 10.

10   Mrs S. Stickney Ellis, *The Daughters of England. Their Position in Society, Character and Responsibilities* (n.d.), p. 223.

11   Mrs S. Stickney Ellis, *Mothers of England, Their Influence and Responsibility* (n.d.), p. 27.

12   For a discussion of the feminist use of this concept see B. Taylor, *Eve and the New Jerusalem. Socialism and Feminism in the Nineteenth Century* (1983).

13   Mrs S. Stickney Ellis, *The Daughters*, p. 318.

14   Mrs S. Stickney Ellis, *Mothers*, p. 348.

15   Mrs S. Stickney Ellis, *The Women*, see the chapter on 'Marriage'.

16   Mrs S. Stickney Ellis, *The Home Life and Letters*, p. 94.

17   J.A.V. Chapple and A. Pollard (eds), *The Letters of Mrs Gaskell* (Manchester, 1966).

18   Mrs S. Stickney Ellis, *The Daughters*, preface.

19   ibid., p. 373; Anon. 'Englishwomen', p. 288.

20   On the Christian tint see J.W. Croker quoted by H. McLeod, *Religion and the People of Western Europe* (Oxford, 1981), p. 107.

21   Mrs Ellis warned against the dangers of women becoming too selfless however. Mrs S. Stickney Ellis, *The Wives* and *The Women*; see also chapter 7.

22   H. Martineau, *Autobiography with Memorials by Maria Weston Chapman*, 3 vols (1877); V.K. Pichanick, *Harriet Martineau. The Woman and Her Work 1802–76* (Ann Arbor, 1980); F.E. Mineka, *The Dissidence of Dissent. The Monthly Repository 1806–38* (North Carolina, 1944).

23   H. Martineau, vol. I, p. 142.

24   On classical liberalism and its treatment of women see A.M. Jaggar, *Feminist Politics and Human Nature* (Brighton, 1984); R.W. Krouse, 'Patriarchal liberalism and beyond: from John Stuart Mill to Harriet Taylor', in J.B. Elshtain (ed.), *The Family in Political Thought* (Brighton, 1984).

25   J. Bentham, *An Introduction to the Principles of Morals and Legislation* (Oxford, 1839), especially pp. 58–9.

26   H. Martineau, vol. 1, p. 253.

27   H. Martineau, vol. 1, p. 401.

28   H. Martineau, vol. 2, p. 225.

29   J.S. Mill, *The Subjection of Women*, and H. Taylor Mill, *Enfranchisement of Women* (1983). See the helpful introduction by K. Soper to these two essays in the Virago edition.

30   H. Martineau, *Household Education* (1848), p. 241.

31   H. Martineau, *Household Education*, p. 244.

32   *The Magazine of Domestic Economy*, I, (1835–6), p. 66; 7 (1841–2), p. 271.

33   H. Martineau, 'The new school for wives', *Household Words*, no. 107 (April 1852); S. Crompton, *Evening Schools for the Education of Women* (Birmingham, 1852).

John Tosh

MEN AND DOMESTICITY

John Tosh, *A Man's Place: Masculinity and the Middle-Class Home in Victorian England* (London: Yale University Press, 1999), 30–4.

Following on from the rise of women's and gender history, there emerged a historiography devoted to studying the history of men as gendered beings. Women's historians had previously argued that most history up to the 1970s had really been about men and complained that masculinity was often treated as the norm against which women were judged. In the late 1980s, some historians (male and female) came to argue that masculinity and manliness had a history that needed discussion in a way that had previously not existed. Their position was often anti-essentialist, arguing that masculinity and femininity are roles that have varied historically and have been deployed diversely in different contexts. Masculinity, which might seem straightforward, they argued, is actually very complex and male power over women (patriarchy) needed to be viewed in historical terms as something constantly changing and being renegotiated. The Victorian period was filled with concerns about appropriate male conduct — from Doctor Arnold's attempt to make Christian gentlemen at Rugby School (captured in Thomas Hughes' *Tom Brown's Schooldays*) to definitions of the male worker who was made virtuous by his skill. The ideals of masculinity were shaped by issues that centred around class as well as, increasingly, race and Empire. Claims about allegedly superior Anglo-Saxon masculinity buttressed Britain's claim to rule large parts of the world.

Early studies focused on all-male environments, such as the army, the Empire and the public school, to consider how boys were socialised into manhood. More recently, there have been attempts to think about masculinity and the history of politics, the emotions and the body. The role of heroes (both real and fictional) has been explored as a way of understanding how society teaches boys to become men.

The emphasis in recent masculinity histories has usually been on men in relation to women (considering, for example, how men were affected by mothers, sisters and wives and vice versa). **John Tosh**'s research has sought to delve into the question of the Victorian middle-class man in his domestic environment. Following the logic of 'separate spheres', the home was considered the woman's domain. Much of the literature had stressed middle-class men's separation from the home as they sought to carve out their niche in the public world of the office, industry or, perhaps, parliament. Tosh, however, insists that domesticity was crucial to middle-class men's visions of themselves and that their public successes were rooted in their home life, where they found respite from the competitive world outside. Tosh argues that, although women were to a great extent charged with shaping this sphere, men also played a crucial role within it. They led family prayers, which emphasised the moral nature of the home. They both indulged and disciplined their children, helping to foster (especially in their sons) the moral fortitude they would need in order to grow into successful adults. They respected and worked with their wives to maintain the home's role as a haven in an increasingly chaotic and competitive world. As we saw in the Introduction, the paterfamilias has always been widely recognised as an emblem of Victorian life but it is Tosh who has really examined this figure and the complexities of his role. Tosh's examination of men's domestic life fills a gap in the new literature on masculinity, which generally focuses on the public man. This extract may be usefully read with the work of **Stefan Collini** on the idea of character elsewhere in this volume (pp. 223–31).

John Tosh is Professor of History at Roehampton University. He is currently researching the relation between masculinity and imperial commitment in Victorian England. Some of this work appears in his most recent book, *Manliness and Masculinities in Nineteenth-Century Britain: Essays on Gender, Family and Empire* (2005).

THE SEPARATION OF HOME AND WORK [. . .] soon acquired psychological and emotional dimensions as well as a physical reality. Just because middle-class men were spared back-breaking manual labour did not mean that their work was congenial or undemanding. The hours were likely to be long; a position in commerce might mean being on one's feet or in the saddle for most of the day. More importantly, as work became detached from home, so its association with a heartless commercial ethic became closer. Early Victorian social comment is full of the chasm between the morality of the home and the morality of business. As Sarah Ellis sadly remarked, the men of her day had 'two sets of consciences . . . one conscience for the sanctuary, and another for the desk and counter'.[1] The world of business was seen as necessary, but morally contaminating. Whatever its rewards in profit, power or reputation, it exacted a heavy price in alienation. After depicting the 'destitution of comfort' endured by the lower middle-class man in warehouses and counting-houses, Ellis asked rhetorically, 'Are these the abodes of free-born and independent men?' Her solution was that men must be made whole again by the comfort and refinement of the properly ordered home.[2] Home provided the refuge from work in all its negativity. It offered bodily repose and human rhythms; it promised the comforts of love and nurture; and it was a reminder of a higher scale of moral values. So many of the treasured attributes of Victorian home life — its seclusion, its intimacy and its elevated morality — owed their appeal to the sense that none of these qualities was to be found in the utterly 'other' world of work. But the healing power did not come cheap: the virtues of home entailed a considerable outlay on the part of the hard-working breadwinner. As W.R. Greg sardonically put it, 'the merchant must be content to purchase the delights of domestic society and unanxious nights at the price of dying fifty thousand pounds poorer than he once expected'.[3] But, viewed as compensation for the emotional and moral costs of economic progress, the outlay was thought to be well worth the price. In reality Victorian bourgeois society included plenty of husbands who spared little time or thought for home life. But admiration for the public achievements of these men was tempered by disapproval of their negligence of the higher things of life.

However, the alienation experienced by Victorian men of the middle class was about more than work. It was not only the process and rhythm of work which exacted their toll. There was the ugliness and noise in which so much of it was located. Middle-class businessmen might live in quiet squares or leafy suburbs, but every day they must pass their waking hours amid the dirt and clatter and smells of an industrial environment. And there was a pervasive sense of social malaise. The changing quality of relations between mill-owner and man, or between master and apprentice, easily became intensified into a troubling sense that all the familiar social landmarks were being swept away in the rapid onset of an urban, individualistic society. Hierarchy and community, ultimately even faith itself, seemed at risk. In this alarming scenario the home, notwithstanding the significant shift in its own structure and function, was cast in the role of 'traditional' bulwark, the last remnant of a vanishing social order. Henry Mayhew remarked that the middle class regarded home as a place where 'all the cares and jealousies of life are excluded' and where reparation was made for 'the petty suspicions and heartlessness of strangers'.[4] Home stood for cooperation and for love, while modern society seemed dedicated to cruel and impersonal competition. In the most ambitious versions of this ideal the ennobling values of the home were destined to suffuse and transform the wider society.[5] Domesticity was a characteristically Victorian response to the damage which entrepreneurial capitalism had wrought on the fabric of human relations. And it was experienced just as keenly by men whose work was largely carried on in the home, as by those who laboured in the market-place.

Much of this sense of opposition between home and society was focused on the city. The early industrial city appeared as the summation of all the anti-social forces which threatened to engulf the Victorians. In the eighteenth century the principal associations of the city had been with economic opportunity and with the pleasure and instruction of society, or 'civility'. These associations persisted, but by the early Victorian period they were giving place to more frightening images. The speed and scale of urbanization had brought together myriads of people who were now apparently removed from the constraining structures of traditional society, and the all too visible extremes of urban destitution and demoralization graphically illustrated where this might lead. The city might be the place where money was made and the world went round, but for many its menacing social problems outweighed its cultural advantages.[6] The well-ordered home, with its welcoming hearth and its solid front door, furnished the most reassuring antidote to the alienation of city life. The Victorians loved to identify with the treasured place which these attributes of home had in the memory of the wanderer, the soldier or the sailor far from home. They continued avidly to read Felicia Hemans's immensely popular 'Domestic Affections' (1812):

> Bower of repose! when, torn from all we love,
> Through toil we struggle, or through distance rove;
> To *thee* we turn, still faithful, from afar —
> Thee, our bright vista! thee, our magnet-star!
> And from the martial field, the troubled sea,
> Unfetter'd thought still roves to bliss and thee!

That penchant for the exile's sensibility was reflected in the homecoming rituals of middle-class homes: the waiting wife and daughters on the threshold, the proffered slippers, the armchair ready at the fireside.[7]

But the most striking testimony to the middle class's ambivalence towards the city was its taste for country trappings. The idealization of the countryside as the realm of the natural and of organic communities originated in the eighteenth century; but the new urban culture of the nineteenth century heightened the appeal of this trope and enlarged its practical consequences. The constant vaunting of home tapped into a profoundly nostalgic longing for the simple, stress-free life of an imagined rural England. For the Victorian middle class the most desirable suburbs were not within walking distance of the centres of commerce, but far enough away to permit space, greenery and quiet. Roads should be leafy and hedge-bound, with open country or woodland within view. [. . .] Since family life was the rationale of the suburb, the ideal features of home and locality closely mirrored each other. Seclusion, refuge and repose in as rural an ambience as possible were the desired characteristics of the middle-class home. Hence the passion for gardening among the English bourgeoisie of this period. The most sought-after property was the villa in its own grounds, set back from the road and approached by a winding drive, with gardens front and rear. Below that every gradation was to be found, down to the small garden at the back of a standard terraced house. Commercially produced garden accessories became widely available, notably the mechanical lawn-mower which was invented in the 1830s and intended for use by the master of the house. Moderately priced instruction manuals came in at the same period. *The Gardener's Magazine* was founded in 1826, followed by *The Horticultural Register* in 1831. The activity of gardening brought a man into closer touch with nature, while the results of his labours refreshed the soul and delighted the eye. That gardening should have been seen in this light is some measure of the emotional needs which the home was called upon to fill.[8]

The place of the home in bourgeois culture could be summed up by the proposition that only at home could a man be truly and authentically himself. While the workplace and the city crippled his moral sense and distorted his human relationships, home gave play to feelings of nurture, love and companionship, as well as 'natural' forms of authority and deference; it nourished the whole man.

Every feature of home life was interpreted in these elevated terms. Samuel Smiles urged the merits of drawing-room music-making as involving all members of the family in an activity which was *harmonious* in both a moral and a literal sense.[9] Particular faith was placed in the healing power of Sunday as a sacred day dedicated to family life. Eliza Wilson employed a familiar trope when urging her fiancé Walter Bagehot to write to her on Sundays: 'Everyone, but especially men, are more themselves on that day; *you* have no Bank to jar you, and one can always go deeper into oneself when one has not been thinking of one's worldly affairs during the day'.[10] Countless writers expressed the belief in the restorative power of the family circle, but perhaps none with more heartfelt conviction than James Anthony Froude in his early novel, *The Nemesis of Faith* (1849):

> When we come home, we lay aside our mask and drop our tools, and are no longer lawyers, sailors, soldiers, statesmen, clergymen, but only men. We fall again into our most human relations . . . We cease the struggle in the race of the world, and give our hearts leave and leisure to love.[11]

Froude's paean to the home implicitly acknowledges the power of the other main constituent of middle-class manhood: occupation. Middle-class men certainly had a great deal invested in doing the kind of responsible and useful work which distinguished them from the supposed idleness of the aristocracy. Moreover they needed to rescue many of their characteristic occupations from the taint of money-grubbing and sharp practice. The work ethic and the emphasis on dignity of calling were an effective counterattack on deep-seated occupational snobbery. But Froude's impassioned comment — echoed by many others — is a reminder that not even prestigious professions like the law or politics offered a wholly secure identity. For the middle-class man work held deeply contradictory associations: on the one hand, pride in climbing the ladder of success, providing for his family, and acquiring the esteem of his peers; on the other, resentment of the time and toil required, fear of failure at the impersonal hands of the market, and revulsion from the morals of the business world. Home served to mitigate the harshness of these reactions. It could not soften the fear of failure. But it did explain and justify the labours of the breadwinner, and perhaps even the moral depths to which he must stoop, in order to sustain his dependants. And, it was claimed on all sides, home offered a morally wholesome environment to ease a man's conscience when ensnared by the corruption of the working world.[12]

Further reading

After writing *A Man's Place*, John Tosh went on to produce a collection of articles about masculinity: *Manliness and Masculinities in Nineteenth-Century Britain: Essays on Gender, Family and Empire* (Harlow: Longman, 2005). The earliest studies of Victorian masculinity were: J.A. Mangan and James Walvin (eds), *Manliness and Morality: Middle-Class Masculinity in Britain and America, 1800–1940* (Manchester: Manchester University Press, 1987); John Tosh and Michael Roper (eds), *Manful Assertions: Masculinities in Britain since 1800* (London: Routledge, 1991). Other studies of Victorian masculinity include: James Eli Adams, *Dandies and Desert Saints: Styles of Victorian Manhood* (Ithaca, NY: Cornell University Press, 1995); Angus McLaren, *The Trials of Masculinity: Policing Sexual Boundaries, 1870–1930* (Chicago, IL: University of Chicago Press, 1997); Kelly Boyd, *Manliness and the Boys' Story Paper in Britain: A Cultural History, 1855–1940* (Basingstoke: Palgrave, 2003); Martin Wiener, *Men of Blood: Violence, Manliness and Criminal Justice in Victorian England* (Cambridge: Cambridge University Press, 2004).

Notes

1   Sarah Ellis, *The Mothers of England*, London, 1843, p. 308.
2   Sarah Ellis, *The Women of England*, London, 1839, p. 243.
3   W.R. Greg, review of W. Johnston, *England As It Is,* in *Edinburgh Review* 93 (1851), p. 326.
4   Henry Mayhew, 'Home Is Home, Be It Never So Homely', in Viscount Ingestre (ed.), *Meliora: Or Better Times to Come*, London, 1852, p. 263.
5   Catherine Gallagher, *The Industrial Reformation of English Fiction*, Chicago, 1985, pp. 115–20.
6   Alexander Welsh, *Dickens and the City*, London, 1971; H.J. Dyos and M. Wolff (eds), *The Victorian City*, 2 vols, London, 1979.
7   Helene Roberts, 'Marriage, Redundancy or Sin: the Painter's View of Women in the First Twenty-Five Years of Victoria's Reign', in Martha Vicinus (ed.), *Suffer and Be Still*, London, 1972, p. 51; John R. Gillis, 'Ritualization of Middle-Class Family Life in Nineteenth-Century Britain', *International Journal of Politics, Culture and Society* 3 (1989), pp. 213–35.
8   Welsh, *Dickens and the City*; Leonore Davidoff and Catherine Hall, *Family Fortunes: Men and Women of the English Middle Class, 1780–1850*, London, 1987, pp. 188–90, 364–74; Leonore Davidoff, *Worlds Between: Historical Perspectives on Gender and Class*, Cambridge, 1995, pp. 46–50, 56–8; Stephen Constantine, 'Amateur Gardening and Popular Recreation in the 19th and 20th Centuries', *Journal of Social History* 14 (1981), p. 389.
9   Samuel Smiles, 'Music in the House', *Eliza Cook's Journal* 6 (1852), pp. 209–11.
10 Eliza Wilson to Walter Bagehot, 21 November 1857, in Mrs R. Barrington (ed.), *The Love-Letters of Walter Bagehot and Eliza Wilson*, London, 1933, p. 44.
11 J.A. Froude, *The Nemesis of Faith*, London, 1849, pp. 112–13.
12 Davidoff and Hall, *Family Fortunes*, ch. 3.

Ellen Ross

WORKING-CLASS FAMILY STRATEGIES

'"Fierce Questions and Taunts": Married Life in Working-Class London, 1870–1914', *Feminist Studies*, 8 (Autumn 1982), 575–602.

Working-class family life in Victorian Britain varied from region to region. In the north of England, where industrial development had most impact, families might see skilled men earn a steady wage. Women entered the workforce in their teens, but might leave after marriage and childbearing. They would supplement their income by taking in boarders, doing laundry or piecework, or co-ordinating the earnings of their husbands and children. In districts where women's work was integral to factory production, however, a different pattern emerged. These areas, mostly in the textile industry, saw women enter the labour force at an early age and seldom leave it again. Even after childbearing, they returned to work, although there was no structure for their advancement. In these households, men might help with some measure of housework and childcare, although generally not openly. The dish 'Lancashire hotpot' has its origins as a stew women could prepare before they left for work, drop off at the local bake shop (as individual homes had no ovens), and pick up on their way home after work. Dishes like fish and chips also emerged from the north, reflecting the constraints on women's time for cooking, as well as their fatigue from work.

The norm in metropolitan areas such as London was somewhat different. In 'Fierce Questions and Taunts', **Ellen Ross** lays out the arguments about the organisation of the working-class family in late Victorian London, which she develops in more depth in *Love and Toil: Motherhood in Outcast London, 1870–1918* (1993). Using a variety of sources from census enumerator records and social surveys to autobiography and court records, she reveals the gender divisions and geographies of the working-class family. Unlike middle-class families, where men were expected to financially support their relations, working-class families were dependent on the skill of mothers to manage household finances, including generating the money for their own and their children's support. These 'family strategies' for survival ranged from the canny use of pawnbroking and knowledge of where to obtain credit, to opportune pilfering of paternal funds when the husband returned home drunk. Rarely based on affection, working-class marital partnerships were a defence against the uncertain labour market and the multiple stresses of large families and cramped quarters. Ross explores the tensions between husbands and wives and the alliances between mothers and children, revealing the tensions inherent in the Victorian working-class family.

Ellen Ross is Professor of History and Women's Studies at Ramapo College of New Jersey where she convenes the Women's/Gender Studies programme. Since publishing *Love and Toil: Motherhood in Outcast London, 1870–1918* in 1993, her research has focused on middle-class slum philanthropists, concentrating on the 'Sisters of the People' of the West London Mission in Soho. In 2007, she will publish an edited anthology entitled: *Slum Travelers: Ladies and London Poverty, 1860–1920.*

There he would sit by the fireside,
Such a chilly man was John:
I hope and trust there's a nice warm fire
Where my old man's gone.
        — "He Was a Good Kind Husband,"
            sung by Vesta Victoria, 1890s

Who sits up when we're out at night? Woman, lovely woman!
Who meets us when we come home tight?
Woman, lovely woman!
By who up the stairs are we carefully led,
And when we're asleep and our senses have fled,
Runs through our pockets, when we are in bed?
Woman, lovely woman!
        — "Woman, Lovely Woman,"
            sung by James Fawn, late 1880s[1]

VICTORIAN AND EDWARDIAN MUSIC HALLS provide vivid commentaries on working-class London's marital and domestic lives. For every song of hopeful young romance, there were half a dozen evoking daily realities, their troubles and antagonisms. As uncovered in music hall lyrics, in autobiographies, and in the observations of contemporary social explorers, cockney culture incorporated distinct attitudes and arrangements toward gender.[2] These patterns diverged strikingly from those of the middle class, and were distinct in some ways too from those of workers in other parts of England. Through pre-World War I public discourse focused on such questions as wifebeating, temperance, prostitution, infant mortality, and divorce, the sexual and marriage patterns of the poor became the subject of rumination and debate.[3] The middle classes had indeed found an "incomprehensible region"[4] where many women were neither ladylike nor deferential, where men struggled to hold on to their authority over them, where "sexual antagonism" was openly acknowledged.[5]

Male domination and exploitation of women do not always lead to overt antagonism between the sexes; women may exhibit proper levels of deference and submissiveness; men may be perfectly satisfied with their degree of control over women. But a number of circumstances made such unchallenged male power relatively rare in large parts of working-class London.

For one thing, the economic basis of men's power was highly precarious for perhaps as many as one-half of London's working husbands. A large portion of London jobs were in the secondary sector — undercapitalized, small-scale, insecure, and not very profitable. Only about one-sixth of London's adult labor force was employed in factories through the 1890s. About 25 percent of adult male workers were unskilled.[6] The building, garment, shoe, furniture, and dockside trades were seasonal; trade slumps, illness, or injury could leave a man dependent on his family for survival. Husbands were supposed to "keep" their families, but everyone knew that in reality they would regularly fail. Few working men would be able to provide for their own or their wives' old age.[7] Children's wage contributions were therefore counted upon, and wives would serve as earners at some point in the life cycle of most families. At all times, wives' skill and energy provided the only real barrier between mere survival and a decent level of comfort.[8] A mother's aptitude for bargaining with the pawnshop assistant, the shopkeepers, and the school board visitors; her domestic arts; her friendship with the landlady — all were worth solid cash, and provided wives with some leverage against husbands. When children went to work, they viewed themselves as "working for" their mothers; their earnings entered the female part of the household exchequer.

Wives' economic importance was enhanced by the supportive presence of neighbors and kin (though the full extent to which matriocal living patterns had already emerged is hard to gauge).[9] Such networks may have developed and sustained concepts of women's material rights and prerogatives. We get a glimpse of their effect in a courtroom scene in the early 1900s in which a large group of women, their prams parked outside, encouraged another: "'You stick to it,' 'Go on wiv' it,' 'Get your separation.'"[10] London mothers of this era, as they are remembered by their children, or described by middle-class acquaintances, had assertive personalities and distinct opinions. [. . .] Thus despite their physical, economic, and legal disadvantages, wives were ready to stand their ground. The result was a culture where husband-wife violence was incredibly frequent, where pubs were regularly invaded by angry wives, where husbands cheated wives, wives stole from husbands, and music halls nightly unfolded new chapters in the domestic struggle for power.

This composite picture of cockney marriage best portrays life among the approximately 30 percent of London's population who lived in "poverty" according to Charles Booth's classification in the late 1880s (those whom he placed in Classes

A through D, "the very poor" and "the poor"), whose means, eighteen to twenty-one shillings a week, were just "barely sufficient for decent independent life." They were concentrated in London's inner ring, in Southwark, Whitechapel, Bethnal Green, and Shoreditch. Much of my discussion also encompasses the larger group, about one-half of London's population, whom Booth placed in Classes E and F ("comfortable working class, including all servants"). Through death, unemployment, or desertion, most of these families also risked periods of poverty.[11]

Chronologically, this study covers the period from 1870 to the First World War, when the cultural and material boundaries shaping family life remained relatively stable for London's working poor. Migration into the metropolis reached a peak in the 1840s, and then began to slow.[12] Though there were streets where transients clustered, most of those who came to London districts like Bethnal Green, Bermondsey, or Poplar in the 1870s and after entered a relatively stable urban culture, and likely encountered families who had lived in the nearby streets for a generation or more.[13] By the 1870s, or earlier, workers lived in neighborhoods from which the middle classes had largely fled. By the last decade of the century, better-off workers like artisans, foremen, and clerks were following their social betters in leaving inner London, moving to new districts supplied by commuter trains. For those who remained in the inner city, neighborhood — even street — endogamy was the rule among the nonservant poor,[14] and local definitions were an unspoken part of each marriage contract, each cohabitation arrangement. London's economy throughout this period continued to provide a great deal of casualized or seasonal labor for women and men trapped in the inner city.[15] Compulsory education, introduced at the start of this period, had meant a radical reorganization of family life for Britain's poor. Families would have to do without major contributions from children under school-leaving age, which was gradually raised throughout this generation. Thus from the 1870s, mothers with young children became more dependent on husbands' earnings, and on their own poorly paid employment. But the added burdens of keeping children clean, clothed, healthy, and punctual for school fell on mothers, settlement worker Anna Martin indignantly observed.[16] Finally, while fertility rates were falling throughout England in the generation before the war, those of the poorest London parishes remained high. While in 1911 there were about 226 births per thousand married women aged fifteen through forty-nine in Bethnal Green, in middle-class Hampstead the rate was only 121. Bethnal Green's ratio of 30.7 births for each 100 wives under forty-five in 1880–81 had fallen only slightly, to 28.3, in 1900–01; the rate in Hampstead at the turn of the century was only 18.3. Class differences in fertility were in fact sharpening in the decade before the war.[17]

Despite the ties of marriage, and their intense economic interdependence, women and men lived in quite separate material worlds organized around their responsibilities in a fairly rigid sexual division of labor. Marriage was not viewed as creating a new social unit: the fissure between wife and children on the one hand, and husband on the other, was accepted as a normal part of it. The fact that children through the early teens moved within "female" space, creates special problems of interpretation in the case of boys, who would have to move from the "woman's" to the "man's" world some time in their late teens. Cockney marriages were also posited on companionship, supervision, and material aid provided by groups outside the couple, neighbors and kin in particular. Goods, services, friendship, and certain spaces — in shops, pubs, doorways, streets — were shared with members of the same sex, and not with spouses.[18]

This sexual separation, however, should not be viewed as a contradiction in the institution of working-class marriage. For the marriage contract as it was understood did not enjoin romantic love or emotional "intimacy" (the latter a term not appropriate until quite recently), although some couples may well have sustained these "unofficially," and a minority had had "romantic" courtships. Despite the dreariness, tensions, and outbursts of violence that characterized much of married life, most women did not focus on the marital relationship, but rather defined wages, children, and kin as more central to their happiness. "Kindness" and efficiency in carrying out appropriate activities were the elements of a good spouse. "Intimacy" was confined within gender-specific spheres: for women, intimacy developed between mothers and children, and encompassed sisters, grandmothers, and neighbors.

The reciprocal obligations of spouses were quite openly acknowledged. Wives' responsibility for childcare and domestic labor are spelled out in numerous ballads and songs. [. . .] The failure of wives to provide such services, even for very good reason — such as a husband's refusal or inability to provide money needed for meals — was looked on by men as a major breach of their marital claims. Those of South London pawnbroker John Small's female customers who demanded quick service because "they had to get the old man's supper ready, or wouldn't they catch it!" were probably not exaggerating.[19]

Husbands' primary obligations were to work, and to hand over a customary amount of their pay to their wives. A wife expected that a husband would "work for" her, and being a husband was synonymous with providing support. [. . .] Women who were not supported by their husbands occasionally assumed that they were no longer married, and got into trouble in bigamy cases when they formed new attachments. One husband's failure to send money for many years was evidence to his wife that he was dead, and she was acquitted in her bigamy case.[20] [. . .] A husband's unemployment thus generated almost intolerable domestic tensions, and seems a factor in a large minority of the Old Bailey assault or murder cases. Unemployed men were angry and frustrated. Their wives' material deprivations could lead to taunting and reproaches. [. . .] When employed men came home with wages badly diminished — usually at the pub — their wives often attacked in sheer despair as they thought of the week ahead. In the 1900s, Margaret Loane reported that she had met a number of wives who did not hesitate to beat up their husbands when they returned home missing "an undue proportion of their week's wages."[21] [. . .] The rowing was not simply a result of weekend drinking, but also of the utterly different hopes, plans, and interests husbands and wives had for the weekly wage packet. Women were under pressure to redeem pawned clothing for the weekend, and to present a hot Sunday meal; their husbands wanted a drink, a visit to the pub.

Household jurisdictions, and even physical spaces, were sharply divided by gender. [. . .] Clean steps, sidewalks, windowsills, hearths, and so on, the work of wives or children, were physical outlines of women's space in households and streets. A young boy entrusted by his mother with domestic chores in his family's home in Wellington Place, Bethnal Green, in the early 1900s, angrily noted that his father and brothers repeatedly violated the household interior's feminine territory, the polished grate and swept-out hearth: "My father used to tap his pipe and empty its contents all over it, and my step-brothers threw their cigarette ends over the hearth."[22] [. . .] Stealing routes also indicate very clearly how spheres within households were demarcated by sex. Exactly because they did not fully share their resources, theft between cohabiting spouses was quite possible. [. . .] In the Jasper family in Hoxton, where the husband gave his wife only seven or eight shillings a week, a small part of his fairly large earnings, the wife stole money regularly from her husband, and so did some of the children. As the son, A.S. Jasper, wrote in his vivid autobiography:

> I remember my father going to his own bed. As he took his trousers off, his money fell out of his pocket. He was so drunk he couldn't bend down to find it. I was going upstairs as this happened and looked in the door and saw some cash on the floor. Knowing he always kept Mum short, I dived under the bed and picked up a two-shilling piece . . . I slid out, found Mum and gave her the two shillings I managed to pick up. She asked me how I came by it, and I explained what had happened. "Good boy," she says, and upstairs she went. Dad was now out to the world, so she had all the silver and left him the coppers.[23]

The internal "wage" system accentuated and dramatized the sexual separation within families. The custom of paying wives "wages" for housekeeping expenses, from which the wage earner's "pocket money" was reserved, was widespread throughout England and Wales by the mid nineteenth century. Possibly it arose as a way of grafting men's wage earning onto older traditions prescribing that wives and children earn most of their own keep.[24] The size of the wife's wage varied. The sum was determined in part by husbands' tastes and habits (teetotalers often gave their wives a few more shillings each week than did moderate drinkers).[25] Power relations within the couple and possibly neighborhood custom also bore on the size of her payment.[26] Wives' wages declined with husbands' underemployment, and disappeared altogether with unemployment, but many arrangements were so formalized that they remained unchanged throughout the wage-earning years, without regard to inflation, the birth of additional children, or special emergencies.[27] [. . .] Many men maintained control over their wages by being secretive about what they earned, and wives used a variety of ways of penetrating the secret, such as listening to street orators during strikes.[28] Actual household spending was entirely in wives' domain. "The custom of leaving the spending of money to the wife," reported Margaret Loane,

> is so deeply-rooted that children always speak of the family income as belonging entirely to her, and will constantly tell you, "Mother has to pay so and so for rent," "Mother is going to afford father this or that," "Mother isn't going to let father work for Mr. — anymore, she says the wages isn't worth the hours."[29]

"Family socialism," the term Loane used to describe the working-class family economy,[30] applied rightly only to the wife/children part of the household. For husbands, even if kindly and well-loved, lived on budgets separate from wives'.

[. . .] Husbands often organized at least some meals and the shopping for them on their own, sending children out, for example, to buy haddock and rewarding them with the head and tail.[31] [. . .] Many husbands bought clothing for themselves out of their pocket money, or provided special items for the household out of their separate funds.

The lower nutritional and caloric levels of wives' and children's diets throughout the prewar period are well documented. The disparity tended to go on outside of the notice of husbands, who exhibited remarkably little curiosity about where, and how, their own meals had been procured — an indifference that is surprising in a period when about two-thirds of workers' earnings were spent on food.[32] In Alice Linton's Shoreditch household, the father ate butter while the rest of the family had margarine. Another East London father ate bacon regularly, "a sign that you was well off" (his daughter observed much later), but the rest of the family went without.[33] Wives did their part to maintain this system, and were often discreet about their poor food. A Poplar woman was in the habit of dining on a "kettle bender," "a cup of crusts with hot water, pepper and salt, and a knob of margarine." "She always had this meal," her daughter remembers, "just before father came in for his."[34] [. . .] Much of the praise of good husbands Anna Martin heard from South London women presupposed a hunger gap as the norm: "All his thought is for his little children," "It's his rule never to eat a mouthful unless I share it," "He would never touch a bit if I and the children were without."[35]

Neighborhood-based "charitable" exchanges were organized predominantly by women, whose friendship and gossip networks implicitly accepted the need for mutual aid, and thus bound households together not only socially, but also materially. [. . .] Neighbors sustained each other through periods of illness, desertion, and un- employment; they contributed to the maintenance of the sick, the old, and women giving birth. Shopkeepers provided credit when employment was scarce.[36] [. . .]

The complexity, and significance to survival, of the neighborhood economy emerges clearly in autobiographies and oral histories, where the tracing of a mother's activities is likely to unwind a long series of connections, both material and personal. Mary Barnes Waters gives a detailed account of her mother's movements in a Hoxton neighborhood off Curtain Road in the early 1900s. Her second "husband" providing her only ten shillings a week, Mrs. Barnes took to selling offal from a basket in the gutter in front of Reid's Butchers near her home. With the butcher's help, Barnes eventually began to sell cooked sheep's heads and pigs' feet at a stall outside the Britannia Theater. Her economies included selling rabbit skins and the remains of the sheep's heads to Ward's, a nearby shop, while her daughter sold rags and jam jars to ragmen. Mrs. Barnes, meanwhile, was giving needy neighbors free meals from her stall: "When they were out of work and told her the tale, she couldn't refuse it," said her daughter years later. On Saturday evenings she regularly distributed her leftovers to those she knew needed the extra food; the odors of the meat stewing for Sunday dinner registered her distinct contribution to her neighbors.[37]

Other elements of the neighborhood economy, as well, belong to "women's sphere." [. . .] Pawning, a crucial link between household and neighborhood economy, was a woman's domain. Women giving depositions at the Worship Street Police Court often reported thefts of pawn tickets, and they appear to have stolen them more than did men. Lent, stolen, or honestly gotten pawn tickets were transferred and traded in complex patterns between groups of women, the court cases show.[38] It required skill and experience to know which shops paid best for pledges of different categories, and how to package them to get maximum value,[39] and women were far more likely to have cultivated this skill. The rings of thieves who used women to pawn their stolen goods paid homage to women's expertise in maneuvering within their neighborhood economies.[40]

A great deal of domestic pawning went on outside the knowledge of men. A boy growing up in Bromley-by-Bow before the war remembers running errands and taking items to the pawnshop for a neighbor who often urged him to hurry "'fore the old man comes in." [. . .] Most family possessions, including men's clothing, were seen as belonging to the mother's jurisdiction simply because of their potential as pawnable goods. When John Blake's father wore his good suit to the pub near their Poplar house, he was sharply instructed by his wife to avoid spilling beer on it, which would lower its value at the counter.[41] Because of its greater value than either women's or children's clothing, men's clothing was prime material for the pawnshop. [. . .] The magnitude, and the gendered character of pawning in the poorest quarters, is vividly illustrated by a Friday night fire at a large St. Giles pawnshop in the 1860s. Neighborhood women by the hundreds had regularly resorted there, many without informing their husbands, and pawning was at its most intense on weekends. The women turned out en masse to help and to treat the firemen with beer, remaining with them throughout the night as the fire continued to burn. Their lack of success led to an epidemic of wifebeatings. [. . .]

As the St. Giles episode shows, husband-wife violence was indeed a "privileged" form in a culture that permitted a wide range of physical expressions of anger, and where violence was a special prerogative of those in authority. Children were slapped and spanked by police, neighbors, and teachers as well as by parents; families feuded violently; fights broke out in pubs and streets not only between men but sometimes between women. Nancy Tomes's rough estimate, for London in a slightly earlier period, the 1850s and 1860s, was that in any neighborhood of two to four hundred houses, ten to twenty men would be convicted of common assaults on women during any year.[42] On a street off Brick Lane in the 1870s, where a coster had attempted to murder his mother-in-law, a slippermaker told a court that he "heard cries of murder, but that being such a common occurence in that neighbourhood I took no notice of it." Cross-examined, he explained that he heard such cries three or four times a week.[43] [. . .]

Community behavior in wifebeating incidents certainly acknowledged the inevitability of violence between spouses, and the "right" of husbands to beat up wives. Outsiders were considerably more likely to intervene when men attacked women with whom they were not living or married.[44] Neighbors in the same house or street were acutely aware of conflict going on nearby, often because they could easily hear or see it. The sound of shouting and blows would cause them to collect on stairs, landings, and at windows, but fights would normally be allowed to continue. Only the presence of a really dangerous weapon, the sight of a lot of blood, or sounds of real terror would get them to intervene. William Hancock's murder of Elizabeth Glover, whom he had probably just met, outside the Black Swan Tavern in Bow Road in January 1879, serves as a dramatic case in point. Hancock threw Glover to the ground repeatedly as a crowd of six or seven gathered. He kept them from interfering by saying, "It's my wife, and I want to take her home, she is drunk" (which Glover was meanwhile loudly denying). A waiter from the tavern and a policeman who had been spectators testified in court that they had avoided interfering "because I thought [said the policeman] they were man and wife . . . ."[45]

Fighting between men, or between women, was usually public and ritualized. Both parties had to agree on the match; coats were removed; seconds were chosen; a place "to spar" was found.[46] Domestic collisions were far less orderly, and more dangerous as a result, especially to women who were usually, though not always, the weaker fighters. The fights normally took place at home. Couples did not decorously exchange punches, but wrestled, slapped, kicked, bit, and threw household objects, while terrified children looked on or tried to intervene. Injuries could be severe. While a few shootings were the result of premeditation, most assaults were products of uncontrollable rage. Both women and men in their court testimony commented on their inability to cope with it. "I got into that way I did not know what I was doing," said one woman who had knifed her husband.[47] The image of wives as delicate and passive, immobile victims of brutal husbands, which dominated nineteenth-century campaigns against wifebeating, and still prevails in today's literature, was probably inaccurate. Cockney men were small and wiry (East London boxing was welterweight and lightweight), while married women tended to be stout, and their very heavy domestic labor developed their shoulders and biceps. Religious visitors' lessons in female patience and meekness met few receptive ears.

Violence itself would not bring wives to the "threshold" of tolerance for marriage or husbands.[48] What did cause women to seek legal separations, or to leave their husbands informally, were threats of murder, physical attacks on the children (very rare according to all observers), refusal to provide income, and sexual insults (but usually not sexual jealousy). "I would forgive anything," a woman told William Fitzsimmons, a police court missionary, "but the filthy names he calls me." At age twenty-three, she had been deafened in one ear and had her nose broken in a long series of attacks by her husband.[49] Wives hated and feared the injuries they received, some of which did indeed leave scars or disabilities. But all the evidence we have on domestic violence in this era suggests that its social meaning was different from today's. If marriage did not enjoin trust, sharing, and partnership, then it was far less surprising that conflict should frequently erupt there. Since men's desire for domination in marriage, and women's to undermine it were openly acknowledged in their culture, it was not unexpected that men might use violent means to obtain wives' obedience. Marriage created no sacred or separate space; there was nothing secret or shameful about a Saturday night fight. Wives' black eyes were one material, and predictable, result of sexual antagonism.

While wifebeating is easily comprehensible in the atmosphere of sexual hostility I have sketched out, sexuality, which today is "officially" associated with emotional intimacy and reciprocity, is far more problematic. Working-class London was considerably more open about sex than was genteel culture, but sexuality nonetheless remained a private and largely invisible realm. As a result, women's rights and privileges were neither defined nor asserted, and, in the realm of sex, male domination remained mostly unchallenged.

The sexual practices of the Victorian working classes are deeply hidden from view and by the latter decades of the century, the sexual taboos of contemporary middle-class observers of the poor coincided with those of their subjects. Poor women were not likely to talk about sex to outsiders, most of whom were male. General and euphemistic statements are difficult to interpret today. Even Anna Martin, an outspoken feminist, only hinted that wives were "subjected, and sometimes deliberately, to injuries of a far worse kind [than wifebeating], as doctors in the leading hospitals can testify."[50] Sexual silence and ignorance provided the backdrop against which the slightly naughty songs of Marie Lloyd ("Please Mr. Porter," "A Little of What You Fancy Does You Good") could be richly appreciated. Colin MacInnis is impressed with the almost complete lack of sexual passion as a theme in music hall lyrics, a strong contrast with contemporary French, German, and Spanish popular music.[51] Prostitutes lived among the poor, every neighborhood had someone who served as an abortionist, and children could see "smutty" acts at penny gaffs, but sexual ignorance was somehow maintained. Adults were careful to avoid sexual subjects in front of children, and children were always sent out during childbirth. Grace Foakes, whose mother had fourteen births, was surprised by each of them, unless she had happened to notice her mother purchasing baby clothes. A Hoxton woman "knew nothing" about sex at her marriage after the war; a woman from Lewisham recently recalled her astonishment at her first childbirth in 1911 when she realized that the baby was not born through her navel as she had supposed. Thus the seventeen-year-old Whitechapel girl whose newborn baby was found dead in a pile of rubbish had some credibility when she told the magistrate that she had had no idea that she was "in the family way."[52]

The public and private silence about sex made this arena one in which it was impossible for wives to develop a collective sense of where their "rights" lay and what their interests were. Women who would fight furiously over a husband's sixpence spent on drink, would yield regretfully to an unwanted sexual advance. As one Rotherhithe woman, then several months pregnant, told Anna Martin in about 1911, "I dreaded your finding out, for I knew how upset you would be; of course it's only bringing poverty and misery into the world, but what is a woman to do when a man's got a drop of drink in him, and she's all alone?"[53] Court missionary William Fitzsimmons implied that wives of men who had contracted venereal diseases feared the infection, but had no choice but to submit to their husbands, so long as they lived together.[54] [. . .]

Pregnancy was assigned squarely to "women's sphere"; it was vaguely blamed on women, though biological fatherhood was surely understood. Music hall songs like "I'm Very Unkind to My Wife" jocularly view the arrival of a pack of children as one of the many annoyances which a wife brings to a man. Lilly Morris sang, "Don't Have Any More, Missus Moore," holding the mother solely responsible it seems for the Moores' twenty children.[55] A Poplar man was overheard by his young daughter complaining to his wife, "I can't hang me trousers on the end of the bed . . . that you're not like that [pregnant]."[56]

The fissures present in the family thus encouraged husbands in their failure to consider sex, or its products — children — a joint responsibility. Another child was generally not "another mouth to feed" for the father, but only for the mother. Abstinence and coitus interruptus, the most common methods of birth control until very recent times, require male cooperation. Some women surely frequently refused intercourse and got away with it. Either they were able and willing to fight for this right, or they had "good" husbands. A few adventurous women may have secretly used sponges, douches, and later, diaphragms without their husbands' knowledge. One Lewisham woman was fitted with a diaphragm at a Marie Stopes clinic in the 1920s. Her husband, she reasoned, "was a bit of a devil, and I thought I'm not having babies for you — give me babies so I could stay in . . . and he could go out on his own." The husband never commented on the small size of their family, two children.[57] [. . .] But for most couples, there is certainly no evidence during the pre-World War I era that sex provided occasions in which tensions between women and men were resolved. It had simply remained an arena in which male dominance was still unquestioned.

It is not my purpose to buttress the now sagging "Whig" theory of family history according to which the antagonisms of Victorian marriage have today been eradicated, replaced by intimate, "companionate" relationships which guarantee equality and minimize hostility between the sexes. Young and Willmott's Bethnal Green study of the children and grandchildren of 'outcast London" in the 1950s reveals few "symmetrical" couples. Most had worked out complex compromises between the demands of spouse and of neighbors, kin, and workmates; between wives' claims and husbands' wages; between public and domestic spaces. [. . .] General concepts like "patriarchy" and "male dominance" can be enormously amplified through examinations of the working balance of daily power between women and men in households, streets, schools, and workplaces. For the power of men to command women's work, their bodies, and their loyalties has been strikingly variable even in Western cultures. Systems of gender relationships are malleable, and the forces shaping them in Victorian London were as complex as that society itself and its class system: the size and regularity of wages for men and for women; the activities of the state and voluntary institutions; patterns of housing and residence; sexual knowledge and attitudes; hopes for social mobility, and so forth. The depressed and sweated labor market described in such detail in *Outcast London* thus provided the external boundaries for London's distinct domestic arrangement. Working-class London's marriages furnish a close look at the domestic side of gender in a single time and place, as well as a lesson in the intertwining of gender systems with the other major systems of the allocation of social power and resources.

Further reading

Ross's article 'Fierce Questions and Taunts' became part of her major study of working-class family life: *Love and Toil: Motherhood in Outcast London, 1870–1918* (Oxford: Oxford University Press, 1993). A good starting point for thinking about the history of the family is Leonore Davidoff *et al.*, *The Family Story: Blood, Contract and Intimacy, 1830–1960* (London: Longman, 1999). For a history of childhood, see: Hugh Cunningham, *The Children of the Poor: Representations of Childhood since the Seventeenth Century* (Oxford: Blackwell, 1991); Anna Davin, *Growing Up Poor: Home, School and Street in London, 1870–1914* (London: Rivers Oram, 1996). Marital violence is treated in A. James Hammerton, *Cruelty and Companionship: Conflict in Nineteenth-Century Married Life* (London: Routledge, 1992).

Notes

1   Christopher Pulling, *They Were Singing* (London: George G. Harrap, 1952): 70–71. I am using the late Victorian and Edwardian music hall as a genuine, if attenuated, expression of London working-class culture, a position convincingly presented in Jacqueline S. Bratton, *The Victorian Popular Ballad* (Totowa, N.J.: Rowman and Littlefield, 1975); and Martha Vicinus, *The Industrial Muse* (London: Croom Helm, 1974): chap. 6.

2   "Cockney" is used here to refer to working-class London. On British family life in this period see Laura Oren, "The Welfare of Women in Labouring Families: England 1860–1950," *Feminist Studies* 1 (Winter-Spring 1973): 107–25; and Standish Meacham, *A Life Apart: The English Working Class 1890–1914* (Cambridge: Harvard University Press, 1977): chap. 2 through 6, which includes generous sections on neighborhood life. On London in particular, see: John R. Gillis, "Servants, Sexual Relations, and the Risks of Illegitimacy in London, 1801–1900," *Feminist Studies* 5 (Spring 1979): 142–73; Patricia Malcolmson, "Getting a Living in the Slums of Victorian Kensington," *London Journal* 1 (May 1975): 28–51; Gareth Stedman Jones, "Working-Class Culture and Working-Class Politics in London 1870–1900: Notes on the Remaking of a Working Class," *Journal of Social History* 7 (Summer 1975): 460–508; Nancy Tomes, "'A Torrent of Abuse': Crimes of Violence between Working-Class Men and Women in London, 1840–1875," *Journal of Social History* 11 (Spring 1978): 329–45.

3   For some recent discussions of nineteenth-century domestic violence, see Janet R. Lambertz, "Male-Female Violence in Late Victorian and Edwardian England" (B.A. thesis, Harvard University, 1979); Margaret May, "Violence in the Family: An Historical Perspective," in *Violence and the Family*, ed. John Powell Martin (New York: John Wiley, 1978); Tomes, "Torrent of Abuse." Two standard works on temperance are Brian Harrison, *Drink and the Victorians: The Temperance Question in England 1815–1872* (London: Faber & Faber, 1971); and A.E. Dingle, *The Campaign for Prohibition in Victorian England* (London: Croom Helm, 1980). Excellent studies of prostitution are: Judith Walkowitz, *Prostitution and Victorian Society: Women, Class, and the State* (New York and Cambridge: Cambridge University Press, 1980); Deborah Gorham, "'The Maiden Tribute of Babylon' Re-Examined: Child Prostitution and the Idea of Childhood in Late-Victorian England," *Victorian Studies* 21 (Spring 1978): 353–79. Infant mortality and the public scrutiny of working-class motherhood are treated in Anna Davin, "Imperialism and Motherhood," *History Workshop* 5 (Spring 1978): 9–65; Carol Dyhouse, "Working-Class Mothers and Infant Mortality in England, 1895–1914," *Journal of Social History* 12 (Winter 1979): 248–67. On divorce, see Iris Minor, "Working-Class Women and Matrimonial Law Reform, 1890–1914," in *Ideology and the Labour Movement*, ed. David E. Martin and David Rubinstein (London: Croom Helm, 1979).

4   C.F.G. Masterman, *The Heart of the Empire* (1901), quoted in Gareth Stedman Jones, *Outcast London: A Study in the Relationship between Classes in Victorian Society* (Harmondsworth, England: Penguin Books, 1971): 326.

5   The term "sexual antagonism" is introduced and illustrated in Marilyn Strathern, *Women in Between* (London and New York: Seminar Press, 1972), especially pp. 296–314; and Ann Whitehead, "Sexual Antagonism in Herefordshire," in *Dependence and Exploitation in Work and Marriage*, ed. D.L. Barker and S. Allen (London: Longman, 1976).

6   Stedman Jones, *Outcast London*, pt. 1, and app. 2, p. 386 (1891 figures).

7   See Michele Barrett and Mary McIntosh, "The 'Family Wage': Some Problems for Socialists and Feminists," *Capital and Class* 11 (Summer 1980): 51–52. On poverty in old age, see Charles Booth, *The Aged Poor in England and Wales* (London: Macmillan, 1894): 14–15.

8   Ada Heather-Bigg, "The Wife's Contribution to the Family Income," *Economic Journal* 4 (1894): 51–58; Henry Higgs, "Workmen's Budgets," *Journal of the Royal Statistical Society* (cited hereafter as *JRSS*) 66 (June 1893): 255–85.

9   In the Katharine Buildings, model dwellings near Tower Bridge opened in 1885, 13 percent of the adult women and 6 percent of the men had kin living in the buildings, according to my rough count of the building records kept by Beatrice Webb and Ella Pycroft for five years ("Received of the Inhabitants," *MS*, London School of Economics [Coll. Misc. 43]). See also, Raphael Samuel, *East End Underworld: Chapters in the Life of Arthur Harding* (London: Routledge & Kegan Paul, 1981): chap. 8; and Hugh McLeod, *Class and Religion in the Late Victorian City* (London: Croom Helm, 1974): 10.

10   John Hasloch Potter, *Inasmuch: The Story of the Police Court Mission, 1876–1926* (London: William & Norgate, 1927): 67–68.

11   Charles Booth, *Life and Labour of the People in London*, 1st ser.: *Poverty*, 5 vols, reprint of the 1902 ed. (New York: Augustus M. Kelley, 1969), 2: 21.

12   Eric E. Lampard, "The Urbanizing World," in *The Victorian City: Images and Realities*, ed. H.J. Dyos and Michael Wolff, 2 vols (London and Boston: Routledge & Kegan Paul, 1973): 13.

13   H.J. Dyos, "The Slums of Victorian London," *Victorian Studies* 11 (September 1967): 5–40.

14   On street and neighborhood endogamy in some selected working-class districts, see McLeod, *Class and Religion*, table 4, pp. 296–97.

15   Stedman Jones, *Outcast London*, p. 322, and chap. 18.

16   Anna Martin, "The Mother and Social Reform," *The Nineteenth Century and After* 73 (May and June 1913): 1060–79, 1235–55.

17   John W. Innes, *Class Fertility Trends in England and Wales, 1876–1934* (Princeton, NJ: Princeton University Press, 1938): app. 2, p. 134 (My thanks to Ros Petchesky for this reference); T.A. Welton, "A Study of Some Portions of the Census of London for 1901," *JRSS* 65 (1902): 447–500, 470–73; T.H.C. Stevenson, "The Fertility of Various Social Classes in England and Wales from the Middle of the Nineteenth Century to 1911," *JRSS* 83 (1920): 401–432, 431.

18   Women's neighborhood ties, and their mutual aid, are the subject of my paper, "Survival Networks: Women's Neighbourhood Sharing in London Before World War One," *History Workshop Journal*, 15 (1983): 4–27.

19   James Greenwood, "Pawnbrokery in London," *Hours at Home* 7 (1868): 109–17, 116. I owe this reference to Janet Lambertz, who cited this article in her "Male-Female Violence."

20   *Old Bailey Trials*, Creighton, vol. 120 (1894): 1196.

21   Margaret Loane, "Husband and Wife Among the Poor," *Contemporary Review* 87 (February 1905): 222–39, 222.

22   George Rushbrook, *Memories* (1974), typescript, Tower Hamlets (London) Local History Library, p. 4.

23   A.S. Jasper, *A Hoxton Childhood* (London: Centerprise Publications, 1974): 31; see also 40, 51.

24   Ivy Pinchbeck, *Women Workers and the Industrial Revolution, 1750–1850* (1930; reprint ed., New York: Augustus M. Kelley, 1960): 1, 312; Alice Clark, *Working Life of Women in the Seventeenth Century* (1919; reprinted., New York: Augustus M. Kelley, 1968): 54.

25   Charles Booth Manuscripts, London School of Economics, ser. B. vol. 352 (George Duckworth's discussion with Constable W.R. Ryland, Hoxton Subdivision of the G Division of the Metropolitan Police, 23 May 1898).

26   On the use of the term "wages" for wives, see Oren, "Welfare of Women": 112–13; Essex Files, no. 368 (a man born in Wapping in 1897, whose father was a docker);

and Elizabeth Roberts, "Working Class Women in the North West," *Oral History* 5 (Autumn 1977): 7–30, 13.

27 Oren, "Welfare of Women": 111–12; Peter N. Stearns, "Working Class Women in Britain, 1890–1914," in *Suffer and Be Still: Women in the Victorian Age*, ed. Martha Vicinus (Bloomington, Ind.: Indiana University Press, 1972): 116; Meacham, *A Life Apart*, chap. 3.

28 H.A. Mess, *Casual Labour at the Docks* (London: G. Bell and Sons, 1916): 35.

29 Loane, "Husband and Wife": 226.

30 Margaret Loane, *The Common Growth* (London: Edward Arnold, 1911): 278.

31 Samuel, *East End Underworld*: 28–29; Jack Harrison (pseud. for a man born in 1884, son of a cabinetmaker who eventually moved to Battersea). Essex Files, no. 225; Hine, 'Poplar Childhood": 35.

32 *Parliamentary Papers* 1905, vol. LXXXIV, pp. 6, 8 (the second part of the Board of Trade Survey of British workers' family budgets).

33 Linton, *Early Memories*, pp. 6, 13; interview by Raphael Samuel with Ethel Wentworth, pseud, for a daughter of a railway employee who grew up on Fulbourne Street in Whitechapel.

34 A woman born on Maroon Street, Limehouse, in 1896, Essex Files, no. 298.

35 Anna Martin, "Mother and Social Reform": 1079.

36 Loane, *Common Growth*: 104; and *An Englishman's Castle* (London: Edward Arnold, 1909): 298; George Sims, *How the Poor Live and Horrible London*, combined ed. (London: Chatto & Windus, 1889): 127.

37 Mary Barnes Waters (pseud. for a woman born in the notorious Norfolk Gardens, off Curtain Road in Hoxton, in 1904), Hackney People's Autobiography typescript, supplied by the interviewer, Anna Davin.

38 *London City Mission Magazine*, October 1864, p. 206 (women at police court because of lost pawn tickets); Mary Blaney, Worship Street Police Court, "May 1874" bundle (a servant who stole three pawn tickets from her landlady and sold two of them to another woman); Sophia Cooper got twenty-one days for stealing three sheets from her landlady, and selling their pawn tickets (Worship Street, "Feb–March, 1874" bundle). Police court depositions from 1855 to 1889 are at the Greater London Record Office, County Hall. Many thanks to the staff of the old Middlesex Record Office, who helped me locate them in 1979, and who have been invariably helpful since then.

39 [Thomas Wright], *The Pinch of Poverty: Sufferings and Heroism of the London Poor* (London: Isbister & Co., 1892): 301.

40 Jasper, *Hoxton Childhood*: 22–23; *Old Bailey Trials*, Perry, Hollingsworth, and Black, vol. 110 (1889): 849 (a Barking case in which a man asked a neighborhood woman to pawn boots he had stolen); Thames Police Court, "Feb-March, 1873" bundle (a mixed-sex group of thieves, in which the women did the group's pawning).

41 John C. Blake, *Memories of Old Poplar* (London: Stepney Books Publications, 1977): 11.

42 Tomes, "Torrent of Abuse": 330.

43 *Old Bailey Trials*, French, vol. 79 (1874): 389–90.

44 Tomes, "Torrent of Abuse": 336–38.

45 *Old Bailey Trials*, Hancock, vol. 89 (1879): 321; Holmes, *Pictures and Problems*: 62–63.

46 Some examples of ritualized fights between men are in Bethnal Green News, 7 September 1895, p. 6; and *Old Bailey Trials*, Onion, vol. 80 (1874): 209.

47 *Old Bailey Trials*, Palmer, vol. 69 (1869): 267.

48 The term "threshold" describing wives' tolerance for domestic violence is developed by Lambertz, in "Male-Female Violence."

49 *Parliamentary Papers 1912–13*, vol. XIX, par. 19, 473f (testimony of William Fitzsimmons).

50   Martin, "Mother and Social Reform": 1077.

51   Colin Macinnis, *Sweet Saturday Night: Songs of the 1890's* (London: MacGibbon & Kee, 1967): 39.

52   Grace Foakes, *Between High Walls: A London Childhood* (London: Shepheard-Walwyn, 1972): 11; interviews with Mr. and Mrs. Kemp (both were pseudonyms; the wife was born in 1905, her husband in 1894), by Raphael Samuel, typescript; Moore (Essex file no. 333, p. 26); "Mrs. N., born 1884, Childbirth at Home — Lewisham, 1911," dittoed excerpts from an interview by Frances Widdowson, Goldsmith's College, University of London; *Bethnal Green News*, 16 March 1895, p. 6.

53   Martin, "Mother and Social Reform": 1061.

54   *Parliamentary Papers 1912–13*, vol. XIX, par. 19, 522.

55   Pulling, *They Were Singing*: 70–71; MacInnis, *Sweet Saturday Night*: 5.

56   Mary Davis (pseud. for a woman born in Canning Town, 1895), Essex Files, no. 126, p. 25. Her mother had nineteen children, of whom only seven survived.

57   "Childbirth in Greenwich Hospital 1930's and Walworth Road Clinic," dittoed interview by Frances Widdowson.

PART 12

Sexuality

I F THE PUBLIC AT LARGE knows anything about the Victorians, it is that they were sexually repressed, unless they were completely depraved; they are seen as hypocrites about the issue of sexual pleasure and the place it took in their society. The Victorians apparently ended the period of sexual licence that we associate with the eighteenth century and with the Regency. They initiated a regime that rendered sex taboo, something that should not be spoken about. The purpose of sexuality was procreation not pleasure. Moreover, the Victorians exemplified (even if they did not invent) the double standard in sexuality: men who exercised their sexuality outside marriage were barely censured whereas women who behaved in the same way were viewed as immoral. The French theorist and historian Michel Foucault, author of a three-volume *History of Sexuality* (published in English 1978– 86), took issue with what he called the 'repressive hypothesis'. He agreed that the Victorians were reluctant to discuss sex openly, but noted there was more literature and legislation relating to sexual behaviour than ever before. He argued that, paradoxically, sexuality was crucial to the way Victorian society functioned and was another way of exerting control and power.

In the 1980s and 1990s sexuality moved to the centre of studies of the Victorians. Nineteenth-century reformers were particularly concerned about prostitution, a very public form of sexuality, as female prostitutes often touted for business on the street (even though it is now accepted that the number of prostitutes was probably not as great as reformers claimed at the time). Historians such as **Judith Walkowitz** demythologised sex workers, viewing them as ordinary working-class women, not, as contemporaries saw them, moral outcasts or degenerates. Prostitution was something that women were forced to do, usually for short periods, because of poverty. There have also been studies of the methods used to discourage masturbation or to suggest that women could not achieve orgasm, examples of the medicalisation of sexuality where the medical profession employed its authority to explain sexuality. Pornography has been examined for its insights into sexual behaviour. Jeffery Weeks demonstrated how homosexuality was a new category in Victorian Britain; a notion of 'same sex sexuality' was only clearly defined (partly through criminal legislation) in the later nineteenth century. The evolution of a gay subculture, particularly in London, was revealed, although other historians have traced its roots much further back. Imaginative research delved into parliamentary reports, social reportage, novels and private diaries to reveal the complexities of sexual behaviour. There were undoubtedly attempts to make sexuality invisible in the public sphere but what also emerged in the late twentieth century was the realisation that a private culture existed in the Victorian period that was more at ease with sexuality than people had thought.

Michael Mason

WORKING-CLASS SEXUALITY

The Making of Victorian Sexuality (Oxford: Oxford University Press, 1995), 139–43.

The late **Michael Mason** provided one of the most extensive discussions of Victorian sexuality to date. In a two-volume study he sought to recover the full complexity of the Victorian relationship with sex. His theme was the 'anti-sensualism' of the Victorian age; in other words, the use of taboos around sexuality. He argued that, although it was true that there was an extensive reticence about sexuality in the nineteenth century, the clichés about repression did not really explain Victorian culture. He distrusted explanations that assumed this anti-sensualism was the product of middle-class prudes who simply imposed these values on the rest of society. Rather, he demonstrated how widely this sexual culture was shared throughout society. He also argued that anti-sensualism was very much seen as progressive and therefore we need to appreciate Victorian sexuality as more complex than the conventional view allows.

Mason explored some common assumptions about the Victorians including the belief that the elite treated adultery with leniency, married women had less freedom than unmarried girls, and middle-class men resorted to prostitutes. He found all these assertions to be overstated. In a discussion of middle-class prudery, he rejected the suggestion that the Victorians were shy when it came to mentioning body parts or physical conditions like pregnancy. Rather, he saw theirs as 'a genuine and deeply rooted commitment to a fineness or purity of tone in respect of sexual matters, a commitment bound up, for example, with national pride'.

In the following Reading, Mason dealt with working-class sexuality and the question of respectability. Middle-class Victorians were concerned about the level of overcrowding in working-class homes, which they feared might lead to sexual degeneracy and even incest. Respectability was one of the most important attributes of the Victorians and many scholars have explored the way it manifested itself (see the Readings by **Ellen Ross** (pp. 324–38), **Peter Bailey** (pp. 380–94), and **Gertrude Himmelfarb** (pp. 209–19)). Mason found that respectability was often situational and noted that all classes strove towards the ideal in their own way. For the poor, it might allow them self-respect and the opportunity for charity. For other classes, sexual respectability garnered them the esteem of their peers and betters. It added to a family's standing in the community on every level. But how did respectability manifest itself on different social levels? Elsewhere in the book, Mason suggested that for the bourgeoisie it meant a degree of trust for young women and men to behave themselves during courtship and the degree to which sexual misconduct (premarital pregnancy) could remove the community's approval. For the working class at all levels, sexual respectability was also admired, and Mason explored how this differed in town and country over time. Sexual self-control, Mason demonstrated, was crucial for all classes, although this does not imply that there was as widespread an ignorance about sex as is often suggested.

Michael Mason (1941–2003) was Professor of Literature at University College, London and a founder of the publishing house Junction Books, later Fourth Estate. Besides *The Making of Victorian Sexuality* and *The Making of Victorian Sexual Attitudes* (both 1994), he also published on Robert Browning, Tennyson and James Joyce.

―――――――――――

S EXUAL MORALISM WAS an important aspect of the ideal of domestic respectability. [. . .] Prostitute funerals in London's East End were apparently liable to be hooted and stoned by 'the virtuous matrons of the neighbourhood' — who, according to Nathaniel Hawthorne's impression, were often a conspicuous if small admixture in slum areas. (By contrast, with no apparent economic rhyme or reason, one London East End court is reported as being on excellent terms with its two resident prostitutes.) William Swan, admittedly a Baptist, twice felt forced to move from lodgings in the Stratford area of London because of the immorality of landladies (in the second house there was 'a married man constantly visiting and the husband not ignorant of it').[1]

The drive to working-class sexual respectability, where it arose, showed a remarkable power to overcome the most important physical constraint in working-class life, namely, domestic crowding. Nineteenth-century middle-class opinion had a strongly environmentalist bias [. . .] and was on the whole incredulous that physical proximity could be other than morally depraving. The belief that individuals who dressed, slept, washed, and excreted very near each other were much more likely to have sexual intercourse seems to have been practically universal. Some otherwise sensible commentators, such as Joseph Kay, dwelt obsessively on the idea of incestuous and freely copulating working-class people in very crowded environments. The proof usually offered of the connection between crowding and sexual licence was simply a kind of thought experiment: high densities of unmarried individuals in beds or bedrooms were alleged, and the reader then invited to draw the supposedly inevitable conclusion about sexual outcomes.

Only occasionally was evidence produced that the worst had happened. Apart from the broad truth of multi-occupied beds and bedrooms the facts mustered by investigators keen to prove the crowding/sexual licence hypothesis now tend to seem strangely feeble. One much cited testimony was that of Riddall Wood, giving evidence in [Edwin] Chadwick's sanitary report. He had visited slum housing in a variety of centres — Manchester, Liverpool, Ashton-under-Lyne, Hull, and Pendelton — and gives several anecdotes of crowding of the sexes, but this was the mouse that emerged when he was asked to summarize his findings on 'persons of different sexes sleeping promiscuously': 'I think I am speaking within bounds when I say I have amongst my memoranda above 100 cases, including, of course, cases of persons of different sexes sleeping in the same room'. Yet these 'memoranda', amounting to very little more than a reiteration of the familiar truth of overcrowding, are endlessly quoted by subsequent commentators as a proof of the fact of general working-class sexual depravity under these conditions.[2]

Riddall Wood does cite a pair of prostitutes who said they had been corrupted by sharing accommodation with married couples. We also have, however, the very words of a prostitute from the Home Counties on this question, and her testimony is oddly half-hearted:

> If it hadn't been that we were all forced to undress ourselves before one another, and five of us to sleep in the same room, I do think — though perhaps that wasn't the only reason — that I should not have been leading this life I now am. If there had been no one else sleeping in the same room, I might perhaps have fallen into this way, but I don't think I should have gone wrong so soon.

A modern historian has concluded from a survey of statements made by unmarried mothers applying to London's Foundling Hospital that 'they throw serious doubt on the idea that housing and working conditions at that time gave the popular classes a broad familiarity with sexual matters'. In the last decades of the century parental reticence on sex in front of children was so great that some working-class sons and daughters in London remained ignorant about basic information into adult life.[3] Examples were reported in the literature of illegitimate births to women who had been made pregnant by men in crowded accommodation, but the general statistics of illegitimacy showed no correlation with density in housing; this was carefully demonstrated in 1862. Marriage rates tended to peak in the autumn and early winter, and, for country districts at least, this may be linked to the high known rates of pre-nuptial pregnancy; in other words, according to a modern study, 'in the crowded housing conditions of the period, courtships involving intimacy would be more likely to occur in the summer than in the winter months'. Mothers' depositions concerning illegitimate births in rural Kent often cite sexual encounters at summer festivities.[4]

This puts the relation between crowding and sexual licence in a startlingly new light — indeed it completely reverses the nineteenth-century wisdom on the question. While it may not have been universally true that courtships were conducted more intensely outdoors [. . .] and while acceptable thresholds of exposure of bodies and bodily functions may have been lower in working-class than in middle-class homes, there is much anecdotal evidence of working-class households trying to mitigate the effects of proximity — so much so that one historian of slum housing has written of her continual surprise at 'the extent to which the poor strove . . . to conform to middle-class standards of morality'.[5] Nineteenth-century observers were so keen to discern depravity that the meaning of their own observations sometimes has to be read against the grain of the surrounding argument. A writer who took refuge early in the morning in a Northumberland cottage, to wait for a coach, gives a vivid and important picture of how decency could be maintained in crowded rural accommodation:

> we were at once astounded, and we will confess it, in some degree amused, to behold one after another of the family creeping forth from some unseen places in the room; some were still asleep; some, a married couple, were having breakfast, and some dressing themselves, thus, the whole of this large family slept, and had their meals in the same room.

But in the same volume this writer fulminates about the 'over-mastering circumstances' which result in incest, and about how it is 'beyond all conception' that 'unutterable horrors' do not take place in crowded cottages, apparently unconscious that he has convincingly described (though as a merely surprising and amusing feature of working-class life) how circumstances were resisted and horrors avoided.[6]

The *Morning Chronicle,* often unfashionable on such topics, gave due weight to the 'praiseworthy effort . . . for the conservation of decency' sometimes to be seen in one-roomed rural houses, and there are many inadvertent glimpses in the literature of very meagre accommodation being exploited for the maximum decorousness: of housewives in Northumberland mining villages running across the street to the 'pantry' (an outdoor foodstore) to change their clothes if a stranger visited, for example, and of expedients even in the lowest multi-occupied rooms in London, such as 'the decency of an old curtain' round a married couple's bed, or a neat separation of personal items showing 'the idea of *meum* and *tuum* . . . some clinging still as to a home'. Parliamentary officialdom too, in its stilted way, acknowledged 'numerous instances . . . of beauty, modesty, and intelligence in girls enduring the intensest cubicular crowding'.

The tenor of the small number of nineteenth-century working-class autobiographies that touch on this subject is that restraints and separations were achieved, even if sexual knowledge was learnt early. In one of these there is an account of two sisters and two brothers, occupying one room in Spitalfields in the 1860s, which beautifully indicates how working-class people strove to maintain standards: 'the men dressed first and came out into the street, or under an archway, while the women rose and dressed'. At one stage in his young life as a colliery worker Thomas Burt had to share a bedroom with six relations; the family were Methodists, and 'we managed, with mutual cordiality and goodwill, to get along very harmoniously'. Laurence Housman has a telling anecdote of how the local poacher's daughter, who shared a bedroom with her three brothers, 'divided from them only by a curtain', one night 'had to flee away in her night-clothes to the home of the man she was to marry'. This suggests both how decorum was fought for at even the lowest rung of rural life, and the degree of sexual self-discipline in rural courtship.[7]

Sharing of beds and bedrooms was the subject of regret and even remorse. Researchers could have difficulty in eliciting the facts because of 'shame' felt by working-class families. Suffolk housewives deplored their own crowded circumstances as 'not respectable or decent . . . hardly bearable'. A Cornish widow pressed on whether she would have enough privacy from the lodger she was to take in retorted 'oh, sir . . . you mustn't think us so bad as we seem; we're drove often to do what we don't like to do, or we wouldn't have a roof at all to cover us.'[8] Even when working-class families were 'drove to do what we don't like to do' in a stronger sense it is apparent, despite the hostility of the contemporary researchers, that they were still trying to achieve the maximum sexual decency consistent with economic constraints. Having a grown-up daughter sleeping with her parents might be a means of avoiding the greater evil of her sharing a room with a mature brother; cases are known of husbands from neighbouring houses in rural areas agreeing to share beds so that their grown-up daughters could have the privacy of a single room. (Investigators never seem to have asked whether families were achieving the greatest *possible* separation of the sexes in the accommodation available — just as it seldom occurred to them that individuals might sleep naked because their limited clothing had been washed for wearing in the morning.)[9]

It would be wrong to suggest that these attitudes and impulses were universal; all that is being claimed is that they had a significant currency even very low on the social scale in nineteenth-century England.

Further reading

For further discussion of Michael Mason's work on sexuality, see Frank Mort, Lynda Nead, Boyd Hilton, Simon Szreter and Michael Mason, 'Roundtable on Michael Mason's *The Making of Victorian Sexuality*', *Journal of Victorian Culture*, 1 (1996), 118–49. Apart from Mason, other revisionist assessments of Victorian sexuality include: Peter Gay's magisterial study of European culture, *The Bourgeois Experience: Victoria to Freud* (5 vols, New York: Oxford University Press, 1984–98); Patricia Anderson, *When Passion Reigned: Sex and the Victorians* (New York: Basic Books, 1995). An excellent starting point particularly for students is Jeffrey Weeks, *Sex, Politics and Society: The Regulation of Sexuality since 1800* (London: Longman, 1989 [1981]). Other studies of Victorian sexuality include: Francoise Barret-Ducrocq, *Love in the Time of Victoria: Sexuality, Class and Gender in Nineteenth-Century London* (London: Verso, 1991); Simon Szreter, *Fertility, Class and Gender in Britain, 1860–1940* (Cambridge: Cambridge University Press, 1996); and the works listed for the other Readings in the Sexuality section.

Notes

1   Allen Clarke ('Ben Adhem'), *Liverpool Weekly Post*, 26 May 1934, p. 2; Frederick
    Rogers, *Labour Life and Literature* (London, 1913): 4; Nathaniel Hawthorne, *Our Old
    Home* (London, 1863): ii. 200–1; Thomas Wright, *The Great Unwashed* (London, 1868):
    142; Guida Swan, *The Journals of Two Poor Dissenters 1786–1880* (London, 1970): 77.
2   Edwin Chadwick, *The Sanitary Condition of the Labouring Population of Great Britain*, ed.
    M.W. Flinn (Edinburgh, 1965): 192–3.
3   *Morning Chronicle*, 28 Oct. 1850, p. 5; Françoise Barret-Ducrocq, *Love in the Time of
    Victoria* (London, 1991): 112; Ellen Ross, '"Fierce Questions and Taunts": Married
    Life in Working-Class London, 1870–1914', *Feminist Studies* 8 (1982): 575–602.
4   W.G. Lumley, 'Observations upon the Statistics of Illegitimacy', *Journal of the [Royal]
    Statistical Society of London* 25 (1862): 219–74; Dennis R. Mills, *Aspects of Marriage*
    (Milton Keynes, 1980): 12–14; Barry Reay, 'Sexuality in Nineteenth-Century England:
    The Social Context of Illegitimacy in Rural Kent', *Rural History* 1 (1990): 219–47.
5   Enid Gauldie, *Cruel Habitations* (London, 1974): 22.
6   Edwin Paxton Hood, *The Age and Its Architects* (London, 1850): 162, 228–9. W.S.
    Gilly, *The Peasantry of the Border* (Berwick-upon-Tweed, 1841): 19, quoted by Hood,
    is similarly self-defeating.
7   P.E. Razzell and R.W. Wainwright, *The Victorian Working Class* (London, 1973): 32;
    J. Ginswick, ed., *Labour and the Poor in England and Wales 1849–51*, (3 vols; London,
    1983): ii. 39; Henry Mayhew, *London Labour and the London Poor* (London, 1861–2):
    i. 135; Montague Gore, *On the Dwellings of the Poor* (2nd ed.; London, 1851): p. x;
    H.J. Hunter, *Inquiry on the State of the Dwellings of Rural Labourers* (Parliamentary Papers
    1865): xxvi, 146; John Burnett, *Destinies Obscure* (London, 1982: 44; Thomas Okey,
    A Basketful of Memories (London, 1930): 147; Thomas Burt, *An Autobiography* (London,
    1924): 91; Laurence Housman, *The Unexpected Years* (London, 1937): 74.
8   *Journal of the [Royal] Statistical Society of London* 5 (1843), 212–21; *Morning Chronicle*,
    5 Dec. 1849, p. 5; 14 Nov 1849, p. 5.
9   *Morning Chronicle*, 17 Nov. 1849, p. 5; Chadwick 1965: 194; Gordon Mingay, 'The
    Rural Slum', in S. Martin Gaskell, ed., *Slums* (Leicester, 1990): 92–43; Theodor
    Fontane, *Theodor Fontane: Von Dreissig bis Achtzig: Sein Leben in seinem Briefen* (Munich,
    1970: i. 127.

Lynda Nead

THE MEANING OF THE PROSTITUTE

Myths of Sexuality: Representations of Women in Victorian Britain (Oxford: Basil Blackwell, 1988), 93–109.

In the nineteenth century the female prostitute became a figure of fascination because she was imagined as the gateway to the criminal underworld. Few figures so unsettled the Victorian conscience, mainly because prostitutes were so visible on the streets and seemed to betray contemporary ideals of womanhood. They represented a very public form of sexuality. While the sexual practices of the respectable remained hidden, seldom written about even in private diaries, and only occasionally being hinted at in divorce proceedings, the prostitute's world could be rediscovered in reports of social investigators (such as Henry Mayhew), in novels (most famously Nancy in *Oliver Twist*), in paintings, in police court records, parliamentary enquiries, medical volumes, and movements such as that against the Contagious Diseases Acts in the 1870s and 1880s.

Lynda Nead has been one of the most important Victorian art historians. The following Reading is drawn from her interdisciplinary study, *Myths of Sexuality* (1988), which examines representations of Victorian sexuality, including that of the prostitute. In this excerpt, she discusses the prostitute's role as catalyst in the debate about national decline. Placing her in the context of discussions about morality and respectability, Nead uncovers the prostitute's centrality in the definition of inappropriate sexual behaviours, which some believed would inevitably bring about the decline of the British Empire. Nead's analysis is informed by the work of Michel Foucault (discussed on p. 24 and in the Introduction to this section, p. 339), but also pays heed to Marxist analyses of value and exchange. She particularly notes the prostitute's unique role as a commodity, which is sold for a limited time only, atypical of systems of value and exchange. *Myths of Sexuality* is concerned with the ways that the Victorians imagined deviancy, whether in the form of the adulteress or the prostitute. These were both seen as 'fallen women', disturbing figures in the Victorian world-view, yet figures who also helped define acceptable forms of sexuality (i.e. married life).

Nead is concerned with the systems of Victorian thought and imagination that made the prostitute a key figure in the social debates of the mid-nineteenth century and the relationship to Victorian sexual culture. In her subsequent book, *Victorian Babylon* (2000), Nead continued her search into Victorian sexuality by examining the sexual geographies of London (the spaces that were associated with sex such as Holywell Street, centre of the pornographic book trade, and Cremorne Gardens where young people would meet for the pleasures of music and courtship) and the different forms of modernity and space that the city offered.

Lynda Nead is Pevsner Professor of History of Art at Birkbeck College, University of London. Her interest in Victorian femininity was developed in the context of metropolitan modernity in *Victorian Babylon: People, Streets and Images in Nineteenth Century London* (2000) and *The Haunted Gallery: Painting, Photography, Film c.1900* (2007). She is currently working on a new project on the visual culture of boxing.

T**HE SPECTRE OF IMPERIAL DECLINE** was a persistent source of anxiety. The concepts of social order and class continuity were not assumed or taken-for-granted but were ideals which were tenuously clung to in the face of the major social changes of the period. Within this context, the general fear of immorality became focused on one particular form — prostitution. Prostitution was defined as the most threatening manifestation of moral degeneration and was regarded as a meta-system which could erode and destroy the nation. Prostitution stood as a metaphor for immorality in general; it represented a nexus of anxieties relating to class, nation and empire. Indeed, publications on prostitution appropriated the language of imperial decline. Prostitution could never be contained as a discrete field of inquiry and discussion constantly spilled over into the social and political ramifications, drawing on the language and debates of social and economic history. This process is clearly demonstrated in the writing of Ralph Wardlaw, a Congregational minister, whose *Lectures on Female Prostitution* were published in 1842; he stated: 'By all historically recorded experience we are borne out in the assertion that the prevalance of this vice [prostitution] tends, in a variety of ways, to the deterioration of national character, — and to the consequent exposure of the nations among whom it abounds to weakness, decline and fall.'[1] It is surely significant that the language of moral and dynastic degeneration is the same: decline and fall; the terms plot both a moral and an imperial narrative and a fall from virtue can symbolize the end of an empire.

Definition of the prostitute

Foucault has shown that definition and categorization are central mechanisms in the organization of sexuality; they work to mark off and differentiate modes of sexual behaviour through definitions of normality and deviancy, acceptability and unacceptability. The term 'prostitute' is an historical construction which works to define and categorize a particular group of women in terms of sex and class. The term should not be seen as an objective description of an already-determined group; rather, it actively constitutes a group which is both socially and economically specific. In the nineteenth century this process of categorization was produced through various social practices, through legal and medical discourses, religious and cultural forms. Visual representations of the prostitute should also be recognized as part of this historical construction, contributing to the definition and regulation of female sexual behaviour.

The category of 'prostitute' was not fixed or internally coherent; it was accommodating and flexible and could define any woman who transgressed the bourgeois code of morality. The prostitute was understood in terms of her difference from the norm of respectable femininity; if the feminine ideal stood for normal, acceptable sexuality, then the prostitute represented deviant, dangerous and illicit sex.

The prostitute, then, was one term within the signifying system of 'woman', and was understood in relation to other terms in this system such as the feminine ideal, the adulteress, the working woman. And yet within the category itself there was little consensus or stability; during the middle decades of the nineteenth century there were continual struggles between competing definitions of prostitution; contradictory explanations of the causes, nature and extent of the practice and an obsessive and persistent attempt to define and contain illicit female behaviour.

The connotations of prostitution were activated through a particular language. Within this system, two terms in particular demand some consideration; these are the 'prostitute' and the 'fallen woman'. The term 'prostitute' connoted a public practice, the regular exchange of sex for money. The combined associations of cash and the public sphere rendered the prostitute powerful and independent — qualities which were the unique privilege of the white, middle-class male. The threat of the prostitute was thus constructed in relation to both gender and class; the prostitute was defined as part of the 'dangerous classes' created by the rapid urbanization and industrialization of nineteenth-century society.[2] Distinct from the respectable classes, she belonged to the 'residuum', that displaced and disinterested mass at the very bottom of the social hierarchy.

The term 'fallen woman' activated significantly different associations. To begin with, the notion of 'fall' implied that she *had been* respectable but had dropped out of respectable society. The term was therefore class specific; unlike the working-class prostitute, the fallen woman came from the respectable classes. A number of these ideas were re-worked in Augustus Egg's [*painting*] *Past and Present* [. . .]. A woman's 'fall' from virtue was frequently attributed to seduction and betrayal which set the scene for her representation as victim. Most importantly, the victimized fallen woman mobilized none of the connotations of power and independence; her deviancy did not involve money and thus, to a certain degree, she retained her femininity, that is, she remained powerless and dependent.[3]

Prostitution was not perceived as an homogeneous category; there were differences within the group, grades of deviancy which could be regulated and ordered. Nineteenth-century surveys usually classified prostitution according to a hierarchy from kept mistresses and courtesans down to soldiers' women and park women; in this way prostitution could be seen as a microcosm of society in general, a hierarchical system organized along lines of social class. At the bottom of the system were the public prostitutes, the female issue of the undeserving poor. At this level, sexual deviancy was defined not only as immoral but also as criminal; describing the lowest ranks of prostitution, James Miller, Professor of Surgery in the University of Edinburgh, referred to the woman who was educated in vice, crime and unchastity and who: 'at the age of ten or twelve, may be both a prostitute and a thief, her lapsed state having proved rather a simple progress than a fall.'[4]

The distinctions between the prostitute and the fallen woman were frequently obscure but writers during the period continually attempted to differentiate and categorize the various forms of illicit behaviour. In his examination of immorality and the modern state, John Stores Smith wished — or needed — to point out to his readers: 'There is a fine distinction between the maiden who submits to the consummation before the ceremony, and her who systematically consents to lend out her body for a consideration.'[5] Furthermore, this separation was reinforced within the institutions. The Magdalen Hospitals — specialized institutions for the treatment and reclamation of prostitutes — maintained special wards for women who had not entered into public prostitution but had been seduced by false promises of marriage and deserted.[6] In this way, the common prostitute was segregated from other forms of female deviancy, a practice which ultimately determined the aims and operation of the Contagious Diseases Acts in the 1860s.

The language of prostitution

By the 1850s the regulation of prostitution had become a dominant feature of Victorian social and political practice. From the end of the eighteenth century prostitution became the target of scrutiny in a wide range of publications: Parliamentary reports and state legislation, police statistics and medical investigation, letters and articles in newspapers and periodicals, evangelical manifestos and religious sermons, novels and poems, paintings and prints. These texts produced a body of knowledge concerning prostitution; they circulated particular attitudes to and images of the prostitute which were repeated and re-formulated at all levels of social and cultural production. In other words, during the nineteenth century the prostitute was defined as a special object of inquiry; she was the subject of social investigation and philanthropic concern and the focus of the developing science of moral statistics.

But this expanding body of information and increase in public discourses on prostitution should not be seen as a progressive uncovering of the issue during the nineteenth century. These texts neither revealed nor distorted the reality of prostitution; instead they actively constructed and defined the category. This entire range of representations can be understood as part of the ceaseless categorization of acceptable and unacceptable forms of behaviour; it worked to re-define respectable and non-respectable individuals and groups and was part of the obsessive attempt to segregate the pure and the impure.

Looking at this range of public and official representations, it is possible to identify certain common structures and shared assumptions. The debates were predicated on the general belief that men demanded sex and women supplied it. In his discussion of the causes of prostitution, William Acton re-presented this model in terms of an economic law of supply and demand:

> Supply, as we all know, is regulated by demand, and demand is the practi-cal expression of an ascertained want . . . the desire for sexual intercourse is strongly felt by the male on attaining puberty, and continues through his life as an ever-present, sensible want . . . this desire of the male is the want that produces the demand, of which prostitution is a result, and which is, in fact, the artificial supply of a natural demand.[7]

Natural male sexual desire is defined as the primary element, the demand, to which female prostitution is the unnatural response. But what kind of artifice is implied here? It is surely both an economic and a sexual imposture; the prostitute transgresses both economic and sexual norms; she is a sham commodity and a counterfeit of respectable femininity.

Marx defines a commodity as an article or object, the product of human labour, which goes to market with a price. Its value has nothing to do with its intrinsic material worth or utility but is part of a social exchange which is expressed in terms of money.[8] The value of a commodity appears to be estimated in relation to different kinds of commodities but is in part conferred in a commodity by the labour involved in its production, its nature being concealed and transformed through its part in the processes of circulation and exchange. Although value is established through the exchange of objects, its origin in labour-time is repressed; value is articulated through prices which conceal the social character of production.

A person can also become a commodity; women may be sold or sell themselves in the market place at a price which is calculated in relation to other kinds of commodities.[9] But how is the value of a prostitute established? How can the price be estimated and how does the value of sex compare with other types of commodities? Within the respectable, public discourses of Victorian Britain, these issues were concealed within a language of public order, health and morality; it is only in the more illicit forms of representation that the economic motif of prostitution is made explicit. Reminiscing about his encounters with prostitutes in the mid-nineteenth century, 'Walter' [*author of the pornographic work, 'My Secret Life'*] continually commented on the prices of these women and sought to fix the comparative value of prostitutes in relation to different kinds of commodities:

> at the time I write of a sovereign would get any woman, and ten shillings as nice a one as you needed. Two good furnished rooms near clubs, could be had by women for from fifteen to twenty shillings per week, a handsome silk dress for five or ten pounds, and other things in proportion. So cunt was a more reasonable article than it now is, and I got quite nice girls from five to ten shilling a poke . . . When but with little money, I used to take out my best silk handkerchiefs, and give them with money, and once or twice I gave nothing else.[10]

For 'Walter' prostitutes are a bargain, cheaper than a silk dress or the same price as a good handkerchief; this is a precise and nuanced sexual economy in which, as Walter states, a woman can discover: 'the ready money-value of her cunt.'[11]

But the prostitute does not behave like any other commodity; she occupies a unique place, at the centre of an extraordinary and nefarious economic system. She is able to represent all the terms within capitalist production; she is the human labour, the object of exchange and the seller at once. She stands as worker, commodity and capitalist and blurs the categories of bourgeois economics in the same way that she tests the boundaries of bourgeois morality. This is the true nature of her deviancy. She is the unnatural supplement to bourgeois femininity and does not even conform to the laws of the market-place. She offers for sale a commodity which can never be completely possessed by the buyer. The prostitute is able to sell her self/sex again and again but she is never owned by being bought and is always available again to be re-sold. This idea of a repeated hiring out was one important way in which prostitution was defined during the period; prostitution was not necessarily constituted as a loss of virtue but as a *repetition* of the act in exchange for money.

As a commodity, therefore, the prostitute both encapsulates and distorts all the classic features of bourgeois economics. This is the full nature of her threat and it is also the key to her power. If male sexuality is seen as an essential and immutable demand, then female prostitution can either satisfy or frustrate this need; it is a potentially powerful and influential system. The stress on degradation and death in official representations of British prostitution was one way of curbing these unsettling associations and of covering over the deficiencies which prostitutes exposed in the dominant bourgeois economic and moral systems.

The prostitute was defined primarily in terms of her difference from the feminine ideal, and, as a system, prostitution was seen as a negation of the respectable system of marriage and procreation. Evangelical writers such as Ralph Wardlaw used this mechanism in order to emphasize the social threat of prostitution; invoking nature and the bible to endorse his argument, Wardlaw reminded his readers:

> nature's way is not the way of indiscriminate promiscuous indulgence, but that of peculiar conjugal appropriation . . . that every man have his own wife, and every woman her own husband . . . the *general barrenness* and unproductiveness of the system of prostitution; the latter distinctly proclaiming its unnaturalness, by its contrariety to nature's admitted end and primary law . . . a law, which, expressed in the terms of holy writ, is 'Be fruitful, and multiply, and replenish the earth'.[12]

In this passage female sexuality is organized around the central polarity of natural/ unnatural with the prostitute and prostitution as the negative terms within the dichotomy.

The image of the prostitute as an unnatural form of femininity was emphasized most strongly in relation to the 'natural' role of motherhood. Statistical surveys were carried out and their results called upon to demonstrate that, on the whole, prostitutes did not, and could not, bear children. In a work of investigative journalism entitled *The Criminal Prisons of London*, Henry Mayhew and John Binny examined the question of female criminality. Observing that prostitutes constituted the main supply of the criminal classes in women's prisons such as Tothill Fields, it was concluded:

'it is a wondrous ordination of Benevolence that such creatures ["public women"] as are absolutely shameless and affectionless should be childless as well.'[13] The 'unnatural' state of the prostitute, therefore, was most strongly registered in terms of her deviation from the functions of the 'natural' feminine ideal. Her sexual deviancy rendered her unfeminine and physiologically unable to fulfil the most 'natural' and elevated role of woman — motherhood.

Prostitution was constituted as a special field of moral and social inquiry through the surveys produced particularly during the 1840s and 1850s and written by doctors, clergymen and social investigators. [. . .] [I]t is [. . .] possible to recognize a common structure, a standard format through which they articulated their findings and analyses. The main issues which they addressed were, in order of discussion: the definition of prostitution; the causes of prostitution; the extent and effects of prostitution; and finally, proposals for the mitigation and prevention of prostitution. In this way, a narrative structure was followed which ordered the argument and gave it meaning. From the definition of prostitution to the prevention of prostitution; these terms set the parameters of the debate. Prostitution was constituted as a 'social' problem which could be defined and cured.

As already seen, the most problematic aspect of this project was to define prostitution. Here, statistics could not be called upon to ratify the argument, and it was in this process of definition that the assumed stability of sexual categories most frequently collapsed and the anxieties concerning female sexuality were revealed. Definitions of prostitution during the period 1840 to 1870 are fragmented and vague and may best be understood as a diverse range of beliefs which work to evade questions of economic causation and displace the subject on to the arena of morality and pathology.

In his 1842 *Lectures*, Wardlaw referred to prostitution as 'illicit intercourse' and specified: 'A prostitute is designation of *character* . . . To form the character, and to justify the designation, there must be the voluntary *repetition of the act*; — *the giving up of the person to criminal indulgence*.'[14] Prostitution is thus defined as a pathological condition produced by repeated indulgence in illicit and deviant sex. Wardlaw entirely sidesteps economic and social issues and represents prostitution as a moral state.

This mechanism was also deployed by William Acton in his polemical second edition of *Prostitution* which was published in 1870 to support the Contagious Diseases legislation. Acton defined the prostitute as a perversion of respectable femininity; made impure by her contact with money, she corrupts and infects the rest of society:

> What is a prostitute? She is a woman who gives for money that which she ought to give only for love; who ministers to passion and lust alone, to the exclusion and extinction of all the higher qualities . . . She is a woman with half the woman gone, and that half containing all that elevates her nature, leaving her a mere instrument of impurity; degraded and fallen she extracts from the sin of others the means of living, corrupt and dependent on corruption, and therefore interested directly in the increase of immorality.[15]

The idea that prostitution was a physical and psychological state which set the prostitute apart from respectable women was also constituted within legal discourse.

The Contagious Diseases Acts were framed to control and regulate the 'common prostitute' but there was a great deal of uncertainty about the definition of this group and in the final instance, the category could only be sustained by assuming common knowledge and shared beliefs; as one public inquiry reported:

> 374. Again, Dr. Brewer asks, What is your definition of a prostitute? To which Mr. Parsons, Visiting Surgeon to the Portsmouth Lock Hospital, replies: Any woman whom there is fair and reasonable ground to believe is, first of all, going to places which are the resorts of prostitutes alone and at times when immoral persons only are usually out. *It is more a question as to mannerism than anything else.*[16] (My italics)

The speaker draws upon dominant beliefs concerning the proper 'sphere' of the respectable woman in order to define the prostitute in terms of her location but, fearing the inadequacy of this definition, Parsons supports this definition in terms of a vague evocation of 'mannerism'. The statement signals a number of the most significant issues raised by the representation of the prostitute in the middle of the nineteenth century. Prostitution was perceived as a threat in terms of its visibility and it was thus the streetwalker who became the symbol for prostitution in general and who was at the centre of the construction of a physical stereotype. This stereotype was circulated and repeated across a wide range of texts; it dominated bourgeois understanding of prostitution [. . .].

The question of the causes of prostitution produced further difficulties. Many of the surveys attempted to divide their analyses into 'Natural' and 'Accidental' or 'Social' causes. In his investigation of prostitution in Edinburgh, the surgeon William Tait defined the two categories as: 'one *natural* to the human mind, and the other *accidental* or arising out of circumstances'.[17] The two groups worked to differentiate moral and environmental causes; vanity, indolence and lust were played off against poverty, lack of education and poor housing with the emphasis on either category constantly shifting. Again and again, the social and economic aspects of prostitution were obscured by notions of individual sin, innate moral weakness and animal desire. Tait devoted an entire chapter of *Magdalenism* to the 'Causes of Prostitution' in which he acknowledged that poverty and unemployment were two primary factors; referring to the conditions of employment for women in Edinburgh, he stated: 'The most distressing causes of prostitution are those which arise from poverty — want of employment — and insufficient remuneration for needle and other kinds of work in which females are employed.'[18] This unequivocal recognition of economic determination was displaced, however, by Tait's subsequent classification of causes. Under the heading of 'Natural Causes' he listed: 'Licentious Inclination — Irritability of Temper — Pride and Love of Dress — Dishonesty and Desire of Property — Indolence'[19] — a curious assortment of moral and psychological conditions which are offered as individual and innate weaknesses.

Tait's attribution of cause was class specific. When speaking of governesses who had become prostitutes, he was unable to find one case that was not caused by seduction but when describing 'sewing-girls', he located them within a specific and distinct working-class morality and concluded: 'there is a looseness in their characters which would lead to the belief that no deception was necessary to decoy them from the path of rectitude.'[20] In this way, the governess — the reduced gentlewoman

— is defined in terms of respectable femininity, lacking sexual desire and therefore the victim of male sexuality and seduction. Sewing-girls and working-class women, however, are classified in terms of an innate licentious inclination. Low wages and unemployment in the textile trades are thus obscured by hegemonic notions of class, gender and sexuality; as Judith Walkowitz comments in *Prostitution and Victorian Society*, middle-class writers were unable to negotiate dominant beliefs concerning respectability and morality with the situation of working-class women:

> For these middle-class writers, working-class culture represented a total negation of culture. From their point of view only a degenerate social milieu that spawned an alienated, anti-social personality provided the setting for women's move into prostitution. For as the studies depicted the types of employment, the social gatherings, and the living conditions that could lead to a woman's downfall, they effectively encompassed the whole of working-class life.[21]

There was considerable disagreement concerning the sexuality of the prostitute; the surveys were unable to reconcile notions of female sexual passivity with the categorization of the prostitute as sexual deviant. Did a woman turn to prostitution through inclination? Was active sexual desire a result or a cause of prostitution? These kinds of questions seriously challenged the dominant definitions of female sexuality and the discourses on prostitution became a crucial site for the production and re-working of ideas concerning femininity and sexuality. In 1843, William Bevan, minister of Newington Chapel, Liverpool, conceded: 'The force of licentious inclination has hurried a greater number into the commission of sin than I was prepared to expect.'[22] But James Miller concluded that if prostitutes were dissolute it was the result rather than the cause of their situation: '1. Is she [the woman] impelled to prostitution by the strength of sexual desire? Sometimes, but, on the whole, rarely. In general, even the furiously lustful prostitute has become so secondarily; by indulgence her passion grew strong; at the first, it was comparatively weak, and quite controllable.'[23] In general, the environmental causes of prostitution were treated as transient conditions which exacerbated the innate moral frailty of the working classes. Social conditions could be constituted as areas for urban 'improvement'; individual sin could be countered by individual redemption.

Surveys of prostitution were part of the larger development of statistical studies during the early-Victorian period.[24] Interest in statistical information was expressed from the late-eighteenth century by Bentham and Malthus who perceived a new science of statistics as part of an examination of population and resources. The first census was taken in 1801 but the statistical movement really expanded in the 1820s and in the 1830s when a number of statistical societies were established in London and the provinces. The movement set out to conduct empirical surveys and to collect standardized data on areas of social life such as health, housing and crime. The constitution of the Statistical Society of London, founded in 1834, stated:

> The Statistical Society of London has been established for the purposes of procuring, arranging and publishing 'Facts calculated to illustrate the Condition and Prospects of Society'. The Statistical Society will consider it to be the first and most essential rule of its conduct to exclude carefully

> all Opinions from its transactions and publications — to confine its
> attention rigorously to facts — and, as far as it may be found possible,
> to facts which can be stated numerically and arranged in tables.[25]

From the beginning the findings of the societies were defined as 'fact'. Statistics
were regarded as objective, truthful and irrefutable, in opposition to the results of
argument and opinion. The ideals of the statistical movement are clearly summarized
by Michael Cullen in *The Statistical Movement in Early Victorian Britain*; he writes: 'the
aim [was] the creation of a virtuous and quiescent working class. Humanitarianism,
class interest and statistics made a powerful reforming brew.'[26] The statisticians
were concerned with the issues of moral decay and political unrest amongst the
working classes. Public health, education and housing were seen as effective strategies
in the reduction of crime and the creation of political stability.

The writers on prostitution appropriated some of the methods and language of
the statisticians. Surveys were frequently conducted at a local level and publications included tables of statistical data relating to prostitution. Numerical figures
and tables imposed an order and meaning on the subject; they were produced and
circulated as truth and fact and set the framework for subsequent social policy. The
language of prostitution should be understood within this context of the emergence
of moral statistics. Arguments and opinion were endorsed by facts and figures; causes
were classified as 'Natural' or 'Accidental' and prostitutes questioned and surveyed
to provide statistical data. Tables were compiled by the police forces and rescue
societies to demonstrate the age distribution, incidence of disease and mortality rate
amongst prostitutes. Statistics formulated a norm of prostitution, a social profile,
which provided official and scientific endorsement of cultural definitions and
stereotypes.

Not surprisingly, since the definition of prostitution produced conflicting and
contradictory statements, estimates of the numbers of prostitutes were equally
wide-ranging;[27] figures for London alone ranged from 8,000 to 80,000 but
irrespective of specific figures, investigators were agreed that prostitution was an
extensive and growing system which threatened the very base of public health,
morality and order.

Statistical information was also used to represent the effects of prostitution. The
consequences of prostitution were understood in terms of both moral and physical conditions and were classified according to those effects felt by the prostitute
herself and those experienced by the rest of society. The prostitute was defined
as a conduit of moral corruption and physical disease and investigators drew on their
findings to recommend ameliorative policies. The recommendations made during
this period can be divided into those which supported and those which opposed
state regulation and legislation of prostitution. Supporters of state regulation argued
that it was the responsibility of the state to minimize the suffering caused by
prostitution. The *laissez-faire* approach of England was unfavourably compared to
the continental system of regulation and police surveillance.[28] Regulation was
presented as a responsible and realistic position which would benefit both the
prostitute and society in general but supporters of state supervision had to answer
the humanitarian arguments of those who opposed legislation and argued that state
registration amounted to official sanction of immorality and debauchery.[29] Religious
writers complained that legislation would turn the women into victims of male lust.

If prostitution was the response to male demand, then the entire system could be eradicated by the adoption of a single standard of moral purity for men and for women. They also recommended early marriages, increased education and better housing for the working classes, an end to intemperance and a general improvement in the moral tone of society. In these ways, it was claimed, prostitution could be repressed rather than regulated.

Across this labyrinth of conflicting arguments and competing analyses, it is possible to identify two dominant images of prostitution. The first representation defined the prostitute as a figure of contagion, disease and death; a sign of social disorder and ruin to be feared and controlled. This construction shifted the focus away from the question of the effects of prostitution on the woman herself and emphasized its effects on respectable society; the prostitute stood as a symbol of the dangerous forces which could bring about anarchy and social disintegration. The second representation displaced these connotations of power and destruction and defined the prostitute as a suffering and tragic figure — the passive victim of a cruel and relentless society. A hopeless outcast, the prostitute was believed to follow a steady, downward progress ending in a premature and tragic death.

But although it is possible to differentiate these two central images, they did not work in opposition to each other. Both worked to define prostitution as deviant and abnormal and sought to separate the prostitute from respectable society through claims concerning her appearance, her habits, her lifestyle and her moral and sexual behaviour. Indeed, both images could be invoked within a single text, thus activating simultaneously complex associations of pity/redemption and fear/threat. In his *History of Prostitution*, published in 1859, W.W. Sanger described the system of prostitution as:

> a malignity which is daily and hourly threatening every man, woman, and child in the community; which for hundreds of years has been slowly but steadily making its way onward, leaving a track marked with broken hopes, ruined frames, and sad recollections of stricken friends; and which now, in the full force of an impetus acquired and aggravated by concealment, almost defies opposition.[30]

This fearful image of a cancerous growth spreading through society and leaving destruction in its wake was set against a representation of the prostitute as a helpless, pitiful figure inviting sympathy and compassion: '[those] truly wretched beings, the outcasts of the outcasts . . . they present most ghastly and heart-rending spectacles . . . subjects for mournful consideration.'[31] Prostitution existed as a powerful and threatening system but at the same time the individual prostitute could be re-defined as a powerless and sympathetic figure intent on self-destruction rather than capable of the destruction of society.

Further reading

On Victorian prostitution, see: Judith R. Walkowitz, *Prostitution and Victorian Society: Women, Class and the State* (Cambridge: Cambridge University Press, 1980); Paul McHugh, *Prostitution and Victorian Social Reform* (London: Croom

Helm, 1980); Linda Mahood, *The Magdalenes: Prostitution in the Nineteenth Century* (London: Routledge, 1990); Paula Bartley, *Prostitution: Prevention and Reform in Britain, 1860–1914* (London: Routlege, 2000). On Victorian pornography, see Lisa Z. Sigel, *Governing Pleasures: Pornography and Social Change in England, 1815–1914* (New Brunswick, NJ: Rutgers University Press, 2002).

Notes

1   Ralph Wardlaw, *Lectures on Female Prostitution*, Glasgow, 1842, p. 65. Also on the theme of prostitution and national decline see J.B. Talbot, *The Miseries of Prostitution*, 1844, p. 2.

2   The prostitute was included in volume 4 of Henry Mayhew's *London Labour and the London Poor* (4 vols, 1861–2) which was devoted to 'Those That Will Not Work' whom the advertisement defined as: 'The Dangerous Classes of the Metropolis'. See also H. Mayhew and John Binny, *The Criminal Prisons of London and Scenes of Prison Life*, 1862, p. 454: 'What theft is to the evil-disposed among men, street-walking is to the same class among women'.

3   The two terms 'prostitute' and 'fallen woman' frequently overlapped and were not consistently held apart as terms of difference; for this reason, I will use the words 'prostitute' and 'prostitution' when referring to the system generally.

4   James Miller, *Prostitution Considered in Relation to Its Cause and Cure*, Edinburgh, 1859, p. 6.

5   John Stores Smith, *Social Aspects*, 1850, p. 107.

6   Referred to in *Special Appeal. The Centenary of the Magdalen Hospital, Blackfriar's Road*, 1858, p. 9.

7   William Acton, *Prostitution Considered in Its Moral, Social, and Sanitary Aspects in London and Other Large Cities and Garrison Towns; with Proposals for the Mitigation and Prevention of Its Attendant Evils*, 2nd edn, 1870, pp. 161–2.

8   For discussion of commodities and commodity fetishism see Karl Marx, *Capital. A Critique of Political Economy. Volume One*, translated by Ben Fowkes, Harmondsworth, 1976, pp. 163–78.

9   Frederick Engels comments on the connection between modern prostitution and the development of capitalist commodity production in *The Origin of the Family, Private Property and the State* (first published Zurich, 1884), New York, 1972, p. 82.

10   'Walter', *My Secret Life*, vol. I, Amsterdam, c.1880, pp. 260–1.

11   'Walter', *My Secret Life*, vol. XI, p. 179.

12   Wardlaw, *Lectures*, p. 70.

13   Mayhew and Binny, *The Criminal Prisons of London*, p. 475.

14   Wardlaw, *Lectures*, pp. 14–45.

15   Acton, *Prostitution*, 2nd edn, 1870, p. 166.

16   Report of the Select Committee on the Contagious Diseases Act, July 1869, quoted in Acton, *Prostitution*, 2nd edn, 1870, p. 2. See also Mr. Jacob Wright, M.P. for Manchester, addressing the House of Commons on the Contagious Diseases Act, 20 July 1870, quoted in William Logan, *The Great Social Evil: Its Causes, Extent, Results and Remedies*, 1871, p. 215: 'The House is aware that the Act professes to be directed against common prostitutes . . . The Act, however, contains no definition of this term. I believe there is a definition in the Police Act. The term there implies women who are seen soliciting in the streets.'

17   William Tait, *Magdalenism: An Inquiry into the Extent, Causes and Consequences of Prostitution*, Edinburgh, 1840, p. 82.

18   Tait, *Magdalenism*, p. 26.

19   Tait, *Magdalenism*, p. 81.

20   Tait, *Magdalenism*, p. 97.

21   Judith Walkowitz, *Prostitution and Victorian Society*, Cambridge, 1980, pp. 38–9.

22   William Bevan, *Prostitution in the Borough of Liverpool*, Liverpool, 1843, p. 7.

23   Miller, *Prostitution*, p. 6.

24   For discussion of the statistical movement see Philip Abrams, *The Origins of British Sociology: 1834–1914*, Chicago, 1968; M. J. Cullen, *The Statistical Movement in Early Victorian Britain, The Foundations of Empirical Social Research*, New York, 1975.

25   Quoted in Abrams, *The Origins of British Sociology*, pp. 14–15.

26   Cullen, *The Statistical Movement in Early Victorian Britain*, p. 137.

27   For a list of the various estimates of numbers of prostitutes in nineteenth-century surveys see Helen Ware, 'Prostitution and the State: The Recruitment, Regulation, and Role of Prostitution in Britain from the Middle of the Nineteenth Century to the Present Day', Ph.D. diss. University of London, 1969, pp. 59–66.

28   See Acton, *Prostitution*, 1857, pp. 74–83; W. R. Greg, 'Prostitution', *The Westminster Review*, vol. 53, 1850, pp. 484–6. Supporters of regulation drew on the findings in A.J.B. Parent Duchâtelet, *De la prostitution dans la ville de Paris considérée sous le rapport de l'hygiène publique, de la morale, et de l'administration* (2 vols, Paris, 1836) in order to support their argument for the state control of prostitution in England.

29   Publications which opposed state registration include Tait, *Magdalenism*; William Sanger, *History of Prostitution: Its Extent, Causes and Effects Throughout the World*, 1859; J. Ewing Ritchie, *The Night Side of London*, 1857.

30   Sanger, *History of Prostitution*, p. 18.

31   Sanger, *History of Prostitution*, p. 565.

Judith Walkowitz

JACK THE RIPPER AND
THE DOCTORS

City of Dreadful Delight: Narratives of Sexual Danger in Late-Victorian London
(London: Virago, 1992), 205–11.

As the works by **Nead** and **Showalter** in this section demonstrate, Victorians feared sexuality and displaced many of their anxieties onto it. Men also feared the increasing numbers of women in public spaces. The spectacle of women walking on the streets without male protection — whether to go to work, to engage in philanthropic activities or to go shopping — disturbed them. Prostitutes were public women who needed to be controlled and policed but were also perceived as the gateway to the criminal underworld. **Judith Walkowitz** has argued that the increasing presence of women in the public sphere led to a series of moral panics in the 1880s around the theme of sexual danger. These took the form of fears about prostitution (particularly child prostitution) and about the regulation of sexuality.

Walkowitz first came to prominence with her book, *Prostitution and Victorian Society* (1980), a key study in the then new discipline of women's history. She examined the impact of the campaign against the Contagious Diseases Acts which became a pivotal moment in the development of female public and political activity, giving women (especially its leader Josephine Butler) a voice and allowing them to talk about the double standards of Victorian sexuality where men who had sex outside marriage were not tarnished but women who did were viewed as immoral.

The following extract comes from her next work, the extremely influential *City of Dreadful Delight* (1992), a powerful study that deployed the full resources of the new cultural history and made the case for thinking seriously about representations. She explores the 'narratives of sexual danger in late Victorian London' allowing the reader to see the new ways of discussing sexuality in this period. For Walkowitz, the reporting and discussion of sexuality in the 1880s shaped the culture in a profound way. Victorians were shocked in 1885 by W.T. Stead's revelations in the *Pall Mall Gazette* about the trade in child prostitution in the East End of London (published under the dramatic title, 'The Maiden Tribute of Modern Babylon'), which overturned any remaining notion that men might be the morally superior sex. Walkowitz showed how Stead seduced his readers by writing within the terms of melodrama, which sensationalised his reporting of the ease with which he was able to procure a child for sexual purposes. The public outcry resulted in the passage of the Criminal Law Amendment Act the same year. This legislation raised the age of female consent from 13 to 16, made brothel-keeping illegal and criminalised homosexual acts between consenting adult men.

In the following Reading, Walkowitz discusses the Jack the Ripper case and employs the techniques of the cultural historian to unpick the meaning of the world's most famous unsolved crime. In 1888 the nation was shocked by a serial killer who killed at least six prostitutes in the East End of London. The murderer was never found but the killings concentrated attention on the poverty of the East End, which was seen as an underworld of crime. The killings were notorious because of their extreme savagery; the bodies of the victims were brutally mutilated. Most of the murders took place on the badly lit streets of Whitechapel. Since that time, the Ripper has been the subject of innumerable books offering to solve the crime (examples of what is called 'Ripperology') as well as films and novels. Walkowitz's study might be seen as an example of 'anti-Ripperology'. It was written in the shadow of the 'Yorkshire Ripper' murders of the early 1980s. Walkowitz avoids the sensationalism of most accounts of the Whitechapel murders in order to demonstrate that the politics of the reporting of violence against women remains contemporary. There is no attempt here to establish the identity of the Ripper; instead, she starts from the position that violent episodes like this were used to restrict and control women's right to enter and participate in the public sphere. She examines the way the incidents were initially portrayed as inevitable in an area of London characterised by poverty and decline and indicative of the criminality of the working class. But she goes on to reveal how the murders fostered anti-Semitism, a fear of medical men and elite visitors, a new vision of male/female relations, and a movement to eradicate common lodging houses among other things.

Walkowitz unravels the different layers of meaning in the moral panic around the Ripper. The extract here focuses on one layer: the way the medical facts of the case served to intensify the horror of the events. For Victorians it recalled Robert Louis Stevenson's recently published *The Strange Case of Dr Jekyll and Mr Hyde* (1886), subject of **Elaine Showalter**'s Reading. Explanations of the brutal crime were also derived from recent psycho-analytic research (particularly Dr Richard Krafft-Ebing's 1886 *Psychopathia Sexualis*). Local working-class people turned against medical men and local elites.

Walkowitz reveals the complexity of reading the Ripper as a cultural event and the way that interpretations were constantly recast. In the moral panic around the Ripper we see the emergence of the serial killer as a celebrity that looks all too familiar. Once more, in the Victorians we find ourselves.

Judith Walkowitz is Professor of History at Johns Hopkins University. She is currently finishing a book on the *Making of Cosmopolitan Soho, 1880–1943*; it investigates the central London district of Soho and the diverse cultures of modernity and modernism that it helped to stage.

———————————

[. . .]

[A]N ALTERNATIVE INQUIRY into the self and the social order materialized in the press. Suspicion [*about the identity of the Ripper*] shifted from the East End to the West End, as representations of the Ripper oscillated from an externalized version of the Other to a variation of the multiple, divided Self.

In "Murder and More to Follow," W.T. Stead, that great crusader against libertine debauchery, was the first journalist to draw attention to the "sexual origins" of the crime and to invoke Dr. Jekyll and Mr. Hyde as a psychological model of the murderer. *The Strange Case of Doctor Jekyll and Mr. Hyde*, Stevenson's enormously popular "shilling shocker" of 1886, had featured a murderer with a divided personality, who encompassed within himself the two social extremes of London: the urbane Dr. Jekyll, who used his scientific knowledge to create another self, the stunted, troglodyte, proletarian Mr. Hyde, as a cover for "secret pleasures" and "nocturnal adventures." Influenced by French writings on the multiple personality as well as Lombrosian theories of criminal anthropology, Stevenson's story represented the "thorough and primitive duality of [urban] man." Despite the author's repeated denials, contemporary readers and reviewers immediately interpreted the undisclosed nocturnal adventures and pleasures of Jekyll/Hyde as illicitly and violently erotic. When the theater version starring Richard Mansfield opened in the West End in August 1888, it adhered to the interpretation of Jekyll/Hyde as a sadistic sex criminal. Mansfield played Hyde as a manifestation of Jekyll's "lust," a creature of infinite sexual drive who, unable to fulfill his desires in conventional heterosexual sex because of his "hideous imagination," "proceeds to satisfy his cravings in violence." To stabilize and fix Hyde's sexual obsession within the boundaries of heterosexuality (the original story remained obscure about the object and aim of Jekyll/Hyde's libidinal desire), the theater version added a new female character, Jekyll's fiancée, murdered by a jealous Hyde, thus injecting heterosexual love and sadism into the closeted professional bachelor world of Jekyll and his friends.[1]

With repeated allusions to Stevenson's story and to evolutionary anthropology, Stead characterized the "real-life" murderer in Whitechapel as an evolutionary throwback and sadist. The crime was a "renewed reminder of the potentialities of revolting barbarity which lie latent in man"; it was committed by a "Mr. Hyde of Humanity," a "Savage of Civilization" from "our slums," as capable of "bathing his hands in blood as any Sioux who ever scalped a foe." Animated by a "mania of bloodthirsty cruelty which sometimes springs from the unbridled indulgence of the worst passions" this midnight murderer might well be a "plebeian Marquis de Sade at large in Whitechapel," who, Stead warned, may not confine his activities to the East End.[2]

"Murder and More to Follow" located the urban savage in London's "teeming" slums. A few days later, however, Stead suggested a more respectable identity and address for the murderer, more akin to Jekyll's urbane appearance and stately West End mansion. In an "Occasional Note," Stead "hoped" that authorities were not confining their attention to those who looked like "horrid ruffians." "Many of the occupants of the Chamber of Horrors look like local preachers, Members of Parliament, or monthly nurses." Even the Marquis de Sade was an "amiable-looking gentleman." In keeping with the case-study approach of Stevenson's *Strange Case*, Stead diagnosed the murderer as a sadistic "victim of erotic mania which often takes the awful shape of an uncontrollable taste for blood."[3]

Thanks to Stead, speculations about the Ripper as a "dual personality," an "amiable-looking gentleman" who was also a "hard ruffian," who "did his bloody work with the lust . . . of a savage, but with the skill of the savant," began to percolate throughout the press. Other dailies took up the "Jekyll and Hyde" theory and fantasized about a "crazed biologist" who took scientific delight in the "details of butchery" or a "mad physiologist looking for living tissue." Indignant correspondents accused Richard Mansfield of being the Ripper because he played his part so convincingly; alternatively, they complained that he provided a role model for some unstable personality. In deference to the public uproar, the play shut down; fittingly the last performance was held as a benefit for night refuges for homeless women.[4]

As Christopher Frayling has observed, the Jekyll and Hyde model represented the most accessible "explanation" of psychopathology for English newspapers to exploit.[5] Nonetheless, Stead's reference to "sadism," as a "mania" from which the murderer was "suffering," invoked the concepts of sexual sadism and lust murder, recently introduced into the medical lexicon by Dr. Richard Krafft-Ebing, professor of psychiatry at the University of Vienna, and a pioneer of sexology, the scientific study of human sexuality.[6] Krafft-Ebing's professional duties included assessing proof of morbidity or "degeneracy" for sexual offenders brought before the court to determine whether they should be held responsible for their actions. Krafft-Ebing collected his case histories and published them in *Psychopathia Sexualis* (1886), a "medico-forensic study" of the "abnormal." Although the most explicit portions were printed in Latin, the book provoked an enormous popular as well as professional response. Krafft-Ebing found himself deluged with confessional letters from sufferers of sexual misery, which he added to his own body of case histories.[7] The appearance of *Psychopathia Sexualis*, observes Jeffrey Weeks, marked the "eruption into print of the speaking pervert, the individual marked or marred by his (or her) sexual impulse."[8]

A series of anxieties about the gendered self and the social order underwrote Krafft-Ebing's assessment of sexual pathology. In *Psychopathia Sexualis*, he produced an elaborate classification scheme, intended to mark off the perverted Other from the normative Self. Nonetheless, the distinctions he drew between natural/ unnatural, normal/abnormal, and progressive/regressive, remained ambiguous.[9] Sexuality, declared Krafft-Ebing, "is the most powerful factor in individual and social existence"; yet all "acts" that deviated from the "purpose of nature" — i.e. propagation of the species — were "perverse."[10] Unfortunately these perversions were "progressively increasing" in advanced societies; they were component parts of progress, telling expressions of the "nervousness of modern society."[11] Both "unnatural habits" and physical degeneracy accounted for their prevalence: they could be a product of acquired vice as well as congenital defect. Only the case-history approach that investigated the "whole personality of the individual and the original impulse leading to the perverse act," could differentiate disease (perversion) from vice (perversity).[12]

Krafft-Ebing's taxonomy highlighted two general categories of sexual degeneracy: perversions committed with members of the opposite sex and those practiced between members of the same sex. In this schema, sexual sadism, rape, and lust murder were heterosexual analogues to homosexuality. Like homosexuality, sadistic sexual crimes were "progressively increasing in modern sexual life"; even more so than homosexuality, they were the acts of men. "Man," Krafft-Ebing explained, has a "more intense sexual appetite than woman"; sadism was nothing else than "an excessive and monstrous pathological intensification of phenomena — possible, too, in normal conditions in rudimentary forms — which accompany the psychical *vita sexualis* particularly in males."[13]

At the time of [*the prostitute Annie*] Chapman's murder, other publicists lent support to the upper-class-maniac theory; they too debated whether the murderer in the Ripper case was mad or vicious, a victim of a disease or a practitioner of "mere debauchery," a "homicidal maniac" bent on violence or an "erotomaniac" bent on sexual satisfaction. In a letter to *the Times* on 12 September Dr. Forbes Winslow hazarded the opinion that the murderer was not of the class of "Leather Apron," [*i.e., working class*] but was instead a "homicidal maniac" of the "upper class of society, as evidenced by the perverted cunning with which the killer had performed the mutilations and evaded justice." Apparently sane on the surface, the murderer was following the "inclination of his morbid imagination" by "wholesale homicide." Winslow based his "method of madness" theory on the assumption that only a cultivated intellect run amok could have committed an act of such enormity. His reference to "morbid imagination" notwithstanding, Winslow proposed that the criminal suffered from "homicidal mania of a religious description," and that he had chosen "the immoral class of society to vent his vengeance upon."[14]

These discussions paved the way for the coroner's "bombshell" at the Chapman inquest on 26 September. Earlier at the inquest, Dr. Phillips, the division surgeon, had described the body as "terribly mutilated," noting "absent portions from the abdomen" (the uterus and appendages had been removed) and "indications of anatomical knowledge." Phillips was reluctant to give the details of the mutilations in open court, and he only agreed to do so after the room had been cleared of women and children. *The Times* pronounced the autopsy report on Annie Chapman "unfit for publication," but the *Lancet* published it in full: "The abdomen had been laid open, the intestines, severed from their mesenteric attachments, had been lifted out of the body and placed on the shoulder of the corpse; whilst from the pelvis, the uterus and its appendages with the upper portion of the vagina and the posterior two-thirds of the bladder had been entirely removed." In the midst of a saturnalia of destruction, Phillips observed, the murderer had stopped to place Chapman's belongings in "order" at her feet, demonstrating what coroner Baxter later termed "reckless daring" and "cool impudence."[15]

In his summary to the jury, Baxter challenged the suggestion circulating in the press "that the criminal was a lunatic with morbid feelings." Resisting the maniac theory, Baxter proposed instead a "rational" pecuniary basis for the crime. "But it is not necessary to assume lunacy. There was a market for that missing organ." A possible motive for the murder, he suggested, was the sale of the organ to American medical schools — recalling the body-snatching crimes of the early nineteenth century.[16]

Baxter's "Burke and Hare theory" alarmed medical authorities who worried that Baxter's "dramatic . . . revelation" might undermine confidence in medical research: "The public mind — ever too ready to cast mud at legitimate research — will hardly fail to be excited to a pitch of animosity against anatomists and curators, which may take a long time to subside." This animosity was already manifested in newspaper correspondence on the "medical question": in a letter appearing in the *Evening News*, for example, "Ex-Medico's Daughter" proposed that the murder may have been committed "in the cause of science" by a "medical maniac," investigating "the mysterious changes that take place in the female sex at about the age of these poor women." Pasteur, she reminded readers, was also a "human vivisectionist."[17]

Speculations about a "medical maniac" researching into the "mysteries" of the "female sex" built on antimedical propaganda produced by feminists, libertarians, and antivivisectionists throughout the 1870s and 1880s. This propaganda had imaginatively connected the fate of animals and women as victims of medical violence, and it widely circulated visual images and narratives of medical sadism and bodily mutilation.[18] Antivivisectionists like Frances Power Cobbe revived the figure of the scientist as a demonic genius: vivisection, Cobbe insisted, fostered "heteropathy," a "new vice of scientific cruelty," which "does not seize the ignorant or hunger-driven or brutalized classes; but the cultivated, the well-fed, the well-dressed, the civilized and (it is said) the otherwise kindly disposed and genial men of science."[19] Cobbe linked vivisection imaginatively to traditional fears of medical men as "bodysnatchers," thus calling into play older popular antagonisms toward anatomists as homicidal maniacs and desecrators of pauper graves. She equipped the "modern" bodysnatcher with the same antisocial associations as his predecessors: libertinism, atheistic materialism, contamination with dark, occult practices and revolutionary ideas gained from study on the Continent. All of these themes figured in *St. Bernard's*, an antivivisection novel published in 1887 and set in the East End, a text that seemed to offer an ominous premonition of the 1888 exploits of Jack the Ripper.[20] Anxiety over the medical "spaying" of women also peaked in 1886, when professional colleagues accused a Liverpool surgeon of performing ovariectomy and oöphorectomy at an excessive rate. By the late 1880s, then, medical spokesmen had good cause to be anxious over Baxter's "dramatic . . . revelation," for recent propaganda, fictional writings, and medical scandals had already cast a dark shadow over medical research into the "mysteries" of the female sex.[21]

The Mad Doctor theory enlarged on all these negative associations. To these, the Ripper formulation added syphilitic madness, introduced into the discussion in early October by Archibald Forbes, the foreign correspondent of the *Daily News*, who suggested that the murderer was a "victim" of a "specific contagion" and was avenging himself. From the "knowledge of anatomy displayed in the murders," Forbes speculated that he was quite possibly a medical student.[22] To be sure, madness had already been identified as a consequence of sexual impurity, and mid-Victorian doctors understood that the tertiary stage of syphilis could attack the brain, among other vital organs; but the specific connection between tertiary syphilis and general paralysis of the insane, or paresis, was only firmly established in the years immediately preceding the Ripper murders.

Scientific progress only partially accounts for the rise of venereal anxiety: as important, argues Corbin, were the propagandist "efforts of the medical profession to develop and exert its authority, first through social hygiene, then through the prevention of disease." Thanks to medical publicity, syphilis assumed a greater cultural significance in this period of biological anxiety, as fears of racial degeneration increasingly obsessed the dominant classes of society.[23] The theory of the Mad Syphilitic Doctor completed the cycle of venereal anxiety: it focused suspicion back on the "anxiety makers"[24] themselves, as deadly materialists soiled by contact with impure bodies.

At the time of the Ripper murders, medical spokesmen were clearly uneasy about the Mad Doctor theory even though they were deeply implicated in its production. It was, after all, Dr. Phillips who had first insisted publicly that the mutilations showed "indications" of "anatomical knowledge." At Chapman's inquest, Dr. Phillips drew a direct comparison between his own skill as a medical man and that of the "miscreant": "I myself could not have performed all the injuries I saw on that woman and effect, even without a struggle, under a quarter of an hour."[25] Claiming specialized knowledge of the "details of butchery" himself, Phillips remained extremely reluctant to share that knowledge with the public at large. By trying to restrict knowledge of the mutilations, yet allowing the full publication of the autopsy report in the *Lancet*, medical authorities enacted a well-established strategy designed to maintain a monopoly of expert knowledge over the body.

Yet this elitist and restrictive strategy clearly backfired: it made doctors publicly suspect as possessors of esoteric and occult knowledge. Moreover, by suppressing information about the mutilations, the medical establishment contributed to an explosion of popular rumors, speculation, and fascination with them. "There was no doubt this time," recalled Dr. Halsted of the London Hospital, that the murderer "had removed certain parts of the body not normally mentioned in polite society and *this perversion* almost *more than the murder itself* excited the frenzy of the large crowd which gathered round the spot during the following day" (emphasis mine).[26] The "frenzy" of the crowd at the prospect of a "woman cut to pieces" stood in stark contrast to the medical language of Chapman's autopsy report, whose Latinate terms ("mesenteric attachments") and detached clinical picture of a body dispossessed of any personal identity (including sexual identity) were rhetorical efforts to sanitize medical engagement with a "grotesque" female body. Taken together, elite and popular responses to the mutilations operated as a twin strategy in a single regime of knowledge, one that simultaneously incited and repressed the "truth" of "sex."[27] The "high" and "low" responses to the mutilations replicated the split "Jekyll and Hyde" personality of the miscreant, the "savage/savant" who also combined behavior of astonishing ferocity with a capacity for rational thought and skill.[28]

Although the mutilations committed on the last Ripper victims seemed to lack any indication of "anatomical knowledge," the Mad Doctor, as the possessor of privileged knowledge and technical skill, would remain the most enduring and publicly compelling member of a cast of privileged villains proposed by the press and by the experts.[29]

Further reading

For responses to *City of Dreadful Delight*, see Martin J. Wiener, John Stokes, Sally Alexander and Judith R. Walkowitz, 'Roundtable on *City of Dreadful Delight*', *Journal of Victorian Culture*, 2 (1997), 302–31. A number of serious studies have been undertaken of the Jack the Ripper case: Christopher Frayling, 'The House that Jack Built' in Sylvana Tomaselli and Roy Porter (eds), *Rape* (Oxford: Basil Blackwell, 1986), 174–215; W.B. Fishman, *East End 1888: A Year in a London Borough Among the Labouring Poor* (London: Duckworth, 1988); L. Perry Curtis, *Jack the Ripper and the London Press* (New Haven, CT: Yale University Press, 2001). On sexual abuse, see: Shani D'Cruze, *Crimes of Outrage: Sex, Violence and Victorian Working Women* (London: UCL Press, 1998); Louise Jackson, *Child Sexual Abuse in Victorian England* (London: Routledge, 2000). On the issue of women's relationship to the city, see Deborah Epstein Nord, *Walking the Victorian Streets: Women, Representation and the City* (Princeton, NJ: Princeton University Press, 1995).

Notes

1   "Murder and More to Follow," *Pall Mall Gazette* [hereafter *PMG*], 8 Sept. 1888; Robert Louis Stevenson, *Doctor Jekyll and Mr. Hyde*, with an introduction by Abraham Rothberg (New York: Bantam, 1967; first edition, 1886), p. 78 (all citations from the novel come from this edition); Paul Wilstach, *Richard Mansfield, the Man and the Actor* (New York: Charles Scribner's Sons, 1908); Harry M. Geduld, Introduction, in Harry M. Geduld, ed., *The Definitive "Dr. Jekyll and Mr. Hyde" Companion* (New York and London: Garland, 1983), p. 12; "Richard Mansfield, vol. 8," Robinson Locke Collection, New York Public Library.

2   "Murder and More to Follow," *PMG*, 8 Sept. 1888.

3   "Occasional Notes," *PMG*, 10 Sept. 1888.

4   *Star*, 16 Sept. 1888; *Daily Telegraph*, 22 Sept. 1888. The *East London Advertiser* pronounced the Jekyll and Hyde theory an "enduring theory" (13 Oct. 1888). On the closing down of the play, see Donald Rumbelow, *The Complete Jack the Ripper* (New York: New American Library, 1975), p. 124.

5   Christopher Frayling, "The House that Jack Built," in Sylvia Tomaselli and Roy Porter, eds, *Rape* (Oxford: Basil Blackwell, 1986), p. 197.

6   Deborah Cameron and Elizabeth Fraser, *Lust to Kill: A Feminist Investigation of Sexual Murder* (New York: New York University Press, 1987), p. 127.

7   *Psychopathia Sexualis* grew from 45 case histories and 110 pages in 1886 to 238 histories and 437 pages by the twelfth edition in 1903. See Jeffrey Weeks, *Sexuality and Its Discontents: Meanings, Myths, and Modern Sexualities* (London: Routledge and Kegan Paul, 1985), p. 67.

8   Weeks, *Sexuality and Its Discontents*, p. 67.

9   Thanks to Susan Maslin for these observations.

10   Dr. R. von Krafft-Ebing, *Psychopathia Sexualis: With Especial Reference to Contrary Sexual Instinct: A Medico-Legal Study*, trans. Charles Gilbert Chaddock (Philadelphia: F.A. Davis, 1891), pp. 1, 56.

11   Ibid., p. 378. As Sander Gilman observes, Krafft-Ebing's view of perversion as intrinsic to modern life differed from the evolutionary view of earlier sexologists, who tended to treat sexual perversions as throwbacks to an earlier sexual primitivism, as "ambiguous

eddies" within a linear history of progress. "Sexology and Psychoanalysis," in J. Edward Chamberlain and Sander Gilman, eds, *Degeneration: The Dark Side of Progress* (New York: Columbia University Press, 1985), pp. 75–79.

12   Krafft-Ebing, *Psychopathia Sexualis*, p. 57.

13   Ibid., pp. 13, 60.

14   Forbes Winslow to the Editor, *The Times*, 12 Sept. 1888; *Recollections of Forty Years* (London: J. Ousley, 1910), p. 270.

15   *Lancet*, excerpted in Elwyn Jones, ed., *Ripper File* (London: Barker, 1975), p. 26; Coroner Baxter, excerpted in ibid., p. 31.

16   Baxter, excerpted in Jones, *Ripper File*, pp. 31, 24, 25.

17   "The Whitechapel Murders," *Lancet*, Sept. 29, 1888:637; "The Whitechapel Murders," *EN*, 17 Sept. 1888.

18   Antivivisection was a campaign with no "landmarks," that reached no great climax, that was fought in the hearts and minds of Victorians with few institutional and legal results. Nonetheless, the amount of propaganda literature churned out by Cobbe's organization is staggering: in 1885 alone, Victoria Street put out 81,672 books, pamphlets, and leaflets (French, *Anti-Vivisection*, pp. 255, 256) Though the press remained overwhelmingly hostile to Cobbe and her fellow agitators, antivivisection tropes and iconography pervaded popular journalism and fiction. Indignant opponents of the "Maiden Tribute," for example, accused Stead of "moral vivisection" for imposing the gynecological examination of Eliza Armstrong. Stead himself made ready use of antivivisectionist rhetoric in his crusades against sexually dangerous men. In 1887, he introduced Edwin Langsworthy to his readers as a privileged sadist who amused himself by torturing cats before he extended his "cruel sport" to his bride, a "refined and cultivated lady." Quoted in Raymond L. Schults, *Crusader in Babylon: W.T. Stead and the Pall Mall Gazette* (Lincoln, Nebraska: University of Nebraska Press, 1972), pp. 212, 213,

19   Frances Power Cobbe, *Life of Frances Power Cobbe*, 2 vols (Boston: Houghton Mifflin, 1895), 2:607.

20   Authored by Edward Berdoe, an East End doctor and close collaborator of Cobbe, *St. Bernard's* was a thinly disguised autobiographical account of Berdoe's own training at the London Hospital. Its publication caused quite a sensation: over fifty reviews of the novel appeared, some denouncing it as a "gross calumny" upon the medical profession, others concerned and appalled by its exposé of doctors as "monsters of cruelty" and of hospitals as "hotbeds of corruption and cruelty," Edward Berdoe, *St. Bernard's: The Romance of a Medical Student* (London: Swan, Sonnenschein, 1887); Edward Berdoe, *Dying Scientifically: A Key to St. Bernard's* (London: Swan Sonnenschein, 1888); Coral Lansbury, *The Old Brown Dog: Women, Workers, and Vivisection in Edwardian England* (Madison: University of Wisconsin Press, 1985), chap. 10.

21   Orvilla Moscucci, *The Science of Woman: Gynecology and Gender in England 1800–1929* (Cambridge: Cambridge University Press, 1990). Already stung by public criticism over lunacy confinement and the medical "rape" of registered prostitutes, doctors responded to this propagandist assault by defending animal experimentation as a sacred cause to be upheld against quacks and religious fanatics. They also countered with their own interpretation of the medical invasion of innocent "feminized" bodies. Medical publicists acknowledged the experimental link between women's bodies and those of laboratory animals, but they defended the violation of the latter to preserve the health of the former. It was precisely *because* the "public" demanded such medical intervention into female bodies that animal experimentation was necessary, declared one gynecologist, Mr. Spencer Wells, who pointed to surgical advances in ovariotomy gained from animal experimentation. Wells complained of public ingratitude: "the public demands of us to save the lives of their wives and daughters and forces upon us operations undreamt of from their very severity even a few years ago" ("Vivisection and Ovariotomy," *BMJ*, 22 Jan. 1881, p. 133). The symbolic struggle between

antivivisectionists and their medical opponents escalated significantly in the 1880s, as did the statistics on antivivisection experiments: in 1879, there were 270 vivisections in Great Britain; ten years later there were 1,417.

However, some doctors remained uneasy about the link between vivisection and ovariotomy. Because the ovaries were deemed the "grand organs" of female identity, medical spokesmen expressed fears that their surgical removal would lead to the "unsexing" of women: there was a widespread feeling, argued the *British Medical Journal* in 1887, that the ovaries of women should be respected because they were "the organs of sexual life, making a woman what she is, fitted for the duties of womanhood, including childbearing." "Normal Ovariotomy: Battey's operation: Tait's operation," *BMJ* 1 (1887): 576–77. Moscuccci, *Science of Woman*, pp. 134, 157.

22   Archibald Forbes to the Editor, *Daily News*, 3 Oct. 1888.
23   This venereal anxiety also coincided with a more explicit thematizing of the danger of "syphilis of the innocents," as expressed in works like Ibsen's *Ghosts* and the New Women novels of the 1890s. Showalter, *Sexual Anarchy*; Alain Corbin, *Women for Hire: Prostitution and Sexuality in France after 1850*, trans. Alan Sheridan (Cambridge, Mass: Harvard University Press, 1990), p. 249.
24   Alex Comfort, *The Anxiety Makers: Some Curious Preoccupations of the Medical Profession* (London: Nelson, 1967).
25   Dr. Phillips, testimony at Chapman's inquest, excerpted in Jones, *Ripper File*, p. 25.
26   D.G. Halsted, *Doctor in the Nineties* (London: Christopher Johnson, 1959), p. 48.
27   Michel Foucault, *The History of Sexuality*, vol. 1, *An Introduction*, translated by Robert Hurley (New York: Pantheon, 1985).
28   As Ludmilla Jordanova observes, because doctors regularly executed tasks which would "in normal circumstances be taboo or emotionally repugnant," they had to renegotiate "body taboos" by presenting themselves "as rational, scientific, in alliance with polite culture and clean." Ludmilla Jordanova, *Sexual Visions* (Madison: University of Wisconsin Press, 1989), p. 138. Thanks to Andrew Bragen and Kim Thompson for some of these observations.
29   In addition, later media coverage "democratized" knowledge by reporting on the extent and nature of the mutilations. *Star*, 1 Oct. 1888; Martin Fido, *The Crimes, Detection, and Death of Jack the Ripper* (London: Weidenfeld and Nicolson, 1987), pp. 70–80.

Elaine Showalter

HOMOSEXUALITY AND LATE VICTORIAN ANXIETY

Sexual Anarchy: Gender and Culture at the Fin-de-Siècle (New York: Viking Penguin, 1990), 105–16.

Elaine Showalter's *Sexual Anarchy* (1990) presents a portrait of late Victorian society comparable to that by **Judith Walkowitz** and can be profitably read alongside *City of Dreadful Delight*. An influential literary critic and cultural historian, Showalter has been one of the leading interdisciplinary figures of her generation. Her body of work typifies the interdisciplinary spirit that has been the hallmark of the New Victorian Studies. She first came to prominence with her rereading of the female voice in Victorian literature, *A Literature of Their Own* (1977), a landmark in feminist approaches to the Victorians. Among other works, she went on to write *The Female Malady* (1986), which examined the way in which hysteria and madness became associated with the feminine in the nineteenth and early twentieth centuries.

Sexual Anarchy emerged as a response to the sexual panics of the late twentieth century. She argued that this was a feature of the ends of centuries and presented a portrait of literature at the end of the nineteenth century struggling to deal with anxieties about sexuality and about the increased visibility of women in the public sphere, leading to images of women as destroyers, demons and femmes-fatales. In the following Reading she unpicks the anxieties that lie underneath Robert Louis Stevenson's *The Strange Case of Dr Jekyll and Mr Hyde*. Most contemporary commentators saw the tale as an allegory about the dangers of science or the division of the self. Showalter demonstrates how it can be read as an exploration of the homosocial world of upper middle-class men, particularly the secret world of homosexuality. As she notes, the time of publication was exactly the moment when a distinctive homosexual subculture was emerging in London and also the moment of its explicit criminalisation. Showalter's Reading is also attuned to the emergence of psychoanalytic categories. The excerpt printed here focuses on the novel itself and its meanings for a contemporary audience, although it is also a fascinating analysis of the way the twentieth century has reshaped the narrative in line with its own anxieties.

Elaine Showalter is Professor Emerita of Princeton University and is currently finishing a literary history of American women writers from 1650 to 2000.

IN JANUARY 1886, the same month that Robert Louis Stevenson published *The Strange Case of Dr. Jekyll and Mr. Hyde*, another strange case of "multiple personality" was introduced to English readers in the pages of *The Journal of Mental Science*. It involved a male hysteric named "Louis V.," a patient at Rochefort Asylum in France whose case of "morbid disintegration" had fascinated French doctors. Louis V.'s hysterical attacks had begun in adolescence, when he underwent a startling metamorphosis. Having been a "quiet, well-behaved, and obedient" street urchin, he abruptly became "violent, greedy, and quarrelsome," a heavy drinker, a political radical, and an atheist. So far his "symptoms" might be those of any teenage boy; but what seems to have upset his doctors particularly was that he tried to caress them. The French physicians attributed his condition to a shock he received from being frightened by a viper, and they cured him through hypnosis so effectively that he could not even remember what he had done.[1]

Stevenson (called "Louis" by his friends) may well have read the case of Louis V.; it had been written up earlier in the *Archives de Neurologie*, and his wife recalled that he had been "deeply impressed" by a "paper he read in French journal on subconsciousness" while he was writing *Jekyll and Hyde*.[2] He was also a friend of Frederic W.H. Myers, who discussed the case for English specialists. But male hysteria was a topic of considerable scientific interest in 1886. Berjon in France published his book, *La grande hystérie chez l'homme*; and in Austria Freud made his debut at the Vienna Medical Society with a controversial paper about male hysteria. While it was recognized in men, hysteria carried the stigma of being a humiliatingly female affliction. Another scholar of male hysteria, Charcot's disciple Emile Bataut, observed that hysterical men in Sâlpetrière's special ward were "timid and fearful men, whose gaze is neither lively nor piercing, but rather, soft, poetic, and languorous. Coquettish and eccentric, they prefer ribbons and scarves to hard manual labor."[3] Later this view of the hysterical man as effeminate would be carried into psychoanalytic theory, where the male hysteric is seen as expressing his bisexuality or homosexuality through the language of the body.

Homosexuality was also a topic of considerable scientific and legal interest in 1886. In January, just as Stevenson published his novel, the Labouchère Amendment criminalizing homosexual acts went into effect, and Krafft-Ebing's *Psychopathia Sexualis* offered some of the first case studies of homosexual men.[4] By the 1880s, such scholars as Jeffrey Weeks and Richard Dellamora have shown, the Victorian homosexual world had evolved into a secret but active subculture, with its own language, styles, practices, and meeting places. For most middle-class inhabitants of this world, homosexuality represented a double life, in which a respectable daytime world often involving marriage and family, existed alongside a night world of homoeroticism. Indeed, the *fin de siècle* was the golden age of literary and sexual doubles. "Late Victorian duality," writes Karl Miller in *Doubles*, "may be identified with the dilemmas, for males, of a choice between male and female roles, or of a possible union of such opposites. The Nineties School of Duality framed a dialect and a dialectic, for the love that dared not speak its name — for the vexed question of homosexuality and bisexuality."[5] J.A. Symonds wrote poignantly in his journals of "the dual life . . . which had been habitual."[6] In Oscar Wilde's *The Importance of Being Earnest*, leading a double life is called "Bunburying" and represents, as one critic notes, "the 'posing' and 'double lives' to which homosexuals were accustomed."[7]

Stevenson was the fin-de-siècle laureate of the double life. In an essay on dreams, he described his passionate aim to "find a body, a vehicle for that strong sense of man's double being" which he had felt as a student in Edinburgh when he dreamed of leading "a double life — one of the day, one of the night."[8] The double life of the day and the night is also the double life of the writer, the split between reality and the imagination. Nonetheless, biographers have long hinted that Stevenson's own double life was more than the standard round of brothels and nighttime bohemia, and have rattled such skeletons in Stevenson's closet as "homosexuality, impotence, a passionate feeling for his stepson, submission to a willful and predatory wife."[9] In particular, Stevenson was the object of extraordinary passion on the part of other men. According to Andrew Lang, he "possessed, more than any man I ever met, the power of making other men fall in love with him."[10] Among the group of friends, both homosexual and heterosexual, in Stevenson's large literary and bohemian circle, "male appreciation of Stevenson was often intensely physical."[11]

Some of this appreciation and sexual ambiguity is vividly conveyed in the portrait, *Robert Louis Stevenson and His Wife* (1885), by one of the artists in Stevenson's circle who led his own double life, John Singer Sargent [. . .] . In the foreground, a slender and anxious-looking Stevenson stares out at the painter, elongated fingers nervously stroking his droopy moustache. On the right, on the very margins of the painting, her body cut off by the picture frame, is the shadowy figure of his wife Fanny reclining on a velvet sofa, wrapped from head to toe in a gilded veil. Between the two is a door in the background wall, opening into a dark closet. For Stevenson himself, the painting was "too eccentric to be exhibited. I am at one extreme corner; my wife, in this wild dress, and looking like a ghost, is at the extreme other end . . . All this is touched in lovely, with that witty touch of Sargent's; but of course, it looks dam queer as a whole." For Sargent, the painting showed Stevenson trapped by domesticity and femininity; it is, he said, "the caged animal lecturing about the foreign specimen in the corner."[12] In his marriage to Fanny, Stevenson wrote to W.E. Henley, he had come out "as limp as a lady's novel . . . the embers of the once gay R.L.S."[13]

Stevenson's real sexuality is much less the issue in *Jekyll and Hyde*, however, than his sense of the fantasies beneath the surface of daylight decorum, the shadow of homosexuality that surrounded Clubland and the nearly hysterical tenor of revealing forbidden emotions between men that constituted the dark side of patriarchy. In many respects, *The Strange Case of Dr. Jekyll and Mr. Hyde* is a case study of male hysteria, not only that of Henry J., but also of the men in the community around him. It can most persuasively be read as a fable of fin-de-siècle homosexual panic, the discovery and resistance of the homosexual self.[14] In contrast to the way it has been represented in film and popular culture, *Jekyll and Hyde* is a story about communities of men. From the moment of its publication, many critics have remarked on the "maleness," even the monasticism, of the story.[15] The characters are all middle-aged bachelors who have no relationships with women except as servants. Furthermore, they are celibates whose major emotional contacts are with each other and with Henry Jekyll. A female reviewer of the book expressed her surprise that "no woman's name occurs in the book, no romance is even suggested in it." Mr. Stevenson, wrote the critic Alice Brown, "is a boy who has no mind to play with girls."[16] The romance of Jekyll and Hyde is conveyed instead through men's names, men's bodies, and men's psyches.

Henry Jekyll is in a sense the odd man of fin-de-siècle literature. Unable to pair off with either a woman or another man, Jekyll divides himself, and finds his only mate in his double, Edward Hyde. Jekyll is thus both odd and even, both single and double. "Man is not truly one, but truly two," he observes, and his need to pursue illicit sexual pleasure and yet to live up to the exacting moral standards of his bleak professional community have committed him to "a profound duplicity of life," accompanied by "an almost morbid sense of shame." Coming to acknowledge his unutterable desires, Jekyll longs to separate his mind and his body: "If each, I told myself, could be housed in separable identities, life would be relieved of all that was unbearable."

Not only the personality of Jekyll, but everything else about the book seems divided and split; Stevenson wrote two drafts of the novel, the Notebook Draft and the Printer's Copy; the fragments or "fractions" of the manuscript are scattered among four libraries (two would obviously be more poetically just, but I cannot tell a lie); and Longmans published two Jekyll-and-Hyde-like simultaneous editions, a paperback shilling shocker and a more respectable cloth-bound volume.[17] Stevenson alludes obliquely to the composition process in the novel itself when Dr. Lanyon discovers the notebook in which Jekyll has recorded his experiments: "Here and there a brief remark was appended to a date, usually no more than a single word: 'double' occurring perhaps six times in a total of several hundred entries; and once very early in the list and followed by several marks of exclamation 'total failure!'" Just as Jekyll searches for the proper dose to fight decomposition, Stevenson hints at his own frustration in composing the narrative of doubles.

Like the stories hysterical women told Freud, full of gaps, inconsistencies, and contradictions, Dr. Jekyll's story is composed of fragments and fractions, told through a series of narratives that the reader must organize into a coherent case history. The central narrator of the story is Gabriel John Utterson, who utters the tale, and eventually inherits Jekyll's estate. More than the others in their social circle, Utterson is a "Jekyll manqué."[18] Like many narrators in late-Victorian fiction, he is a lawyer, a spokesman for the Law of the Father and the social order, and "a lover of the sane and customary sides of life." His demeanor is muted and sober; "scanty and embarrassed in discourse"; "undemonstrative" and "backward in sentiment," austere and self-denying, he spends evenings alone drinking gin "to mortify a taste for vintages," or reading "a volume of some dry divinity"; although he likes the theater, he has not "crossed the doors of one for twenty years." He has almost a dread of the fanciful, a fear of the realm of the anarchic imagination.

Yet like Jekyll, Utterson also has an unconventional side to keep down; indeed, his self-mortification seems like an effort to stay within the boundaries of masculine propriety. Utterson's fantasies take the form of vicarious identification with the high spirits and bad fortune of "down-going men," for whom he is often the last respectable friend. "I incline to Cain's heresy," he is wont to say; "I let my brother go to the devil in his own way." Utterson, too, has a particular male friend, the younger "man about town" Richard Enfield, whom he sees every Sunday for an excursion that is the "chief jewel of every week," although "it was a nut to crack for many, what these two could see in each other." In another scene, he shares an intimate evening with his clerk Mr. Guest, his own confidant; at least "there was no man from whom he kept fewer secrets." Perhaps because his own life is so involved with repression and fantasy, Utterson becomes "enslaved" to the mystery of Hyde: "If he be Mr. Hyde . . . I shall be Mr. Seek." He begins to haunt the "by street" near Jekyll's house and to have rape fantasies of a faceless figure who opens the door to the room where Jekyll lies sleeping, pulls back the curtains of the bed, and forces Jekyll to rise and do his bidding.

Fin-de-siècle images of forced penetration through locked doors into private cabinets, rooms and closets permeate Utterson's narrative; as Stephen Heath notes, "the organizing image for this narrative is the breaking down of doors, learning the secret behind them."[19] The narrators of Jekyll's secret attempt to open up the mystery of another man, not by understanding or secret sharing, but by force. "Make a clean breast of this [to me] in confidence," Utterson pleads with Jekyll, who rebuffs him: "it isn't what you fancy; it is not so bad as that." Jekyll cannot open his heart or his breast even to his dearest male friends. Thus they must spy on him to enter his mind, to get to the bottom of his secrets. The first chapter is called "The Story of the Door," and while Hyde, as the text repeatedly draws to our attention, has a key to Jekyll's house, Utterson makes violent entries, finally breaking down the door to Jekyll's private closet with an axe, as if into what Jekyll calls "the very fortress of identity."

One of the secrets behind these doors is that Jekyll has a mirror in his cabinet, a discovery almost as shocking to Utterson and the butler Poole as the existence of Hyde. "This glass has seen some queer doings," Poole exclaims in the manuscript (changed to "strange things" in the text).[20] The mirror testifies not only to Jekyll's scandalously unmanly narcissism, but also to the sense of the mask and the Other that has made the mirror an obsessive symbol in homosexual literature. Behind Jekyll's red baize door, Utterson sees his own mirrored face, the image of the painfully repressed desires that the cane and the axe cannot wholly shatter and destroy.

The agitation and anxiety felt by the bachelor friends of Jekyll's circle reflects their mutual, if tacit and unspoken, understanding of Jekyll's "strange preference" for Edward Hyde. Utterson, Enfield, and Lanyon initially think that Jekyll is keeping Hyde. What they see is that their rich friend Harry Jekyll has willed his very considerable estate to a loutish younger man, who comes and goes as he pleases, has expensive paintings and other gifts from Jekyll in his Soho apartment, gives orders to the servants, and cashes large checks Jekyll has signed. However unsuitable, this young man is Jekyll's "favorite," a term that, as Vladimir Nabokov noted in his lecture on the novel, "sounds almost like *minion*."[21] Even when Hyde is suspected of a crime, Jekyll attempts to shield him, and begs Utterson to protect him: "I do sincerely take a great, a very great interest in that young man."

Jekyll's apparent infatuation with Hyde reflects the late-nineteenth-century upper-middle-class eroticization of working-class men as the ideal homosexual objects. "The moving across the class barrier," Weeks points out, "on the one hand the search for 'rough trade,' and on the other the reconciling effect of sex across class lines, was an important and recurrent theme in the homosexual world."[22] Edward Carpenter dreamed of being loved by "the thick-thighed hot coarse-fleshed young bricklayer with the strap round his waist," while E.M. Forster fantasized about "a strong young man of the working-class."[23] Furthermore, prostitution was "an indispensable part of the male homosexual life . . . with participants beginning usually in their mid-teens and generally leaving the trade by their mid-twenties." The "kept boy" was as common as the rough trade picked up on the streets; when he is "accosted" by the "aged and beautiful" M.P., Sir Danvers Carew, late at night in the dark streets by the river and beats him to death, Hyde both strikes at a father figure and suggests a male prostitute mugging a client on the docks.

Furthermore, Enfield calls Jekyll's abode "Blackmail House" on "Queer Street" and speculates that Jekyll is "an honest man paying through the nose for some of the capers of his youth." While Enfield explicitly does not want to pursue these implications   "the more it looks like Queer Street, the less I ask" — the butler Poole has also noted "something queer" about Hyde. As a number of scholars have noted, the homosexual significance of "queer" had entered English slang by 1900.[24] "'Odd,' 'queer,' 'dark,' 'fit,' 'nervous,'" notes Karl Miller, "these are the bricks which had built the house of the double."[25] For contemporary readers of Stevenson's novel, moreover, the term "blackmail" would have immediately suggested homosexual liaisons. Originating in sixteenth-century Scotland, it was generally associated with accusations of buggery.[26] Furthermore, the vision of blackmail as the penalty for homosexual sin was intensified by the Labouchère Amendment [*which criminalized homosexuality as part of the Criminal Law Amendment Act of 1885*].While homosexual men had long been vulnerable to blackmail, the new law, as Edward Carpenter noted, "opened wider than ever before the door to a real, most serious social evil and crime — that of blackmailing."[27] Popularly known as the "Blackmailer's Charter," the Labouchère Amendment put closeted homosexual men like Wilde and J.A. Symonds at particular risk. It made a major contribution to that "blackmailability" that Sedgwick sees as a crucial component of the "leverage of homophobia."[28]

In his original draft of the manuscript, Stevenson was more explicit about the sexual practices that had driven Jekyll to a double life. Jekyll has become "from an early age . . . the slave of certain appetites," vices which are "at once criminal in the sight of the law and abhorrent in themselves. They cut me off from the sympathy of those whom I otherwise respected."[29] While these passages were omitted in the published version, Stevenson retained the sense of abhorrence and dread that surrounds Hyde. The metaphors associated with Hyde are those of abnormality, criminality, disease, contagion, and death. The reaction of the male characters to Hyde is uniformly that of "disgust, loathing, and fear," suggestive of the almost hysterical homophobia of the late nineteenth century. In the most famous code word of Victorian homosexuality, they find something *unspeakable* about Hyde "that gave a man a turn," something "surprising and revolting." Indeed, the language surrounding Hyde is almost uniformly negative, although when Jekyll first takes the drug, he feels "younger, lighter, happier in body." Hyde is represented as apelike, pale, and inexpressibly deformed, echoing the imagery of syphilitic afflictions in nineteenth-century medical texts, and Utterson speculates that Jekyll may have contracted a disease from Hyde, "one of those maladies that both torture and deform the sufferer," for which he is seeking the drug as an antidote. Meditating on Jekyll's possible youthful crime, Utterson fears "the cancer of some concealed disgrace; punishment coming, *pede claudo*." Along with the imagery of disease and retribution, the Latin phrase (literally "on halting foot") suggests a bilingual pun on "pederasty."

The male homosexual body is also represented in the narrative in a series of images suggestive of anality and anal intercourse. Hyde travels in the "chocolate-brown fog" that beats about the "back-end of the evening"; while the streets he traverses are invariably "muddy" and "dark," Jekyll's house, with its two entrances, is the most vivid representation of the male body. Hyde always enters it through the blistered back door, which, in Stevenson's words, is "equipped with neither bell nor knocker" and which bears the "marks of prolonged and sordid negligence."

Finally, the suicide which ends Jekyll's narrative is the only form of narrative closure thought appropriate to the Gay Gothic, where the protagonist's death is both martyrdom and retribution. To learn Jekyll-Hyde's secret leads to death; it destroys Dr. Lanyon, for example, as later, Dorian Gray also causes the suicides of a number of young men and then kills himself. While Jekyll tries to convince himself that his desire is merely an addiction, a bad habit that he can overcome whenever he wants, he gradually comes to understand that Hyde is indeed part of him. In a final spasm of homophobic guilt, Jekyll slays his other "hated personality." Death is the only solution to the "illness" of homosexuality. As A.E. Housman would write in *A Shropshire Lad*:

> Shot? so quick, so clean an ending?
> Oh that was right, lad, that was brave:
> Yours was not an ill for mending,
> 'Twas best to take it to the grave.

Jekyll is a "self-destroyer," Utterson concludes, not only because he has killed himself, but because it is self-destructive to violate the sexual codes of one's society.[30]

In the multiplication of narrative viewpoints that makes up the story, however, one voice is missing: that of Hyde himself. We never hear his account of the events, his memories of his strange birth, his pleasure and fear. Hyde's story would disturb the sexual economy of the text, the sense of panic at having liberated an uncontrollable desire. Hyde's hysterical narrative comes to us in two ways: in the representation of his feminine behavior, and in the body language of hysterical discourse. As William Veeder points out, "despite all his 'masculine' traits of preternatural strength and animal agility, Hyde is prey to what the nineteenth century associated primarily with women."[31] He is seen "wrestling against the approaches of hysteria," and heard "weeping like a woman." Hyde's reality breaks through Jekyll's body in the shape of his hand, the timbre of his voice, and the quality of his gait.

In representing the effects of splitting upon the male body, Stevenson drew upon the advanced medical science of his day. In the 1860s the French neuroanatomist Paul Broca had first established the concept of the double brain and of left cerebral dominance. Observing that language disorders resulted from left-brain injuries, he hypothesized that the left frontal brain lobes, which controlled the right side of the body, were the seat of the intellectual and motor skills. Thus the left brain was more important than the right and virtually defined the distinction between the animal and the human. The right frontal brain lobes, which controlled the left side of the body, were subordinate; they were the seat of lesser, non-verbal traits. Individuals in whom the right hemisphere predominated had to be low on the human evolutionary scale. In describing or imagining the operations of the double brain, European scientists were influenced by their cultural assumptions about duality, including gender, race and class. They characterized one side of the brain and body as masculine, rational, civilized, European, and highly evolved, and the other as feminine, irrational, primitive, and backward. Many scientists argued that the intellectual inferiority and social subordination of women and blacks could be attributed to their weak left brains. Furthermore, when mental disturbances occurred, as one physician noted in 1887, there must be a terrible struggle "between the left personality and the right personality, or in other more familiar terms, between the good and the bad side."[32]

These ideas about the brain were strongly related to late-nineteenth-century ideas about handedness, since handedness was usually inversely related to brain dominance; and considerable effort was made to get left-handed children to change. Freud's close friend Wilhelm Fliess, however, argued that all human beings were bisexual, with the dominant side of the brain representing the dominant gender, and the other the repressed gender. Thus Fliess believed that normal, heterosexual people would be right-handed, while "effeminate men and masculine women are entirely or partly left-handed."[33]

The imagery of hands is conspicuous in the text of *Jekyll and Hyde* and has also been dramatically put to use in the various film versions, where Hyde's hands seem almost to have a life of their own. It draws upon ideas of the double brain and hand, as well as upon other social and sexual meanings. As a child, Jekyll recalls, he had "walked with my father's hand," suggesting that he had taken on the bodily symbols of the "right" — or proper — hand of patriarchal respectabilities and constraint. Hyde seems to be the sinister left hand of Jekyll, the hand of the rebellious and immoral son. Suddenly Jekyll discovers that he cannot control the metamorphosis; he wakes up to find that his own hand, the hand of the father, the "large, firm, white and comely" hand of the successful professional, has turned into the "lean, corded, knuckly," and hairy hand of Hyde. The implied phallic image here also suggests the difference between the properly socialized sexual desires of the dominant society and the twisted, sadistic, and animal desires of the other side. Jekyll's "hand" also means his handwriting and signature, which Hyde can forge, although his own writing looks like Jekyll's with a different slant. As Frederic W.H. Myers wrote to Stevenson, "Hyde's writing might look like Jekyll's, done *with the left hand*."[34] Finally, the image draws upon the Victorian homosexual trope of the left hand of illicit sexuality. Jekyll tells Lanyon that in the days of their Damon and Pythias friendship, he would have sacrificed "my left hand to help you." In his secret memoirs, Symonds, too, uses the figure of the useless hand "clenched in the grip of an unconquerable love" to express his double life and the sublimation of his homosexual desires.[35]

Some men, like Symonds and Wilde, may have read the book as a signing to the male community. "Viewed as an allegory," Symonds wrote to Stevenson, "it touches upon one too closely. Most of us at some epoch of our lives have been upon the verge of developing a Mr. Hyde."[36] Wilde included an anecdote in "The Decay of Lying" about "a friend of mine, called Mr. Hyde" who finds himself eerily reliving the events in Stevenson's story. But most Victorian and modern readers ignored such messages or evaded them. While there have been over seventy films and television versions of *Dr. Jekyll and Mr. Hyde*, for example, not one tells the story as Stevenson wrote it — that is, as a story about men. All of the versions add women to the story and either eliminate the homoerotic elements or suggest them indirectly through imagery and structural elements. [. . .]

Further reading

On late Victorian sexual anxiety see: Daniel Pick, *Faces of Degeneration: A European Disorder, c.1848–1914* (Cambridge: Cambridge University Press, 1989); Judith Walkowitz, *City of Dreadful Delight: Narratives of Sexual Danger in Late-Victorian London* (London: Virago, 1992); Rebecca Stott, *Fabrication of the Late Victorian Femme Fatale: Kiss of Death* (London: Macmillan, 1992); Lucy Bland, *Banishing the Beast: English Feminism and Sexual Morality, 1885–1914* (London: Penguin, 1995); Frank Mort, *Dangerous Sexualities: Medico-Moral Politics in England since 1830* (London: Routledge, 2000 [1987]). On homosexuality, see: Harry Cocks, *Nameless Offences: Homosexual Desire in the Nineteenth Century* (London: I.B. Tauris, 1993); Matt Cook, *London and the Culture of Homosexuality, 1885–1914* (Cambridge: Cambridge University Press, 2003).

Notes

1   Frederic W.H. Myers, "Multiplex Personality," *The Nineteenth Century* (November 1886): 648–66.
2   Mrs. R.L. Stevenson, "Note," in *Works of Robert Louis Stevenson: Skerryvore Edition* (London: Heinemann, 1924), 4:xvii–xvii.
3   Emile Batault, *Contribution à l'étude de l'hystérie chez l'homme*, (Paris, 1885), author's translation.
4   See Wayne Koestenbaum, "The Shadow Under the Bed: Dr. Jekyll, Mr. Hyde, and the Labouchère Amendment," *Critical Matrix* 1 (Spring 1988): 31–55.
5   Karl Miller, *Doubles: Studies in Literary History* (London: Oxford University Press, 1987), p. 216.
6   Phyllis Grosskurth, ed. *The Memoirs of John Addington Symonds: The Secret Homosexual Life of a Leading Nineteenth-Century Man of Letters* (Chicago: University of Chicago Press, 1984), p. 122.
7   Regenia Gagnier, *Idylls of the Marketplace: Oscar Wilde and the Victorian Public* (Stanford: Stanford University Press, 1986), p. 158.
8   "A Chapter on Dreams," in *The Works of Robert Louis Stevenson* (London 1922), p. 247.
9   Miller, *Doubles*, p. 213. For discussions of Stevenson's homosociality/homosexuality, see William Veeder's brilliant essay, "Children of the Night: Stevenson and Patriarchy," in *Dr. Jekyll and Mr. Hyde after One Hundred Years*, (Chicago: University of Chicago Press, 1988), William Veeder and Gordon Hirsch, eds, especially pp. 159–60; and Wayne Koestenbaum, *Double Talk: The Erotics of Male Literary Collaboration* (New York and London: Routledge, 1989), pp. 145–51.
10   Andrew Lang, "Recollections of Robert Louis Stevenson," *Adventures Among Books* (London: Longmans, Green, and Co., 1903), p. 51.

11   Jenni Calder, *Robert Louis Stevenson: A Life Study* (New York: Oxford University Press, 1980), p. 65.

12   Quoted in Stanley Olson, *John Singer Sargent* (New York: St. Martin's Press, 1986), pp. 115, 114.

13   Malcolm Elwin, *The Strange Case of Robert Louis Stevenson* (London: Macdonald, 1950), p. 198; quoted in Koestenbaum, *Double Talk*, p. 150

14   Eve Kosofsky Sedgwick has called the genre to which Stevenson's novel belongs "the paranoid Gothic." According to Sedgwick, "the Gothic novel crystallized for English audiences the terms of a dialectic between male homosexuality and homophobia, in which homophobia appeared thematically in paranoid plots," (*Between Men: English Literature and Male Homosocial Desire* (New York: Columbia University Press, 1985), p. 92). Such texts involved doubled male figures, one of whom feels obsessed by or persecuted by the other; and the central image of the unspeakable secret. I am indebted also to Paul Zablocki, and to John Perry's unpublished senior thesis, "Novel as Homotext: A Gay Critical Approach to Narrative" Princeton University, 1987.

15   See, for example, the excellent essay by Stephen Heath, "Psychopathia sexualis: Stevenson's *Strange Case*," *Critical Quarterly* 28 (1986), p. 2.

16   Julia Wedgwood, *Contemporary Review* 49 (April 1886): 594–95; and Alice Brown, *Study of Stevenson* (Boston: Copeland and Day, 1895) quoted in Koestenbaum, *Double Talk*, p. 145.

17   For the manuscripts and publishing history of the novel, see William Veeder, "The Texts in Question," and Veeder and Hirsch, eds, "Collated Fragments of the Manuscript Drafts of *Strange Case of Dr. Jekyll and Mr. Hyde*," in *Dr. Jekyll and Mr. Hyde*, pp. 3–58.

18   James Twitchell, *Dreadful Pleasures: An Anatomy of Modern Horror* (New York: Oxford University Press, 1985), p. 236.

19   Heath, "Psychopathia sexualis," p. 95.

20   Veeder and Hirsch, *Dr. Jekyll and Mr. Hyde*, p. 55.

21   Vladimir Nabokov, "The Strange Case of Dr. Jekyll and Mr. Hyde," *Lectures on Literature*, ed. Fredson Bowers (New York: Harcourt Brace Jovanovich, 1980), p. 194.

22   Jeffrey Weeks, *Sex, Politics, and Society* (New York and London: Longman, 1981), p. 113.

23   Weeks, *Sex, Politics, and Society*, p. 113.

24   See Veeder, "Children of the Night," in *Dr. Jekyll and Mr. Hyde*, p. 159.

25   Miller, *Doubles*, p. 241.

26   Alexander Welsh, *George Eliot and Blackmail* (Cambridge: Harvard University Press, 1985), p. 9.

27   Edward Carpenter, *The Intermediate Sex*, p. 79; quoted in Jeffrey Weeks, *Coming Out: Homosexual Politics in Britain from the Nineteenth Century to the Present* (London: Quartet, 1977), p. 21.

28   Sedgwick, *Between Men*, p. 88.

29   Veeder, "Collated Fragments," pp. 34–35.

30   Thanks to Paul Zablocki and Gary Sunshine, students in my course on the *fin de siècle*, for their comments on "homotextuality" and suicide.

31   Veeder, "Children of the Night," p. 149. Thanks to Phil Pearson.

32   Anne Harrington, *Medicine, Mind, and the Double Brain* (Princeton: Princeton University Press, 1987), p. 170.

33   Harrington, *Medicine, Mind, and the Double Brain*, p. 94.

34   Paul Maixner, *Robert Louis Stevenson: The Critical Heritage* (London: Routledge Kegan Paul, 1981), p. 215.

35   See Christopher Craft, "'Descend and Touch and Enter': Tennyson's Strange Manner of Address," *Genders* 1 (Spring 1988): 91–92.

36   J.A. Symonds to Stevenson, 3 March 1886, in *Letters of J.A. Symonds*, eds Herbert M. Schueller and Robert L. Peters (Detroit: Wayne State University Press, 1968), pp. 120–21.

Peter Bailey

SEXUALITY AND THE PUB

Popular Culture and Performance in the Victorian City (Cambridge: Cambridge University Press, 1998), 151–6, 163–71.

The historiography of Victorian popular culture has had relatively little to say about sexuality. This is a surprising omission, which **Peter Bailey** challenges in the following Reading. His examination of the Victorian barmaid is an enormously creative piece that allows us to understand what was at stake in the sexual politics of metropolitan culture. Note how Bailey is concerned to examine the images of the barmaid but also to set these within the context of the lived experience of barmaids and their relationship to Victorian society. This Reading is an example of the productive interdisiplinarity found in modern Victorian Studies. Bailey's discussion of 'para-sexuality' is extremely innovative and captures the characteristics not only of Victorian sexuality but also of a particularly British form of sexual culture.

Peter Bailey has been the foremost historian of British popular culture. The great theme of Victorian popular culture historiography has been the rise of mass culture: entertainments made for the people by entrepreneurs rather than culture made by the people. Examples of mass culture would include the music hall (where Bailey's work has been crucial) and seaside resorts, forms of commercialised leisure that grew in popularity in the later nineteenth century. Marxist historians argued that these forms of popular culture were fundamentally conservative and induced greater conformity among the working class after the stormy days of Chartism in the 1840s. In other words, popular culture acted as a form of social control and helped explain why there was no revolution in Britain during the nineteenth century. Peter Bailey on the other hand has insisted that popular culture was often disorderly and untamed, particularly when we look at music halls or that popular institution, which persisted despite the disapproval of much of polite society, the pub. In a remarkable series of essays (published in 1998 as *Popular Culture and Performance in the Victorian City*), he traced the different forms of pleasure available to the urban population. Bailey sees more continuity than change and emphasises how consumers of mass culture were never passive. Identities such as 'respectability' were simply masks that could be adopted or discarded in different circumstances. Bailey's Victorians are not stern moralists but ordinary people in search of 'fun' (a word he takes very seriously).

Peter Bailey is Professor Emeritus of the University of Manitoba. He is currently completing a book on the social and cultural history of British music hall 1840–1960; his article entitled 'Languages of Pleasure from Belle Epoque to New Jerusalem' is due to appear in the *Revue français de civilisation britannique* (2007).

S EXUALITY, WE ARE NOW TOLD, plausibly enough, is everywhere.[1] Yet recent scholarship, for all its advances, has done little to register or interpret this ubiquity. The history of sexuality which sees the nineteenth century as the crucial era in creating its modern sensibility has concentrated on certain areas: the submerged histories of 'deviant' groups; the ideology of written texts; controversies over regulation; and individual cases of that remarkable phenomenon, closet *hetero-sexuality*.[2] These emphases on the wilder and more esoteric reaches of sexuality reinforce the construct of separate terrains by focusing on the (unacceptable) public face and the (secretive) private face in civil society. What is missing is an illumination of the 'middle' ground of sexuality, not as another exclusive territory, but as an extensive ensemble of sites, practices and occasions that mediate across the frontiers of the putative public/private divide.[3] Arguably it is here — in such everyday settings as the pub, the expanding apparatus of the service industries, and a commercialised popular culture — that capitalism and its patriarchal managers construct a new form of open yet licit sexuality that I propose to term *parasexuality,* a form whose visual code is known to us as the familiar but largely unexamined phenomenon of glamour.

Parasexuality? The prefix combines two otherwise discrete meanings: first, in the sense of 'almost' or 'beside', denoting a secondary, or modified form of sexuality (cf. paramedic); second, the counter sense of being 'against', denoting a form of protection from, or prevention of sexuality (cf. parachute). However here the function argued is conceived somewhat differently, as an inoculation in which a little sexuality is encouraged as an antidote to its subversive properties. Parasexuality then is sexuality that is deployed but contained, carefully channelled rather than fully discharged; in vulgar terms it might be represented as 'everything but'.

Everything but what? What is the prime form of sexuality for which parasexuality is taken to offer a modification or antidote? The language of discharge bespeaks a fundamentally male or phallocentric concept of sexuality — the hydraulic model — in which sex is a limited but powerful energy system, a spermatic economy whose force must always be either fully released or suppressed, its prime expression being the male orgasm. While the upheaval in sexual politics in our own day has taught us to recognise other less oppressive forms, this was a powerful model of sexuality in nineteenth century Britain and, however rebarbative it may be, it remains on the historical agenda.[4] The objectification of women as spectacle and commodity examined below is now understood as a projection of male hegemony and has been further defined in the pathologies of scopophilia and fetishism; yet while we recognise the saliency of such features in modern capitalism their formation is still underexplored.[5]

Parasexuality identifies a significant historical initiative as a *managed* version of the fraught imperatives of release or suppression in orthodox bourgeois sexuality. Management is an appropriate term in the increasingly rationalised operations of an emergent leisure industry in the nineteenth century, and is taken here to denote not only systematic direction, but also the proper utilisation of resources. In the pub, the music hall and the popular theatre, unlike the home, the courts and legislature, sexuality was a natural resource rather than a natural enemy. Thus while parasexuality was certainly a form of control, it started from a point of acknowledgment and accommodation rather than denial and punishment — in this sense it might be said to reverse Foucault's couplet of regulation as production.

Of course, management of any kind is rarely as efficient a process as the word implies, and this was certainly true of the business of pleasure which was in any case marked by its own distinctive practices. Paradoxically, if unsurprisingly, the normalisation of sexuality that was parasexuality proved to be controversial and was much contested by vigilante groups as a threat to established values. In exploring the limits of normative tolerance a new breed of capitalist cultural managers could therefore be represented as challenging the dominant ideology, yet the impression remains that whatever the charges made against them, these men were interested only in flexing not transgressing such limits. Parasexuality may be understood therefore as an exercise in framed liminality or contained licence that constituted a reworking rather than a dismantling of hegemony.[6] At the same time, the definition of limits was not just an issue between an industry and its critics, but a matter of everyday negotiation among front line participants, whose exchanges constituted an informal process of management that made its own contribution to the repatterning of nineteenth-century sexuality. History is also made by the people in pubs.

And so to the barmaid, a seemingly unproblematical social type, and an unlikely subject for any kind of historical theorising. For the unreconstructed male she is an instant cue for the knowing smile; for the feminist she is the classic token woman.[7] Both perspectives register the barmaid's role with its obvious but safely anchored sexuality as a timelessly familiar feature of the British pub. This essay is concerned to show that the barmaid was not always taken for granted, but has a specific and indeed sensational history of her own in the Victorian era, one of whose important themes is her glamorous embodiment of a distinct form of modernity — parasexuality.

What follows is an attempt to locate this specific strategy of cultural management within the popular discourse of pub sexuality by relating rather than merely juxtaposing the modes of social history and cultural or critical studies. The history of the barmaid is examined first in relation to the modernisation of the Victorian pub. [. . .] [T]he essay then situates pub sexuality and its controversies in the material context of female barwork. It concludes with a brief speculative reconnaissance of the barmaid's membership in the larger constituency of young women service workers, notes some further representations of their type, and considers the implications for sexual politics in the critical years of the late Victorian period.

The modern barmaid was a product of the transformation of the urban public house from the 1830s, when the tavern was superseded by the so-called gin palace with its dramatic innovations of scale, plan, management and style.[8] The new pub was devised to service the increasing volume of custom in the expanding towns, and to hold its market share in the face of heightened competition in the licensed trade. Many old pubs were little more than the parlours or kitchens of private houses catering to a familiar neighbourhood clientele. In catering to the more numerous, transitory and anonymous urban crowd, the new pubs were much bigger, and sales were made across a bar counter which separated customers from the drink supply and made for a more efficient and secure operation. Capacity was maximised by doing away with chairs and tables which also ensured a more rapid turnover in customers. Any feeling of congestion was relieved by the upward spaciousness of high ceilings and the illusory roominess contrived by the generous use of mirrors and plate glass, for the gin palace sought to attract the new generation of 'perpendicular drinkers' by the lavishness of its amenities. The new pubs needed the barmaid both as staff behind the counters of its enlarged premises and as a further item of allurement among its mirrors and mahogany, its brassware and coloured tile.[9]

There was, of course, nothing new in the employment of women and their attractions in the serving of drink. The older alehouse had commonly been a family enterprise wherein the service of wives and daughters was routinely exploited as an extension of their domestic duties. The alewife who ran the business in the absence of her husband was variously rough or motherly, but dependent upon an outgoing manner as a social stock in trade, while daughters or maidservants often added a fresher allure.[10] What was new about the barmaid of the 1830s was the redefinition of her traditional role brought by changes in the social logistics of the pub. Most importantly, she was now physically separated from the public by the novel device of the bar counter, part of the pub's duplication of the apparatus of the retail shop which formalised selling and began the conversion of its clientele from guests to customers.[11] The bar was now also a boundary or cordon sanitaire which kept the barmaid almost literally out of reach of the customer (or vice versa), and met the publican's new concern for respectability to protect his licence and greater business investment in a time of tighter licensing controls and reform hostility.

Yet if the roaming wanton of the alehouse had now become contained within the closed territory of the serving area, the configuration that secured her separation from the public house made her role there more conspicuous and seductive. The bar counter with its newly sumptuous fittings was the visual as well as transactional focus of the pub-gin palace and provided a framing effect that gave it the dramatic properties of a stage, thus heightening the presence of its attendants as social actors and objects of display. This theatrical aura was amplified by the flaring quality of the new gas lighting and the reflections of the pub's numerous mirrors. Moreover, the new barmaid shared her stage with a concentration of the commodities that the pub sold, suggesting that she herself might be an article for purchase and consumption.

The impact of the barmaid as spectacle was registered in significant terms from her earliest appearance in the new setting. Thus in the 1820s Thompsons, of Holborn

Hill, London, was 'particularly noted' for retaining 'four handsome, sprightly and neatly dressed young females, but of modest deportment . . . An opportunity of casting a scrutinising glance at the so-highly spoken of barmaids operated as a spell, and myriads . . . were drawn in thither'.[12] There was renewed attention to the modern barmaid during the Crimean War, when a fashionable pub in the City hired women to make good the loss of men to the services. Such was the reported sensation at their appearance that other houses rapidly copied the practice, while barmaids had also been noted in the 1840s serving behind the refreshment counters of railway stations.[13]

The number of pubs grew steadily from the 1830s, but there was also growth in other forms of catering as well as the railway system; thus music halls, theatres, hotels, restaurants, and exhibitions provided more newly conspicuous jobs in barwork from the third quarter of the century. Of the Oxford music hall that opened in 1861 as the first purpose-built hall in the West End, it was recorded that 'the brightest, most glittering, and most attractive thing about the bars was the barmaids,' and Billy Holland's barmaid contests at various other London venues provided steady publicity in the 1860s and 1870s.[14]

Most renowned of London barmaids were the nine hundred or so employed by Spiers and Pond, pioneers of large-scale commercial catering, with extensive interests that included the sumptuous Criterion in Piccadilly where the barmaids operated in shifts: 'one corps would march out from behind the bars and others would walk in and relieve them like soldiers relieving the sentry.' Kaiser William II was said to have insisted on an incognito trip to a branch of Spiers and Pond on his first London visit, and was delighted by its spectacle of well-drilled pretty women.[15]

Foreigners were particularly impressed by the English barmaid, for her occupation and setting were virtually unique to Britain and the colonies of Australia and New Zealand.[16] English barmaids excited great attention in the English pub-restaurant at the Paris Exhibition in 1867.[17] The story was told of the American visitor to England who, on being asked what had struck him most, replied without hesitation, 'Barmaids!', an exclamation that reformers took to be one of horror.[18] Some of his more enthusiastic countrymen sought to exploit such a novelty by replicating an English bar and its barmaids in New York in the 1890s, but fell foul of legislation prohibiting the employment of women in public saloons.[19] Thus the barmaid attracted controversy and attention both at home and abroad.

As these accounts suggest, much of the impact of the barmaid lay in her enhanced public visibility, her staged openness to the 'scrutinizing glance.' What is significant here is not just, as we now conventionally say, the woman as sex object, but the woman as bearer of *glamour,* arguably a distinctively modern visual property, and central to parasexuality in its practice of managed arousal.

The most familiar usage of the word is in its description of the Hollywood stars of the 1930s and after — the 'glamour girls' of screen and pin-ups — and a film historian defines glamour in this context as 'alluring charm or fascination, often based on illusion, that transforms or glorifies a person or thing.'[20] Previous usage in the nineteenth century was confined to a poetic vocabulary, as introduced by Sir Walter Scott to denote a magical or fictitious beauty.[21] There is considerable significance in the word's debut in Scott's novels, for in its application to the world of the past that was the setting for his work, we can identify a further property of glamour, implicit but unacknowledged in other definitions yet crucial to its operation as parasexuality — that of distance. Distance not only sustains and protects the magical property that is commonly recognised in glamour, but also heightens desire through the tension generated by the separation of the glamour object and the beholder, a separation that also functions to limit the expression or consummation of desire. Distance may be secured in a variety of ways: by time and history as in Scott's usage; by putting the loved one up a tower as in the conventions of courtly love; by the traditional device of the stage; more recently by the shop window or the distance inherent in the mechanical representations of photography, film and television; or, by a bar. Thus it is the bar that constitutes the necessary material and symbolic distance that simultaneously heightens and contains the sexual attractiveness of the barmaid and qualifies her as a glamour figure. It may be that something of the enigmatic property of glamour lies in its asexuality, but glamour here is conceived as a dramatically enhanced yet distanced style of sexual representation, display or address, primarily visual in appeal.[22] [. . .]

Who was the Victorian barmaid? What were the actualities of barwork, and how did they sustain or confound the[ir] glamorous images [. . .] ? What else can we learn of sexuality in the sub-culture of the pub and the perceptions of drink sellers, customers and reform critics?[23]

In England the greatest concentration of women barworkers was in London, but they were common enough in the big provincial cities and larger towns. They were much less common in Scotland and Ireland where employment was restricted to big city hotels. (In Scotland, as a type, they were referred to with suspicion as 'London barmaids'). Reliable numbers cannot be established, but in the improved categories of the 1901 census the number of barmaids was returned as 27,707 for England and Wales, of whom 7,632 were employed in London; the licensed trade habitually claimed higher figures, and argued for a count of 100,000 barmaids in England's public houses during the reform agitation of 1907–8.[24] On the most generous arithmetic, the barmaid was a minor calling compared with the nearly one and a half million female domestic servants enumerated in 1901, but her distribution as well as her setting made her a significant minority.

A wide variety of conditions obtained in the licensed trade and its numerous outlets, but by the 1890s if not before a broad distinction was recognised between the 'mere' or 'old-fashioned barmaid', and the 'young lady in the public line of business' or 'modern barmaid'. Recruitment, remuneration, duties and prospects differed accordingly.[25] The first category was a daughter of the working class who started work early as a housemaid in a small working-class pub before graduating to service at the bar. Though not found in the roughest of houses, she was likely to spend her career in working-class pubs and might keep in employment into her late thirties. The second category came from a higher social background, entering the business in the late-teens and passing immediately to work behind the bar in a public house catering predominantly to the upper and middle class. As a saloon or lounge barmaid she could also find employment in theatre, music hall, railway and restaurant bars. From the start she was paid more than her working-class sister, proceeded more quickly to a full wage and had some prospects of advancement to a supervisory post with a big company. In general, however, the career of the saloon barmaid was finished by her mid-twenties.

There were far many more women seeking employment than there were placements. Recruits were said to come from every grade of the working and lower middle class, while the majority of entrants to the London trade enlisted from 'the country'. At all levels of entry, there was a substantial number of women already socialised in the trade as daughters or relatives of publicans. Yet even the publican's daughter, for whom choice was so obviously predetermined by family, seemed anxious to use her insider's knowledge to break away from family. In this she conformed to a common characterisation of newcomers to the trade as free spirits, for while some were undoubtedly outcasts and casualties to start with, the majority were said to be impatient to escape from the monotony of more conventional jobs and locations, and were drawn to barwork as an avenue to the big city and a fuller life. By the 1890s, too, it seems that the trade was drawing more entrants from a higher social class. There are cases of women who preferred bar work to clerking or governessing, occupations which had disappointed in either remuneration or social interest, and Spiers and Pond were said to receive numerous applications from parents in the clergy and professional classes seeking employment for their daughters. With allowance for status inflation and the defensiveness of the trade, there does seem some plausibility, if a dubious exactitude, to the claim that 1,178 of the barmaids working in London in 1892 were the 'daughters of gentlemen'.[26]

In turn of the century London, the basic wage for a barmaid was 8–10s a week. In addition the employer provided board and lodging, though deductions for laundry and breakages (a controversial item) chopped as much as two shillings off, and the maintenance of a smart appearance could be expensive. Extra income from tips was mostly prohibited. A full weekly wage for the experienced saloon barmaid in a thriving pub might reach 15s, though the big London music halls, followed by the theatres, paid more. Wages and terms of work were notably inferior in the provinces, but in general, taking into account the provision of board and lodging, the barmaid's earnings were high compared to other semi-skilled female occupations.[27]

Whatever the sector of the trade, barmaid's work was long and demanding. London pubs were licensed to be open for 123½ hours per week in the 1890s and a barmaid might be on duty for more than a hundred of those, but the most reliable report of the period recorded a standard working day of some 12 hours or so, making up a 70–80 hour week.[28] The day ran from early morning to past midnight with 4 or 5 hours off for meals, dressing and rest. Opening hours were shorter on Sunday, the usual day off for the barmaid; after a year she might take a week's holiday, and up to a month thereafter, in some cases with pay. During working hours a barmaid was habitually on her feet, and though male staff did the heavier work, the physical regimen of the bar was punishing. In addition to serving drink and food — and remaining civil — there was cleaning up after closing time, which could be particularly onerous on Saturday night. [. . .]

Although the division into old-fashioned and modern or saloon barmaids indicates a clear distinction in status and function, attention to the particular circumstances of barwork suggests a more complex picture. In single-handed berths at the cheap end of the market a barmaid was little better than a maid of all work, with dismal food and accommodation, yet it was in the smaller establishments that a barmaid might find herself welcomed as one of the family.[29] The best conditions were found with the big companies, notably Spiers and Pond who were widely respected as model employers. Employees here lived in company dormitories and visitors pronounced them well housed, well fed and well looked after. Yet there were complaints from one branch of bad food on the table and dead rats under the floor, and the paternalist regime could be irksome.[30] A further variable in the trade was the high rate of turnover and mobility among women bar workers. One unavoidable constant was a working environment heavily polluted by gas and tobacco fumes, conditions found at their worst in the underground railway bars.

The sense of the evidence is that the barmaid maintained a considerable degree of self-respect and independence in the often testing conditions of her trade. In working-class pubs, she was low caste even in her own class,[31] but the saloon barmaid had a high regard for her status and considered herself superior to other service workers such as domestics and shopclerks.[32] Though also subordinate and in some cases closely regulated, it was no requirement of her job that she be either deferential, anonymous, or invisible. Indeed on her own territory the barmaid enjoyed a certain authority: 'behind the bar,' said one observer, 'she is the mistress of the situation . . . and an absolute despot.'[33] There was considerable social contact on the job, if much of it was conventionalised and almost exclusively male. In big establishments there was the company of other working women, while in the single-handed berth, which probably accounted for the majority of situations, there was the presence, if not always the support, of the publican's wife. Gossip across the bar provided a bush-telegraph that kept even the solitary barmaid aware of conditions elsewhere in the trade and made her a stubborn defender of her basic terms of employment.[34] The rapid turnover was in part an index to the publican's hunger for fresh faces but may have also been a further expression of the barmaid's confidence in pursuit of her calling.

If the level of earnings and the common requirement of living-in disallowed complete independence, barmaids were reputedly among those best placed to take the traditional avenue to supposed escape and fulfilment, for it was the popular myth that barmaids always married, and almost always married well. Premises in the centre of London afforded a high concentration of wealthy upper class males, and there were many tales of erstwhile barmaids transported by marriage from some West End bar to a suburban mansion. Furthermore, barmaids were said to prosper in marriage; not only were they sociable creatures but, as the myth went, their schooling behind the bar made them shrewd judges of men.[35]

Such a benign account of the barmaid's expectations of living happily ever after was dismissed by a growing lobby of reformers for whom the barmaid constituted a most serious problem of physical and moral welfare. Dating from the mid 1880s, the reform campaign was part of the more general movement for social purity. Its impetus came from various evangelical rescue organisations and branches of the temperance movement. Its membership was predominantly that of churchmen and middle-class women, with the support of a number of politicians, mostly Labour MPs and Progressive members of the London County Council. The reformers were particularly active in London, but there were organised campaigns in other big cities, notably Manchester and Glasgow. The earliest initiatives sought to provide social centres and services for those out of work, or who wished to live off licensed premises, and a series of Parliamentary bills were introduced (unsuccessfully) from 1890 on, calling for a reduction in hours and the improvement of working conditions.[36] The campaign then moved to call for an end to the employment of women in the bar, and recorded some success in the Licensing Act of 1904, which gave Justices of the Peace discretionary power to forbid such employment in granting new licences. A new licensing bill in 1908 required the phased but ultimately total prohibition of barwork for women (other than members of the publican's family), but the measure failed.[37]

Though the references are obscure, barmaids were reported to have gone on strike in 1889, and they made further attempts to organise themselves in the early 1890s,[38] but in a trade that was difficult to unionise, most active worker participation there was supported the employers' counter attack against the reformers and their demand for the elimination of the barmaid. In this highly controversial issue, the reform proposals of the 1908 bill were also contested by the radical suffragists, Esther Roper and Eva Gore-Booth, who rallied support from the trade in their Manchester-based Barmaids' Political Defence League, which defended the women's right to work.[39]

In their attack on 'the Moloch of the drink trade', reformers cast the barmaid as the physical victim of a sweated industry, but they were often more exercised by her plight as a moral casualty, fatally vulnerable to drink, seduction and worse. Drink was the very raison d'être of the barmaid's occupation, but formal constraints upon her personal consumption were well advertised by the trade. House regulations commonly forbade treating by customers, and the larger businesses often demanded abstinence during working hours. Private opinion in the trade varied considerably on the extent of the barmaid's temperance or otherwise, but two of them interviewed by the Parliamentary investigator Eliza Orme in 1892 maintained that 'the variety and amusement of the life lessens the propensity to drink.'[40] For reformers, however, the bar automatically constituted a permanent temptation; they remained convinced that regulations were habitually set at nought by surreptitious drinking to counter fatigue, and quoted rising insurance premiums as evidence of general intemperance in a trade they pronounced more hazardous than that of filemakers and lead workers.[41] In reform logic, drink also inevitably increased the moral risks of bar work by softening resistance to seduction.

Reformers conceded that the women drawn to bar work were not themselves necessarily of a low character, but maintained that the pub environment was inevitably corrupting. In their view, 'the variety and amusement' of bar life meant the inescapable sexualisation of social encounter; accordingly, the 'banter' and 'chaff' of conventional account translated in reform terms to 'bad language . . . [that] tends to the insidious weakening of the barrier of modest and maidenly shame in which her [the barmaid's] strength resides.'[42] Reformers were convinced of the publican's sexual as well as economic exploitation of young women. For evidence they referred to the advertisements for vacancies in the trade which targeted the under-20s and commonly called for photographs (the carte de visite) of applicants. The reform conclusion was that the barmaid 'is employed by the publican as a decoy for men, and her very existence depends on her ability to attract.'[43] When her novelty as the siren of the bar wore off, she was likely to be dismissed, and numerous personal testimonies to prison chaplains and police court missionaries were adduced to demonstrate how easy was the subsequent descent to prostitution.[44]

As it managed the flow of drink, the trade also managed the flow of sexuality, though this was territory harder to police. Some house rules expressly forbade the shaking of hands across the bar as part of a general prohibition on physical contact between server and customer and reform investigators found the relative broadness of bar counters worth report.[45] Dress was also formally regulated. By the 1890s 'except in very small houses the rule is universal that barmaids . . . must wear black dresses . . . and a large apron of the same material'. With this occupational uniform went white collars and cuffs, but no further relief or distraction was allowed, and employers proscribed false hair and busts.[46] It was and has remained a truism in the trade that the plain rather than the showy barmaid was the better choice. In any case, where trade was habitually brisk there was little time for dalliance. A French visitor in the 1860s who noted the prettiness of English barmaids suggested that they were 'protected from all human seductions behind the imposing serenity and the Olympian majesty of business.'[47] Thus the ritualisation of the task as well as its busyness may have reinforced the sexual controls of pub protocol.

Who were typical customers, and what were their likely perceptions of the barmaid and her glamorised sexuality? It was the saloon or lounge barmaid who was most obviously meant to be attractive. Her customers were middle to lower-middle class and, of course, almost exclusively male. Most reports from City and West End premises suggest two broad though overlapping categories of clientele: the habitual 'lounger', from the leisured man about town to the more raffish 'horsey' type; and the 'business man' of varying rank, from the banker down to the clerk and the shopman.[48] Whatever the actual provenance of its customers, the saloon preserved the fiction of catering to gentlemen.

It seems plausible enough that the erotic charge for the male habitue derived in part from the piquant inflections of the conventional gentleman-maidservant relationship, restaged away from home in the liminoid space and time of the pub.[49] Thus the business-like, even officious manner of the barmaid noted above reversed the normal roles of authority relationships for the middle-class male to whom most women, and certainly those in service, were habitually deferential. It is a commonplace that watching other people work is fascinating, but how much more so would this have been for middle-class males who did so little of it themselves, and for whom the extensive female labour and service that supported their life-style was usually either honorific or invisible? There seems to be little need to argue at length for the attractions of the austere livery of the dress-uniform. Here, practises meant to register distance exercised their own fascination. At the same time enduring associations of the nurturing role of the nanny or nursemaid could make the barmaid a figure of comfort as well as power, particularly in the case of the older woman who survived in suburban public houses and was plainly valued for her maternal-confessional role.[50]

What the graphic texts [*contemporary illustrations discussed in the original version of this article*] also demonstrate is the vital role men ascribed to the barmaid in the bidding for, and bestowal of, recognition. The considerable emotional investment in the winning of the woman's gaze that these attempts signify, strongly suggests the degree of anonymity and competition in the pub crowd that had to be bid against. In consequence men, too, put themselves on display. The hunger for a privileged acknowledgment from the woman behind the bar also suggests a further prize for the male ego, given the intimate terrain of the pub, its eroticised associations of drink and the night, and the fascination the barmaid might hold as the stranger of uncertain background. She was respectable, yes; she was the girl whom a chap might just marry, by Jove; she was also the girl who just might . . . without one having to marry her — perhaps the typical male reading of parasexuality. It may be then that together with perhaps nobler sentiments — there was another male perception at play, half fantasy and half calculation — that of the barmaid as potential mistress or 'kept woman'. Indeed, she may have functioned as a collectively kept woman in the male social psyche. With all these attractions in play, the wonder is not that men had to be lured into pubs, but that they were ever persuaded to leave.

Spokesmen for the licensed trade habitually disclaimed any intentions of even the mildest sexual exploitation of women workers. They preferred women over men not because they were 'attractive', but because they were less expensive, less clumsy, less wasteful and less corruptible. Such valued workers were necessarily treated well by their employers, while the presence of women in licensed premises was said to have a civilising influence, an argument made by the barmaids themselves in defending their occupation against elimination in 1908.[51] The licensed victuallers proclaimed the respectability of their trade, their barmaids, and their customers who, according to one spokesman in 1906 'are the fathers and brothers of other respectable middle class girls.'[52] The trade thus addressed the world from a moving escalator of respectability such that the gaudy temptress of reformers' accounts was always dismissed as a figure from the periphery of the trade or its unimproved past.[53]

Some employers, however, did manifestly stoke the fires of the 'amorous furnace.' 'In many houses in the West End and the City used by clerks, lawyers and shopmen', according to an account of the mid '70s 'landlords find it greatly to their interest to have handsome, fine, showy, attractive and talkative young ladies behind the bar.' These women were dressed by their employers, served only in peak hours, and were most likely to be trapped as mistresses.[54] Neither adventures nor misadventures were necessarily resolved in marriage — 'men in pubs', observed one commentator tartly, 'are not the marrying kind' — and a combination of low wages and sweet talk undoubtedly led some barmaids into destructive relationships. Muriel Perry, the mistress but never the wife of J.R. Ackerley's businessman father — was seduced by the latter when a barmaid at the Tavistock in Covent Garden in 1909.[55] Whatever the various controls at work, barmaids were women at risk.

In all of this there remains the important but elusive matter of the barmaid's perception of her role and its sexual dimension — the view from behind. There is little direct testimony but the foregoing evidence does strongly suggest that young women were partly drawn to barwork by its promise of excitement, in which sexual opportunity was a strong element as a prelude to marriage. And while employers denied that the barmaid was as a decoy, it was an acknowledged part of her job that she make herself 'agreeable'.[56]

But how did the barmaid comply with this requirement? There is some significant indication that the barmaid protected herself from the beeriness and leeriness of the pub's sexual culture by her own manipulation of its particular parameters of distance and intimacy. George Moore catches this in his characterisation of Lizzie Baker, the Spiers and Pond heroine in *Spring Days: A Realistic Novel* (1888):

> Lizzie had her bar manners and her town manners, and she slipped on the former as she would an article of clothing, when she lifted the slab and passed behind. They consisted principally of cordial smiles, personal observations, and a look of vacancy which she assumed when the

conversation became coarse. From behind the bar she spoke authorita-
tively, she was secure, it was different — it was behind the bar; and she
spoke with a cheek and a raciness that at other times were quite foreign
to her . . . what she heard and said in the bar remained not a moment
on her mind, she appeared to accept it all as part of the business of the
place.[57]

The crucial function of the bar comes across plainly here, as does Lizzie's modern
consciousness of barwork as role-playing, and there is corroborative testimony in
the words of some of Miss Orme's barmaid-respondents who ridiculed any idea that
they were flattered by the customers' chat: 'If they only knew it,' they said, 'we
regard them no more than a set of bottles.'[58]

Parasexuality in the Victorian pub was very much the product of a male agenda
and male management, yet its women subjects were accomplished managers too.
Certainly the anti-barmaid reformers had a case, for barwork could be squalid
drudgery and its rewards disappointing. There were also real dangers of sexual
corruption. Yet compared with prostitution, parasexuality was mostly safe sex, and
the evidence suggests that in general the Victorian barmaid was not [. . .] an alienated
whore, but an assertive and competent modernist; there may in fact have been more
alienation on the other side of the bar. [. . .]

Further reading

On popular culture, see the other articles in Peter Bailey, *Popular Culture and
Performance in the Victorian City* (Cambridge: Cambridge University Press, 1998).
Gareth Stedman Jones has written two very important studies of working-class
culture: 'Working-Class Culture and Working-Class Politics in London, 1870–1914:
Notes on the Remaking of a Working Class' in his *Languages of Class: Studies in
English Working-Class History, 1832–1982* (Cambridge: Cambridge University
Press, 1983), 179–238; 'The "Cockney" and the Nation, 1780–1988' in David
Feldman and Gareth Stedman Jones (eds), *Metropolis London: Histories and
Representations since 1800* (London: Routledge, 1989), 272–324. For discussions
of the historiography of popular culture, see Peter Bailey: 'The Politics and Poetics
of Modern British Leisure — A Late Twentieth Century Review', *Rethinking History*,
3(2) (1999), 131–75; Emma Griffin, 'Popular Culture in Industrializing England',
Historical Journal, 45 (2002), 619–35. Other works on late Victorian popular
culture include: Chris Waters, *British Socialists and the Politics of Popular Culture,
1884–1914* (Manchester: Manchester University Press, 1990); Gavin Weightman,
Bright Lights, Big City: London Entertained, 1830–1950 (London: Collins, 1992);
Dagmar Kift, *The Victorian Music Hall: Culture, Class and Conflict* (Cambridge:
Cambridge University Press, 1996); Andrew Horrall, *Popular Culture in London,
c.1890–1918: The Transformation of Entertainment* (Manchester: Manchester
University Press, 2001).

Notes

1   Jeff Hearn and Wendy Parkin, *'Sex' at 'Work': The Power and Paradox of Organisation Sexuality* (Brighton, 1987), p. 3.

2   See R.A. Padgug, 'Sexual matters: on conceptualising sexuality in history', *Radical History Review*, 20 (1974), pp. 3–23; M. Vicinus, 'Sexuality and power: a review of current work in the history of sexuality', *Feminist Studies*, 8 (Spring 1982), pp. 133–56; Jeffrey Weeks, *Sex, Politics and Society: The Regulation of Sexuality since 1800* (London, 1981 and 1989) offers an admirable synthesis, and of more recent work I note P. Gay, *The Bourgeois Experience: Victoria to Freud*, vol. I, *Education of the Senses*; vol. II, *The Tender Passion* (Oxford University Press, New York, 1985, 1986) and Catherine Gallagher and Thomas Laqueur (eds), *The Making of the Modern Body: Sexuality and Society in the Nineteenth Century* (Berkeley, CA, 1987); Michael Mason, *The Making of Victorian Sexuality* (Oxford, 1994).

3   On the complexities of this divide see Janet Wolff, 'The culture of separate spheres: the role of culture in nineteenth century public and private life', in Wolff and John Seed (eds), *The Culture of Capital: Art, Power and the Nineteenth Century Middle Class* (Manchester, 1988), pp. 117–34.

4   For critiques, see Carroll Smith-Rosenberg, 'The female world of love and ritual: relations between women in nineteenth century America', *Signs*, 1 (Autumn 1975), pp. 1–29; Vicinus, 'Sexuality and power', pp. 136–7.

5   Colin Mercer, 'A poverty of desire: pleasure and popular politics', in *Formations of Pleasure* (London, 1983), p. 97.

6   Bernice Martin, *A Sociology of Contemporary Cultural Change* (Oxford, 1981), p. 243; Victor Turner, 'Comment', in B.A. Babcock (ed.), *The Reversible World: Symbolic Inversion in Art and Society*, (Ithaca, N.Y., 1978), pp. 286–7.

7   Cf. M. Cleave, The greater British barmaid', in A. McGill (ed.), *The Pub: A Celebration* (London, 1969), pp. 131–48 and Valerie Hey, *Patriarchy and Pub Culture* (London, 1986), pp. 43–4, who is valuable on contemporary pub sexuality.

8   Peter Clark, *The English Alehouse: A Social History, 1200–1830* (London, 1983), ch. 12; Brian Harrison, *Drink and the Victorians: The Temperance Question in England, 1815–1872* (London, 1975), pp. 45, 66; Mark Girouard, *Victorian Pubs* (New Haven, CT, 1975), pp. 19–32.

9   For photographic illustrations of typical interiors [. . .] , see Girouard, *Victorian Pubs.*

10 On women as proprietors and servants, see Clark, *English Alehouse*, pp. 83–6, 206; Leonore Davidoff and Catherine Hall, *Family Fortunes: Men and Women of the English Middle Class, 1780–1850* (London, 1987), pp. 299–301; *Notes and Queries*, 7, 21 March 1914.

11 Girouard, *Victorian Pubs*, p. 26; Clark, *English Alehouse*, pp. 275–6.

12 *Observer, The Gin Shop: History of Inherent Evils, Special Influences, Deceptive Allurements and Demoralising Nature of the Worship of the Ginshop* (London, 1837).

13 *Note and Queries*, 21 February 1914; Barbara Drake, 'The barmaid', *Women's Industrial News*, 65 (April 1914), pp. 221–38; Francis Bond Head, *Stokers and Pokers or the London North Western Railway* (1849) (Newton Abbott, 1968), pp. 86–7.

14 Emily Soldene, *My Theatrical and Musical Recollections* (London, 1897), pp. 41–2; M. Willson Disher, *The Pleasures of London* (London, 1950), pp. 296–7.

15 On Spiers and Pond, see Robert Thorne, 'Places of refreshment in the nineteenth-century city', in A.D. King (ed.), *Buildings and Society* (London, 1980), pp. 240–3. The quote is from Royal Commission on the employment of women, *Parliamentary Papers (PP)* (Victoria, Australia), 2 (1983), 1.1382. For the Kaiser, see *The Barmaid*, 17 December 1891.

16 For Australia see also Royal Commission on the employment of women; report of Inquiry into intoxicating drink to New South Wales Legislative Council (1887); John

Freeman, *Lights and Shadows of Melbourne Life* (London, 1888), pp. 46–53; (C.A. Wright), *Caddie: The Autobiography of a Sydney Barmaid* (London, 1953); Keith Dunstan, *Wowsers* (Australia, 1968), pp. 72–84. For New Zealand, see Jock Phillips, *A Man's Country? The Image of the Pakeha Male: A History* (Auckland, 1988), pp. 65–6. A cross-cultural study of the barmaid would be useful.

17   *Era*, 12 April 1867.

18   Joint Committee on the Employment of Barmaids, *The Barmaid Problem* (London, 1904).

19   Final report of Royal Commission on Liquor Licensing Laws, *PP*, 36 (1898), q. 31807.

20   Larry Carr, *Four Fabulous Faces* (New York, 1970), p. 3.

21   *Oxford English Dictionary*, 1933.

22   For historical distance in legitimising Victorian erotic art, see Gay, *Education of the Senses*, pp. 379–402; for the shop window as barrier and transparency, see Rachel Bowlby, *Just Looking: Consumer Culture in Dreiser, Gissing and Zola* (London, 1985), pp. 332–4.

23   The evidence for such considerations is sketchy and diffuse. The most authoritative and systematic source, including interview material, is that of Eliza Orme, 'Report on conditions of work of barmaids', to Royal Commission on Labour, *PP*, 37 (1893–4), pp. 197–229. For Orme, a prominent Liberal, feminist, and middle-class professional woman (who liked a good cigar), see Leslie Howsam, '"Sound-minded women": Eliza Orme and the study and practice of law in late-Victorian England', *Atlantis*, 15 (Autumn 1989), pp. 44–55. Later pamphlet and periodical treatments drew heavily on Orme while often ignoring her judicious approach. For material on bar*men*, see Booth Mss. B135, London School of Economics; Dr. V. Padmavathy of Miami University, Oxford, Ohio has completed her thesis on the politics of the barmaid question, and Professor David Gutzke of Southwest Missouri State University, is working on a much-needed history of the licensed trade, 1840–1940. I am grateful to both for sharing references and ideas.

24   National British Women's Temperance Association, *Facts about Barmaids* (December 1907); Eva Gore-Booth, Sarah Dickenson and Esther Roper, *Barmaids Political Defence League* (Manchester, n.d.), for the higher counter estimate.

25   Barbara Drake, 'The barmaid', *Women's Industrial News*, April 1914, pp. 222–38; The girl workers of London, II. The barmaid', *The Young Woman: An Illustrated Monthly Magazine*, 6 (1897–8), pp. 52–4.

26   *Women and Work*, 19 December 1874; *Barmaid*, 17 December 1891; Orme, 'Report on conditions', pp. 205, 208–210; W.H. Wilkins, 'A plea for the barmaid', *Humanitarian* (June 1896), pp. 423–34; cutting, 5 February 1898 in the Philip Norman collection, London Inns and Taverns, Guildhall Library; Drake, 'The barmaid'.

27   Orme, 'Report on conditions', pp. 200, 204; Norman Collection cutting, 5 February 1898. For Birmingham, see 'Prisoners at the Bar', *Cassell's Saturday Journal*, 4 March 1911.

28   Orme, 'Report on conditions', pp. 198–203.

29   *Ibid.*, pp. 200, 204.

30   Report of Select Committee of House of Commons on the Shop Hours Bill, *PP*, 17 (1892), qq. 5453, 5375–82, 5485.

31   George Gissing, *The Nether World* (London, 1903), p. 23; M. Powell, *My Mother and I* (London, 1972), p. 107.

32   Orme, 'Report on conditions', p. 207.

33   *Entr'acte*, 27 October 1877.

34   Drake, 'The barmaid'.

35   Among many references, see F. Freeman, 'Barmaids', *Weekly Despatch*, 4 February 1883.

36   For an early note of the issue see Select Committee of the House of Lords on Intemperance, *PP,* (1878), qq. 118–19. See also *Toilers in London: An Enquiry Concerning Female Labour in the Metropolis* (London, 1889), pp. 205–14; *Barmaid*, 14 January 1892.

Joint Committee, *The Barmaid Problem*, details the later, more concerted campaign and its legislative proposals.

37   On the campaign for prohibition, see *The Times*, 19, 21, 28 December 1903; correspondence with the Home Secretary, Herbert Gladstone, from the Countess Carlisle, President of the British Women's Temperance Association, and from Ramsay MacDonald, British Museum Additional Ms. 46065 f. 208, 1 April 1908 and Add. ms. 45986 f. 102, 8 April 1908 respectively. For the LCC, see also George Foster, *The Spice of Life: Sixty Five Years in the Glamour World* (London, 1939), pp. 172–7. For the defence, see below.

38   *Ally Sloper's Half-Holiday*, 11 May 1889, 24 October 1891.

39   See Gore-Booth *et al.*, *Barmaids Defence League*; Gifford Lewis, *Eva Gore-Booth and Esther Roper: A Biography* (London, 1988), pp. 103–6; *Licensing World*, 16 March 1907, 4 April 1908; *Brewing Trade Review*, 1 July 1908.

40   Orme, 'Report on conditions', pp. 207–8.

41   *Manchester Guardian*, 11 July 1906.

42   Joint Committee, *The Barmaid Problem*.

43   'The prisoner at the bar', *Cassell's Saturday Journal*, 7 January 1911; Carlisle to Gladstone, add. ms.

44   Drake, 'The barmaid'.

45   Norman Collection cutting, 5 February 1898; Orme, 'Report on conditions', p. 197.

46   *Barman and Barmaid*, 12 July 1879; A.B. Deane (ed.), *Licensed Victuallers Official Annual for the Year 1895*, (London, 1895), pp. 159–60.

47   A. Esquiros, *The English at Home* (London, 1861–3), vol. I, p. 272.

48   Representative evidence in *Toilers in London*, pp. 209–10; 'The girl workers of London', p. 54; *Young Girls in Drinking Bars: A Narrative of the Facts*, pamphlet reprinted from Church of England Temperance Chronicle (n.d.); *Licensed World*, 17 September 1904.

49   Leonore Davidoff, 'Class and gender in Victorian England: the diaries of Arthur J. Munby and Hannah Cullwick', *Feminist Studies*, 5 (1979), pp. 89–141; Peter Stallybrass and Allon White, *The Politics and Poetics of Transgression* (London, 1986), pp. 149–70.

50   *Barman and Barmaid*, 12 July 1879; Frederick Willis, *101 Jubilee Road: A Book of London Yesterdays* (London, 1948), p. 57; Willis, *London General* (London, 1953), pp. 50–7; Hey, *Patriarchy and Pub Culture*, p. 44.

51   Select Committee on Shop Hours (1892), q. 3276; *Licensed World*, 16 March 1907. Cf. Davidoff, *Family Fortunes*, p. 301.

52   *Manchester Guardian*, 13 July 1906.

53   Deane, *Licensed Victuallers Annual*, p. 159.

54   *Women and Work*, 19 December 1874. See also *Rosa Grey: The Life of a Barmaid* (London, n.d.), Lilly Collection, University of Indiana.

55   Diana Petre, *The Secret Orchard of Roger Ackerley* (London, 1985), pp. 38–9.

56   Report of Royal Commission on Liquor Licensing Laws, *PP*, 36 (1898), p. 308.

57   George Moore, *Spring Days: A Realistic Novel* (London, 1888), p. 308.

58   Orme, 'Report on Conditions', p. 209.

PART 13

Monarchy

John Plunkett

RESTORING THE POPULARITY OF THE MONARCHY

Queen Victoria: First Media Monarch (Oxford: Oxford University Press, 2003), 13–15, 16–18, 35–46, 67.

Although the history of monarchs went out of fashion among scholars in the post-war period (despite their continuing sales), it became clear in the 1980s that the institution of monarchy in Victorian Britain could not be ignored. Previously, historians had wanted to get away from the notion that Albert and Victoria epitomised and defined their age even though the political power of the monarchy waned. Instead, they sought to reconstruct the diversity and complexity of nineteenth-century life. However, the continuing appeal of the British monarchy in the late twentieth century meant that historians could not ignore its Victorian roots. In a brilliant article, David Cannadine memorably showed how the monarchy was not very popular in the early nineteenth century but regained a following in the later nineteenth century through the invention of tradition and new forms of pomp and circumstance. In other words, the Victorian period witnessed the emergence of a modern form of monarchy based not on executive power but on ceremonial and on representations of the royals as an ideal family that managed also to rule the Empire. For Cannadine, the Jubilees of 1887 and 1897 were integral to this process, as was the rebuilding of central London as a stage for royal and imperial spectacle.

John Plunkett demonstrates, however, that the monarchy had wide popular appeal from early in the Queen's reign. A new kind of monarchy emerged under Victoria that was based around her appeal as a woman, a wife and a mother. Even the Chartists were not immune to her appeal. In *Queen Victoria: First Media Monarch* (2003), Plunkett epitomises the new interdisciplinarity. With a background in Literature, he is also sensitive to the use of visual sources and develops an almost anthropological approach to the complexities of Victorian material culture. In the following extract, Plunkett uses the term 'civic publicness' to understand this new kind of monarchy and examines the spectacle of the royal visits that Victoria undertook in the early years of her reign. Elsewhere in the book, he discusses engravings, cartoons, photography and reportage to demonstrate how the expansion of print culture and the mass media provided the institution of monarchy with a new lease of life.

John Plunkett is Lecturer in Victorian Literature and Culture at the University of Exeter. He is the author of *Queen Victoria — First Media Monarch* (2003), co-editor with Andrew King of *Popular Print Media 1820–1900* (2004) and *Victorian Print Media — A Reader* (2005), and co-editor with James Lyons of *Multimedia Histories: From the Magic Lantern to the Internet* (2006). He is working on a study of nineteenth-century optical recreations, including panoramas, dioramas, peep-shows, and magic lanterns.

> Assuredly, the reign of Victoria will be known as the reign of royal visits: it seems to have established an era of royal and imperial sociability.
>
> (*Illustrated London News*, June 1844)[1]

WHAT DOES A BRITISH constitutional monarch do? Month on month, year on year, what provides worthy employment for a sovereign, particularly one supposedly above the machinations of party politics? In the profession of royalty, the public engagement reigns supreme. Whether patronizing diverse charities, touring countries in the Commonwealth, or honouring the latest newly built hospital or battleship, civic visits loom large in the modern conception of royal duties. This chapter argues that Queen Victoria and Prince Albert, through the impact of a burgeoning print and visual culture, set the model for the serious duties and pleasurable diversions that we have come to expect from a constitutional monarchy. They undertook an unprecedented number of regional tours, foreign visits, and civic engagements, forging a role that would be successfully followed by future British monarchs. Their work ranged from an earnest social concern, as in Albert assuming the Presidency of the Society for Improvement of the Labouring Classes in 1848, to the more enlivening nature of their marine jaunts to Louis-Philippe and Napoleon III in 1843 and 1855 respectively.

The thread that binds together the diverse activities of Victoria and Albert is the extensive attention that they received. Royal occasions, whether an exclusive court levee at Windsor or one of the many parish dinners given to commemorate the monarch's birthday, had traditionally occupied a privileged position in the official calendar of national events. Industrialism and mass society wrought vast changes to the make-up of nineteenth-century Britain. Yet the cumulative regularity of Victoria and Albert's activities, along with the media attention they received, ensured that the monarchy continued to dominate the public sphere. Royal events were increasingly indivisible from the way in which they were experienced through their media coverage. There was a new style of royalty that was as much inaugurated around Victoria and Albert as by them. The roles they created were inseparable from the modernity of their lives existing as royal news, disseminated as never before by prints, periodicals, and newspapers.

The engagements carried out by Victoria and Albert were keyed into the simultaneous development of popular weekly newspapers and the first periodicals devoted primarily to graphic news. *The News of the World, Lloyd's Weekly Newspaper,* and the *Weekly Times,* along with the more expensive 6*d.* illustrated periodicals such as the *Illustrated London News* and the *Illustrated Times,* all commenced publication during the 1840s. The reduction in Stamp Duty in 1855 and the repeal of paper tax in 1860 meant that the circulation of metropolitan daily newspapers also underwent a significant jump. These well-known changes in print culture, a shift not only in quantity but in kind, became bound up with a new style of monarchy. They did so because in contrast to Victoria's consultations with her ministers — which invariably took place behind closed doors — her tours and visits took place as a series of specifically 'public' duties. There was a crucial symbiotic relationship between the civic publicness of Victoria and the publicity that these events received. The very nature of the events fostered the royal news coverage that facilitated the domination of the public sphere. Tellingly, one of the most common truisms concerning Victoria was that her political influence was greater than was commonly realized. Only brief episodes bought to light her proactive relationship with her governments and threatened to interrupt the procession of tours and visits. Instead of loyalty towards the Crown being played out primarily through the customary local ceremonies, the movements of Victoria and Albert provided an ever-greater individual focus on their lives.

Attacks and commentary upon the nineteenth-century monarchy as an institution have to be continually set against the much larger number of column inches engendered by the Queen's engagements. By its *ipso facto* success, Victoria and Albert's civic publicness set the agenda for a royalist popular politics. Publicness is used here in the sense defined by John Thompson, meaning not just making visible but the making of the experience of an event available to an audience not immediately present.[2] Coinciding with the aftermath of the Reform Bill turmoil and the changing balance of power between the Crown, the Lords, and the Commons, royal civic activities were invested with the discourse of popular constitutionalism. They were integral to the coterminous creation of Victoria as both a popular and a constitutional monarch, defining her royal role as well as producing a label that inspired endless platitudes. [. . .]

One of the most oft-repeated platitudes concerning Victoria was that she had overseen the transition to a constitutional monarchy. At Victoria's death in January 1901, even the republican *Reynolds's Newspaper* felt able to assert that she was 'the example of a constitutional ruler and the founder of the Modern British Monarchy . . . she reduced meddling to the lowest terms and never imposed her will in an arrogant manner on her Ministers'.[3] As the monarch who had elevated the Crown above party politics, Victoria basked in the long afterglow of the Magna Carta and the Glorious Revolution. Later, the Reform Acts of 1832, 1867, and 1884 became part of the same constitutional mythology. This was a narrative whose potent hold was political, imaginative, historic. Moreover, it is vital to emphasize that it seeped into every aspect of Victoria's role. It was through the interlinked discourses around the People and the constitution that Victoria's first tours and visits were endlessly played out. Their prominence established her role as a national figurehead and simultaneously downplayed the high politics between Victoria and her ministers.

The populist invention of the British monarchy is often dated from the latter years of Victoria's reign. David Cannadine has contrasted the lack of grandiose royal ritual in the first half of the reign with the imperial extravaganzas of Victoria's Golden and Diamond Jubilees (1887, 1897), and the coronation of Edward VII (1902).[4] The pomp and circumstance of these late set-pieces is taken to exemplify Victoria's apotheosis as an imperial and national figurehead. Such an interpretation invariably downplays the significance of the Queen's activities during the first twenty years of the reign. In my view, the years between 1837 and 1861 were crucial in creating a successful model for the month-to-month duties of the British monarch. Pervading the multitudinous reports of the royal engagements of this period is the discourse of popular constitutionalism. Tours and visits were cast as a recognition of reliance on the approval of her subjects, a celebration of the inclusivity and participation of the People in the political nation. Time and time again, the freely given support of the People was placed over and against the role of the organized pageantry. The large crowds in attendance at royal occasions were turned into a confirmation of the strength of support enjoyed by the monarchy. Royal events between 1837 and 1861 had an imaginative potency precisely because they were not overladen with militaristic or aristocratic ceremony.

Although Victoria was certainly a well-supported monarch, a weighty ideological significance was ascribed to her popular status. The term 'royal populism' is thus used throughout this chapter to describe the meanings attached to Victoria's public role. One defining index to the importance of royal populism during the 1840s and 1850s is the extent to which its claims were contested by a range of radicals, republicans, and Chartists. Victoria and Albert's civic publicness was conceived as being the monarchy maintaining its position in the face of its declining political and social importance. Tours and visits were perceived to be reliant on a restricted and pre-defined political participation: radicals criticized the way in which royal populism prescribed the position of the People for them. Good old plebeian John Bull was often portrayed as the most loyal of royals. And there was certainly no shortage of deep-rooted deference and long-standing customs. Conversely, anti-monarchists frequently argued that the discourse of the People was used to overdetermine the meaning of royal occasions. Victoria's support was cast as heavily populist; it was both manipulated and exaggerated, rather than the genuine expression of cross-class feeling. Opposition to royal events was only partially motivated by an outright republicanism. This is important because it indicates that these protests formed part of a larger battle over the role of citizenship and the nature of participation in popular politics. Whether to be passive subjects or active citizens was the issue.

The press played a key role in creating a sense of participation or alienation around Victoria's tours and visits. Radical journals attacked the way most newspapers celebrated Victoria's visits as a validation of the existing political status quo. In 1855, *Reynolds's Newspaper* declared, albeit with a large element of self-promotion, that it was the 'only paper in the kingdom that has the courage to speak the truth in regard to royalty — the only one that dares to look the execrable tyranny in the face'.[5]

Newspapers and prints, already conceived of as a foundational element of the public sphere, were caught up in a contest over the meaning of royal events, where the role of print media was an integral part of the struggle.

It is in the first three years of Victoria's reign that we can see the contours of royal populism begin to take shape. Victoria's coronation and marriage were both significant departures from precedent and aroused a large degree of controversy. Examining the tension around Victoria's coronation and marriage locates the civic publicness of the 1840s and 1850s within a reformist trajectory that the earlier two events had helped to initiate. The weight of constitutional discourse around Victoria's tours and visits was such that it actually migrated back into a broad conception of the monarch's constitutional role. In Walter Bagehot's *The English Constitution*, a treatise notable for its subsequent status, we can trace the impact of Victoria's media making upon Bagehot's conception of the Queen's political function. [. . .]

Slowly emerging out of the tension of Victoria's coronation and marriage, and the political turmoil of the 1830s, was a new role for royalty. It is the reinvented publicness of Victoria's coronation and marriage, and their corresponding association with a reforming populism, which provides the discursive framework through which we can understand the potency of Victoria's activities during the 1840s and 1850s. In a recent book, Frank Prochaska has argued that much scholarship on the monarchy has neglected its substantive role in civil society. Prochaska's work focuses on the creation of what he describes as the welfare monarchy — the vital role played by royal philanthropy through the patronage of numerous charities and individuals. Given the importance of a paternalistic *noblesse oblige* at a time when the role of government remained limited, the good causes adopted by Victoria and Albert were an uncontentious way of demonstrating their compassion and concern for their subjects. Victoria was a patron of, and not just a contributor to, 150 institutions, three times as many as George IV. Between 1831 and 1871, donations to institutions and individuals were equivalent to 15 per cent of Victoria's income from the Privy Purse.[6]

Charity work nevertheless comprised only part of the revivified prominence that Victoria and Albert enjoyed. The initial excitement occasioned by the new reign, which had been fostered by a regular procession of royal events, settled down only in the sense that the Queen's marriage did not see any diminution in her high-profile role. Between 1840 and 1861, it is crucial to the whole style of Victoria's monarchy that she undertook a wide range of public engagements, and that she was seen to be doing them. Royal ceremonial may have been downsized but amongst radicals and Tories alike there was a desire for Victoria and Albert to adopt an industrious public role. For Tories, royal visits harked back to the progresses of Elizabeth I, a reinforcement of the monarch's traditional pre-eminence in the midst of disorientating change. For Benthamite critics, they satisfied the demand for a more utilitarian monarchy: one that was at least being put to work for its handsome remuneration. As the *Penny Satirist* declared in 1843: 'She is kept by the nation as a spectacle and it is right that she should be seen. In fact it is her duty to come out and show herself, that we may have value for our money; and if she should do anything very ridiculous so much the better.'[7] Royal visits provided an outlet for municipal pride in conjunction with an endorsement of Britain's new industrial achievements. Above all, they were an enactment of the reciprocal interest present between Victoria and her subjects. As the *Illustrated London News* fawningly put it on the Queen's first tour of Scotland: 'Abstractedly, the desire of a sovereign to hold communion with all classes of her people without regard to local or national distinctions, is an indication of a love of justice, and of that beautiful maternal affection which, in domestic life, cherishes no favourite in a family, but sheds its holy love on all alike.'[8] The comment is exemplary of the populist discourse attached to the Queen's activities. In 1843, *The Times* similarly declared that Victoria's visits 'cement the union between the Crown and the people by a reciprocity of confidence'.[9] Again and again and again, royal visits were made to signify a popular constitutionalism — the monarch willingly placing herself before her People. Furthermore, it is significant that the *Illustrated London News* saw the visits as an extension of Victoria's maternal beneficence. The feelings inscribed into the visits are intimate and personal rather than a form of state duty. Instead of any contradiction between Victoria's femininity and her 'public' role, they are conflated together by the *Illustrated London News* so that each becomes the rationale of the other. Making the monarchy available to the People gave royal events an inclusive rhetoric that mitigated much potential criticism.

The majority of the metropolitan and provincial press echoed the *Illustrated London News*'s sentiments. The extensiveness of the discourse of royal populism cannot be underestimated. On Victoria's tour of the midlands in November 1843, the *News of the World* claimed that her visits were only nominally visits to Sir Robert Peel, the Duke of Devonshire, and the Duke of Rutland. They were in fact 'intended as visits to the people — all the working people as well as the burgesses in the different localities'.[10] For the *News of the World*, it was the Queen's most agreeable pleasure to see and to be seen. The *News of the World* itself had only begun publication in October 1843. It was one of the first of the new 3*d*. Sunday newspapers aimed at a broad readership unwilling to afford a metropolitan daily paper or without the leisure time to read one. Predominantly liberal in outlook, the royal coverage of the new weekly press was far removed from the radicalism of the *Northern Star* or the scabrous satire of the *Satirist*. Publications like the *News of the World* and the *Illustrated London News* were replacing the Regency-inspired style of the *Satirist*. The latter finally ceased publication in 1846. *The Northern Star*, too, was at its most influential with the growth of Chartism in the late 1830s and early 1840s.

The *News of the World*'s comments upon Victoria's midlands tour are from its reporting of the first significant royal event to take place following its commencement. They exemplify much of the future coverage given to Victoria by papers like *Lloyd's Weekly Newspaper* and the *Weekly Times*, which began publication in January 1843 and January 1847 respectively. Upon Victoria's visit to Louis Napoleon in 1855, for example, *Lloyd's Weekly Newspaper*, which had a predominantly artisan readership, made the typical declaration that 'it is not Victoria who visits Louis Napoleon, but England who visits France. It is not potentate embracing potentate, but people grasping people.'[11] The coverage of these weekly newspapers is all the more significant because they were amongst the most widely circulated of the period. By 1855, the *Illustrated London News* was selling 155,000 copies a week, the *News of the World* 110,000, *Lloyd's Weekly Newspaper* 92,000, and the *Weekly Times* 76,000.[12] These figures place them in advance of the majority of daily newspapers. Only *The Times* and, after 1855, the *Daily Telegraph* remotely approached such circulation. In 1861, the daily circulation of *The Times* was approximately 65,000 copies and the *Daily Telegraph* 141,000.[13]

The almost wholly supportive coverage of the monarchy by the new Sunday newspapers, the new illustrated press, and the existing metropolitan daily newspapers was crucial for materially embodying the discursive claims of royal populism. Victoria's visits shaped a civic role for the monarchy but they were equally important through being turned into pleasurable reading or viewing matter. Francis Mulhern has argued that communities are 'not places but *practices* of collective identification'.[14] Reading about the monarchy in a newspaper, or viewing a print or photograph, were increasingly important everyday practices of collective identification. The promotion of Victoria's relationship with the People; the assertion of an unprecedented bond of intimacy between her and her subjects; the placing of her at the centre of an imagined national community — all these were achieved, at least partially, through the extensive coverage that was given to Victoria. There was a mutually supportive reciprocity between the cultural work carried out by the growth of newspapers, prints, and periodicals, and the political claims of royal populism. Newspapers and periodicals had an essentially self-fulfilling function; they constantly enacted what they claimed simply to describe.

The number of newspapers commencing in the 1840s accentuated the impact of the number of engagements undertaken by Victoria and Albert. It is important to emphasize that their activities were a significant departure from those of the previous three monarchs. The madness of George III had ensured his long closeting away at Windsor. George IV had visited Dublin in 1821 and toured Scotland in 1822. Ill health and unpopularity, however, meant his last years were notable for a similar reclusiveness. Although George IV had been an enthusiastic supporter of art and architecture, his patronage was never couched within the same framework of moral and civic progress as that of Victoria and Albert. Exhibiting more of a dilettante indulgence than a concern with industrialism and the manufacturing poor, projects such as the Brighton Pavilion seemed only to guarantee more courtly extravagance and debt. The Queen Caroline affair and the debacle of his coronation hardly encouraged the type of civic visits undertaken by Victoria. William IV did not plumb the same depths of unpopularity as George IV but he ascended the throne in 1830 at the age of 65. His age and his involvement in the Reform Bill prevented the type of popular constitutionalism that became so significant in Victoria's reign.

Commentators in the 1840s frequently used Victoria's visits to substantiate the break between her sovereignty and that of her Hanoverian predecessors. Comparing the movements of Victoria with their seclusion, the *Illustrated London News* was typical in its approval of the new royal openness: 'the people of England had for many years been accustomed to look to their Sovereign as a fixture, which it would have been something astounding to have found out of its place, or moving out of its orbit, which was the rather circumscribed one, including Windsor, Buckingham Palace, St James, or now and then, Ascot.[15] Instead of confining the court to a single location, Victoria was lauded for bringing its economic benefits, and sharing its attractiveness, with her subjects. In conjunction with the development of an illustrated and a popular press, Victoria and Albert inaugurated a new style of royalty. A young couple touring different areas of the nation without the trappings of pageantry, frequently accompanied by their infant family, their visits could be invested with a heady mixture of romantic sentiment, family propriety, royal patronage, and local civic pride. And, of course, it was all broadcast as a constant stream of royal news. As indeed it still is.

The Queen's first tour of Scotland, including visits to Perth, Stirling, Taymouth, and Edinburgh, took place in September 1842, the same year in which the *Illustrated London News* began publication. Much of the success of these first tours was due to their novelty. In September 1843, when it was announced that Victoria and Albert were to make an impending visit to Louis-Philippe, the reaction was one of surprise, bewilderment, and uneasiness. The *Illustrated London News*'s commentary on the startling nature of the announcement sums up the general response:

> The speculations of the learned waxed many, and were mysteriously inquisitive mid the general amaze. Was it not contrary to the principle of the English constitution that Her Majesty should leave her dominions without the consent of parliament? And, on the other hand, was not her Parliament prorogued? Had she even applied for the permission of Her Privy Council? Could she go? Rumours were afloat that the Duke of Wellington and others high in office had strongly, but respectfully, protested against the step.[16]

The last reigning sovereign to leave British shores had been George IV in 1821 on a coronation visit to Hanover, the British Crown then still being joined with that of the German state. The visit of Victoria and Albert to a traditional enemy was unprecedented, the first since Henry VIII met Francis I at the Field of the Cloth of Gold in 1520. Given that Victoria was meeting Louis-Philippe at Chateau D'Eu, his country retreat in Normandy, it was also a visit without any of the trappings of state. The *Illustrated London News* described it as an episode of royal adventure that assumed 'the friendly call on a neighbour whom she knows and respects'.[17] The tours were so successful because they were not ostensibly motivated by royal statecraft: they were pleasurable diversions from politics and not its source.

Despite the praise heaped upon her first engagements, it is important to emphasize that they did not simply emerge as fully fledged successes. Their novelty afflicted the participants as much as the spectators. Alex Tyrell and Yvonne Ward have noted that Victoria's first tours were characterized by numerous incidents where the royal couple exhibited a marked reluctance to fulfil the duties expected of them.[18] On their first visit to Edinburgh, the Queen's party arrived unexpectedly early. They passed quickly through the empty streets and went straight to their temporary residence at Dalkeith Castle. Many of the city's inhabitants were dismayed that their elaborate preparations had been so bypassed. Members of the Town Council went to see Robert Peel, who was travelling with the Queen's party, and a reluctant Victoria was persuaded to progress through the streets two days later. Similar incidents occurred on a marine tour around the south coast in 1843, when Victoria declined to receive addresses from various port towns.

The political pressure was very much upon the Crown to perform a worthwhile role. The making and the receiving of state visits, along with a plethora of minor civic engagements, consequently came to dominate the public activities of Victoria and Albert throughout the 1840s and 1850s. Given that their nine children were also born during this period, their domesticity combined with their diligence in a wholesome mixture to which the newspaper and periodical press gave fulsome attention. The couple established a precedent of royal duties, consisting of civic visits, military reviews, meetings, and benevolent charity work. They set a successful model for the duties of a British constitutional monarch. Visits and engagements followed on from one another in quick succession. The latter half of 1844 was typical in that there was a second tour of the Scottish highlands in September, closely followed by the return visit of Louis-Philippe and the opening of the new Royal Exchange in October. November then saw an excursion to Burghley House and a tour of Northampton and the surrounding district.

In addition to the visits to and from Louis-Philippe, the first half of the 1840s saw visits from the Kings of Saxony, Belgium, Prussia, and the Czar of Russia, along with a visit to Saxe-Coburg by Victoria and Albert. A wryly amused *Punch* noted Victoria's propensity for visitations by publishing, in two separate articles, a list of the prospective marine excursions and distinguished visitors over the next five years.[19] Marine journeys were to include calling on St Petersburg, New York, and the South Pole, while projected visitors ranged from Mehmet Ali in 1847 to the Emperor of Lapland in 1852. A full-page engraving captures the packed schedule of Victoria and Albert and *Punch*'s breathless attempts to keep up with their movements. Produced upon Victoria and Albert's return from Saxe-Coburg in 1845, the engraving neatly combines their travels with their tender regard for the royal hearth.

One of the most notable features of the tours was the sheer labour that they involved. Each tour could last for a week or more, with an itinerary packed full of receptions, addresses, and dinners. The visit to the midlands in 1843 was typical in that it lasted for nine days and took in Nottingham, Derby, Chesterfield, Belvoir Castle, Lichfield Cathedral, Coventry, and Leicester. There was also an excursion to Birmingham for Prince Albert, which managed to cram in guided tours of six factories before moving on to visit the town hall and the Free Grammar School.[20] Significantly, the visit was one of the first occasions on which Victoria and Albert travelled by train. The number of subsequent tours, and the number of places they were able to visit on those tours, was, in part, a product of the railways' ability to transport the Queen with relative rapidity. Industrial precision allowed a carefully orchestrated series of receptions as Victoria would be briefly cheered at every station along the route.

Simply on her midlands train trip from Watford to Tamworth in 1843, Victoria passed through seven stations. And at each station the concourse was thronged. Crowds gathered near the railway line just to watch the royal train pass. At Weedon station the buildings were decorated with flags bearing inscriptions such as 'Victoria, England's Hope'. The national anthem was played as the train approached and, in the four minutes that it took for the engine to take on water, the soldiers lining the platform presented arms. There would be countless such four minutes in the years ahead. The concurrent development of the electronic telegraph meant that the Queen's arrival and departure at each location were transmitted back to London, where newspaper offices eagerly awaited the succession of royal bulletins. (It is apt that the first news story carried by telegraph was the birth of the Queen's second son, Prince Alfred, in August 1844.)[21] Victoria and Albert did more than place themselves on the side of progress through their patronage of manufacturing: they were the unconscious beneficiaries of its forces.

The visit to the midlands in 1843 is indicative of what was seen to be the Queen's willingness to patronize every part of the nation with her presence, honouring the industrial areas of Britain as well as the inhabitants of London and Windsor. Each tour of a manufacturing area was given a weighty political symbolism on top of the more pragmatic pleasures of a general holiday for many of the local inhabitants. The opening of the Royal Exchange in 1844 by Victoria and Albert was seen as one of their many acknowledgements of the power of commerce. Their tour of Lancashire in late 1851 accorded the same respect to northern industrialism. The tour of Lancashire, which took in Salford, Liverpool, Carlisle, and Manchester, shows that these visits were enormous occasions for those cities so graced. Manchester had only been incorporated in 1838 and would be made a city in 1852. Being honoured by a royal visit was an important episode in these cities' sense of their own status and development. When Victoria opened Leeds Town Hall in 1858, the corporation wore civic robes for the first time in their history.[22]

The scale of preparations attendant upon a royal visit is indicative of the importance with which they were regarded. Banners, grandstands, triumphal arches, and illuminations were the staple components of any royal visit. In a crucial shift of emphasis, local committees and dignitaries provided the pageantry on these occasions rather than the court. In 1851, Manchester spent between £100,000 and £150,000 on its entertainment for the Queen.[23] The Queen had visited Liverpool only a few days previously and, with the local rivalry between the two cities, Manchester was determined to outdo the greeting that Liverpool had given to the Queen. One member of the Manchester Corporation allegedly declared that for each thousand pounds spent by Liverpool they would spend ten.[24] Many local mayors were knighted for their loyal efforts on these occasions, a fact that must have encouraged the enthusiasm of the local corporation. A brief survey of Manchester's decorations testifies to the effort and time involved. The four miles of the Queen's route through Manchester were decorated with banners, transparencies, wreaths, and emblematic devices. Numerous triumphal arches were built, the largest of which was 60 ft high, while the arch in St Anne's Square was decorated with 4,000 variegated oil lamps. Viewing platforms were constructed on the line of the route, each of which could hold several hundred people. Many of the streets through which Victoria would pass were also repainted and repaved. As a final touch, Manchester's reception included the gathering together of 80,000 local Sunday school scholars in Peel Park to sing the national anthem to Victoria.[25] Civic pride replaced aristocratic ceremony in the consolidation of a mode of royal publicness that was clearly emerging out of the disputes around Victoria's coronation and marriage.

The impact of Victoria and Albert's civic publicness is particularly evident in the way their visits helped to forge a local consensus around the Crown. The provincial press's coverage of Victoria's visits to their own locality emphasizes the iterative nature of royal populism. On Victoria and Albert's aforementioned visit to Birmingham in 1843, the *Birmingham Journal* declared that their presence would 'hardly fail to operate favourably on the somewhat conflicting materials that have, for a long time, constituted that capital's population'.[26] Radical, Tory, and Whig came together to organize the welcome to the Prince. Similarly, when Victoria and Albert visited Birmingham again in June 1858, this time to open Aston Park, the *Birmingham Daily Post* took great pride in declaring that 'The most democratic town in England must also be the most orderly in its loyalty'.[27] The very contrariness of the comment is telling. Birmingham's consciousness of its own civic pride meant that it went out of its way to prove its loyalty. In a situation that is akin to the Chartist demonstrations of their enlightened loyalty at Victoria's coronation, Birmingham's feting of Victoria confirmed not its deference but the dignity of its democratic civic identity.

The various local prints and newspapers produced to commemorate a royal visit were never simply representations of the event. They were part of the communicative encounter between the monarchy and the press that helped to shape the nature of the monarchy itself. In the days before Victoria's visits in 1858, the *Birmingham Daily Post* was full of adverts for commemorative sonnets and lithographic prints of Aston Hall. There was even a satire, *The Great Avatar*, providing anecdotes of the local dignitaries and promising to be 'incomparably more entertaining than any newspaper details can possibly be'.[28] As well as giving fulsome coverage to the event itself, the *Birmingham Daily Post* produced an extra commemorative edition in order to meet the enormous demand for an account of the occasion. Although the print-run of the commemorative edition was double the normal run of the newspaper, all copies were sold by four o'clock on the day of publication. The narrative consequently had to be inserted in its evening journal.[29] With a national press not yet in existence, the prominence of the provincial press was vital for perpetuating the narrative of royal populism. Tellingly, the only point of dissent around the opening of Aston Hall was a protest by members of the council against their being coerced into wearing ceremonial robes.[30] Feelings were strong enough for a petition to be presented to the Mayor, signed by thirty-six Alderman and Councillors. The reluctance to adopt any form of pomp and circumstance emphasizes the continuing importance of the style in which Victoria and Albert made their visits. The more the barriers of aristocratic ceremony were perceived to have been removed, the greater the ostensible transparency of the relationship between Victoria and the People.

One particularly revealing example of the social compact symbolized by these civic engagements is a speech made by Prince Albert at his inauguration of the Grimsby Docks in April 1849. Congratulating the great spirit of English commercial enterprise for undertaking the project, Albert noted that it also shared another prominent national trait:

> that other feature so peculiar to the enterprise of Englishmen, that strongly attached as they were to the institutions of the country, gratefully acknowledging the protection of those laws under which those enterprises commenced and prospered, they loved to connect them in some manner with the authority of the Crown and the person of the Sovereign, and it is the appreciation of this circumstance which has impelled me to respond to your call, as the readiest mode of testifying to you how strongly her Majesty the Queen values and reciprocates this feeling.[31]

The desire to bask in a warm royal glow meant that Victoria and Albert entered a mutually beneficial compact with the achievements of industrialism, and with the men who ran it. Their presence acknowledged the economic and social power of manufacturing, while the still expanding industrial cities reciprocated the compliment by deferentially acknowledging the continued centrality of the monarchy. Each performed a symbolic touching of the forelock.

The particular importance of municipal pride in this period meant that Victoria's visits were far from being frivolously decorative. They were constitutive of Victoria and Albert's role. In terms that prefigure those of Bagehot in the *English Constitution*, *The Times* saw Albert's opening of the Royal Exchange in 1844 as an essential part of the post-Reform Bill political landscape: 'These great occasions are not far from being an integral part of our constitution. To the middle-classes, who may now almost be considered the ruling class of England, it has become nearly a right . . . that the great men of the country should pay them the compliment — we might say the homage — of appearing periodically.'[32] *The Times* is typical of the way in which these royal events were signified as a new position for the Crown, an *entente cordial* between the monarchy and the middle class. Moreover, as *The Times* unconsciously expresses, thanks to the newspapers and journals, the monarchy did indeed appear periodically (*sic*). Albert's involvement with the Great Exhibition and Victoria's opening of the event was only the crowning glory of a constitutional role that encompassed a multitude of dinners, reviews, and meetings. Ranging from enormous set-piece occasions to the briefest passing through of the royal train and the receiving of yet another platitudinous address from local dignitaries, the dutiful labour of Victoria and Albert was being never-endingly displayed for all to see. [. . .]

By the end of Victoria's reign, the civic publicness of the royal family had become the accepted model for the role of the monarch as a national figurehead. After the death of Albert in 1861, Victoria's own long seclusion only served to accentuate the importance of her previous industry. It is no coincidence that republicanism was at its strongest during the late 1860s and early 1870s when Victoria was perceived as receiving large amounts of money from the Civil List without performing any duties in return. Royal populism and the role of the crowd also continued as the dominant narrative at royal occasions. At the Thanksgiving Service for the recovery of the Prince of Wales from typhoid fever in 1872, *Lloyd's Weekly Newspaper* commented that the enthusiasm of the crowd demonstrated not a blind sycophancy but 'the wisdom, the moderation, and the sound heart'[33] which merited their enfranchisement. Whereas Victoria's creation as the Empress of India in 1876 added an imperial hauteur to her position, the subsequent decline of the British Empire and the slow fading of the Commonwealth has entailed the monarchy losing its imperial gloss. What has nevertheless remained is the round of public functions and philanthropic work. The value of each individual royal is now often measured according to the number of engagements he or she carries out. Indeed, the recent casting of Diana, Princess of Wales, as the 'People's Princess' merely serves to underline the continuing hold of the rhetoric of royal populism. At the same time as the civic publicness of Victoria and Albert was an important part of the development of a constitutional monarchy, the attention they received was a reinvention of the monarchy's aristocratic prominence.

Further reading

The most influential work on the modern commemoration of monarchy remains David Cannadine, 'The Context, Performance and Meaning of Ritual: The British Monarchy and the "Invention of Tradition", c.1820–1977' in Eric Hobsbawm and Terence Ranger (eds), *The Invention of Tradition* (Cambridge: Cambridge University Press, 1983), 101–64. Like Plunkett, Paul Pickering also argues that the monarchy was extremely popular in the early Victorian period: see his '"The Hearts of the Millions": Chartism and Popular Monarchism in the 1840s', *History*, 88 (2003), 227–48. On republicanism, see David Nash and Antony Taylor (eds), *Republicanism in Victorian Society* (Stroud: Sutton, 2000). A useful article for thinking about the image of royalty is Judith Williamson, 'Royalty and Representation' in her *Consuming Passions: The Dynamics of Popular Culture* (London: Marion Byars, 1987), 75–89.

Notes

1   'The Royal Guests', *Illustrated London News*, 8 June 1844, 361.
2   John Thompson, *The Media and Modernity* (Cambridge: Polity, 1995), 120–5.
3   'Our Glorious Constitution', *Reynolds's Newspaper*, 27 Jan. 1901, 4.
4   David Cannadine, 'The Context, Performance and Meaning of Ritual: The British Monarchy and the "Invention of Tradition", c.1820–1977', in E. Hobsbawm and T. Ranger (eds), *The Invention of Tradition* (Cambridge: Cambridge University Press, 1983), 101–64.
5   'Monarchs and their Rights — Divine or Diabolical? Which?', *Reynolds's Newspaper*, 9 Sept. 1855, 8.
6   Frank Prochaska, *Royal Bounty* (New Haven: Yale University Press, 1995), 77.
7   'The Royal Visitations, and Learned Foolery', *Penny Satirist*, 18 Nov. 1843, 2.
8   'The Royal Visit to Scotland', *Illustrated London News*, 3 Sept. 1842, 257.
9   Quoted in Richard Williams, *The Contentious Crown* (Aldershot: Ashgate, 1997), 198.
10 'The Queen's Visit to Her People', *News of the World*, 3 Dec. 1843, 4.
11 'England Meets France', *Lloyd's Weekly Newspaper*, 19 Aug. 1855, 1.
12 Quoted in Peter Sinnema, *Dynamics of the Printed Page: Representing the Nation in the Illustrated London News* (Aldershot: Ashgate, 1998), 16.
13 Lucy Brown, *Victorian News and Newspapers* (Oxford: Clarendon Press, 1985), 52.
14 Quoted in Terry Eagleton, *The Idea of Culture* (Oxford: Blackwell, 2000), 80.
15 'Royal Visits', *Illustrated London News*, 31 Aug. 1844, 128.
16 'The Queen's Visit to France', *Illustrated London News*, 2 Sept. 1843, 155.
17 Ibid. 155.
18 Alex Tyrell and Yvonne Ward, 'God Bless Her Little Majesty: The Popularity of Monarchy in the 1840s', *National Identities*, 2.2 (2000), 109–26.
19 'Victoria's Voyages for the Next Ten Years', *Punch*, 5 (1843), 128; 'The Queen's Illustrious Visitors', *Punch*, 7 (1844), 182.
20 'Visit of Prince Albert to Birmingham', *Illustrated London News*, 2 Dec. 1843, 362.
21 Donald Read, *The Power of News: The History of Reuters 1849–1989* (Oxford: Oxford University Press, 1992), 7.
22 See Williams, *Contentious Crown*, 97.
23 'Great Reception of Her Majesty at Manchester', *Illustrated London News*, 18 Oct. 1851, 478.
24 Ibid. 478.

25   'Preparations in Salford', *Manchester Guardian*, 11 Oct. 1851, 5.

26   'Saturday, December 2', *Birmingham Journal*, 2 Dec. 1843, 4.

27   'The Royal Visit', *Birmingham Daily Post*, 11 June 1858, 2.

28   'The Great Avatar', *Birmingham Daily Post*, 10 June 1858, 2.

29   'To Our Readers', *Birmingham Daily Post*, 14 June 1858, 2.

30   'The Royal Visit', *Birmingham Daily Post*, 11 June 1858, 2.

31   Prince Albert, *Addresses delivered on Different Public Occasions by HRH Prince Albert* (London: Society of Arts, 1857), 27.

32   Quoted in Williams, *Contentious Crown*, 196.

33   Quoted in Williams, *Contentious Crown*, 48.

PART 14

Race, Empire and national identity

Catherine Hall

BRINGING THE EMPIRE BACK IN

Civilising Subjects: Metropole and Colony in the English Imagination, 1830–1867 (London: Polity, 2002), 267–85, 289.

The reduction of interest in class in the later twentieth century led to renewed focus on other Victorian identities. The continued appeal of Margaret Thatcher in the 1980s (particularly following the Falklands conflict in 1982) and the revival of nationalist struggles in Europe following the end of the cold war put issues of national identity on the agenda. Any discussion of British national identity required extended reflection on the role of the British Empire, as it had played a vital role in the ways that the British saw themselves. The Empire was significant not least because it had bequeathed a set of attitudes about race. As Britain became an increasingly multicultural society, it was necessary to reflect on the origins of attitudes, which assumed that white people were inherently superior to non-white peoples. However, the history of the Empire had largely been conducted separately from the domestic history of Britain, generating two lines of inquiry; they rarely connected or addressed each other.

In the 1990s, a new agenda emerged which was determined to rethink British history by bringing the Empire back in. One of the most prominent advocates of this approach was **Catherine Hall**. Commencing with a series of articles, she demonstrated how assumptions about race and Empire underpinned such issues as the construction of masculinity. The mid-nineteenth century saw a shift from the universalist assumptions of the anti-slavery movement, which assumed a common humanity between blacks and whites, towards, in the 1860s, a new, allegedly scientific racism derived from Darwinism. In *Defining the Victorian Nation* (2000), Hall demonstrated how even an unlikely subject such as the passing of the 1867 Reform

Act had an imperial dimension and was underpinned by assumptions about race (a clear contrast to standard political histories of the coming of Reform). Implicit in Hall's work is the argument that race has no scientific basis; it is culturally constructed in different historical contexts. The following Reading comes from her major study, *Civilising Subjects* (2002), which treats the relationship between Birmingham and Jamaica. She demonstrates how the two were connected not only through economic ties but also through the work of Birmingham-based Baptist missionaries, and how Englishness was partly defined through colonial connections and encounters. This extract has been chosen because it demonstrates how we can see an urban centre such as Birmingham in a completely different way when we adopt the lens of race and Empire. Even in the midst of Birmingham's energetic commerce and industry, Hall is able to uncover representations not only of Empire but also of a new understanding of racial difference, which began to underpin Victorian Britain's understanding of itself as an imperial nation. Birmingham helped shape the Empire — and was shaped by it. Hall's evidence includes newspapers, exhibitions, Kashmir shawls and even that great icon of Britishness, the cup of tea. Her form of local history is anything but local.

Catherine Hall is Professor of Modern British Social and Cultural History at University College, London. Her current research interests focus on the ways in which nation and Empire were imagined and conceptualised in the nineteenth century with a particular focus on the life and work of Thomas Babington Macaulay. In addition to *Civilising Subjects: Metropolis and Colony in the English Imagination, 1830–1867* (2002), her works on race and nation include (with Jane Rendall and Keith McClelland) *Defining the Victorian Nation: Class, Race, Gender and the British Reform Act of 1867* (2000) and (as editor) *Cultures of Empire: Colonisers in Britain and the Empire in the Nineteenth and Twentieth Centuries* (2000).

LIVING IN A THRIVING ENGLISH TOWN shaped men's identities and imaginations as surely as living in a colony. If Jamaica was known for its plantations, sugar and slavery, Birmingham was known for its manufactories, commodities and 'sooty artisans'.[1] Whereas white travellers to Jamaica were riveted by black bodies, travellers to Birmingham were transfixed by industry. Birmingham commodities could be found across the empire, linking the town to its markets and consumers in the most material way. 'The Australian', as a *Morning Chronicle* correspondent argued in a special series on the town,

> ploughs his fields with a Birmingham ploughshare, shoes his horses with Birmingham shoes, and hangs a Birmingham bell around the necks of his cattle, that they may not stray too far from home on the hills or the rich pasture lands of that country. The savage in Africa exchanges his gold dust, his ivory, and his spices for Birmingham muskets. The boor of the Cape shoots elephants with a gun expressly made for his purpose by the

Birmingham manufactures. The army, the navy, and the East India Company's service draw from Birmingham their principal supplies of the weapons of destruction — the sword, the pistol and the musket. The riflemen of the backwoods of Canada and the Hudson's Bay territories would be deprived for a while of the means of trade or sport, if Birmingham should cease its fabrication of gun barrels and locks . . . The negroes of the West Indies . . . cut down the sugar cane with Birmingham matchetts; and grass is mowed and corn is reaped, in England and the Antipodes, by scythes and sickles of its manufacture.[2]

The first ports of call for visitors to the town were its manufactories and its workshops. In the late eighteenth century travellers would go to Soho to wonder at the engines of Boulton and Watt. When the princes of Oude, the Indian principality, visited Birmingham in 1857, only months before the news of the 'Mutiny', they were conducted, as all significant visitors were, around local manufactories, the plate for the official dinner being provided by a Birmingham firm.[3] But the town was widely seen as 'uninviting and monotonous' in its outward appearance. It had no decent river, no mountains, 'nothing but a dull, and endless succession of house after house, and street after street'.[4] The improving middle-class men of Birmingham may well have been galled at these descriptions, busy as they were with the construction of public buildings from the town hall to the market hall and the free library, the endowment of new churches and chapels, the clearing of overcrowded streets, the establishment of philosophical institutions and botanical and horticultural societies, the creation of what they liked to call the 'midland metropolis'.[5] But the fact remained: Birmingham was known for its industries.

[. . .] Birmingham specialised in finishing work and had a relatively high number of skilled workers; the initial stages in iron manufacture were usually done in the towns of the coal and iron fields. It focused on newer industries, designed for luxury markets both at home and abroad — anything that required 'the exercise of taste, skill and science' in the course of its conception and completion.[6] Birmingham trades were built on export markets: a complex network of merchants and agents operated not only in the town but also in Liverpool, London and abroad, to organise the movement of goods to European, American and African markets.[7] Developments in banking and canals and transport made this possible. The town was renowned for its inventive activities: products and raw materials were changed and adapted, tools and scientific instruments improved (though the basic tools remained the hammer, the lathe, the stamp and the press), new divisions of labour were introduced. The restructuring of the labour force, in both large and small firms, involved an expansion in female and child labour, an increasing division and specialisation by sex and age, and a drastic intensification of the pace of work. The dominance of small workshop production, which has been seen as central to the particular character of the town, associated with a tradition of cooperation between masters and men, was lessening by the 1840s, as steam power and capital investment encouraged the emergence of larger firms upon which the small masters became increasingly dependent.[8] Birmingham's economic success has been connected with the lack of institutional regulation in the town, its traditions of religious toleration, of skill and of artisanal co-operation. [. . .]

Birmingham had all the accoutrements of a flourishing industrial town by the 1830s. It was relatively well supplied with churches and chapels, in part because of the strong evangelical presence. It boasted a general hospital and dispensary alongside specialist orthopaedic and eye hospitals, the new town hall, of which residents were inordinately proud, taverns and hotels, schools, including the well-known Free Grammar School, and a fine new market hall. Its print culture was vibrant, with booksellers, publishers, circulating and scientific libraries, local newspapers and magazines. Its main shopping areas were being improved, and trains ran to London. It had a public office, a mechanics institute, banks, a society of arts and school of design, a theatre, an institution for the deaf and dumb, a philosophical institution, penitentiaries, a school of medicine and surgery, innumerable philanthropic societies, a town mission, a fine botanical garden and a fire office. Its triennial music festival was famous throughout the region. It was lit with gas, and its water was piped in. By the 1840s it had a splendid corn exchange, an ambitious drainage scheme had begun, and there was talk not only of a library but also a lunatic asylum. The comfortable new suburb of Edgbaston was burgeoning within walking distance of the town. Birmingham's club culture was extensive, its political culture energetic: dominated by radicals and reformers of every variety, it was, particularly in the 1830s, a place of meetings, petitions and demonstrations, a place of activity.[9]

[. . .] [Birmingham] produced the necessary commodities for a civilised life — the life that Baptist missionaries in Jamaica [the main subject of Hall's book] longed for their flocks to desire. Towns, as Adam Smith had argued, contributed to 'improvement and cultivation' by the market they provided for rural produce, by the spirited economic activities of their merchants, and by the forms of good government which they developed. Towns were progressive by their very nature.[10] Furthermore, Birmingham produced the commodities which encouraged people to move from a state of subsistence to one of civilisation. Civilisation for the political economists was characterised by 'artificial wants' — luxuries, which encouraged the development of an aesthetic, comforts which went beyond bare necessities. The failure to want such material goods was seen as a mark of backwardness, whether in the negroes of the West Indies or the Irish in Manchester.[11] Birmingham goods and things epitomised such 'artificial wants'; they improved those who utilised them, making them into new, civilised subjects. [. . .]

By the mid-1860s townsmen were proud to be able to claim that within a radius of about thirty miles, 'nearly the whole of the hardware wants of the world are practically supplied'.[12] These goods all had their origins in the workshops of Birmingham. Such items were required the world over, and colonies provided a particularly significant market for Birmingham entrepreneurs. Australia and New Zealand, for example, were the most important markets for doorknobs, while India led the sales of iron padlocks. The lock-makers were confident of their future. The opening-up of fresh fields of commerce in our colonies', it was argued, 'augur well for this department of local industry . . . the demand for locks and keys must necessarily extend with the growth of civilisation.'[13] Australia and India provided excellent markets for chains, cables and anchors.[14] 'There are few civilised countries which do not import English hollow-ware,' noted William Kenrick, a major manufacturer in that field and well-known Birmingham figure, 'but the best foreign markets are, as a rule, found in the British colonies.'[15] Australia was second only to Britain for the jewellery and gilt toy trades, while iron and brass bed manufacturers depended both on the colonies and dependencies of the British empire. Vast quantities of cut nails found their way to India and Australia, alongside patent wrought-iron hinges which also did well in the West Indies, Canada, New Zealand and the Cape.[16] Settlers in Australia and the Cape swore by Birmingham saddlery, and there was a flourishing market for this in India.[17]

Birmingham manufacturers were clearly proud of their sound and practical goods. They could rely on their kin across the Anglo-Saxon globe to carry their products with them, metallic symbols of the civilisation associated with commerce, private property and domesticity, signifiers of progress in the liberal mind. The empire, its colonies and dependencies were part of the everyday world of Birmingham men and women in the nineteenth century. Birmingham was not an imperial city in any obvious sense.[18] It did not depend on slavery or on raw materials from the colonies. It had no black population of any size, no dockers or sailors, unlike London, Liverpool or Cardiff, no East India Docks Road or Hyderabad Barracks.[19] There were both visitors and residents of colour: [*Writer and anti-slavery advocate Olaudah*] Equiano visited in 1789, the Jamaican William Davidson lived there briefly in the early nineteenth century, a missionary sighted three lodging-houses for Asians in the town in 1869.[20] But these were all unusual enough to be matters of note: black missionaries or entertainers were commented on in the local press.[21] The peoples of the empire were rarely seen in the midland metropolis. Even the Irish population, from that very special 'metropolitan colony', was small in comparison with that of a place like Manchester, for it was skilled labour which was in demand in the town.[22] [. . .]

Yet Birmingham was *of* the empire, situated within the empire, defining itself as a town through its relation to nation and empire, imbricated with empire, long before Joseph Chamberlain articulated its political identity as imperial in the late nineteenth century. By the mid-nineteenth century its export market was closely linked to the colonies, its citizens formed a diaspora across those colonies, many of them closely maintaining their connections with their home town, families and friends. New Zealand boasted three Birminghams, Australia five, Canada ten, and even Jamaica had its New Birmingham.[23] The political, cultural and indeed domestic life of the midland metropolis was inflected with issues of race, nation and empire.

Manufacturers and merchants were ever aware of commercial imperatives. When John Bright was proposed as a parliamentary candidate by Birmingham Liberals in 1857, his candidature was unsuccessfully opposed by a Mr Dalziel on the grounds that Bright's well-known views on the desirability of peace were hardly appropriate to a town whose trading interests (in this instance their guns as well as all the other paraphernalia of military metallic supplies) depended on war.[24] But commerce with empire was only one of the multiple ways in which that empire figured in the minds and imagined landscapes of Birmingham people.

Newspaper readers, for example, could enter the imagined community of nation and empire, as well as that of the town, as they read of strange doings elsewhere and reflected on their own different and not so different daily lives. Englishmen and Brummagems did not have the same 'peculiarities of character' as 'the Hindoo', and were not locked in prejudice like 'the Sepoy'. Readers of the national periodicals which circulated amongst predominantly middle-class publics also had frequent opportunities to learn of colonial lands and peoples, as did those readers of fiction whose colonial frame of reference has been so extensively analysed.[25] John MacKenzie was the first to draw attention to the myriad ways in which empire was propagandised from the late nineteenth century through a host of popular forms from the press, postcards and cigarette cards to the exhibitions, theatre productions and music-hall performances which all played a part in the circulation of ideas about empire.[26] The work that has been carried out in this area since, from the detailed analysis of exhibitions to the deconstruction of advertisements and popular fiction, has done much to open up the imagined worlds of writers, editors, theatre managers and the makers of advertisements.[27]

We know little, however, of what people made of this plethora of representations, and, as [Roger] Chartier argued, it is in the spaces between production and consumption that meanings are produced.[28] An analysis which focuses on a particular public, that of a town, can perhaps begin the task of connecting these discourses and cultural forms to their consumption. The work of historians such as Christine Bolt has told us a great deal about the particular histories of the abolitionists and the ways in which they were framed by, and constitutive of, shifts in racial thinking.[29] Meanwhile cultural critics have greatly enriched our understanding of the cultural practices of particular authors and the complex links made in their texts between race, nation and empire. But the task of connecting these two sites of analysis — the task of the cultural historian — has only just begun. The men and women of Birmingham learned about the colonial order of things through a multiplicity of forms. Here was no consolidated vision of empire, but rather a cacophony of sounds: abolitionists contending with 'scientific racists', would-be colonisers competing with the more cautious voices of those who saw empire as an unnecessary expense, exhibitors rivalling missionaries in the advertising of their wares.

But what were the many and varied sites, each with its specific audience, for the production and circulation of these representations of difference in a nineteenth-century town? And how were the identities of the men and women of Birmingham framed in this process? One site was the press. [. . .] Birmingham had two weekly papers: *Aris's Birmingham Gazette,* established in 1741, and the *Birmingham Journal.* The readership of the latter has been estimated as one in four of the adult population of both sexes in the town in the heady political days of the 1830s. The town's first daily was established in 1855, soon to be followed by the very successful *Birmingham Daily Post*.[30] Local newspapers reported regularly on events in the empire, often with excerpts from national newspapers and editorial comment; they reviewed the new books of explorers and travellers, and commented in myriad ways on the differences between 'them' and 'us'. A reading of the *Birmingham Journal*, originally a Tory paper but transformed into a powerful vehicle for reform in the early 1830s, reveals a regular diet of imperial issues.[31] From November 1845 to June 1846, for example, coverage included debates on the emancipated peoples of the West Indies, with particular reference to the sugar duties and the importation of 'coolie labour'; news of the Sikh war in India and the discovery of Sikhs as brave tribal fighters, a depiction that was contrasted with that of the 'Hindoo'; comment on the beginnings of the famine in Ireland, inflected with racialised representations of the Irish as indolent and living only for the moment; advice about settling in South Australia, news of wars in New Zealand, features on exploration and the strange rituals and rites of native peoples, reports of missionary speeches.[32] Similarly, in the first three months of 1866, there was extensive coverage of the events in Jamaica following Morant Bay, continuing anxieties about India in the aftermath of 1857, much comment on

Fenian activity in Ireland and the United States, reflections on the difficulties which settlers faced in New Zealand and on the troubles of the Cape, together with reviews of missionary and anthropological works.[33]

The *Birmingham Journal* saw it as part of its task to educate its readers on matters colonial, and provided special features, sometimes with maps included, for those who were not sure where such places as the principality of Oude or the region of the Punjab were. The editors confidently characterised peoples, placing them in relation to their own assumptions about nation and civilisation. 'All India', they instructed their readership during the Sikh wars of the mid-1840s,

> from the Himalayas to the southern extremity of Ceylon, and from the Gulph of Cutch, on the west, to the Mouths of the Ganges, on the east, may be said to belong to England; for the states that claim independence are so surrounded by English states, that they are comparatively powerless. The population exceeds one hundred millions; the British force is under forty thousand. But these latter are multiplied by that peculiarity of the Hindoo character which makes it easy to train him into an instrument for holding his own country in subjection. He has scarcely the idea of a country to fight for . . . the Sepoys . . . are found nearly as efficient as troops entirely British; and so long as nothing is done to shock their religion and prejudices, they are equally faithful.[34]

This was the character of the 'Hindoo' and the 'Sepoy': easy to train as 'an instrument for holding his own country in subjection', likely to be as solid as 'troops entirely British' as long as 'their religion and prejudices' were not disturbed.

Canada was another colony about which it was assumed that readers needed instruction. A feature on the Hudson's Bay Company appeared in the *Birmingham Journal* only weeks before Robert Knox's lectures on 'The Races of Men' (later to be published as his celebrated book) were delivered in the town.[35] [*Robert Knox was a famous surgeon who became a promoter of the idea that climate influenced racial difference.*] Knox was fierce on the atrocious dangers of 'miscegenation', but this article carried a quite contrary view. 'The Company's servants are principally Scotch and Canadians', the writer informed his readers,

> but there is also a great number of half-breeds, children of the company's servants and Indian women. These are generally a well-featured race, ingenious, athletic and remarkably good horsemen; the men make excellent trappers, and women, who frequently marry officers of the Company, make clever, faithful and attentive wives; they are ingenious needlewomen, and good managers.[36]

Journalistic representations of racial difference operated within a field which was continually being reworked. There were always different voices, sometimes juxtaposed. Racial representation has its own history, but it was not a closed system, rather it operated in relation with historical events, playing a part in the constitution of meaning in those events, but also being reconstituted in these moments. While stereotypical elements of these representations — as, for example, that of the negro as indolent — continually reappeared, reworked in particular forms, they never stood uncontested. Representation, in other words, was a process, a process which was central to the construction of identities, the making of self and other. At its heart was ambivalence, rooted in the twin dynamics of identification and disavowal, desire and repudiation, both key to the marking of difference. While journalists, ethnographers, missionaries and others attempted to fix 'the peculiarity of the Hindoo', for example, to know it, to name it and classify it, to write of the character of 'the race' as particular and recognisable, they were marking the continuous attempt to construct binaries, make hierarchies of difference. This was part of the effort to construct consent around particular readings of racial difference and to stabilise the field. At moments, in certain conjunctures, particular representations won wide enough consent to become hegemonic and legitimate political conse-quences. But these binaries were just as continuously being dissolved, the 'essential' characteristics of different peoples slipping away as times changed; the negro was no longer represented as a victim, the sepoy no longer loyal, and the imagined map of the peoples and races of the empire was reworked.

Birmingham's institutions, products of the rapid development of a new predominantly middle-class and artisan public sphere in the late eighteenth and early nineteenth centuries, were another significant source of knowledge of empire. The missionary and anti-slavery societies, for example, were devoted to the cause of disseminating information and building support. They held innumerable meetings, hosted lectures, and produced pamphlets and magazines in furtherance of their cause. Speakers from afar had an entertainment value in a Victorian town. In February 1846, for example, residents of Birmingham could hear the Rev. Peter Jones, a converted American-Indian chief, give a lecture at Ebenezer Chapel, a lecture that, as so often, was enlivened by an exhibition of idols. He had come to England to raise money for the establishment of industrial schools, aware that unless his people were 'taught to work as well as to read and write, they would remain in a half-civilised state and soon become extinct'.[37] In that same year, Frederick Douglass [*former American slave and leading abolitionist*], travelling the country on a spectacularly successful lecture tour, spoke at the Livery Street chapel, one of the first African-Americans to be celebrated in this way in Victorian Birmingham.[38] A range of other societies and institutions debated matters imperial in a variety of ways: while 'ladies' were usually welcomed to public meetings, there were a large number of men-only venues. In 1848 the Eclectic Society discussed whether colonies were beneficial to the mother country.[39] The Mechanics Institute and the Philosophical Institution hosted lectures on colonies and on questions of race, and taught geography and history through the lens of empire. A favourite public speaker was Charles Dickens, who visited Birmingham several times and gave three Christmas readings in 1853 in support of the campaign to launch the Birmingham and Midland Institute, an ambitious educational venture, initially designed for men. 'Erect in Birmingham', he argued,

> a great educational institution — properly educational — educational
> of the feeling as well as of the reason — to which all orders of Birmingham
> men contribute; in which all orders of Birmingham men meet; wherein
> all orders of Birmingham men are faithfully represented; and you will
> erect a temple of concord here which will be a model edifice to the
> whole of England.[40]

Dickens's vision of concord, eloquently spoken of in *A Christmas Carol*, which he read to a packed and appreciative town hall, was a vision of domestic harmony, both at home and in the nation, which depended on keeping the boundaries of race firmly in place. The eyes of England's mothers should be on their children, not on Africa, as he had memorably laid out in *Bleak House*.[41] The establishment of the Midland Institute meant another public space for lectures, and imperial topics were favourites, with India dominating in the years after the 'Mutiny'.[42] The immensely popular minister and lecturer George Dawson ran a series of classes on English history in the late 1860s, especially for ladies, a novel idea. The first lecture was on the English [sic] colonies, and used as its text Caroline Bray's *The British Empire*. Participants were invited to bring a map of the British empire, coloured in red, to their first class.[43]

A national ethnological society had been founded in 1843, and by the mid-1850s lectures on ethnology in Birmingham were attracting large, respectable and 'influential' audiences. In October and November 1856, for example, Dr Latham lectured on 'The Races of Men' to a crowded auditorium, and his lectures were reproduced in the local press. Latham was concerned to defend the new discipline of ethnology (*racial science*) as a proper science, its founders Linnaeus, Buffon, Blumenbach and Prichard providing a worthy intellectual lineage. He had published a major ethnological survey in 1850, concerned with the narrow classification of human species.[44] 'Linnaeus has been the first to point out in a scientific manner the characteristics of man as a species,' he argued; Buffon had looked at the moral peculiarities of different races, Blumenbach at the anatomical. 'Our countryman, the late Dr. Prichard, continued these observations with those of the philologists, and thus laid the foundation of ethnology as it exists at the present day.' Latham was a strong supporter of Prichard, a believer in the unity of mankind and the unbridgeable gap between apes and humans.[45] Following in his mentor's footsteps, he insisted on the practical importance of the subject,

> especially of the question whether the differences between the races of men, such as the negro and European, are specific differences, like those between the fox and the dog, or whether they are merely the result of circumstances operating through great lengths of time, and producing varieties of one species as the shepherd's dog, and the greyhound are varieties of the species dog.

Latham alluded, as the report put it, to 'the bearing of this upon the question of negro slavery, and upon our views of the future destinies of nations', and declared that he would reserve his own opinions until he had presented 'the facts upon which such opinions must be founded'.[46]

Latham was well aware of the challenges to a monogenist view of the world by the mid-1850s: the discovery of new chronologies of human existence, the increasing scientific investigation of human diversity, the work on comparative philology — all tested the orthodoxy best expressed, as Stocking argues, in the visual metaphor of the tree with its common root and many branches. Knox had explicitly targeted Prichard in the second edition of his book, and insisted that he was using the word 'race' in a new sense, 'to designate physical entities unchanged since the beginning of recorded time'.[47] Latham adopted a Dickensian strategy for his lectures, relying on unresolved climaxes to bring his audience back for more. En route, he reported (*Charles*) Lyell's conviction, for example, that 'American negroes had a better physical conformation than those of Africa, and that the better instructed and fed negroes of Africa in many cases approached the European type. If this were the case they would certainly have something like evidence of inferior organisations being capable of improvement.'[48] He himself, however, declined to give an opinion on the subject at that stage. He built up to the declaration in his final lecture of his commitment to the doctrine of the unity of the species. The changes which took place over time convinced him that 'the dominant races' — those who colonised, the European races and the more civilised races of Asia — would slowly spread themselves over the world and would 'obliterate' Aboriginals in Australia, Hottentots and Bushmen in South Africa, and the Indians of North America. 'The minor varieties of the human race', as he put it, 'would be gradually displaced.' 'Upon the whole', he concluded, 'there was an approach to something like unity in the physical and moral characteristics of our race, a good deal in the way of unity of language and creed.' Dr Latham then took leave of his subject 'by impressing on the audience the relation which ethnology had to other sciences, the necessity of guarding against hasty statements respecting the principles of the science he had endeavoured to explain, and in individuals being moderate in their views upon it'.[49] [. . .]

Exhibitions provided another form of education and entertainment about empire. 'The most Extraordinary Exhibition of Aborigines ever seen in Europe!' was announced in April 1847. Since it was only in Birmingham for a few days, the 'Man of Science' and the 'Student in Zoology' were enjoined to hurry to the Athenaeum on Temple Street. Entry was only one shilling, and private interviews could be arranged for *2s 6d*. 'The Aborigines consist', the potential audience were informed, 'of two Men, two Women and a Baby, of the Bush Tribe, from the interior of South Africa, belonging to a race that, from their wild habits, could never before be induced to visit a place of civilisation.' The interest excited by their appearance had been unprecedented in Liverpool and Manchester, and thousands had been disappointed by failing to obtain admission. The people of Birmingham should hurry if their curiosity was to be gratified. The newspaper advertisement for this exhibition was followed by an extract from the celebrated South African missionary, Moffat's, commentary on the terrible fate of the Bushmen, 'hunted like partridges in the mountains . . . deprived of what nature had made their own'. To the thinking mind', concluded the editor, 'these people afford ample food for reflection; they are the very last degree of humanity.'[50] A month later *The Times* commented on this same group who were then being exhibited at the Egyptian Hall in London. The tone was significantly more hostile than that of the liberal *Birmingham Journal*:

> In appearance they are little above the monkey tribe, and scarcely better than the mere brutes of the field. They are continually crouching, warming themselves by the fire, chattering or growling, smoking, etc. They are sullen, silent, and savage — mere animals in propensity, and worse than animals in appearance. The exhibition is, however, one that will and ought to attract. The admirers of 'pure nature' can confirm their speculations on unsophisticated man, and woman also, or repudiate them, by a visit to these specimens. They are well calculated to remove prejudices, and make people think aright of the times when 'wild in his

woods the noble savage ran'. In short, a more miserable set of human beings — for human they are, nevertheless — was never seen.[51]

The Times correspondent might have attended the lecture on Bushmen given by Robert Knox this same week and concluded that 'these specimens' were certainly destined to extinction. This event, which took place at Exeter Hall, usually the home of abolitionists and evangelicals, was advertised (no doubt with that in mind) as dealing with 'the great question of race, and the probable extinction of the Aboriginal races, the progress of the Anglo-African Empire, and the all important questions of Christian mission and human civilization in that quarter of the globe'.[52] Birmingham viewers of the exhibition had had the chance to listen to Knox's series of lectures three months previously.[53]

Exhibitions, as Altick has argued, provided an alternative medium to print; 'through them, the vicarious became the immediate, the theoretical and general became the concrete and specific'.[54] Their claim to educate as well as to entertain ensured a varied audience until well into the 1860s, by which time developments in engraving and photography had displaced the painted panoramas and dioramas which had enchanted their publics. The Shakespeare Rooms in Birmingham provided a regular diet of visual pleasures. In the late 1840s, for example, they offered both panoramas and dioramas on the late war in India.[55] In 1856 Professor Millar was laying on a diorama of India at the music hall. The advert promised 'a charming and colossal art production, admirably managed, and enhanced by the clever introduction of mechanical effects and coloured lights'. There were

> Ninety-five unequalled views, Displaying the magnificent Cities and Palaces, Manners and Customs, of the Inhabitants of the East, for the distance of 2,000 miles; painted on 30,000 square feet of canvas, by Phillips, Haghe, (Painters to the Queen) and Knell; being the largest diorama in the world; universally acknowledged to be the best Exhibition ever seen in Birmingham.

The diorama was complemented by 'a clever illustrated lecture' from a Mr Watkins, who had been connected with the diplomatic service in India and who spoke on Eastern life and habits.[56] By 1853 the proprietor of the Shakespeare Rooms, J.W. Reimers, had started competing with the Athenaeum and was advertising an anatomical and ethnological museum. There were critics of this exhibit, but Reimers insisted that, 'thanks to the universal diffusion of intellectual knowledge', the inhabitants of Birmingham were far too enlightened to be prejudiced. 'We are now in an age of progression and improvement,' he argued, 'where the engines of terror, superstition, and bigotry are being shattered by the iron rod of science.' Museums of anatomy and ethnology played their part in this story of progress.[57]

Birmingham theatre-goers could encounter these issues in other ways. Sometimes this meant seeing black actors on stage. 'The African Roscius', for example — otherwise known as Ira Aldridge — enjoyed a season in the town, performing Othello amongst other roles. The son of an African-American minister, Aldridge had come to England, where opportunities were known to be better for black actors. His marriage to a white woman in the 1820s increased the attention of hostile pro-slavery advocates, and he was the victim of a press campaign against him in 1833.

Driven out of London, he settled in the provinces, relying on small theatres for work.[58] Presented in Birmingham as the son of an African prince who had become a clergyman, he was congratulated on his 'modest and unassuming manner', guaranteed to win him consideration.[59] *Uncle Tom's Cabin*, 'a Drama of powerful interest, thrilling situations, peculiar and novel characters and extraordinary scenic effects', was playing at the Theatre Royal in May 1853, months after the spectacular success of the best-selling novel, and to coincide with the visit to the town of Harriet Beecher Stowe. Her visit attracted much comment, and was significant in its public celebration of a woman author, though, as was the norm, Mrs Stowe relied on her husband to speak on her behalf in public.[60] Meanwhile, at the concert hall, 'the Living Tableaux illustrative of Uncle Tom's Cabin' was showing, a much cheaper spectacle than that at the theatre. The same week — and this was Whit week so there were holiday novelties — there was an 'entirely new Vocal and Pictorial Entertainment' at the Odd Fellows' Hall, entitled 'An Emigrant's Voyage to and Travels in Australia' which included the songs 'Onward Oh!', 'Hurrah for a Life in the Bush', 'The Australian Settler' and 'The Gambler's Hut'.[61] Ten years later, at a time when both town and nation were divided over the question of the American Civil War, *Uncle Tom's Cabin* was playing again at the Theatre Royal alongside Christy's Minstrels, demonstrating, according to one reviewer, that slave life had its bright side, exhibiting 'that practical and demonstrative humour which seems inseparable from the race, and which one can scarcely imagine to co-exist with a condition of unmitigated misery'.[62] [. . .]

Issues regarding empire inflected (Birmingham's) public political life directly and indirectly. Chartism had its own implicit maps of empire, while the Colonisation Society was formed to intervene directly in matters colonial. In 1843 the emigration movement in Warwickshire called a public meeting at the town hall to hear a deputation from the Colonisation Society, protagonists of Edward Gibbon Wakefield's plan for 'a systematic method of emigration to various parts of our colonial empire'. Times were hard in Birmingham, and unemployment high. The intention was to encourage hard-working men to emigrate and thus solve the problem of poverty at home and lack of labour in Australia and New Zealand at one and the same time. The meeting was well attended, despite taking place at midday. One of the local aristocrats, Lord Lyttleton, was in the chair, and on the platform were a collection of clergymen and gentlemen, together with the two MPs for Birmingham, William Scholefield and G.F. Muntz. Francis Scott, one of the members of the deputation, insisted that they had simply come to state the facts and open the eyes of the men of Birmingham to the importance of their subject. He wanted to show them that

> the want of labour in Australia was so great that the employers had been obliged to resort to the South Sea islands, and take savages to do that which was the birthright of the labouring poor of that country. [Hear] He thought that British soil should belong to British subjects — that the soil should be tilled by British hands, and that British industry should be employed in the possessions of the British Crown. [Loud cheers]

Another member of the deputation, Walter Wrottesley, spoke from personal experience as an emigrant. He had lived and travelled in New South Wales, which, 'sixty years ago was inhabited only by the black man, and boasted not of an animal fit for human food'. Now it had become 'one of the most important colonies any country ever possessed'. Birmingham men should turn their attention to this colony. Emigration was a law of nature. America had been transformed, and now Australia was following suit. 'It was boasted', he said, that 'on Britain's dominions the sun never set, and therefore when a man left his home in this country for another on a distant shore, there met him the old English habits and customs, not amongst strangers but amongst friends, men speaking their own language and believing their own faith'.

Australia, in other words, was presented as home from home. Indeed, in some respects it was better than home. As Arthur Hodgson, a resident of South Australia for ten years and another member of the Colonisation Society put it, he regarded Australia, with its space, its 'heavenly climate' and its 'extraordinary resources' as 'a country intended by Providence to receive the surplus population of the mother land'. It was 'the Eden' 'to which they might go to have their hopes, their antici- pations, their dreams realised'. William Scholefield, one of the Birmingham MPs, was not prepared to let this pass. He 'could not concur with those that thought there was any surplus population in this country [hear, hear, and loud cheering]'. However, he 'saw in emigration a most important means of benefitting the industrious classes, and in colonisation one of the very best means for extending the markets of this country'. Muntz, the other MP, went farther. He announced himself no friend to emigration or colonisation, believing them both to be expensive and injurious, 'the excrescence of an attempt to make up for a bad system of government [hear, hear]'. Despite this, he applauded the fact that the meeting had taken place and that information about the Society and its efforts had been made available.[63]

At the end of the 1840s, the European revolutions provoked much excitement in Birmingham, and European nationalisms were the galvanising topic of the 1850s, turning attention from universal brotherhood to the white brotherhood of Europe, until the 'Indian Mutiny' of 1857 transfixed both town and nation. Race returned as a central political preoccupation, played out over India, the American Civil War and Morant Bay, only displaced by the reform movement, which focused on the reconstitution of the nation in 1867.

If public life was entwined with empire, so too was private. The foods that people ate, the clothes they wore, the articles in their homes, the plants in their gardens, their psychic lives — all were marked by empire.[64] By the eighteenth century sugar, for example, had become a part of the everyday life of the English, necessary for a proper cup of tea and for the wide array of puddings for which the English were famous.[65] It was in every kitchen cupboard by the 1780s, and the abolition movement was well aware of the importance of transforming it from the simple commodity, West Indian sugar, to an item the production of which was casting a stain upon the nation. It was the women abolitionists who were in the forefront of making the consumption of sugar in the domestic environment into a moral and political question. As Clare Midgley has shown, the campaign to abstain from slave sugar was a way of bringing home to British people their personal involvement in slavery and creating an anti-slavery domestic culture. The Society for the Abolition of the Slave Trade had Cowper's poem 'Pity the Poor Africans' reprinted on fine-quality paper and distributed by the thousands with the recommendation that it made an excellent subject for conversation at the teatable. Eighteenth-century coffee sets showing the enslaved serving white couples were displaced by anti-slavery tea sets. Sugar basins were produced bearing the motto 'East India sugar not made by slaves'. The cameo image of the kneeling slave appeared on bracelets and hairpins. The representation of the black person as commodity featured in eighteenth-century portraits as a symbol of status, comments Midgley, was replaced by the black person as victim.[66]

If the West Indies was primarily associated with sugar in the mind of the English consumer, India featured first as the land of Kashmir shawls. The Kashmir shawl was introduced from the mid-eighteenth century, and became a desirable fashion item for the wealthy woman, generating home-based production of shawls on Indian motifs and a demand for 'sale and exchange'.[67] Mrs Gaskell was well aware of the status of the Indian shawl as an item of luxury and beauty. Her heroine Margaret Hale in *North and South*, attending her cousin's wedding, helps to show off the shawls which are part of the trousseau, 'snuffing up their spicy Eastern smell' and showing off their 'gorgeous' qualities and 'brilliant colours'.[68] Indian fabrics, the lightweight muslins and silks, became fashionable, the names of the places they came from part of the conversation of middle-class women. At the same time memsahibs were publishing recipes for curry and rice in popular periodicals and modifying 'the food habits of many middle-class Britons'. Indian condiments and pickles, chutneys and spices, became a part of British cuisine, with Mrs Beeton particularly recommending the use of leftover fish and meat in curries.[69]

[. . .] The midland metropolis was industrial in its character, yet civilising in its nature, producing commodities which improved manners and refined many. It was irredeemably provincial, dominated by middle-class men and, with no resident aristocracy, not part of the educated world in which the classics dominated, far from the court and Parliament, from society, and what was seen as the effeminacy and corruption of London. It liked to imagine itself as a moving power, leading the industrial world in things progressive. Not only was it said, for example, that one of its own shows inspired Prince Albert's vision of the Great Exhibition, but Birmingham had provided the glass and iron for the Crystal Palace and for the crystal fountain placed at the heart of the exhibition.[70] Birmingham was 'a town of the future rather than of the past'.[71] Yet Birmingham's provincialism had its metropolitan dimension: for the town was imbricated with empire. Town dwellers encountered the empire in multiple ways: in their newspapers and their novels, in their museums and their lectures, in their shows and their chapels, in their theatres and their public meetings, in their food and their clothes, in their homes and their gardens, in the worlds of their families and friends. But in those encounters and that cacophony of sounds, some voices had more weight than others. At key moments choices were made, for one view of 'the negro' rather than another, for one notion of empire rather than another. In that process identities were articulated in ways that spoke to and for significant numbers of men and women, naming the residents of Birmingham in ways that resonated with town, nation and empire.

Further reading

For responses to *Civilizing Subjects*, see David Feldman, Alan Lester, Jean Besson, David Killingray and Catherine Hall, 'Roundtable on *Civilising Subjects*', *Journal of Victorian Culture,* 9 (2004), 235–58. For studies that attempt to bring the Empire back into Britain's domestic history, see: John McKenzie, *Propaganda and Empire: The Manipulation of British Public Opinion, 1880–1960* (Manchester: Manchester University Press, 1984); Antoinette Burton, *Burdens of History: British Feminists, Indian Women, and Imperial Culture, 1865–1915* (Chapel Hill, NC: University of North Carolina Press, 1994); Raphael Samuel, 'Empire Stories: The Imperial and the Domestic' in his *Island Stories: Unravelling Britain* (London: Verso, 1998), 74–97; Catherine Hall, Keith McClelland and Jane Rendall, *Defining the Victorian Nation: Class, Race, Gender and the Reform Act of 1867* (Cambridge: Cambridge University Press, 2000); Andrew Thompson, *The Empire Strikes Back?: The Impact of Imperialism on Britain from the Mid-Nineteenth Century* (London: Longman, 2005). Bernard Porter, in *The Absent-Minded Imperialists: Empire, Society and Culture in Britain* (Oxford: Oxford University Press, 2004), argues that the British people were never much interested in Empire. On race and the Victorians, see: Nancy Stepan, *The Idea of Race in Science: Great Britain, 1800–1960* (London: Macmillan, 1982); Evelleen Richards, 'The "Moral Anatomy" of Robert Knox: The Interplay between Biological and Social Thought in Victorian Scientific Naturalism', *Journal of the History of Biology,* 22 (1989), 373–436; Clare Midgley, *Women against Slavery: The British Campaigns, 1780–1870* (London: Routledge, 1992); David Feldman, *Englishmen and Jews: Social Relations and Political Culture, 1840–1914* (New Haven, CT: Yale University Press, 1994); Shearer West (ed.), *The Victorians and Race* (Aldershot: Scolar Press, 1996).

Notes

1   The phrase was Carlyle's, quoted in *Showell's Dictionary of Birmingham* (Walter Showell, Birmingham, 1885), p. 31.

2   'Labour and the Poor — Birmingham', letter 1: Parochial and Moral Statistics, *Morning Chronicle,* 7 Oct. 1850.

3   *Birmingham Journal (BJ),* 4 Apr. 1857.

4   J.G. Kohl, *Ireland, Scotland and England* (Chapman and Hall, London, 1844), pp. 8–9.

5   *BJ,* 17 June 1865. On the gender implications of this new public sphere see Leonore Davidoff and Catherine Hall, *Family Fortunes: Men and Women of the English Middle Class, 1780–1867* (Hutchison, London, 1987), ch. 10.

6   William Hawkes Smith, *Birmingham and its Vicinity as a Manufacturing and Commercial District* (J. Drake, Birmingham, 1836), p. 2.

7   Pat Hudson, *The Industrial Revolution* (Edward Arnold, London, 1992), esp. pp. 121–6; Davidoff and Hall, *Family Fortunes;* Conrad Gill, *History of Birmingham,* vol. 1: *Manor and Borough to 1865* (Oxford University Press, Oxford, 1952); Victoria County History, *History of Warwick,* vol. 7: *The City of Birmingham,* ed. R.B. Pugh (Oxford University Press, Oxford, 1964).

8   Asa Briggs, *Victorian Cities* (Odhams, London, 1963); Clive Behagg, 'Masters and Manufacturers: Social Values and the Smaller Unit of Production in Birmingham, 1800–1850', in G. Crossick and H.G. Haupt (eds), *Shopkeepers and Master Artisans in Nineteenth Century Europe* (Routledge, London, 1995), pp. 137–54; ibid., *Politics and Production in the Early Nineteenth Century* (Routledge, London, 1990).

9   James Drake, *The Picture of Birmingham* (J. Drake, Birmingham, 1825); William Smith, *A New and Compendious History of the County of Warwick from the Earliest Period to the Present Time* (W. Emans, Birmingham, 1830); John Alfred Langford, *Modern Birmingham*

and its Institutions: A Chronicle of Local Events, from 1841–1871, 2 vols (Osborne Birmingham, 1873).

10   Adam Smith, *The Wealth of Nations*, 2 vols, 1st edn 1776 (Dent, London, 1964), vol. 1, pp. 362–3.

11   On the 'barbaric' nature of the Irish in Manchester see James Phillips Kay, *The Moral and Physical Condition of the Working Classes Employed in the Cotton Manufacturies in Manchester*, 1st edn. 1832 (Cass, London, 1970).

12   Samuel Timmins (ed.), *The Resources, Products and Industrial History of Birmingham and the Midland Hardware District* (Robert Hardwicke, London, 1866), preface, p. 222.

13   J.E. Tildesley, 'Locks and Lockmaking', in Timmins (ed.), *Resources*, p. 90.

14   John Jones, 'South Staffordshire Manufactures: Chains, Cables and Anchors', in Timmins (ed.), *Resources*, pp. 99–102.

15   William Kenrick, 'Cast-iron Hollow-ware, Tinned and Enamelled, and Cast-Ironmongery', in Timmins (ed.), *Resources*, p. 108.

16   J.S. Wright, 'The Jewellery and Gilt-Toy Trades'; E. Peyton, 'Manufacture of Iron and Brass Bedsteads'; R.F. Martineau, 'Cut Nails'; F.E. Martineau, 'Patent Wrought Iron Hinges'; in Timmins (ed.), *Resources*, pp. 452–62, 624–7, 613–16, 610–12.

17   Thomas Middlemore, 'The Birmingham Saddlery Trade', in Timmins (ed.), *Resources*, pp. 463–76, 472.

18   On more classic imperial cities see Felix Driver and David Gilbert (eds), *Imperial Cities. Landscape, Display and Identity* (Manchester University Press, Manchester, 1999), esp. John MacKenzie on Glasgow; Jonathan Schneer, *London 1900. The Imperial Metropolis* (Yale University Press, New Haven, 1999).

19   On the black and South Asian population in Britain in the nineteenth century see Peter Fryer, *Staying Power: The History of Black People in Britain* (Pluto Press, London, 1984); Rozina Visram, *Ayahs, Lascars and Princes. Indians in Britain, 1700–1947* (Pluto Press, London, 1986); Folarin Shyllon, *Black People in Britain 1555–1833* (Oxford University Press, Oxford, 1977). Shyllon argues that the eighteenth-century black population was never more than 10,000, and that the number fell in the nineteenth century as black domestics were displaced and some black people were assimilated through intermarriage: pp. 102, 159–61.

20   Fryer, *Staying Power*, pp. 110, 215, 262.

21   e.g. *BJ*, 22 Nov. 1845, 3 Jan. 1846.

22   The phrase is R.F. Foster's in *Paddy and Mr Punch: Connections in Irish and English History* (Penguin, Harmondsworth, 1993), p. 86.

23   *Showell's Dictionary of Birmingham*, p. 22.

24   William Robertson, *Life and Times of the Right Honourable John Bright* (Cassell, London, 1883), p. 345.

25   See, e.g., Patrick Brantlinger, *Rule of Darkness: British Literature and Imperialism 1830–1914* (Cornell University Press, Ithaca, NY, 1988); Edward Said, *Culture and Imperialism* (Chatto and Windus, London, 1993); Cora Kaplan, '"A heterogeneous thing": Female Childhood and the Rise of Racial Thinking in Victorian Britain', in Diana Fuss (ed.), *Human, All Too Human* (Routledge, New York, 1996), pp. 169–202.

26   John MacKenzie, *Propaganda and Empire* (Manchester University Press, Manchester, 1984).

27   Annie E. Coombes, *Reinventing Africa. Museums, Material Culture and Popular Imagination* (Yale University Press, London, 1994), and Anne McClintock, *Imperial Leather: Race, Gender and Sexuality in the Colonial Context* (Routledge, New York, 1995).

28   Cited in Lynn Hunt (ed.), *The New Cultural History* (University of California Press, Berkeley, 1989), p. 161.

29   Christine Bolt, *The Anti-Slavery Movement and Reconstruction. A Study in Anglo-American Cooperation 1833–77* (Oxford University Press, Oxford, 1969); ibid., *Victorian Attitudes to Race* (Routledge and Kegan Paul, London, 1971).

30   H.E.G. Whates, *The Birmingham Post 1857–1957* (Birmingham Post and Mail, Birmingham, 1957), p. 13.

31   Asa Briggs, *Press and Public in Early Nineteenth Century Birmingham*, Dugdale Society Occasional Papers no. 8 (Dugdale Society, Oxford, 1949).

32   *BJ*, 1 Nov. 1845–13 June 1846.

33   *BJ*, 6 Jan. 3 Mar. 1866.

34   *BJ*, 28 Feb. 1846.

35   *BJ*, 16 Jan. 1847.

36   *BJ*, 14 Mar. 1846.

37   *BJ*, 2 Feb. 1846.

38   Langford, *Modern Birmingham*, vol. 1, p. 57; Fryer, *Staying Power*, p. 433.

39   George Dawson Collection, vol. 11: Lectures 1845–50, Birmingham Reference Library 260167.

40   Langford, *Modern Birmingham*, vol. 1, p. 265.

41   Charles Dickens, *A Christmas Carol*, 1st edn 1843 (Oxford University Press, Oxford, 1988); ibid., *Bleak House*, 1st edn 1853 (Penguin, Harmondsworth, 1979).

42   Langford, *Modern Birmingham*, vol. 1, pp. 293–304.

43   George Dawson Collection, vol. 12: Lectures 1851–76; Caroline Bray, *The British Empire: A Sketch of the Geography, Natural and Political Features of the United Kingdom, its Colonies and Dependencies* (Longman, Green, Roberts, Longman and Green, London, 1863).

44   Philip D. Curtin, *The Image of Africa British Ideas and Action 1780–1850* (University of Wisconsin Press, Madison, 1964), vol. 2, p. 337.

45   George W. Stocking Jr., *Victorian Anthropology* (Free Press, New York, 1987), p. 53.

46   *BJ*, 22 Oct. 1856.

47   Stocking Jr., *Victorian Anthropology*, pp. 49–65. The quotation from Knox is on p. 65.

48   *BJ*, 5 Nov. 1856.

49   *BJ*, 12 Nov. 1856.

50   *BJ*, 17 Apr. 1847.

51   *The Times*, 19 May 1847, cited in Richard D. Altick, *The Shows of London* (The Belknap Press of Harvard University Press, Cambridge, Mass., 1978), p. 280.

52   Altick, *Shows of London*, p. 280.

53   *BJ*, 16 Jan. 1847.

54   Altick, *Shows of London*, p. 1; there are many other stories which could be told about the exhibiting of peoples in Birmingham. See, e.g., David Sampson, 'Strangers in a Strange Land: The 1868 Aborigines and other Indigenous Performers in Mid-Victorian Britain', Ph.D., University of Technology, Sydney, 2001.

55   *BJ*, 13 June 1846, 9 Dec. 1848.

56   *BJ*, 29 Oct. 1856.

57   *BJ*, 7 May 1853.

58   Shyllon, *Black People*, pp. 204–10; Fryer, *Staying Power*, pp. 252–6.

59   *BJ*, 22 Nov. 1845.

60   Ladies' Negro Friend Society, *Twenty-eighth Report 1853* (Hudson, Birmingham, 1853), pp. 18–21.

61   *BJ*, 7 May 1853.

62   *BJ*, 28 Mar. 1863.

63   *BJ*, 16 Dec. 1848.

64   On gardens see Rebecca Preston, '"The scenery of the torrid zone": Imagined Travels and the Culture of the Exotic in Nineteenth Century British Gardens', in Driver and Gilbert (eds), *Imperial Cities*, pp. 191–214. On psychic lives — a much under-researched area — see Leonore Davidoff, 'Class and Gender in Victorian England', in Judith L. Newton, Mary P. Ryan and Judith R. Walkowitz (eds), *Sex and Class in Women's History* (Routledge and Kegan Paul, London, 1983), pp. 16–71, and McClintock, *Imperial Leather*.

65 Sidney W Mintz, *Sweetness and Power: The Place of Sugar in Modern History* (Viking, New York, 1985), p. 6.

66 This paragraph is heavily dependent on Clare Midgley, 'Slave Sugar Boycotts, Female Activism and the Domestic Base of British Anti-Slavery Culture', *Slavery and Abolition*, 17/3 (Dec. 1996), pp. 137–62; see also Lynne Walker and Vron Ware, 'Political Pincushions: Decorating the Abolitionist Interior', in Inga Bryden and Janet Floyd (eds), *Domestic Space. Reading the Nineteenth-Century Interior* (Manchester University Press, Manchester, 1999), pp. 58–93.

67 Nupur Chaudhuri, 'Shawls, Jewellery, Curry, and Rice in Victorian Britain', in Nupur Chaudhuri and Margaret Strobel (eds), *Western Women and Imperialism: Complicity and Resistance* (Indiana University Press, Bloomington, 1992), pp. 231–46.

68 Mrs Gaskell, *North and South*, 1st edn 1854–5 (Penguin, Harmondsworth, 1970), p. 39.

69 Chaudhuri, 'Shawls, Jewellery, Curry, and Rice', pp. 238, 241.

70 *Showell's Dictionary*, p. 71; Langford, *A Century of Birmingham Life* (Osborne, Birmingham, 1868), vol. 2, p. 395.

71 Rev. George Dawson, *Daily Gazette*, 5 May 1853.

Index

In this index, spellings have been standardised to UK usage.

Abel, Dr Clarke 272
Acton, William 21, 351, 353
Adcock, St John 122
Africa and Africans 4, 52, 296, 414–15,
    420–5
Age of Equipoise, the 3, 18, 240
agriculture 19, 53, 54, 67, 83, 86–8, 115,
    214, 236
Albert, Prince *see* Victoria, Queen
alcohol 102, 103, 383, 388; *see also*
    barmaids
Alice in Wonderland (TV version, 1966) 14
Alison, Archibald 193
Altick, Richard 9, 20, 423
Amies, Hardy 14
Anderson, Perry 86
Anglicans and Anglicanism 170, 172, 233,
    237–8, 244, 256, 259, 261–3, 293
animal magnetism *see* Mesmer, Franz
    Anton, and mesmerism
Anti-Corn Law League 3, 196
anti-Victorianism 6, 10, 209
aristocracy *see* elites, aristocratic
Arnold, Matthew 74, 213, 283
Arnold, Thomas 8, 70, 74, 77, 213, 318
Art and the Industrial Revolution (F.
    Klingender) 20
Ashley, Laura 14

Ashley, Viscount *see* Shaftesbury, Seventh
    Earl of
Ashton, T.S. 17
Attlee, Clement 13
Attwood, Thoms 182
Australia 20, 384, 414, 416–18, 422,
    424–5

Baer, Karl Ernst von 273–5
Bagehot, Walter 1, 9, 89, 226, 322, 401,
    408
banking 27, 83, 89, 121; *see also* financial
    sector and services
barmaids 159, 380–91
Barretts of Wimpole Street, The (R. Besier)
    9–10
Barry, Martin 274
Barton, Margaret 9
Bates, Alan 14
Baudrillard, Jean 133–4
BBC radio, 'Third Programme' series on
    nineteenth-century life and culture 12
BBC television series 15
Beardsley, Aubrey 7
Beatles, The 14
Bell, Vanessa 8
Bentham, Jeremy 7, 290, 308, 313, 355,
    401

Besier, Rudolf 9
Best, Geoffrey 3
Bevan, William 355
Birmingham 152, 154–6, 158–60, 179, 182–3, 198–9, 308, 315–16, 405–7, 414–26
births out of wedlock 216, 343
Blake, Peter 14
Bloomsbury Group 6, 8–10, 12
Boer War 4, 13
Bolt, Christine 418
Booth, Charles 13, 326–7
Bosanquet, Helen 224
Bourdieu, Pierre 160
Bray, Caroline 421
breadwinner wages 31, 194, 201, 306, 320, 322
Brewster, Rev. Patrick 196
Briggs, Asa, Lord Briggs 3, 5, 17–19, 28, 35, 97, 107, 178, 183
Bright, John 55, 130, 174, 229, 417
British Empire and imperialism 1, 4, 13, 23, 25, 31–7, 56, 61, 70, 78–9, 83–6, 91–2, 100, 113, 170, 283, 286, 308, 318–19, 322, 347, 348, 397, 408, 413–26
Broca, Paul 376
Brocklehurst, 'Fitz' 72
Brooks, Peter 33
Brown, Alice 373
Browning, Elizabeth Barrett 9
Browning, Robert 9, 342
Brunel, Isambard Kingdom 1, 76
Buckley, Jerome 19
Burn, W.L. 3, 18
Butler, Samuel 6

Cain, Peter 28, 83–92, 110, 115
Camus, Albert 211
Canada 415, 417, 419
Canning, Lord 172, 173
capitalism 17, 20, 27–8, 73–4, 83, 106, 110, 193, 196, 320, 381–2; development of 13; effects of 19; and periodisation 54; romance of 15, 20; see also Gentlemanly Capitalism
Captain Swing 7, 19
Cardiff 417
Cardwell, Edward, Lord Cardwell 168
Carlyle, Thomas 3, 157, 179, 180, 211–12, 217, 223
Carpenter, Edward 375
Carpenter, William 274–5

Carroll, Lewis 14, 283
Castoriadis, Cornelius 132–3
Catholic Emancipation 137, 141–2, 145, 172
Catholics and Catholicism 172, 233, 236, 239, 247–8, 293; see also Catholic Emancipation; Ireland and the Irish
Chadwick, Edwin 138, 343
Chamberlain, Joseph 7, 55, 174, 417
Chambers, Anne 270, 275
Chambers, Robert 33, 260–1, 268–78
character 26, 75, 78, 103, 113, 157–9, 169–71, 196, 215, 224–9, 297
Charge of the Light Brigade, The (film, 1968) 14
Chartier, Roger 418
Chartism 3, 19, 29, 30, 57, 177–88, 191–201, 240, 380, 402, 424; see also women
Chesterfield, Lord 210
children 1, 4, 10, 14–15, 18, 26, 31, 61, 69, 72, 76, 78, 123, 136, 139, 186, 194, 197, 199, 213, 215–17, 248–9, 270–7 passim, 306, 309–19 passim, 324–34, 343, 352, 364, 377, 404, 419, 421
cholera 137, 143, 145, 239–40
Christie, Julie 14
Churchill, Sir Winston 13
cinema 10, 33, 36, 112
Clapham, Sir John 11, 53, 67
Clapham Sect 56
Clarendon Commission 75
Clark, Alice 56
Clark, George Kitson 16, 18
class see social class
Cobbe, Frances Power 365
Cobden, Richard 72, 91, 174
Cole, G.D.H. and Margaret 7, 183
Colmore, G. 120
Combe, George 270, 271, 273, 275, 278
commercial society, elites and revolution 51–5, 70, 73–4, 76, 78, 83, 85–7, 89–91, 101, 103–4, 106, 113, 116, 119, 169–70, 172–3, 228, 240, 264, 319, 407, 417
Communist Party Historians Group 16–18
Conan Doyle, Sir Arthur 4
'Condition of England' question 3, 138, 179
consumerism 2, 14, 25, 97–123, 307

Contagious Diseases Acts 22, 57, 61, 347, 350, 354, 360
Cooper, Thomas 182
Corn Laws 27, 71, 144–5, 178, 186, 313
Corn Laws, Repeal of (1846) 27, 71, 144–5, 178, 186, 313
Costello, Dudley 273
Country Diary of an Edwardian Lady, The (E. Holden) 15
Cowper, William 309, 425
Cremorne Pleasure Gardens, London 10
Crimean War 14, 384
Criminal Law Amendment Act (1885) 361, 375
Crosland, T.W.H. 119
Crossick, Geoffrey 115, 121
Crossman, Richard 12
Crystal Palace, London 13, 426
Cullen, Michael 356
cultural history 23, 25, 28, 32–3, 128, 131, 268, 288, 360
Culture and Society (R. Williams) 20
Cuvier, Georges 260–1

Darwin, Charles 3, 32–3, 209, 212, 239, 253, 255–64, 268, 277
Darwin, Erasmus 272, 285
Davidoff, Leonore 31, 191, 307–8, 316
Davidson, William 417
Dawson, George 421
Dellamora, Richard 371
Dicey, Albert Venn 11
Dickens, Charles 1, 3, 5, 7, 8, 11, 70, 158, 211, 238, 290, 420–1
Dickens' England (G.M. Young) 11
Dickens World, The (H. House) 11
discourse 23, 25, 130, 132, 137, 143, 227, 326, 349, 350–1, 353, 355, 373, 399–402, 418
Disraeli, Benjamin, later Lord Beaconsfield 1, 3, 9, 168, 240
divorce 326, 328–9, 332, 347
Doctor Who (TV series) 15
Dolléans, Edouard 182
domesticity 31, 105, 139, 192, 200, 211, 276, 308, 309–10, 312, 315, 372, 404, 417; and class 312; democratisation of 312; and men 318–22; 'militant' 199; rhetoric of 201; working-class 193–7
Douglass, Frederick 420
Dracula 14

Duncombe, Thomas 178
duty 26, 104, 117–18, 169, 213, 224, 244, 311, 401

Earle, Peter 56
Early Victorian England (ed. G.M. Young) 11
economic history 11–12, 16, 18, 23, 28, 51–2, 67, 79, 85, 91, 97, 316, 348
Economic History of Modern Britain (J. Clapham) 11
Edinburgh 228, 245, 247, 258, 260, 270, 273, 275, 350, 354, 372, 404
education: scientific 75–6, 171; women's 199, 310–16; working-class 137, 144, 198, 249, 327, 354, 357; see also public schools
Egg, Augustus 349
Eliot, George 22, 158, 211, 213, 282
elites 19, 71, 106, 115–16, 144, 170, 193, 237; Anglican 262; aping aristocratic display 118–21; aristocratic ideals/values of 72, 77; attitude towards lower classes 240–1; in Birmingham 424, 426; capitalist and commercial 54, 83, 84; and culture 69; education of 75, 79; and fashion 110, 113–17, 123; governing 168, 173; intellectual 122, 256, 290; and Jack the Ripper 364, 366; landed 55, 87; leisured 151; London 387; morality of 61, 193, 341; persistence of 28, 67, 69, 116; and popular culture 294; professional 361; and religion 235, 236; transformation of 72; upper class 70, 72, 75–6, 79; withdrawal from common culture 294
elites, aristocratic 4, 27, 258, 306; Anglican, response to Darwin 256; anti-capitalism 74; and change 257; and the City 89; clothing frowned on 157; cultural values 71, 92, 116; decline of 91; defined 161; depicted in melodrama 193–6; and 'economic irrationality' 90; and education 70; and gentlemanly capitalism 83; and ideals of honour 78; idleness of 322; and landed capitalism 87; and politics 28, 55, 59, 138, 167, 172, 179, 186; pre-capitalist 86; reaction against 225, 294; and royalty 400, 406–8
Elliotson, John 289–300

Ellis, Mrs Sarah Stickney 309–12, 315, 319

Eminent Victorians (L. Strachey) 8, 11

Engels, Friedrich 3, 71, 153, 155, 179, 180

Englishness 30, 70, 143, 414

entrepreneurialism 1, 19, 31, 51, 72, 88–9, 91, 120, 320

Equiano, Oulaudah 417

Escott, T.H.S. 73, 117–18

eugenics 4, 253, 288

Evaluation, Age of 12–22

evangelicals and evangelicalism 55–7, 123, 169, 193, 224–5, 233, 238–9, 241–2, 248–50, 292–3, 307, 312, 315, 350, 352, 387, 416, 423

evolution 32–3, 212, 239, 253, 255–61, 264, 268–73, 277, 282–4, 286, 362, 377

family 1, 6, 10, 30–1, 55–7, 61, 89, 101, 160, 174, 192–201, 215–17, 248, 275–7, 307–16, 318–22, 324–34, 342, 344–5, 388, 402–3

Far from the Madding Crowd (film, 1967) 14

Father and Son (E. Gosse) 6

Fawn, James 325

feminism 2, 21, 22, 58, 61, 131, 193, 305, 314

femme fatale 33

financial sector and services 27–8, 36, 54–5, 83–4, 86, 89–90, 92, 102, 112, 115–16, 120, 136

'fiscal-military' state 54–5

flagellation 212

flâneurs 25–6, 123, 151

Flashman 14

Fletcher, John 274–5

Fliess, Wilhelm 377

Foakes, Grace 333

Fordyce, James 56

Forster, E.M. 121, 375

Forsyte Saga, The (J. Galsworthy) 70

Forsyte Saga, The (TV series) 15

Foucault, Michel 21, 24, 129, 136, 339, 347, 349, 382

Fowles, John 14

Fraser, George MacDonald 14

Frayling, Christopher 363

French Lieutenant's Woman, The (J. Fowles) 14

Freud, Sigmund 8–10, 14, 289, 345, 371, 373, 377

Froude, James Anthony 322

Gallagher, John 85

Gammage, R.G. 182–4

Gash, Norman 173

Gaskell, Mrs Elizabeth 3, 179, 312, 426

Gaslight (P. Hamilton) 10

Gavin, Hector 138

Gay, Peter 4, 345

Gay Victorians, The (R. Nevill) 10

gender history 30, 318

Gentlemanly Capitalism 28, 54, 83–92

gentlemen, education of 74–9, 88, 90

Geoffroy Saint-Hilaire, Etienne 260, 273

George IV 401, 403–4

Gilbert, Sandra 22

Gilbert and Sullivan 4

Gladstone, William Ewart 1, 9, 20, 76, 100, 165, 168, 173, 211–12, 229, 236–7

Glasgow 192–4, 198–200, 244–50, 387

globalisation and the global marketplace 2, 23, 28, 36–7, 84

golf 270, 275

Good Old Days, The (TV series) 14–15

Goodway, David 196

Gordon, General Charles Edward, of Khartoum 8

Gosse, Edmund 6

Gosse, Philip Henry 6

Grant, Robert 259–63, 290

Great Exhibition 1, 3, 13, 253, 408, 426

Greg, W.R. 320

Grossmith, George and Weedon 118

Gubar, Susan 22

Guinness, Alec 14

Habbakuk, H.J. 72

Haggard, H. Rider 112

Halévy, Elie 7

Hall, Catherine 31, 56, 191–2, 307, 308, 413–14

Hall, Stuart 18

Hamer, D.A. 174

Hamilton, Patrick 10

Hammond, J.L. and Barbara 3, 7

Hapgood, Lynn 112–13

Hardy, Thomas 14, 282
Harlow, Vincent T. 85
Harney, George Julian 194
Harrington, James 88
Hartington, Lord 168
Hartwell, R.M. 17
Harvey, D.W. 200
Haupt, H.G. 115
Headmasters' Conference 75, 79
Hemans, Felicia 321
Henley, W.E. 372
heritage 15, 30, 87, 192
Herschel, John 276
Hewitt, Martin 5, 35, 61, 162
Himmelfarb, Gertrude 26, 209–10,
    342
Hobbes, Thomas 210, 214, 313
Hobsbawm, Eric 17–19
Hoggart, Richard 18
Holmes, Sherlock 1
Holywell Street, London 10, 348
homosexuality 61, 340, 364, 370–8
Hood, Edwin Paxton 1
Hopkins, A.G. 28, 83–92, 110, 115
Hoppen, K. Theodore 3
Houghton, Walter 19
House, Humphrey 11
Housman, Laurence 345
Hovell, Mark 183, 184
Humboldt, Wilhelm von 285
Hutton, R.H. 283
Huxley, Thomas Henry 76, 256,
    278
hypocrisy 6, 8–9, 12, 26, 200, 209,
    211–14

Ibsen, Henrik 7
illegitimacy 216, 343
India and Indians 4, 32, 121, 408,
    415–26 passim
industrialisation 7, 24, 31, 53, 54, 71,
    85–6, 180, 182, 194, 307, 349
Industrial Revolution 5, 11–12,
    17–20, 27, 28, 51, 53, 67, 86–8,
    91, 97, 182, 191, 263; class society,
    and the emergence of 51; and
    domestic ideology 57; standard of
    living 67; women 31
'In Queen Victoria's Ampler Days'
    (revue sketch) 9
insurance 83, 89, 388; see also financial
    sector and services
intellectual history 166, 223–4, 229

interdisciplinarity 5, 6, 11, 18, 20, 25,
    36, 136, 223, 397
Ireland and the Irish: in Birmingham 417;
    Catholicism 170, 172, 233, 236, 247;
    Liberalism 172–3; in Manchester
    136–46, 416; Nationalists 173; potato
    famine 236; racialised 418
Irish Home Rule 4
Irving, Edward 292

Jack the Ripper 1, 360–6
Jamaica 414, 416–18
Jasper, A.S. 329
Jessop, Andrew 122
Jim Crow 295
Jones, Gareth Stedman 29, 177–8, 191,
    223, 391
Joseph, Sir Keith 26
Joyce, Patrick 29, 128–30
juvenile literature 32

Kanner, Barbara 21
Kay, James Phillips (later Kay-
    Shuttleworth) 137–46
Kind Hearts and Coronets (film, 1949)
    13–14
Kingsley, Charles 284
Kinsey, Alfred 21
Kipling, Rudyard 112
Klingender, Francis 20
Knox, Robert 258–9, 419, 421, 423
Krafft-Ebing, Richard 363–4, 371
Kuhn, Thomas 33

laissez-faire 27, 356
Lamarck, Jean-Baptiste, and Lamarckism
    256, 258–62, 264, 272–4
Lanchester, Elsa 9
Lang, Andrew 372
La Rochefoucauld, François 211
Laughton, Charles 10
'Law and Literature' movement 25
Law and Public Opinion in England (A.V.
    Dicey) 11
Layard, G.S. 120
Leavis, F.R. 19
Lee, Christopher 14
Lee, J.M. 72
Leeds 152, 154–6, 158–60, 198, 406
lesbians 34
Lewes, G.H. 211, 285
Liberalism 27, 30, 129, 167–74, 226,
    228–9, 269, 313

linguistic turn 23, 52, 128–9, 131
Linton, Alice 330
Liverpool 78, 89, 155, 247, 343, 355, 365, 406, 415, 417, 422
Lloyd, Marie 333
Loane, Margaret 328–9
London 1, 9–10, 13, 54–6, 74, 78, 83, 89–90, 92, 99–100, 111, 113, 118, 120, 122, 152–3, 157, 182–3, 192, 194–7, 255, 259–61, 291, 293–5, 300, 310; and barmaids 383–7; and family life 325–34; and sexual behaviour 342–4, 355–6, 361–3, 366; shopping in 100–6
Londonderry, third marquis of 58
London in the Sixties ('One of the Old Brigade') 10
London Missionary Society 310
Lord, Perceval 273–5
Lovett, William 182, 196, 199
Lyell, Charles, Sir 239, 272, 422

Macaulay, Lord 30, 179–80
McCulloch, John 241
Machen, Arthur 10
MacInnis, Colin 333
MacQueen Pope, W. 116, 122–3
Madwoman in the Attic, The (S. Gilbert and S. Gubar) 22
Magna Charta 57, 399
Making of the English Working Class, The (E.P. Thompson) 18, 132, 165, 184, 191
Malthus, Thomas, and Malthusian ideas 137, 143, 187, 194, 239–40, 257–8, 313, 355
Manchester 3, 32, 72, 78, 137, 141, 152–60, 179, 199, 343, 387–8, 406, 416–17, 422
Manning, Cardinal 8
manufacturers and manufacturing 23, 27, 53, 68–9, 73, 83, 88–9, 91, 139, 144–5, 158, 240, 312, 406–7, 415–17
Marcus, Steven 14, 21
marriage 90, 104, 120, 195, 199, 211–12, 309–15, 324, 326–8, 332–4, 343, 350, 352, 357, 360, 372, 387, 390, 401, 423
Marshall, Alfred 224, 226
Marshall, John 72
Martin, Anna 327, 330
Martin, John 9

Martineau, Harriet 309–15
Marx, Karl 13, 16, 23, 32, 71, 351
Marxism 13, 16–18, 20, 22–4, 28–9, 71, 85, 91, 115–16, 129, 131–2, 166, 177, 179–80, 184–5, 188, 347, 351, 380
masculinity 31, 114, 159, 192, 194, 196–7, 201, 318–19, 413
Massey, Gerald 193
Matthew, Patrick 259–60
Maurice, Frederick Denison 237, 242
Mayhew, Henry 34, 320, 347, 352
Melbourne, Lord 212
melodrama and the 'melodramatic turn' 33–4, 122, 138, 193–4, 196, 294, 361
mentalities 23, 29
Mesmer, Franz Anton, and mesmerism 33, 288–300, 308
Methodism 7
middle class 4; attitude towards royalty 408; Chartism 179; consumerism 98–9, 104–5, 110; defined 171; education 78; gender 31, 55–6, 307–8, 309–16, 318–22; and the gentleman 72, 75, 86; imperialism 426; influence of 27–9, 51–5, 71; masculinity 318–22; men and fashion 116–23; national identity 69; popular politics 186–7; and the professions 73, 259; and the public sphere 152–61, 192; religion 56, 169, 213, 236–7, 241, 245, 247–8; values 19, 127, 138, 145, 193, 195–6, 199, 210, 214–16
Middlemarch (G. Eliot) 18, 286
Miles, Andrew 114
Mill, John Stuart 3, 20, 70, 209, 211–12, 223, 226, 285, 314
Miller, James 350, 355
Miller, Jonathan 14, 20
Miller, Karl 372
Mills, W.H. 158
Milton, John 210, 282
modernity and modernisation 12–13, 17, 24, 28, 36, 70, 106, 112, 122, 180, 182, 210, 226, 348, 362, 382, 399
monarchy 1, 5, 30, 179, 259, 398–408
Monboddo, Lord 272
Moore, George 390
Moran, Joe 5
Morant, Sir Robert 79
More, Hannah 56, 308–12, 315

Mulhern, Francis 403
multi-disciplinarity 5, 11
music hall 9, 15, 32, 120, 161, 294, 297,
    325–6, 333, 380, 382, 384–6, 423
Myers, Frederic W.H. 371, 377
My Secret Life ('Walter') 21, 351

Nairn, Tom 86
national identity 25, 30, 32, 36, 69, 84,
    137, 138, 141, 168, 233, 413
Neagle, Anna 10
Nef, J.U. 53
Nevill, Lady Dorothy 10
Nevill, Ralph 10
Newbould 174
New Historicism 25, 282
New Statesman, The 26
New Zealand 384, 416–19 *passim*, 424
Nichol, John Pringle 270–1, 275–6, 278
Nightingale, Florence 8, 56
nostalgia 14–15, 79, 286

Oastler, Richard 194
O'Connor, Feargus 182–3, 201
O'Gorman, Frank 59
O'Key, Elizabeth and Jane 289–300
Onedin Line, The (TV series) 15
'One of the Old Brigade' 10
'On Liberty' 3
Origin of Species (C. Darwin) 3, 212,
    255–6, 272, 277–8, 282
Orme, Eliza 388
Owenism and Owenites 185, 187, 193;
    and feminism 193, 200, 305

Palmerston, Lord 172–3
parasexuality 380–2, 384, 390–1
paterfamilias 4, 6, 9, 10, 31, 277, 319
patriotism 30
pawnbroking 325–6, 328, 330–1
Paxton, Joseph 13
Pearsall, Ronald 21
Peel, Sir Robert 142, 237, 402, 404
performativity 23, 33
periodisation 3, 18, 36, 51–2, 85
Perkin, Harold 18, 19, 31, 71, 73, 120
Pertwee, Roland 10
philanthropy 26, 56, 209, 401
Phillips, John 59
Pink String and Sealing Wax (R. Pertwee) 10
Pocock, J.G.A. 223
political history 17, 29, 165–7, 177, 191,
    270

popular culture 11, 32, 34, 58, 153, 161,
    244, 248, 373, 380–1
pornography 10, 358
'Portrait of an Age' (G.M. Young) 11
Post-Colonial Studies 32
post-modernism 23, 131, 134
Pound, Ezra 2
Pre-Raphaelites 1
Price, Richard 3, 35, 51–2, 84
private sphere 24, 31, 56, 99, 101, 102,
    227, 308
Prochaska, Frank 401
professionalism 19, 55, 70, 73–4, 76–7,
    87, 116–18, 120–2, 133, 158, 161,
    169, 174, 229, 253, 256, 259, 261,
    295, 297, 298, 310, 312, 362–3, 365,
    373, 377, 386
prostitution 2, 61, 103, 154–6, 209, 326,
    339, 347–57, 348–57, 360–1, 375,
    388, 391
public schools 74–9
public sphere 20, 31, 55–6, 100–1, 104,
    192, 228, 307, 340, 349, 360–1, 399,
    401, 420

Queen Caroline affair 57, 403

race and racism 23–4, 32, 34, 61, 137,
    140–1, 143–4, 270, 273, 296, 306,
    318, 377, 413–14, 417–25
Reaganism 23
reality television 35
Recrimination, Age of 6
Reform Act (1832) 27
Reform Act (1867) 4, 165, 167
Reid, Alastair 114
religion 7, 56; and doctrinal belief
    236–42; and evolution 278, 292; and
    gender 293, 310, 312–13, 315; and
    race 419; and urban populations
    245–50
Religious Census of 1851 213, 234, 244
rentier capital 83, 87–8
Representations, Age of 22
respectability 1, 4, 31, 73, 117, 121, 123,
    143, 146, 154–9, 195, 210–11, 213,
    215, 217, 236, 249, 277, 341–2, 347,
    355, 383, 390
Richardson, R.J. 200
Richardson, Tony 14
Riley, Denise 134, 306
Ritchie, Leitch 273
Robert and Elizabeth (musical) 10

Robinson, Ronald 85
Roche, Daniel 112
Rostow, W.W. 17
Rousseau, Jean-Jacques 56
Rowntree, Seebohm 13
Rubinstein, W.D. 27, 55, 79, 84, 92
Rudé, George 19
Ruskin, John 9, 56, 70, 84, 211, 223
Russell, Bertrand 13, 72
Russell, Lord John 171–3

Samuel, Raphael 15
Sanger, W.W. 357
Sargent, John Singer 372
Schlesinger, John 14
Schroeder, Baron von 72
Schumpeter, Joseph 86
science and technology 3, 6, 15, 23–5,
    32–3, 36, 69, 74–7, 90, 110, 117,
    134, 136, 171, 212, 238–9, 253;
    before Darwin 256–64, 270–8; and
    the imagination 282–6; and Jack the
    Ripper 365; and pseudo-science
    288–306; and race 421–3; and *The
    Strange Case of Dr Jekyll and Mr Hyde*
    370, 376
Scott, Joan W. 134, 306
Scott, Sir Walter 30, 269–70, 384–5
Secord, James 260
secularisation 33, 167, 213, 233–4,
    244–50, 256
Sedgwick, Reverend Adam 278
Self-Help (S. Smiles) 3, 26
Selfridge, Gordon 99
Sennett, Richard 158
separate spheres 2, 31, 56, 192–3,
    307–16, 319
Sergeant Pepper's Lonely Hearts Club Band
    (The Beatles) 14
sexuality, history of 9–10, 14, 21–2, 24,
    61, 159, 315, 332, 339–40; and Jack
    the Ripper 360–6; working-class
    341–5
Shaftesbury, Seventh Earl of 138
Shannon, Richard 174
shopping 99–106, 330, 360
Showalter, Elaine 22, 360–1, 370
Silvester, Bernard 285
Sitwell, Osbert 9
Sixty Glorious Years (film, 1938) 10
Skinner, Quentin 223
Smiles, Samuel 3, 26, 224–5, 228–9, 322
Smith, Reginald 118

Snow, C.P. 70
social class 12, 152, 174, 181, 350, 386:
    and education 76; and fashion history
    111; and political power 54; *see also*
    elites; middle class; working classes
social history 7, 12, 16–18, 21–4, 28–9,
    114, 127, 131, 134, 136, 165, 178,
    258, 262, 305, 382
socialism 2, 4, 27, 29, 58, 88, 193; family
    329; Owenite 187
Society for the Promotion of Christian
    Knowledge 274
Spenser, Edmund 285, 286
Stamp, Terence 14
Standage, Tom 36
statistics 136, 353–6
Stead, W.T. 362–3
Stephen, Leslie 213
Stephens, Reverend Joseph Rayner 197,
    199
Stevenson, Robert Louis 362, 371–8
Stoker, Bram 14
Stowe, Harriet Beecher 424
Strachey, Lytton 8, 11–12, 14
Strange Case of Dr Jekyll and Mr Hyde, The
    (R.L. Stevenson) 10, 370–8
Structure of Scientific Revolutions, The (T.
    Kuhn) 33
Sturge, Joseph 182
Suffer and Be Still (M. Vicinus) 21
Sweet, Matthew 34
Swinburne, Algernon Charles 9
'Swinging Sixties' 14
Symonds, J.A. 372, 375, 377

Taine, Hippolyte 213
Tait, William, 354
Taunton Commission 75, 78
Taylor, Ann 309, 314–15
Taylor, Harriet 211
Taylor, Isaac 309
Teddy boys 14
Tennyson, Alfred Lord 9, 30, 284,
    342
Thackeray, William 210
Thatcher, Margaret 26, 35, 210, 211,
    216, 413
Thatcherism 23, 26–7, 70
Thomas, Keith 18
Thompson, E.P. 16–18, 24, 57–8, 127,
    132, 134, 165, 184–5, 191
Thompson, F.M.L. 19, 72
Thompson, John 399

Tichborne Claimant 57
Tiedemann, Friedrich 273
Tomes, Nancy 331
Tosh, John 31, 192, 319
Toynbee, Arnold 17
Treitschke, Heinrich 216
Turner, J.M.W. 9
Tyrell, Alex 404

United States 4, 10, 20, 21, 36, 67, 85, 210, 419
University College Hospital 292
Upstairs, Downstairs (TV series) 15
urban history 5, 17

Veblen, Thorstein 86–7, 97
Verne, Jules 15
Vernon, James 59, 135
Vestiges of the Natural History of Creation (R. Chambers) 33, 260, 268–78
Vicinus, Martha 21
Victoria, Queen 1, 9–10, 18, 30, 34, 236, 306, 397–408; and Prince Albert, 13, 34
Victorian frame of mind 19, 33, 235
Victorian Studies 12
Victoria the Great (film, 1937) 10
Victorian values 26, 27, 210–11, 214–17, 236
Vincent, David 114
Vincent, John 165, 174

Wahrman, Dror 28–9
Wakley, Thomas 297–300
Walkowitz, Judith 158, 339, 355
Wallerstein, Immanuel 85
'Walter' 21, 351–2
Ward, Yvonne 404
Wardlaw, Ralph 348, 352–3
Waterhouse, John William 9
Waters, Mary Barnes 330
Waters, Sarah 34
Watson, Hewett 259
Watts, James 72
Waugh, Edwin 130
Way of All Flesh, The (S. Butler) 6
Webb, R.K. 20
Webb, Sidney and Beatrice 7, 59
Weber, Max 16, 88–9, 115
Weeks, Jeffrey 340, 363, 371, 375

Wellesley Index to Victorian Periodicals 20
Wells, H.G. 7, 15, 112, 121
West Indies 415–18, 426
Whiteing, Richard 112–15
Whiteley, William 99–106
Wiener, Martin 28, 69–79, 84, 86, 110, 116
wifebeating 331–3
Wilberforce, William 56
Wilde, Oscar 4, 6–7, 88, 159, 211, 372, 375, 377
Wilkes, John 57, 60, 185
Willey, Basil 12
William of Wykeham 210
Williams, Raymond 18, 20, 224
Williams-Wynn, Charlotte 242
Willis, Frederick 122
Wolff, Michael 17
Wollstonecraft, Mary 313–14
women 4, 13–14, 21–2, 30–1, 33–4, 55–7, 158, 213, 215–16, 244, 273, 305–6, 319, 324, 326, 363–4; Chartism 191–201; family strategies 325–34; politics 127, 166; as prostitutes 155; in public 159; respectable 156–7; and separate spheres 307–18; sexuality 339, 341–5, 360–1; shopping 99–106; and space 151, 154; and work 142–3
women's history 21, 30–1, 191, 305, 307–8, 360
Woodard, Nathaniel 78
Woolf, Virginia 8, 283
working classes 3, 12–13, 16, 18–19, 73, 127, 131, 187, 210, 214; Chartism 179, 181, 184, 186, 192–3; cleanliness 216; as a concept 29, 57, 132, 161, 165, 171, 185, 186; culture of 132; divisions in 114; family life 327; Jack the Ripper 364; in Manchester 137–40, 144; political education of 177; prostitution 356–7; religion 234, 244–5, 247–8; respectability 217; sexuality 332, 342, 355; shopping 98; 'social control' 214; standard of living of 67, 120; Victorian values 214–15; *see also* barmaids
Worm in the Bud, The (R. Pearsall) 21

Young, G.M. 11, 16, 229

Routledge History

The Routledge Companion to Britain in the Nineteenth Century, 1815–1914

Chris Cook

The Routledge Companion to Britain in the Nineteenth Century, 1815–1914 is an accessible and indispensable compendium of essential information on the Victorian era. Arranged in four key sections – political; social and religious; economic; and foreign affairs, defence and empire – this clear and concise book provides a comprehensive guide to modern British history from the end of the Napoleonic Wars to the outbreak of the First World War. Using chronologies, maps, glossaries, an extensive bibliography, a wealth of statistical information and nearly two hundred biographies of key figures, this book is an ideal reference resource for students and teachers alike.

As well as the key areas of political, economic and social development of the era, this book also covers the increasingly emergent themes of sexuality, leisure, gender and the environment, exploring in detail the following aspects of the 19th century:

- Parliamentary and political reform
- Chartism, radicalism and popular protest
- The Irish Question
- The rise of Imperialism
- The regulation of sexuality and vice
- The development of organised sport and leisure
- The rise of consumer society.

Hb ISBN10 0–415–35969–4   ISBN13 978–0–415–35969–6
Pb ISBN10 0–415–35970–8   ISBN13 978–0–415–35970–2

Available at all good bookshops
For ordering and further information please visit:
www.routledge.com

Routledge History

The Routledge Atlas of British History
4th edition
Martin Gilbert

This new edition of *The Routledge Atlas of British History* uses maps to focus on the economic and social history which tells the changing story of England, Ireland, Scotland and Wales.

This compelling 4th edition atlas now includes:

- politics: from the Saxon kingdoms to the Commonwealth and Europe
- war and conflict: the Viking attacks, World Wars I and II and 21st century war in Iraq
- trade and industry: from the post-Norman economy and international trade routes
- religion: from the Saxon church to the reformation
- society and economics: Roman Britain and Agricultural revolutions
- immigration: growth of immigrant communities.

Hb ISBN10 0–415–36950-X   ISBN13 978–0-415–39550–2
Pb ISBN10 0–415–39551–8   ISBN13 978–0-415–39551–9

Available at all good bookshops
For ordering and further information please visit:
www.routledge.com

Routledge History

Gladstone

Michael Partridge

Gladstone is one of the most important political figures in modern British history. He held the office of Prime Minister four times during a turbulent and changing time in Britain's history.

Michael Partridge provides a new survey of Gladstone's life and career, placing him firmly in the context of nineteenth-century Britain, and covering both his intriguing private life and his public career. Surveying a broad range of source material, Partridge begins by looking at Gladstone's early life, education and entry to Parliament, before looking at his marriage and service with Peel. He goes on to look in detail at Gladstone's terms as prime minister concluding with his fourth ministry, when Gladstone, by now in his eighties, returned to power. He tried and failed to resolve the problems of Ireland, which had become his great obsession, for the last time and eventually retired from politics in 1894 and died a few years later.

Hb ISBN10 0–415–21626–5   ISBN13 978–0-415–21626–5
Pb ISBN10 0–415–21627–3   ISBN13 978–0-415–21627–2

Available at all good bookshops
For ordering and further information please visit:
www.routledge.com

Routledge History

Sir Robert Peel
2nd edition
Eric Evans

Sir Robert Peel provides an accessible and concise introduction to the life and career of one of the most political leaders of the nineteenth century. Perhaps best known for seeing through the Repeal of the Corn Laws, Peel had an enormous impact on political life of his age and beyond. Eric J. Evans reassesses Peel's career, arguing that although Peel's executive and administrative strengths were great, his arrogance, lack of empathy with the development of political parties and his inflexible commitment to economic liberalism presented political problems which he was incapable of solving.

This expanded and fully revised second edition:

- fully engages with the extensive new historical work on Sir Robert Peel published since the first edition appeared fifteen years ago
- includes a glossary of key terms plus an updated and expanded bibliography, including listing useful websites.

Sir Robert Peel is the perfect introduction for all students of nineteenth-century history.

Hb ISBN10 0–415–36615–1   ISBN13 978–0–415–36615–1
Pb ISBN10 0–415–36616-X   ISBN13 978–0–415–36616–8

Available at all good bookshops
For ordering and further information please visit:
www.routledge.com

Routledge History

Britishness since 1870
Paul Ward

What does it mean to be British? It is now recognized that being British is not innate, static or permanent, but that national identities within Britain are constantly constructed and reconstructed. *Britishness since 1870* examines this definition and redefinition of the British national identity since the 1870s.

Paul Ward argues that British national identity is a resilient force, and looks at how Britishness has adapted to changing circumstances.

Taking a thematic approach, *Britishness since 1870* examines the forces that have contributed to a sense of Britishness, and considers how Britishness has been mediated by other identities such as class, gender, region, ethnicity and the sense of belonging to England, Scotland, Wales and Ireland.

Hb ISBN10 0–415–22016–5   ISBN13 978–0-415–22016–3
Pb ISBN10 0–415–22017–3   ISBN13 978–0-415–22017–0

Routledge History

The First Industrial Nation
The Economic History from Britain 1700–1914

Peter Mathias

This celebrated and seminal text examines the industrial revolution, from its genesis in pre-industrial Britain, through its development and into maturity. A chapter-by-chapter analysis explores topics such as economic growth, agriculture, trade finance, labour and transport.

First published in 1969, *The First Industrial Nation* is widely recognised as a classic text for students of the industrial revolution.

Pb ISBN10 0–415–26672–6   ISBN13 978–0–415–26672–7

Available at all good bookshops
For ordering and further information please visit:
www.routledge.com